T0198387

MACHINE LEARNING
FOR BUSINESS ANALYTICS

MACHINE LEARNING FOR BUSINESS ANALYTICS

Concepts, Techniques, and Applications in R

Second Edition

GALIT SHMUELI
National Tsing Hua University

PETER C. BRUCE
statistics.com

PETER GEDECK
Collaborative Drug Discovery

INBAL YAHAV
Tel Aviv University

NITIN R. PATEL
Cytel, Inc.

This edition first published 2023
© 2023 John Wiley & Sons, Inc.

The right of Galit Shmueli, Peter C. Bruce, Peter Gedeck, Inbal Yahav, and Nitin R. Patel to be identified as the authors of this work has been asserted in accordance with law.

Registered Offices
John Wiley & Sons, Inc., 111 River Street, Hoboken, NJ 07030, USA

For details of our global editorial offices, customer services, and more information about Wiley products visit us at www.wiley.com.

Wiley also publishes its books in a variety of electronic formats and by print-on-demand. Some content that appears in standard print versions of this book may not be available in other formats.

Library of Congress Cataloging-in-Publication Data applied for

Hardback: 9781119835172

Cover Design: Wiley
Cover Image: © Hiroshi Watanabe/Getty Images

Set in 11.5/14.5pt BemboStd by Straive, Chennai, India

SKY10063169_122023

The beginning of wisdom is this:
Get wisdom, and whatever else you get, get insight.

רֵאשִׁית חָכְמָה, קְנֵה חָכְמָה;   וּבְכָל-קִנְיָנְךָ, קְנֵה בִינָה.

–Proverbs 4:7

Contents

PART II DATA EXPLORATION AND DIMENSION REDUCTION

CHAPTER 3 Data Visualization   63

CHAPTER 4 Dimension Reduction   101

PART III PERFORMANCE EVALUATION

CHAPTER 5 Evaluating Predictive Performance 129

PART IV PREDICTION AND CLASSIFICATION METHODS

CHAPTER 6 Multiple Linear Regression 167

CHAPTER 7 k-Nearest Neighbors (kNN) 193

CHAPTER 8 The Naive Bayes Classifier 207

CHAPTER 9 Classification and Regression Trees 225

CHAPTER 12 Discriminant Analysis

CHAPTER 13 Generating, Comparing, and Combining Multiple Models

PART V INTERVENTION AND USER FEEDBACK

CHAPTER 14 Interventions: Experiments, Uplift Models, and Reinforcement Learning

PART VII   FORECASTING TIME SERIES

CHAPTER 17   Handling Time Series   455

CHAPTER 18   Regression-Based Forecasting   469

CHAPTER 19   Smoothing and Deep Learning Methods for   499
                 Forecasting

PART VIII DATA ANALYTICS

CHAPTER 20 Social Network Analytics   527

CHAPTER 21 Text Mining   549

CHAPTER 22 **Responsible Data Science** — 573

PART IX **CASES**

CHAPTER 23 **Cases** — 603

Foreword by Ravi Bapna

Converting data into an asset is the new business imperative facing modern managers. Each day the gap between what analytics capabilities make possible and companies' absorptive capacity of creating value from such capabilities increases. In many ways, data is the new gold—and mining this gold to create business value in today's context of a highly networked and digital society requires a skillset that we haven't traditionally delivered in business or statistics or engineering programs on their own. For those businesses and organizations that feel overwhelmed by today's Big Data, the phrase *you ain't seen nothing yet* comes to mind. Yesterday's three major sources of Big Data—the 20+ years of investment in enterprise systems (ERP, CRM, SCM, etc.), the three billion plus people on the online social grid, and the close to five billion people carrying increasingly sophisticated mobile devices—are going to be dwarfed by tomorrow's smarter physical ecosystems fueled by the Internet of Things (IoT) movement.

The idea that we can use sensors to connect physical objects such as homes, automobiles, roads, and even garbage bins and streetlights to digitally optimized systems of governance goes hand in glove with bigger data and the need for deeper analytical capabilities. We are not far away from a smart refrigerator sensing that you are short on, say, eggs, populating your grocery store's mobile app's shopping list, and arranging a Task Rabbit to do a grocery run for you. Or the refrigerator negotiating a deal with an Uber driver to deliver an evening meal to you. Nor are we far away from sensors embedded in roads and vehicles that can compute traffic congestion, track roadway wear and tear, record vehicle use, and factor these into dynamic usage-based pricing, insurance rates, and even taxation. This brave new world is going to be fueled by analytics and the ability to harness data for competitive advantage.

Business Analytics is an emerging discipline that is going to help us ride this new wave. This new Business Analytics discipline requires individuals who are grounded in the fundamentals of business such that they know the right questions to ask; who have the ability to harness, store, and optimally process vast datasets from a variety of structured and unstructured sources; and who can then use an array of techniques from machine learning and statistics to uncover new insights for decision-making. Such individuals are a rare commodity today, but their creation has been the focus of this book for a decade now. This book's forte is that it relies on explaining the core set of concepts required for today's business analytics professionals using real-world data-rich cases in a hands-on manner, without sacrificing academic rigor. It provides a modern-day foundation for Business Analytics, the notion of linking the x's to the y's of interest in a predictive sense. I say this with the confidence of someone who was probably the first adopter of the zeroth edition of this book (Spring 2006 at the Indian School of Business).

The updated R version is much awaited. R is used by a wide variety of instructors in our MS-Business Analytics program. The open-innovation paradigm used by R is one key part of the analytics perfect storm, the other components being the advances in computing and the business appetite for data-driven decision-making.

The new addition also covers causal analytics as experimentation (often called A/B testing in the industry), which is now becoming mainstream in the tech companies. Further, the authors have added a new chapter on Responsible Data Science, a new part on AutoML, more on deep learning and beefed up deep learning examples in the text mining and forecasting chapters. These updates make this new edition "state of the art" with respect to modern business analytics and AI.

I look forward to using the book in multiple fora, in executive education, in MBA classrooms, in MS-Business Analytics programs, and in Data Science bootcamps. I trust you will too!

RAVI BAPNA
Carlson School of Management, University of Minnesota, 2022

Foreword by Gareth James

The field of statistics has existed in one form or another for 200 years and by the second half of the 20th century, had evolved into a well-respected and essential academic discipline. However, its prominence expanded rapidly in the 1990s with the explosion of new, and enormous, data sources. For the first part of this century, much of this attention was focused on biological applications, in particular, genetics data generated as a result of the sequencing of the human genome. However, the last decade has seen a dramatic increase in the availability of data in the business disciplines and a corresponding interest in business-related statistical applications.

The impact has been profound. Fifteen years ago, when I was able to attract a full class of MBA students to my new statistical learning elective, my colleagues were astonished because our department struggled to fill most electives. Today, we offer a Masters in Business Analytics, which is the largest specialized masters program in the school and has application volume rivaling those of our MBA programs. Our department's faculty size and course offerings have increased dramatically, yet the MBA students are still complaining that the classes are all full. Google's chief economist, Hal Varian, was indeed correct in 2009 when he stated that "the sexy job in the next 10 years will be statisticians."

This demand is driven by a simple, but undeniable, fact. Business analytics solutions have produced significant and measurable improvements in business performance, on multiple dimensions, and in numerous settings, and as a result, there is a tremendous demand for individuals with the requisite skill set. However, training students in these skills is challenging given that, in addition to the obvious required knowledge of statistical methods, they need to understand business-related issues, possess strong communication skills, and be comfortable dealing with multiple computational packages. Most statistics texts concentrate on abstract training in classical methods, without much emphasis on practical, let alone business, applications.

This book has by far the most comprehensive review of business analytics methods that I have ever seen, covering everything from classical approaches such as linear and logistic regression to modern methods like neural networks, bagging and boosting, and even much more business-specific procedures such as social network analysis and text mining. If not the bible, it is at the least a definitive manual on the subject. However, just as important as the list of topics, is the way that they are all presented in an applied fashion using business applications. Indeed the last chapter is entirely dedicated to 10 separate cases where business analytics approaches can be applied.

In this latest edition, the authors have added an important new dimension in the form of the R software package. Easily the most widely used and influential open source statistical software, R has become the go-to tool for such purposes. With literally hundreds of freely available add-on packages, R can be used for almost any business analytics related problem. The book provides detailed descriptions and code involving applications of R in numerous business settings, ensuring that the reader will actually be able to apply their knowledge to real-life problems.

I would strongly recommend this book. I'm confident that it will be an indispensable tool for any MBA or business analytics course.

GARETH JAMES

Goizueta Business School, Emory University, 2022

Preface to the Second R Edition

This textbook first appeared in early 2007 and has been used by numerous students and practitioners and in many courses, including our own experience teaching this material both online and in person for more than 15 years. The first edition, based on the Excel add-in Analytic Solver Data Mining (previously XLMiner), was followed by two more Analytic Solver editions, a JMP edition, an R edition, a Python edition, a RapidMiner edition, and now this new R edition, with its companion website, www.dataminingbook.com.

This new R edition, which relies on the free and open source R software, presents output from R, as well as the code used to produce that output, including specification of a variety of packages and functions. Unlike computer-science or statistics-oriented textbooks, the focus in this book is on machine learning concepts and how to implement the associated algorithms in R. We assume a basic familiarity with R.

For this new R edition, a new co-author, Peter Gedeck, comes on board bringing extensive data science experience in business.

The new edition provides significant updates both in terms of R and in terms of new topics and content. In addition to updating R code and routines that have changed or become available since the first edition, the new edition provides the following:

- A stronger focus on model selection using cross-validation with the use of the `caret` package

- Streamlined data preprocessing using tidyverse style

- Data visualization using `ggplot`

- Names of R packages, functions, and arguments are highlighted in the text, for easy readability.

This edition also incorporates updates and new material based on feedback from instructors teaching MBA, MS, undergraduate, diploma, and executive courses, and from their students. Importantly, this edition includes several new topics:

- A dedicated section on *deep learning* in Chapter 11, with additional deep learning examples in text mining (Chapter 21) and time series forecasting (Chapter 19).

- A new chapter on *Responsible Data Science* (Chapter 22) covering topics of fairness, transparency, model cards and datasheets, legal considerations, and more, with an illustrative example.

- The *Performance Evaluation* exposition in Chapter 5 was expanded to include further metrics (precision and recall, F1).

- A new chapter on *Generating, Comparing, and Combining Multiple Models* (Chapter 13) that covers ensembles, AutoML, and explaining model predictions.

- A new chapter dedicated to *Interventions and User Feedback* (Chapter 14), that covers A/B tests, uplift modeling, and reinforcement learning.

- A new case (Loan Approval) that touches on regulatory and ethical issues.

A note about the book's title: The first two editions of the book used the title *Data Mining for Business Intelligence*. *Business intelligence* today refers mainly to reporting and data visualization ("what is happening now"), while *business analytics* has taken over the "advanced analytics," which include predictive analytics and data mining. Later editions were therefore renamed *Data Mining for Business Analytics*. However, the recent AI transformation has made the term *machine learning* more popularly associated with the methods in this textbook. In this new edition, we therefore use the updated terms *Machine Learning* and *Business Analytics*.

Since the appearance of the (Analytic Solver-based) second edition, the landscape of the courses using the textbook has greatly expanded: whereas initially the book was used mainly in semester-long elective MBA-level courses, it is now used in a variety of courses in business analytics degrees and certificate programs, ranging from undergraduate programs to postgraduate and executive education programs. Courses in such programs also vary in their duration and coverage. In many cases, this textbook is used across multiple courses. The book is designed to continue supporting the general "predictive analytics" or "data mining" course as well as supporting a set of courses in dedicated business analytics programs.

A general "business analytics," "predictive analytics," or "machine learning" course, common in MBA and undergraduate programs as a one-semester elective, would cover Parts I–III, and choose a subset of methods from Parts IV and V. Instructors can choose to use cases as team assignments, class discussions, or projects. For a two-semester course, Part VII might be considered, and we recommend introducing Part VIII (Data Analytics).

For a set of courses in a dedicated business analytics program, here are a few courses that have been using our book:

Predictive Analytics—Supervised Learning: In a dedicated business analytics program, the topic of predictive analytics is typically instructed across a set of courses. The first course would cover Parts I–III, and instructors typically choose a subset of methods from Part IV according to the course length. We recommend including Part VIII: Data Analytics.

Predictive Analytics—Unsupervised Learning: This course introduces data exploration and visualization, dimension reduction, mining relationships, and clustering (Parts II and VI). If this course follows the Predictive Analytics: Supervised Learning course, then it is useful to examine examples and approaches that integrate unsupervised and supervised learning, such as Part VIII on Data Analytics.

Forecasting Analytics: A dedicated course on time series forecasting would rely on Part VI.

Advanced Analytics: A course that integrates the learnings from predictive analytics (supervised and unsupervised learning) can focus on Part VIII: Data Analytics, where social network analytics and text mining are introduced, and responsible data science is discussed. Such a course might also include Chapter 13, Generating, Comparing, and Combining Multiple Models from Part IV, as well as Part V, which covers experiments, uplift modeling, and reinforcement learning. Some instructors choose to use the cases (Chapter 23) in such a course.

In all courses, we strongly recommend including a project component, where data are either collected by students according to their interest or provided by the instructor (e.g., from the many machine learning competition datasets available). From our experience and other instructors' experience, such projects enhance the learning and provide students with an excellent opportunity to understand the strengths of machine learning and the challenges that arise in the process.

GALIT SHMUELI, PETER C. BRUCE, PETER GEDECK, INBAL YAHAV, AND NITIN R. PATEL

2022

Acknowledgments

We thank the many people who assisted us in improving the book from its inception as *Data Mining for Business Intelligence* in 2006 (using XLMiner, now Analytic Solver), its reincarnation as *Data Mining for Business Analytics*, and now *Machine Learning for Business Analytics*, including translations in Chinese and Korean and versions supporting Analytic Solver Data Mining, R, Python, SAS JMP, and RapidMiner.

Anthony Babinec, who has been using earlier editions of this book for years in his data mining courses at Statistics.com, provided us with detailed and expert corrections. Dan Toy and John Elder IV greeted our project with early enthusiasm and provided detailed and useful comments on initial drafts. Ravi Bapna, who used an early draft in a data mining course at the Indian School of Business, and later at University of Minnesota, has provided invaluable comments and helpful suggestions since the book's start.

Many of the instructors, teaching assistants, and students using earlier editions of the book have contributed invaluable feedback both directly and indirectly, through fruitful discussions, learning journeys, and interesting data mining projects that have helped shape and improve the book. These include MBA students from the University of Maryland, MIT, the Indian School of Business, National Tsing Hua University, and Statistics.com. Instructors from many universities and teaching programs, too numerous to list, have supported and helped improve the book since its inception.

Several professors have been especially helpful with the first R edition: Hayri Tongarlak, Prashant Joshi (UKA Tarsadia University), Jay Annadatha, Roger Bohn, Sridhar Vaithianathan, Travis Greene, and Dianne Cook provided detailed comments and/or R code files for the companion website; Scott Nestler has been a helpful friend of this book project from the beginning.

Kuber Deokar, instructional operations supervisor at Statistics.com, has been unstinting in his assistance, support, and detailed attention. We also thank Anuja Kulkarni, Poonam Patil, and Shweta Jadhav, assistant teachers. Valerie Troiano has shepherded many instructors and students through the Statistics.com courses that have helped nurture the development of these books.

Colleagues and family members have been providing ongoing feedback and assistance with this book project. Vijay Kamble at UIC and Travis Greene at NTHU have provided valuable help with the section on reinforcement learning. Boaz Shmueli and Raquelle Azran gave detailed editorial comments and suggestions on the first two editions; Bruce McCullough and Adam Hughes did the same for the first edition. Noa Shmueli provided careful proofs of the third edition. Ran Shenberger offered design tips. Ken Strasma, founder of the microtargeting firm HaystaqDNA and director of targeting for the 2004 Kerry campaign and the 2008 Obama campaign, provided the scenario and data for the section on uplift modeling. We also thank Jen Golbeck, Professor in the College of Information Studies at the University of Maryland and author of *Analyzing the Social Web*, whose book inspired our presentation in the chapter on social network analytics. Randall Pruim contributed extensively to the chapter on visualization.

Marietta Tretter at Texas A&M shared comments and thoughts on the time series chapters, and Stephen Few and Ben Shneiderman provided feedback and suggestions on the data visualization chapter and overall design tips.

Susan Palocsay and Mia Stephens have provided suggestions and feedback on numerous occasions, as has Margret Bjarnadottir. We also thank Catherine Plaisant at the University of Maryland's Human–Computer Interaction Lab, who helped out in a major way by contributing exercises and illustrations to the data visualization chapter. Gregory Piatetsky-Shapiro, founder of KDNuggets.com, was generous with his time and counsel in the early years of this project.

We thank colleagues at the Sloan School of Management at MIT for their support during the formative stage of this book—Dimitris Bertsimas, James Orlin, Robert Freund, Roy Welsch, Gordon Kaufmann, and Gabriel Bitran. As teaching assistants for the data mining course at Sloan, Adam Mersereau gave detailed comments on the notes and cases that were the genesis of this book, Romy Shioda helped with the preparation of several cases and exercises used here, and Mahesh Kumar helped with the material on clustering.

Colleagues at the University of Maryland's Smith School of Business: Shrivardhan Lele, Wolfgang Jank, and Paul Zantek provided practical advice and comments. We thank Robert Windle and University of Maryland MBA students Timothy Roach, Pablo Macouzet, and Nathan Birckhead for invaluable datasets. We also thank MBA students Rob Whitener and Daniel Curtis for the heatmap and map charts.

Anand Bodapati provided both data and advice. Jake Hofman from Microsoft Research and Sharad Borle assisted with data access. Suresh Ankolekar and Mayank Shah helped develop several cases and provided valuable pedagogical comments. Vinni Bhandari helped write the Charles Book Club case.

We are grateful to colleagues at UMass Lowell's Manning School of Business for their encouragement and support in developing data analytics courses at the undergraduate and graduate levels that led to the development of this edition: Luvai Motiwalla, Harry Zhu, Thomas Sloan, Bob Li, and Sandra Richtermeyer. We also thank Michael Goul (late), Dan Power (late), Ramesh Sharda, Babita Gupta, Ashish Gupta, and Haya Ajjan from the Association for Information System's Decision Support and Analytics (SIGDSA) community for ideas and advice that helped the development of the book.

We would like to thank Marvin Zelen, L. J. Wei, and Cyrus Mehta at Harvard, as well as Anil Gore at Pune University, for thought-provoking discussions on the relationship between statistics and data mining. Our thanks to Richard Larson of the Engineering Systems Division, MIT, for sparking many stimulating ideas on the role of data mining in modeling complex systems. Over two decades ago, they helped us develop a balanced philosophical perspective on the emerging field of machine learning.

Lastly, we thank the folks at Wiley for this successful journey of nearly two decades. Steve Quigley at Wiley showed confidence in this book from the beginning and helped us navigate through the publishing process with great speed. Curt Hinrichs' vision, tips, and encouragement helped bring the first edition of this book to the starting gate. Jon Gurstelle guided us through additional editions and translations. Brett Kurzman has taken over the reins and is now shepherding the project. Becky Cowan, Sarah Lemore, Kathleen Pagliaro, Katrina Maceda, and Kavya Ramu greatly assisted us in pushing ahead and finalizing this and the earlier R edition. We are also especially grateful to Amy Hendrickson, who assisted with typesetting and making this book beautiful.

## PART I

Preliminaries

## CHAPTER 1

Introduction

1.1 WHAT IS BUSINESS ANALYTICS?

Business Analytics (BA) is the practice and art of bringing quantitative data to bear on decision-making. The term means different things to different organizations.

Consider the role of analytics in helping newspapers survive the transition to a digital world. One tabloid newspaper with a working-class readership in Britain had launched a web version of the paper and did tests on its home page to determine which images produced more hits: cats, dogs, or monkeys. This simple application, for this company, was considered analytics. By contrast, the *Washington Post* has a highly influential audience that is of interest to big defense contractors: it is perhaps the only newspaper where you routinely see advertisements for aircraft carriers. In the digital environment, the *Post* can track readers by time of day, location, and user subscription information. In this fashion, the display of the aircraft carrier advertisement in the online paper may be focused on a very small group of individuals—say, the members of the House and Senate Armed Services Committees who will be voting on the Pentagon's budget.

Business Analytics, or more generically, *analytics*, include a range of data analysis methods. Many powerful applications involve little more than counting, rule-checking, and basic arithmetic. For some organizations, this is what is meant by analytics.

The next level of business analytics, now termed *Business Intelligence* (BI), refers to data visualization and reporting for understanding "what happened and what is happening." This is done by use of charts, tables, and dashboards to display, examine, and explore data. BI, which earlier consisted mainly of generating static reports, has evolved into more user-friendly and effective tools and practices, such as creating interactive dashboards that allow the user not only to

Machine Learning for Business Analytics: Concepts, Techniques, and Applications in R, Second Edition.
Galit Shmueli, Peter C. Bruce, Peter Gedeck, Inbal Yahav, and Nitin R. Patel
© 2023 John Wiley & Sons, Inc. Published 2023 by John Wiley & Sons, Inc.

access real-time data, but also to directly interact with it. Effective dashboards are those that tie directly into company data and give managers a tool to quickly see what might not readily be apparent in a large complex database. One such tool for industrial operations managers displays customer orders in a single two-dimensional display, using color and bubble size as added variables, showing customer name, type of product, size of order, and length of time to produce.

Business Analytics now typically includes BI as well as sophisticated data analysis methods, such as statistical models and machine learning algorithms used for exploring data, quantifying and explaining relationships between measurements, and predicting new records. Methods like regression models are used to describe and quantify "on average" relationships (e.g., between advertising and sales), to predict new records (e.g., whether a new patient will react positively to a medication), and to forecast future values (e.g., next week's web traffic).

Readers familiar with earlier editions of this book may have noticed that the book title has changed from *Data Mining for Business Intelligence* to *Data Mining for Business Analytics* and, finally, in this edition to *Machine Learning for Business Analytics*. The first change reflected the advent of the term BA, which overtook the earlier term BI to denote advanced analytics. Today, BI is used to refer to data visualization and reporting. The second change reflects how the term *machine learning* has overtaken the older term *data mining*.

WHO USES PREDICTIVE ANALYTICS?

The widespread adoption of predictive analytics, coupled with the accelerating availability of data, has increased organizations' capabilities throughout the economy. A few examples are as follows:

Credit scoring: One long-established use of predictive modeling techniques for business prediction is credit scoring. A credit score is not some arbitrary judgment of creditworthiness; it is based mainly on a predictive model that uses prior data to predict repayment behavior.

Future purchases: A more recent (and controversial) example is Target's use of predictive modeling to classify sales prospects as "pregnant" or "not-pregnant." Those classified as pregnant could then be sent sales promotions at an early stage of pregnancy, giving Target a head start on a significant purchase stream.

Tax evasion: The US Internal Revenue Service found it was 25 times more likely to find tax evasion when enforcement activity was based on predictive models, allowing agents to focus on the most-likely tax cheats (Siegel, 2013).

The Business Analytics toolkit also includes statistical experiments, the most common of which is known to marketers as A/B testing. These are often used for pricing decisions:

- Orbitz, the travel site, found that it could price hotel options higher for Mac users than Windows users.

- Staples online store found it could charge more for staplers if a customer lived far from a Staples store.

Beware the organizational setting where analytics is a solution in search of a problem: a manager, knowing that business analytics and machine learning are hot areas, decides that her organization must deploy them too, to capture that hidden value that must be lurking somewhere. Successful use of analytics and machine learning requires both an understanding of the business context where value is to be captured and an understanding of exactly what the machine learning methods do.

1.2 WHAT IS MACHINE LEARNING?

In this book, machine learning (or data mining) refers to business analytics methods that go beyond counts, descriptive techniques, reporting, and methods based on business rules. While we do introduce data visualization, which is commonly the first step into more advanced analytics, the book focuses mostly on the more advanced data analytics tools. Specifically, it includes statistical and machine learning methods that inform decision-making, often in an automated fashion. Prediction is typically an important component, often at the individual level. Rather than "what is the relationship between advertising and sales," we might be interested in "what specific advertisement, or recommended product, should be shown to a given online shopper at this moment?" Or we might be interested in clustering customers into different "personas" that receive different marketing treatment and then assigning each new prospect to one of these personas.

The era of Big Data has accelerated the use of machine learning. Machine learning methods, with their power and automaticity, have the ability to cope with huge amounts of data and extract value.

1.3 MACHINE LEARNING, AI, AND RELATED TERMS

The field of analytics is growing rapidly, both in terms of the breadth of applications and in terms of the number of organizations using advanced analytics. As a result, there is considerable overlap and inconsistency of definitions. Terms have also changed over time.

The older term *data mining* itself means different things to different people. To the general public, it may have a general, somewhat hazy and pejorative meaning of digging through vast stores of (often personal) data in search of something interesting. *Data mining*, as it refers to analytic techniques, has largely been superseded by the term *machine learning*. Other terms that organizations use are *predictive analytics*, *predictive modeling*, and most recently *machine learning* and *artificial intelligence (AI)*.

Many practitioners, particularly those from the IT and computer science communities, use the term *AI* to refer to all the methods discussed in this book. AI originally referred to the general capability of a machine to act like a human, and, in its earlier days, existed mainly in the realm of science fiction and the unrealized ambitions of computer scientists. More recently, it has come to encompass the methods of statistical and machine learning discussed in this book, as the primary enablers of that grand vision, and sometimes the term is used loosely to mean the same thing as *machine learning*. More broadly, it includes generative capabilities such as the creation of images, audio, and video.

Statistical Modeling vs. Machine Learning

A variety of techniques for exploring data and building models have been around for a long time in the world of statistics: linear regression, logistic regression, discriminant analysis, and principal components analysis, for example. However, the core tenets of classical statistics—computing is difficult and data are scarce—do not apply in machine learning applications where both data and computing power are plentiful.

This gives rise to Daryl Pregibon's description of "data mining" (in the sense of machine learning) as "statistics at scale and speed" (Pregibon, 1999). Another major difference between the fields of statistics and machine learning is the focus in statistics on inference from a sample to the population regarding an "average effect"—for example, "a $1 price increase will reduce average demand by 2 boxes." In contrast, the focus in machine learning is on predicting individual records—"the predicted demand for person i given a $1 price increase is 1 box, while for person j it is 3 boxes." The emphasis that classical statistics places on inference (determining whether a pattern or interesting result might have happened by chance in our sample) is absent from machine learning. Note also that the term *inference* is often used in the machine learning community to refer to the process of using a model to make predictions for new data, also called *scoring*, in contrast to its meaning in the statistical community.

In comparison with statistics, machine learning deals with large datasets in an open-ended fashion, making it impossible to put the strict limits around the question being addressed that classical statistical inference would require. As a result, the general approach to machine learning is vulnerable to the danger of *overfitting*, where a model is fit so closely to the available sample of data that it describes not merely structural characteristics of the data, but random peculiarities as well. In engineering terms, the model is fitting the noise, not just the signal.

In this book, we use the term *machine learning algorithm* to refer to methods that learn directly from data, especially local patterns, often in layered or iterative fashion. In contrast, we use *statistical models* to refer to methods that apply global structure to the data that can be written as a simple mathematical equation. A simple example is a linear regression model (statistical) vs. a k-nearest neighbors algorithm (machine learning). A given record would be treated by linear regression in accord with an overall linear equation that applies to *all* the records. In k-nearest neighbors, that record would be classified in accord with the values of a small number of nearby records.

1.4 BIG DATA

Machine learning and Big Data go hand in hand. *Big Data* is a relative term—data today are big by reference to the past and to the methods and devices available to deal with them. The challenge Big Data presents is often characterized by the four V's—volume, velocity, variety, and veracity. *Volume* refers to the amount of data. *Velocity* refers to the flow rate—the speed at which it is being generated and changed. *Variety* refers to the different types of data being generated (time stamps, location, numbers, text, images, etc.). *Veracity* refers to the fact that data is being generated by organic distributed processes (e.g., millions of people signing up for services or free downloads) and not subject to the controls or quality checks that apply to data collected for a study.

Most large organizations face both the challenge and the opportunity of Big Data because most routine data processes now generate data that can be stored and, possibly, analyzed. The scale can be visualized by comparing the data in a traditional statistical analysis (say, 15 variables and 5000 records) to the Walmart database. If you consider the traditional statistical study to be the size of a period at the end of a sentence, then the Walmart database is the size of a football field. Moreover, that probably does not include other data associated with Walmart—social media data, for example, which comes in the form of unstructured text.

If the analytical challenge is substantial, so can be the reward:

- OKCupid, the online dating site, uses statistical models with their data to predict what forms of message content are most likely to produce a response.
- Telenor, a Norwegian mobile phone service company, was able to reduce subscriber turnover 37% by using models to predict which customers were most likely to leave and then lavishing attention on them.
- Allstate, the insurance company, tripled the accuracy of predicting injury liability in auto claims by incorporating more information about vehicle type.

The above examples are from Eric Siegel's book *Predictive Analytics* (2013, Wiley).

Some extremely valuable tasks were not even feasible before the era of Big Data. Consider web searches, the technology on which Google was built.

In early days, a search for "Ricky Ricardo Little Red Riding Hood" would have yielded various links to the *I Love Lucy* TV show, other links to Ricardo's career as a band leader, and links to the children's story of Little Red Riding Hood. Only once the Google database had accumulated sufficient data (including records of what users clicked on) would the search yield, in the top position, links to the specific *I Love Lucy* episode in which Ricky enacts, in a comic mixture of Spanish and English, Little Red Riding Hood for his infant son.

1.5 DATA SCIENCE

The ubiquity, size, value, and importance of Big Data has given rise to a new profession: the *data scientist*. *Data science* is a mix of skills in the areas of statistics, machine learning, math, programming, business, and IT. The term itself is thus broader than the other concepts we discussed above, and it is a rare individual who combines deep skills in all the constituent areas. In their book *Analyzing the Analyzers* (Harris et al., 2013), the authors describe the skill sets of most data scientists as resembling a "T"—deep in one area (the vertical bar of the T) and shallower in other areas (the top of the T).

At a large data science conference session (Strata+Hadoop World, October 2014), most attendees felt that programming was an essential skill, though there was a sizable minority who felt otherwise. Also, although Big Data is the motivating power behind the growth of data science, most data scientists do not actually spend most of their time working with terabyte-size or larger data.

Data of the terabyte or larger size would be involved at the deployment stage of a model. There are manifold challenges at that stage, most of them IT and programming issues related to data handling and tying together different components of a system. Much work must precede that phase. It is that earlier piloting and prototyping phase on which this book focuses—developing the statistical and machine learning models that will eventually be plugged into a deployed system. What methods do you use with what sorts of data and problems? How do the methods work? What are their requirements, their strengths, their weaknesses? How do you assess their performance?

1.6 WHY ARE THERE SO MANY DIFFERENT METHODS?

As can be seen in this book or any other resource on machine learning, there are many different methods for prediction and classification. You might ask yourself why they coexist and whether some are better than others. The answer is that each method has advantages and disadvantages. The usefulness of a method can depend on factors such as the size of the dataset, the types of patterns that exist in the data, whether the data meet some underlying assumptions of the method, how noisy the data are, and the particular goal of the analysis. A small illustration is shown in Figure 1.1, where the goal is to find a combination of *household income level* and *household lot size* that separates buyers (solid circles) from nonbuyers (hollow circles) of riding mowers. The first method (left panel) looks only for horizontal and vertical lines to separate buyers from nonbuyers, whereas the second method (right panel) looks for a single diagonal line.

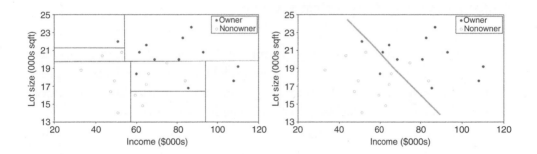

FIGURE 1.1   TWO METHODS FOR SEPARATING OWNERS FROM NONOWNERS

Different methods can lead to different results, and their performance can vary. It is therefore customary in machine learning to apply several different methods and select the one that appears most useful for the goal at hand.

1.7 TERMINOLOGY AND NOTATION

Because of the hybrid parentry of data science, its practitioners often use multiple terms to refer to the same thing. For example, in the machine learning and artificial intelligence fields, the variable being predicted is the *output variable* or *target variable*. A categorical target variable is often called a *label*. To a statistician or social scientist, the variable being predicted is the *dependent variable* or the *response*. Here is a summary of terms used:

Algorithm A specific procedure used to implement a particular machine learning technique: classification tree, discriminant analysis, and the like.

Attribute see **Predictor**.

Case see **Observation**.

Categorical variable A variable that takes on one of several fixed values, e.g., a flight could be on-time, delayed, or canceled.

Confidence A performance measure in association rules of the type "IF A and B are purchased, THEN C is also purchased." Confidence is the conditional probability that C will be purchased IF A and B are purchased.

Confidence also has a broader meaning in statistics (*confidence interval*), concerning the degree of error in an estimate that results from selecting one sample as opposed to another.

Dependent variable see **Response**.

Estimation see **Prediction**.

Factor variable see **Categorical variable**

Feature see **Predictor**.

Holdout data (or **Holdout set**) A sample of data not used in fitting a model, but instead used only at the end of the model building and selection process to assess how well the final model might perform on new data. This book uses the term *holdout set* instead of *validation set* and *test set*.

Inference In statistics, the process of accounting for chance variation when making estimates or drawing conclusions based on samples; in machine learning, the term often refers to the process of using a model to make predictions for new data (see *Score*).

Input variable see **Predictor**.

Label A categorical variable being predicted in supervised learning.

Model An algorithm as applied to a dataset, complete with its settings (many of the algorithms have parameters that the user can adjust).

Observation The unit of analysis on which the measurements are taken (a customer, a transaction, etc.), also called *instance*, *sample*, *example*, *case*, *record*, *pattern*, or *row*. In spreadsheets, each row typically represents a record; each column, a variable. Note that the use of the term "sample" here is different from its usual meaning in statistics, where it refers to a collection of observations.

Outcome variable see **Response**.

Output variable see **Response**.

$P(A \mid B)$ The conditional probability of event A occurring given that event B has occurred, read as "the probability that A will occur given that B has occurred."

Prediction The prediction of the numerical value of a continuous output variable; also called *estimation*.

Predictor A variable, usually denoted by X, used as an input into a predictive model, also called a *feature*, *input variable*, *independent variable*, or, from a database perspective, a *field*.

Profile A set of measurements on an observation (e.g., the height, weight, and age of a person).

Record see **Observation**.

Response A variable, usually denoted by Y, which is the variable being predicted in supervised learning, also called *dependent variable*, *output variable*, *target variable*, or *outcome variable*.

Sample In the statistical community, "sample" means a collection of observations. In the machine learning community, "sample" means a single observation.

Score A predicted value or class. *Scoring new data* means using a model developed with training data to predict output values in new data.

Success class The class of interest in a binary outcome (e.g., *purchasers* in the outcome *purchase/no purchase*); the outcome need not be favorable.

Supervised learning The process of providing an algorithm (logistic regression, classification tree, etc.) with records in which an output variable of interest is known, and the algorithm "learns" how to predict this value for new records where the output is unknown.

Target see **Response**.

Test data (or **Test set**) Sometimes used to refer to the portion of the data used only at the end of the model building and selection process to assess how well the final model might perform on new data. This book uses the term *holdout set* instead and uses the term *validation* to refer to certain validation checks (e.g., *Cross-Validation*) during the model-tuning phase.

Training data (or **Training set**) The portion of the data used to fit a model.

Unsupervised learning An analysis in which one attempts to learn patterns in the data other than predicting an output value of interest.

Validation data (or **Validation set**) The portion of the data used to assess how well the model fits, to adjust models, and to select the best model from among those that have been tried.

Variable Any measurement on the records, including both the input (X) variables and the output (Y) variable.

1.8 ROAD MAPS TO THIS BOOK

The book covers many of the widely used predictive and classification methods as well as other machine learning tools. Figure 1.2 outlines machine learning from a process perspective and where the topics in this book fit in. Chapter numbers are indicated beside the topic. Table 1.1 provides a different perspective: it organizes supervised and unsupervised machine learning procedures according to the type and structure of the data.

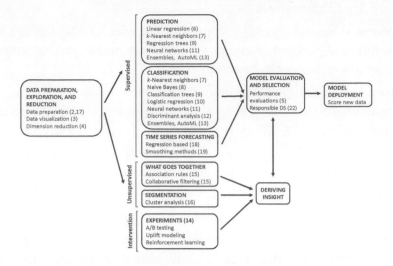

FIGURE 1.2   MACHINE LEARNING FROM A PROCESS PERSPECTIVE. NUMBERS IN PARENTHESES
INDICATE CHAPTER NUMBERS

TABLE 1.1   ORGANIZATION OF MACHINE LEARNING METHODS IN THIS BOOK, ACCORDING TO
THE NATURE OF THE DATA[a]

	Supervised		Unsupervised
	Continuous response	Categorical response	No response
Continuous predictors	Linear regression (6) Neural nets (11) k-Nearest neighbors (7)	Logistic regression (10) Neural nets (11) Discriminant analysis (12)	Principal components (4) Cluster analysis (16) Collaborative filtering (15)
	Ensembles (13)	k-Nearest neighbors (7) Ensembles (13)	
Categorical predictors	Linear regression (6) Neural nets (11)	Neural nets (11) Classification trees (9)	Association rules (15) Collaborative filtering (15)
	Regression trees (9) Ensembles (13)	Logistic regression (10) Naïve Bayes (8) Ensembles (13)	

[a]Numbers in parentheses indicate the chapter number.

Order of Topics

The book is divided into nine parts: Part I (Chapters 1 and 2) gives a general overview of machine learning and its components. Part II (Chapters 3 and 4) focuses on the early stages of data exploration and dimension reduction.

Part III (Chapter 5) discusses performance evaluation. Although it contains only one chapter, we discuss a variety of topics, from predictive performance metrics to misclassification costs. The principles covered in this part are crucial for the proper evaluation and comparison of supervised learning methods.

Part IV includes eight chapters (Chapters 6–13), covering a variety of popular supervised learning methods (for classification and/or prediction). Within this part, the topics are generally organized according to the level of sophistication of the algorithms, their popularity, and ease of understanding. The final chapter introduces ensembles and combinations of methods.

Part V (Chapter 14) introduces the notions of experiments, intervention, and user feedback. This single chapter starts with A/B testing and then its use in uplift modeling and finally expands into reinforcement learning, explaining the basic ideas and formulations that utilize user feedback for learning best treatment assignments.

Part VI focuses on unsupervised mining of relationships. It presents association rules and collaborative filtering (Chapter 15) and cluster analysis (Chapter 16).

Part VII includes three chapters (Chapters 17–19), with the focus on forecasting time series. The first chapter covers general issues related to handling and understanding time series. The next two chapters present two popular forecasting approaches: regression-based forecasting and smoothing methods.

Part VIII presents two broad data analytics topics: social network analysis (Chapter 20) and text mining (Chapter 21). These methods apply machine learning to specialized data structures: social networks and text. The final chapter on responsible data science (Chapter 22) introduces key issues to consider for when carrying out a machine learning project in a responsible way.

Finally, Part IX includes a set of cases.

Although the topics in the book can be covered in the order of the chapters, each chapter stands alone. We advise, however, to read Parts I–III before proceeding to chapters in Parts IV–V. Similarly, Chapter 17 should precede other chapters in Part VI.

USING R AND RSTUDIO

To facilitate a hands-on machine learning experience, this book uses R, a free software environment for statistical computing and graphics, and RStudio, an integrated development environment (IDE) for R. The R programming language is widely used in academia and industry for machine learning and data analysis. R offers a variety of methods for analyzing data, provided by a variety of separate packages. Among the numerous packages, R has extensive coverage of statistical and machine learning techniques for classification, prediction, mining associations and text, forecasting, and data exploration and reduction. It offers a variety of supervised machine learning tools: neural nets, classification and regression trees, k-nearest-neighbor classification, naive Bayes, logistic regression, linear regression, and discriminant analysis, all for predictive modeling. R's packages also cover unsupervised algorithms: association rules, collaborative filtering, principal components analysis, k-means clustering, and hierarchical clustering, as well as visualization tools and data-handling utilities. Often, the same method is implemented in multiple packages, as we will discuss throughout the book. The illustrations, exercises, and cases in this book are written in relation to R.

Download: To download R and RStudio, visit www.r-project.org and www.rstudio. com/products/RStudio and follow the instructions there.

Installation: Install both R and RStudio. Note that R releases new versions fairly often. When a new version is released, some packages might require a new installation of R (this is rare).

Use: To start using R, open RStudio, then open a new script under *File > New File > R Script*. RStudio contains four panels as shown in Figure 1.3: Script (top left), Console (bottom left), Environment (top right), and additional information, such as plot and help (bottom right). To run a selected code line from the Script panel, press *ctrl+r*. Code lines starting with # are comments.

Package Installation: To start using an R package, you will first need to install it. Installation is done via the information panel (tab "packages") or using command *install.packages()* . New packages might not support old R versions and require a new R installation.

Source Code Availability: The code is available from the accompanying web sites https://www.dataminingbook.com/ and https://github.com/gedeck/mlba-R-code; data are available in the R package `mlba`.

FIGURE 1.3   RSTUDIO SCREEN

CHAPTER 2

Overview of the Machine Learning Process

In this chapter, we give an overview of the steps involved in machine learning (ML), starting from a clear goal definition and ending with model deployment. The general steps are shown schematically in Figure 2.1. We also discuss issues related to data collection, cleaning, and preprocessing. We introduce the notion of *data partitioning*, where methods are trained on a set of training data and then their performance is evaluated on a separate set of holdout data, as well as explain how this practice helps avoid overfitting. Finally, we illustrate the steps of model building by applying them to data.

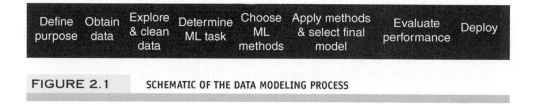

FIGURE 2.1   SCHEMATIC OF THE DATA MODELING PROCESS

2.1 INTRODUCTION

In Chapter 1, we saw some very general definitions of business analytics and machine learning. In this chapter, we introduce a variety of machine learning methods. The core of this book focuses on what has come to be called *predictive analytics*, the tasks of classification and prediction as well as pattern discovery, which have become key elements of a "business analytics" function in most large firms. These terms are described next.

Machine Learning for Business Analytics: Concepts, Techniques, and Applications in R, Second Edition.
Galit Shmueli, Peter C. Bruce, Peter Gedeck, Inbal Yahav, and Nitin R. Patel.
© 2023 John Wiley & Sons, Inc. Published 2023 by John Wiley & Sons, Inc.

2.2 CORE IDEAS IN MACHINE LEARNING

Classification

Classification is perhaps the most basic form of predictive analytics. The recipient of an offer can respond or not respond. An applicant for a loan can repay on time, repay late, or declare bankruptcy. A credit card transaction can be normal or fraudulent. A packet of data traveling on a network can be benign or threatening. A bus in a fleet can be available for service or unavailable. The victim of an illness can be recovered, still be ill, or be deceased.

A common task in machine learning is to examine data where the classification is unknown or will occur in the future, with the goal of predicting what that classification is or will be. Similar data where the classification is known are used to develop rules, which are then applied to the data with the unknown classification.

Prediction

Prediction is similar to classification, except that we are trying to predict the value of a numerical variable (e.g., amount of purchase) rather than a class (e.g., purchaser or nonpurchaser). Of course, in classification we are trying to predict a class, but the term *prediction* in this book refers to the prediction of the value of a continuous numerical variable.

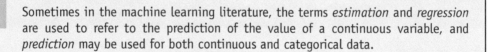

Sometimes in the machine learning literature, the terms *estimation* and *regression* are used to refer to the prediction of the value of a continuous variable, and *prediction* may be used for both continuous and categorical data.

Association Rules and Recommendation Systems

Large databases of customer transactions lend themselves naturally to the analysis of associations among items purchased, or "what goes with what." *Association rules*, or *affinity analysis*, is designed to find such general associations patterns between items in large databases. The rules can then be used in a variety of ways. For example, grocery stores can use such information for product placement. They can use the rules for weekly promotional offers or for bundling products. Association rules derived from a hospital database on patients' symptoms during consecutive hospitalizations can help find "which symptom is followed by what other symptom" to help predict future symptoms for returning patients.

Online recommendation systems, such as those used on Amazon and Netflix, use *collaborative filtering*, a method that uses individual users' preferences and tastes given their historic purchase, rating, browsing, or any other measurable behavior indicative of preference, as well as other users' history. In contrast to *association rules* that generate rules general to an entire population, collaborative filtering generates "what goes with what" at the individual user level. Hence, collaborative filtering is used in many recommendation systems that aim to deliver personalized recommendations to users with a wide range of preferences.

Predictive Analytics

Classification, prediction, and, to some extent, association rules and collaborative filtering constitute the analytical methods employed in *predictive analytics*. The term predictive analytics is sometimes used to also include data pattern identification methods such as clustering.

Data Reduction and Dimension Reduction

The performance of some machine learning algorithms is often improved when the number of variables is limited, and when large numbers of records can be grouped into homogeneous groups. For example, rather than dealing with thousands of product types, an analyst might wish to group them into a smaller number of groups and build separate models for each group. Or a marketer might want to classify customers into different "personas" and must therefore group customers into homogeneous groups to define the personas. This process of consolidating a large number of records (or cases) into a smaller set is termed *data reduction*. Methods for reducing the number of cases are often called *clustering*.

Reducing the number of variables is typically called *dimension reduction*. Dimension reduction is a common initial step before deploying machine learning methods, intended to improve predictive power, manageability, and interpretability.

Data Exploration and Visualization

One of the earliest stages of engaging with data is exploring it. Exploration is aimed at understanding the global landscape of the data and detecting unusual values. Exploration is used for data cleaning and manipulation as well as for visual discovery and "hypothesis generation."

Methods for exploring data include looking at various data aggregations and summaries, both numerically and graphically. This includes looking at each variable separately as well as looking at relationships among variables. The purpose is to discover patterns and exceptions. Exploration by creating charts and dashboards is called *data visualization* or *visual analytics*. For numerical variables, we use histograms and boxplots to learn about the distribution of their values, to detect outliers (extreme observations), and to find other information that is relevant to the analysis task. Similarly, for categorical variables, we use bar charts. We can also look at scatter plots of pairs of numerical variables to learn about possible relationships, the type of relationship, and, again, to detect outliers. Visualization can be greatly enhanced by adding features such as color and interactive navigation.

Supervised and Unsupervised Learning

A fundamental distinction among machine learning techniques is between supervised and unsupervised methods. *Supervised learning algorithms* are those used in classification and prediction. We must have data available in which the value of the outcome of interest (e.g., purchase or no purchase) is known. Such data are also called "labeled data," since they contain the label (outcome value) for each record. The use of the term "label" reflects the fact that the outcome of interest for a record may often be a characterization applied by a human: a document may be labeled as relevant, or an object in an X-ray may be labeled as malignant. These *training data* are the data from which the classification or prediction algorithm "learns," or is "trained," about the relationship between predictor variables and the outcome variable. Once the algorithm has learned from the training data, it is then applied to another sample of data (the *validation data*) where the outcome is known, to see how well it does in comparison to other models (either a different algorithm or different parameter values of the same algorithm). If many different models are being tried out, it is prudent to save a third sample, which also includes known outcomes (the *holdout data*) to use with the model finally selected to predict how well it will do. The model can then be used to classify or predict the outcome of interest in new cases where the outcome is unknown.

Simple linear regression is an example of a supervised learning algorithm (although rarely called that in the introductory statistics course where you probably first encountered it). The Y variable is the (known) outcome variable, and the X variable is a predictor variable. A regression line is drawn to minimize the sum of squared deviations between the actual Y values and the values predicted by this line. The regression line can now be used to predict Y values for new values of X for which we do not know the Y value.

Unsupervised learning algorithms are those used where there is no outcome variable to predict or classify. Hence, there is no "learning" from cases where such an outcome variable is known. Association rules, dimension reduction methods, and clustering techniques are all unsupervised learning methods.

Supervised and unsupervised methods are sometimes used in conjunction. For example, unsupervised clustering methods are used to separate loan applicants into several risk-level groups. Then, supervised algorithms are applied separately to each risk-level group for predicting propensity of loan default.

SUPERVISED LEARNING REQUIRES GOOD SUPERVISION

In some cases, the value of the outcome variable (the "label") is known because it is an inherent component of the data. Web logs will show whether a person clicked on a link or not. Bank records will show whether a loan was paid on time or not. In other cases, the value of the known outcome must be supplied by a human labeling process to accumulate enough data to train a model. E-mail must be labeled as spam or legitimate, documents in legal discovery must be labeled as relevant or irrelevant. In either case, the machine learning algorithm can be led astray if the quality of the supervision is poor.

Gene Weingarten reported in the January 5, 2014 *Washington Post* magazine how the strange phrase "defiantly recommend" is making its way into English via autocorrection. "Defiantly" is closer to the common misspelling *definatly* than *definitely*, so Google, in the early days, offered it as a correction when users typed the misspelled word "definatly" on google.com. In the ideal supervised learning model, humans guide the autocorrection process by rejecting *defiantly* and substituting *definitely*. Google's algorithm would then learn that this is the best first-choice correction of "definatly." The problem was that too many people were lazy, just accepting the first correction that Google presented. All these acceptances then cemented "defiantly" as the proper correction.

2.3 THE STEPS IN A MACHINE LEARNING PROJECT

This book focuses on understanding and using machine learning algorithms (Steps 4–7 below). However, some of the most serious errors in analytics projects result from a poor understanding of the problem—an understanding that must be developed before we get into the details of algorithms to be used. Here is a list of steps to be taken in a typical machine learning effort:

1. *Develop an understanding of the purpose of the machine learning project*: How will the stakeholder use the results? Who will be affected by the results? Will the analysis be a one-shot effort or an ongoing procedure?

2. *Obtain the data to be used in the analysis*: This often involves random sampling from a large database to capture records to be used in an analysis. How well this sample reflects the records of interest affects the ability of the machine learning results to generalize to records outside of this sample. It may also involve pulling together data from different databases or sources. The databases could be internal (e.g., past purchases made by customers) or external (credit ratings). While machine learning deals with very large databases, usually the analysis to be done requires only thousands or tens of thousands of records.

3. *Explore, clean, and preprocess the data*: This step involves verifying that the data are in reasonable condition. How should missing data be handled? Are the values in a reasonable range, given what you would expect for each variable? Are there obvious outliers? The data are reviewed graphically: for example, a matrix of scatterplots showing the relationship of each variable with every other variable. We also need to ensure consistency in the definitions of fields, units of measurement, time periods, and so on. In this step, new variables are also typically created from existing ones. For example, "duration" can be computed from start and end dates.

4. *Reduce the data dimension, if necessary*: Dimension reduction can involve operations such as eliminating unneeded variables, transforming variables (e.g., turning "money spent" into "spent $> \$100$" vs. "spent $\leq \$100$"), and creating new variables (e.g., a variable that records whether at least one of several products was purchased). Make sure that you know what each variable means and whether it is sensible to include it in the model.

5. *Determine the machine learning task (classification, prediction, clustering, etc.)*: This involves translating the general question or problem of Step 1 into a more specific machine learning question.

6. *Partition the data (for supervised tasks)*: If the task is supervised (classification or prediction), randomly partition the dataset into three parts: training, validation, and holdout datasets.

7. *Choose the machine learning techniques to be used (regression, neural nets, hierarchical clustering, etc.)*.

8. *Use algorithms to perform the task*: This is typically an iterative process— trying multiple variants and often using multiple variants of the same algorithm (choosing different variables or parameter settings within the algorithm). Where appropriate, feedback from the algorithm's performance on validation data is used to refine the parameter settings.

9. *Interpret the results of the algorithms*: This involves making a choice as to the best algorithm to deploy, and where possible, testing the final choice on the holdout data to get an idea as to how well it will perform. (Recall that each algorithm may also be tested on the validation data for tuning purposes; in this way, the validation data become a part of the fitting process and are likely to underestimate the error in the deployment of the model that is finally chosen.)

10. *Deploy the model*: This step involves integrating the model into operational systems and running it on real records to produce decisions or actions. For example, the model might be applied to a purchased list of possible customers, and the action might be "include in the mailing if the

predicted amount of purchase is >$10." A key step here is "scoring" the new records, or using the chosen model to predict the outcome value ("score") for each new record.

The foregoing steps encompass the steps in SEMMA, a methodology developed by the software company SAS:

Sample Take a sample from the dataset; partition into training, validation, and holdout datasets.

Explore Examine the dataset statistically and graphically.

Modify Transform the variables and impute missing values.

Model Fit predictive models (e.g., regression tree, neural network).

Assess Compare models using a validation dataset.

IBM SPSS Modeler (previously SPSS-Clementine) has a similar methodology, termed CRISP-DM (CRoss-Industry Standard Process for Data Mining). All these frameworks include the same main steps involved in predictive modeling.

2.4 PRELIMINARY STEPS

Organization of Data

Datasets are nearly always constructed and displayed so that variables are in columns and records are in rows. In the example shown in Section 2.6 (home values in West Roxbury, Boston, in 2014), 14 variables are recorded for over 5000 homes. The spreadsheet is organized so that each row represents a home—the first home's assessed value was $344,200, its tax was $4430, its size was 9965 ft^2, it was built in 1880, and so on. In supervised learning situations, one of these variables will be the outcome variable, typically listed in the first or last column (in this case, it is TOTAL.VALUE, in the first column).

Predicting Home Values in the West Roxbury Neighborhood

The Internet has revolutionized the real estate industry. Realtors now list houses and their prices on the web, and estimates of house and condominium prices have become widely available, even for units not on the market. In 2014, Zillow (www.zillow.com), a popular online real estate information site in the United States,[1] purchased its major rival, Trulia. By 2015, Zillow had become the dominant platform for checking house prices and, as such, the dominant

---

[1]Harney, K., "Zestimates may not be as right as you'd like", *Washington Post*, Feb. 7, 2015, p. T10.

online advertising venue for realtors. By 2021, another competitor, Redfin, had eclipsed Zillow in market capitalization, largely via its strategy of employing its own agents directly on a salaried basis. What used to be a comfortable 6% commission structure for independent realtors, affording them a handsome surplus (and an oversupply of realtors), was being rapidly eroded by an increasing need to pay for advertising on Zillow and by competition from Redfin. (This, in fact, was the original key to Zillow's business model—redirecting the 6% commission away from realtors and to itself.)

Zillow gets much of the data for its "Zestimates" of home values directly from publicly available city housing data, used to estimate property values for tax assessment. A competitor seeking to get into the market would likely take the same approach. So might realtors seeking to develop an alternative to Zillow.

A simple approach would be a naive, model-less method—just use the assessed values as determined by the city. Those values, however, do not necessarily include all properties, and they might not include changes warranted by remodeling, additions, etc. Moreover, the assessment methods used by cities may not be transparent or always reflect true market values. However, the city property data can be used as a starting point to build a model, to which additional data (such as that collected by large realtors) can be added later.

Let's look at how Boston property assessment data, available from the city of Boston, might be used to predict home values. The data in *mlba::WestRoxbury* includes information on single family owner-occupied homes in West Roxbury, a neighborhood in southwest Boston, MA, in 2014. The data include values for various predictor variables and for an outcome—assessed home value ("total value"). This dataset has 14 variables and includes 5802 homes. A sample of the data[2] is shown in Table 2.1, and the "data dictionary" describing each variable[3] is in Table 2.2.

As we saw earlier, below the header row, each row in the data represents a home. For example, the first home was assessed at a total value of $344.2 thousand (TOTAL.VALUE). Its tax bill was $4330. It has a lot size of 9965 square feet (ft^2), was built in the year 1880, has two floors, six rooms, and so on.

Loading and Looking at the Data in R

To load data into R, we will typically want to have the data available as a .csv (comma separated values) file. If the data are in an .xls or .xlsx file, we can save that same file in Excel as a csv file: go to File > Save as > Save as type: CSV (Comma delimited) ($\star$.csv) > Save.

---

[2]The data are a slightly cleaned version of the Property Assessment FY2014 data at https://data.boston.gov/dataset/property-assessment (accessed December 2017).
[3]The full data dictionary provided by the City of Boston is available at https://data.boston.gov/dataset/property-assessment; we have modified a few variable names.

| TABLE 2.1 | | FIRST 10 RECORDS IN THE WEST ROXBURY HOME VALUES DATASET | | | | | | | | | | | |

TOTAL VALUE	TAX	LOT SQ FT	YR BUILT	GROSS AREA	LIVING AREA	FLOORS	ROOMS	BED ROOMS	FULL BATH	HALF BATH	KIT CHEN	FIRE PLACE	REMODEL
344.2	4330	9965	1880	2436	1352	2	6	3	1	1	1	0	None
412.6	5190	6590	1945	3108	1976	2	10	4	2	1	1	0	Recent
330.1	4152	7500	1890	2294	1371	2	8	4	1	1	1	0	None
498.6	6272	13773	1957	5032	2608	1	9	5	1	1	1	1	None
331.5	4170	5000	1910	2370	1438	2	7	3	2	0	1	0	None
337.4	4244	5142	1950	2124	1060	1	6	3	1	0	1	1	Old
359.4	4521	5000	1954	3220	1916	2	7	3	1	1	1	0	None
320.4	4030	10000	1950	2208	1200	1	6	3	1	0	1	0	None
333.5	4195	6835	1958	2582	1092	1	5	3	1	0	1	1	Recent
409.4	5150	5093	1900	4818	2992	2	8	4	2	0	1	0	None

TABLE 2.2	DESCRIPTION OF VARIABLES IN WEST ROXBURY (BOSTON) HOME VALUE DATASET
TOTAL.VALUE	Total assessed value for property, in thousands of USD
TAX	Tax bill amount based on total assessed value multiplied by the tax rate, in USD
LOT SQ FT	Total lot size of parcel in square feet
YR BUILT	Year the property was built
GROSS AREA	Gross floor area
LIVING AREA	Total living area for residential properties (ft^2)
FLOORS	Number of floors
ROOMS	Total number of rooms
BEDROOMS	Total number of bedrooms
FULL BATH	Total number of full baths
HALF BATH	Total number of half baths
KITCHEN	Total number of kitchens
FIREPLACE	Total number of fireplaces
REMODEL	When the house was remodeled (recent/old/none)

Note: When dealing with .csv files in Excel, beware of two things:

- Opening a .csv file in Excel strips off leading 0's, which corrupts zip code data.
- Saving a .csv file in Excel saves only the digits that are displayed; if you need precision to a certain number of decimals, you need to ensure they are displayed before saving.

Once we have R and RStudio installed on our machine and the *WestRoxbury.csv* file saved as a csv file, we can run the code in Table 2.3 to load the data into R.

Data from a .csv file is stored in R as a *data frame* (e.g., *housing.df*). A data frame is the fundamental object almost all analyses begin with in R. A data frame has rows and columns. The rows are the observations for each case (e.g., house), and the columns are the variables of interest (e.g., TOTAL.VALUE, TAX).

TABLE 2.3	WORKING WITH FILES IN R

To start, open RStudio, go to File > New File > R Script. It opens a new tab.
Then save your Untitled1.R file into the directory where your csv is saved. Give it the name WestRoxbury.R.
From the Menu Bar, go to Session > Set Working Directory > To Source File Location; this sets the working directory as the place where both the R file and csv file are saved.

 code for loading and creating subsets from the data

```
housing.df <- read.csv('WestRoxbury.csv') # load data from file
housing.df <- mlba::WestRoxbury # load data from mlba package
dim(housing.df)  # find the dimension of data frame
head(housing.df)  # show the first six rows
View(housing.df)  # show all the data in a new tab

# Practice showing different subsets of the data
housing.df[1:10, 1]  # show the first 10 rows of the first column only
housing.df[1:10, ]  # show the first 10 rows of each of the columns
housing.df[5, 1:10]  # show the fifth row of the first 10 columns
housing.df[5, c(1:2, 4, 8:10)]  # show the fifth row of some columns
housing.df[, 1]  # show the whole first column
housing.df$TOTAL.VALUE  # a different way to show the whole first column
housing.df$TOTAL.VALUE[1:10]  # show the first 10 rows of the first column
length(housing.df$TOTAL.VALUE) # find the length of the first column
mean(housing.df$TOTAL.VALUE) # find the mean of the first column
summary(housing.df)  # find summary statistics for each column
```

If our .csv file has column headers, these headers get automatically stored as the column names of our data.

The code[4] in Table 2.3 walks you through some basic steps you will want to perform prior to doing any analysis: finding the size and dimension of your data (number of rows and columns), viewing all the data, displaying only selected rows and columns, and computing summary statistics for variables of interest. Note that comments are preceded with the # symbol.

While we provide all datasets used in the book with the `mlba` package in R, it is useful to know how to load datasets in various formats. The function *read.csv* and its variations have a large number of arguments that control how the text file is parsed. If something goes wrong, check the documentation.[5]

Sampling from a Database

Quite often, we want to perform our modeling on less than the total number of records that are available. Machine learning algorithms will have varying

---

[4]Code available at www.dataminingbook.com and https://github.com/gedeck/mlba-R-code; data available in R package **mlba**.

[5]Note: The upgrade of R from version 3 to 4 changed the way strings are handled on import. In the older versions, strings were automatically converted to factors. This is no longer the case and can break older R code you might come across. To restore the old behavior, use *stringAsFactors=TRUE*.

TABLE 2.4   **SAMPLING IN R**

 code for sampling and over/undersampling

```
housing.df <- mlba::WestRoxbury

# random sample of 5 observations
s <- sample(row.names(housing.df), 5)
housing.df[s,]

# oversample houses with over 10 rooms
s <- sample(row.names(housing.df), 5, prob=ifelse(housing.df$ROOMS>10, 0.9, 0.01))
housing.df[s,]

# rebalance
housing.df$REMODEL <- factor(housing.df$REMODEL)
table(housing.df$REMODEL)
upsampled.df <- caret::upSample(housing.df, housing.df$REMODEL, list=TRUE)$x
table(upsampled.df$REMODEL)
```

Output

```
> table(housing.df$REMODEL)
  None    Old Recent
  4346    581    875
> table(upsampled.df$REMODEL)
  None    Old Recent
  4346   4346   4346
```

limitations on what they can handle in terms of the numbers of records and variables, limitations that may be specific to computing power and capacity as well as software limitations. Even within those limits, many algorithms will execute faster with smaller samples.

Accurate models can often be built with as few as several thousand records. Hence, we will want to sample a subset of records for model building. Table 2.4 provides code for sampling in R. Throughout this book, we will use R's *sample()* function for sampling. We will also make use of the *caret::createDataPartition()* function for stratified sampling, which aims to preserve the distribution of the outcome variable in each data partition.

Oversampling Rare Events in Classification Tasks

If the event we are interested in classifying is rare, such as customers purchasing a product in response to a mailing, or fraudulent credit card transactions, sampling a random subset of records may yield so few events (e.g., purchases) that we have little information on them. We would end up with lots of data on nonpurchasers and non-fraudulent transactions but little on which to base a model that distinguishes purchasers from nonpurchasers or fraudulent from non-fraudulent. In such cases, we would want our sampling procedure to overweight the rare class (purchasers or frauds) relative to the majority class (nonpurchasers, non-frauds) so that our sample would end up with a healthy complement of purchasers or frauds. In R, this can be done with the functions *sample()* or *upSample()* in the `caret` package (see Table 2.4).

Assuring an adequate number of responder or "success" cases to train the model is just part of the picture. A more important factor is the costs of misclassification. Whenever the response rate is extremely low, we are likely to attach more importance to identifying a responder than to identifying a nonresponder. In direct-response advertising (whether by traditional mail, email, web, or mobile advertising), we may encounter only one or two responders for every hundred records—the value of finding such a customer far outweighs the costs of reaching him or her. In trying to identify fraudulent transactions, or customers unlikely to repay debt, the costs of failing to find the fraud or the nonpaying customer are likely to exceed the cost of more detailed review of a legitimate transaction or customer.

If the costs of failing to locate responders are comparable to the costs of misidentifying responders as non-responders, our models would usually achieve highest overall accuracy if they identified everyone as a non-responder (or almost everyone, if it is easy to identify a few responders without catching many nonresponders). In such a case, the misclassification rate is very low—equal to the rate of responders—but the model is of no value.

More generally, we want to train our model with the asymmetric costs in mind so that the algorithm will catch the more valuable responders, probably at the cost of "catching" and misclassifying more non-responders as responders than would be the case if we assume equal costs. This subject is discussed in detail in Chapter 5.

Preprocessing and Cleaning the Data

Types of Variables   There are several ways of classifying variables. Variables can be numerical or text (character/string). They can be continuous (able to assume any real numerical value, usually in a given range), integer (taking only integer values), categorical (assuming one of a limited number of values), or date–time (able to assume date and time values). Categorical variables can be either coded as numerical $(1, 2, 3)$ or text (payments current, payments not current, bankrupt). Categorical variables can also be unordered (called *nominal variables*) with categories such as North America, Europe, and Asia; or they can be ordered (called *ordinal variables*) with categories such as high value, low value, and nil value. Date–time variables can have values denoting either date or time, or both.

Continuous variables can be handled by most machine learning routines with the exception of the naive Bayes classifier, which deals exclusively with categorical predictor variables. The roots of machine learning grew out of problems with categorical outcomes; the roots of statistics lie in the analysis of continuous variables. Sometimes, it is desirable to convert continuous variables to categorical variables. This is done most typically in the case of outcome variables, where the numerical variable is mapped to a decision (e.g., credit scores above a certain threshold mean "grant credit," a medical test result above a certain threshold means "start treatment").

For the West Roxbury data, Table 2.5 presents some R statements to review the variables and determine what type R thinks they are. We see that the

---

TABLE 2.5   **REVIEWING VARIABLES IN R**

 code for reviewing variables

```
library(tidyverse)

# get overview
str(housing.df)

# make REMODEL a factor variable
housing.df$REMODEL <- factor(housing.df$REMODEL)
str(housing.df$REMODEL)
levels(housing.df$REMODEL) # show factor's categories (levels)

# use tidyverse to load and preprocess data in one statement
# the %>% operator inserts the result of the expression on the left
# as the first argument into the function on the right
housing.df <- mlba::WestRoxbury %>%
  mutate(REMODEL=factor(REMODEL))
```

Partial Output

```
> str(housing.df)
'data.frame':       5802 obs. of  14 variables:
 $ TOTAL.VALUE: num  344 413 330 499 332 ...
 $ TAX        : int  4330 5190 4152 6272 4170 4244 4521 4030 4195 5150 ...
 $ LOT.SQFT   : int  9965 6590 7500 13773 5000 5142 5000 10000 6835 5093 ...
 $ YR.BUILT   : int  1880 1945 1890 1957 1910 1950 1954 1950 1958 1900 ...
 $ GROSS.AREA : int  2436 3108 2294 5032 2370 2124 3220 2208 2582 4818 ...
 $ LIVING.AREA: int  1352 1976 1371 2608 1438 1060 1916 1200 1092 2992 ...
 $ FLOORS     : num  2 2 2 1 2 1 2 1 1 2 ...
 $ ROOMS      : int  6 10 8 9 7 6 7 6 5 8 ...
 $ BEDROOMS   : int  3 4 4 5 3 3 3 3 3 4 ...
 $ FULL.BATH  : int  1 2 1 1 2 1 1 1 1 2 ...
 $ HALF.BATH  : int  1 1 1 1 0 0 1 0 0 0 ...
 $ KITCHEN    : int  1 1 1 1 1 1 1 1 1 1 ...
 $ FIREPLACE  : int  0 0 0 1 0 1 0 0 1 0 ...
 $ REMODEL    : chr  "None" "Recent" "None" "None" ...

> str(housing.df$REMODEL)
 Factor w/ 3 levels "None","Old","Recent": 1 3 1 1 1 2 1 1 3 1 ...
> levels(housing.df$REMODEL)
[1] "None"    "Old"     "Recent"
```

REMODEL variable is of type *chr*, BEDROOMS is an integer (*int*) variable, and total_value is a numerical (*num*) variable. We then convert REMODEL to a categorical variable (called a *factor* variable in R) using the *factor* function. The resulting factor has three categories (levels). Table 2.5 also demonstrates how to use `tidyverse` to combine all preprocessing steps into a pipeline using the %>% operator.

Handling Categorical Variables   Categorical variables can also be handled by most machine learning routines, but often require special handling. If the categorical variable is ordered (age group, degree of creditworthiness, etc.), we can sometimes code the categories numerically (1, 2, 3, ...) and treat the variable as if it were a continuous variable. The smaller the number of categories, and the less they represent equal increments of value, the more problematic this approach becomes, but it often works well enough.

Nominal categorical variables, however, often cannot be used as is. In many cases, they must be decomposed into a series of binary variables, called *dummy variables*. For example, a single categorical variable that can have possible values of "student," "unemployed," "employed," or "retired" would be split into four separate dummy variables:

Student—1/0
Unemployed—1/0
Employed—1/0
Retired—1/0

In some algorithms (e.g., regression models), only three of the dummy variables should be used; if the values of three are known, the fourth is also known. For example, given that these four values are the only possible ones, we can know that if a person is neither student, unemployed, nor employed, he or she must be retired. In fact, due to this redundant information, linear regression and logistic regression algorithms will produce incorrect results or fail if you use all four variables. Yet, in other algorithms (e.g., *k*-nearest neighbors), we must include all four dummy variables. This is called *one-hot encoding*. Note, also, that typical methods of creating dummy variables will leave the original categorical variable intact; obviously you should not use both the original variable and the dummies. In R, we can use the `fastDummies` package to create dummies from a categorical (factor) variable. An example using this package is shown in Table 2.6, resulting in two new dummies for REMODEL.

Variable Selection   More is not necessarily better when it comes to selecting variables for a model. Other things being equal, parsimony, or compactness, is a desirable feature in a model. For one thing, the more variables we include, the greater the number of records we will need to assess relationships among the

TABLE 2.6   CREATING DUMMY VARIABLES IN R

 code for creating binary dummies (indicators)

```
library(fastDummies)
library(tidyverse)

housing.df <- dummy_cols(mlba::WestRoxbury,
                remove_selected_columns=TRUE,   # remove the original column
                remove_first_dummy=TRUE)  # removes the first created dummy variable
housing.df %>% head(2)
```

Output

```
  TOTAL.VALUE  TAX LOT.SQFT YR.BUILT GROSS.AREA LIVING.AREA FLOORS ROOMS BEDROOMS
1       344.2 4330     9965     1880       2436        1352      2     6        3
2       412.6 5190     6590     1945       3108        1976      2    10        4
  FULL.BATH HALF.BATH KITCHEN FIREPLACE REMODEL_Old REMODEL_Recent
1         1         1       1         0           0              0
2         2         1       1         0           0              1
```

variables. Fifteen records may suffice to give us a rough idea of the relationship between Y and a single predictor variable X. If we now want information about the relationship between Y and 15 predictor variables $X_1, \ldots, X_{15}$, 15 records will not be enough (each estimated relationship would have an average of only one record's worth of information, making the estimate very unreliable). In addition, models based on many variables are often less robust, as they require the collection of more variables in the future, are subject to more data quality and availability issues, and require more data cleaning and preprocessing. The process of variable selection is also called *feature selection*.

How Many Variables and How Much Data?   Statisticians give us procedures to learn with some precision how many records we would need to achieve a given degree of reliability with a given dataset and a given model. These are called "power calculations" and are intended to assure that an average population effect will be estimated with sufficient precision from a sample. Predictive analytics needs are usually different, because the focus is not on identifying an average effect but rather on predicting individual records. This purpose typically requires larger samples than those used for statistical inference. A good rule of thumb is to have 10 records for every predictor variable. Another rule, used by Delmaster and Hancock (2001, p. 68) for classification procedures, is to have at least $6 \times m \times p$ records, where m is the number of outcome classes and p is the number of variables.

In general, compactness or parsimony is a desirable feature in a machine learning model. Even when we start with a small number of variables, we often end up with many more after creating new variables (such as converting a categorical variable into a set of dummy variables). Data visualization and dimension reduction methods help reduce the number of variables so that redundancies and information overlap are reduced.

Even when we have an ample supply of data, there are good reasons to pay close attention to the variables that are included in a model. Someone with domain knowledge (i.e., knowledge of the business process and the data) should be consulted, as knowledge of what the variables represent is typically critical for building a good model and avoiding errors and legal violations.

For example, suppose we're trying to predict the total purchase amount spent by customers, and we have a few predictor columns that are coded $X_1, X_2, X_3, \ldots$, where we don't know what those codes mean. We might find that X_1 is an excellent predictor of the total amount spent. However, if we discover that X_1 is the amount spent on shipping, calculated as a percentage of the purchase amount, then obviously a model that uses shipping amount cannot be used to predict purchase amount, because the shipping amount is not known until the transaction is completed. This is known as *target leakage*. Another example is if we are trying to predict loan default at the time a customer applies for a loan. If our dataset includes only information on approved loan applications, we will not have information about what distinguishes defaulters from non-defaulters among denied applicants. A model based on approved loans alone can therefore not be used to predict defaulting behavior at the time of loan application, but rather only once a loan is approved. Finally, in certain applications (e.g., credit scoring), attributes such as gender and race are legally prohibited.

Outliers   The more data we are dealing with, the greater the chance of encountering erroneous values resulting from measurement error, data-entry error, or the like. If the erroneous value is in the same range as the rest of the data, it may be harmless. If it is well outside the range of the rest of the data (a misplaced decimal, for example), it may have a substantial effect on some of the machine learning procedures we plan to use.

Values that lie far away from the bulk of the data are called *outliers*. The term *far away* is deliberately left vague because what is or is not called an outlier is an arbitrary decision. Analysts use rules of thumb such as "anything over three standard deviations away from the mean is an outlier," but no statistical rule can tell us whether such an outlier is the result of an error. In this statistical sense, an outlier is not necessarily an invalid data point; it is just a distant one.

The purpose of identifying outliers is usually to call attention to values that need further review. We might come up with an explanation looking at the data—in the case of a misplaced decimal, this is likely. We might have no explanation, but know that the value is wrong—a temperature of 178°F for a sick person. We might conclude that the value is within the realm of possibility and leave it alone. Or, it might be that the outliers are what we are looking for—unusual financial transactions or travel patterns. All these are judgments best made by someone with *domain knowledge*, knowledge of the particular application being considered: direct mail, mortgage finance, and so on, as opposed to technical knowledge of statistical or machine learning procedures. Statistical procedures can do little beyond identifying the record as something that needs review.

If manual review is feasible, some outliers may be identified and corrected. In any case, if the number of records with outliers is very small, they might be treated as missing data. How do we inspect for outliers? One technique is to sort the records by the first column (e.g., using the R function *order()*), then review the data for very large or very small values in that column. Then repeat for each successive column. Another option is to examine the minimum and maximum values of each column using R's *min()* and *max()* functions. For a more automated approach that considers each record as a unit, rather than each column in isolation, clustering techniques (see Chapter 16) could be used to identify clusters of one or a few records that are distant from others. Those records could then be examined.

Missing Values   Typically, some records will contain missing values. If the number of records with missing values is small, those records might be omitted. However, if we have a large number of variables, even a small proportion of missing values can affect a lot of records. Even with only 30 variables, if only 5% of the values are missing (spread randomly and independently among records and variables), almost 80% of the records would have to be omitted from the analysis. (The chance that a given record would escape having a missing value is $0.95^{30} = 0.215$.)

An alternative to omitting records with missing values is to replace the missing value with an imputed value, based on the other values for that variable across all records. For example, among 30 variables, if household income is missing for a particular record, we might substitute the mean household income across all records. Doing so does not, of course, add any information about how household income affects the outcome variable. It merely allows us to proceed with the analysis and not lose the information contained in this record for the other 29 variables. Note that using such a technique will understate the variability in a dataset. However, we can assess variability and the performance of our machine learning technique using the holdout data, and therefore this need not present a major problem. One option is to replace missing values using fairly simple substitutes (e.g., mean, median). More sophisticated procedures do exist—for example, using linear regression, based on other variables, to fill in the missing values. These methods have been elaborated mainly for analysis of medical and scientific studies, where each patient or subject record comes at great expense. In machine learning, where data are typically plentiful, simpler methods usually suffice. Table 2.7 shows some R code to illustrate the use of the median to replace missing values using function *replace_na()* . Since the data are complete to begin with, the first step is an artificial one of creating some missing records for illustration purposes. The median is used for imputation, rather than the mean, to preserve the integer nature of the counts for BEDROOMS.

TABLE 2.7   IMPUTING MISSING DATA

---

 code for imputing missing data with median

```
# To illustrate missing data procedures, we first convert a few entries for
# BEDROOMS to NA's. Then we impute these missing values using the median of the
# remaining values.
rows.to.missing <- sample(row.names(housing.df), 10)
housing.df[rows.to.missing,]$BEDROOMS <- NA
summary(housing.df$BEDROOMS)
# Now we have 10 NA's and the median of the remaining values is 3.

# replace the missing values using the median of the remaining values
# use median() with na.rm=TRUE to ignore missing values when computing the median.
housing.df <- housing.df %>%
  replace_na(list(BEDROOMS=median(housing.df$BEDROOMS, na.rm=TRUE)))

summary(housing.df$BEDROOMS)
```

After adding missing values

```
> summary(housing.df$BEDROOMS)
   Min. 1st Qu.  Median   Mean 3rd Qu.    Max.    NA's
   1.00    3.00    3.00    3.23    4.00    9.00      10
```

After replacing missing values using median

```
> summary(housing.df$BEDROOMS)
   Min. 1st Qu.  Median   Mean 3rd Qu.    Max.
   1.00    3.00    3.00    3.23    4.00    9.00
```

Some datasets contain variables that have a very large number of missing values. In other words, a measurement is missing for a large number of records. In that case, dropping records with missing values will lead to a large loss of data. Imputing the missing values might also be useless, as the imputations are based on a small number of existing records. An alternative is to examine the importance of the predictor. If it is not very crucial, it can be dropped. If it is important, perhaps a proxy variable with fewer missing values can be used instead. When such a predictor is deemed central, the best solution is to invest in obtaining the missing data.

Significant time may be required to deal with missing data, as not all situations are susceptible to automated solutions. In a messy dataset, for example, a "0" might mean two things: (1) the value is missing, or (2) the value is actually zero. In the credit industry, a "0" in the "past due" variable might mean a customer who is fully paid up or a customer with no credit history at all—two very different situations. Human judgment may be required for individual cases or to determine a special rule to deal with the situation.

Normalizing (Standardizing) and Rescaling Data   Some algorithms require that the data be normalized before the algorithm can be implemented effectively. To normalize a variable, we subtract the mean from each value and then divide by the standard deviation. This operation is also sometimes called *standardizing* or *z-transformation*. In R, function *scale()* performs the z-transform operation. In effect, we are expressing each value as the "number of standard deviations away from the mean," also called a *z-score*.

Normalizing is one way to bring all variables to the same scale. Another popular approach is rescaling each variable to a [0,1] range. This is done by subtracting the minimum value and then dividing by the range. Subtracting the minimum shifts the variable origin to zero. Dividing by the range shrinks or expands the data to the range [0,1]. This is sometimes called *range transformation*. In R, the different types of rescaling can be done using function *rescale()* in the `scales` package.

To consider why normalizing or scaling to [0,1] might be necessary, consider the case of clustering. Clustering typically involves calculating a distance measure that reflects how far each record is from a cluster center or from other records. With multiple variables, different units will be used: days, dollars, counts, and so on. If the dollars are in the thousands and everything else is in the tens, the dollar variable will come to dominate the distance measure. Moreover, changing units from, say, days to hours or months, could alter the outcome completely.

Some machine learning software provide an option to normalize the data in those algorithms where it may be required. It is an option rather than an automatic feature of such algorithms, because there are situations where we want each variable to contribute to the distance measure in proportion to its original scale.

2.5 PREDICTIVE POWER AND OVERFITTING

In supervised learning, a key question presents itself: how well will our prediction or classification model perform when we apply it to new data? We are particularly interested in comparing the performance of various models so that we can choose the one we think will do the best when it is implemented in practice. A key concept is to make sure that our chosen model generalizes beyond the dataset that we have at hand. To assure generalization, we use the concept of *data partitioning* and try to avoid *overfitting*. These two important concepts are described next.

Overfitting

The more variables we include in a model, the greater the risk of overfitting the particular data used for modeling. What is overfitting?

In Table 2.8, we show hypothetical data about advertising expenditures in one time period and sales in a subsequent time period. A scatter plot of the data is shown in Figure 2.2. We could connect up these points with a smooth but complicated function, one that interpolates all these data points perfectly and leaves no error (residuals). This can be seen in Figure 2.3. However, we can see that such a curve is unlikely to be accurate, or even useful, in predicting future sales on the basis of advertising expenditures. For instance, it is hard to believe that increasing expenditures from $400 to $500 will actually decrease revenue.

A basic purpose of building a model is to represent relationships among variables in such a way that this representation will do a good job of predicting future outcome values on the basis of future predictor values. Of course, we want the model to do a good job of describing the data we have, but we are more interested in its performance with future data.

In the hypothetical advertising example, a simple straight line might do a better job than the complex function in terms of predicting future sales on the basis of advertising. Instead, we devised a complex function that fits the data perfectly, and in doing so, we overreached. We ended up modeling some variation in the data that is nothing more than chance variation. We mistreated the noise in the data as if it were a signal.

Similarly, we can add predictors to a model to sharpen its performance with the data at hand. Consider a database of 100 individuals, half of whom have contributed to a charitable cause. Information about income, family size, and zip code might do a fair job of predicting whether or not someone is a contributor. If we keep adding additional predictors, we can improve the performance of the model with the data at hand and reduce the misclassification error to a negligible level. However, this low error rate is misleading, because it probably includes spurious effects, which are specific to the 100 individuals, but not beyond that sample.

For example, one of the variables might be height. We have no basis in theory to suppose that tall people might contribute more or less to charity, but if there are several tall people in our sample and they just happened to contribute heavily to charity, our model might include a term for height—the taller you

TABLE 2.8	HYPOTHETICAL DATA ON ADVERTISING EXPENDITURES AND SUBSEQUENT SALES	
Advertising		**Sales**
239		514
364		789
602		550
644		1386
770		1394
789		1440
911		1354

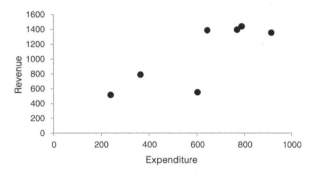

FIGURE 2.2   SCATTER PLOT FOR ADVERTISING AND SALES DATA

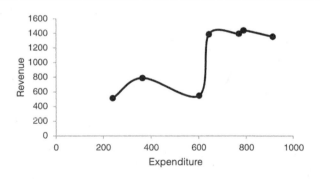

FIGURE 2.3   OVERFITTING: THIS FUNCTION FITS THE DATA WITH NO ERROR

are, the more you will contribute. Of course, when the model is applied to additional data, it is likely that this will not turn out to be a good predictor.

If the dataset is not much larger than the number of predictor variables, it is very likely that a spurious relationship like this will creep into the model. Continuing with our charity example, with a small sample just a few of whom are tall, whatever the contribution level of tall people may be, the algorithm is tempted to attribute it to their being tall. If the dataset is very large relative to the number of predictors, this is less likely to occur. In such a case, each predictor must help predict the outcome for a large number of cases, so the job it does is much less dependent on just a few cases, which might be flukes.

Somewhat surprisingly, even if we know for a fact that a higher-degree curve is the appropriate model, if the model-fitting dataset is not large enough, a lower-degree function (that is not as likely to fit the noise) is likely to perform better in terms of predicting new values. Overfitting can also result from the application of many different models, from which the best performing model is selected.

Creating and Using Data Partitions

At first glance, we might think it best to choose the model that did the best job of classifying or predicting the outcome variable of interest with the data at hand. However, when we use the same data both to develop the model and to assess its performance, we introduce an "optimism" bias. This is because when we choose the model that works best with the data, this model's superior performance comes from two sources:

- A superior model
- Chance aspects of the data that happen to match the chosen model better than they match other models

The latter is a particularly serious problem with techniques (such as trees and neural nets) that do not impose linear or other structure on the data, and thus end up overfitting it.

To address the overfitting problem, we simply divide (partition) our data and develop our model using only one of the partitions. After we have a model, we try it out on another partition and see how it performs, which we can measure in several ways. In a classification model, we can count the proportion of held-back records that were misclassified. In a prediction model, we can measure the residuals (prediction errors) between the predicted values and the actual values. This evaluation approach in effect mimics the deployment scenario, where our model is applied to data that it hasn't "seen."

We typically deal with two or three partitions: a training set, a validation set, and sometimes an additional holdout set. Partitioning the data into training, validation, and holdout sets is done either randomly according to predetermined proportions or by specifying which records go into which partition according to some relevant variable (e.g., in time series forecasting, the data are partitioned according to their chronological order). In most cases, the partitioning should be done randomly to minimize the chance of getting a biased partition. Note the varying nomenclature—the training partition is nearly always called "training" but the names for the other partitions can vary and overlap.

Training Partition   The training partition, typically the largest partition, contains the data used to build the various models we are examining. The same training partition is generally used to develop multiple models.

Validation Partition   The validation partition (sometimes called the *test partition*) is used to assess the predictive performance of each model so that you can compare models and choose the best one. In some algorithms (e.g., classification and regression trees, *k*-nearest neighbors), the validation partition may be used in an automated fashion to tune parameters and improve the model.

Holdout Partition   The holdout partition (sometimes called the *test partition* or *evaluation partition*) is used to assess the performance of the chosen model with new data.

Why have both a validation and a holdout partition? When we use the validation data to assess multiple models and then choose the model that performs best with the validation data, we again encounter another (lesser) facet of the overfitting problem—chance aspects of the validation data that happen to match the chosen model better than they match other models. In other words, by using the validation data to choose one of several models, the performance of the chosen model on the validation data will be overly optimistic.

The random features of the validation data that enhance the apparent performance of the chosen model will probably not be present in new data to which the model is applied. Therefore, we may have overestimated the accuracy of our model. The more models we test, the more likely it is that one of them will be particularly effective in modeling the noise in the validation data. Applying the model to the holdout data, which it has not seen before, will provide an unbiased estimate of how well the model will perform with new data. Figure 2.4 shows the three data partitions and their use in the machine learning process applied to the West Roxbury dataset. When we are concerned mainly with finding the best model and less with exactly how well it will do, we might use only

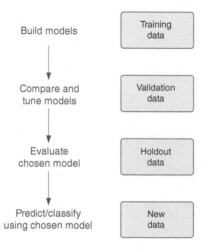

FIGURE 2.4   THREE DATA PARTITIONS AND THEIR ROLE IN THE MACHINE LEARNING PROCESS

training and validation partitions. Table 2.9 shows R code to partition the West
Roxbury data into two sets (training and validation) or into three sets (training,
validation, and test). This is done by first drawing a random sample of records
into the training set, then assigning the remaining records as validation. In the
case of three partitions, the validation records are chosen randomly from the
data after excluding the records already sampled into the training set. The function *createDataPartition()* from the `caret` package samples in such a way that the
distribution of the outcome variable is reproduced in the partitions.

TABLE 2.9   DATA PARTITIONING IN R

 code for partitioning the West Roxbury data into training, (validation), and
holdout sets

```
housing.df <- mlba::WestRoxbury %>%
  mutate(REMODEL=factor(REMODEL))

# use set.seed() to get the same partitions when re-running the R code.
set.seed(1)

## partitioning into training (60%) and holdout (40%)
# randomly sample 60% of the row IDs for training; the remaining 40% serve
# as holdout
train.rows <- sample(rownames(housing.df), nrow(housing.df)*0.6)
# collect all the columns with training row ID into training set:
train.df <- housing.df[train.rows, ]
# assign row IDs that are not already in the training set, into holdout
holdout.rows <- setdiff(rownames(housing.df), train.rows)
holdout.df <- housing.df[holdout.rows, ]

## partitioning into training (50%), validation (30%), holdout (20%)
# randomly sample 50% of the row IDs for training
train.rows <- sample(rownames(housing.df), nrow(housing.df)*0.5)

# sample 30% of the row IDs into the validation set, drawing only from records
# not already in the training set
# use setdiff() to find records not already in the training set
valid.rows <- sample(setdiff(rownames(housing.df), train.rows),
              nrow(housing.df)*0.3)

# assign the remaining 20% row IDs serve as holdout
holdout.rows <- setdiff(rownames(housing.df), union(train.rows, valid.rows))

# create the 3 data frames by collecting all columns from the appropriate rows
train.df <- housing.df[train.rows, ]
valid.df <- housing.df[valid.rows, ]
holdout.df <- housing.df[holdout.rows, ]

## partitioning into training (60%) and holdout (40%) using caret
set.seed(1)
idx <- caret::createDataPartition(housing.df$TOTAL.VALUE, p=0.6, list=FALSE)
train.df <- housing.df[idx, ]
holdout.df <- housing.df[-idx, ]
```

Note that with some algorithms, such as nearest-neighbor algorithms, records in the validation and holdout partitions, and in new data, are compared to records in the training data to find the nearest neighbor(s). As k-nearest neighbors is discussed in this book, the use of two partitions is an essential part of the classification or prediction process, not merely a way to improve or assess it. Nonetheless, we can still interpret the error in the validation data in the same way that we would interpret error from any other model.

Cross-Validation   When the number of records in our sample is small, data partitioning might not be advisable as each partition will contain too few records for model building and performance evaluation. Furthermore, some machine learning methods are sensitive to small changes in the training data, so that a different partitioning can lead to different results. An alternative to data partitioning is cross-validation, which is especially useful with small samples. Cross-validation, or *k-fold cross-validation*, is a procedure that starts with partitioning the data into "folds," or non-overlapping subsamples. Often we choose $k = 5$ folds, meaning that the data are randomly partitioned into five equal parts, where each fold has 20% of the observations. A model is then fit k times. Each time, one of the folds is used as the validation set and the remaining $k - 1$ folds serve as the training set. The result is that each fold is used once as the validation set, thereby producing predictions for every observation in the dataset. We can then combine the model's predictions on each of the k validation sets in order to evaluate the overall performance of the model. Sometimes cross-validation is built into a machine learning algorithm, with the results of the cross-validation used for choosing the algorithm's parameters (see, e.g., Chapter 9). The R package `caret` contains general functionality to validate models using cross-validation. We will demonstrate this in subsequent chapters.

2.6 BUILDING A PREDICTIVE MODEL

Let us go through the steps typical to many machine learning tasks using a familiar procedure: multiple linear regression. This will help you understand the overall process before we begin tackling new algorithms.

Modeling Process

We now describe in detail the various model stages using the West Roxbury home values example.

1. *Determine the purpose*: Let's assume that the purpose of our machine learning project is to predict the value of homes in West Roxbury for new records.

2. *Obtain the data*: We will use the 2014 West Roxbury housing data. The dataset in question is small enough that we do not need to sample from it—we can use it in its entirety.

3. *Explore, clean, and preprocess the data*: Let's look first at the description of the variables, also known as the "data dictionary," to be sure that we understand them all. These descriptions are available in Table 2.2. The variable names and descriptions in this dataset all seem fairly straightforward, but this is not always the case. Often variable names are cryptic, and their descriptions may be unclear or missing.

   It is useful to pause and think about what the variables mean and whether they should be included in the model. Consider the variable TAX. At first glance, we consider that the tax on a home is usually a function of its assessed value, so there is some circularity in the model—we want to predict a home's value using TAX as a predictor, yet TAX itself is determined by a home's value. TAX might be a very good predictor of home value in a numerical sense, but would it be useful if we wanted to apply our model to homes whose assessed value might not be known? For this reason, we will exclude TAX from the analysis.

   At this point we would also search for missing data and decide whether to remove rows or columns where data are missing, or impute the missing values.

   It is also useful to check for outliers that might be errors. For example, suppose that the column FLOORS (number of floors) looked like the one in Table 2.10, after sorting the data in descending order based on floors. We can tell right away that the 15 is in error—it is unlikely

TABLE 2.10	OUTLIER IN WEST ROXBURY DATA
FLOORS	**ROOMS**
15	8
2	10
1.5	6
1	6

   that a home has 15 floors. Since all other values are between 1 and 2 the decimal was probably misplaced and the value should be 1.5.

   Lastly, we create dummy variables for categorical variables. Here, we have one categorical variable: REMODEL, which has three categories. We will keep only two of the dummies because we plan to use a regression model. Table 2.11 shows the R code for all these preprocessing steps.

4. *Reduce the data dimension*: The West Roxbury dataset has been prepared for presentation with fairly low dimension—it has only 13 variables, and

TABLE 2.11   CLEANING AND PREPROCESSING DATA

 code for cleaning and preprocessing the West Roxbury dataset

```
library(tidyverse)
library(mlba)
library(fastDummies)

housing.df <- mlba::WestRoxbury %>%
  # remove rows with missing values
  drop_na() %>%
  # remove column TAX
  select(-TAX) %>%
  # make REMODEL a factor and convert to dummy variables
  mutate(REMODEL=factor(REMODEL)) %>%
  dummy_cols(select_columns=c('REMODEL'),
            remove_selected_columns=TRUE, remove_first_dummy=TRUE)
```

the single categorical variable considered has only three categories (and hence adds two dummy variables when used in a linear regression model). If we had many more variables, at this stage, we might want to apply a variable reduction technique, such as condensing multiple categories into a smaller number, or applying principal component analysis to consolidate multiple similar numerical variables (e.g., LIVING AREA, ROOMS, BEDROOMS, BATH, HALF BATH) into a smaller set.

5. *Determine the machine learning task*: The specific task is to predict the value of TOTAL.VALUE using the predictor variables. This is a supervised prediction task. For simplicity, we excluded several additional variables present in the original dataset, which have many categories (BLDG TYPE, ROOF TYPE, and EXT FIN). We therefore use all the numerical variables (except TAX) and the dummies created for the remaining categorical variables.

6. *Partition the data (for supervised tasks)*: In this case, we divide the data into two partitions: training and holdout (see Table 2.9). The training partition is used to build the model, and the holdout partition is used to see how well the model does when applied to new data. We need to specify the percent of the data used in each partition. *Note*: Although not used here, a validation partition might also be used when comparing models.

7. *Choose the technique*: In this case, it is multiple linear regression. Having divided the data into training and holdout partitions, we can build a multiple linear regression model with the training data. We want to predict the value of a house in West Roxbury on the basis of all the other predictors (except TAX).

8. *Use the algorithm to perform the task*: In R, we use the *lm()* function to predict house value with the training data, then use the same model to predict values for the holdout data. Chapter 6 on linear regression goes into more detail. Table 2.12 shows how the linear regression is trained on the training data (based on the 60–40 training/holdout partitions from Table 2.9), and then used to predict values for the records in the training data. These predictions are shown along with the actual values and the residuals (prediction errors). Note that the predicted values are often called the *fitted values*, since they are for the records to which the model was fit. The results for the holdout data are shown in Table 2.13.

TABLE 2.12   **TRAINING A REGRESSION MODEL AND GENERATING PREDICTIONS (FITTED VALUES) FOR THE TRAINING DATA**

 code for fitting a regression model to training data and obtaining fitted values

```
reg <- lm(TOTAL.VALUE ~ ., data=train.df)
train.res <- data.frame(actual=train.df$TOTAL.VALUE, predicted=reg$fitted.values,
                        residuals=reg$residuals)
head(train.res)
```

Partial Output

```
  actual predicted  residuals
1  344.2  384.4206 -40.220638
4  498.6  546.4628 -47.862759
5  331.5  347.9170 -16.417031
12 344.5  380.4297 -35.929727
13 315.5  313.1879   2.312083
15 326.2  345.3751 -19.175064
```

TABLE 2.13   **GENERATING PREDICTIONS FOR THE HOLDOUT DATA**

 code for applying the regression model to predict the holdout set (West Roxbury)

```
pred <- predict(reg, newdata=holdout.df)
holdout.res <- data.frame(actual=holdout.df$TOTAL.VALUE, predicted=pred,
                          residuals=holdout.df$TOTAL.VALUE - pred)
head(holdout.res)
```

Partial Output

```
  actual predicted  residuals
2  412.6  460.2777 -47.677744
3  330.1  359.3920 -29.291958
6  337.4  290.0277  47.372303
7  359.4  402.5332 -43.133242
8  320.4  314.0683   6.331652
9  333.5  339.8206  -6.320582
```

The prediction errors for the training and holdout data are compared in Table 2.14. Prediction error can be aggregated in several ways. Five common measures are shown in Table 2.14. The first is *mean error (ME)*, simply the average of the residuals (errors). In both cases, it is quite small relative to the units of TOTAL.VALUE, indicating that, on balance, predictions average about right—our predictions are "unbiased." Of course, this simply means that the positive and negative errors balance out. It tells us nothing about how large these errors are.

TABLE 2.14	PREDICTION ERROR METRICS FOR TRAINING AND HOLDOUT DATA (ERROR FIGURES ARE IN THOUSANDS OF $)

 code for computing model evaluation metrics

```
library(caret)
# compute metrics on training set
data.frame(
    ME = round(mean(train.res$residuals), 5),
    RMSE = RMSE(pred=train.res$predicted, obs=train.res$actual),
    MAE = MAE(pred=train.res$predicted, obs=train.res$actual)
)

# compute metrics on holdout set
data.frame(
    ME = round(mean(holdout.res$residuals), 5),
    RMSE = RMSE(pred=holdout.res$predicted, obs=holdout.res$actual),
    MAE = MAE(pred=holdout.res$predicted, obs=holdout.res$actual)
)
```

Output

```
# Training set
  ME     RMSE      MAE
1  0 42.14665 31.98717

# Holdout set
        ME     RMSE      MAE
1 -1.04237 43.90381 33.05476
```

The *RMS error* (root-mean-squared error, RMSE) is more informative of the error magnitude: it takes the square root of the average squared error, so it gives an idea of the typical error (whether positive or negative) in the same scale as that used for the original outcome variable. As we might expect, the RMS error for the holdout data ($43.9K), which the model is seeing for the first time in making these predictions, is slightly worse than that for the training data ($42.2K), which were used in training the model. However, both values here are close, which is a good indication the model is not overfitting the data. Additional measures are discussed in Chapter 5.

9. *Interpret the results*: At this stage, we would typically try other prediction algorithms (e.g., regression trees) and see how they do error-wise. We might also try different "settings" on the various models (e.g., we could use the *best subsets* option in multiple linear regression to choose a reduced set of variables that might perform better with the validation data). For this purpose of model comparison and model tuning, we should use the validation dataset instead of the holdout data. After choosing the best model—typically, the model with the lowest error on the validation data while also recognizing that "simpler is better"—we use that model to predict the output variable in fresh data. These steps are covered in more detail in the analysis of cases.

10. *Deploy the model*: After the best model is chosen, it is applied to new data to predict TOTAL.VALUE for homes where this value is unknown. This was, of course, the original purpose. Predicting the output value for new records is called *scoring*. For predictive tasks, scoring produces predicted numerical values. For classification tasks, scoring produces classes and/or propensities. Table 2.15 shows an example of a data frame with three homes to be scored using our linear regression model. Note that all the required predictor columns are present, and the output column is absent.

TABLE 2.15   DATA FRAME WITH THREE RECORDS TO BE SCORED

```
# new.data can be read from a csv file, or defined directly in R.

new.data
  TOTAL.VALUE LOT.SQFT YR.BUILT GROSS.AREA LIVING.AREA FLOORS ROOMS BEDROOMS
1       303.5     4200     1960       2670        1710    2.0    10        4
2       301.4     6444     1940       2886        1474    1.5     6        3
3       339.9     5035     1925       3264        1523    1.0     6        2
  FULL.BATH HALF.BATH KITCHEN FIREPLACE REMODEL_Old REMODEL_Recent
1         1         1       1         1           0              0
2         1         1       1         1           0              0
3         1         0       1         0           0              1
pred <- predict(reg, newdata = new.data)
pred
       1        2        3
390.0638 377.1395 348.3657
```

2.7   USING R FOR MACHINE LEARNING ON A LOCAL MACHINE

An important aspect of the machine learning process is that the heavy-duty analysis does not necessarily require a huge number of records. The dataset to be analyzed may have millions of records, or be part of a regular ongoing flow, but in applying multiple linear regression or applying a classification tree, the use of a sample of 20,000 is likely to yield as accurate an answer as that obtained when using the entire dataset. The principle involved is the same as the principle behind polling: if sampled judiciously, 2000 voters can give an estimate of the entire population's opinion within one or two percentage points. (See "How Many Variables and How Much Data" in Section 2.4 for further discussion.)

Therefore, in most cases, the number of records required in each partition (training, validation, and holdout) can be accommodated within the memory limit allowed in R, (to check and increase memory limit in R, use function *memory.limit()*).

When we apply Big Data analytics in R, it might be useful to remove unused objects (function *rm()*) and call the garbage collection (function *gc()*) afterwards.

2.8 AUTOMATING MACHINE LEARNING SOLUTIONS[6]

Automating machine learning solutions is often termed "machine learning operations" ("MLOps"), or "AI engineering." In most supervised machine learning applications, the goal is not a static, one-time analysis of a particular dataset. Rather, we want to develop a model that can be used on an ongoing basis to predict or classify new records. Our initial analysis will be in prototype mode, while we explore and define the problem and test different models. We will follow all the steps outlined earlier in this chapter.

At the end of that process, we will typically want our chosen model to be deployed in automated fashion. For example, the US Internal Revenue Service (IRS) receives several hundred million tax returns per year—it does not want to have to pull each tax return out into an Excel sheet or other environment separate from its main database to determine the predicted probability that the return is fraudulent. Rather, it would prefer that determination be made as part of the normal tax filing environment and process. Music streaming services, such as Pandora or Spotify, need to determine "recommendations" for next songs quickly for each of millions of users; there is no time to extract the data for manual analysis.

In practice, this is done by building the chosen algorithm into the computational setting in which the rest of the process lies. A tax return is entered directly into the IRS system by a tax preparer, a predictive algorithm is immediately applied to the new data in the IRS system, and a predicted classification is decided by the algorithm. Business rules would then determine what happens with that classification. In the IRS case, the rule might be "if no predicted fraud,

---

[6]This section copyright 2021 Peter Bruce, Galit Shmueli, and Victor Diloreto; used by permission.

continue routine processing; if fraud is predicted, alert an examiner for possible audit."

This flow of the tax return from data entry, into the IRS system, through a predictive algorithm, then back out to a human user is an example of a "data pipeline." The different components of the system communicate with one another via application programming interfaces (APIs) that establish locally valid rules for transmitting data and associated communications. An API for a machine learning algorithm would establish the required elements for a predictive algorithm to work—the exact predictor variables, their order, data formats, and so on. It would also establish the requirements for communicating the results of the algorithm. Algorithms to be used in an automated data pipeline will need to be compliant with the rules of the APIs where they operate.

Finally, once the computational environment is set and functioning, the machine learning work is not done. The environment in which a model operates is typically dynamic, and predictive models often have a short shelf life—one leading consultant finds they rarely continue to function effectively for more than a year. So, even in a fully deployed state, models must be periodically checked and reevaluated. Once performance flags, it is time to return to prototype mode and see if a new model can be developed.

As you can imagine, these computational environments are complex, and, as of 2022, large companies are only beginning to construct them. They are often driven to do so by the force of circumstance. In the following section, we describe two examples of such environments.

Predicting Power Generator Failure[6]

Sira-Kvina, a major hydro-electric power company that supplies 7% of Norway's power, found that generator failures were taking a long time to diagnose, leading to lengthy offline periods and loss of revenue and customer dissatisfaction. The company was using an engineering checklist approach: imagine a more complex version of the troubleshooting guide that comes with a fancy appliance, or the advice you encounter when trying to fix a software problem. Such an approach, however, could not begin to make use of all the data that comes in from hundreds of sensors producing tens of thousands of readings per day. A team from Elder Research investigated one particularly lengthy and costly outage and, after much data wrangling, visualization, and analysis, identified a set of separate events which, when they happened together, caused the failure.

---

[6]Thanks to Victor Diloreto, Chief Technical Officer of Elder Research, Inc., who wrote portions of this segment.

Moreover, generator failures were often preceded by a set of defined temperature spikes in one specific sensor (you can read a summary of the analysis at www. statistics.com/sira-kvina-hydro-power-the-case-of-the-faulty-generator). But an after-the-fact detective hunt is inherently unsatisfactory, since the generator down-time has already occurred. What is really needed is *proactive preventive maintenance*, triggered by advance warnings that are predictive of failure. Elder built such a system for Sira-Kvina. Machine learning models that predict generator failure are the key analytical component, but they are embedded in a system that must also handle, in addition to training and fitting a model, the following tasks:

- collecting and ingesting data from sensors
- transforming data (especially aggregating and disaggregating granular time series data)
- passing alerts from models to humans and other elements of the system
- providing visualization tools for analysts
- applying case management of anomalies
- adding manual labels applied by analysts, to facilitate further training.

Dozens of tools are involved in this structure. Figure 2.5 illustrates how different layers of tools contribute to this process.

FIGURE 2.5   **LAYERS OF TOOLS SUPPORTING MACHINE LEARNING AUTOMATION**

The "Infrastructure" base layer provides base computing capability, memory, and networking, either on-premises or in the cloud. The next layer up supports basic services for the layers above it. "Security" provides user admin capabilities, permission levels, and networking and access rules. "Monitoring" ingests logs, implements needed thresholds, and issues alerts. "Automation" has a more limited meaning than the overall topic of this section: it refers to bringing up, configuring, and tearing down tools and infrastructure as needed.

"Resource management" provides the oversight of the various resources used throughout the stack. This area is closely coupled to monitoring: understanding what resources could be coming close to exhaustion is important for maintenance purposes.

"Testing/debugging" is self-explanatory, while the "data collection" layer refers primarily to the data store (data warehouse, data lake, or data lake house). In the Sira–Kvina case, there is a raw immutable data store (IDS) where all source data is collected, plus an analytic base table (ABT) that holds derivatives of the main data store needed for analysis. The "data ETL" (Extract, Transform, Load) layer provides the tools to create these derivatives. The verification step within this layer checks that the transformations, aggregations, or any formula used to take a raw piece of data and convert it to something else is doing the job we think it's supposed to do. This verification function is wired into the monitoring capability of the system, which flags any issue with an alert to maintainers of the system. The modeling layer contains the model(s) that make predictions (i.e., the primary focus of this book) and is accompanied by the model-monitoring section, which checks that the model is performing to expectations. Tools in the latter are tied into the lower-level infrastructure monitoring to generate alerts when a model is missing on expectations. Finally, the "delivery" layer is the user window into the system, and can represent simple things like a spreadsheet or a text file, or be as elaborate as an enterprise-wide tool like Tableau or Power BI.

From the above, you can see that Sira–Kvina's predictive models occupy only a small part of the data pipeline through which sensor data could flow and, when needed, trigger alerts to operators about system components that need attention. For a more far-reaching structure, consider Uber.

Uber's Michelangelo

Uber, which provides ride-sharing, meal delivery services, and more, uses real-time predictive models for several purposes including:

- matching the optimal driver for a customer ride request
- predicting customer pickup time
- predicting ride duration
- estimating pricing (including which peak pricing tier applies)
- predicting Uber Eats delivery time.

To integrate model-building with deployment, Uber built its own machine learning (ML) structure (MLOps) called Michelangelo. Prior to Michelangelo, in Uber's words, "the impact of ML at Uber was limited to what a few data scientists and engineers could build in a short time frame with mostly open source tools. Specifically, there were no systems in place to build reliable, uniform, and reproducible pipelines for creating and managing training and prediction data at scale."

Uber is a company essentially built on data science; at more traditional companies, the model deployment challenge is exacerbated by the fact that data science and data engineering are often considered separate jobs and disciplines. One major retailer described the problem as follows: "Our highly trained data scientists would build great models, give them to the engineers, who would say 'thank you very much, now we will need to build it again from scratch'."

Uber's Michelangelo is a development and deployment environment that Uber's data scientists use for a variety of models. It provides integration with the company's data stores and standard tools to build pipelines to ingest data. It has tools to split data into training and validation partitions and to ensure that new data to be predicted follows the same format.

Some of Uber's goals (e.g., predicting the restaurant prep time component of Uber Eats delivery time) are not extremely time-sensitive, and batch processing can be used. Others (e.g., finding a driver) require nearly instantaneous action ("low-latency" response). Michelangelo supports both batch processing and real-time low-latency processing (Uber calls it "online"). Uber is constantly adding huge amounts of granular customer and driver data to its data store, so Michelangelo must have sufficient compute, data storage, and data flow capacity to scale efficiently. It also provides a facility to standardize feature definition and storage, so that data can be shared easily across users. It provides visualization and exploration tools for the prototyping and prep phases. Finally, it collects and makes available (via APIs and via a web user interface) standard information about each model[7]:

- Who trained the model
- Start and end times of the training job
- Full model configuration (features used, hyperparameter values, etc.)
- Reference to training and test datasets
- Distribution and relative importance of each feature
- Model accuracy metrics
- Standard charts and graphs for each model type (e.g., ROC curve, PR curve, and confusion matrix for a binary classifier)
- Full learned parameters of the model
- Summary statistics for model visualization.

---

[7]This list is from the Uber Engineering blog at https://eng.uber.com/michelangelo-machine-learning-platform; see also the discussion of "Model Cards" in Chapter 22.

Finally, to ensure that model performance does not degrade over time, Michelangelo has facilities for periodically storing a sample of predictions, comparing predictions to outcomes, and sending signals to operators when the margin exceeds a certain standard.

A variety of tools, both proprietary and open source, can be used to build the MLOps pipeline. In the Sira-Kvina case, the infrastructure layer was built in the cloud using Amazon Web Services Cloud Development Kit (AWS CDK). AWS's Simple Notification Service (SNS) was used to transmit verification and monitoring messages between layers. Uber built Michelangelo with open source tools such as the Cassandra distributed database system and Kafka brokers to stream verification and monitoring messages.

In this book, our focus will be on the prototyping phase—all the steps that go into properly defining the model and developing and selecting a model. You should be aware, though, that most of the actual work of implementing a machine learning solution lies in the automated deployment phase. Much of this work is not in the analytic domain; rather, it lies in the domains of databases and computer engineering, to assure that detailed nuts and bolts of an automated dataflow all work properly. Nonetheless, some familiarity with the requirements and components of automated pipelines will benefit the data scientist, as it will facilitate communication with the engineers who must ultimately deploy their work.

2.9 Ethical Practice in Machine Learning

Prior to the advent of Internet-connected devices, the biggest source of big data was public interaction on the Internet. Social media users, as well as shoppers and searchers on the Internet, have made an implicit deal with the big companies that provide these services: users can take advantage of powerful search, shopping, and social interaction tools for free, and, in return, the companies get access to user data. Since the first edition of this book was published in 2007, ethical issues in machine learning and data science have received increasing attention, and new rules and laws have emerged. As a business analytics professional or data scientist, you must be aware of the rules and follow them, but you must also think about the implications and use of your work once it goes beyond the prototyping phase. It is now common for businesses, governments, and other organizations to require the explicit incorporation of ethical principles and audits into machine learning and AI applications. Chapter 22, Responsible Data Science, covers this topic in more detail.

MACHINE LEARNING SOFTWARE TOOLS:
THE STATE OF THE MARKET

by Herb Edelstein

Over time, three things are steadily increasing: the amount of data available for analysis, the power of the computing environment, and the number of organizations taking advantage of the first two changes for a widening variety of analytical and predictive goals. Software products for machine learning must deliver more comprehensive coverage than ever before. The term "data science" has become ubiquitous and covers the spectrum of tasks required for business analytics, starting with data engineering (including data gathering, building databases, and making the data suitable for analytics) and machine learning. Machine learning starts with describing and understanding the data, often utilizing advanced visualization techniques followed by sophisticated model building. After the models are constructed, they must be efficiently deployed, so an organization can meet its goals. At the same time, the amount of data collected today presents a great opportunity to tease out subtle relationships that allow precise predictions while unfortunately making it easy to find spurious relationships or statistically significant results that have no practical value. The range of users that must be supported has also increased. Software must support people with diverse backgrounds, ranging from extensive education in machine learning, statistics, and programming to professionals performing such tasks as sales and marketing, risk analysis, fraud detection, reliability prediction, and engineering and scientific analysis. One of the biggest contributors to the hardware environment for machine learning is the spread of high-powered GPU's (Graphic Processing Units). While originally intended for accelerating 3D graphics, meeting the computational requirements for fast 3D graphics also significantly accelerates machine learning. The algorithms used by the major cloud vendors all take advantage of GPUs. However, not all GPUs have the same interface and therefore not all stand-alone software will necessarily take advantage of the GPUs on your computer. Machine learning has also improved model building. As you read this book, you will see that the various algorithms have a plethora of tuning options to help you build the best model. While many experienced model builders can do a good job of manual tuning, it is impossible to try all the combinations of parameters that control the learning process (called hyperparameters) by hand, so an increasing number of products offer the ability to automatically tune the hyperparameters. The more hyperparameters, the larger the number of combinations to be searched. Autotuning can be particularly useful in building the neural networks used for deep learning.

R and Python

One of the most common open source statistical analysis and machine learning software languages is R. It is the successor to a Bell Labs program called S, which was commercialized as S+. Widely used in the academic community, R has become one of the most popular machine learning tools. New algorithms are frequently available first in R. It includes an enormous collection of machine learning algorithms contained in what are known as "packages," along with an abundance of statistical algorithms, data management tools, and visualization tools. Over 10,000 packages are in the CRAN (Comprehensive R Archive Network) library, and there are numerous packages outside of CRAN. This large number provides a great deal of choice. There are multiple packages that will perform essentially the same task, allowing the user to choose the one they think is most appropriate. However, there is a downside to all these options in that there is no uniformity in the R community. For example, in addition to the base R graphing tools, there are the packages Lattice, ggplot2, Plotly, and others. Because it is essentially a special-purpose programming language, R has enormous flexibility but a steeper learning curve than many of the Graphical User Interface (GUI)-based tools. The most common tool used with R is RStudio, an interactive development environment that facilitates the use of R. RStudio has also created a collection of packages called the "tidyverse" which are designed to enhance the ability of R to manipulate and graph data. These have become widely used in the R community. In particular, R has excelled in creating publication quality visualizations using the ggplot2 package (part of the tidyverse) which is based on Leland Wilkinson's groundbreaking book *The Grammar of Graphics*. Some GUIs for R try to improve its usability. R Commander is the oldest of these and like R is extensible with add-on packages. Its creator views it as a gateway to writing R code for more complex analyses. BlueSky is a more recent interface that not only is more comprehensive than R Commander but also allows the user to create their own dialogs to add R functionality.

Python is a widely used general programming language (developed in the 1980s by Guido van Rossum and named after the British comedy group Monty Python) that has overtaken R as the most popular machine learning package. This is due in part to its speed advantage over R, its data-wrangling capabilities, and its better functionality as a programming language. Furthermore, there is an interface to R that allows you to access R functionality should you need to. Pandas is an open source Python library that provides extensive data-wrangling capabilities. Scikit-Learn is another open source Python library that provides a very comprehensive suite of tools for machine learning that is widely used in the Python community. Python is more often used for deep neural networks than R. While R is still dominating in academia, Python appears to be dominating in commercial applications.

Stand-Alone Machine Learning Software

Many stand-alone software packages have appeared that are intended to simplify the process of creating machine learning models. The number of machine learning packages has grown considerably in response to the increasing demand. IBM offers two machine learning platforms: Watson and SPSS Modeler. Watson is cloud based and offers the same ability to utilize GPUs as the other major cloud providers. SPSS Modeler is aimed at local implementation. However, Watson Studio includes Modeler which can run under Studio. In addition to running on IBM's cloud servers, Watson is also available to run on local computers. SAS is the largest company specializing in statistical software. Recognizing the growing importance of machine learning, SAS added Enterprise Miner, a workflow drag-and-drop software, in 1999 to address this need. More recently, SAS created Viya

Machine Learning. SAS Enterprise Miner has multiple client interfaces, whereas Viya's interface is a unified HTML5 interface. While both Enterprise Miner and Viya can operate in the cloud, Viya has a wider range of interfaces to the major cloud providers. It is aimed more directly at the data science and machine learning communities. SAS's JMP Pro has a comprehensive set of machine learning tools. It is widely used in the science and engineering world, but also competes in commercial and government settings. It has a unique GUI that is centered on what you are trying to accomplish. For example, to analyze data, you go to the Analyze menu, choose Predictive Modeling, and then select a modeling method (which JMP calls a platform). JMP has its own scripting language, JSL, for tasks that are more complicated than can be accomplished through the GUI, but it also interfaces with R and Python.

Analytic Solver Data Mining (ASDM) is an add-in for Microsoft Excel that provides access to a suite of machine learning tools as well as data engineering capabilities without the need for programming. It is widely used in MBA programs because of its accessibility to students, but it is also used in industry, especially with its cloud interface to Microsoft's Azure. The original version (XLMiner) was developed by one of the authors of this book (Patel). It provides not only traditional machine learning tools such as tree-based learning and neural nets, but also a variety of ensemble methods which have become central to accurate prediction. Additionally, ASDM provides text mining capabilities.

Drag-and-Drop Workflow Interfaces

Since machine learning solutions are typically deployed in workflow pipelines (data ingestion > model fitting > model assessment > data scoring), some software use a drag-and-drop icon and arrows interface, where icons represent different stages of the process, and arrows connect different stages. While there are a variety of such software, we'll mention a few: IBM Modeler is based on the SPSS Clementine program, which had one of the first workflow-based interfaces. This style of interface links the data engineering, exploration, machine learning, model evaluation, and deployment steps together. Modeler has a wide range of statistical and machine learning algorithms and provides interfaces to Watson, Python, and R for additional functionality.

RapidMiner Studio was originally developed in Germany in 2001 (the original name was YALE) and has grown into a widely used platform for machine learning. It has a workflow drag-and-drop interface that supports data import, data cleansing, graphics, a large variety of machine learning tools, and model evaluation. One of the most difficult problems in building good models is feature selection. RapidMiner provides a number of tools including genetic algorithms for feature selection. Its Turbo Prep and Auto Model interfaces offer support for data preparation tasks and auto-tuning hyperparameters for standard machine learning algorithms, respectively. RapidMiner also has integration with R and Python to extend its capabilities. Orange is a visual interface for Python and Scikit-Learn using wrappers designed to make analysis easier. Developed at the University of Ljubljana in Slovenia, Orange is an open-source software that uses a workflow interface to provide a greatly improved way to use Python for analysis.

Cloud Computing Cloud-computing vendors are actively promoting their services for machine learning. These products are oriented more toward application developers than machine learning prototypers and business analysts. A big part of the attraction of machine learning in the cloud is the ability to store and manage enormous amounts of data without requiring the expense and complexity of building an in-house capability. This can also enable a more rapid implementation of large distributed multi-user applications. Many of the non-cloud-based machine learning vendors provide interfaces to cloud storage to enable their tools to work with mammoth amounts of data. For example, RapidMiner offers a product RapidMiner AI Hub (formerly RapidMiner Server) that leverages the standard cloud computing platforms (Amazon AWS, Google Cloud, MS Azure) for automation and deployment of machine learning models. Amazon has several machine learning services. SageMaker is a machine learning platform that provides developers with functionality including acquiring and wrangling data, building models based on its large collection of algorithms, and deploying the resulting models. Models can be used with data stored in Amazon Web Services (AWS) or exported for use in local environments. There is also an automatic machine learning process that will choose the appropriate algorithm and create the model. AWS also has what it calls Deep Learning AMI's (Amazon Machine Images) that are preconfigured virtual machines with deep learning frameworks such as TensorFlow.

Google is very active in cloud analytics with its Vertex AI. The user can either custom train models or use Vertex AI's AutoML which will automatically build models based on your selected targets. Unfortunately, this is not a transparent process, and there is a limitation in the size of the data—100 GB or 100 million rows of tabular data. Models such as TensorFlow deep learning models can be exported for use in local environments. Microsoft is an active player in cloud analytics with its Azure Machine Learning. Azure ML also supports a workflow interface making it more accessible to the nonprogrammer data scientist. Along with Amazon and Google, Azure Machine Learning also supports an automated machine learning mode. ASDM's cloud version is based on Microsoft Azure. Machine learning plays a central role in enabling many organizations to optimize everything from manufacturing and production to marketing and sales. New storage options and analytical tools promise even greater capabilities. The key is to select technology that's appropriate for an organization's unique goals and constraints. As always, human judgment is the most important component of a machine learning solution. The focus of *Machine Learning for Business Analytics* is on a comprehensive understanding of the different techniques and algorithms used in machine learning, and less on the data management requirements of real-time deployment of machine learning models.

***

Herb Edelstein is president of Two Crows Consulting (www.twocrows.com), a leading machine learning consulting firm near Washington, DC. He is an internationally recognized expert in machine learning and data warehousing, a widely published author on these topics, and a popular speaker.
©2015–2022 Herb Edelstein.

PROBLEMS

2.1 Assuming that machine learning techniques are to be used in the following cases, identify whether the task required is supervised or unsupervised learning.

  a. Deciding whether to issue a loan to an applicant based on demographic and financial data (with reference to a database of similar data on prior customers).

  b. In an online bookstore, making recommendations to customers concerning additional items to buy based on the buying patterns in prior transactions.

  c. Identifying a network data packet as dangerous (virus, hacker attack) based on comparison to other packets whose threat status is known.

  d. Identifying segments of similar customers.

  e. Predicting whether a company will go bankrupt based on comparing its financial data to those of similar bankrupt and nonbankrupt firms.

  f. Estimating the repair time required for an aircraft based on a trouble ticket.

  g. Automated sorting of mail by zip code scanning.

  h. Printing of custom discount coupons at the conclusion of a grocery store checkout based on what you just bought and what others have bought previously.

2.2 Describe the difference in roles assumed by the validation partition and the holdout partition.

2.3 Consider the sample from a database of credit applicants in Table 2.16. Comment on the likelihood that it was sampled randomly and whether it is likely to be a useful sample.

TABLE 2.16   SAMPLE FROM A DATABASE OF CREDIT APPLICATIONS

OBS	CHECK ACCT	DURATION	HISTORY	NEW CAR	USED CAR	FURNITURE	RADIO TV	EDUC	RETRAIN	AMOUNT	SAVE ACCT	RESPONSE
1	0	6	4	0	0	0	1	0	0	1169	4	1
8	1	36	2	0	1	0	0	0	0	6948	0	1
16	0	24	2	0	0	0	1	0	0	1282	1	0
24	1	12	4	0	1	0	0	0	0	1804	1	1
32	0	24	2	0	0	1	0	0	0	4020	0	1
40	1	9	2	0	0	0	1	0	0	458	0	1
48	0	6	2	0	1	0	0	0	0	1352	2	1
56	3	6	1	1	0	0	0	0	0	783	4	1
64	1	48	0	0	0	0	0	0	1	14421	0	0
72	3	7	4	0	0	0	1	0	0	730	4	1
80	1	30	2	0	0	1	0	0	0	3832	0	1
88	1	36	2	0	0	0	0	1	0	12612	1	0
96	1	54	0	0	0	0	0	0	1	15945	0	0
104	1	9	4	0	0	1	0	0	0	1919	0	1
112	2	15	2	0	0	0	0	1	0	392	0	1

2.4 Consider the sample from a bank database shown in Table 2.17; it was selected randomly from a larger database to be the training set. *Personal Loan* indicates whether a solicitation for a personal loan was accepted and is the response variable. A campaign is planned for a similar solicitation in the future and the bank is looking for a model that will identify likely responders. Examine the data carefully and indicate what your next step would be.

TABLE 2.17   SAMPLE FROM A BANK DATABASE

OBS	AGE	EXPERIENCE	INCOME	ZIP CODE	FAMILY	CC AVG	EDUC	MORTGAGE	PERSONAL LOAN	SECURITIES ACCT
1	25	1	49	91107	4	1.6	1	0	0	1
4	35	9	100	94112	1	2.7	2	0	0	0
5	35	8	45	91330	4	1	2	0	0	0
9	35	10	81	90089	3	0.6	2	104	0	0
10	34	9	180	93023	1	8.9	3	0	1	0
12	29	5	45	90277	3	0.1	2	0	0	0
17	38	14	130	95010	4	4.7	3	134	1	0
18	42	18	81	94305	4	2.4	1	0	0	0
21	56	31	25	94015	4	0.9	2	111	0	0
26	43	19	29	94305	3	0.5	1	97	0	0
29	56	30	48	94539	1	2.2	3	0	0	0
30	38	13	119	94104	1	3.3	2	0	1	0
35	31	5	50	94035	4	1.8	3	0	0	0
36	48	24	81	92647	3	0.7	1	0	0	0
37	59	35	121	94720	1	2.9	1	0	0	0
38	51	25	71	95814	1	1.4	3	198	0	0
39	42	18	141	94114	3	5	3	0	1	1
41	57	32	84	92672	3	1.6	3	0	0	1

2.5 Using the concept of overfitting, explain why when a model is fit to training data, zero error with those data is not necessarily good.

2.6 In fitting a model to classify prospects as purchasers or nonpurchasers, a certain company drew the training data from internal data that include demographic and purchase information. Future data to be classified will be lists purchased from other sources, with demographic (but not purchase) data included. It was found that "refund issued" was a useful predictor in the training data. Why is this not an appropriate variable to include in the model?

2.7 A dataset has 1000 records and 50 variables with 5% of the values missing, spread randomly throughout the records and variables. An analyst decides to remove records with missing values. About how many records would you expect to be removed?

2.8 Normalize the data in Table 2.18, showing calculations.

TABLE 2.18

Age	Income ($)
25	49,000
56	156,000
65	99,000
32	192,000
41	39,000
49	57,000

2.9 Statistical distance between records can be measured in several ways. Consider Euclidean distance, measured as the square root of the sum of the squared differences. For the first two records in Table 2.18, it is

$$\sqrt{(25 - 56)^2 + (49{,}000 - 156{,}000)^2}.$$

Can normalizing the data change which two records are farthest from each other in terms of Euclidean distance?

2.10 Two models are applied to a dataset that has been partitioned. Model A is considerably more accurate than model B on the training data, but slightly less accurate than model B on the validation data. Which model are you more likely to consider for final deployment?

2.11 The dataset *mlba::ToyotaCorolla* contains data on used cars on sale during the late summer of 2004 in the Netherlands. It has 1436 records containing details on 38 variables, including *Price*, *Age*, *Kilometers*, *HP*, and other specifications. We plan to analyze the data using various data mining techniques described in future chapters.

  a. The dataset has two categorical variables, *Fuel_Type* and *Color*. Describe how you would convert these to binary variables. Confirm this using R's functions to transform categorical variables into dummies. What would you do with the variable *Model*?

  b. Prepare the dataset (as factored into dummies) for machine learning techniques of supervised learning by creating partitions in R. Select variables, and use default values for the random seed and partitioning percentages for training (50%), validation (30%), and holdout (20%) sets. Describe the roles that these partitions will play in modeling.

2.12 [For class or group discussion:] Sort the West Roxbury data (*mlba::WestRoxbury*) by YR BUILT and report any anomalies. Discuss the implications for the analysis done in this chapter and possible steps to take.

## PART II

Data Exploration and Dimension Reduction

## CHAPTER 3

Data Visualization

In this chapter, we describe a set of plots that can be used to explore the multidimensional nature of a dataset. We present basic charts (bar charts, line graphs, and scatter plots), distribution plots (boxplots and histograms), and different enhancements that expand the capabilities of these plots to visualize more information. We focus on how the different visualizations and operations can support machine learning tasks, from supervised tasks (prediction, classification, and time series forecasting) to unsupervised tasks, and provide a few guidelines on specific visualizations to use with each machine learning task. We also describe the advantages of interactive visualization over static plots. This chapter concludes with a presentation of specialized plots suitable for data with special structure (hierarchical, network, and geographical).

3.1 USES OF DATA VISUALIZATION[1]

The popular saying "a picture is worth a thousand words" refers to the ability to condense diffused verbal information into a compact and quickly understood graphical image. In the case of numbers, data visualization and numerical summarization provide us with both a powerful tool to explore data and an effective way to present results.

Where do visualization techniques fit into the machine learning process, as described so far? They are primarily used in the preprocessing portion of the machine learning process. Visualization supports data cleaning by finding incorrect values, (e.g., patients whose age is 999 or −1), missing values, duplicate rows, columns with all the same value, and the like. Visualization techniques are

---

[1] Randall Pruim assisted with the ggplot code in this chapter. This section copyright © 2019 Datastats, LLC, Galit Shmueli, and Peter Bruce.

Machine Learning for Business Analytics: Concepts, Techniques, and Applications in R, Second Edition.
Galit Shmueli, Peter C. Bruce, Peter Gedeck, Inbal Yahav, and Nitin R. Patel
© 2023 John Wiley & Sons, Inc. Published 2023 by John Wiley & Sons, Inc.

also useful for variable derivation and selection: they can help determine which variables to include in the analysis and which might be redundant. They can also help with determining appropriate bin sizes, should binning of numerical variables be needed, (e.g., a numerical outcome variable might need to be converted to a binary variable if a yes/no decision is required). They can also play a role in combining categories as part of the data reduction process. Finally, if the data have yet to be collected and collection is expensive (as with the Pandora project at its outset; see Chapter 7), visualization methods can help determine, using a sample, which variables and metrics are useful.

In this chapter, we focus on the use of graphical presentations for the purpose of *data exploration*, particularly with relation to predictive analytics. Although our focus is not on visualization for the purpose of data reporting, this chapter offers ideas as to the effectiveness of various graphical displays for the purpose of data presentation. These offer a wealth of useful presentations beyond tabular summaries and basic bar charts, which are currently the most popular form of data presentation in the business environment. For an excellent discussion of using plots to report business data, see Few (2012). In terms of reporting machine learning results graphically, we describe common graphical displays elsewhere in the book, some of which are technique-specific [e.g., dendrograms for hierarchical clustering (Chapter 16), network charts for social network analysis (Chapter 20), and tree charts for classification and regression trees (Chapter 9)] while others are more general [e.g., receiver operating characteristic (ROC) curves and lift charts for classification (Chapter 5) and profile plots and heatmaps for clustering (Chapter 16)].

Note: The term "graph" has two meanings in statistics. It can refer, particularly in popular usage, to any of a number of figures to represent data (e.g., line chart, bar plot, histogram, etc.). In a more technical use, it refers to the data structure and visualization in networks (see Chapter 20). Using the terms "chart" and "plot" for the visualizations we explore in this chapter avoids this confusion.

Data exploration is a mandatory initial step whether or not more formal analysis follows. Graphical exploration can support free-form exploration for the purpose of understanding the data structure, cleaning the data (e.g., identifying unexpected gaps or "illegal" values), identifying outliers, discovering initial patterns (e.g., correlations among variables and surprising clusters), and generating interesting questions. Graphical exploration can also be more focused, geared toward specific questions of interest. In the machine learning context, a combination is needed: free-form exploration performed with the purpose of supporting a specific goal.

Graphical exploration can range from generating very basic plots to using operations such as filtering and zooming interactively to explore a set of interconnected visualizations that include advanced features such as color and multiple panels. This chapter is not meant to be an exhaustive guidebook on visualization techniques, but instead discusses main principles and features that support data exploration in a machine learning context. We start by describing varying levels of sophistication in terms of visualization and show the advantages of different features and operations. Our discussion is from the perspective of how visualization supports the subsequent machine learning goal. In particular, we distinguish between supervised and unsupervised learning; within supervised learning, we also further distinguish between classification (categorical outcome variable) and prediction (numerical outcome variable).

Base R or ggplot?

The `ggplot2` package by Hadley Wickham has become the most popular dedicated graphics package in R for creating presentation-quality visualization in a wide variety of contexts. The "gg" in ggplot refers to "Grammar of Graphics," a term coined by Leland Wilkinson to define a system of plotting theory and nomenclature. Learning ggplot effectively means becoming familiar with this philosophy and technical language of plotting. This brings with it flexibility and power. It also entails a non-trivial learning curve. If you are likely to be using data visualizations on a regular basis in communicating with others with high-quality graphics, it is worth the time and effort to get up to speed on ggplot. If your uses of visualization are likely to be exploratory and informal, perhaps as an initial part of analysis that will not be formally written up, you may decide not to undertake the investment of learning ggplot.

In this chapter, which is primarily an introduction, we present both base R and ggplot syntax for nearly all the visualizations. The Figures were all created using `ggplot2`.[2]

3.2 DATA EXAMPLES

To illustrate data visualization, we use two datasets used in additional chapters in the book.

Example 1: Boston Housing Data

The Boston Housing data contain information on census tracts in Boston[3] for which several measurements are taken (e.g., crime rate, pupil/teacher ratio). It has 14 variables. A description of each variable is given in Table 3.1, and a sample of the first nine records is shown in Table 3.2. In addition to the original

---

[2]The code is available from the accompanying web sites https://www.dataminingbook.com/ and https://github.com/gedeck/mlba-R-code; data are available in the R package `mlba`.

[3]The Boston Housing dataset was originally published by Harrison and Rubinfeld in "Hedonic prices and the demand for clean air," *Journal of Environmental Economics & Management*, vol. 5, p. 81–102, 1978. A census tract includes 1200–8000 homes.

TABLE 3.1	DESCRIPTION OF VARIABLES IN BOSTON HOUSING DATASET
CRIM	Crime rate
ZN	Percentage of residential land zoned for lots over 25,000 ft^2
INDUS	Percentage of land occupied by nonretail business
CHAS	Does tract bound Charles River (= 1 if tract bounds river, = 0 otherwise)
NOX	Nitric oxide concentration (parts per 10 million)
RM	Average number of rooms per dwelling
AGE	Percentage of owner-occupied units built prior to 1940
DIS	Weighted distances to five Boston employment centers
RAD	Index of accessibility to radial highways
TAX	Full-value property tax rate per $10,000
PTRATIO	Pupil-to-teacher ratio by town
LSTAT	Percentage of lower status of the population
MEDV	Median value of owner-occupied homes in $1000s
CAT.MEDV	Is median value of owner-occupied homes in tract above $30,000 (CAT.MEDV = 1) or not (CAT.MEDV = 0)

TABLE 3.2	FIRST NINE RECORDS IN THE BOSTON HOUSING DATA

 code for opening the Boston Housing data and viewing the first nine records

```
housing.df <- mlba::BostonHousing
head(housing.df, 9)
```

Partial Output

```
> head(housing.df, 9)
     CRIM   ZN INDUS CHAS   NOX    RM   AGE    DIS RAD TAX PTRATIO LSTAT MEDV CAT.MEDV
1 0.00632 18.0  2.31    0 0.538 6.575  65.2 4.0900   1 296    15.3  4.98 24.0        0
2 0.02731  0.0  7.07    0 0.469 6.421  78.9 4.9671   2 242    17.8  9.14 21.6        0
3 0.02729  0.0  7.07    0 0.469 7.185  61.1 4.9671   2 242    17.8  4.03 34.7        1
4 0.03237  0.0  2.18    0 0.458 6.998  45.8 6.0622   3 222    18.7  2.94 33.4        1
5 0.06905  0.0  2.18    0 0.458 7.147  54.2 6.0622   3 222    18.7  5.33 36.2        1
6 0.02985  0.0  2.18    0 0.458 6.430  58.7 6.0622   3 222    18.7  5.21 28.7        0
7 0.08829 12.5  7.87    0 0.524 6.012  66.6 5.5605   5 311    15.2 12.43 22.9        0
8 0.14455 12.5  7.87    0 0.524 6.172  96.1 5.9505   5 311    15.2 19.15 27.1        0
9 0.21124 12.5  7.87    0 0.524 5.631 100.0 6.0821   5 311    15.2 29.93 16.5        0
```

13 variables, the dataset contains the variable CAT.MEDV, which has been created by categorizing median value (MEDV) into two categories: high and low.

We consider three possible tasks:

1. A supervised predictive task, where the outcome variable of interest is the median value of a home in the tract (MEDV).

2. A supervised classification task, where the outcome variable of interest is the binary variable CAT.MEDV that indicates whether the home value is above or below $30,000.

3. An unsupervised task, where the goal is to cluster census tracts.

(MEDV and CAT.MEDV are not used together in any of the three cases).

Example 2: Ridership on Amtrak Trains

Amtrak, a US railway company, routinely collects data on ridership. Here we focus on forecasting future ridership using the series of monthly ridership between January 1991 and March 2004. The data and their source are described in Chapter 17. Hence our task here is (numerical) time series forecasting.

3.3 BASIC CHARTS: BAR CHARTS, LINE CHARTS, AND SCATTER PLOTS

The three most effective basic charts are bar charts, line charts, and scatter plots. These plots are easy to create in R and are the plots most commonly used in the current business world, in both data exploration and presentation (unfortunately, pie charts are also popular, although they are usually ineffective visualizations). Basic charts support data exploration by displaying one or two columns of data (variables) at a time. This is useful in the early stages of getting familiar with the data structure, the amount and types of variables, the volume and type of missing values, etc.

The nature of the machine learning task and domain knowledge about the data will affect the use of basic charts in terms of the amount of time and effort allocated to different variables. In supervised learning, there will be more focus on the outcome variable. In scatter plots, the outcome variable is typically associated with the y-axis. In unsupervised learning (for the purpose of data reduction or clustering), basic plots that convey relationships (such as scatter plots) are preferred.

The top-left panel in Figure 3.1 displays a line chart for the time series of monthly railway passengers on Amtrak. Line graphs are used primarily for showing time series. The choice of time frame to plot, as well as the temporal scale, should depend on the horizon of the forecasting task and on the nature of the data.

Bar charts are useful for comparing a single statistic (e.g., average, count, percentage) across groups. The height of the bar (or length in a horizontal display) represents the value of the statistic, and different bars correspond to

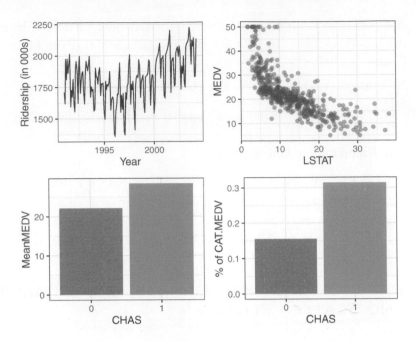

BASIC PLOTS: LINE GRAPH (TOP LEFT), SCATTER PLOT (TOP RIGHT), BAR CHART FOR NUMERICAL VARIABLE (BOTTOM LEFT), AND BAR CHART FOR CATEGORICAL VARIABLE (BOTTOM RIGHT)

different groups. Two examples are shown in the bottom panels in Figure 3.1. The left panel shows a bar chart for a numerical variable (MEDV), and the right panel shows a bar chart for a categorical variable (CAT.MEDV). In each, separate bars are used to denote tracts in Boston that are near the Charles River vs. those that are not (thereby comparing the two categories of CHAS). The chart with the numerical output MEDV (bottom left) uses the average MEDV on the y-axis. This supports the predictive task: the numerical outcome is on the y-axis, and the x-axis is used for a potential categorical predictor.[4] (Note that the x-axis on a bar chart must be used only for categorical variables, because the order of bars in a bar chart should be interchangeable.) For the classification task (bottom right), the y-axis indicates the percent of tracts with median value above $30K, and the x-axis is a binary variable indicating proximity to the Charles. This plot shows us that the tracts bordering the Charles are much more likely to have median values above $30K.

The top-right panel in Figure 3.1 displays a scatter plot of MEDV vs. LSTAT. This is an important plot in the prediction task. Note that the output

---

[4]We refer here to a bar chart with vertical bars. The same principles apply if using a bar chart with horizontal lines, except that the x-axis is now associated with the numerical variable and the y-axis with the categorical variable.

R code for creating Figure 3.1

```
# Amtrak data
library(forecast)
Amtrak.df <- mlba::Amtrak
ridership.ts <- ts(Amtrak.df$Ridership, start=c(1991, 1), end=c(2004, 3), freq=12)

# Boston housing data
housing.df <- mlba::BostonHousing
# compute mean MEDV per CHAS = (0, 1)
MEDV.per.CHAS  <- aggregate(housing.df$MEDV, by=list(housing.df$CHAS), FUN=mean)
names(MEDV.per.CHAS) <- c("CHAS", "MeanMEDV")
MEDV.per.CHAS$CHAS <- factor(MEDV.per.CHAS$CHAS)
# compute % mean CAT.MEDV
CATMEDV.per.CHAS <- aggregate(housing.df$CAT.MEDV, by=list(housing.df$CHAS), FUN=mean)
names(CATMEDV.per.CHAS) <- c("CHAS", "MeanCATMEDV")
CATMEDV.per.CHAS$CHAS <- factor(CATMEDV.per.CHAS$CHAS)
```

Base-R version

```
## line chart for the Amtrak data
plot(ridership.ts, xlab="Year", ylab="Ridership (in 000s)", ylim=c(1300, 2300))

## scatter plot with axes names for Boston housing data
plot(housing.df$MEDV ~ housing.df$LSTAT, xlab="LSTAT", ylab="MEDV")

## barchart of CHAS vs. mean MEDV
barplot(MEDV.per.CHAS$MeanMEDV,  names.arg=MEDV.per.CHAS$CHAS,
        xlab="CHAS", ylab="Avg. MEDV")

## barchart of CHAS vs. % CAT.MEDV
barplot(CATMEDV.per.CHAS$MeanCATMEDV * 100,  names.arg=CATMEDV.per.CHAS$CHAS,
        xlab="CHAS", ylab="% of CAT.MEDV")
```

ggplot2 version

```
library(ggplot2)
library(gridExtra)

g1 <- autoplot(ridership.ts) +
  xlab("Year") + ylab("Ridership (in 000)")

## scatter plot with axes names
g2 <- ggplot(housing.df) +
  geom_point(aes(x=LSTAT, y=MEDV), colour="navy", alpha=0.5)

g3 <- ggplot(MEDV.per.CHAS) +
  geom_bar(aes(x=CHAS, y=MeanMEDV, fill=CHAS), stat="identity")

g4 <- ggplot(CATMEDV.per.CHAS) +
  geom_bar(aes(x=CHAS, y=MeanCATMEDV, fill=CHAS), stat="identity") +
  ylab("% of CAT.MEDV")

grid.arrange(g1, g2, g3, g4, ncol=2, nrow=2)
```

MEDV is again on the y-axis (and LSTAT on the x-axis is a potential predictor). Because both variables in a basic scatter plot must be numerical, it cannot be used to display the relation between CAT.MEDV and potential predictors for the classification task (but we can enhance it to do so—see Section 3.4). For unsupervised learning, this particular scatter plot helps study the association between two numerical variables in terms of information overlap, as well as identifying clusters of observations.

All three basic plots highlight global information such as the overall level of ridership or MEDV, as well as changes over time (line chart), differences between subgroups (bar chart), and relationships between numerical variables (scatter plot).

Distribution Plots: Boxplots and Histograms

Before moving on to more sophisticated visualizations that enable multidimensional investigation, we note two important plots that are usually not considered "basic charts" but are very useful in statistical and machine learning contexts. The *boxplot* and the *histogram* are two plots that display the entire distribution of a numerical variable. Although averages are very popular and useful summary statistics, there is usually much to be gained by looking at additional statistics such as the median and standard deviation of a variable and even more so by examining the entire distribution. Whereas bar charts can only use a single aggregation, boxplots and histograms display the entire distribution of a numerical variable. Boxplots are also effective for comparing subgroups by generating side-by-side boxplots or for looking at distributions over time by creating a series of boxplots.

Distribution plots are useful in supervised learning for determining potential machine learning methods and variable transformations. For example, skewed numerical variables might warrant transformation (e.g., moving to a logarithmic scale) if used in methods that assume normality (e.g., linear regression, discriminant analysis).

A histogram represents the frequencies of all x values with a series of vertical connected bars. For example, in the left panel of Figure 3.2, there are over 150 tracts where MEDV is between \$20K and \$25K.

A boxplot represents the variable being plotted on the y-axis (although the plot can potentially be turned in a $90°$ angle, so that the boxes are parallel to the x-axis). In the right panel of Figure 3.2, there are two boxplots (called a side-by-side boxplot). The box encloses 50% of the data—for example, in the right-hand box half of the tracts have MEDVs between \$20,000 and \$33,000. The horizontal line inside the box represents the median (50th percentile). The top and bottom of the box represent the 75th and 25th percentiles, respectively. Lines extending above and below the box cover the rest of the data range; outliers may be depicted as points or circles. Sometimes, the average is marked by a + (or similar) sign. Comparing the average and the median helps in assessing how

| FIGURE 3.2 | DISTRIBUTION PLOTS FOR NUMERICAL VARIABLE MEDV. LEFT: HISTOGRAM AND RIGHT: BOXPLOT |

 code for creating Figure 3.2

```
## histogram of MEDV
hist(housing.df$MEDV, xlab="MEDV")

## boxplot of MEDV for different values of CHAS
boxplot(housing.df$MEDV ~ housing.df$CHAS, xlab="CHAS", ylab="MEDV")
```

ggplot2 version

```
ggplot(housing.df) + geom_histogram(aes(x=MEDV), bins=9) + ylab("Count")

ggplot(housing.df) + geom_boxplot(aes(x=as.factor(CHAS), y=MEDV)) + xlab("CHAS")
```

skewed the data are. Boxplots are often arranged in a series with a different plot for each of the various values of a second variable, shown on the x-axis.

Because histograms and boxplots are geared toward numerical variables, their basic form is useful for *prediction* tasks. Boxplots can also support *unsupervised learning* by displaying relationships between a numerical variable (y-axis) and a categorical variable (x-axis). For example, the histogram of MEDV in the left panel in Figure 3.2 reveals a skewed distribution. Transforming the output variable to log(MEDV) would likely improve results of a linear regression predictor.

Compare the side-by-side boxplot in Figure 3.2 to the bottom-left bar chart in Figure 3.1 that only displays the average values. We see that not only is the average MEDV for river-bounding tracts (CHAS = 1) higher than the non-river-bounding tracts (CHAS = 0), the entire distribution is higher (median, quartiles, and whiskers). We can also see that all river-bounding tracts have MEDV above $10 thousand, unlike non-river-bounding tracts. This information is useful for identifying the potential importance of this predictor (CHAS) and for choosing machine learning methods that can capture the non-overlapping area between the two distributions (e.g., trees).

Boxplots and histograms applied to numerical variables can also provide directions for deriving new variables; for example, they can indicate how to bin a numerical variable (for example, binning a numerical outcome in order to use a naive Bayes classifier, or in the Boston Housing example, choosing the cutoff to convert MEDV to CAT.MEDV).

Finally, side-by-side boxplots are useful in classification tasks for evaluating the potential of numerical predictors. This is done by using the x-axis for the categorical outcome and the y-axis for a numerical predictor. An example is shown in Figure 3.3, where we can see the effects of four numerical predictors on CAT.MEDV. The pairs that are most separated (e.g., PTRATIO and INDUS) indicate potentially useful predictors.

The main weakness of basic charts and distribution plots in their basic form (that is, using position in relation to the axes to encode values), is that they

FIGURE 3.3   SIDE-BY-SIDE BOXPLOTS FOR EXPLORING THE CAT.MEDV OUTPUT VARIABLE BY DIFFERENT NUMERICAL PREDICTORS. IN A SIDE-BY-SIDE BOXPLOT, ONE AXIS IS USED FOR A CATEGORICAL VARIABLE AND THE OTHER FOR A NUMERICAL VARIABLE. PLOTTING A CATEGORICAL OUTCOME VARIABLE AND A NUMERICAL PREDICTOR COMPARES THE PREDICTOR'S DISTRIBUTION ACROSS THE OUTCOME CATEGORIES. PLOTTING A NUMERICAL OUTCOME VARIABLE AND A CATEGORICAL PREDICTOR DISPLAYS THE DISTRIBUTION OF THE OUTCOME VARIABLE ACROSS DIFFERENT LEVELS OF THE PREDICTOR

 code for creating Figure 3.3

```
## side-by-side boxplots
# use par() to split the plots into panels.
par(mfcol=c(1, 4))
boxplot(housing.df$NOX ~ housing.df$CAT.MEDV, xlab="CAT.MEDV", ylab="NOX")
boxplot(housing.df$LSTAT ~ housing.df$CAT.MEDV, xlab="CAT.MEDV", ylab="LSTAT")
boxplot(housing.df$PTRATIO ~ housing.df$CAT.MEDV, xlab="CAT.MEDV", ylab="PTRATIO")
boxplot(housing.df$INDUS ~ housing.df$CAT.MEDV, xlab="CAT.MEDV", ylab="INDUS")
```

ggplot2 version

```
g1 <- ggplot(housing.df, aes(x=factor(CAT.MEDV), y=NOX)) + geom_boxplot()
g2 <- ggplot(housing.df, aes(x=factor(CAT.MEDV), y=LSTAT)) + geom_boxplot()
g3 <- ggplot(housing.df, aes(x=factor(CAT.MEDV), y=PTRATIO)) + geom_boxplot()
g4 <- ggplot(housing.df, aes(x=factor(CAT.MEDV), y=INDUS)) + geom_boxplot()
grid.arrange(g1, g2, g3, g4, ncol=4, nrow=1)
```

can only display two variables and therefore cannot reveal high-dimensional information. Each of the basic charts has two dimensions, where each dimension is dedicated to a single variable. In machine learning, the data are usually multivariate by nature, and the analytics are designed to capture and measure multivariate information. Visual exploration should therefore also incorporate this important aspect. In the next section, we describe how to extend basic charts (and distribution plots) to multidimensional data visualization by adding features, employing manipulations, and incorporating interactivity. We then present several specialized plots that are geared toward displaying special data structures (Section 3.5).

Heatmaps: Visualizing Correlations and Missing Values

A *heatmap* is a graphical display of numerical data where color is used to denote values. In a machine learning context, heatmaps are especially useful for two purposes: for visualizing correlation tables and for visualizing missing values in the data. In both cases the information is conveyed in a two-dimensional table. A correlation table for p variables has p rows and p columns. A data table contains p columns (variables) and n rows (observations). If the number of rows is huge, then a subset can be used. In both cases, it is much easier and faster to scan the color-coding rather than the values. Note that heatmaps are useful when examining a large number of values, but they are not a replacement for more precise graphical display, such as bar charts, because color differences cannot be perceived accurately.

An example of a correlation table heatmap is shown in Figure 3.4, displaying all the pairwise correlations between 13 variables (MEDV and 12 predictors). Darker shades correspond to stronger (positive or negative) correlation, making it easy to quickly spot the high and low correlations. Adding color—here red and blue—can be used to distinguish positive and negative values.

In a missing value heatmap, rows correspond to records and columns to variables. We use a binary coding of the original dataset where 1 denotes a missing value and 0 otherwise. This new binary table is then colored such that only missing value cells (with value 1) are colored. Figure 3.5 shows an example of a missing value heatmap for a dataset on motor vehicle collisions. The missing data heatmap helps visualize the level and amount of "missingness" in the merged data file. Some patterns of "missingness" easily emerge: variables that are missing for nearly all observations and clusters of rows (countries) that are missing many values. Variables with little missingness are also visible. This information can then be used for determining how to handle the missingness (e.g., dropping some variables, dropping some records, imputing, or via other techniques).

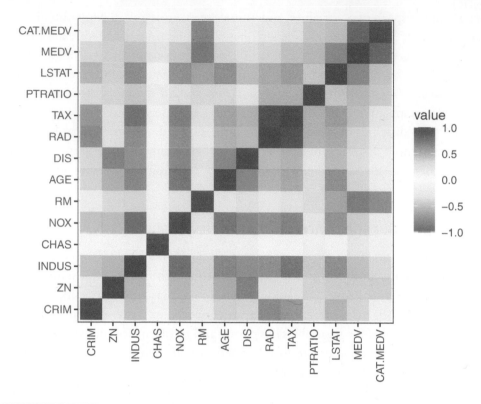

FIGURE 3.4   HEATMAP OF A CORRELATION TABLE. DARK RED VALUES DENOTE STRONG
POSITIVE CORRELATION AND DARK BLUE STRONG NEGATIVE CORRELATION

 code for creating Figure 3.4

```
## simple heatmap of correlations (without values)
heatmap(cor(housing.df), Rowv=NA, Colv=NA)

## heatmap with values
library(gplots)
heatmap.2(cor(housing.df), Rowv=FALSE, Colv=FALSE, dendrogram="none",
        cellnote=round(cor(housing.df),2),
        notecol="black", key=FALSE, trace="none", margins=c(10,10))
```

ggplot2 version

```
library(reshape) # to generate input for the plot
cor.mat <- round(cor(housing.df), 2) # rounded correlation matrix
melted.cor.mat <- melt(cor.mat)
ggplot(melted.cor.mat, aes(x=X1, y=X2, fill=value)) +
  geom_tile() + xlab("") + ylab("") +
  scale_fill_distiller(palette="RdBu", limits=c(-1, 1))
```

code for generating a heatmap of missing values

```
# replace dataFrame with your data.
dataFrame = mlba::NYPDMotorVehicleCollisions

# we treat empty strings as missing values
# is.na() returns a Boolean (TRUE/FALSE) output indicating the location of missing
# values.
# multiplying the Boolean value by 1 converts the output into binary (0/1).
missing = dataFrame
missing[missing == ""] = NA
missing = 1 * is.na(missing)
heatmap(missing, Rowv=NA, Colv=NA)
```

ggplot2 version

```
library(ggplot2)
library(reshape) # to generate input for the plot
melted.missing <- melt(missing)
ggplot(melted.missing, aes(x=X1, y=X2, fill=value)) +
  geom_tile(show.legend=FALSE) +
  scale_fill_gradient(low="white", high="#666666") +
  scale_x_continuous(expand=c(0, 0))
```

3.4 MULTIDIMENSIONAL VISUALIZATION

Basic plots can convey richer information with features such as color, size, and multiple panels, and by enabling operations such as rescaling, aggregation, and interactivity. These additions allow looking at more than one or two variables at a time. The beauty of these additions is their effectiveness in displaying complex information in an easily understandable way. Effective features are based on understanding how visual perception works [see Few (2021) for a discussion]. The purpose is to make the information more understandable, not just to represent the data in higher dimensions (such as three-dimensional plots that are usually ineffective visualizations).

Adding Variables: Color, Size, Shape, Multiple Panels, and Animation

In order to include more variables in a plot, we must consider the type of variable to include. To represent additional categorical information, the best way is to use hue, shape, or multiple panels. For additional numerical information, we can use color intensity or size. Temporal information can be added via animation.

Incorporating additional categorical and/or numerical variables into the basic (and distribution) plots means that we can now use all of them for both prediction and classification tasks. For example, we mentioned earlier that a basic scatter plot cannot be used for studying the relationship between a categorical outcome and predictors (in the context of classification). However, a very effective plot for classification is a scatter plot of two numerical predictors color-coded by the categorical outcome variable. An example is shown in the top panel of Figure 3.6, with color denoting CAT.MEDV.

In the context of prediction, color-coding supports the exploration of the conditional relationship between the numerical outcome (on the y-axis) and a numerical predictor. Color-coded scatter plots then help assess the need for creating interaction terms (for example, is the relationship between MEDV and LSTAT different for tracts near vs. away from the river?).

Color can also be used to include further categorical variables into a bar chart, as long as the number of categories is small. When the number of categories is large, a better alternative is to use multiple panels. Creating multiple panels (also called "trellising") is done by splitting the observations according to a categorical variable and creating a separate plot (of the same type) for each category. An example is shown in the right-hand panel of Figure 3.6, where a bar chart of average MEDV by RAD is broken down into two panels by CHAS. We see that the average MEDV for different highway accessibility levels (RAD) behaves differently for tracts near the river (lower panel) compared to tracts away from the river (upper panel). This is especially salient for RAD = 1. We also see that there are no near-river tracts in RAD levels 2, 6, and 7. Such information might lead us to create an interaction term between RAD and CHAS and to consider condensing some of the bins in RAD. All these explorations are useful for prediction and classification.

A special plot that uses scatter plots with multiple panels is the *scatter plot matrix*. In it, all pairwise scatter plots are shown in a single display. The panels in a matrix scatter plot are organized in a special way, such that each column and

FIGURE 3.6   ADDING CATEGORICAL VARIABLES BY COLOR-CODING AND MULTIPLE PANELS. LEFT: SCATTER PLOT OF TWO NUMERICAL PREDICTORS, COLOR-CODED BY THE CATEGORICAL OUTCOME CAT.MEDV. RIGHT: BAR CHART OF MEDV BY TWO CATEGORICAL PREDICTORS (CHAS AND RAD), USING MULTIPLE PANELS FOR CHAS

 code for creating Figure 3.6

```
## color scatter plot
par(xpd=TRUE) # allow legend to be displayed outside of plot area
plot(housing.df$NOX ~ housing.df$LSTAT, ylab="NOX", xlab="LSTAT",
     col=ifelse(housing.df$CAT.MEDV == 1, "blue", "red"))
legend("topleft", inset=c(0, -0.2), legend=c("CAT.MEDV = 1", "CAT.MEDV = 0"),
       col=c("blue", "red"), pch=1, cex=0.5)


## panel plots
# compute mean MEDV per RAD and CHAS
# In aggregate() use argument drop = FALSE to include all combinations
# (exiting and missing) of RAD X CHAS.
data.for.plot <- aggregate(housing.df$MEDV, by=list(housing.df$RAD, housing.df$CHAS),
                           FUN=mean, drop=FALSE)
names(data.for.plot) <- c("RAD", "CHAS", "meanMEDV")
# plot the data
par(mfcol=c(2,1))
barplot(height=data.for.plot$meanMEDV[data.for.plot$CHAS == 0],
        names.arg=data.for.plot$RAD[data.for.plot$CHAS == 0],
        xlab="RAD", ylab="Avg. MEDV", main="CHAS = 0")
barplot(height=data.for.plot$meanMEDV[data.for.plot$CHAS == 1],
        names.arg=data.for.plot$RAD[data.for.plot$CHAS == 1],
        xlab="RAD", ylab="Avg. MEDV", main="CHAS = 1")
```

ggplot version

```
g1 <- ggplot(housing.df, aes(x=LSTAT, y=NOX, color=factor(CAT.MEDV))) +
  labs(color="CAT.MEDV") + geom_point(alpha=0.6)

g2 <- ggplot(data.for.plot) +
  geom_bar(aes(x=factor(RAD), y=meanMEDV), stat="identity") +
  labs(x="RAD", y="Avg. MEDV") +
  facet_grid(CHAS ~ .)

grid.arrange(g1, g2, ncol=2)
```

each row correspond to a variable, thereby the intersections create all the possible pairwise scatter plots. The scatter plot matrix is useful in unsupervised learning for studying the associations between numerical variables, detecting outliers, and identifying clusters. For supervised learning, it can be used for examining pairwise relationships (and their nature) between predictors to support variable transformations and variable selection (see Correlation Analysis in Chapter 4). For prediction, it can also be used to depict the relationship of the outcome with the numerical predictors.

An example of a scatter plot matrix is shown in Figure 3.7, with MEDV and three predictors. Below the diagonal are the scatter plots. Variable name

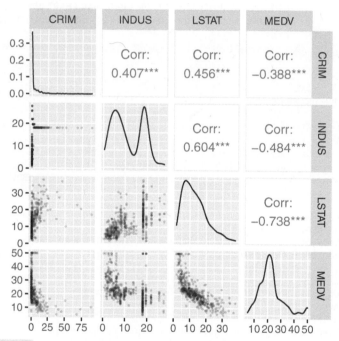

FIGURE 3.7   SCATTER PLOT MATRIX FOR MEDV AND THREE NUMERICAL PREDICTORS

 code for creating Figure 3.7

```
## simple plot
# use plot() to generate a matrix of 4X4 panels with variable name on the diagonal,
# and scatter plots in the remaining panels.
plot(housing.df[, c(1, 3, 12, 13)])
```

ggplot2 version

```
library(GGally)
ggpairs(housing.df[, c(1, 3, 12, 13)],
  lower=list(continuous=wrap("points", alpha=0.25, size=0.3)))
```

indicates the y-axis variable. For example, the plots in the bottom row all have MEDV on the y-axis (which allows studying the individual outcome–predictor relations). We can see different types of relationships from the different shapes (e.g., an exponential relationship between MEDV and LSTAT and a highly skewed relationship between CRIM and INDUS), which can indicate needed transformations. Along the diagonal, where just a single variable is involved, the frequency distribution for that variable is displayed. Above the diagonal are the correlation coefficients corresponding to the two variables.

Once hue is used, further categorical variables can be added via shape and multiple panels. However, one must proceed cautiously in adding multiple variables, as the display can become over-cluttered and then visual perception is lost.

Adding a numerical variable via size is useful especially in scatter plots (thereby creating "bubble plots"), because in a scatter plot points represent individual observations. In plots that aggregate across observations (e.g., boxplots, histograms, bar charts), size and hue are not normally incorporated.

Finally, adding a temporal dimension to a plot to show how the information changes over time can be achieved via animation. A famous example is Rosling's animated scatter plots showing how world demographics changed over the years (www.gapminder.org). However, while animations of this type work for "statistical storytelling," they are not very effective for data exploration.

Manipulations: Rescaling, Aggregation and Hierarchies, Zooming, Filtering

Most of the time spent in machine learning projects is spent in data preprocessing. Typically, considerable effort is expended getting all the data in a format that can actually be used in the machine learning software. Additional time is spent processing the data in ways that improve the performance of the machine learning procedures. This preprocessing step includes variable transformation and derivation of new variables to help models perform more effectively. Transformations include changing the numeric scale of a variable, binning numerical variables, and condensing categories in categorical variables. The following manipulations support the preprocessing step and the choice of adequate machine learning methods. They do so by revealing patterns and their nature.

Rescaling   Changing the scale in a display can enhance the plot and illuminate relationships. For example, in Figure 3.8, we see the effect of changing both axes of the scatter plot (top) and the y-axis of a boxplot (bottom) to logarithmic (log) scale. Whereas the original plots (left) are hard to understand, the patterns become visible in log scale (right). In the scatter plots, the nature of the relationship between MEDV and CRIM is hard to determine in the original scale, because too many of the points are "crowded" near the y-axis. The rescaling removes this crowding and allows a better view of the linear relationship

FIGURE 3.8   RESCALING CAN ENHANCE PLOTS AND REVEAL PATTERNS. LEFT: ORIGINAL SCALE
AND RIGHT: LOGARITHMIC SCALE

 code for creating Figure 3.8

```
options(scipen=999) # avoid scientific notation

## scatter plot: regular and log scale
plot(housing.df$MEDV ~ housing.df$CRIM, xlab="CRIM", ylab="MEDV")
# to use logarithmic scale set argument log = to either 'x', 'y', or 'xy'.
plot(housing.df$MEDV ~ housing.df$CRIM,
    xlab="CRIM", ylab="MEDV", log="xy")


## boxplot: regular and log scale
boxplot(housing.df$CRIM ~ housing.df$CAT.MEDV,
    xlab="CAT.MEDV", ylab="CRIM")
boxplot(housing.df$CRIM ~ housing.df$CAT.MEDV,
    xlab="CAT.MEDV", ylab="CRIM", log="y")
```

ggplot2 version

```
## scatter plot: regular and log scale
# alternative log-scale plot with ggplot
g1 <- ggplot(housing.df) + geom_point(aes(x=CRIM, y=MEDV))
g2 <- g1 +
  scale_x_log10(breaks=10^(-2:2),
    labels=format(10^(-2:2), scientific=FALSE, drop0trailing=TRUE))
  scale_y_log10(breaks=c(5, 10, 20, 40))

## boxplot: regular and log scale
g3 <- ggplot(housing.df, aes(x=factor(CAT.MEDV), y=CRIM)) + geom_boxplot()
g4 <- g3 + scale_y_log10()

grid.arrange(g1, g2, g3, g4, ncol=2)
```

between the two log-scaled variables (indicating a log–log relationship). In the boxplot displaying the crowding toward the x-axis in the original units does not allow us to compare the two box sizes, their locations, lower outliers, and most of the distribution information. Rescaling removes the "crowding to the x-axis" effect, thereby allowing a comparison of the two boxplots.

Aggregation and Hierarchies   Another useful manipulation of scaling is changing the level of aggregation. For a temporal scale, we can aggregate by different granularity (e.g., monthly, daily, hourly) or even by a "seasonal" factor of interest such as month of year or day of week. A popular aggregation for time series is a moving average, where the average of neighboring values within a given window size is plotted. Moving average plots help reveal a global trend (see Chapter 17).

Non-temporal variables can be aggregated if some meaningful hierarchy exists: geographical (tracts within a zip code in the Boston Housing example), organizational (people within departments within business units), etc. Figure 3.9 illustrates two types of aggregation for the railway ridership time series. The original monthly series is shown in the top-left panel. Seasonal aggregation (by month-of-year) is shown in the top-right panel, where it is easy to see the peak in ridership in July–August and the dip in January–February. The bottom-right panel shows temporal aggregation, where the series is now displayed in yearly aggregates. This plot reveals the global long-term trend in ridership and the generally increasing trend from 1996 on.

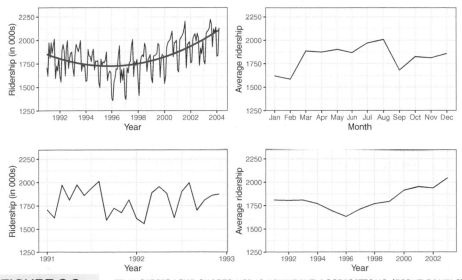

FIGURE 3.9   TIME SERIES LINE CHARTS USING DIFFERENT AGGREGATIONS (RIGHT PANELS), ADDING CURVES (TOP-LEFT PANEL), AND ZOOMING IN (BOTTOM-LEFT PANEL)

R code for creating Figure 3.9

```
library(forecast)
Amtrak.df <- mlba::Amtrak
ridership.ts <- ts(Amtrak.df$Ridership, start=c(1991, 1), end=c(2004, 3), freq=12)
## fit curve
ridership.lm <- tslm(ridership.ts ~ trend + I(trend^2))

plot(ridership.ts, xlab="Year", ylab="Ridership (in 000s)", ylim=c(1300, 2300))
lines(ridership.lm$fitted, lwd=2)

## zoom in, monthly, and annual plots
ridership.2yrs <- window(ridership.ts, start=c(1991,1), end=c(1992,12))
plot(ridership.2yrs, xlab="Year", ylab="Ridership (in 000s)", ylim=c(1300, 2300))
monthly.ridership.ts <- tapply(ridership.ts, cycle(ridership.ts), mean)
plot(monthly.ridership.ts, xlab="Month", ylab="Average ridership",
    ylim=c(1300, 2300), type="l", xaxt="n")
## set x labels
axis(1, at=c(1:12), labels=c("Jan","Feb","Mar", "Apr","May","Jun",
                             "Jul","Aug","Sep",  "Oct","Nov","Dec"))

annual.ridership.ts <- aggregate(ridership.ts, FUN=mean)
plot(annual.ridership.ts, xlab="Year", ylab="Average ridership",
    ylim=c(1300, 2300))
```

ggplot2 version

```
g1 <- autoplot(ridership.ts) + ylim(1300, 2300) +
  labs(x="Year", y="Ridership (in 000s)") +
  geom_smooth(formula=y ~ poly(x, 2), method="lm",
              colour="navy", se=FALSE, na.rm=TRUE) +
  scale_x_continuous(n.breaks=10)

## zoom in, monthly, and annual plots
g2 <- autoplot(window(ridership.ts, start=c(1991,1), end=c(1992,12))) +
  ylim(1300, 2300) +
  labs(x="Year", y="Ridership (in 000s)")

months=c("Jan", "Feb", "Mar", "Apr", "May", "Jun",
         "Jul", "Aug", "Sep", "Oct", "Nov", "Dec")
df <- data.frame(
  monthly.ridership=tapply(ridership.ts, cycle(ridership.ts), mean),
  month=factor(months, levels=months))
g3 <- ggplot(df, aes(x=month, y=monthly.ridership)) + ylim(1300, 2300) +
  geom_line(group=1) +
  labs(x="Month", y="Average ridership")

annual.ridership.ts <- aggregate(ridership.ts, FUN=mean)
g4 <- autoplot(annual.ridership.ts) + ylim(1300, 2300) +
  labs(x="Year", y="Average ridership")
```

Examining different scales, aggregations, or hierarchies supports both supervised and unsupervised tasks in that it can reveal patterns and relationships at various levels and can suggest new sets of variables with which to work.

Zooming and Panning   The ability to zoom in and out of certain areas of the data on a plot is important for revealing patterns and outliers. We are often interested in more detail on areas of dense information or of special interest. Panning refers to the operation of moving the zoom window to other areas (popular in mapping applications such as Google Maps). An example of zooming is shown in the bottom-left panel of Figure 3.9, where the ridership series is zoomed in to the first two years of the series.

Zooming and panning support supervised and unsupervised methods by detecting areas of different behavior, which may lead to creating new interaction terms, new variables, or even separate models for data subsets. For example, a major US power distributor, long frustrated in its efforts to diagnose and predict transmission failures, was able to identify troubling anomalies in electrical frequency data only after zooming in to an extremely micro scale. In addition, zooming and panning can help choose between methods that assume global behavior (e.g., regression models) and data-driven methods (e.g., exponential smoothing forecasters and k-nearest neighbors classifiers) and indicate the level of global/local behavior (as manifested by parameters such as k in k-nearest neighbors, the size of a tree, or the smoothing parameters in exponential smoothing).

Filtering   Filtering means removing some of the observations from the visualization. The purpose of filtering is to focus the attention on certain data while eliminating "noise" created by other data. Filtering supports supervised and unsupervised learning in a similar way to zooming and panning: it assists in identifying different or unusual local behavior.

Reference: Trend Lines and Labels

Trend lines and using in-plot labels also help detect patterns and outliers. Trend lines serve as a reference and allow us to more easily assess the shape of a pattern. Although linearity is easy to visually perceive, more elaborate relationships such as exponential and polynomial trends are harder to assess by eye. Trend lines are useful in line charts and in scatter plots. An example is shown in the top-left panel of Figure 3.9, where a polynomial curve is overlaid on the original line chart (see also Chapter 17).

In displays that are not overcrowded, the use of in-plot labels can be useful for better exploration of outliers and clusters. An example is shown in Figure 3.10. The figure shows different utilities on a scatter plot that compares fuel cost with

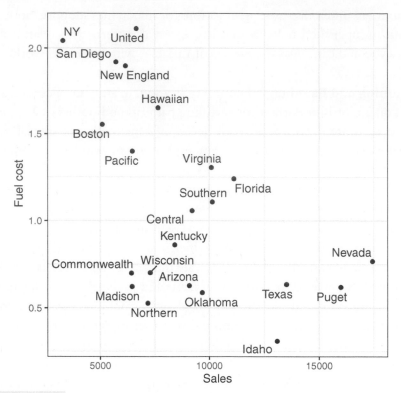

FIGURE 3.10   SCATTER PLOT WITH LABELED POINTS

R code for creating Figure 3.10

```
utilities.df <- mlba::Utilities

plot(utilities.df$Fuel_Cost ~ utilities.df$Sales,
     xlab = "Sales", ylab = "Fuel cost", xlim = c(2000, 20000))
text(x = utilities.df$Sales, y = utilities.df$Fuel_Cost,
     labels = utilities.df$Company, pos = 4, cex = 0.8, srt = 20, offset = 0.2)
```

alternative with ggplot

```
library(ggrepel)
ggplot(utilities.df, aes(y = Fuel_Cost, x = Sales)) +
  geom_point() +
  geom_text_repel(aes(label=Company)) +
  labs(x="Sales", y="Fuel cost")
```

total sales. We might be interested in clustering the data and using clustering algorithms to identify clusters of utilities that differ markedly with respect to fuel cost and sales. Figure 3.10, with the labels, helps visualize these clusters and their members (e.g., Nevada and Puget are part of a clear cluster with low fuel costs and high sales). For more on clustering and on this example, see Chapter 16.

Scaling Up to Large Datasets

When the number of observations (rows) is large, plots that display each individual observation (e.g., scatter plots) can become ineffective. Aside from using aggregated charts such as boxplots, some alternatives are:

1. Sampling—drawing a random sample and using it for plotting

2. Reducing marker size

3. Using more transparent marker colors and removing fill

4. Breaking down the data into subsets (e.g., by creating multiple panels)

5. Using aggregation (e.g., bubble plots where size corresponds to number of observations in a certain range)

6. Using jittering (slightly moving each marker by adding a small amount of noise).

An example of the advantage of plotting a sample over the large dataset is shown in Figure 12.2 in Chapter 12, where a scatter plot of 5000 records is plotted alongside a scatter plot of a sample. Figure 3.11 illustrates an improved plot of the full dataset by using smaller markers, using jittering to uncover overlaid points, and more transparent colors. We can see that larger areas of the plot are dominated by the light blue class, the dark blue class is mainly on the right, while there is a lot of overlap in the high-income area.

Multivariate Plot: Parallel Coordinates Plot

Another approach toward presenting multidimensional information in a two-dimensional plot is via specialized plots such as the *parallel coordinates plot*. In this plot a vertical axis is drawn for each variable. Then each observation is represented by drawing a line that connects its values on the different axes, thereby creating a "multivariate profile." An example is shown in Figure 3.12 for the Boston Housing data. In this display, separate panels are used for the two values of CAT.MEDV, in order to compare the profiles of tracts in the two classes (for a classification task). We see that the more expensive tracts (bottom panel) consistently have low CRIM, low LSAT, and high RM compared with cheaper tracts (top panel), which are more mixed on CRIM, and LSAT, and have a medium level of RM. This observation gives indication of useful predictors and suggests possible binning for some numerical predictors.

Parallel coordinates plots are also useful in unsupervised tasks. They can reveal clusters, outliers, and information overlap across variables. A useful manipulation is to reorder the columns to better reveal observation clusterings.

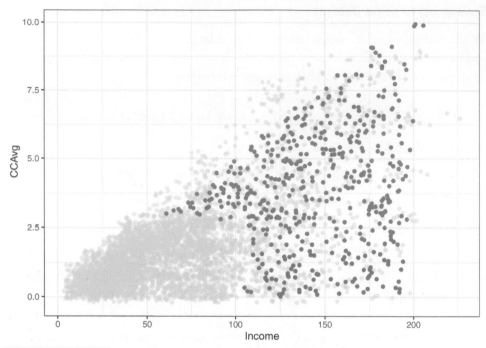

FIGURE 3.11   SCATTER PLOT OF LARGE DATASET WITH REDUCED MARKER SIZE, JITTERING, AND
MORE TRANSPARENT COLORING

 code for creating Figure 3.11

```
# use function alpha() in library scales to add transparent colors
library(scales)
universal.df <- mlba::UniversalBank
no_personal_loan <- subset(universal.df, Personal.Loan == 0)
personal_loan <- subset(universal.df, Personal.Loan == 1)
plot(jitter(no_personal_loan$CCAvg, 1) ~ jitter(no_personal_loan$Income, 1),
    col=alpha("lightblue", 0.5), pch=20, xlab="Income", ylab="CCAvg")
points(jitter(personal_loan$CCAvg, 1) ~ jitter(personal_loan$Income, 1),
    col="steelblue", pch=20, xlab="Income", ylab="CCAvg")
```

alternative with ggplot

```
ggplot(universal.df, aes(x=Income, y=CCAvg)) +
    geom_jitter(data=no_personal_loan, width=5, height=0.2, alpha=0.5,
                color="lightblue") +
    geom_jitter(data=personal_loan, width=5, height=0.2, color="steelblue") +
    labs(colour="Personal\nLoan")
```

FIGURE 3.12   PARALLEL COORDINATES PLOT FOR BOSTON HOUSING DATA. EACH OF THE
VARIABLES (SHOWN ON THE HORIZONTAL AXIS) IS SCALED TO 0–100%. PANELS
ARE USED TO DISTINGUISH CAT.MEDV (TOP PANEL = HOMES BELOW $30,000)

code for creating Figure 3.12

```
library(MASS)
par(mfcol = c(2,1))
parcoord(housing.df[housing.df$CAT.MEDV == 0, -14], main = "CAT.MEDV = 0")
parcoord(housing.df[housing.df$CAT.MEDV == 1, -14], main = "CAT.MEDV = 1")
```

ggplot version using GGally package

```
library(GGally)

ggparcoord(subset(housing.df, select=-CAT.MEDV), scale="uniminmax", alpha=0.3) +
  facet_wrap(vars(housing.df$CAT.MEDV), nrow=2) +
  labs(x="Variable", y="Value")
```

Interactive Visualization

Similar to the interactive nature of the machine learning process, interactivity is key to enhancing our ability to gain information from graphical visualization. In the words of Stephen Few (2021), an expert in data visualization:

> We can only learn so much when staring at a static visualization such as a printed graph . . . If we can't interact with the data . . . we hit the wall.

By interactive visualization, we mean an interface that supports the following principles:

1. Making changes to a chart is *easy, rapid, and reversible*.
2. Multiple concurrent charts and tables can be easily combined and displayed on a single screen.
3. A set of visualizations can be linked so that operations in one display are reflected in the other displays.

Let us consider a few examples where we contrast a static plot generator (e.g., Excel or ggplot2) with an interactive visualization interface.

Histogram Rebinning   Consider the need to bin a numerical variables and using a histogram for that purpose. A static histogram would require replotting for each new binning choice. If the user generates multiple plots, then the screen becomes cluttered. If the same plot is recreated, then it is hard to compare different binning choices. In contrast, an interactive visualization would provide an easy way to change bin width interactively (see, e.g., the slider below the histogram in Figure 3.13), and then the histogram would automatically and rapidly replot as the user changes the bin width.

Aggregation and Zooming   Consider a time series forecasting task, given a long series of data. Temporal aggregation at multiple levels is needed for determining short and long term patterns. Zooming and panning are used to identify unusual periods. A static plotting software requires the user to compute new variables for each temporal aggregation (e.g., aggregate daily data to obtain weekly aggregates). Zooming and panning requires manually changing the min and max values on the axis scale of interest (thereby losing the ability to quickly move between different areas without creating multiple charts). An interactive visualization would provide immediate temporal hierarchies which the user can easily switch between. Zooming would be enabled as a slider near the axis (see, e.g., the sliders on the top-left panel in Figure 3.13), thereby allowing direct manipulation and rapid reaction.

Combining Multiple Linked Plots That Fit in a Single Screen   To support a classification task, multiple plots are created of the outcome variable vs. potential categorical and numerical predictors. These can include side-by-side

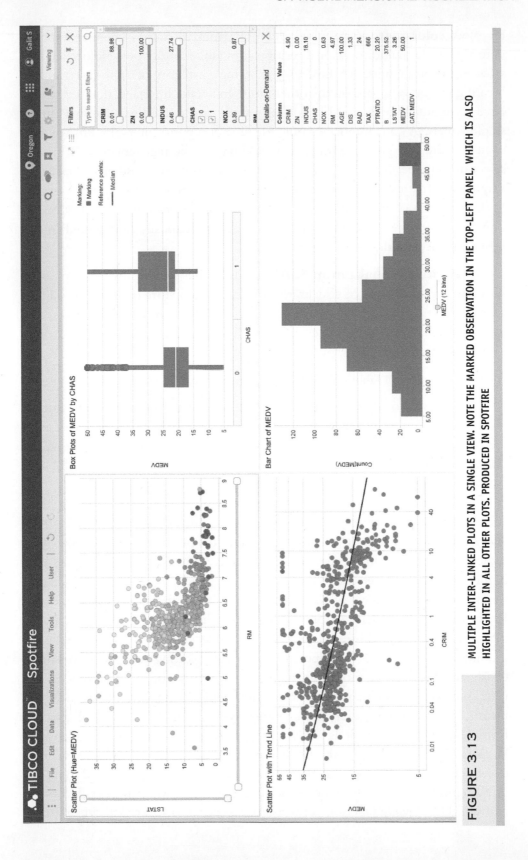

FIGURE 3.13   MULTIPLE INTER-LINKED PLOTS IN A SINGLE VIEW. NOTE THE MARKED OBSERVATION IN THE TOP-LEFT PANEL, WHICH IS ALSO HIGHLIGHTED IN ALL OTHER PLOTS. PRODUCED IN SPOTFIRE

boxplots, color-coded scatter plots, and multipanel bar charts. The user wants to detect possible multidimensional relationships (and identify possible outliers) by selecting a certain subset of the data (e.g., a single category of some variable) and locating the observations on the other plots. In a static interface, the user would have to manually organize the plots of interest and resize them to fit within a single screen. A static interface would usually not support inter-plot linkage, and even if it did, the entire set of plots would have to be regenerated each time a selection is made. In contrast, an interactive visualization would provide an easy way to automatically organize and resize the set of plots to fit within a screen. Linking the set of plots would be easy, and in response to the users selection on one plot, the appropriate selection would be automatically highlighted in the other plots (see example in Figure 3.13).

Interactive Visualization Software In earlier sections, we used plots to illustrate the advantages of visualizations, because "a picture is worth a thousand words." The advantages of an interactive visualization are even harder to convey in words. As Ben Shneiderman, a well-known researcher in information visualization and interfaces, puts it:

> A picture is worth a thousand words. An interface is worth a thousand pictures.

The ability to interact with plots and link them together turns plotting into an analytical tool that supports continuous exploration of the data. Several commercial visualization tools provide powerful capabilities along these lines; two very popular ones are Spotfire (spotfire.tibco.com) and Tableau (www.tableausoftware.com). Figure 3.13 was generated using Spotfire.

Tableau and Spotfire have spent hundreds of millions of dollars on software R&D and review of interactions with customers to hone interfaces that allow analysts to interact with their data via plots smoothly and efficiently. It is difficult to replicate in a programming language like R the sophisticated and highly engineered user interface required for rapid progression through different exploratory views of the data. The need is there, however, and the R community is moving to provide the capability to provide interactivity in plots. The widespread use of javascript in web development has led some programmers to provide R wrappers for javascript plotting tools such as Highcharts and Plotly. For more information, see "JavaScript for R" from Coene (2021) at https://book.javascript-for-r.com/ and "Interactive Charts in R" at https://www.r-graph-gallery.com/interactive-charts.html. The tool `ggvis`, from Hadley Wickham at RStudio, also provides interactivity capabilities for R plots. `Plotly` is one of the popular packages to create interactive visualizations (see "Interactive web-based data visualization with R, plotly, and shiny" at https://plotly-r.com/). It supports zooming, panning, and getting detailed information. The *ggplotly* function converts every *ggplot* into a `plotly` visualization.

```
library(plotly)
g <- ggplot(housing.df) + geom_point(aes(x=CRIM, y=MEDV))
ggplotly(g)
```

With **Shiny** (https://shiny.rstudio.com/gallery/), it is possible to create complex interactive visualizations that support filtering and linking between different plots. Other noteworthy packages are `liminal` for interactive multi-dimensional data exploration and `tsibbletalk` for linked brushing between multiple graphs. R programmers have now the tools to develop custom interactive plots that can be deployed and used by other non-programming analysts in the organization.

3.5 SPECIALIZED VISUALIZATIONS

In this section, we mention a few specialized visualizations that are able to capture data structures beyond the standard time series and cross-sectional structures—special types of relationships that are usually hard to capture with ordinary plots. In particular, we address hierarchical data, network data, and geographical data—three types of data that are becoming increasingly available.

Visualizing Networked Data

Network analysis techniques were spawned by the explosion of social and product network data. Examples of social networks are networks of sellers and buyers on eBay and networks of Facebook users. An example of a product network is the network of products on Amazon (linked through the recommendation system). Network data visualization is available in various network-specialized software and also in general-purpose software.

A network diagram consists of actors and relations between them. "Nodes" are the actors (e.g., users in a social network or products in a product network) and represented by circles. "Edges" are the relations between nodes and are represented by lines connecting nodes. For example, in a social network such as Facebook, we can construct a list of users (nodes) and all the pairwise relations (edges) between users who are "Friends." Alternatively, we can define edges as a posting that one user posts on another user's Facebook page. In this setup, we might have more than a single edge between two nodes. Networks can also have nodes of multiple types. A common structure is networks with two types of nodes. An example of a two-type node network is shown in Figure 3.14, where we see a set of transactions between a network of sellers and buyers on the online auction site www.eBay.com [the data are for auctions selling Swarovski beads and took place during a period of several months; from Jank and Yahav (2010)]. The dark blue circles represent sellers, and the light blue circles represent

FIGURE 3.14   NETWORK PLOT OF EBAY SELLERS (DARK BLUE CIRCLES) AND BUYERS (LIGHT
BLUE CIRCLES) OF SWAROVSKI BEADS

R code for creating Figure 3.14

```
library(igraph)
ebay.df <- mlba::eBayNetwork

# transform node ids to factors
ebay.df[,1] <- as.factor(ebay.df[,1])
ebay.df[,2] <- as.factor(ebay.df[,2])

graph.edges <- as.matrix(ebay.df[,1:2])
g <- graph.edgelist(graph.edges, directed=FALSE)
isBuyer <- sapply(V(g)$name, function(node){ node %in% ebay.df[,2] })

plot(g, vertex.label=NA, vertex.color=ifelse(isBuyer,  "lightblue", "steelblue"),
     vertex.size=ifelse(isBuyer, 7, 10))
```

ggplot version using ggnetwork

```
library(ggnetwork)
g = set_vertex_attr(g, "isBuyer", value=ifelse(isBuyer, "buyer", "seller"))
ggplot(g, aes(x=x, y=y, xend=xend, yend=yend)) +
    geom_edges(color="grey50") +
    geom_nodes(aes(color=isBuyer, size=isBuyer)) +
    scale_color_manual(values = c("buyer"="lightblue", "seller"="steelblue")) +
    scale_size_manual(values = c("buyer"=2, "seller"=5)) +
    theme_blank(legend.position="none")
```

buyers. We can see that this marketplace is dominated by three or four high-volume sellers. We can also see that many buyers interact with a single seller. The market structures for many individual products could be reviewed quickly in this way. Network providers could use the information, for example, to identify possible partnerships to explore with sellers.

Figure 3.14 was produced using R's `igraph` and `ggnetwork` packages. Another useful package, especially for social network analysis, is `sna`. Using these packages, networks can be imported from social network websites such as Twitter and Facebook. The plot's appearance can be customized and various features are available such as filtering nodes and edges, 3D visualization, altering the plot's layout, finding clusters of related nodes, calculating network metrics, and performing network analysis (see Chapter 20 for details and examples).

Network plots can be potentially useful in the context of association rules (see Chapter 15). For example, consider a case of mining a dataset of consumers' grocery purchases to learn which items are purchased together ("what goes with what"). A network can be constructed with items as nodes and edges connecting items that were purchased together. After a set of rules is generated by the machine learning algorithm (which often contains an excessive number of rules, many of which are unimportant), the network plot can help visualize different rules for the purpose of choosing the interesting ones. For example, a popular "beer and diapers" combination would appear in the network plot as a pair of nodes with very high connectivity. An item which is almost always purchased regardless of other items (e.g., milk) would appear as a very large node with high connectivity to all other nodes.

Visualizing Hierarchical Data: Treemaps

We discussed hierarchical data and the exploration of data at different hierarchy levels in the context of plot manipulations. *Treemaps* are useful visualizations specialized for exploring large datasets that are hierarchically structured (tree-structured). They allow exploration of various dimensions of the data while maintaining the hierarchical nature of the data. An example is shown in Figure 3.15, which displays a large set of auctions from eBay.com,[5] hierarchically ordered by item category, subcategory, and brand. The levels in the hierarchy of the treemap are visualized as rectangles containing sub-rectangles. Categorical variables can be included in the display by using hue. Numerical variables can be included via rectangle size and color intensity (ordering of the rectangles is sometimes used to reinforce size). In the example in Figure 3.15, size is used to represent the average closing price (which reflects item value), and color

---

[5]We thank Sharad Borle for sharing this dataset.

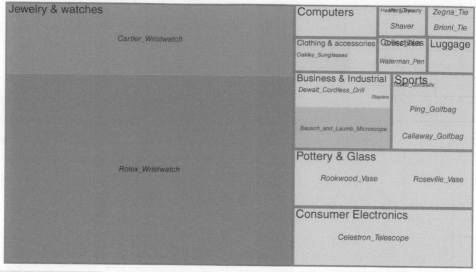

FIGURE 3.15   TREEMAP SHOWING NEARLY 11,000 EBAY AUCTIONS, ORGANIZED BY ITEM CATEGORY, SUBCATEGORY, AND BRAND. RECTANGLE SIZE REPRESENTS AVERAGE CLOSING PRICE (REFLECTING ITEM VALUE). SHADE REPRESENTS PERCENTAGE OF SELLERS WITH NEGATIVE FEEDBACK (DARKER = HIGHER)

 code for creating Figure 3.15

```
library(treemapify)
# load data and add column for negative feedback
tree.df <- mlba::eBayTreemap
tree.df$negative.feedback <- 1* (tree.df$Seller.Feedback < 0)
data <- aggregate(. ~ Brand + Category + Sub.Category, data=tree.df, mean)

ggplot(data, aes(area=High.Bid, subgroup=Category, fill=-negative.feedback,
                label=Brand)) +
    geom_treemap() + geom_treemap_subgroup_border() +
    geom_treemap_subgroup_text(place="topleft", colour="black",
                               min.size=5, size=12) +
    geom_treemap_text(fontface="italic", colour="black", place="centre",
                      min.size=5, size=8) +
    scale_fill_gradient(low="#0396CC", high="#ABDCFF")
```

intensity represents the percent of sellers with negative feedback (a negative seller feedback indicates buyer dissatisfaction in past transactions and is often indicative of fraudulent seller behavior). Consider the task of classifying ongoing auctions in terms of a fraudulent outcome. From the treemap, we see that the highest proportion of sellers with negative ratings (darker blue) is concentrated in expensive item auctions (Rolex and Cartier wristwatches).

Ideally, treemaps should be explored interactively, zooming to different levels of the hierarchy. One example of an interactive online application of treemaps is currently available at www.drasticdata.nl. One of their treemap examples displays player-level data from the 2014 World Cup, aggregated to team level. The user can choose to explore players and team data.

Visualizing Geographical Data: Map Charts

Many datasets used for machine learning now include geographical information. Zip codes are one example of a categorical variable with many categories, where it is not straightforward to create meaningful variables for analysis. Plotting the data on a geographic map can often reveal patterns that are harder to identify otherwise. A map chart uses a geographical map as its background; then color, hue, and other features are used to include categorical or numerical variables. Besides specialized mapping software, maps are now becoming part of general-purpose software, and Google Maps provides application programming interfaces (APIs) that allow organizations to overlay their data on a Google map. While Google Maps is readily available, resulting map charts (such as Figure 3.16) are somewhat inferior in terms of effectiveness compared to map charts in dedicated interactive visualization software.

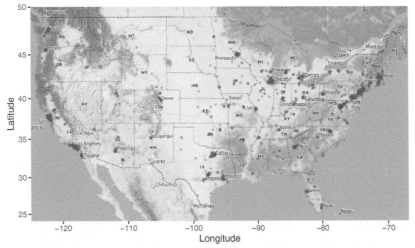

FIGURE 3.16   MAP CHART OF STATISTICS.COM STUDENTS' AND INSTRUCTORS' LOCATIONS ON A STAMEN MAP (MAP TILES BY STAMEN DESIGN, UNDER CC BY 3.0. DATA BY OPENSTREETMAP, UNDER ODBL)

 code for creating Figure 3.16

```
library(ggmap)
us <- c(left=-125, bottom=24, right=-67, top=50)
SCstudents <- mlba::SCstudents
map <- get_stanmenmap(us, zoom=5)
ggmap(map) +
  geom_point(aes(x=longitude, y=latitude), data=SCstudents,
    alpha=0.4, colour="red", size=0.75) +
  labs(x="Longitude", y="Latitude")
```

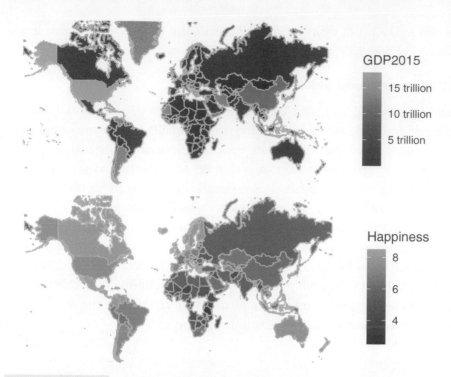

FIGURE 3.17   WORLD MAPS COMPARING "WELL-BEING" (TOP) TO GDP (BOTTOM). SHADING BY
AVERAGE "GLOBAL WELL-BEING" SCORE (TOP) OR GDP (BOTTOM) OF COUNTRY.
LIGHTER CORRESPONDS TO HIGHER SCORE OR LEVEL.

code for creating Figure 3.17

```
library(mosaic)

gdp.df <- mlba::GDP
names(gdp.df)[5] <- "GDP2015"
happiness.df <- mlba::Veerhoven

# gdp map
g1 <- mWorldMap(gdp.df, key="Country.Name", fill="GDP2015") + coord_map()

# well-being map
g2 <- mWorldMap(happiness.df, key="Nation", fill="Score") + coord_map() +
  scale_fill_continuous(name="Happiness")
grid.arrange(g1, g2, nrow=2)
```

Figure 3.17 shows two world map charts comparing countries' "well-being"
(according to a 2006 Gallup survey) in the top map, to gross domestic product
(GDP) in the bottom map.[6] Lighter shade means higher value.

---

[6]Data from Veenhoven, R., World Database of Happiness, Erasmus University Rotterdam. Available
at http://worlddatabaseofhappiness.eur.nl

3.6 SUMMARY: MAJOR VISUALIZATIONS AND OPERATIONS, BY MACHINE LEARNING GOAL

Prediction

- Plot outcome on the y-axis of boxplots, bar charts, and scatter plots.
- Study relation of outcome to categorical predictors via side-by-side boxplots, bar charts, and multiple panels.
- Study relation of outcome to numerical predictors via scatter plots.
- Use distribution plots (boxplot, histogram) for determining needed transformations of the outcome variable (and/or numerical predictors).
- Examine scatter plots with added color/panels/size to determine the need for interaction terms.
- Use various aggregation levels and zooming to determine areas of the data with different behavior and to evaluate the level of global vs. local patterns.

Classification

- Study relation of outcome to categorical predictors using bar charts with the outcome on the y-axis.
- Study relation of outcome to pairs of numerical predictors via color-coded scatter plots (color denotes the outcome).
- Study relation of outcome to numerical predictors via side-by-side boxplots. Plot boxplots of a numerical variable by outcome. Create similar displays for each numerical predictor. The most separable boxes indicate potentially useful predictors.
- Use color to represent the outcome variable on a parallel coordinates plot.
- Use distribution plots (boxplot, histogram) for determining needed transformations of numerical predictor variables.
- Examine scatter plots with added color/panels/size to determine the need for interaction terms.
- Use various aggregation levels and zooming to determine areas of the data with different behavior and to evaluate the level of global vs. local patterns.

Time Series Forecasting

- Create line charts at different temporal aggregations to determine types of patterns.
- Use zooming and panning to examine various shorter periods of the series to determine areas of the data with different behavior.

- Use various aggregation levels to identify global and local patterns.
- Identify missing values in the series (that will require handling).
- Overlay trend lines of different types to determine adequate modeling choices.

Unsupervised Learning

- Create scatter plot matrices to identify pairwise relationships and clustering of observations.
- Use heatmaps to examine the correlation table.
- Use various aggregation levels and zooming to determine areas of the data with different behavior.
- Generate a parallel coordinates plot to identify clusters of observations.

PROBLEMS

3.1 **Shipments of Household Appliances: Line Graphs.** The dataset *mlba::ApplianceShipments* contains the series of quarterly shipments (in millions of dollars) of US household appliances between 1985 and 1989.

a. Create a well-formatted time plot of the data using R.

b. Does there appear to be a quarterly pattern? For a closer view of the patterns, zoom in to the range of 3500–5000 on the y-axis.

c. Using R, create one chart with four separate lines, one line for each of Q1, Q2, Q3, and Q4. In R, this can be achieved by generating a data.frame for each quarter Q1, Q2, Q3, and Q4, and then plotting them as separate series on the line graph. Zoom in to the range of 3500–5000 on the y-axis. Does there appear to be a difference between quarters?

d. Using R, create a line graph of the series at a yearly aggregated level (i.e., the total shipments in each year).

3.2 **Sales of Riding Mowers: Scatter Plots.** A company that manufactures riding mowers wants to identify the best sales prospects for an intensive sales campaign. In particular, the manufacturer is interested in classifying households as prospective owners or nonowners on the basis of Income (in $1000s) and Lot Size (in 1000 ft^2). The marketing expert looked at a random sample of 24 households, given in the dataset *mlba::RidingMowers*.

Using R, create a scatter plot of Lot Size vs. Income, color-coded by the outcome variable owner/nonowner. Make sure to obtain a well-formatted plot (create legible labels and a legend, etc.).

3.3 **Laptop Sales at a London Computer Chain: Bar Charts and Boxplots.** The dataset *mlba::LaptopSalesJanuary2008* contains data for all sales of laptops at a computer chain in London in January 2008. This is a subset of the full dataset that includes data for the entire year.

a. Create a bar chart, showing the average retail price by store. Which store has the highest average? Which has the lowest?

b. To better compare retail prices across stores, create side-by-side boxplots of retail price by store. Now compare the prices in the two stores from (a). Does there seem to be a difference between their price distributions?

3.4 **Laptop Sales at a London Computer Chain: Interactive Visualization.** *The next exercises are designed for using an interactive visualization tool.* The dataset *mlba::LaptopSales* contains nearly 300,000 rows. ENBIS (the European Network for Business and Industrial Statistics) provided these data as part of a contest organized in the fall of 2009.

Scenario: Imagine that you are a new analyst for a company called Acell (a company selling laptops). You have been provided with data about products and sales. You need to help the company with their business goal of planning a product strategy and pricing policies that will maximize Acell's projected revenues in 2009. Using an interactive visualization tool, answer the following questions.

a. Price Questions:

    i. At what price are the laptops actually selling?

    ii. Does price change with time? (*Hint*: Make sure that the date column is recognized as such. The software should then enable different temporal aggregation choices, e.g., plotting the data by weekly or monthly aggregates or even by day of week.)

   iii. Are prices consistent across retail outlets?

   iv. How does price change with configuration?

b. Location Questions:

    i. Where are the stores and customers located?

    ii. Which stores are selling the most?

   iii. How far would customers travel to buy a laptop?

      ○ *Hint 1*: You should be able to aggregate the data, for example, plot the sum or average of the prices.

      ○ *Hint 2*: Use the coordinated highlighting between multiple visualizations in the same page, for example, select a store in one view to see the matching customers in another visualization.

      ○ *Hint 3*: Explore the use of filters to see differences. Make sure to filter in the zoomed out view. For example, try to use a "store location" slider as an alternative way to dynamically compare store locations. This might be more useful to spot outlier patterns if there were 50 store locations to compare.

   iv. Try an alternative way of looking at how far customers traveled. Do this by creating a new data column that computes the distance between customer and store.

c. Revenue Questions:

    i. How do the sales volume in each store relate to Acell's revenues?

    ii. How does this relationship depend on the configuration?

d. Configuration Questions:

    i. What are the details of each configuration? How does this relate to price?

    ii. Do all stores sell all configurations?

## CHAPTER 4

Dimension Reduction

In this chapter, we describe the important step of dimension reduction. The dimension of a dataset, which is the number of variables, must be reduced for the machine learning algorithms to operate efficiently. This process is part of the pilot/prototype phase of supervised learning and is done before deploying a model. We present and discuss several dimension reduction approaches: (1) incorporating domain knowledge to remove or combine categories, (2) using data summaries to detect information overlap between variables (and remove or combine redundant variables or categories), (3) using data conversion techniques such as converting categorical variables into numerical variables, and (4) employing automated reduction techniques, such as principal component analysis (PCA), where a new set of variables (which are weighted averages of the original variables) is created. These new variables are uncorrelated, and a small subset of them usually contains most of their combined information. Hence, we can reduce dimension by using only a subset of the new variables. Finally, we mention supervised learning methods such as regression models and classification and regression trees, which can be used for removing redundant variables and for combining "similar" categories of categorical variables.

4.1 INTRODUCTION

In machine learning, one often encounters situations where there is a large number of variables in the database. Even when the initial number of variables is small, this set quickly expands in the data preparation step, where new derived variables are created (e.g., dummies for categorical variables and new forms of existing variables). In such situations, it is likely that subsets of variables are highly correlated with each other. Including highly correlated variables in a classification or prediction model or including variables that are unrelated to the

Machine Learning for Business Analytics: Concepts, Techniques, and Applications in R, Second Edition.
Galit Shmueli, Peter C. Bruce, Peter Gedeck, Inbal Yahav, and Nitin R. Patel
© 2023 John Wiley & Sons, Inc. Published 2023 by John Wiley & Sons, Inc.

outcome of interest, can lead to overfitting, and prediction accuracy and relia-bility can suffer. A large number of variables also poses computational problems for some supervised and unsupervised algorithms (aside from questions of cor-relation). In model deployment, superfluous variables can increase costs due to the collection and processing of these variables.

4.2 CURSE OF DIMENSIONALITY

The *dimensionality* of a model is the number of predictors or input variables used by the model. The *curse of dimensionality* is the affliction caused by adding vari-ables to multivariate data models. As variables are added, the data space becomes increasingly sparse, and classification and prediction models fail because the avail-able data are insufficient to provide a useful model across so many variables. An important consideration is the fact that the difficulties posed by adding a variable increase exponentially with the addition of each variable. One way to think of this intuitively is to consider the location of an object on a chessboard. It has two dimensions and 64 squares or choices. If you expand the chessboard to a cube, you increase the dimensions by 50%—from two dimensions to three dimen-sions. However, the location options increase by 800%, to 512 ($8 \times 8 \times 8$). In statistical distance terms, the proliferation of variables means that nothing is close to anything else anymore—too much noise has been added, and patterns and structure are no longer discernible. The problem is particularly acute in Big Data applications, including genomics, where, for example, an analysis might have to deal with values for thousands of different genes. One of the key steps in machine learning, therefore, is finding ways to reduce dimensionality with minimal sacrifice of accuracy. In the artificial intelligence literature, dimension reduction is often referred to as *factor selection*, *feature selection*, or *feature extraction*.

4.3 PRACTICAL CONSIDERATIONS

Although machine learning prefers automated methods over domain knowl-edge, it is important at the first step of data exploration to make sure that the variables measured are reasonable for the task at hand. The integration of expert knowledge through a discussion with the data provider (or user) will probably lead to better results. Practical considerations include: which variables are most important for the task at hand, and which are most likely to be useless? Which variables are likely to contain much error? Which variables will be available for measurement (and what will it cost to measure them) in the future if the analysis is repeated? Which variables can actually be measured before the outcome (tar-get) occurs? For example, if we want to predict the closing price of an ongoing online auction, we cannot use the number of bids as a predictor because this will not be known until the auction closes.

Example 1: House Prices in Boston

We return to the Boston Housing example introduced in Chapter 3. For each neighborhood, a number of variables are given, such as the crime rate, the student/teacher ratio, and the median value of a housing unit in the neighborhood. A description of all 14 variables is given in Table 4.1. The first nine records of the data are shown in Table 4.2. The first row represents the first neighborhood, which had an average per capita crime rate of 0.006, 18% of the residential land zoned for lots over 25,000 ft^2, 2.31% of the land devoted to nonretail business, no border on the Charles River, and so on.

TABLE 4.1   DESCRIPTION OF VARIABLES IN THE BOSTON HOUSING DATASET

CRIM	Crime rate
ZN	Percentage of residential land zoned for lots over 25,000 ft^2
INDUS	Percentage of land occupied by nonretail business
CHAS	Does tract bound Charles River? (= 1 if tract bounds river, = 0 otherwise)
NOX	Nitric oxide concentration (parts per 10 million)
RM	Average number of rooms per dwelling
AGE	Percentage of owner-occupied units built prior to 1940
DIS	Weighted distances to five Boston employment centers
RAD	Index of accessibility to radial highways
TAX	Full-value property tax rate per $10,000
PTRATIO	Pupil-to-teacher ratio by town
LSTAT	Percentage of lower status of the population
MEDV	Median value of owner-occupied homes in $1000s
CAT.MEDV	Is median value of owner-occupied homes in tract above $30,000 (CAT.MEDV = 1) or not (CAT.MEDV = 0)?

TABLE 4.2   FIRST NINE RECORDS IN THE BOSTON HOUSING DATA

CRIM	ZN	INDUS	CHAS	NOX	RM	AGE	DIS	RAD	TAX	PTRATIO	LSTAT	MEDV	CAT.MEDV
0.00632	18.0	2.31	0	0.538	6.575	65.2	4.09	1	296	15.3	4.98	24.0	0
0.02731	0.0	7.07	0	0.469	6.421	78.9	4.9671	2	242	17.8	9.14	21.6	0
0.02729	0.0	7.07	0	0.469	7.185	61.1	4.9671	2	242	17.8	4.03	34.7	1
0.03237	0.0	2.18	0	0.458	6.998	45.8	6.0622	3	222	18.7	2.94	33.4	1
0.06905	0.0	2.18	0	0.458	7.147	54.2	6.0622	3	222	18.7	5.33	36.2	1
0.02985	0.0	2.18	0	0.458	6.43	58.7	6.0622	3	222	18.7	5.21	28.7	0
0.08829	12.5	7.87	0	0.524	6.012	66.6	5.5605	5	311	15.2	12.43	22.9	0
0.14455	12.5	7.87	0	0.524	6.172	96.1	5.9505	5	311	15.2	19.15	27.1	0
0.21124	12.5	7.87	0	0.524	5.631	100.0	6.0821	5	311	15.2	29.93	16.5	0

4.4 DATA SUMMARIES

As we have seen in the chapter on data visualization, an important initial step of data exploration is getting familiar with the data and their characteristics through summaries and graphs. The importance of this step cannot be overstated. The better you understand the data, the better the results from the modeling or mining process.

Numerical summaries and graphs of the data are very helpful for data reduction. The information that they convey can assist in combining categories of a categorical variable, in choosing variables to remove, in assessing the level of information overlap between variables, and more. Before discussing such strategies for reducing the dimension of a dataset, let us consider useful summaries and tools.

Summary Statistics

R has several functions and facilities that assist in summarizing data. The function *summary()* gives an overview of the entire set of variables in the data. The functions *mean()*, *sd()*, *min()*, *max()*, *median()*, and *length()* are also very helpful for learning about the characteristics of each variable. First, they give us information about the scale and type of values that the variable takes. The min and max functions can be used to detect extreme values that might be errors. The mean and median give a sense of the central values of that variable, and a large deviation between the two also indicates skew. The standard deviation gives a sense of how dispersed the data are (relative to the mean). Further options, such as *sum(is.na(variable))*, which gives the number of null values, can alert us about missing values.

Table 4.3 shows summary statistics (and R code) for the Boston Housing example. We immediately see that the different variables have very different ranges of values. We will soon see how variation in scale across variables can distort analyses if not treated properly. Another observation that can be made based on the variable distribution is that the mean of the first variable, CRIM (as well as several others), is much larger than the median, indicating right skew. None of the variables have missing values. There also do not appear to be indications of extreme values that might result from typing errors.

Next, we summarize relationships between two or more variables. For numerical variables, we can compute a complete matrix of correlations between each pair of variables, using the R function *cor()*. Table 4.4 shows the correlation matrix for the Boston Housing variables. We see that most correlations are low and that many are negative. Recall also the visual display of a correlation matrix via a heatmap (see Figure 3.4 in Chapter 3 for the heatmap corresponding to this correlation table). We will return to the importance of the correlation matrix soon, in the context of correlation analysis.

Aggregation and Pivot Tables

Another very useful approach for exploring the data is aggregation by one or more variables. For aggregation by a single variable, we can use *table()*.

TABLE 4.3   SUMMARY STATISTICS FOR THE BOSTON HOUSING DATA

code for summary statistic

```
boston.housing.df <- mlba::BostonHousing
head(boston.housing.df, 9)
summary(boston.housing.df)

# compute mean, standard dev., min, max, median, length, and missing values of CRIM
mean(boston.housing.df$CRIM)
sd(boston.housing.df$CRIM)
min(boston.housing.df$CRIM)
max(boston.housing.df$CRIM)
median(boston.housing.df$CRIM)
length(boston.housing.df$CRIM)

# find the number of missing values of variable CRIM
sum(is.na(boston.housing.df$CRIM))

# compute mean, standard dev., min, max, median, length, and missing values for all
# variables
data.frame(mean=sapply(boston.housing.df, mean),
           sd=sapply(boston.housing.df, sd),
           min=sapply(boston.housing.df, min),
           max=sapply(boston.housing.df, max),
           median=sapply(boston.housing.df, median),
           length=sapply(boston.housing.df, length),
           miss.val=sapply(boston.housing.df,
                       function(x) sum(length(which(is.na(x))))))
```

Partial Output

```
> data.frame(mean=sapply(boston.housing.df, mean),
+            sd=sapply(boston.housing.df, sd),
+            min=sapply(boston.housing.df, min),
+            max=sapply(boston.housing.df, max),
+            median=sapply(boston.housing.df, median),
+            length=sapply(boston.housing.df, length)
+            miss.val=sapply(boston.housing.df,
             function(x) sum(length(which(is.na(x)))))
                     mean          sd       min       max    median length  miss.val
CRIM         3.61352356   8.6015451   0.00632   88.9762   0.25651    506         0
ZN          11.36363636  23.3224530   0.00000  100.0000   0.00000    506         0
INDUS       11.13677866   6.8603529   0.46000   27.7400   9.69000    506         0
CHAS         0.06916996   0.2539940   0.00000    1.0000   0.00000    506         0
NOX          0.55469506   0.1158777   0.38500    0.8710   0.53800    506         0
RM           6.28463439   0.7026171   3.56100    8.7800   6.20850    506         0
AGE         68.57490119  28.1488614   2.90000  100.0000  77.50000    506         0
DIS          3.79504269   2.1057101   1.12960   12.1265   3.20745    506         0
RAD          9.54940711   8.7072594   1.00000   24.0000   5.00000    506         0
TAX        408.23715415 168.5371161 187.00000  711.0000 330.00000    506         0
PTRATIO     18.45553360   2.1649455  12.60000   22.0000  19.05000    506         0
LSTAT       12.65306324   7.1410615   1.73000   37.9700  11.36000    506         0
MEDV        22.53280632   9.1971041   5.00000   50.0000  21.20000    506         0
CAT.MEDV     0.16600791   0.3724560   0.00000    1.0000   0.00000    506         0
```

TABLE 4.4	CORRELATION TABLE FOR BOSTON HOUSING DATA

```
round(cor(boston.housing.df),2)
```

	CRIM	ZN	INDUS	CHAS	NOX	RM	AGE	DIS	RAD	TAX	PTRATIO	LSTAT	MEDV	CAT.MEDV
CRIM	1.00	-0.20	0.41	-0.06	0.42	-0.22	0.35	-0.38	0.63	0.58	0.29	0.46	-0.39	-0.15
ZN	-0.20	1.00	-0.53	-0.04	-0.52	0.31	-0.57	0.66	-0.31	-0.31	-0.39	-0.41	0.36	0.37
INDUS	0.41	-0.53	1.00	0.06	0.76	-0.39	0.64	-0.71	0.60	0.72	0.38	0.60	-0.48	-0.37
CHAS	-0.06	-0.04	0.06	1.00	0.09	0.09	0.09	-0.10	-0.01	-0.04	-0.12	-0.05	0.18	0.11
NOX	0.42	-0.52	0.76	0.09	1.00	-0.30	0.73	-0.77	0.61	0.67	0.19	0.59	-0.43	-0.23
RM	-0.22	0.31	-0.39	0.09	-0.30	1.00	-0.24	0.21	-0.21	-0.29	-0.36	-0.61	0.70	0.64
AGE	0.35	-0.57	0.64	0.09	0.73	-0.24	1.00	-0.75	0.46	0.51	0.26	0.60	-0.38	-0.19
DIS	-0.38	0.66	-0.71	-0.10	-0.77	0.21	-0.75	1.00	-0.49	-0.53	-0.23	-0.50	0.25	0.12
RAD	0.63	-0.31	0.60	-0.01	0.61	-0.21	0.46	-0.49	1.00	0.91	0.46	0.49	-0.38	-0.20
TAX	0.58	-0.31	0.72	-0.04	0.67	-0.29	0.51	-0.53	0.91	1.00	0.46	0.54	-0.47	-0.27
PTRATIO	0.29	-0.39	0.38	-0.12	0.19	-0.36	0.26	-0.23	0.46	0.46	1.00	0.37	-0.51	-0.44
LSTAT	0.46	-0.41	0.60	-0.05	0.59	-0.61	0.60	-0.50	0.49	0.54	0.37	1.00	-0.74	-0.47
MEDV	-0.39	0.36	-0.48	0.18	-0.43	0.70	-0.38	0.25	-0.38	-0.47	-0.51	-0.74	1.00	0.79
CAT.MEDV	-0.15	0.37	-0.37	0.11	-0.23	0.64	-0.19	0.12	-0.20	-0.27	-0.44	-0.47	0.79	1.00

For example, Table 4.5 shows the number of neighborhoods that bound the Charles River vs. those that do not (the variable CHAS is chosen as the grouping variable). It appears that the majority of neighborhoods (471 of 506) do not bound the river.

TABLE 4.5	NUMBER OF NEIGHBORHOODS THAT BOUND THE CHARLES RIVER VS. THOSE THAT DO NOT

```
boston.housing.df <- mlba::BostonHousing
table(boston.housing.df$CHAS)

# tidyverse version
boston.housing.df %>% count(CHAS)

  0    1
471   35
```

The *aggregate()* function can be used for aggregating by one or more variables and computing a range of summary statistics (count, average, percentage, etc.). For categorical variables, we obtain a breakdown of the records by the combination of categories. For instance, in Table 4.6, we compute the average MEDV by CHAS and RM. Note that the numerical variable RM (the average number of rooms per dwelling in the neighborhood) should be first grouped into bins of size 1 (0–1, 1–2, and so on). Note the empty values, denoting that there are no neighborhoods in the dataset with those combinations (e.g., bounding the river and having on average three rooms).

Another useful set of functions are *melt()* and *cast()* in the **reshape** package, which allow the creation of pivot tables. *melt()* takes a set of columns and stacks them into a single column. *cast()* then reshapes the single column into multiple

TABLE 4.6	AVERAGE MEDV BY CHAS AND RM

 code for aggregating MEDV by CHAS and RM

```
# create bins of size 1
boston.housing.df <- boston.housing.df %>%
  mutate(RM.bin = cut(RM, c(1:9), labels=FALSE))

# compute the average of MEDV by (binned) RM and CHAS
# in aggregate() use the argument by= to define the list of aggregating variables,
# and FUN= as an aggregating function.
aggregate(boston.housing.df$MEDV, by=list(RM=boston.housing.df$RM.bin,
        CHAS=boston.housing.df$CHAS), FUN=mean)

# tidyverse version
boston.housing.df %>%
  group_by(RM.bin, CHAS) %>%
  summarise(mean(MEDV))
```

Output

```
   RM CHAS        x
1   3    0 25.30000
2   4    0 15.40714
3   5    0 17.2000
4   6    0 21.76917
5   7    0 35.96444
6   8    0 45.70000
7   5    1 22.21818
8   6    1 25.91875
9   7    1 44.06667
10  8    1 35.95000
```

columns by the aggregating variables of our choice. For example, Table 4.7 computes the average of MEDV by CHAS and RM and presents it as a pivot table.

In classification tasks, where the goal is to find predictor variables that distinguish between two classes, a good exploratory step is to produce summaries for each class. This can assist in detecting useful predictors that display some separation between the two classes. Data summaries are useful for almost any machine learning task and are therefore an important preliminary step for cleaning and understanding the data before carrying out further analyses.

4.5 CORRELATION ANALYSIS

In datasets with a large number of variables (which are likely to serve as predictors), there is usually much overlap in the information covered by the set of

TABLE 4.7	PIVOT TABLES IN R

 code for creating pivot tables using functions *melt()* and *cast()*

```
# use install.packages("reshape") the first time the package is used
library(reshape)
boston.housing.df <- mlba::BostonHousing
# create bins of size 1
boston.housing.df <- boston.housing.df %>%
  mutate(RM.bin = cut(RM, c(1:9), labels=FALSE))

# use melt() to stack a set of columns into a single column of data.
# stack MEDV values for each combination of (binned) RM and CHAS
mlt <- melt(boston.housing.df, id=c("RM.bin", "CHAS"), measure=c("MEDV"))
head(mlt, 5)

# use cast() to reshape data and generate pivot table
cast(mlt, RM.bin ~ CHAS, subset=variable=="MEDV",
     margins=c("grand_row", "grand_col"), mean)

# tidyverse version
boston.housing.df %>%
  group_by(RM.bin, CHAS) %>%
  summarize(mean=mean(MEDV)) %>%
  spread(CHAS, mean)
```

Output

```
% melt
  RM.bin CHAS variable value
1      6    0     MEDV  24.0
2      6    0     MEDV  21.6
3      7    0     MEDV  34.7
4      6    0     MEDV  33.4
5      7    0     MEDV  36.2

% cast - RM.bin in rows, CHAS in columns
  RM.bin        0        1     (all)
1      3 25.30000      NaN 25.30000
2      4 15.40714      NaN 15.40714
3      5 17.20000 22.21818 17.55159
4      6 21.76917 25.91875 22.01599
5      7 35.96444 44.06667 36.91765
6      8 45.70000 35.95000 44.20000
7  (all) 22.09384 28.44000 22.53281
```

variables. One simple way to find redundancies is to look at a correlation matrix. This shows all the pairwise correlations between variables. Pairs that have a very strong (positive or negative) correlation contain a lot of overlap in information and are good candidates for data reduction by removing one of the variables. Removing variables that are strongly correlated to others is useful for avoiding multicollinearity problems that can arise in various models. (*Multicollinearity* is the presence of two or more predictors sharing the same linear relationship with the outcome variable; R handles this automatically in regression.)

Correlation analysis is also a good method for detecting duplications of variables in the data. Sometimes, the same variable appears accidentally more than once in the dataset (under a different name) because the dataset was merged from multiple sources, the same phenomenon is measured in different units, and so on. Using correlation table heatmaps, as shown in Chapter 3, can make the task of identifying strong correlations easier.

4.6 REDUCING THE NUMBER OF CATEGORIES IN CATEGORICAL VARIABLES

When a categorical variable (i.e., having a nominal type) has many categories, and this variable is destined to be a predictor, many machine learning methods will require converting it into many dummy variables. In particular, a variable with m categories will be transformed into either m or $m - 1$ dummy variables (depending on the method). This means that even if we have very few original categorical variables, they can greatly inflate the dimension of the dataset. One way to handle this is to reduce the number of categories by combining close or similar categories. Combining categories requires incorporating expert knowledge and common sense. Pivot tables are useful for this task: we can examine the sizes of the various categories and how the outcome variable behaves in each category. Generally, categories that contain very few observations are good candidates for combining with other categories. Use only the categories that are most relevant to the analysis, and label the rest as "other." In classification tasks (with a categorical outcome variable of nominal type, i.e., class label), a pivot table broken down by the outcome classes can help identify categories that do not separate the classes. Those categories too are candidates for inclusion in the "other" category. An example is shown in Figure 4.1, where the distribution of outcome variable CAT.MEDV is broken down by ZN (treated here as a categorical variable). We can see that the distribution of CAT.MEDV is identical for ZN = 17.5, 90, 95, and 100 (where all neighborhoods have CAT.MEDV = 1). These four categories can then be combined into a single category. Similarly, categories ZN = 12.5, 25, 28, 30, and 70 can be combined. Further combination is also possible based on similar bars.

In a time series context where we might have a categorical variable denoting season (such as month, or hour of day) that will serve as a predictor, reducing categories can be done by examining the time series plot and identifying similar periods. For example, the time plot in Figure 4.2 shows the quarterly revenues of

FIGURE 4.1   DISTRIBUTION OF CAT.MEDV (BLACK DENOTES CAT.MEDV = 0) BY ZN. SIMILAR BARS INDICATE LOW SEPARATION BETWEEN CLASSES AND CAN BE COMBINED

 code for creating Figure 4.1

```
boston.housing.df <- mlba::BostonHousing

tbl <- table(boston.housing.df$CAT.MEDV, boston.housing.df$ZN)
prop.tbl <- prop.table(tbl, margin=2)
barplot(prop.tbl, xlab="ZN", ylab="", yaxt="n",main="Distribution of CAT.MEDV by ZN")
axis(2, at=(seq(0,1, 0.2)), paste(seq(0,100,20), "%"))

library(tidyverse)
df <- data.frame(prop.tbl)
ggplot(df, aes(x=Var2, y=Freq, group=Var1, fill=Var1)) +
  geom_bar(stat="identity", color="grey", width=1) +
  scale_y_continuous(labels = scales::percent, expand=expansion()) +
  scale_fill_manual("CAT.MEDV", values=c("0"="#eeeeee", "1"="darkgrey")) +
  labs(x="ZN", y="", title="Distribution of CAT.MEDV by ZN")
```

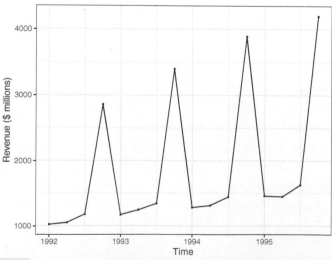

FIGURE 4.2   QUARTERLY REVENUES OF TOYS "R" US, 1992–1995

Toys "R" Us between 1992 and 1995. Only quarter 4 periods appear different, and therefore, we can combine quarters 1–3 into a single category.

4.7 CONVERTING A CATEGORICAL VARIABLE TO A NUMERICAL VARIABLE

Sometimes the categories in a categorical variable represent intervals. Common examples are age group or income bracket. If the interval values are known (e.g., category 2 is the age interval 20–30), we can replace the categorical value ("2" in the example) with the mid-interval value (here "25"). The result will be a numerical variable which no longer requires multiple dummy variables.

4.8 PRINCIPAL COMPONENT ANALYSIS

Principal component analysis (PCA) is a useful method for dimension reduction, especially when the number of variables is large. PCA is especially valuable when we have subsets of measurements that are measured on the same scale and are highly correlated. In that case, it provides a few variables (often as few as three) that are weighted linear combinations of the original variables and that retain the majority of the information of the full original set. PCA is intended for use with numerical variables. For categorical variables, other methods such as correspondence analysis are more suitable.

Example 2: Breakfast Cereals

Data were collected on the nutritional information and consumer rating of 77 breakfast cereals.[1] The consumer rating is a rating of cereal "healthiness" for consumer information (not a rating by consumers). For each cereal, the data include 13 numerical variables, and we are interested in reducing this dimension. For each cereal, the information is based on a bowl of cereal rather than a serving size, because most people simply fill a cereal bowl (resulting in constant volume, but not weight). A snapshot of these data is given in Figure 4.3, and the description of the different variables is given in Table 4.8.

We focus first on two variables: *calories* and *consumer rating*. These are given in Table 4.9. The average calories across the 77 cereals is 106.88, with standard deviation of 19.48. The average consumer rating is 42.67 with standard deviation 14.05. The two variables are strongly correlated with a negative correlation of −0.69.

---

[1] The data are available at https://dasl.datadescription.com/datafile/cereals/.

Cereal Name	mfr	type	calories	protein	fat	sodium	fiber	carbo	sugars	potass	vitamins
100% Bran	N	C	70	4	1	130	10	5	6	280	25
100% Natural Bran	Q	C	120	3	5	15	2	8	8	135	0
All-Bran	K	C	70	4	1	260	9	7	5	320	25
All-Bran with Extra Fiber	K	C	50	4	0	140	14	8	0	330	25
Almond Delight	R	C	110	2	2	200	1	14	8		25
Apple Cinnamon Cheerios	G	C	110	2	2	180	1.5	10.5	10	70	25
Apple Jacks	K	C	110	2	0	125	1	11	14	30	25
Basic 4	G	C	130	3	2	210	2	18	8	100	25
Bran Chex	R	C	90	2	1	200	4	15	6	125	25
Bran Flakes	P	C	90	3	0	210	5	13	5	190	25
Cap'n'Crunch	Q	C	120	1	2	220	0	12	12	35	25
Cheerios	G	C	110	6	2	290	2	17	1	105	25
Cinnamon Toast Crunch	G	C	120	1	3	210	0	13	9	45	25
Clusters	G	C	110	3	2	140	2	13	7	105	25
Cocoa Puffs	G	C	110	1	1	180	0	12	13	55	25
Corn Chex	R	C	110	2	0	280	0	22	3	25	25
Corn Flakes	K	C	100	2	0	290	1	21	2	35	25
Corn Pops	K	C	110	1	0	90	1	13	12	20	25
Count Chocula	G	C	110	1	1	180	0	12	13	65	25
Cracklin' Oat Bran	K	C	110	3	3	140	4	10	7	160	25

FIGURE 4.3   SAMPLE FROM THE 77 BREAKFAST CEREALS DATASET

TABLE 4.8   DESCRIPTION OF THE VARIABLES IN THE BREAKFAST CEREAL DATASET

Variable	Description
mfr	Manufacturer of cereal (American Home Food Products, General Mills, Kellogg, etc.)
type	Cold or hot
calories	Calories per serving
protein	Grams of protein
fat	Grams of fat
sodium	Milligrams of sodium
fiber	Grams of dietary fiber
carbo	Grams of complex carbohydrates
sugars	Grams of sugars
potass	Milligrams of potassium
vitamins	Vitamins and minerals: 0, 25, or 100, indicating the typical percentage of FDA recommended
shelf	Display shelf (1, 2, or 3, counting from the floor)
weight	Weight in ounces of one serving
cups	Number of cups in one serving
rating	Rating of the cereal calculated by consumer reports

Roughly speaking, 69% of the total variation in both variables is actually "co-variation," or variation in one variable that is duplicated by similar variation in the other variable. Can we use this fact to reduce the number of variables while making maximum use of their unique contributions to the overall variation? Since there is redundancy in the information that the two variables contain, it might be possible to reduce the two variables to a single variable without losing too much information. The idea in PCA is to find a linear combination of the

TABLE 4.9   CEREAL CALORIES AND RATINGS

Cereal	Calories	Rating	Cereal	Calories	Rating
100% Bran	70	68.40297	Just Right Fruit & Nut	140	36.471512
100% Natural Bran	120	33.98368	Kix	110	39.241114
All-Bran	70	59.42551	Life	100	45.328074
All-Bran with Extra Fiber	50	93.70491	Lucky Charms	110	26.734515
Almond Delight	110	34.38484	Maypo	100	54.850917
Apple Cinnamon Cheerios	110	29.50954	Muesli Raisins, Dates & Almonds	150	37.136863
Apple Jacks	110	33.17409	Muesli Raisins, Peaches & Pecans	150	34.139765
Basic 4	130	37.03856	Mueslix Crispy Blend	160	30.313351
Bran Chex	90	49.12025	Multi-Grain Cheerios	100	40.105965
Bran Flakes	90	53.31381	Nut&Honey Crunch	120	29.924285
Cap'n'Crunch	120	18.04285	Nutri-Grain Almond-Raisin	140	40.69232
Cheerios	110	50.765	Nutri-grain Wheat	90	59.642837
Cinnamon Toast Crunch	120	19.82357	Oatmeal Raisin Crisp	130	30.450843
Clusters	110	40.40021	Post Nat. Raisin Bran	120	37.840594
Cocoa Puffs	110	22.73645	Product 19	100	41.50354
Corn Chex	110	41.44502	Puffed Rice	50	60.756112
Corn Flakes	100	45.86332	Puffed Wheat	50	63.005645
Corn Pops	110	35.78279	Quaker Oat Squares	100	49.511874
Count Chocula	110	22.39651	Quaker Oatmeal	100	50.828392
Cracklin' Oat Bran	110	40.44877	Raisin Bran	120	39.259197
Cream of Wheat (Quick)	100	64.53382	Raisin Nut Bran	100	39.7034
Crispix	110	46.89564	Raisin Squares	90	55.333142
Crispy Wheat & Raisins	100	36.1762	Rice Chex	110	41.998933
Double Chex	100	44.33086	Rice Krispies	110	40.560159
Froot Loops	110	32.20758	Shredded Wheat	80	68.235885
Frosted Flakes	110	31.43597	Shredded Wheat 'n'Bran	90	74.472949
Frosted Mini-Wheats	100	58.34514	Shredded Wheat spoon size	90	72.801787
Fruit & Fibre Dates, Walnuts & Oats	120	40.91705	Smacks	110	31.230054
Fruitful Bran	120	41.01549	Special K	110	53.131324
Fruity Pebbles	110	28.02577	Strawberry Fruit Wheats	90	59.363993
Golden Crisp	100	35.25244	Total Corn Flakes	110	38.839746
Golden Grahams	110	23.80404	Total Raisin Bran	140	28.592785
Grape Nuts Flakes	100	52.0769	Total Whole Grain	100	46.658844
Grape-Nuts	110	53.37101	Triples	110	39.106174
Great Grains Pecan	120	45.81172	Trix	110	27.753301
Honey Graham Ohs	120	21.87129	Wheat Chex	100	49.787445
Honey Nut Cheerios	110	31.07222	Wheaties	100	51.592193
Honey-comb	110	28.74241	Wheaties Honey Gold	110	36.187559
Just Right Crunchy Nuggets	110	36.52368			

two variables that contains most, even if not all, of the information so that this new variable can replace the two original variables. Information here is in the sense of variability: what can explain the most variability *among* the 77 cereals? The total variability here is the sum of the variances (squared standard deviations) of the two variables, which in this case is $19.48^2 + 14.05^2 = 577$. This means that *calories* accounts for $66\% = 19.48^2/577$ of the total variability and *rating* for the remaining 34%. If we drop one of the variables for the sake of dimension reduction, we lose at least 34% of the total variability. Can we redistribute the total variability between two new variables in a more polarized way? If so, it might be possible to keep only the one new variable that (hopefully) accounts for a large portion of the total variation.

Figure 4.4 shows a scatter plot of *rating* vs. *calories*. The line z_1 is the direction in which the variability of the points is largest. It is the line that captures the most variation in the data if we decide to reduce the dimensionality of the data from two to one. Among all possible lines, it is the line for which, if we project the points in the dataset orthogonally to get a set of 77 (one-dimensional) values, the variance of the z_1 values will be maximum. This is called the *first principal component* (PC). It is also the line that minimizes the sum-of-squared perpendicular distances from the line. The z_2-axis is chosen to be perpendicular to the z_1-axis. In the case of two variables, there is only one line that is perpendicular to z_1, and it has the second largest variability, but its information is uncorrelated with z_1. This is called the *second principal component*. In general, when we have more than two variables, once we find the direction z_1 with the

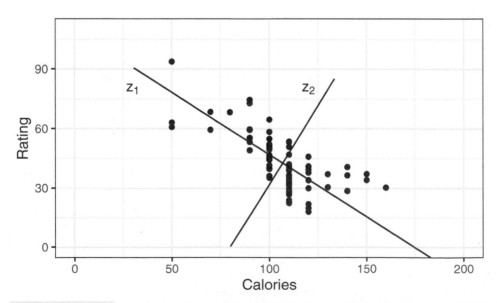

FIGURE 4.4   SCATTER PLOT OF *RATING* VS. *CALORIES* FOR 77 BREAKFAST CEREALS, WITH THE TWO PRINCIPAL COMPONENT DIRECTIONS

largest variability, we search among all the orthogonal directions to z_1 for the one with the next-highest variability. That is z_2. The idea is then to find the coordinates of these lines and to see how they redistribute the variability.

Running PCA in R is done with the function *prcomp()* . Table 4.10 shows the output from running PCA on the two variables *calories* and *rating*. The value *.rot* of this function is the rotation matrix, which gives the weights that are used to project the original points onto the two new directions. The weights for z_1 are given by (0.847, −0.532), and for z_2 they are given by (0.532, 0.847). The function *summary()* gives the reallocated variance: z_1 accounts for 86% of the total variability and z_2 for the remaining 14%. Therefore, if we drop z_2, we still maintain 86% of the total variability.

The weights are used to compute principal component scores, which are the projected values of *calories* and *rating* onto the new axes (after subtracting the

TABLE 4.10   **PCA ON THE TWO VARIABLES *CALORIES* AND *RATING***

 code for running PCA

```
library(tidyverse)
cereals.df <- mlba::Cereals %>% select(calories, rating)
# compute PCs on two dimensions
pcs <- prcomp(cereals.df %>% select(calories, rating))
summary(pcs)
pcs$rot
scores <- pcs$x
head(scores, 5)
```

Output

```
> summary(pcs)
Importance of components:
                          PC1    PC2
Standard deviation     22.3165 8.8844
Proportion of Variance  0.8632 0.1368
Cumulative Proportion   0.8632 1.0000

> pcs$rot
               PC1         PC2
calories   0.8470535  0.5315077
rating    -0.5315077  0.8470535

> scores <- pcs$x
> head(scores, 5)
           PC1         PC2
[1,] -44.921528   2.1971833
[2,]  15.725265  -0.3824165
[3,] -40.149935  -5.4072123
[4,] -75.310772  12.9991256
[5,]   7.041508  -5.3576857
```

means). In R, scores for the two dimensions are depicted by the PCA value pcs$x. The first column is the projection onto z_1 using the weights (0.847, −0.532). The second column is the projection onto z_2 using the weights (0.532, 0.847). For example, the first score for the 100% Bran cereal (with 70 calories and a rating of 68.4) is $(0.847)(70 − 106.88) + (−0.532)(68.4 − 42.67) = −44.92$.

Note that the means of the new variables z_1 and z_2 are zero, because we've subtracted the mean of each variable. The sum of the variances var(z_1)+var(z_2) is equal to the sum of the variances of the original variables, var(*calories*) + var(*rating*). Furthermore, the variances of z_1 and z_2 are 498 and 79, respectively, so the first principal component, z_1, accounts for 86% of the total variance. Since it captures most of the variability in the data, it seems reasonable to use one variable, the first principal score, to represent the two variables in the original data. Next, we generalize these ideas to more than two variables.

Principal Components

Let us formalize the procedure described above so that it can easily be generalized to $p > 2$ variables. Denote the original p variables by $X_1, X_2, \ldots, X_p$. In PCA, we are looking for a set of new variables $Z_1, Z_2, \ldots, Z_p$ that are weighted averages of the original variables (after subtracting their mean):

$$Z_i = a_{i,1}(X_1 − \bar{X}_1) + a_{i,2}(X_2 − \bar{X}_2) + \cdots + a_{i,p}(X_p − \bar{X}_p), \quad i = 1, \ldots, p \tag{4.1}$$

where each pair of Z's has correlation = 0. We then order the resulting Z's by their variance, with Z_1 having the largest variance and Z_p having the smallest variance. The software computes the weights $a_{i,j}$, which are then used in computing the principal component scores.

A further advantage of the principal components compared with the original data is that they are uncorrelated (correlation coefficient = 0). If we construct regression models using these principal components as predictors, we will not encounter problems of multicollinearity.

Let us return to the breakfast cereal dataset with all 15 variables and apply PCA to the 13 numerical variables. The resulting output is shown in Table 4.11. Note that the first three components account for more than 96% of the total variation associated with all 13 of the original variables. This suggests that we can capture most of the variability in the data with less than 25% of the original dimensions in the data. In fact, the first two principal components alone capture 92.6% of the total variation. However, these results are influenced by the scales of the variables, as we describe next.

TABLE 4.11	PCA OUTPUT USING ALL 13 NUMERICAL VARIABLES IN THE BREAKFAST CEREALS DATASET. THE TABLE SHOWS RESULTS FOR THE FIRST FIVE PRINCIPAL COMPONENTS

```
# load and preprocess the data
cereals.df <- mlba::Cereals %>%
  column_to_rownames("name") %>%
  select(-c(mfr, type)) %>%
  drop_na()

pcs <- prcomp(cereals.df)
summary(pcs)
pcs$rotation[,1:5]
```

Output

```
> pcs <  prcomp(cereals.df)
> summary(pcs)

Importance of components:
                          PC1      PC2       PC3       PC4      PC5      PC6      PC7
Standard deviation     83.7641  70.9143  22.64375  19.18148  8.42323  2.09167  1.69942
Proportion of Variance  0.5395   0.3867   0.03943   0.02829  0.00546  0.00034  0.00022
Cumulative Proportion   0.5395   0.9262   0.96560   0.99389  0.99935  0.99968  0.99991
                          PC8      PC9      PC10     PC11     PC12      PC13
Standard deviation      0.77963  0.65783  0.37043  0.1864   0.06302  5.334e-08
Proportion of Variance  0.00005  0.00003  0.00001  0.0000   0.00000  0.000e+00
Cumulative Proportion   0.99995  0.99999  1.00000  1.0000   1.00000  1.000e+00

> pcs$rotation[,1:5]

                   PC1            PC2            PC3            PC4           PC5
calories    0.0779841812   0.0093115874  -0.6292057595  -0.6010214629   0.454958508
protein    -0.0007567806  -0.0088010282  -0.0010261160   0.0031999095   0.056175970
fat        -0.0001017834  -0.0026991522  -0.0161957859  -0.0252622140  -0.016098458
sodium      0.9802145422  -0.1408957901   0.1359018583  -0.0009680741   0.013948118
fiber      -0.0054127550  -0.0306807512   0.0181910456   0.0204721894   0.013605026
carbo       0.0172462607   0.0167832981  -0.0173699816   0.0259482087   0.349266966
sugars      0.0029888631   0.0002534853  -0.0977049979  -0.1154809105  -0.299066459
potass     -0.1349000039  -0.9865619808  -0.0367824989  -0.0421757390  -0.047150529
vitamins    0.0942933187  -0.0167288404  -0.6919777623   0.7141179984  -0.037008623
shelf      -0.0015414195  -0.0043603994  -0.0124888415   0.0056471836  -0.007876459
weight      0.0005120017  -0.0009992138  -0.0038059565  -0.0025464145   0.003022113
cups        0.0005101111   0.0015910125  -0.0006943214   0.0009853800   0.002148458
rating     -0.0752962922  -0.0717421528   0.3079471212   0.3345338994   0.757708025
```

Normalizing the Data

A further use of PCA is to understand the structure of the data. This is done by examining the weights to see how the original variables contribute to the different principal components. In our example, it is clear that the first principal component is dominated by the sodium content of the cereal: it has the highest (in this case, positive) weight. This means that the first principal component is in fact measuring how much sodium is in the cereal. Similarly, the second principal component seems to be measuring the amount of potassium. Since both these variables are measured in milligrams, whereas the other nutrients are measured in grams, the scale is obviously leading to this result. The variances of potassium and sodium are much larger than the variances of the other variables, and thus the total variance is dominated by these two variances. A solution is to normalize the data before performing the PCA. Normalization (or standardization) means replacing each original variable by a standardized version of the variable that has unit variance. This is easily accomplished by dividing each variable by its standard deviation. The effect of this normalization is to give all variables equal importance in terms of variability.

When should we normalize the data like this? It depends on the nature of the data. When the units of measurement are common for the variables (e.g., dollars), and when their scale reflects their importance (sales of jet fuel, sales of heating oil), it is probably best not to normalize (i.e., not to rescale the data so that they have unit variance). If the variables are measured in different units so that it is unclear how to compare the variability of different variables (e.g., dollars for some, parts per million for others) or if for variables measured in the same units, scale does not reflect importance (earnings per share, gross revenues), it is generally advisable to normalize. In this way, the differences in units of measurement do not affect the principal components' weights. In the rare situations where we can give relative weights to variables, we multiply the normalized variables by these weights before doing the PCA.

Thus far, we have calculated principal components using the covariance matrix. An alternative to normalizing and then performing PCA is to perform PCA on the correlation matrix instead of the covariance matrix. Most software programs allow the user to choose between the two. Remember that using the correlation matrix means that you are operating on the normalized data.

Returning to the breakfast cereal data, we normalize the 13 variables due to the different scales of the variables and then perform PCA (or equivalently, we use PCA applied to the correlation matrix). The output is given in Table 4.12.

Now we find that we need seven principal components to account for more than 90% of the total variability. The first two principal components account for only 52% of the total variability, and thus reducing the number of variables to two would mean losing a lot of information. Examining the weights, we see that the first principal component measures the balance between two quantities: (1) calories and cups (large positive weights) vs. (2) protein, fiber, potassium, and consumer rating (large negative weights). High scores on principal component 1 mean that the cereal is high in calories and the amount per bowl while it is low in protein and potassium. Unsurprisingly, this type of cereal is associated with a low consumer rating. The second principal component is most affected by the weight of a serving, and the third principal component by the carbohydrate

TABLE 4.12   PCA OUTPUT USING ALL *NORMALIZED* 13 NUMERICAL VARIABLES IN THE BREAKFAST CEREALS DATASET. THE TABLE SHOWS RESULTS FOR THE FIRST FIVE PRINCIPAL COMPONENTS

```
# Use function prcomp() with scale. = T to run PCA on normalized data
pcs.cor <- prcomp(cereals.df, scale. = T)

summary(pcs.cor)
pcs.cor$rotation[,1:5]

Output
```

```
> pcs.cor <- prcomp(cereals.df, scale. = T)
> summary(pcs.cor)

Importance of components:
                         PC1     PC2     PC3     PC4     PC5     PC6      PC7      PC8
Standard deviation     1.9062  1.7743  1.3818  1.00969  0.9947  0.84974  0.81946  0.64515
Proportion of Variance 0.2795  0.2422  0.1469  0.07842  0.0761  0.05554  0.05166  0.03202
Cumulative Proportion  0.2795  0.5217  0.6685  0.74696  0.8231  0.87861  0.93026  0.96228
                         PC9     PC10    PC11    PC12     PC13
Standard deviation     0.56192 0.30301 0.25194 0.13897  1.499e-08
Proportion of Variance 0.02429 0.00706 0.00488 0.00149  0.000e+00
Cumulative Proportion  0.98657 0.99363 0.99851 1.00000  1.000e+00

> pcs.cor$rotation[,1:5]

                  PC1          PC2          PC3          PC4          PC5
calories   0.29954236   0.3931479  -0.114857453   0.20435870   0.20389885
protein   -0.30735632   0.1653233  -0.277281953   0.30074318   0.31974897
fat        0.03991542   0.3457243   0.204890102   0.18683311   0.58689327
sodium     0.18339651   0.1372205  -0.389431009   0.12033726  -0.33836424
fiber     -0.45349036   0.1798119  -0.069766079   0.03917361  -0.25511906
carbo      0.19244902  -0.1494483  -0.562452458   0.08783547   0.18274252
sugars     0.22806849   0.3514345   0.355405174  -0.02270716  -0.31487243
potass    -0.40196429   0.3005442  -0.067620183   0.09087843  -0.14836048
vitamins   0.11598020   0.1729092  -0.387858660  -0.60411064  -0.04928672
shelf     -0.17126336   0.2650503   0.001531036  -0.63887859   0.32910135
weight     0.05029930   0.4503085  -0.247138314   0.15342874  -0.22128334
cups       0.29463553  -0.2122479  -0.139999705   0.04748909   0.12081645
rating    -0.43837841  -0.2515389  -0.181842433   0.03831622   0.05758420
```

content. We can continue labeling the next principal components in a similar fashion to learn about the structure of the data.

When the data can be reduced to two dimensions, a useful plot is a scatter plot of the first vs. second principal scores with labels for the observations (if the dataset is not too large). To illustrate this, Figure 4.5 displays the first two principal component scores for the breakfast cereals.

We can see that as we move from left (bran cereals) to right, the cereals are less "healthy" in the sense of high calories, low protein and fiber, and so on. Also, moving from bottom to top, we get heavier cereals (moving from puffed rice to raisin bran). These plots are especially useful if interesting clusters of

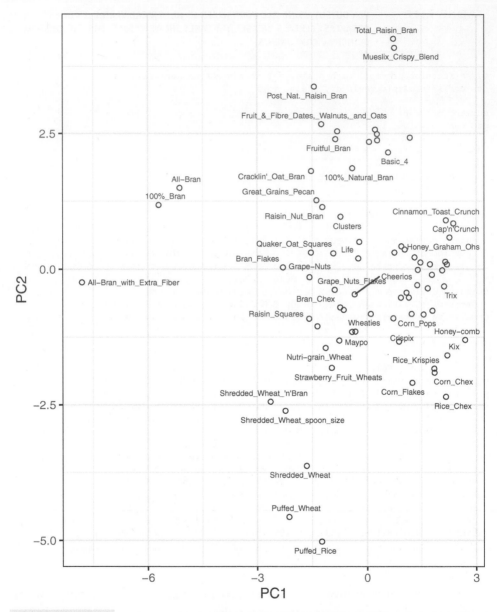

FIGURE 4.5   SCATTER PLOT OF THE SECOND VS. FIRST PRINCIPAL COMPONENTS SCORES FOR
THE NORMALIZED BREAKFAST CEREAL OUTPUT

observations can be found. For instance, we see here that children's cereals are close together on the middle-left part of the plot.

Using Principal Components for Classification and Prediction

When the goal of the data reduction is to have a smaller set of variables that will serve as predictors, we can proceed as follows: apply PCA to the predictors using the training data. Use the output to determine the number of principal components to be retained. The predictors in the model now use the (reduced number of) principal scores columns. For the holdout set, we can use the weights computed from the training data to obtain a set of principal scores by applying the weights to the variables in the holdout set. These new variables are then treated as the predictors.

One disadvantage of using a subset of principal components as predictors in a supervised task is that we might lose predictive information that is nonlinear (e.g., a quadratic effect of a predictor on the outcome variable or an interaction between predictors). This is because PCA produces linear transformations, thereby capturing linear relationships between the original variables.

4.9   DIMENSION REDUCTION USING REGRESSION MODELS

In this chapter, we discussed methods for reducing the number of columns using summary statistics, plots, and PCA. All these are considered exploratory methods. Some of them completely ignore the outcome variable (e.g., PCA), whereas in other methods we informally try to incorporate the relationship between the predictors and the outcome variable (e.g., combining similar categories, in terms of their outcome variable behavior). Another approach to reducing the number of predictors, which directly considers the predictive or classification task, is by fitting a regression model. For prediction, a linear regression model is used (see Chapter 6), and for classification, a logistic regression model is used (see Chapter 10). In both cases, we can employ subset selection procedures that algorithmically choose a subset of predictor variables among the larger set (see details in the relevant chapters).

Fitted regression models can also be used to further combine similar categories: categories that have coefficients that are not statistically significant (i.e., have a high p-value) can be combined with the reference category, because their distinction from the reference category appears to have no significant effect on the outcome variable. Moreover, categories that have similar coefficient values (and the same sign) can often be combined, because their effect on the outcome variable is similar. See the example in Chapter 10 on predicting delayed flights for an illustration of how regression models can be used for dimension reduction.

4.10   DIMENSION REDUCTION USING CLASSIFICATION AND REGRESSION TREES

Another method for reducing the number of columns and for combining categories of a categorical variable is by applying classification and regression trees (see Chapter 9). Classification trees are used for classification tasks and regression trees for prediction tasks. In both cases, the algorithm creates binary splits on the predictors that best classify/predict the outcome variable (e.g., above/below age 30). Although we defer the detailed discussion to Chapter 9, we note here that the resulting tree diagram can be used for determining the important predictors. Predictors (numerical or categorical) that do not appear in the tree can be removed. Similarly, categories that do not appear in the tree can be combined.

PROBLEMS

4.1 **Breakfast Cereals.** Use the data for the breakfast cereals example in Section 4.8 to explore and summarize the data as follows:

    a. Which variables are quantitative/numerical? Which are ordinal? Which are nominal?

    b. Compute the mean, median, min, max, and standard deviation for each of the quantitative variables. This can be done through R's *sapply()* function (e.g., *sapply(data, mean, na.rm=TRUE)*).

    c. Use R to plot a histogram for each of the quantitative variables. Based on the histograms and summary statistics, answer the following questions:

        i. Which variables have the largest variability?

        ii. Which variables seem skewed?

        iii. Are there any values that seem extreme?

    d. Use R to plot a side-by-side boxplot comparing the calories in hot vs. cold cereals. What does this plot show us?

    e. Use R to plot a side-by-side boxplot of consumer rating as a function of the shelf height. If we were to predict consumer rating from shelf height, does it appear that we need to keep all three categories of shelf height?

    f. Compute the correlation table for the quantitative variable (function *cor()*). In addition, generate a matrix plot for these variables (function *plot(data)*).

        i. Which pair of variables is most strongly correlated?

        ii. How can we reduce the number of variables based on these correlations?

        iii. How would the correlations change if we normalized the data first?

    g. Consider the first PC of the analysis of the 13 numerical variables in Table 4.11. Describe briefly what this PC represents.

4.2 **University Rankings.** The dataset on American college and university rankings (available as dataset *mlba::Universities*) contains information on 1302 American colleges and universities offering an undergraduate program. For each university, there are 17 measurements that include continuous measurements (such as tuition and graduation rate) and categorical measurements (such as location by state and whether it is a private or a public school).

    a. Remove all categorical variables. Then remove all records with missing numerical measurements from the dataset.

    b. Conduct a principal component analysis on the cleaned data and comment on the results. Should the data be normalized? Discuss what characterizes the components you consider key.

4.3 **Chemical Features of Wine.** Table 4.13 shows the PCA output on data (non-normalized) in which the variables represent chemical characteristics of wine, and each case is a different wine.

    a. The data are in the *mlba::Wine* dataset. Consider the rows labeled "Proportion of Variance." Explain why the value for PC1 is so much greater than that of any other column.

    b. Comment on the use of normalization (standardization) in part (a).

TABLE 4.13	PRINCIPAL COMPONENTS OF NON-NORMALIZED WINE DATA

 code for running PCA on the wine data

```
wine.df <- mlba::Wine %>% select(-Type)
pcs.cor <- prcomp(wine.df)
summary(pcs.cor)
pcs.cor$rotation[,1:4]
```

Output

```
> summary(pcs.cor)

importance of components:
                          PC1      PC2      PC3      PC4      PC5
Standard deviation    314.9632 13.13527 3.07215 2.23409 1.10853
Proportion of Variance  0.9981  0.00174 0.00009 0.00005 0.00001
Cumulative Proportion   0.9981  0.99983 0.99992 0.99997 0.99998
                          PC6      PC7      PC8      PC9     PC10
Standard deviation    0.91710  0.5282  0.3891  0.3348  0.2678
Proportion of Variance 0.00001 0.0000  0.0000  0.0000  0.0000
Cumulative Proportion  0.99999 1.0000  1.0000  1.0000  1.0000
                         PC11    PC12     PC13
Standard deviation    0.1938  0.1452  0.09057
Proportion of Variance 0.0000  0.0000  0.00000
Cumulative Proportion  1.0000  1.0000  1.00000

> pcs.cor$rotation[,1:4]

                               PC1             PC2           PC3           PC4
Alcohol              -0.0016592647 -0.00120340617 -0.016873809   0.141446778
Malic_Acid            0.0006810156 -0.00215498184 -0.122003373   0.160389543
Ash                  -0.0001949057 -0.00459369254 -0.051987430  -0.009772810
Ash_Alcalinity        0.0046713006 -0.02645039303 -0.938593003  -0.330965260
Magnesium            -0.0178680075 -0.99934418606  0.029780248  -0.005393756
Total_Phenols        -0.0009898297 -0.00087796215  0.040484644  -0.074584656
Flavanoids           -0.0015672883  0.00005185073  0.085443339  -0.169086724
Nonflavanoid_Phenols  0.0001230867  0.00135447892 -0.013510780   0.010805561
Proanthocyanins      -0.0006006078 -0.00500440040  0.024659382  -0.050120952
Color_Intensity      -0.0023271432 -0.01510035300 -0.291398464   0.878893693
Hue                  -0.0001713800  0.00076267312  0.025977662  -0.060034945
OD280_OD315          -0.0007049316  0.00349536431  0.070323969  -0.178200254
Proline              -0.9998229365  0.01777380946 -0.004528682  -0.003112916
```

4.4   **Sales of Toyota Corolla Cars.** The *mlba::ToyotaCorolla* dataset contains data on used cars (Toyota Corollas) on sale during late summer of 2004 in the Netherlands. It has 1436 records containing details on 38 variables, including Price, Age, Kilometers, HP, and other specifications. The goal will be to predict the price of a used Toyota Corolla based on its specifications.

    a. Identify an outlier observation, possibly caused due to a data entry error. This can be done by analyzing the data summary. Filter out this observation for the subsequent analysis.

    b. Identify the categorical variables.

c. Explain the relationship between a categorical variable and the series of binary dummy variables derived from it.

d. How many dummy binary variables are required to capture the information in a categorical variable with N categories?

e. Use R to convert the categorical variables in this dataset into dummy variables, and explain in words, for one record, the values in the derived binary dummies.

f. Use R to produce a correlation matrix and matrix plot. Comment on the relationships among variables.

## PART III

Performance Evaluation

## CHAPTER 5

Evaluating Predictive Performance

In this chapter, we discuss how the predictive performance of machine learning methods can be assessed. We point out the danger of overfitting to the training data and the need to test model performance on data that were not used in the training step. We discuss popular performance metrics. For prediction, metrics include average error, mean absolute percentage error (MAPE), and root mean squared error (RMSE) (based on the holdout data). For classification tasks, metrics based on the confusion matrix include overall accuracy, specificity and sensitivity, and metrics that account for misclassification costs. We also show the relation between the choice of threshold value and classification performance and present the receiver operating characteristic (ROC) curve, which is a popular chart for assessing method performance at different threshold values. When the goal is to accurately classify the most interesting or important records, called *ranking*, rather than accurately classify the entire sample (e.g., the 10% of customers most likely to respond to an offer or the 5% of claims most likely to be fraudulent), cumulative gains and lift charts are used to assess performance. We also discuss the need for oversampling rare classes and how to adjust performance metrics for the oversampling. Finally, we mention the usefulness of comparing metrics based on the holdout data with those based on the training data for the purpose of detecting overfitting. While some differences are expected, extreme differences can be indicative of overfitting.

Evaluating Performance in R

The main R packages used in this chapter are `caret`, `ROCR`, and `gains` for performance metrics and charts.

Machine Learning for Business Analytics: Concepts, Techniques, and Applications in R, Second Edition.
Galit Shmueli, Peter C. Bruce, Peter Gedeck, Inbal Yahav, and Nitin R. Patel
© 2023 John Wiley & Sons, Inc. Published 2023 by John Wiley & Sons, Inc.

5.1   INTRODUCTION

In supervised learning, we are interested in predicting the outcome variable for new records. Three main types of outcomes of interest are:

Predicted numerical value: when the outcome variable is numerical (e.g., house price)

Predicted class membership: when the outcome variable is categorical (e.g., buyer/nonbuyer)

Propensity: the probability of class membership, when the outcome variable is categorical (e.g., the propensity to default).

Prediction methods are used for generating numerical predictions, while classification methods ("classifiers") are used for generating propensities and, using a threshold value on the propensities, we can generate predicted class memberships.

A subtle distinction to keep in mind is the two distinct predictive uses of classifiers: one use, *classification*, is aimed at predicting class membership for new records. The other, *ranking*, is detecting among a set of new records the ones most likely to belong to a class of interest.

Let's now examine the approach for judging the usefulness of a prediction method used for generating numerical predictions (Section 5.2), a classifier used for classification (Section 5.3), and a classifier used for ranking (Section 5.4). In Section 5.5, we'll look at evaluating performance under the scenario of oversampling.

5.2   EVALUATING PREDICTIVE PERFORMANCE

First, let us emphasize that predictive accuracy is not the same as goodness of fit. Classical statistical measures of performance are aimed at finding a model that fits well to the data on which the model was trained. In machine learning, we are interested in models that have high predictive accuracy when applied to *new* records. Measures such as R^2 and standard error of estimate are common metrics in classical regression modeling, and residual analysis is used to gauge goodness of fit in that situation. However, these measures do not tell us much about the ability of the model to predict new records.

For assessing prediction performance, several measures are used. In all cases, the measures are based on the holdout set, which serves as a more objective ground than the training set to assess predictive accuracy. This is because records in the holdout set are more similar to the future records to be predicted, in the sense that they are not used to select predictors or to estimate the model parameters. Models are trained on the training data, applied to the holdout data, and measures of accuracy then use the prediction errors on that holdout set.

Naive Benchmark: The Average

The benchmark criterion in prediction is using the average outcome value (thereby ignoring all predictor information). In other words, the prediction for a new record is simply the average across the outcome values of the records in the training set ($\bar{y}$). This is sometimes called a naive benchmark. A good predictive model should outperform the benchmark criterion in terms of predictive accuracy.

Prediction Accuracy Measures

The prediction error for record i is defined as the difference between its actual outcome value and its predicted outcome value: $e_i = y_i - \hat{y}_i$. A few popular numerical measures of predictive accuracy are as follows:

MAE (mean absolute error/deviation) = $\frac{1}{n}\sum_{i=1}^{n}|e_i|$. This gives the magnitude of the average absolute error.

Mean error = $\frac{1}{n}\sum_{i=1}^{n}e_i$. This measure is similar to MAE except that it retains the sign of the errors so that negative errors cancel out positive errors of the same magnitude. It therefore gives an indication of whether the predictions are on average over- or underpredicting the outcome variable.

MPE (mean percentage error) = $100 \times \frac{1}{n}\sum_{i=1}^{n}e_i/y_i$. This gives the percentage score of how predictions deviate from the actual values (on average), taking into account the direction of the error.

MAPE (mean absolute percentage error) = $100 \times \frac{1}{n}\sum_{i=1}^{n}|e_i/y_i|$. This measure gives a percentage score of how predictions deviate (on average) from the actual values.

RMSE (root mean squared error) = $\sqrt{\frac{1}{n}\sum_{i=1}^{n}e_i^2}$. This is similar to the standard error of estimate in linear regression, except that it is computed on the holdout data rather than on the training data. It has the same units as the outcome variable.

Such measures can be used to compare models and to assess their degree of prediction accuracy. Note that all these measures are influenced by outliers. To check outlier influence, we can compute median-based measures (and compare to the above mean-based measures) or simply plot a histogram or boxplot of the errors. Plotting the prediction errors' distribution is in fact very useful and can highlight more information than the metrics alone.

To illustrate the use of predictive accuracy measures and charts of prediction error distribution, consider the error metrics and charts shown in Table 5.1 and

TABLE 5.1	PREDICTION ERROR METRICS FROM A MODEL FOR TOYOTA CAR PRICES. TRAINING AND HOLDOUT

 code for accuracy measure

```
library(tidyverse)
set.seed(1)

# load and preprocess file
car.df <- mlba::ToyotaCorolla %>%
    select(-one_of("Id", "Model", "Fuel_Type", "Color")) %>%
    drop_na()


# randomly generate training and holdout sets
idx <- caret::createDataPartition(car.df$Price, p=0.6, list=FALSE)
train.df <- car.df[idx, ]
holdout.df <- car.df[-idx, ]

# run linear regression model
reg <- lm(Price~., data=train.df)
pred_t <- predict(reg)
pred_h <- predict(reg, newdata=holdout.df)

## evaluate performance
# training
caret::RMSE(pred_t, train.df$Price)
# holdout
caret::RMSE(pred_h, holdout.df$Price)
# use utility function from the mlba package to calculate various metrics at once
rbind(
  Training=mlba::regressionSummary(pred_t, train.df$Price),
  Holdout=mlba::regressionSummary(pred_h, holdout.df$Price)
)
```

Partial Output

	ME	RMSE	MAE	MAPE
Training	0.000	1045.999	778.976	7.674176
Holdout	126.6309	1395.578	915.0846	8.99556

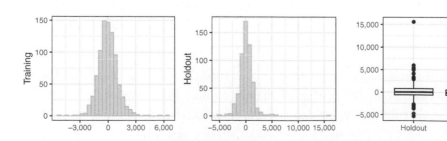

FIGURE 5.1	HISTOGRAMS AND BOXPLOTS OF TOYOTA PRICE PREDICTION ERRORS, FOR TRAINING AND HOLDOUT SETS

Figure 5.1. These are the result of fitting a certain predictive model to prices of used Toyota Corolla cars. The training set includes 600 cars and the holdout set includes 400 cars. Results are displayed separately for the training and holdout sets. We can see from the histogram and boxplot corresponding to the holdout set that most errors are in the $[-1000, 1000]$ range, with a few large positive (under-prediction) errors.

Comparing Training and Holdout Performance

Errors that are based on the training set tell us about model fit, whereas those that are based on the holdout set (called "prediction errors") measure the model's ability to predict new data (predictive performance). We expect training errors to be smaller than the holdout errors (because the model was fitted using the training set), and the more complex the model, the greater the likelihood that it will *overfit* the training data (indicated by a greater difference between the training and holdout errors). In an extreme case of overfitting, the training errors would be zero (perfect fit of the model to the training data), and the holdout errors would be non-zero and non-negligible. For this reason, it is important to compare the error plots and metrics (RMSE, MAE, etc.) of the training and holdout sets. Table 5.1 illustrates this comparison: the training set performance measures appear much lower (better) than those for the holdout set. However, the charts reveal more than the metrics alone: looking at the charts in Figure 5.1, the discrepancies are most likely due to some outliers in the holdout set, especially the asymmetric outliers in the holdout set. The positive holdout errors (under-predictions) are slightly larger than the training errors, as reflected by the medians and outliers.

Cumulative Gains and Lift Charts

In some applications, the goal is to search, among a set of new records, for a subset of records that gives the highest cumulative predicted values. In such cases, a graphical way to assess predictive performance is through the *cumulative gains chart* and *lift chart*. This compares the model's predictive performance to a baseline model that has no predictors.[1] Cumulative gains and lift charts for a continuous response are relevant only when we are searching for a set of records that gives the highest cumulative predicted values. Such charts are not relevant if we are interested in predicting the outcome value for *each* new record.

To illustrate this type of goal, called *ranking*, consider a car rental firm that renews its fleet regularly so that customers drive late-model cars. This entails

---

[1]The terms *lift* and *gains* are occasionally used interchangeably; to avoid confusion we use the prevalent definitions in which *cumulative gains* refers to the sum of outcome values for the top cases identified by a model, and *lift* to the ratio of that sum to the sum obtained through random selection.

disposing of a large quantity of used vehicles on a continuing basis. Since the firm is not primarily in the used car sales business, it tries to dispose of as much of its fleet as possible through volume sales to used car dealers. However, it is profitable to sell a limited number of cars through its own channels. Its volume deals with the used car dealers allow it flexibility to pick and choose which cars to sell in this fashion, so it would like to have a model for selecting cars for resale through its own channels. Since all cars were purchased some time ago and the deals with the used car dealers are for fixed prices (specifying a given number of cars of a certain make and model class), the cars' costs are now irrelevant, and the dealer is interested only in maximizing revenue. This is done by selecting for its own resale, the cars likely to generate the most revenue. The lift chart in this case gives the predicted lift for revenue.

The cumulative gains and lift charts are based on ordering the set of records of interest (typically holdout data) by their predicted value, from high to low. Then, we accumulate the actual values and plot their cumulative value (=gains) on the y-axis as a function of the number of records accumulated (the x-axis value). This is the *cumulative gains* curve. This curve is compared with assigning a naive prediction ($\bar{y}$) to each record and accumulating these average values, which results in a diagonal line. The further away the cumulative gains curve from the diagonal benchmark line, the better the model is doing in separating records with high value outcomes from those with low value outcomes. The same information can be presented in a decile lift chart, where the ordered records are grouped into 10 deciles, and for each decile, the chart presents the ratio of model gains to naive benchmark gains, which is called *lift*.

Figure 5.2 shows a cumulative gains chart and decile lift chart based on fitting a linear regression model to the Toyota data. The charts are based on the holdout data of 573 cars. It can be seen that the model's predictive performance in terms of gains is better than the baseline model, since its cumulative gains curve is higher than that of the baseline model. The charts in Figure 5.2 would be useful in the following scenario: choosing the top 10% of the cars that gave the highest predicted sales, for example, we would gain 1.85 times the amount of revenue, compared with choosing 10% of the cars at random. This lift number can also be computed from the cumulative gains chart by comparing the sales for 57 random cars (the value of the baseline curve at $x = 57$), which is \$619,401 (= the sum of the actual sales for the 573 validation set cars divided by 10), with the actual sales of the 57 cars that have the highest predicted values (the value of the cumulative gains curve at $x = 57$), which is \$1,137,362. The ratio between these numbers is 1.85.

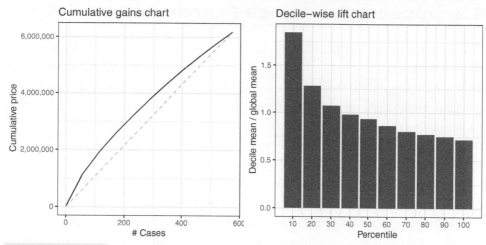

FIGURE 5.2   CUMULATIVE GAINS CHART (LEFT) AND DECILE LIFT CHART (RIGHT) FOR CONTINUOUS OUTCOME VARIABLE (SALES OF TOYOTA CARS)

code for generating a cumulative gains chart and decile-wise lift chart for the regression model from Table 5.1

```
library(ggplot2)
library(gridExtra)

# load package gains, compute gains (we will use package caret for categorical y later)
library(gains)
price <- holdout.df$Price
gain <- gains(price, pred_h)

# cumulative lift chart
# we will compute the gain relative to price
df <- data.frame(
  ncases=c(0, gain$cume.obs),
  cumPrice=c(0, gain$cume.pct.of.total * sum(price))
)
g1 <- ggplot(df, aes(x=ncases, y=cumPrice)) +
  geom_line() +
  geom_line(data=data.frame(ncases=c(0, nrow(holdout.df)), cumPrice=c(0, sum(price))),
            color="gray", linetype=2) + # adds baseline
  labs(x="# Cases", y="Cumulative price", title="Cumulative gains chart") +
  scale_y_continuous(labels = scales::comma)

# Decile-wise lift chart
df <- data.frame(
  percentile=gain$depth,
  meanResponse=gain$mean.resp / mean(price)
)
g2 <- ggplot(df, aes(x=percentile, y=meanResponse)) +
  geom_bar(stat="identity") +
  labs(x="Percentile", y="Decile mean / global mean", title="Decile-wise lift chart")

grid.arrange(g1, g2, ncol=2)
```

5.3 JUDGING CLASSIFIER PERFORMANCE

The need for performance measures arises from the wide choice of classifiers and predictive methods. Not only do we have several different methods, but even within a single method there are usually many options that can lead to completely different results. A simple example is the choice of predictors used within a particular predictive algorithm. Before we study these various algorithms in detail and face decisions on how to set these options, we need to know how we will measure success.

A natural criterion for judging the performance of a classifier is the probability of making a *misclassification error*. Misclassification means that the record belongs to one class but the model classifies it as a member of a different class. A classifier that makes no errors would be perfect, but we do not expect to be able to construct such classifiers in the real world due to "noise" and not having all the information needed to classify records precisely. Is there a minimal probability of misclassification that we should require of a classifier?

Benchmark: The Naive Rule

A very simple rule for classifying a record into one of m classes, ignoring all predictor information $(x_1, x_2, \ldots, x_p)$ that we may have, is to classify the record as a member of the majority class. In other words, "classify as belonging to the most prevalent class." The *naive rule* is used mainly as a baseline or benchmark for evaluating the performance of more complicated classifiers. Clearly, a classifier that uses external predictor information (on top of the class membership allocation) should outperform the naive rule. There are various performance measures based on the naive rule that measure how much better than the naive rule a certain classifier performs.

Similar to using the sample mean $(\bar{y})$ as the naive benchmark in the numerical outcome case, the naive rule for classification relies solely on the y information and excludes any additional predictor information.

Class Separation

If the classes are well separated by the predictor information, even a small dataset will suffice in finding a good classifier, whereas if the classes are not separated at all by the predictors, even a very large dataset will not help. Figure 5.3 illustrates this for a two-class case. The top panel includes a small dataset ($n = 24$ records) where two predictors (income and lot size) are used for separating owners from nonowners [we thank Dean Wichern for this example, described in Johnson and Wichern (2002)]. Here, the predictor information seems useful in that it separates the two classes (owners/nonowners). The bottom panel shows a much larger dataset ($n = 5000$ records) where the two predictors (income and monthly

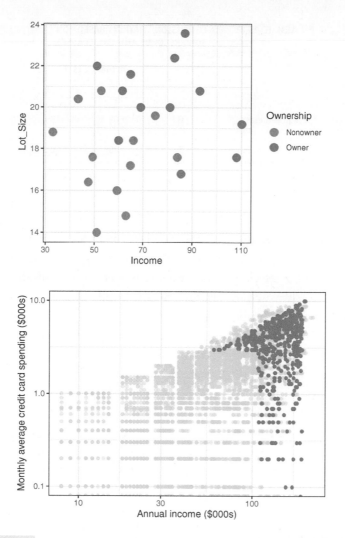

FIGURE 5.3   HIGH (TOP) AND LOW (BOTTOM) LEVELS OF SEPARATION BETWEEN TWO CLASSES, USING TWO PREDICTORS

average credit card spending) do not separate the two classes well in most of the higher ranges (loan acceptors/nonacceptors).

The Confusion (Classification) Matrix

In practice, most accuracy measures are derived from the *confusion matrix*, also called *classification matrix*. This matrix summarizes the correct and incorrect classifications that a classifier produced for a certain dataset. Rows and columns of the confusion matrix correspond to the predicted and true (actual) classes, respectively. Table 5.2 shows an example of a classification (confusion) matrix for a two-class (0/1) problem resulting from applying a certain classifier to 3000

TABLE 5.2	CONFUSION MATRIX BASED ON 3000 RECORDS AND TWO CLASSES		
		Actual class	
		0	1
Predicted class	0	2689	85
	1	25	201

records. The two diagonal cells (upper left, lower right) give the number of correct classifications, where the predicted class coincides with the actual class of the record. The off-diagonal cells give counts of misclassification. The top right cell gives the number of class 1 members that were misclassified as 0's (in this example, there were 85 such misclassifications). Similarly, the lower-left cell gives the number of class 0 members that were misclassified as 1's (25 such records). In R, we can obtain a confusion matrix using the function *confusionMatrix()* in the **caret** package. This function creates the cross-tabulation of actual and predicted classes. We will see an example later in this chapter.

The confusion matrix gives estimates of the true classification and misclassification rates. Of course, these are estimates and they can be incorrect, but if we have a large enough dataset and neither class is very rare, our estimates will be reliable. Sometimes, we may be able to use public data such as US Census data to estimate these proportions. However, in most business settings, we will not know them.

Using the Holdout Data

To obtain an honest estimate of future classification error, we use the confusion matrix that is computed from the *holdout data*. In other words, we first partition the data into training and holdout sets by random selection of records. We then construct a classifier using the training data and then apply it to the holdout data. This will yield the predicted classifications for records in the holdout set (see Figure 2.4 in Chapter 2). We then summarize these classifications in a confusion matrix. Although we can summarize our results in a confusion matrix for training data as well, the resulting confusion matrix is not useful for getting an honest estimate of the misclassification rate for new data due to the danger of overfitting.

In addition to examining the holdout data confusion matrix to assess the classification performance on new data, we compare the training data confusion matrix with the holdout data confusion matrix, in order to detect overfitting: although we expect somewhat inferior results on the holdout data, a large discrepancy in training and holdout performance might be indicative of overfitting.

Accuracy Measures

Different accuracy measures can be derived from the classification matrix. Consider a two-class case with classes C_1 and C_2 (e.g., buyer/non-buyer). The schematic confusion matrix in Table 5.3 uses the notation $n_{i,j}$ to denote the number of records that are class C_i members and were classified as C_j members. Of course, if $i \neq j$, these are counts of misclassifications. The total number of records is $n = n_{1,1} + n_{1,2} + n_{2,1} + n_{2,2}$.

TABLE 5.3   CONFUSION MATRIX: MEANING OF EACH CELL

		Actual class	
		C_1	C_2
Predicted class	C_1	$n_{1,1}$ = number of C_1 records classified correctly	$n_{2,1}$ = number of C_2 records classified incorrectly as C_1
	C_2	$n_{1,2}$ = number of C_1 records classified incorrectly as C_2	$n_{2,2}$ = number of C_2 records classified correctly

A main accuracy measure is the *estimated misclassification rate*, also called the *overall error rate*. It is given by

$$\text{err} = \frac{n_{1,2} + n_{2,1}}{n},$$

where n is the total number of records in the holdout dataset. In the example in Table 5.2, we get $\text{err} = (25 + 85)/3000 = 3.67\%$.

We can measure accuracy by looking at the correct classifications—the full half of the cup—instead of the misclassifications. The *overall accuracy* of a classifier is estimated by

$$\text{accuracy} = 1 - \text{err} = \frac{n_{1,1} + n_{2,2}}{n}.$$

In the example, we have $(201 + 2689)/3000 = 96.33\%$.

Propensities and Threshold for Classification

The first step in most classification algorithms is to estimate the probability that a record belongs to each of the classes. These probabilities are also called *propensities*. Propensities are typically used either as an interim step for generating predicted class membership (classification) or for rank-ordering the records by their probability of belonging to a class of interest. Let us consider their first use in this section. The second use is discussed in Section 5.4.

If overall classification accuracy (involving all the classes) is of interest, the record can be assigned to the class with the highest probability. In many contexts, a single class is of special interest, which is also called the *positive class*. So we will focus on that particular class and compare the propensity of belonging to that class to a *threshold value* (or *cutoff value*) set by the analyst. This approach can be used with two classes or more than two classes, though it may make sense in such cases to consolidate classes so that you end up with two: the class of interest and all other classes. If the probability of belonging to the class of interest is above the cutoff, the record is assigned to that class.

The default threshold value in two-class classifiers is 0.5. Thus, if the probability of a record being a class C_1 member is greater than 0.5, that record is classified as a C_1. Any record with an estimated probability of less than 0.5 would be classified as a C_2. It is possible, however, to use a threshold that is either higher or lower than 0.5. A threshold greater than 0.5 will end up classifying fewer records as C_1's, whereas a threshold less than 0.5 will end up classifying more records as C_1. Typically, the misclassification rate will rise in either case.

Consider the data in Table 5.4, showing the actual class for 24 records, sorted by the probability that the record is an "owner" (as estimated by a machine learning algorithm). If we adopt the standard 0.5 as the threshold, our misclassification rate is 3/24, whereas if we instead adopt a threshold of 0.25, we classify more records as owners, and the misclassification rate goes up (comprising more nonowners misclassified as owners) to 5/24. Conversely, if we adopt a threshold of 0.75, we classify fewer records as owners. The misclassification rate goes up (comprising more owners misclassified as nonowners) to 6/24. All this can be seen in the confusion matrices in Table 5.5. Note that R's *confusionMatrix()* output uses the term "Reference" for the actual class.

To see the entire range of threshold values and how the accuracy or misclassification rates change as a function of the threshold, we can plot the performance measure of interest vs. the threshold. The results for the riding-mowers example are shown in Figure 5.4. We can see that the accuracy level is pretty stable around 0.8 for threshold values between 0.2 and 0.8.

TABLE 5.4	24 RECORDS WITH THEIR ACTUAL CLASS AND THE PROBABILITY (PROPENSITY) OF THEM BEING CLASS "OWNER" MEMBERS, AS ESTIMATED BY A CLASSIFIER

Actual class	Probability of class "owner"	Actual class	Probability of class "owner"
Owner	0.9959	Owner	0.5055
Owner	0.9875	Nonowner	0.4713
Owner	0.9844	Nonowner	0.3371
Owner	0.9804	Owner	0.2179
Owner	0.9481	Nonowner	0.1992
Owner	0.8892	Nonowner	0.1494
Owner	0.8476	Nonowner	0.0479
Nonowner	0.7628	Nonowner	0.0383
Owner	0.7069	Nonowner	0.0248
Owner	0.6807	Nonowner	0.0218
Owner	0.6563	Nonowner	0.0161
Nonowner	0.6224	Nonowner	0.0031

TABLE 5.5	CONFUSION MATRICES BASED ON THRESHOLDS OF 0.5, 0.25, AND 0.75 (RIDING-MOWERS EXAMPLE)

```
# note: function confusionMatrix requires library caret
library(caret)
owner.df <- mlba::OwnerExample
## threshold = 0.5
confusionMatrix(factor(ifelse(owner.df$Probability>0.5, "owner", "nonowner")),
                owner.df$Class)$table
# note: "reference" = "actual"
## threshold = 0.25
confusionMatrix(factor(ifelse(owner.df$Probability>0.25, "owner", "nonowner")),
                owner.df$Class)$table
## threshold = 0.75
confusionMatrix(factor(ifelse(owner.df$Probability>0.75, "owner", "nonowner")),
                owner.df$Class)$table
```

Partial Output

```
## threshold = 0.5
> confusionMatrix(ifelse(owner.df$Probability>0.5, "owner", "nonowner"), owner.df$Class)
# note: "reference" = "actual"
Confusion Matrix and Statistics

          Reference
Prediction nonowner owner
  nonowner       10     1
  owner           2    11

               Accuracy : 0.875

## threshold = 0.25
> confusionMatrix(ifelse(owner.df$Probability>0.25, "owner", "nonowner"), owner.df$Class)
Confusion Matrix and Statistics

          Reference
Prediction nonowner owner
  nonowner        8     1
  owner           4    11

               Accuracy : 0.7916667

## threshold = 0.75
> confusionMatrix(ifelse(owner.df$Probability>0.75, "owner", "nonowner"), owner.df$Class)
Confusion Matrix and Statistics

          Reference
Prediction nonowner owner
  nonowner       11     5
  owner           1     7

               Accuracy : 0.75
```

FIGURE 5.4   **PLOTTING ACCURACY AND OVERALL ERROR AS A FUNCTION OF THE THRESHOLD VALUE (RIDING-MOWERS EXAMPLE)**

 code for creating Figure 5.4

```
# replace data.frame with your own
df <- mlba::LiftExample

# compute accuracy per threshold
result = data.frame()
for (cut in seq(0,1,0.1)){
  cm <- confusionMatrix(factor(1 * (df$prob > cut), levels=c(0,1)),
                        factor(df$actual, levels=c(0,1)))
  result <- bind_rows(result,
                      c(Threshold=cut, cm$overall["Accuracy"]))
}
result$Error <- 1 - result$Accuracy

# plot accuracy and error rate
ggplot(result, aes(x=Threshold)) +
  geom_line(aes(y=Accuracy, linetype="Accuracy")) +
  geom_line(aes(y=Error, linetype="Overall error"), color="gray") +
  labs(x="Threshold value", y="", linetype="Legend")
```

Why would we want to use threshold values different from 0.5 if they increase the misclassification rate? The answer is that it might be more important to classify owners properly than nonowners, and we would tolerate a greater misclassification of the latter. Or the reverse might be true; in other words, the costs of misclassification might be asymmetric. We can adjust the threshold value in such a case to classify more records as the high-value class, that is, accept more misclassifications where the misclassification cost is low. Keep in mind that we are doing so after the machine learning model has already been selected—we are not changing that model. It is also possible to incorporate costs into the picture before deriving the model. These subjects are discussed in greater detail below.

THRESHOLD VALUES FOR TRIAGE

In some cases, it is useful to have two thresholds and allow a "cannot say" option for the classifier. In a two-class situation, this means that for a record, we can make one of three predictions: the record belongs to C_1, or the record belongs to C_2, or we cannot make a prediction because there is not enough information to pick C_1 or C_2 confidently. Records that the classifier cannot classify are subjected to closer scrutiny either by using expert judgment or by enriching the set of predictor variables by gathering additional information that is perhaps more difficult or expensive to obtain. An example is classification of documents found during legal discovery (reciprocal forced document disclosure in a legal proceeding). Under traditional human-review systems, qualified legal personnel are needed to review what might be tens of thousands of documents to determine their relevance to a case. Using a classifier and a triage outcome, documents could be sorted into clearly relevant, clearly not relevant, and the gray area documents requiring human review. This substantially reduces the costs of discovery.

Performance in Case of Unequal Importance of Classes

Suppose that it is more important to predict membership correctly in class C_1 than in class C_2. An example is predicting the financial status (bankrupt/solvent) of firms. It may be more important to predict correctly a firm that is going bankrupt than to predict correctly a firm that is going to remain solvent. The classifier is essentially used as a system for detecting or signaling bankruptcy. In such a case, the overall accuracy is not a good measure for evaluating the classifier. Suppose that the important class is C_1. The following pair of accuracy measures are the most popular:

The sensitivity (also termed *recall*) of a classifier is its ability to detect the important class members correctly. This is measured by $n_{1,1}/(n_{1,1} + n_{1,2})$, the percentage of C_1 (positive) members that are correctly classified. Sensitivity is also called the *True Positive Rate (TPR)*.

The specificity of a classifier is its ability to rule out C_2 (negative class) members correctly. This is measured by $n_{2,2}/(n_{2,1} + n_{2,2})$, the percentage of C_2 (negative) members that are correctly classified. Specificity is also called the *True Negative Rate (TNR)*.

It can be useful to plot these measures against the threshold value in order to find a threshold value that balances these measures.

ROC Curve   A more popular method for plotting the two measures is through *ROC* (Receiver Operating Characteristic) *curves*. Starting from the lower left, the ROC curve plots the pairs {sensitivity, specificity} as the threshold value descends from 1 to 0. (A typical alternative presentation is to plot 1-specificity on the x-axis, which allows 0 to be placed on the left end of the axis and 1 on the right.) Better performance is reflected by curves that are closer to the top-left corner. The comparison curve is the diagonal, which reflects the average performance of a guessing classifier that has no information about the predictors or outcome variable. This guessing classifier guesses that a proportion α of the records is 1's and therefore assigns each record an equal probability $P(Y = 1) = \alpha$. In this case, on average, a proportion α of the 1's will be correctly classified (Sensitivity = α), and a proportion α of the 0's will be correctly classified (1–Specificity = α). As we increase the threshold value α from 0 to 1, we get the diagonal line Sensitivity = 1–Specificity. Note that the naive rule is one point on this diagonal line, where α = proportion of actual 1's.

A common metric to summarize an ROC curve is "area under the curve (AUC)," which ranges from 1 (perfect discrimination between classes) to 0.5 (no better than random guessing). AUC is commonly used to compare models, especially when there are many models and algorithms under consideration. It has the advantage of simplicity and can be compared across datasets with different positive class rates. However, the AUC has several critical deficiencies arising from the fact that it considers all misclassifications (negatives as positives and positives as negatives) as being of equal value. For example, some areas of

---

COMPUTING RATES: FROM WHOSE POINT OF VIEW?

Sensitivity and specificity measure the performance of a classifier from the point of view of the "classifying agency" (e.g., a company classifying customers or a hospital classifying patients). They answer the question "how well does the classifier segregate the important class members?" It is also possible to measure accuracy from the perspective of the entity being classified (e.g., the customer or the patient), who asks "given my predicted class, what is my chance of actually belonging to that class?" The terms "false discovery rate" and "false omission rate" are measures of performance from the perspective of the individual entity. If C_1 is the important (positive) class, then they are defined as

The false discovery rate (FDR) is the proportion of C_1 predictions that are wrong, equal to $n_{2,1}/(n_{1,1} + n_{2,1})$. Note that this is a ratio within the row of C_1 predictions (i.e., it uses only records that were classified as C_1).

The false omission rate (FOR) is the proportion of C_2 predictions that are wrong, equal to $n_{1,2}/(n_{1,2} + n_{2,2})$. Note that this is a ratio within the row of C_2 predictions (that is, it uses only records that were classified as C_2).

the ROC curve may be irrelevant (e.g., if extremely low sensitivity is unacceptable). AUC comparisons across models can be misleading: when ROC curves of different algorithms cross, a larger AUC value might correspond to poorer performance over almost the entire range of threshold values (Hand, 2009). For further issues, see Lobo et al. (2008). We therefore advocate not using AUC as a single performance metric for selecting a model.

The ROC curve for the owner/nonowner example and its corresponding AUC are shown in Figure 5.5.

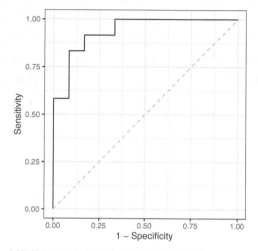

FIGURE 5.5   ROC CURVE FOR RIDING-MOWERS EXAMPLE

 code for generating ROC curve and computing AUC

```
library(ROCR)
predob <- prediction(df$prob, df$actual)
perf <- performance(predob, "tpr", "fpr")
perf.df <- data.frame(
  tpr=perf@x.values[[1]],
  fpr=perf@y.values[[1]]
)
ggplot(perf.df, aes(x=tpr, y=fpr)) +
  geom_line() +
  geom_segment(aes(x=0, y=0, xend=1, yend=1), color="grey", linetype="dashed") +
  labs(x="1 - Specificity", y="Sensitivity")

# get the AUC value
performance(predob, measure="auc")@y.values[[1]]
```

Output

```
> performance(predob, measure="auc")@y.values[[1]]
[1] 0.9375
```

Precision and Recall In addition to sensitivity and specificity, there is another performance measure called *precision* that is often considered in tandem with recall (sensitivity):

The **precision** of a classifier is its ability to correctly detect only the important (positive) class members. This is measured by $n_{1,1}/(n_{1,1} + n_{0,1})$, the percentage of correctly classified positive (C_1) members among all those classified as positive.

For a two-class classifier, there tends to be a tradeoff between precision and recall. While precision is a measure of *exactness* (what percentage of members classified as C_1 actually belong to C_1), recall is a measure of *completeness* (what percentage of C_1 members are classified as such). Depending on the business context, precision may be more important than recall, and vice versa. For example, for credit card fraud detection (positive class = fraudulent), we would want recall close to 1 since we want to find *all* transactions that are truly fraudulent, and we can accept low precision (mistakenly classifying non-fraudulent transactions as fraudulent) if the cost of such misclassification is not too high. The threshold value can be selected based on whether precision or recall is a more important consideration.

A metric called *F1-score* is used to combine precision and recall values into a single measure, giving them equal weights. F1-score is given by

$$F1 = \frac{2 \times \text{precision} \times \text{recall}}{(\text{precision} + \text{recall})}.$$

We can plot precision, recall, and F1-score against the threshold to see the precision–recall tradeoff as a function of threshold values. The results for the riding-mowers example are shown in Figure 5.6. We can see that recall is relatively stable around 0.9 for threshold values between 0.2 and 0.6, while precision is generally increasing. The highest F1-score 0.88 is at threshold value of 0.5.

Asymmetric Misclassification Costs

Implicit in our discussion of the lift curve, which measures how effective we are in identifying the members of one particular class, is the assumption that the error of misclassifying a record belonging to one class is more serious than for the other class. For example, misclassifying a household as unlikely to respond to a sales offer when it belongs to the class that would respond incurs a greater cost (the opportunity cost of the foregone sale) than the converse error. In the former case, you are missing out on a sale worth perhaps tens or hundreds of dollars. In the latter, you are incurring the costs of contacting someone who will not purchase. In such a scenario, using the misclassification rate as a criterion can be misleading.

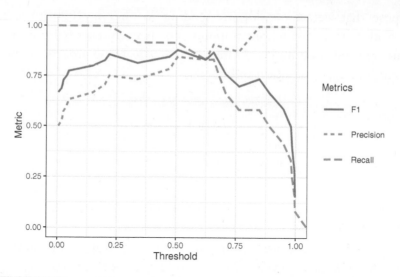

FIGURE 5.6   PRECISION, RECALL, AND F1-SCORE AS A FUNCTION OF THE THRESHOLD VALUE

Note that we are assuming that the cost (or benefit) of making correct classifications is zero. At first glance, this may seem incomplete. After all, the benefit (negative cost) of classifying a buyer correctly as a buyer would seem substantial. Also, in other circumstances (e.g., using our classification algorithm to score fresh data to implement our decisions), it will be appropriate to consider the actual net dollar impact of each possible classification (or misclassification). Here, however, we are attempting to assess the value of a classifier in terms of classification error, so it greatly simplifies matters if we can capture all cost/benefit information in the misclassification cells. So, instead of recording the benefit of classifying a respondent household correctly, we record the cost of failing to classify it as a respondent household. It amounts to the same thing, and our goal becomes the minimization of costs, whether the costs are actual costs or missed benefits (opportunity costs).

Consider the situation where the sales offer is mailed to a random sample of people for the purpose of constructing a good classifier. Suppose that the offer is accepted by 1% of those households. For these data, if a classifier simply classifies every household as a non-responder, it will have an error rate of only 1% but it will be useless in practice. A classifier that misclassifies 2% of buying households as nonbuyers and 20% of the nonbuyers as buyers would have a higher error rate but would be better if the profit from a sale is substantially higher than the cost of sending out an offer. In these situations, if we have estimates of the cost of both types of misclassification, we can use the confusion matrix to compute the expected cost of misclassification for each record in the holdout data. This enables us to compare different classifiers using overall expected costs (or profits) as the criterion.

Suppose that we are considering sending an offer to 1000 more people, where on average 1% of whom respond (1). Naively classifying everyone as a 0 has an error rate of only 1%. Using a machine learning process, suppose that we can produce these classifications:

	Actual 0	Actual 1
Predicted 0	970	2
Predicted 1	20	8

These classifications have an error rate of $100 \times (20 + 2)/1000 = 2.2\%$—higher than the naive rate.

Now suppose that the profit from a responder is $10 and the cost of sending the offer is $1. Classifying everyone as a 0 still has a misclassification rate of only 1% but yields a profit of $0. Using the machine learning process, despite the higher misclassification rate, yields a profit of $60.

The matrix of profit is as follows (nothing is sent to the predicted 0's so there are no costs or sales in that row):

Profit	Actual 0	Actual 1
Predicted 0	0	0
Predicted 1	− $20	$80

Looked at purely in terms of costs, when everyone is classified as a 0, there are no costs of sending the offer; the only costs are the opportunity costs of failing to make sales to the ten 1's = $100. The cost (actual costs of sending the offer plus the opportunity costs of missed sales) of using the machine learning process to select people to send the offer to is only $48:

Costs	Actual 0	Actual 1
Predicted 0	0	$20
Predicted 1	$20	$8

However, this does not improve the actual classifications themselves. A better method is to change the classification rules (and hence the misclassification rates) as discussed in the preceding section, to reflect the asymmetric costs.

A popular performance measure that includes costs is the *average misclassification cost*, which measures the average cost of misclassification per classified record. Denote by q_1 the cost of misclassifying a class C_1 record (as belonging to class C_2) and by q_2 the cost of misclassifying a class C_2 record (as belonging to class C_1). The average misclassification cost is

$$\frac{q_1 n_{1,2} + q_2 n_{2,1}}{n}.$$

Thus, we are looking for a classifier that minimizes this quantity. This can be computed, for instance, for different threshold values.

It turns out that the optimal parameters are affected by the misclassification costs only through the ratio of these costs. This can be seen if we write the foregoing measure slightly differently:

$$\frac{q_1 n_{1,2} + q_2 n_{2,1}}{n} = \frac{n_{1,2}}{n_{1,1} + n_{1,2}} \frac{n_{1,1} + n_{1,2}}{n} q_1 + \frac{n_{2,1}}{n_{2,1} + n_{2,2}} \frac{n_{2,1} + n_{2,2}}{n} q_2.$$

Minimizing this expression is equivalent to minimizing the same expression divided by a constant. If we divide by q_1, it can be seen clearly that the minimization depends only on q_2/q_1 and not on their individual values. This is very practical, because in many cases it is difficult to assess the costs associated with misclassifying a C_1 member and a C_2 member, but estimating the ratio is easier.

This expression is a reasonable estimate of future misclassification cost if the proportions of classes C_1 and C_2 in the sample data are similar to the proportions of classes C_1 and C_2 that are expected in the future. If, instead of a random sample, we draw a sample such that one class is oversampled (as described in the next section), then the sample proportions of C_1's and C_2's will be distorted compared with the future or population. We can then correct the average misclassification cost measure for the distorted sample proportions by incorporating estimates of the true proportions (from external data or domain knowledge), denoted by $p(C_1)$ and $p(C_2)$, into the formula

$$\frac{n_{1,2}}{n_{1,1} + n_{1,2}} p(C_1)\, q_1 + \frac{n_{2,1}}{n_{2,1} + n_{2,2}} p(C_2)\, q_2.$$

Using the same logic as above, it can be shown that optimizing this quantity depends on the costs only through their ratio (q_2/q_1) and on the prior probabilities only through their ratio $[p(C_2)/p(C_1)]$. This is why software packages that incorporate costs and prior probabilities might prompt the user for ratios rather than actual costs and probabilities.

Generalization to More Than Two Classes

All the comments made above about two-class classifiers extend readily to classification into more than two classes. Let us suppose that we have m classes $C_1, C_2, \ldots, C_m$. The confusion matrix has m rows and m columns. The misclassification cost associated with the diagonal cells is, of course, always zero. Incorporating prior probabilities of the various classes (where now we have m such numbers) is still done in the same manner. However, evaluating misclassification costs becomes much more complicated: for an m-class case, we have $m(m-1)$ types of misclassifications. Constructing a matrix of misclassification costs thus becomes prohibitively complicated.

5.4   Judging Ranking Performance

We now turn to the predictive goal of detecting, among a set of new records, the ones most likely to belong to a class of interest. Recall that this differs from the goal of predicting class membership for each new record.

Cumulative Gains and Lift Charts for Binary Data

We already introduced cumulative gains charts and lift charts in the context of a numerical outcome (Section 5.2). We now describe these charts for a binary outcome. This is a more common usage than for predicted continuous outcomes. The gains and lift charts help us determine how effectively we can "skim the cream" by selecting a relatively small number of records and getting a relatively large portion of the responders.[2] The input required to construct these charts is a validation dataset that has been "scored" by appending to each record the propensity that it will belong to a given class.

Let's continue with the case in which a particular class is relatively rare and of much more interest than the other class: tax cheats, debt defaulters, or responders to a mailing. We would like our classification model to sift through the records and sort them according to which ones are most likely to be tax cheats, responders to the mailing, and so on. We can then make more informed decisions. For example, we can decide how many and which tax returns to examine if looking for tax cheats. The model will give us an estimate of the extent to which we will encounter more and more non-cheaters as we proceed through the sorted data starting with the records most likely to be tax cheats. Or we can use the sorted data to decide to which potential customers a limited-budget mailing should be targeted. In other words, we are describing the case when our goal is to obtain a rank ordering among the records according to their class membership propensities.

Sorting by Propensity   To construct a cumulative gains chart, we sort the set of records by propensity, in descending order. This is the propensity to belong to the important class, say, C_1. Then, in each row, we compute the cumulative number of C_1 members (Actual Class = C_1) or, if we use the ratio,

---

[2]The terms *lift* and *gains* are occasionally used interchangeably; to avoid confusion we use the prevalent definitions in which *gains* refers to total numbers or percentages of cases of interest identified by a model and *lift* to the ratio of such cases to those found through random targeting.

TABLE 5.6	RECORDS SORTED BY PROPENSITY OF OWNERSHIP (HIGH TO LOW) FOR THE MOWER EXAMPLE

Obs	Propensity of 1	Actual class	Cumulative actual class
1	0.995976726	1	1
2	0.987533139	1	2
3	0.984456382	1	3
4	0.980439587	1	4
5	0.948110638	1	5
6	0.889297203	1	6
7	0.847631864	1	7
8	0.762806287	0	7
9	0.706991915	1	8
10	0.680754087	1	9
11	0.656343749	1	10
12	0.622419543	0	10
13	0.505506928	1	11
14	0.471340450	0	11
15	0.337117362	0	11
16	0.217967810	1	12
17	0.199240432	0	12
18	0.149482655	0	12
19	0.047962588	0	12
20	0.038341401	0	12
21	0.024850999	0	12
22	0.021806029	0	12
23	0.016129906	0	12
24	0.003559986	0	12

the cumulative sensitivity (or TPR). For example, Table 5.6 shows the 24 records ordered in descending class "1" propensity. The right-most column accumulates the number of actual 1's.

Cumulative Gains Chart   The cumulative gains chart then plots this cumulative column against the number of records or their ratio.

In R, there are multiple packages for creating lift charts. Three useful options include the ROCR package, which allows creating a variety of charts besides the gains chart. We've already seen it being used for ROC curves (see Figure 5.5). The second option is with the caret package, which is easy to use, but select-ing the important class can be tricky, and furthermore it cannot be used for a numerical outcome variable. The third option is using the gains package. We will mostly use the gains package for gains and lift charts in this book. Figure 5.7 shows cumulative gains charts (and R code) for all three methods. Note that the gains package uses counts instead of percentage on both axes.

Interpreting the Cumulative Gains Chart   What is considered good or bad performance? The ideal ranking performance would place all the 1's at the

FIGURE 5.7   **CUMULATIVE GAINS CHARTS FOR THE MOWER EXAMPLE USING** ROCR, CARET, **AND** GAINS **PACKAGES (LEFT TO RIGHT)**

The shown ROCR graph was created using *ggplot*. See accompanying source code for details.

 code for creating a cumulative gains chart: three options

```
df <- mlba::LiftExample %>%
  mutate(actual=relevel(factor(actual), ref="1"))

# first option with 'ROCR' library:
pred <- prediction(df$prob, df$actual)
perf <- performance(pred, "tpr", "rpp")
plot(perf, xlab="Ratio of cases", ylab="Ratio of samples found")
lines(c(0, 1), c(0, 1), lty='dashed')

# second option with 'caret' library:
# load data and make actual a factor variable with 1 as the reference class
lift.example <- caret::lift(actual ~ prob, data=df)
ggplot(lift.example, plot = "gain") +
  labs(x="# Samples tested", y="# Samples found")

# third option with 'gains' library:
library(gains)
df <- mlba::LiftExample
gain <- gains(df$actual, df$prob, groups=nrow(df))
result <- data.frame(
  ncases=c(0, gain$cume.obs),
  cumulative=sum(df$actual)*c(0, gain$cume.pct.of.total)
)
ggplot(result, aes(x=ncases, y=cumulative)) +
  geom_line() +
  geom_segment(aes(x=0, y=0, xend=nrow(df), yend=sum(df$actual)),
               color="gray", linetype=2) + # adds baseline
  labs(x="# Cases", y="# Samples found")
```

beginning (the actual 1's would have the highest propensities and be at the top of the table) and all the 0's at the end. A curve corresponding to this ideal case would be a diagonal line with slope 1, using a graph with actual counts, which turns into a horizontal line (once all the 1's were accumulated). In the example, the curve for the best possible classifier—a classifier that makes no errors—would overlap the existing curve at the start, continue with a slope of

1 until it reached all the twelve 1's (or 50%), and then continue horizontally to the right. In Figure 5.7, this is the top dotted grey line in the middle plot.

In contrast, a useless model would be one that randomly assigns propensities (shuffling the 1's and 0's randomly in the Actual Class column). Such behavior would increase the cumulative number of 1's, on average, by $\frac{\#1's}{n}$ in each row. In fact, this is the diagonal dotted line joining the points $(0,0)$ to $(24,12)$[3] seen in Figure 5.7. This serves as a reference line. For any given number of records (the x-axis value), it represents the expected ratio of 1 classifications (=gains) if we did not have a model but simply selected records at random. It provides a benchmark against which we can evaluate the ranking performance of the model. In this example, although our model is not perfect, it seems to perform much better than the random benchmark.

How do we read a cumulative gains chart? For a given number of records (x-axis), the cumulative gains curve value on the y-axis tells us how much better we are doing compared with random assignment. For example, looking at the right panel in Figure 5.7, if we use our model to target the top 10 records (40%), the cumulative gains curve tells us that we would be right for about nine of them (or for 75% of them as shown in the left and center panels). If we simply target 10 records at random, we expect to be right for $10 \times 12/24 = 5$ records (or about 40%). The model gives us a "lift" in detecting class 1 members of 9/5 = 1.8. The lift will vary with the number of records we choose to act on. A good classifier will give us a high lift when we act on only a few records. As we include more records, the lift will decrease.

Decile-wise Lift Charts

Lift charts are a modified view of the cumulative gains information. They focus on *lift*, which is the ratio between the gains of the model relative to the random benchmark.

The information from the cumulative gains chart can be portrayed as a *decile-wise lift chart*[4], as shown in Figure 5.8, which is widely used in direct marketing predictive modeling. The decile-wise lift chart aggregates all the gains information into 10 buckets. The bars show, on the y-axis, the factor by which our model outperforms a random assignment of 0's and 1's, taking one decile at a time. Reading the bar on the left, we see that taking 8% of the records that are ranked by the model as "the most probable 1's" (having the highest propensities) yields twice as many 1's as would a random selection of 8% of the records. In this example, the decile-wise lift chart indicates that we can even use the model to

---

[3]This is the value for counts. If ratios are used, the top-right point is (100%, 100%).
[4]Note that the *lift* object in the **gains** package provides *cumulative lift* rather than lift. Interpreting cumulative lift is less straightforward, and therefore we advocate decile-wise lift charts.

FIGURE 5.8   DECILE-WISE LIFT CHART

 code for creating a decile lift chart

```
df <- mlba::LiftExample

# use gains() to compute deciles.
gain <- gains(df$actual, df$prob)
barplot(gain$mean.resp / mean(df$actual), names.arg=seq(10, 100, by=10),
        xlab="Percentile", ylab="Decile mean / global mean")
```

select the top 30% records with the highest propensities and still perform twice as well as random. However, adding another 10% records will only give a selection of records with a success rate that is equivalent to random (lift = 1).

Beyond Two Classes

A lift chart cannot be used with a multiclass classifier unless a single "important class" is defined and the classifications are reduced to "important" and "unimportant" classes (or, equivalently, *positive* and *negative* classes).

Gains and Lift Charts Incorporating Costs and Benefits

When the benefits and costs of correct and incorrect classifications are known or can be estimated, the lift chart is still a useful presentation and decision tool. As before, we need a classifier that assigns to each record a propensity that it belongs to a particular class. The procedure is then as follows:

1. Sort the records in descending order of predicted probability of success (where *success* = belonging to the class of interest).

2. For each record, record the cost (benefit) associated with the actual outcome.

3. For the highest propensity (i.e., first) record, its x-axis value is 1, and its y-axis value is its cost or benefit (computed in Step 2) on the cumulative gains curve.

4. For the next record, again calculate the cost (benefit) associated with the actual outcome. Add this to the cost (benefit) for the previous record. This sum is the y-axis coordinate of the second point on the cumulative gains curve. Its x-axis value is 2.

5. Repeat Step 4 until all records have been examined. Connect all the points, and this is the cumulative gains curve.

6. The reference line is a straight line from the origin to the point $y =$ total net benefit and $x = n$ ($n =$ number of records).

Note: It is entirely possible for a reference line that incorporates costs and benefits to have a negative slope if the net value for the entire dataset is negative. For example, if the cost of mailing to a person is \$0.65, the value of a responder is \$25, and the overall response rate is 2%, the expected net value of mailing to a list of 10,000 is $(0.02 \times \$25 \times 10{,}000) - (\$0.65 \times 10{,}000) = \$5000 - \$6500 = -\$1500$. Hence, the y-value at the far right of the cumulative gains curve ($x = 10{,}000$) is -1500, and the slope of the reference line from the origin will be negative. The optimal point will be where the cumulative gains curve is at a maximum (i.e., mailing to about 3000 people) in Figure 5.9.

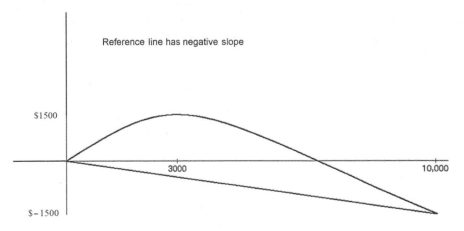

FIGURE 5.9   **CUMULATIVE GAINS CURVE INCORPORATING COSTS**

Cumulative Gains as a Function of Threshold

We could also plot the cumulative gains as a function of the threshold value. The only difference is the scale on the x-axis. When the goal is to select the top records based on a certain budget, the cumulative gains vs. number of records is preferable. In contrast, when the goal is to find a threshold that distinguishes well between the two classes, the cumulative gains vs. threshold value is more useful. To get a cumulative gains vs. threshold graph with `caret`'s *lift()* function, use the following:

```
plot(caret::lift(actual ~ prob, data=df), plot="lift")
```

5.5 OVERSAMPLING

As we saw briefly in Chapter 2, when classes are present in very unequal proportions, simple random sampling may produce too few of the rare class to yield useful information about what distinguishes them from the dominant class. In such cases, stratified sampling is often used to oversample the records from the rarer class and improve the performance of classifiers. It is often the case that the rarer events are the more interesting or important ones: responders to a mailing, those who commit fraud, defaulters on debt, and the like. This same stratified sampling procedure is sometimes called *weighted sampling* or *undersampling*, the latter referring to the fact that the more plentiful class is undersampled, relative to the rare class. We shall stick to the term *oversampling*.

> In all discussions of *oversampling*, we assume the common situation in which there are two classes, one of much greater interest than the other. Data with more than two classes do not lend themselves to this procedure.

Consider the data in Figure 5.10, where × represents non-responders and ○, responders. The two axes correspond to two predictors. The dashed vertical line does the best job of classification under the assumption of equal costs: it results in just one misclassification (one ○ is misclassified as an ×).

If we incorporate more realistic misclassification costs—let's say that failing to catch a ○ is five times as costly as failing to catch an ×—the costs of misclassification jump to 5. In such a case, a horizontal line as shown in Figure 5.11 does a better job: it results in misclassification costs of just 2.

Oversampling is one way of incorporating these costs into the training process. In Figure 5.12, we can see that classification algorithms would automatically determine the appropriate classification line if four additional ○'s were present at each existing ○. We can achieve appropriate results either by taking five times as many ○'s as we would get from simple random sampling (by sampling with replacement if necessary) or by replicating the existing ○'s 4-fold.

Oversampling without replacement in accord with the ratio of costs (the first option above) is the optimal solution, but may not always be practical. There may

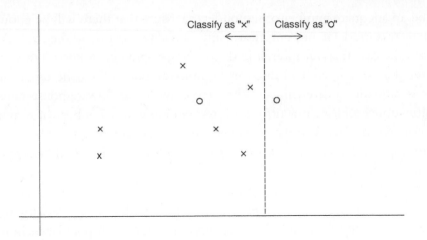

FIGURE 5.10   CLASSIFICATION ASSUMING EQUAL COSTS OF MISCLASSIFICATION

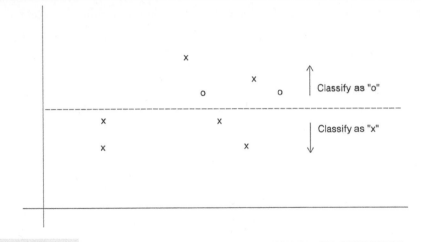

FIGURE 5.11   CLASSIFICATION ASSUMING UNEQUAL COSTS OF MISCLASSIFICATION

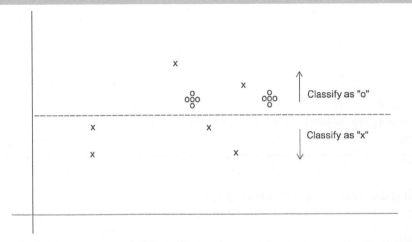

FIGURE 5.12   CLASSIFICATION USING OVERSAMPLING TO ACCOUNT FOR UNEQUAL COSTS

not be an adequate number of responders to assure that there will be enough of them to fit a model if they constitute only a small proportion of the total. Also, it is often the case that our interest in discovering responders is known to be much greater than our interest in discovering non-responders, but the exact ratio of costs is difficult to determine. When faced with very low response rates in a classification problem, practitioners often sample equal numbers of responders and non-responders as a relatively effective and convenient approach.

In `caret`, the functions *downSample* and *upSample* balance a dataset to either the size of the minority or the majority class, respectively. *upSample* increases the minority class by sampling with replacement from the minority class records. Alternatively, an algorithmic approach may be considered for oversampling the rare class to match the number of majority class records. A popular technique is SMOTE (Synthetic Minority Over-sampling Technique) proposed by Chawla et al. (2002). This technique involves synthetically generating records for the minority class. First, a record from the rare class is randomly selected, and k records similar to it are found using the k-nearest-neighbors algorithm (see Chapter 7). One of these neighbors is selected, and then synthetic records are generated through a combination of these two records. A suitable implementation can be found in the `ROSE` package.

Whatever approach is used, when it comes time to assess and predict model performance, we will need to adjust for the oversampling in one of two ways:

1. Score the model to a holdout set that has been selected without oversampling (i.e., via simple random sampling), or

2. Score the model to an oversampled holdout set, and reweight the results to remove the effects of oversampling.

The first method is more straightforward and easier to implement. We describe how to oversample and how to evaluate performance for each of the two methods.

When classifying data with very low response rates, practitioners typically:
- train models on data that are 50% responder and 50% non-responder
- validate the models with an unweighted (simple random) sample from the original data.

Creating an Over-sampled Training Set

How is weighted sampling done? When responders are sufficiently scarce that you will want to use all of them, one common procedure is as follows:

1. The response and non-response data are separated into two distinct sets, or *strata*.

2. Records are then randomly selected for the training set from each stratum. Typically, one might select half the (scarce) responders for the training set and then an equal number of non-responders.

3. The remaining responders are put in the validation set.

4. Non-responders are randomly selected for the validation set in sufficient numbers to maintain the original ratio of responders to non-responders.

5. If a holdout set is required, it can be taken randomly from the validation set.

Evaluating Model Performance Using a Non-oversampled Holdout Set

Although the oversampled data can be used to train models, they are often not suitable for evaluating model performance, because the number of responders will (of course) be exaggerated. The most straightforward way of gaining an unbiased estimate of model performance is to apply the model to regular data (i.e., data not oversampled). In short, train the model on oversampled data, but validate it with regular data.

Evaluating Model Performance If Only Oversampled Holdout Set Exists

In some cases, very low response rates may make it more practical to use over-sampled data not only for the training data but also for the holdout data. This might happen, for example, if an analyst is given a dataset for exploration and prototyping that is already oversampled to boost the proportion with the rare response of interest (perhaps because it is more convenient to transfer and work with a smaller dataset). In such cases, it is still possible to assess how well the model will do with real data, but this requires the oversampled holdout set to be reweighted, in order to restore the class of records that were underrepresented in the sampling process. This adjustment should be made to the confusion matrix and to the cumulative gains chart in order to derive good accuracy measures. These adjustments are described next.

I. Adjusting the Confusion Matrix for Oversampling   Suppose that the response rate in the data as a whole is 2% and that the data were oversampled, yielding a sample in which the response rate is 25 times higher (50% responders). The relationship is as follows:

Responders: 2% of the whole data; 50% of the sample

Non-responders: 98% of the whole data, 50% of the sample

Each responder in the whole data is worth 25 responders in the sample (50/2). Each non-responder in the whole data is worth 0.5102 non-responders in the sample (50/98). We call these values *oversampling weights*.

Assume that the holdout confusion matrix looks like this

CONFUSION MATRIX, OVERSAMPLED DATA (HOLDOUT)

	Actual 0	Actual 1	Total
Predicted 0	390	80	470
Predicted 1	110	420	530
Total	500	500	1000

At this point, the misclassification rate appears to be $(80 + 110)/1000 = 19\%$, and the model ends up classifying 53% of the records as 1's. However, this reflects the performance on a sample where 50% are responders.

To estimate predictive performance when this model is used to score the original population (with 2% responders), we need to undo the effects of the oversampling. The actual number of responders must be divided by 25, and the actual number of non-responders divided by 0.5102:

The revised confusion matrix is as follows:

CONFUSION MATRIX, REWEIGHTED

	Actual 0	Actual 1	Total
Predicted 0	390/0.5102 = 764.4	80/25 = 3.2	
Predicted 1	110/0.5102 = 215.6	420/25 = 16.8	
Total	980	20	1000

The adjusted misclassification rate is $(3.2 + 215.6)/1000 = 21.9\%$. The model ends up classifying $(215.6 + 16.8)/1000 = 23.24\%$ of the records as 1's, when we assume 2% responders.

II. Adjusting the Cumulative Gains Chart for Oversampling   The cumulative gains curve is likely to be a more useful measure in low-response situations, where our interest lies not so much in classifying all the records correctly as in finding a model that guides us toward those records most likely to contain the response of interest (under the assumption that scarce resources preclude examining or contacting all the records). Typically, our interest in such a case is in maximizing value or minimizing cost, so we will show the adjustment process incorporating the benefit/cost element. The following procedure can be used:

1. Sort the holdout records in order of the predicted probability of success (where success = belonging to the class of interest).

2. For each record, record the cost (benefit) associated with the actual outcome.

3. Divide that value by the oversampling rate. For example, if responders are overweighted by a factor of 25, divide by 25.

4. For the highest probability (i.e., first) record, the value above is the y-coordinate of the first point on the cumulative gains chart. The x-coordinate is index number 1.

5. For the next record, again calculate the adjusted value associated with the actual outcome. Add this to the adjusted cost (benefit) for the previous record. This sum is the y-coordinate of the second point on the cumulative gains curve. The x-coordinate is index number 2.

6. Repeat Step 5 until all records have been examined. Connect all the points, and this is the cumulative gains curve.

7. The reference line is a straight line from the origin to the point y = total net benefit and $x = n$ (n = number of records).

PROBLEMS

5.1   A machine learning process has been applied to a transaction dataset and has classified 88 records as fraudulent (30 correctly so) and 952 as non-fraudulent (920 correctly so). Construct the confusion matrix and calculate the overall error rate.

5.2   Suppose that this process has an adjustable threshold (cutoff) mechanism by which you can alter the proportion of records classified as fraudulent. Describe how moving the threshold up or down would affect the following:

  a. The classification error rate for records that are truly fraudulent.

  b. The classification error rate for records that are truly non-fraudulent.

5.3   Consider Figure 5.13, the decile-wise lift chart for the transaction data model, applied to new data.

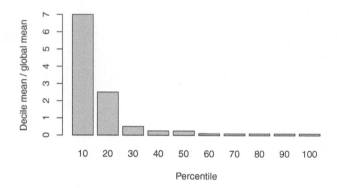

FIGURE 5.13   DECILE-WISE LIFT CHART FOR TRANSACTION DATA

  a. Interpret the meaning of the first and second bars from the left.

  b. Explain how you might use this information in practice.

  c. Another analyst comments that you could improve the accuracy of the model by classifying everything as non-fraudulent. If you do that, what is the error rate?

  d. Comment on the usefulness, in this situation, of these two metrics of model performance (error rate and lift).

5.4   FiscalNote is a startup founded by a Washington, DC entrepreneur and funded by a Singapore sovereign wealth fund, the Winklevoss twins of Facebook fame, and others. It uses machine learning and machine learning techniques to predict for its clients whether legislation in the US Congress and in US state legislatures will pass or not. The company reports 94% accuracy (*Washington Post*, November 21, 2014, "Capital Business").

Considering just bills introduced in the US Congress, do a bit of Internet research to learn about numbers of bills introduced and passage rates. Identify the possible types of misclassifications, and comment on the use of overall accuracy as a metric. Include a discussion of other possible metrics and the potential role of propensities.

5.5   A large number of insurance records are to be examined to develop a model for predicting fraudulent claims. Of the claims in the historical database, 1% were judged to be fraudulent. A sample is taken to develop a model, and oversampling is used to provide a balanced sample in light of the very low response rate. When applied to this sample ($n = 800$), the model ends up correctly classifying 310 frauds and 270 non-frauds. It missed 90 frauds and classified 130 records incorrectly as frauds when they were not.

a. Produce the confusion matrix for the sample as it stands.

b. Find the adjusted misclassification rate (adjusting for the oversampling).

c. What percentage of new records would you expect to be classified as fraudulent?

5.6 A firm that sells software services has been piloting a new product and has records of 500 customers who have either bought the services or decided not to. The target value is the estimated gross profit from each sale (excluding sales costs). The global mean is about $2128. However, the cost of the sales effort is not cheap—the company figures it comes to $2500 for each of the 500 customers (whether they buy or not). The firm developed a predictive model in hopes of being able to identify the top spenders in the future. The cumulative gains and decile-wise lift charts for the holdout set are shown in Figure 5.14.

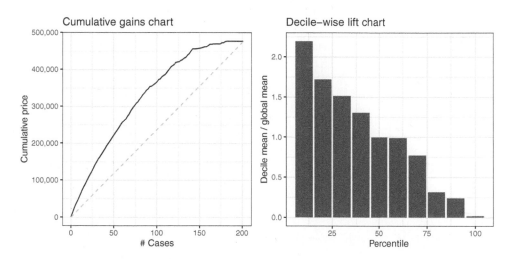

FIGURE 5.14   CUMULATIVE GAINS AND DECILE-WISE LIFT CHARTS FOR SOFTWARE SERVICES PRODUCT SALES (HOLDOUT SET)

a. If the company begins working with a new set of 1000 leads to sell the same services, similar to the 500 in the pilot study (except the company has not tried to sell the services to the new leads before), without any use of predictive modeling to target sales efforts, what is the estimated gross profit?

b. If the firm wants the average gross profit on each sale to roughly double the sales effort cost and applies an appropriate threshold with this predictive model to a new set of 1000 leads, how far down the new list of 1000 should it proceed (how many deciles)?

c. Still considering the new list of 1000 leads, if the company applies this predictive model with a lower threshold of $2500, how far should it proceed down the ranked leads, in terms of deciles?

    d. Why use this two-stage process for predicting sales—why not simply develop a model for predicting profit for the 1000 new leads?

5.7   Table 5.7 shows a small set of predictive model holdout results for a classification model, with both actual values and propensities.

    a. Calculate error rates, sensitivity, and specificity using thresholds of 0.25, 0.5, and 0.75.

    b. Create a decile-wise lift chart in R.

TABLE 5.7	PROPENSITIES AND ACTUAL CLASS MEMBERSHIP FOR HOLDOUT DATA

Propensity of 1	Actual
0.03	0
0.52	0
0.38	0
0.82	1
0.33	0
0.42	0
0.55	1
0.59	0
0.09	0
0.21	0
0.43	0
0.04	0
0.08	0
0.13	0
0.01	0
0.79	1
0.42	0
0.29	0
0.08	0
0.02	0

Prediction and Classification Methods

## CHAPTER 6

Multiple Linear Regression

In this chapter, we introduce linear regression models for the purpose of prediction. We discuss the differences between fitting and using regression models for the purpose of inference (as in classical statistics) and for prediction. A predictive goal calls for evaluating model performance cross-validation and on a holdout set and for using predictive metrics. We then raise the challenges of using many predictors and describe variable selection algorithms that are often implemented in linear regression procedures. Finally, we introduce regularized regression techniques, which are particularly useful for datasets with a large number of highly-correlated predictors.

Linear Regression in R

The main R function introduced in this chapter is *lm* in the `caret` package. We also use package `fastDummies` for creating dummies and `leaps` and `glmnet` for variable selection.

6.1 INTRODUCTION

The most popular model for making predictions is the *multiple linear regression model* encountered in most introductory statistics courses and textbooks. This model is used to fit a relationship between a numerical *outcome variable* Y (also called the *response*, *target*, or *dependent variable*) and a set of *predictors* $X_1, X_2, \ldots, X_p$ (also referred to as *independent variables*, *input variables*, *regressors*, or *covariates*). The assumption is that the following function approximates the relationship between the predictors and outcome variable:

$$Y = \beta_0 + \beta_1 x_1 + \beta_2 x_2 + \cdots + \beta_p x_p + \epsilon, \tag{6.1}$$

Machine Learning for Business Analytics: Concepts, Techniques, and Applications in R, Second Edition.
Galit Shmueli, Peter C. Bruce, Peter Gedeck, Inbal Yahav, and Nitin R. Patel
© 2023 John Wiley & Sons, Inc. Published 2023 by John Wiley & Sons, Inc.

where $\beta_0, \ldots, \beta_p$ are *coefficients* and ϵ is the *noise* or *unexplained* part. Data are then used to estimate the coefficients and to quantify the noise. In predictive modeling, the data are also used to evaluate model performance.

Regression modeling means not only estimating the coefficients but also choosing which predictors to include and in what form. For example, a numerical predictor can be included as is, or in logarithmic form $[\log(X)]$, or in a binned form (e.g., age group). Choosing the right form depends on domain knowledge, data availability, and needed predictive power.

Multiple linear regression is applicable to numerous predictive modeling situations. Examples are predicting customer activity on credit cards from their demographics and historical activity patterns, predicting expenditures on vacation travel based on historical frequent flyer data, predicting staffing requirements at help desks based on historical data and product and sales information, predicting sales from cross-selling of products from historical information, and predicting the impact of discounts on sales in retail outlets.

6.2 EXPLANATORY VS. PREDICTIVE MODELING

Before introducing the use of linear regression for prediction, we must clarify an important distinction that often escapes those with earlier familiarity with linear regression from courses in statistics. In particular, the two popular but different objectives behind fitting a regression model are as follows:

1. Explaining or quantifying the average effect of inputs on an outcome (explanatory or descriptive task, respectively).

2. Predicting the outcome value for new records, given their input values (predictive task).

The classical statistical approach is focused on the first objective. In that scenario, the data are treated as a random sample from a larger population of interest. The regression model estimated from this sample is an attempt to capture the *average* relationship in the larger population. This model is then used in decision-making to generate statements such as "a unit increase in service speed (X_1) is associated with an average increase of 5 points in customer satisfaction (Y), all other factors $(X_2, X_3, \ldots, X_p)$ being equal." If X_1 is known to *cause* Y, then such a statement indicates actionable policy changes—this is called explanatory modeling. When the causal structure is unknown, then this model quantifies the degree of *association* between the inputs and outcome variable, and the approach is called descriptive modeling.

In predictive analytics, however, the focus is typically on the second goal: predicting new individual records. Here, we are not interested in the coefficients themselves, nor in the "average record," but rather in the predictions that this model can generate for new records. In this scenario, the model is used for micro-decision-making at the record level. In our previous example, we would use the regression model to predict customer satisfaction for each new customer of interest.

Both explanatory and predictive modeling involve using a dataset to fit a model (i.e., to estimate coefficients), checking model validity, assessing its performance, and comparing with other models. However, the modeling steps and performance assessment differ in the two cases, usually leading to different final models. Therefore, the choice of model is closely tied to whether the goal is explanatory or predictive.

In explanatory and descriptive modeling, where the focus is on modeling the average record, we try to fit the best model to the data in an attempt to learn about the underlying relationship in the population. In contrast, in predictive modeling (machine learning), the goal is to find a regression model that best predicts new individual records. A regression model that fits the existing data too well is not likely to perform well with new data. Hence, we look for a model that has the highest predictive power by evaluating it on a holdout set and using predictive metrics (see Chapter 5).

Let us summarize the main differences in using a linear regression in the two scenarios:

1. A good explanatory model is one that fits the data closely, whereas a good predictive model is one that predicts new records accurately. Choices of input variables and their form can therefore differ.

2. In explanatory models, the entire dataset is used for estimating the best-fit model, to maximize the amount of information that we have about the hypothesized relationship in the population. When the goal is to predict outcomes of new individual records, the data are typically split into a training set and a holdout set. The training set is used to estimate the model, and the validation or *holdout set*[1] is used to assess this model's predictive performance on new, unobserved data.

3. Performance measures for explanatory models measure how close the data fit the model (how well the model approximates the data) and how strong the average relationship is, whereas in predictive models performance is measured by predictive accuracy (how well the model predicts new individual records).

4. In explanatory models, the focus is on the coefficients (β), whereas in predictive models the focus is on the predictions ($\hat{y}$).

---

[1]In practice, a validation set is used when the model is adjusted for selecting the model with the best performance, while a separate holdout set is used to assess the performance of the "best model" on new, unobserved data before model deployment.

For these reasons, it is extremely important to know the goal of the analysis before beginning the modeling process. A good predictive model can have a looser fit to the data on which it is based, and a good explanatory model can have low prediction accuracy. In the remainder of this chapter, we focus on predictive models because these are more popular in machine learning and because most statistics textbooks focus on explanatory modeling.

6.3 ESTIMATING THE REGRESSION EQUATION AND PREDICTION

Once we determine the predictors to include and their form, we estimate the coefficients of the regression formula from the data using a method called *ordinary least squares* (OLS). This method finds values $\hat{\beta}_0, \hat{\beta}_1, \hat{\beta}_2, \ldots, \hat{\beta}_p$ that minimize the sum of squared deviations between the actual outcome values (Y) and their predicted values based on that model $(\hat{Y})$.

To predict the value of the outcome variable for a record with predictor values $x_1, x_2, \ldots, x_p$, we use the equation

$$\hat{Y} = \hat{\beta}_0 + \hat{\beta}_1 x_1 + \hat{\beta}_2 x_2 + \cdots + \hat{\beta}_p x_p. \tag{6.2}$$

Predictions based on this equation are the best predictions possible in the sense that they will be unbiased (equal to the true values on average) and will have the smallest mean squared error compared with any unbiased estimates *if* we make the following assumptions:

1. The noise ϵ (or equivalently, Y) follows a normal distribution.
2. The choice of predictors and their form is correct (*linearity*).
3. The records are independent of each other.
4. The variability in the outcome values for a given set of predictors is the same regardless of the values of the predictors (*homoskedasticity*).

An important and interesting fact for the predictive goal is that *even if we drop the first assumption and allow the noise to follow an arbitrary distribution, these estimates are very good for prediction,* in the sense that among all linear models, as defined by Equation (6.1), the model using the least squares estimates, $\hat{\beta}_0, \hat{\beta}_1, \hat{\beta}_2, \ldots, \hat{\beta}_p$, will have the smallest mean squared errors. The assumption of a normal distribution is required in explanatory modeling, where it is used for constructing confidence intervals and statistical tests for the model parameters.

Even if the other assumptions are violated, it is still possible that the resulting predictions are sufficiently accurate and precise for the purpose they are intended for. The key is to evaluate predictive performance of the model, which is the main priority. Satisfying assumptions is of secondary interest, and residual analysis can give clues to potential improved models to examine.

Example: Predicting the Price of Used Toyota Corolla Cars

A large Toyota car dealership offers purchasers of new Toyota cars the option to buy their used car as part of a trade-in. In particular, a new promotion promises to pay high prices for used Toyota Corolla cars for purchasers of a new car. The dealer then sells the used cars for a small profit. To ensure a reasonable profit, the dealer needs to be able to predict the price that the dealership will get for the used cars. For that reason, data were collected on all previous sales of used Toyota Corollas at the dealership. The data include the sales price and other information on the car, such as its age, mileage, fuel type, and engine size. A description of each of these variables is given in Table 6.1. A sample of this dataset is shown in Table 6.2. The total number of records in the dataset is 1000 cars (we use the first 1000 cars from the dataset *mlba::ToyotaCorolla*). After partitioning the data into training (60%) and holdout (40%) sets, we fit a multiple linear regression model between price (the outcome variable) and the other variables (as predictors) using only the training set. Table 6.3 shows the estimated coefficients. Notice that the Fuel Type predictor has three categories (Petrol, Diesel, and CNG). We therefore have two dummy variables in the model: Fuel_TypePetrol (0/1) and Fuel_TypeDiesel (0/1); the third, for CNG (0/1), is redundant given the information on the first two dummies. Including the redundant dummy would cause the regression to fail, since the redundant dummy will be a perfect linear combination of the other two; R's *lm* routine handles this issue automatically.

TABLE 6.1	VARIABLES IN THE TOYOTA COROLLA EXAMPLE

Variable	Description
Price	Offer price in Euros
Age	Age in months as of August 2004
Kilometers	Accumulated kilometers on odometer
Fuel Type	Fuel type (*Petrol, Diesel, CNG*)
HP	Horsepower
Metallic	Metallic color? (Yes = 1, No = 0)
Automatic	Automatic (Yes = 1, No = 0)
CC	Cylinder volume in cubic centimeters
Doors	Number of doors
QuartTax	Quarterly road tax in Euros
Weight	Weight in kilograms

TABLE 6.2			PRICES AND ATTRIBUTES FOR USED TOYOTA COROLLA CARS (SELECTED ROWS AND COLUMNS ONLY)							

Price	Age	Kilometers	Fuel Type	HP	Metallic	Auto-matic	CC	Doors	Quart Tax	Weight
13500	23	46986	Diesel	90	1	0	2000	3	210	1165
13750	23	72937	Diesel	90	1	0	2000	3	210	1165
13950	24	41711	Diesel	90	1	0	2000	3	210	1165
14950	26	48000	Diesel	90	0	0	2000	3	210	1165
13750	30	38500	Diesel	90	0	0	2000	3	210	1170
12950	32	61000	Diesel	90	0	0	2000	3	210	1170
16900	27	94612	Diesel	90	1	0	2000	3	210	1245
18600	30	75889	Diesel	90	1	0	2000	3	210	1245
21500	27	19700	Petrol	192	0	0	1800	3	100	1185
12950	23	71138	Diesel	69	0	0	1900	3	185	1105
20950	25	31461	Petrol	192	0	0	1800	3	100	1185
19950	22	43610	Petrol	192	0	0	1800	3	100	1185
19600	25	32189	Petrol	192	0	0	1800	3	100	1185
21500	31	23000	Petrol	192	1	0	1800	3	100	1185
22500	32	34131	Petrol	192	1	0	1800	3	100	1185
22000	28	18739	Petrol	192	0	0	1800	3	100	1185
22750	30	34000	Petrol	192	1	0	1800	3	100	1185
17950	24	21716	Petrol	110	1	0	1600	3	85	1105
16750	24	25563	Petrol	110	0	0	1600	3	19	1065
16950	30	64359	Petrol	110	1	0	1600	3	85	1105
15950	30	67660	Petrol	110	1	0	1600	3	85	1105
16950	29	43905	Petrol	110	0	1	1600	3	100	1170
15950	28	56349	Petrol	110	1	0	1600	3	85	1120
16950	28	32220	Petrol	110	1	0	1600	3	85	1120
16250	29	25813	Petrol	110	1	0	1600	3	85	1120
15950	25	28450	Petrol	110	1	0	1600	3	85	1120
17495	27	34545	Petrol	110	1	0	1600	3	85	1120
15750	29	41415	Petrol	110	1	0	1600	3	85	1120
11950	39	98823	CNG	110	1	0	1600	5	197	1119

The regression coefficients are then used to predict prices of individual used Toyota Corolla cars based on their age, mileage, and so on. Table 6.4 shows a sample of predicted prices for 20 cars in the holdout set, using the estimated model. It gives the predictions and their errors (relative to the actual prices) for these 20 cars. Below the predictions, we have overall measures of predictive accuracy. Note that for this holdout data, RMSE= $1423 and the mean absolute error (MAE) is $1054.

TABLE 6.3	LINEAR REGRESSION MODEL OF PRICE VS. CAR ATTRIBUTES

 code for fitting a regression model

```
library(caret)
car.df <- mlba::ToyotaCorolla
# select variables for regression
outcome <- "Price"
predictors <- c("Age_08_04", "KM", "Fuel_Type", "HP", "Met_Color", "Automatic",
                "CC", "Doors", "Quarterly_Tax", "Weight")
# reduce data set to first 1000 rows and selected variables
car.df <- car.df[1:1000, c(outcome, predictors)]

# partition data
set.seed(1)  # set seed for reproducing the partition
idx <- createDataPartition(car.df$Price, p=0.6, list=FALSE)
train.df <- car.df[idx, ]
holdout.df <- car.df[-idx, ]

# use lm() to run a linear regression of Price on all 11 predictors in the
# training set.
# use . after ~ to include all the remaining columns in train.df as predictors.
car.lm <- lm(Price ~ ., data = train.df)
# use options() to ensure numbers are not displayed in scientific notation.
options(scipen = 999)
summary(car.lm)
```

Output

```
> summary(car.lm)

Call:
lm(formula = Price ~ ., data = train.df)

Residuals:
   Min    1Q Median    3Q    Max
 -9047   -831     -6   832   6057

Coefficients:
                   Estimate  Std. Error  t value            Pr(>|t|)
(Intercept)     -3725.59270  1913.92374    -1.95            0.05206 .
Age_08_04        -133.98649     4.92047   -27.23 < 0.0000000000000002 ***
KM                 -0.01741     0.00231    -7.53 0.00000000000019238 ***
Fuel_TypeDiesel  1179.18603   724.71141     1.63            0.10425
Fuel_TypePetrol  2173.64897   729.55378     2.98            0.00301 **
HP                 36.34253     4.75838     7.64 0.00000000000008997 ***
Met_Color          -7.60255   119.54320    -0.06            0.94931
Automatic         276.55860   267.85985     1.03            0.30227
CC                  0.01517     0.09440     0.16            0.87236
Doors               2.28016    62.30556     0.04            0.97082
Quarterly_Tax       9.64453     2.60048     3.71            0.00023 ***
Weight             15.25566     1.81726     8.39 0.00000000000000035 ***
---
Signif. codes:  0 '***' 0.001 '**' 0.01 '*' 0.05 '.' 0.1 ' ' 1

Residual standard error: 1340 on 589 degrees of freedom
Multiple R-squared:  0.869,      Adjusted R-squared:  0.867
F-statistic:  356 on 11 and 589 DF,  p-value: <0.0000000000000002
```

TABLE 6.4	PREDICTED PRICES (AND ERRORS) FOR 20 CARS IN HOLDOUT SET AND SUMMARY PREDICTIVE MEASURES FOR ENTIRE HOLDOUT SET

 code for prediction and measuring accuracy

```
# use predict() to make predictions on a new set.
pred <- predict(car.lm, holdout.df)

options(scipen=999, digits=0)
data.frame(
  'Predicted' = pred[1:20],
  'Actual' = holdout.df$Price[1:20],
  'Residual' = holdout.df$Price[1:20] - pred[1:20]
)
options(scipen=999, digits = 3)

# calculate performance metrics
rbind(
  Training=mlba::regressionSummary(predict(car.lm, train.df), train.df$Price),
  Holdout=mlba::regressionSummary(pred, holdout.df$Price)
)
```

Output

	Predicted	Actual	Residual
1	16652	13500	-3152
14	19941	21500	1559
15	19613	22500	2887
16	20424	22000	1576
18	16553	17950	1397
19	15247	16750	1503
20	15006	16950	1944
21	14949	15950	1001
22	16917	16950	33
24	16063	16950	887
25	16040	16250	210
26	16530	15950	-580
30	16163	17950	1787
32	16034	15750	-284
36	15370	15750	380
37	15817	15950	133
39	14866	15750	884
40	15506	14750	-756
41	15800	13950	-1850
45	17475	16950	-525

	RMSE	MAE
Training	1329	1009
Holdout	1423	1054

A histogram of the residuals (Figure 6.1) shows that most of the errors are between ±$2500. This error magnitude might be small relative to the car price but should be taken into account when considering the profit. Another observation of interest is the large positive residuals (under-predictions), which may or may not be a concern, depending on the application. Measures such as RMSE and MAE are used to assess the predictive performance of a model and to compare models.

 code for plotting histogram of holdout errors

```
library(ggplot2)
pred <- predict(car.lm, holdout.df)
all.residuals <- holdout.df$Price - pred

ggplot() +
    geom_histogram(aes(x=all.residuals), fill="lightgray", color="grey") +
    labs(x="Residuals", y="Frequency")
```

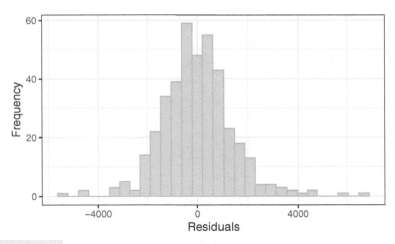

FIGURE 6.1   HISTOGRAM OF MODEL ERRORS (BASED ON HOLDOUT SET)

Cross-validation and `caret`

In the previous section, the model was validated using a single random split into training and holdout sets. Cross-validation (see Section 2.5) gives a better estimate of the predictive performance. While many R packages come with specialized implementations for cross-validation, `caret` provides a consistent interface to do cross-validation for a large variety of machine learning methods. Table 6.5 describes a 5-fold cross-validation of a linear regression model of the Toyota Corolla dataset. Across the five cross-validation folds, RMSE averages $1949 and MAE $1086. Following the cross-validation, `caret` trains a model

---

TABLE 6.5   CROSS-VALIDATION IN TOYOTA COROLLA EXAMPLE

 code for 5-fold cross-validation using caret

```
set.seed(1)
library(caret)
# define 5-fold
trControl <- caret::trainControl(method="cv", number=5, allowParallel=TRUE)
model <- caret::train(Price ~ ., data=car.df,
                      method="lm",  # specify the model
                      trControl=trControl)
model
coef(model$finalModel)
```

Output

```
> model
Linear Regression

1000 samples
  10 predictor

No pre-processing
Resampling: Cross-Validated (5 fold)
Summary of sample sizes: 799, 801, 800, 799, 801
Resampling results:

  RMSE  Rsquared  MAE
  1949  0.753     1086

Tuning parameter 'intercept' was held constant at a value of TRUE
> coef(model$finalModel)
    (Intercept)       Age_08_04               KM Fuel_TypeDiesel Fuel_TypePetrol
     -6419.2947       -132.4105          -0.0187        654.4718       2536.4747
             HP       Met_Color        Automatic              CC           Doors
        35.0697         58.8612         239.5717         -0.0210        -69.0173
   Quarterly_Tax          Weight
        15.9124         17.4002
```

Predict

```
predict(model, car.df[1:3,])

    1     2     3
16892 16408 16858
```

---

using the full dataset and returns this in the value *finalModel*. The trained model can be used to predict new data.

6.4 VARIABLE SELECTION IN LINEAR REGRESSION

Reducing the Number of Predictors

A frequent problem in machine learning is that of using a regression equation to predict the value of a dependent variable when we have many variables available to choose as predictors in our model. Given the high speed of modern algorithms for multiple linear regression calculations, it is tempting in such a situation to take a kitchen-sink approach: why bother to select a subset? Just use all the variables in the model.

Another consideration favoring the inclusions of numerous variables is the hope that a previously hidden relationship will emerge. For example, a company found that customers who had purchased anti-scuff protectors for chair and table legs had lower credit risks. However, there are several reasons for exercising caution before throwing all possible variables into a model:

- It may be expensive or not feasible to collect a full complement of predictors for future predictions.

- We may be able to measure fewer predictors more accurately (e.g., in surveys).

- The more predictors, the higher the chance of missing values in the data. If we delete or impute records with missing values, multiple predictors will lead to a higher rate of record deletion or imputation.

- *Parsimony* is an important property of good models. We obtain more insight into the influence of predictors in models with few parameters.

- Estimates of regression coefficients are likely to be unstable, due to *multicollinearity* in models with many variables. (Multicollinearity is the presence of two or more predictors sharing the same linear relationship with the outcome variable.) Regression coefficients are more stable for parsimonious models. One very rough rule of thumb is to have a number of records n larger than $5(p + 2)$, where p is the number of predictors.

- It can be shown that using predictors that are uncorrelated with the outcome variable increases the variance of predictions.

- It can be shown that dropping predictors that are actually correlated with the outcome variable can increase the average error (bias) of predictions.

The last two points mean that there is a trade-off between too few and too many predictors. In general, accepting some bias can reduce the variance in predictions. This *bias–variance trade-off* is particularly important for large numbers of predictors, because in that case, it is very likely that there are variables in the model that have small coefficients relative to the standard deviation of the noise and also exhibit at least moderate correlation with other variables. Dropping such variables will improve the predictions, as it reduces the prediction variance. This type of bias–variance trade-off is a basic aspect of most machine learning procedures for prediction and classification. In light of this, methods for reducing the number of predictors p to a smaller set are often used.

How to Reduce the Number of Predictors

The first step in trying to reduce the number of predictors should always be to use domain knowledge. It is important to understand what the various predictors are measuring and why they are relevant for predicting the outcome variable. With this knowledge, the set of predictors should be reduced to a sensible set that reflects the problem at hand. Some practical reasons for predictor elimination are the expense of collecting this information in the future, inaccuracy, high correlation with another predictor, many missing values, or simply irrelevance. Also helpful in examining potential predictors are summary statistics and graphs, such as frequency and correlation tables, predictor-specific summary statistics and plots, and missing value counts.

The next step makes use of computational power and statistical performance metrics. In general, there are two types of methods for reducing the number of predictors in a model. The first is an *exhaustive search* for the "best" subset of predictors by fitting regression models with all the possible combinations of predictors.

The exhaustive search approach is not practical in many applications, and implementation in R can be tedious and unstable. The second approach is to search through a partial set of models. We describe these two approaches next.

Exhaustive Search   The idea here is to evaluate all subsets of predictors. Since the number of subsets for even moderate values of p is very large, after the algorithm creates the subsets and runs all the models, we need some way to examine the most promising subsets and to select from them. The challenge is to select a model that is not too simplistic in terms of excluding important parameters (the model is *underfit*), nor overly complex thereby modeling random noise (the model is *overfit*). Several criteria for evaluating and comparing models are based on metrics computed from the training data:

One popular criterion is the *adjusted* R^2, which is defined as

$$R^2_{\text{adj}} = 1 - \frac{n-1}{n-p-1}(1 - R^2), \tag{6.3}$$

where R^2 is the proportion of explained variability in the model (in a model with a single predictor, this is the squared correlation). Like R^2, higher values of R^2_{adj} indicate better fit. Unlike R^2, which does not account for the number of predictors used, R^2_{adj} uses a penalty on the number of predictors. This avoids the artificial increase in R^2 that can result from simply increasing the number of predictors but not the amount of information. It can be shown that using R^2_{adj} to choose a subset is equivalent to choosing the subset that minimizes the training RMSE.

A second popular set of criteria for balancing underfitting and overfitting are the *Akaike Information Criterion (AIC)* and Schwartz's *Bayesian Information*

Criterion (BIC). *AIC* and *BIC* measure the goodness of fit of a model but also include a penalty that is a function of the number of parameters in the model. As such, they can be used to compare various models for the same dataset. *AIC* and *BIC* are estimates of prediction error based on information theory. For linear regression, *AIC* and *BIC* can be computed from the formulas:

$$AIC = n \ln(SSE/n) + n(1 + \ln(2\pi)) + 2(p+1) \tag{6.4}$$

$$BIC = n \ln(SSE/n) + n(1 + \ln(2\pi)) + \ln(n)(p+1) \tag{6.5}$$

where SSE is the model's sum of squared errors. In general, models with smaller *AIC* and *BIC* values are considered better.

A third criterion often used for subset selection is *Mallow's C_p* (see formula below[2]). This criterion assumes that the full model (with all predictors) is unbiased, although it may have predictors that if dropped would reduce prediction variability. With this assumption, we can show that if a subset model is unbiased, the average C_p value equals $p + 1$ (= number of predictors + 1), the size of the subset. So a reasonable approach to identifying subset models with small bias is to examine those with values of C_p that are near $p + 1$. Good models are those that have values of C_p near $p + 1$ and that have small p (i.e., are of small size). C_p is computed from the formula

$$C_p = \frac{\text{SSE}}{\hat{\sigma}^2_{\text{full}}} + 2(p+1) - n, \tag{6.6}$$

where $\hat{\sigma}^2_{\text{full}}$ is the estimated value of σ^2 (MSE) in the full model that includes all predictors. It is important to remember that the usefulness of this approach depends heavily on the reliability of the estimate of σ^2 for the full model. Getting this reliable estimate requires that the training set contain a large number of records relative to the number of predictors.

Note: It can be shown that for linear regression, in large samples Mallow's C_p is equivalent to *AIC*.

Finally, a useful point to note is that for a fixed size of subset, R^2, R^2_{adj}, C_p, *AIC*, and *BIC* all select the same subset. In fact, there is no difference between them in the order of merit they ascribe to subsets of a fixed size. This is good to know if comparing models with the same number of predictors, but often we want to compare models with different numbers of predictors.

Table 6.6 gives the results of applying an exhaustive search on the Toyota Corolla price data (with the 11 predictors) using the R package `regsubsets`.

It reports the best model with a single predictor, two predictors, and so on. It can be seen that the R^2_{adj} increases until eight predictors are used (number of

---

[2]Mallow's C_p is unrelated to the CP, or complexity parameter, used in classification and regression trees, described in Chapter 9.

TABLE 6.6	EXHAUSTIVE SEARCH FOR REDUCING PREDICTORS IN TOYOTA COROLLA EXAMPLE

 code for best subset

```
# use regsubsets() in package leaps to run an exhaustive search.
# unlike with lm, categorical predictors must be turned into dummies manually.
library(leaps)
library(fastDummies)

# create dummies for fuel type
leaps.train.df <- dummy_cols(train.df, remove_first_dummy=TRUE,
                           remove_selected_columns=TRUE)
search <- regsubsets(Price ~ ., data=leaps.train.df, nbest=1,
                   nvmax=ncol(leaps.train.df), method="exhaustive")
sum <- summary(search)

# show models
sum$which

# show metrics
sum$rsq
sum$adjr2
sum$cp
```

Output

```
> sum$which
   (Intercept) Age_08_04    KM    HP Met_Color Automatic    CC Doors Quarterly_Tax Weight
1         TRUE      TRUE FALSE FALSE     FALSE     FALSE FALSE FALSE         FALSE  FALSE
2         TRUE      TRUE FALSE  TRUE     FALSE     FALSE FALSE FALSE         FALSE  FALSE
3         TRUE      TRUE FALSE  TRUE     FALSE     FALSE FALSE FALSE         FALSE   TRUE
4         TRUE      TRUE  TRUE  TRUE     FALSE     FALSE FALSE FALSE         FALSE   TRUE
5         TRUE      TRUE  TRUE  TRUE     FALSE     FALSE FALSE FALSE          TRUE   TRUE
6         TRUE      TRUE  TRUE  TRUE     FALSE     FALSE FALSE FALSE          TRUE   TRUE
7         TRUE      TRUE  TRUE  TRUE     FALSE     FALSE FALSE FALSE          TRUE   TRUE
8         TRUE      TRUE  TRUE  TRUE     FALSE      TRUE FALSE FALSE          TRUE   TRUE
9         TRUE      TRUE  TRUE  TRUE     FALSE      TRUE  TRUE FALSE          TRUE   TRUE
10        TRUE      TRUE  TRUE  TRUE      TRUE      TRUE  TRUE FALSE          TRUE   TRUE
11        TRUE      TRUE  TRUE  TRUE      TRUE      TRUE  TRUE  TRUE          TRUE   TRUE
   Fuel_TypeDiesel Fuel_TypePetrol
1            FALSE           FALSE
2            FALSE           FALSE
3            FALSE           FALSE
4            FALSE           FALSE
5            FALSE           FALSE
6            FALSE            TRUE
7             TRUE            TRUE
8             TRUE            TRUE
9             TRUE            TRUE
10            TRUE            TRUE
11            TRUE            TRUE

> sum$rsq
 [1] 0.773 0.816 0.848 0.865 0.866 0.868 0.869 0.869 0.869 0.869 0.869

> sum$adjr2
 [1] 0.773 0.815 0.847 0.864 0.865 0.867 0.867 0.867 0.867 0.867 0.867

> sum$cp
 [1] 422.90 234.33  92.94  17.09  14.05   5.73   5.20   6.03   8.01  10.00  12.00
```

coefficients = 9) and then stabilizes. The C_p indicates that a model with seven to eight predictors is good. The dominant predictor in all models is the age of the car, with horsepower and mileage playing important roles as well.

Popular Subset Selection Algorithms   The second method of finding the best subset of predictors relies on a partial, iterative search through the space of all possible regression models. The end product is one best subset of predictors (although there do exist variations of these methods that identify several close-to-best choices for different sizes of predictor subsets). This approach is computationally cheaper, but it has the potential of missing "good" combinations of predictors. None of the methods guarantee that they yield the best subset for any criterion, such as R^2_{adj}. They are reasonable methods for situations with a large number of predictors, but for a moderate number of predictors, the exhaustive search is preferable.

Three popular iterative search algorithms are *forward selection, backward elimination*, and *stepwise regression*. In *forward selection*, we start with no predictors and then add predictors one by one. Each predictor added is the one (among all predictors) that has the largest contribution on top of the predictors that are already in it. The algorithm stops when the contribution of additional predictors is not useful. The main disadvantage of this method is that the algorithm will miss pairs or groups of predictors that perform very well together but perform poorly as single predictors. This is similar to interviewing job candidates for a team project one by one, thereby missing groups of candidates who perform superiorly together ("colleagues"), but poorly on their own or with non–colleagues.

In *backward elimination*, we start with all predictors and then at each step, eliminate the least useful predictor. The algorithm stops when all the remaining predictors have significant contributions. The weakness of this algorithm is that computing the initial model with all predictors can be time-consuming and unstable. *Stepwise regression* is like forward selection except that at each step, we consider dropping predictors that are not useful as in backward elimination.

The marginal usefulness of a predictor, for purposes of adding or dropping it from a model, can be measured in different ways. R has several libraries with stepwise functions: function *regsubsets()* in the `leaps` package implements (in addition to exhaustive search) forward selection, backward elimination, and stepwise regression. Predictors are added/dropped based on R^2, R^2_{adj}, or C_p. In contrast, function *step()* in the `stats` package and function *stepAIC()* in the MASS package perform model selection using the *AIC* criterion (*stepAIC* offers a wider range of object classes).

`caret` provides an interface to the *stepAIC* implementation in *MASS::stepAIC*. Table 6.7 shows the results for backward elimination, forward selection, and stepwise regression for the Toyota Corolla example. All approaches lead here to the same seven-predictor model which is identical to

TABLE 6.7   SUBSET SELECTION ALGORITHMS REDUCING PREDICTORS IN TOYOTA COROLLA EXAMPLE

 code for backward elimination (top), forward selection (middle), and stepwise regression (bottom)

Backward elimination

```
# as model performance is estimated using AIC, we don't need to use cross-validation
trControl <- caret::trainControl(method="none")
model <- caret::train(Price ~ ., data=train.df, trControl=trControl,
                      # select backward elmination
                      method="glmStepAIC", direction='backward')

coef(model$finalModel)
```

Partial output

```
  (Intercept)         Age_08_04                 KM Fuel_TypeDiesel Fuel_TypePetrol
    -4129.823          -133.367             -0.017        1147.855        2193.712
           HP      Quarterly_Tax             Weight
       35.927             9.602             15.673
```

Forward selection

```
model <- caret::train(Price ~ ., data=train.df, trControl=trControl,
                      method="glmStepAIC", direction='forward')

coef(model$finalModel)
```

Partial output

```
    (Intercept)         Age_08_04                 HP            Weight               KM
      -4129.823          -133.367             35.927            15.673           -0.017
  Quarterly_Tax   Fuel_TypePetrol    Fuel_TypeDiesel
          9.602          2193.712           1147.855
```

Stepwise regression

```
model <- caret::train(Price ~ ., data=train.df, trControl=trControl,
                      method="glmStepAIC", direction='both')

coef(model$finalModel)
```

Partial output

```
  (Intercept)         Age_08_04                 KM Fuel_TypeDiesel Fuel_TypePetrol
    -4129.823          -133.367             -0.017        1147.855        2193.712
           HP      Quarterly_Tax             Weight
       35.927             9.602             15.673
```

Performance metrics

```
rbind(Training=mlba::regressionSummary(predict(model, train.df), train.df$Price),
      Holdout=mlba::regressionSummary(predict(model, holdout.df), holdout.df$Price))

          RMSE MAE
Training  1331 1010
Holdout   1423 1054
```

the best model chosen by the exhaustive search. It is also possible to use the implementation in the `leaps` package.

Finally, additional ways to reduce the dimension of the data are by using principal components (Chapter 4) and regression trees (Chapter 9).

Regularization (Shrinkage Models)

Selecting a subset of predictors is equivalent to setting some of the model coefficients to zero. This approach creates an interpretable result—we know which predictors were dropped and which are retained. A more flexible alternative called *regularization* or *shrinkage*, "shrinks" the coefficients toward zero. Recall that adjusted R^2 incorporates a penalty according to the number of predictors p. Shrinkage methods also impose a penalty on the model fit, except that the penalty is not based on the *number* of predictors but rather on some aggregation of the coefficient values (typically predictors are first standardized to have the same scale).

The reasoning behind constraining the magnitude of $\hat{\beta}$ coefficients is that highly correlated predictors will tend to exhibit coefficients with high standard errors, since small changes in the training data might radically shift which of the correlated predictors gets emphasized. This instability (high standard errors) leads to poor predictive power. By constraining the combined magnitude of the coefficients, this variance is reduced because the variance is a function of the coefficients' magnitudes.

The two most popular shrinkage methods are *ridge regression* and *lasso*. They differ in terms of the penalty used: in ridge regression, the penalty is based on the sum of squared coefficients $\sum_{j=1}^{p} \beta_j^2$ (called L2 penalty or L2 regularization), whereas lasso uses the sum of absolute values $\sum_{j=1}^{p} |\beta_j|$ (called L1 penalty or L1 regularization), for p predictors (excluding an intercept). It turns out that the lasso penalty effectively shrinks some of the coefficients to zero, thereby resulting in a subset of predictors.

Whereas in linear regression coefficients are estimated by minimizing the training data sum of squared errors (SSE), in ridge regression and lasso the coefficients are estimated by minimizing the training data SSE

$$\text{SSE} = \sum_{i=1}^{N} \left(y_i - b_0 - \sum_{j=1}^{p} \beta_j x_{ij} \right)$$

subject to the penalty term.

Lasso: L1 regularization
$$\text{SSE} + \lambda \sum_{j=1}^{p} |\beta_j|$$

Ridge regression: L2 regularization
$$\text{SSE} + \lambda \sum_{j=1}^{p} \beta_j^2$$

The λ parameter controls the amount or strength of regularization applied to the model and can have values ≥ 0. When $\lambda = 0$, no regularization is applied, yielding ordinary linear regression.

The L1 and L2 regularization can be combined in an approach called *elastic net*.

Elastic net: L1 and L2 regularization $\text{SSE} + \lambda \left[\alpha \sum_{j=1}^{p} |\beta_j| + \frac{1}{2}(1 - \alpha) \sum_{j=1}^{p} \beta_j^2 \right]$

The parameter α controls the penalty distribution between the L1 and L2 penalties and can have a value between 0 and 1. *Ridge regression* model is obtained with $\alpha = 0$ (only L2 penalty), while a *lasso* model is obtained with $\alpha = 1$ (only L1 penalty). Choosing $0 < \alpha < 1$ produces a model that is a combination of L1 and L2 penalties. As above, the λ parameter controls the amount or strength of regularization applied to the model.

In R, *elastic net* (which includes ridge and lasso regression as special cases) is implemented in the *generalized linear model* package `glmnet` and can be used through `caret`. Table 6.8 shows the training of a ridge regression model and Table 6.9 that of a lasso model. The possible values for α and λ are specified using the *tuneGrid* argument. We set the α parameter to 0 for ridge and to 1 for lasso regression. Rather than choosing a specific value for λ, we select a set of values and search for the optimal value within this set. For example, here the λ parameter is specified using an exponential sequence (for example, for ridge we chose 31 values from 100 to 100,000) and combined with the α value using *expand.grid*. If both parameters are specified as sequences, *expand.grid* will create all possible combinations.

The optimal parameter combination is determined using 5-fold cross-validation and selecting the parameter set that has the lowest RMSE value. Figure 6.2 shows the cross-validated RMSE as a function of the λ parameter. The parameters for the *best* model are accessible with the *bestTune* field: for ridge regression, $\lambda = 1000$ is best, and for lasso, it is $\lambda = 158$. Figure 6.2 clearly shows why an exponential sequence is required to explore the λ parameter.

In comparison to the linear regression model of Table 6.3, the coefficients of both models are reduced. The best lasso model has only four non-zero coefficients: Age_08_04, mileage (KM), horsepower (HP), and Weight. Despite the reduction, the performance of the models is comparable with the full model.

Finally, we compare the different variable selection approaches in Table 6.10. We see that in this case all models perform very closely both on the training and the holdout sets. Yet, they differ in terms of computational intensity and in terms of the number of predictors (11 for the full model, 7 for exhaustive search and stepwise methods, and 4 for lasso).

TABLE 6.8   RIDGE REGRESSION FOR SHRINKING PREDICTORS IN TOYOTA COROLLA EXAMPLE

---

 code for ridge regression using caret

```
set.seed(1)
library(caret)
trControl <- caret::trainControl(method='cv', number=5, allowParallel=TRUE)
tuneGrid <- expand.grid(lambda=10^seq(5, 2, by=-0.1), alpha=0)
model <- caret::train(Price ~ ., data=train.df,
                method='glmnet',
                family='gaussian',  # set the family for linear regression
                trControl=trControl,
                tuneGrid=tuneGrid)
model$bestTune
coef(model$finalModel, s=model$bestTune$lambda)
```

Output

```
> model$bestTune
   alpha lambda
41     0   1000
> coef(model$finalModel, s=model$bestTune$lambda)
12 x 1 sparse Matrix of class "dgCMatrix"
                            1
(Intercept)       -2658.9954
Age_08_04          -100.9073
KM                   -0.0223
Fuel_TypeDiesel      -8.4115
Fuel_TypePetrol     266.9359
HP                   33.9810
Met_Color            97.2147
Automatic           195.7619
CC                    0.0726
Doors                99.6551
Quarterly_Tax         6.5570
Weight               14.7082
```

Performance metrics

```
rbind(
  Training=mlba::regressionSummary(predict(model, train.df), train.df$Price),
  Holdout=mlba::regressionSummary(predict(model, holdout.df), holdout.df$Price)
)

          RMSE MAE
Training   1423 1061
Holdout    1590 1162
```

TABLE 6.9	LASSO REGRESSION FOR REDUCING PREDICTORS IN TOYOTA COROLLA EXAMPLE

R code for lasso regression using caret

```
set.seed(1)
tuneGrid <- expand.grid(lambda=10^seq(4, 0, by=-0.1), alpha=1)
model <- caret::train(Price ~ ., data=train.df,
                method='glmnet',
                family='gaussian',  # set the family for linear regression
                trControl=trControl,
                tuneGrid=tuneGrid)
model$bestTune
coef(model$finalModel, s=model$bestTune$lambda)
```

Output

```
> model$bestTune
   alpha lambda
33     1    158
> coef(model$finalModel, s=model$bestTune$lambda)
12 x 1 sparse Matrix of class "dgCMatrix"
                       1
(Intercept)      368.168
Age_08_04       -132.917
KM                -0.015
Fuel_TypeDiesel     .
Fuel_TypePetrol     .
HP                30.759
Met_Color           .
Automatic           .
CC                  .
Doors               .
Quarterly_Tax       .
Weight            14.536
```

Performance metrics

```
rbind(
  Training=mlba::regressionSummary(predict(model, train.df), train.df$Price),
  Holdout=mlba::regressionSummary(predict(model, holdout.df), holdout.df$Price)
)

         RMSE MAE
Training 1372 1026
Holdout  1557 1112
```

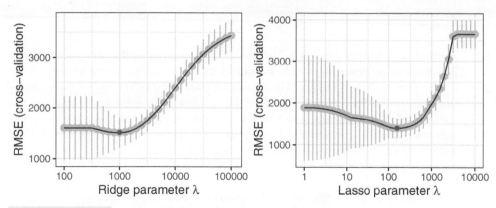

FIGURE 6.2   CROSS-VALIDATED RMSE OF TOYOTA PRICE PREDICTION MODELS AS A FUNCTION OF THE TUNING PARAMETER FOR THE RIDGE (LEFT) AND LASSO (RIGHT) REGRESSION. THE ERROR BARS ARE ± STANDARD DEVIATION BASED ON THE RMSE VALUES FROM THE CROSS-VALIDATION FOLDS

TABLE 6.10   COMPARING PERFORMANCE OF THE DIFFERENT VARIABLE SELECTION METHODS WITH THE FULL MODEL

	Cross-validation		Training		Holdout		No. of predictors
	RMSE	MAE	RMSE	MAE	RMSE	MAE	
Full	1949	1086	1344	1009	1366	1030	11
Exhaustive	1379	1031	1343	1012	1373	1034	7
Stepwise	1379	1031	1343	1012	1373	1034	7
Ridge	1507	1092	1423	1061	1590	1162	11
Lasso	1396	1039	1372	1026	1557	1112	4

PROBLEMS

6.1 Predicting Boston Housing Prices. The dataset *mlba::BostonHousing* contains information collected by the US Bureau of the Census concerning housing in the area of Boston, Massachusetts. The dataset includes information on 506 census housing tracts in the Boston area. The goal is to predict the median house price in new tracts based on information such as crime rate, pollution, and number of rooms. The dataset contains 13 predictors, and the response is the median house price (MEDV). Table 6.11 describes each of the predictors and the response.

TABLE 6.11	**DESCRIPTION OF VARIABLES FOR BOSTON HOUSING EXAMPLE**
CRIM	Per capita crime rate by town
ZN	Proportion of residential land zoned for lots over 25,000 ft^2
INDUS	Proportion of nonretail business acres per town
CHAS	Charles River dummy variable (= 1 if tract bounds river; = 0 otherwise)
NOX	Nitric oxide concentration (parts per 10 million)
RM	Average number of rooms per dwelling
AGE	Proportion of owner-occupied units built prior to 1940
DIS	Weighted distances to five Boston employment centers
RAD	Index of accessibility to radial highways
TAX	Full-value property-tax rate per $10,000
PTRATIO	Pupil/teacher ratio by town
LSTAT	Percentage lower status of the population
MEDV	Median value of owner-occupied homes in $1000s

a. Why should the data be partitioned into training and holdout sets? What will the training set be used for? What will the holdout set be used for?

b. Fit a multiple linear regression model to the median house price (MEDV) as a function of CRIM, CHAS, and RM. Write the equation for predicting the median house price from the predictors in the model.

c. Using the estimated regression model, what median house price is predicted for a tract in the Boston area that does not bound the Charles River, has a crime rate of 0.1, and where the average number of rooms per house is 6?

d. Reduce the number of predictors:

    i. Which predictors are likely to be measuring the same thing among the 13 predictors? Discuss the relationships among INDUS, NOX, and TAX.

    ii. Compute the correlation table for the 12 numerical predictors, and search for highly correlated pairs. These have potential redundancy and can cause multicollinearity. Choose which ones to remove based on this table.

    iii. Use stepwise regression with the three options (*backward, forward,* and *both*) to reduce the remaining predictors as follows: Run stepwise on the training set. Choose the top model from each stepwise run. Then use each of these models separately to predict the holdout set. Compare RMSE and mean absolute error, as well as lift charts. Finally, describe the best model.

6.2 Predicting Software Reselling Profits. Tayko Software is a software catalog firm that sells games and educational software. It started out as a software manufacturer and then added third–party titles to its offerings. It recently revised its collection of items in a new catalog, which it mailed out to its customers. This mailing yielded 2000 purchases. Based on these data, Tayko wants to devise a model for predicting the spending amount that a purchasing customer will yield. The dataset *mlba::Tayko* contains information on 2000 purchases. Table 6.12 describes the variables to be used in the problem (the dataset contains additional variables).

TABLE 6.12   DESCRIPTION OF VARIABLES FOR TAYKO SOFTWARE EXAMPLE

Freq	Number of transactions in the preceding year
last_update_days_ago	Number of days since last update to customer record
Web.order	Whether customer purchased by Web order at least once
Gender.male	Male or female
Address_is_res	Whether it is a residential address
US	Whether it is a US address
Spending (response)	Amount spent by customer in test mailing ($)

a. Explore the spending amount by creating a pivot table for the categorical variables and computing the average and standard deviation of spending in each category.

b. Explore the relationship between spending and each of the two continuous predictors by creating two scatterplots (Spending vs. Freq, and Spending vs. last_update_days_ago). Does there seem to be a linear relationship?

c. To fit a predictive model for Spending:

   i. Partition the 2000 records into training and holdout sets.

   ii. Run a multiple linear regression model for Spending vs. all six predictors. Give the estimated predictive equation.

   iii. Based on this model, what type of purchaser is most likely to spend a large amount of money?

   iv. If we used backward elimination to reduce the number of predictors, which predictor would be dropped first from the model?

   v. Show how the prediction and the prediction error are computed for the first purchase in the holdout set.

   vi. Evaluate the predictive accuracy of the model by examining its performance on the holdout set.

   vii. Create a histogram of the model residuals. Do they appear to follow a normal distribution? How does this affect the predictive performance of the model?

6.3 **Predicting Airfare on New Routes.** The following problem takes place in the United States in the late 1990s, when many major US cities were facing issues with airport congestion, partly as a result of the 1978 deregulation of airlines. Both fares and routes were freed from regulation, and low-fare carriers such as Southwest (SW) began competing on existing routes and starting nonstop service on routes that previously lacked it. Building completely new airports is generally not feasible, but sometimes decommissioned military bases or smaller municipal airports can be reconfigured as regional or larger commercial airports. There are numerous players and interests involved in the issue (airlines, city, state and federal authorities, civic groups, the military, airport operators), and an aviation consulting firm is seeking advisory contracts with these players. The firm needs predictive models to support its consulting service. One thing the firm might want to be able to predict is fares, in the event a new airport is brought into service. The firm starts with the dataset *mlba::Airfares*, which contains real data that were collected between Q3-1996 and Q2-1997. The variables in these data are listed in Table 6.13 and are believed to be important in predicting FARE. Some airport-to-airport data are available, but most data are at the city-to-city level. One question that will be of interest in the analysis is the effect that the presence or absence of Southwest has on FARE.

TABLE 6.13   **DESCRIPTION OF VARIABLES FOR AIRFARE EXAMPLE**

S_CODE	Starting airport's code
S_CITY	Starting city
E_CODE	Ending airport's code
E_CITY	Ending city
COUPON	Average number of coupons (a one-coupon flight is a nonstop flight, a two-coupon flight is a one-stop flight, etc.) for that route
NEW	Number of new carriers entering that route between Q3-1996 and Q2-1997
VACATION	Whether (Yes) or not (No) a vacation route
SW	Whether (Yes) or not (No) Southwest Airlines serves that route
HI	Herfindahl index: measure of market concentration
S_INCOME	Starting city's average personal income
E_INCOME	Ending city's average personal income
S_POP	Starting city's population
E_POP	Ending city's population
SLOT	Whether or not either endpoint airport is slot-controlled (this is a measure of airport congestion)
GATE	Whether or not either endpoint airport has gate constraints (this is another measure of airport congestion)
DISTANCE	Distance between two endpoint airports in miles
PAX	Number of passengers on that route during period of data collection
FARE	Average fare on that route

a. Explore the numerical predictors and response (FARE) by creating a correlation table and examining some scatterplots between FARE and those predictors. What seems to be the best single predictor of FARE?

b. Explore the categorical predictors (excluding the first four) by computing the percentage of flights in each category. Create a pivot table with the average fare in each category. Which categorical predictor seems best for predicting FARE?

c. Find a model for predicting the average fare on a new route:

   i. Convert categorical variables into dummy variables. Then, partition the data into training and holdout sets. The model will be fit to the training data and evaluated on the holdout set.

   ii. Use stepwise regression to reduce the number of predictors. You can ignore the first four predictors (S_CODE, S_CITY, E_CODE, E_CITY). Report the estimated model selected.

   iii. Repeat (ii) using exhaustive search instead of stepwise regression. Compare the resulting best model to the one you obtained in (ii) in terms of the predictors that are in the model.

   iv. Repeat (ii) using Lasso regression. Compare the resulting best model for Lasso regression to the one you obtained in (ii) and (iii) in terms of the predictors that are in the model.

   v. Compare the predictive accuracy of models (ii), (iii) and (iv) using measures such as RMSE and average error and lift charts.

vi. Using model (iii), predict the average fare on a route with the following characteristics: COUPON = 1.202, NEW = 3, VACATION = No, SW = No, HI = 4442.141, S_INCOME = $28,760, E_INCOME = $27,664, S_POP = 4,557,004, E_POP = 3,195,503, SLOT = Free, GATE = Free, PAX = 12,782, DISTANCE = 1976 miles.

vii. Predict the reduction in average fare on the route in (vi) if Southwest decides to cover this route [using model (iii)].

viii. In reality, which of the factors will not be available for predicting the average fare from a new airport (i.e., before flights start operating on those routes)? Which ones can be estimated? How?

ix. Select a model that includes only factors that are available before flights begin to operate on the new route. Use an exhaustive search to find such a model.

x. Use the model in (ix) to predict the average fare on a route with characteristics COUPON = 1.202, NEW = 3, VACATION = No, SW = No, HI = 4442.141, S_INCOME = $28,760, E_INCOME = $27,664, S_ POP = 4,557,004, E_POP = 3,195,503, SLOT = Free, GATE = Free, PAX = 12,782, DISTANCE = 1976 miles.

xi. Compare the predictive accuracy of this model with model (iii). Is this model good enough, or is it worthwhile reevaluating the model once flights begin on the new route?

d. In competitive industries, a new entrant with a novel business plan can have a disruptive effect on existing firms. If a new entrant's business model is sustainable, other players are forced to respond by changing their business practices. If the goal of the analysis was to evaluate the effect of Southwest Airlines' presence on the airline industry rather than predicting fares on new routes, how would the analysis be different? Describe technical and conceptual aspects.

6.4 **Predicting Prices of Used Cars.** The dataset *mlba::ToyotaCorolla* contains data on used cars (Toyota Corolla) on sale during late summer of 2004 in the Netherlands. It has 1436 records containing details on 38 variables, including Price, Age, Kilometers, HP, and other specifications. The goal is to predict the price of a used Toyota Corolla based on its specifications. (The example in Section 6.3 is a subset of this dataset.)

Split the data into training (60%) and holdout (40%) datasets.

Run a multiple linear regression with the outcome variable Price and predictor variables Age_08_04, KM, Fuel_Type, HP, Automatic, Doors, Quarterly_Tax, Mfr_Guarantee, Guarantee_Period, Airco, Automatic_airco, CD_Player, Powered_Windows, Sport_Model, and Tow_Bar.

a. What appear to be the three or four most important car specifications for predicting the car's price?

b. Using metrics you consider useful, assess the performance of the model in predicting prices.

c. Train lasso and ridge regression models, and compare their performance to the multiple linear regression model. Tune the λ parameter using 5-fold cross-validation.

d. Repeat (c) using the full dataset. Compare the training, cross-validation, and holdout performance for all three models. You will need to use cross-validation for the linear regression model as well. Which model would you select based on the results and why?

k-Nearest Neighbors (k-NN)

In this chapter, we describe the k-nearest neighbors (k-NN) algorithm that can be used for classification (of a categorical outcome) or prediction (of a numerical outcome). To classify or predict a new record, the method relies on finding "similar" records in the training data. These "neighbors" are then used to derive a classification or prediction for the new record by voting (for classification) or averaging (for prediction). We explain how similarity is determined, how the number of neighbors is chosen, and how a classification or prediction is computed. k-NN is a highly automated data-driven method. We discuss the advantages and weaknesses of the k-NN method in terms of performance and practical considerations such as computational time.

k-NN in R

The main R function introduced in this chapter is *knn* in the **caret** package.

7.1 THE k-NN CLASSIFIER (CATEGORICAL OUTCOME)

The idea in k-NN methods is to identify k records in the training dataset that are similar to a new record that we wish to classify. We then use these similar (neighboring) records to classify the new record into a class, assigning the new record to the predominant class among these neighbors. Denote the values of the predictors for this new record by $x_1, x_2, \ldots, x_p$. We look for records in our training data that are similar or "near" the record to be classified in the predictor space (i.e., records that have values close to $x_1, x_2, \ldots, x_p$). Then, based on the classes to which those proximate records belong, we assign a class to the record that we want to classify.

Machine Learning for Business Analytics: Concepts, Techniques, and Applications in R, Second Edition.
Galit Shmueli, Peter C. Bruce, Peter Gedeck, Inbal Yahav, and Nitin R. Patel
© 2023 John Wiley & Sons, Inc. Published 2023 by John Wiley & Sons, Inc.

Determining Neighbors

The k-NN algorithm is a classification method that does not make assumptions about the form of the relationship between the class membership (Y) and the predictors $X_1, X_2, \ldots, X_p$. This is a nonparametric method because it does not involve estimation of parameters in an assumed function form, such as the linear form assumed in linear regression (Chapter 6). Instead, this method draws information from similarities between the predictor values of the records in the dataset.

A central question is how to measure the distance between records based on their predictor values. The most popular measure of distance is the Euclidean distance. The Euclidean distance between two records $(x_1, x_2, \ldots, x_p)$ and $(u_1, u_2, \ldots, u_p)$ is

$$\sqrt{(x_1 - u_1)^2 + (x_2 - u_2)^2 + \cdots + (x_p - u_p)^2}. \qquad (7.1)$$

You will find a host of other distance metrics in Chapters 12 and 16 for both numerical and categorical variables. However, the k-NN algorithm relies on many distance computations (between each record to be predicted and every record in the training set), and therefore the Euclidean distance, which is computationally cheap, is the most popular in k-NN.

To equalize the scales that the various predictors may have, note that in most cases, predictors should first be standardized before computing a Euclidean distance. Also note that the means and standard deviations used to standardize new records are those of the *training* data, and the new record is not included in calculating them. The holdout data, like new data, are also not included in this calculation.

Classification Rule

After computing the distances between the record to be classified and existing records, we need a rule to assign a class to the record to be classified, based on the classes of its neighbors. The simplest case is $k = 1$, where we look for the record that is closest (the nearest neighbor) and classify the new record as belonging to the same class as its closest neighbor. It is a remarkable fact that this simple, intuitive idea of using a single nearest neighbor to classify records can be very powerful when we have a large number of records in our training set. It turns out that the misclassification error of the 1-nearest neighbor scheme has a misclassification rate that is no more than twice the error when we know exactly the probability density functions for each class.

The idea of the *1-nearest neighbor* (1-NN) can be extended to $k > 1$ neighbors as follows:

1. Find the nearest k neighbors to the record to be classified.
2. Use a majority decision rule to classify the record, where the record is classified as a member of the majority class of the k neighbors.

Example: Riding Mowers

A riding–mower manufacturer would like to find a way of classifying families in a city into those likely to purchase a riding mower and those not likely to buy one. A pilot random sample is undertaken of 12 owners and 12 nonowners in the city. The data are shown in Table 7.1. We first partition the data into training data (14 households) and holdout data (10 households). Obviously, this dataset is too small for partitioning, which can result in unstable results, but we will continue with this partitioning for illustration purposes. A scatter plot of the training data is shown in Figure 7.1.

TABLE 7.1	LOT SIZE, INCOME, AND OWNERSHIP OF A RIDING MOWER FOR 24 HOUSEHOLDS		
Household number	Income ($000s)	Lot size (000s ft^2)	Ownership of riding mower
1	60.0	18.4	Owner
2	85.5	16.8	Owner
3	64.8	21.6	Owner
4	61.5	20.8	Owner
5	87.0	23.6	Owner
6	110.1	19.2	Owner
7	108.0	17.6	Owner
8	82.8	22.4	Owner
9	69.0	20.0	Owner
10	93.0	20.8	Owner
11	51.0	22.0	Owner
12	81.0	20.0	Owner
13	75.0	19.6	Nonowner
14	52.8	20.8	Nonowner
15	64.8	17.2	Nonowner
16	43.2	20.4	Nonowner
17	84.0	17.6	Nonowner
18	49.2	17.6	Nonowner
19	59.4	16.0	Nonowner
20	66.0	18.4	Nonowner
21	47.4	16.4	Nonowner
22	33.0	18.8	Nonowner
23	51.0	14.0	Nonowner
24	63.0	14.8	Nonowner
25	60.0	20.0	?

Now consider a new household with $60,000 income and 20,000 ft^2 lot size (also shown in Figure 7.1). Among the households in the training set, the one closest to the new household (in Euclidean distance after normalizing income and lot size) is household 9, with $69,000 income and 20,000 ft^2 lot size. If we use a 1–NN classifier, we would classify the new household as an owner, like household 9. If we use $k = 3$, the three nearest households are 9, 14, and 1, as can be seen visually in the scatter plot and as computed by the software (see output in Table 7.2). Two of these neighbors are owners of riding mowers, and the last is a nonowner. The majority vote is therefore *owner*, and the new household would be classified as an owner (see bottom of output in Table 7.2).

> **R** code for loading and partitioning the riding mower data, and plotting scatter
> plot

```
library(ggrepel)
mowers.df <- mlba::RidingMowers
set.seed(35)

idx <- sample(nrow(mowers.df), 0.6*nrow(mowers.df))
train.df <- mowers.df[idx, ]
holdout.df <- mowers.df[-idx, ]
## new household
new.df <- data.frame(Income = 60, Lot_Size = 20)

ggplot(mapping=aes(x=Income, y=Lot_Size, shape=Ownership, color=Ownership)) +
  geom_point(data=train.df) +
  geom_text_repel(aes(label=rownames(train.df)), data=train.df, show.legend = FALSE) +
  geom_point(data=cbind(new.df, Ownership='New'))
```

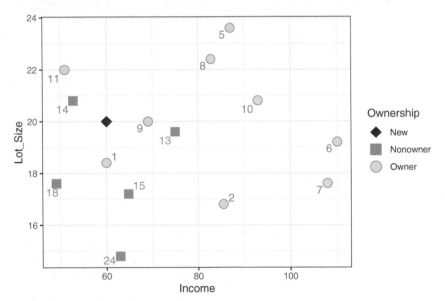

FIGURE 7.1   SCATTER PLOT OF LOT SIZE VS. INCOME FOR THE 14 HOUSEHOLDS IN THE
TRAINING SET AND THE NEW HOUSEHOLD TO BE CLASSIFIED

Choosing k

The advantage of choosing $k > 1$ is that higher values of k provide smoothing that reduces the risk of overfitting due to noise in the training data. Generally speaking, if k is too low, we may be fitting to the noise in the data. However, if k is too high, we will miss out on the method's ability to capture the local structure in the data, one of its main advantages. In the extreme, $k = n =$ the number of records in the training dataset. In that case, we simply assign all records to the majority class in the training data, irrespective of the values of $(x_1, x_2, \ldots, x_p)$, which coincides with the naive rule! This is clearly a case of oversmoothing in the absence of useful information in the predictors about

TABLE 7.2   RUNNING k-NN

 code for training a k-NN model and finding nearest neighbors

```
library(caret)
# train k-NN model with k=3
model <- train(Ownership ~ ., data=train.df,
               method="knn",  # specify the model
               preProcess=c("center", "scale"),  # normalize data
               tuneGrid=expand.grid(k=3),
               trControl=trainControl(method="none"))
model

# predict new data point
predict(model, new.df)

# determine nearest neighbors to new data point
train.norm.df <- predict(model$preProcess, train.df)
new.norm.df <- predict(model$preProcess, new.df)
distances <- apply(train.norm.df[, 1:2], 1,
                   function(d){ sqrt(sum((d - new.norm.df)^2)) })
rownames(train.df)[order(distances)][1:3]
```

Output

```
> model
k-Nearest Neighbors

14 samples
 2 predictor
 2 classes: 'Nonowner', 'Owner'

Pre-processing: centered (2), scaled (2)
Resampling: None

> predict(model, new.df)
[1] Owner
Levels: Nonowner Owner

> rownames(train.df)[order(distances)][1:3]
[1] "9"  "14"  "1"
```

the class membership. In other words, we want to balance between overfitting to the predictor information and ignoring this information completely. A balanced choice greatly depends on the nature of the data. The more complex and irregular the structure of the data, the lower the optimum value of k. Typically, values of k fall in the range 1–20. We will use odd numbers to avoid ties.

So how is k chosen? Answer: We choose the k with the best estimated classification performance. We use cross-validation with the training data and compute accuracies for various choices of k. For our example, if we choose $k = 1$, we will classify in a way that is very sensitive to the local characteristics of the training data. On the other hand, if we choose a large value of k, such as $k = 18$, we would simply predict the most frequent class in the dataset in all cases. This is a very stable prediction, but it completely ignores the information in the predictors. To find a balance, we examine the accuracy (of cross-validation predictions in the training set) that results from different choices of k between 1 and 13 (see Table 7.3). For an even number k, if there is a tie in classifying a household, the tie is broken randomly.[1] Looking at the results in Table 7.3, we would choose $k = 7$, which maximizes our accuracy in cross-validation.[2] Note, however, that

TABLE 7.3   ACCURACY (OR CORRECT RATE) OF *k*-NN PREDICTIONS IN VALIDATION SET FOR VARIOUS CHOICES OF *k*

 code for measuring the accuracy of different *k* values

```
# use leave-one-out cross-validation for small dataset
trControl <- trainControl(method="loocv", number=5, allowParallel=TRUE)
model <- train(Ownership ~ ., data=train.df,
               method="knn",
               preProcess=c("center", "scale"),
               tuneGrid=expand.grid(k=seq(1, 13, 2)),
               trControl=trControl)
model
```

Output

```
k-Nearest Neighbors

14 samples
 2 predictor
 2 classes: 'Nonowner', 'Owner'

Pre-processing: centered (2), scaled (2)
Resampling: Leave-One-Out Cross-Validation
Summary of sample sizes: 13, 13, 13, 13, 13, 13, ...
Resampling results across tuning parameters:

  k   Accuracy  Kappa
   1  0.429     0
   3  0.643     0
   5  0.643     0
   7  0.714     0
   9  0.571     0
  11  0.643     0
  13  0.643     0

Accuracy was used to select the optimal model using the largest value.
The final value used for the model was k = 7.
```

---

[1]If you are interested in reproducibility of results, consider only odd values for k, as shown in Table 7.3.
[2]For such a small dataset, we use leave-one-out cross-validation. Partitioning the dataset into larger folds can lead to unstable performance, because different choices of folds can lead to different choices of optimal k. For instance, if you use 5-fold cross-validation, you might obtain a different "optimal" k under different partitionings into 5 folds. For larger datasets, leave-one-out cross-validation becomes impractical and it is better to use 5-fold or 10-fold cross-validation.

because the training data was used for selecting k, the cross-validation accuracy is over-optimistic. We would therefore want a separate holdout set to evaluate the performance of the method on data that it did not see.

Once k is chosen, we rerun the algorithm on the combined training and holdout sets to generate classifications of new records. An example is shown in Table 7.4, where the seven nearest neighbors are used to classify the new household.

TABLE 7.4   **CLASSIFYING A NEW HOUSEHOLD USING THE "BEST K" = 7**

 code for running the *k-NN algorithm to classify the new household*

```
model <- train(Ownership ~ ., data=mowers.df,
               method="knn",
               preProcess=c("center", "scale"),
               tuneGrid=expand.grid(k=7),
               trControl=trainControl(method="none"))
predict(model, new.df)
```

Partial Output

```
> predict(model, new.df)
[1] Owner
Levels: Nonowner Owner
```

Weighted k-NN

In using a majority vote approach, k-NN assigns equal weight to each of the k neighbors. For example, with $k = 3$, each neighbor's vote has a weight = 1/3. Weighted k-NN improves the k-NN algorithm by using an incredibly simple yet powerful idea that the closer the neighbor, the heavier its weight in the overall vote. Each neighbor's weight is determined by the inverse of its distance from the record to be predicted (normalized by the sum of inverse distances of all k neighbors). Thus, given $d_1, d_2, \ldots, d_k$ distances to each of the k neighbors, the weight for neighbor 1 is computed as

$$w_1 = \frac{1/d_1}{\left(1/d_1 + 1/d_2 + \cdots + 1/d_k\right)}. \tag{7.2}$$

Then, to compute the probability of belonging to a certain class, we sum up the weights of the neighbors with that class.

For example, returning to our example with $k = 3$, suppose the distances from the new record to its three nearest neighbors (and their labels) were $d_1 = 0.5$ (Nonowner), $d_2 = 0.2$ (Nonowner), and $d_3 = 0.1$ (Owner). Using

Equation (7.2), we get weights $w_1 = 0.12$, $w_2 = 0.29$, and $w_3 = 0.59$. The probability of belonging to the Owner class is then 0.59 (and for belonging to Nonowner class is $0.12 + 0.29 = 0.41$). Assuming a 0.5 threshold, the predicted class for the record would be `Owner` even though the majority vote is `Nonowner`. *Note:* The *kknn* method in `caret` uses the package `kknn`, which implements weighted *k*-NN using a variety of weighting schemes.

Setting the Cutoff Value

k-NN uses a majority decision rule to classify a new record, where the record is classified as a member of the majority class of the k neighbors. The definition of "majority" is directly linked to the notion of a cutoff value applied to the class membership probabilities. Let us consider a binary outcome case. For a new record, the proportion of class 1 members among its neighbors is an estimate of its propensity (probability) of belonging to class 1. In the riding-mowers example with $k = 7$, we found that the seven nearest neighbors to the new household (with income = \$60,000 and lot size = 20,000 ft^2) are households 9, 14, 1, 13, 11, 18, and 15.[3] Since three of these are owners and the other four are nonowners, we can estimate for the new household a probability of $3/7 = 0.43$ of being an owner (and 0.57 for being a nonowner). Using a simple unweighted majority rule is equivalent to setting the cutoff value to 0.5. This 0.5 cutoff assigns class *Nonowner* to this record.

Had we used $k = 8$, then household 8 would be added as a neighbor, resulting in 4 of the neighbors being owners while the other 4 are nonowners. This gives a probability of 0.5 of being an owner (and 0.5 for being a nonowner) for the new record. In a case like this, the software will break the tie by (randomly) assigning a class. The prediction will therefore vary randomly between *Owner* and *Nonowner*.

As mentioned in Chapter 5, changing the cutoff value affects the confusion matrix (and the error rates). Hence, in some cases, we might want to choose a cutoff other than the default 0.5 for the purpose of maximizing accuracy or for incorporating misclassification costs. This is particularly likely to be the case when the class of primary interest is relatively rare, and the threshold for classifying records as members of that class must be lowered. For more on the use of cutoff value in classification with a single class of interest, see Chapter 5.

---

[3]The *k*-NN implementation described earlier does not provide a way to get the neighbor IDs. We found these using a manual computation of distances—see code in Table 7.2.

k-NN with More Than Two Classes

The *k*-NN classifier can easily be applied to an outcome with m classes, where $m > 2$. The "majority rule" means that a new record is classified as a member of the majority class of its *k* neighbors. An alternative, when there is a specific class that we are interested in identifying (and are willing to "overidentify" records as belonging to this class), is to calculate the proportion of the *k* neighbors that belong to this class of interest, use that as an estimate of the probability (propensity) that the new record belongs to that class, and then refer to a user-specified cutoff value to decide whether to assign the new record to that class.

Converting Categorical Variables to Binary Dummies

It usually does not make sense to calculate Euclidean distance between two non-numeric categories (e.g., cookbooks and maps, in a bookstore). Therefore, before *k*-NN can be applied, categorical variables must be converted to binary dummies. In contrast to the situation with statistical models such as regression, all m binaries should be created and used with *k*-NN. While mathematically this is redundant, since $m-1$ dummies contain the same information as m dummies, this redundant information does not create the multicollinearity problems that it does for linear models. Moreover, in *k*-NN, the use of $m-1$ dummies can yield different classifications than the use of m dummies and lead to an imbalance in the contribution of the different categories to the model. The *knn* method in `caret` handles dummy creation automatically.

7.2 *k*-NN FOR A NUMERICAL OUTCOME

The idea of *k*-NN can readily be extended to predicting a continuous value (as is our aim with multiple linear regression models). The first step of determining neighbors by computing distances remains unchanged. The second step, where a majority vote of the neighbors is used to determine class, is modified such that we take the average outcome value of the *k*-nearest neighbors to determine the prediction. Often, this average is a weighted average, with the weight decreasing with increasing distance from the point at which the prediction is required. In R, we can use the methods *knn* and *kknn* in `caret` to compute *k*-NN numerical predictions for the holdout set.

Another modification is in the error metric used for determining the "best *k*." Rather than the overall error rate used in classification, RMS error or another prediction error metric should be used in prediction (see Chapter 5). `Caret` will use RMSE by default for k-NN with a numerical outcome.

PANDORA

Pandora is an Internet music radio service that allows users to build customized "stations" that play music similar to a song or artist that they have specified. When it started, Pandora used a k-NN style clustering/classification process called the Music Genome Project to locate new songs or artists that are close to the user-specified song or artist.

Pandora was the brainchild of Tim Westergren, who worked as a musician and a nanny when he graduated from Stanford in the 1980s. Together with Nolan Gasser, who was studying medieval music, he developed a "matching engine" by entering data about a song's characteristics into a spreadsheet. The first result was surprising—a Beatles song matched to a Bee Gees song, but they built a company around the concept. The early days were hard—Westergren racked up over $300,000 in personal debt, maxed out 11 credit cards, and ended up in the hospital once due to stress-induced heart palpitations. A venture capitalist finally invested funds in 2004 to rescue the firm, and it eventually went public.

In simplified terms, the process works roughly as follows for songs:

1. Pandora established hundreds of variables on which a song can be measured on a scale from 0 to 5. Four such variables from the beginning of the list are

   - Acid Rock Qualities
   - Accordion Playing
   - Acousti-Lectric Sonority
   - Acousti-Synthetic Sonority

2. Pandora pays musicians to analyze tens of thousands of songs and rate each song on each of these atributes. Each song will then be represented by a row vector of values between 0 and 5, for example, for Led Zeppelin's Kashmir:

   Kashmir 4 0 3 3 ... (high on acid rock variable, no accordion, etc.)

   This step represents a significant investment and lies at the heart of Pandora's value because these variables have been tested and selected because they accurately reflect the essence of a song and provide a basis for defining highly individualized preferences.

3. The online user specifies a song that s/he likes (the song must be in Pandora's database).

4. Pandora then calculates the statistical distance[1] between the user's song and the songs in its database. It selects a song that is close to the user-specified song and plays it.

5. The user then has the option of saying "I like this song," "I don't like this song," or saying nothing.

6. If "like" is chosen, the original song and the new song are merged into a 2-song cluster[2] that is represented by a single vector comprising means of the variables in the original two song vectors.

7. If "dislike" is chosen, the vector of the song that is not liked is stored for future reference. (If the user does not express an opinion about the song, in our simplified example here, the new song is not used for further comparisons.)

8. Pandora looks in its database for a new song, one whose statistical distance is close to the "like" song cluster[3] and not too close to the "dislike" song. Depending on the user's reaction, this new song might be added to the "like" cluster or "dislike" cluster.

Over time, Pandora develops the ability to deliver songs that match a particular taste of a particular user. A single user might build up multiple stations around different song clusters. Clearly, this is a less limiting approach than selecting music in terms of which "genre" it belongs to.

While the process described above is a bit more complex than the basic "classification of new data" process described in this chapter, the fundamental process—classifying a record according to its proximity to other records—is the same at its core. Note the role of domain knowledge in this machine learning process—the variables have been tested and selected by the project leaders, and the measurements have been made by human experts. In another sense, this human role represented the achilles heel of Pandora—it was costly and constituted a bottleneck obstructing the flow of new songs into the system.

Music streaming services later came to omit this step of pre-labeling songs and to rely on machine learning algorithms that get input only from users. Collaborative filtering, for example, recommends songs that are liked by other people who share your tastes (i.e., like the same songs); see Chapter 15 for more on collaborative filtering. Deep learning networks (which were not practically available at Pandora's inception) can take the sound waves in songs and derive features from them, in the same way that these networks derive features from images. These derived features can then be used to predict user choices. See Chapter 11 for more on neural networks.

Pandora was a pioneer in licensed music streaming but was later eclipsed by Spotify and Apple Music, which offered features that Pandora's "customized radio station" model did not, such as the ability to play a specific song on demand and the ability to download music.

Further reading: See www.pandora.com, Wikipedia's article on the Music Genome Project, and Joyce John's article "Pandora and the Music Genome Project," *Scientific Computing*, vol. 23, no. 10: 14, pp. 40–41, Sep. 2006.

---

[1] See Section 12.5 in Chapter 12 for an explanation of statistical distance.

[2] See Chapter 16 for more on clusters.

[3] See Case 23.6 "Segmenting Consumers of Bath Soap" for an exercise involving the identification of clusters, which are then used for classification purposes.

7.3 ADVANTAGES AND SHORTCOMINGS OF *k*-NN ALGORITHMS

The main advantage of *k*-NN methods is their simplicity and lack of parametric assumptions. In the presence of a large enough training set, these methods perform surprisingly well, especially when each class is characterized by multiple combinations of predictor values. For instance, in real estate databases, there are likely to be multiple combinations of {home type, number of rooms, neighborhood, asking price, etc.} that characterize homes that sell quickly vs. those that remain for a long period on the market.

There are three difficulties with the practical exploitation of the power of the *k*-NN approach. First, although no time is required to estimate parameters from the training data (as would be the case for parametric models such as regression), the time to find the nearest neighbors in a large training set can be prohibitive. A number of ideas have been implemented to overcome this difficulty. The main ideas are as follows:

- Reduce the time taken to compute distances by working in a reduced dimension using dimension reduction techniques such as principal components analysis (Chapter 4).

- Use sophisticated data structures such as search trees to speed up identification of the nearest neighbor. This approach often settles for an "almost nearest" neighbor to improve speed. An example is using *bucketing*, where the records are grouped into buckets so that records within each bucket are close to each other. For a to-be-predicted record, buckets are ordered by their distance to the record. Starting from the nearest bucket, the distance to each of the records within the bucket is measured. The algorithm stops when the distance to a bucket is larger than the distance to the closest record thus far.

Second, the number of records required in the training set to qualify as large increases exponentially with the number of predictors p. This is because the expected distance to the nearest neighbor goes up dramatically with p unless the size of the training set increases exponentially with p. This phenomenon is known as the *curse of dimensionality*, a fundamental issue pertinent to all classification, prediction, and clustering techniques. This is why we often seek to reduce the number of predictors through methods such as selecting subsets of the predictors for our model or by combining them using methods such as principal components analysis, singular value decomposition, and factor analysis (see Chapter 4).

Third, *k*-NN is a "lazy learner": the time-consuming computation is deferred to the time of prediction. For every record to be predicted, we compute its distances from the entire set of training records only at the time of prediction. This behavior prohibits using this algorithm for real-time prediction of a large number of records simultaneously.

PROBLEMS

7.1 Calculating Distance with Categorical Predictors. This exercise with a tiny dataset illustrates the calculation of Euclidean distance and the creation of binary dummies. The online education company Statistics.com segments its customers and prospects into three main categories: IT professionals (IT), statisticians (Stat), and other (Other). It also tracks, for each customer, the number of years since first contact (years). Consider the following customers; information about whether they have taken a course or not (the outcome to be predicted) is included:

  Customer 1: Stat, 1 year, did not take course
  Customer 2: Other, 1.1 year, took course

a. Consider now the following new prospect:

  Prospect 1: IT, 1 year

Using the above information on the two customers and one prospect, create one dataset for all three with the categorical predictor variable transformed into two binaries and a similar dataset with the categorical predictor variable transformed into three binaries.

b. For each derived dataset, calculate the Euclidean distance between the prospect and each of the other two customers. (*Note:* while it is typical to normalize data for k-NN, this is not an iron-clad rule, and you may proceed here without normalization.)

c. Using k-NN with $k = 1$, classify the prospect as taking or not taking a course using each of the two derived datasets. Does it make a difference whether you use two or three dummies?

7.2 Personal Loan Acceptance. Universal Bank is a relatively young bank growing rapidly in terms of overall customer acquisition. The majority of these customers are liability customers (depositors) with varying sizes of relationship with the bank. The customer base of asset customers (borrowers) is quite small, and the bank is interested in expanding this base rapidly to bring in more loan business. In particular, it wants to explore ways of converting its liability customers to personal loan customers (while retaining them as depositors).

A campaign that the bank ran last year for liability customers showed a healthy conversion rate of over 9% success. This has encouraged the retail marketing department to devise smarter campaigns with better target marketing. The goal is to use k-NN to predict whether a new customer will accept a loan offer. This will serve as the basis for the design of a new campaign.

The dataset *mlba::UniversalBank* contains data on 5000 customers. The data include customer demographic information (age, income, etc.), the customer's relationship with the bank (mortgage, securities account, etc.), and the customer response to the last personal loan campaign (Personal Loan). Among these 5000 customers, only 480 (= 9.6%) accepted the personal loan that was offered to them in the earlier campaign.

Partition the data into training (60%) and holdout (40%) sets.

a. Consider the following customer:

  Age = 40, Experience = 10, Income = 84, Family = 2, CCAvg = 2, Education = 2, Mortgage = 0, Securities Account = 0, CD Account = 0, Online = 1, and Credit Card = 1. Perform a k-NN classification with all predictors except ID and ZIP code using $k = 1$. Remember to define categorical predictors with more than two categories as factors (for *k*–NN, to automatically handle categorical predictors). Use the default cutoff value of 0.5. How would this customer be classified?

b. What is a choice of k that balances between overfitting and ignoring the predictor information? Use 5-fold cross-validation to find the best k.

c. Show the confusion matrix for the holdout data that results from using the best k.

d. Consider the following customer: Age = 40, Experience = 10, Income = 84, Family = 2, CCAvg = 2, Education = 2, Mortgage = 0, Securities Account = 0, CD Account = 0, Online = 1 and Credit Card = 1. Classify the customer using the best k.

7.3   **Predicting Housing Median Prices.** The dataset *mlba::BostonHousing* contains information on over 500 census tracts in Boston, where for each tract multiple variables are recorded. The last column (CAT.MEDV) was derived from median value (MEDV) such that it obtains the value 1 if MEDV > 30 and 0 otherwise. Consider the goal of predicting the MEDV of a tract, given the information in the first 12 columns.

Partition the data into training (60%) and holdout (40%) sets.

a. Perform a *k*-NN prediction with all 12 predictors (ignore the CAT.MEDV column), trying values of k from 1 to 5. Use `caret` with 5-fold cross-validation to find the best k. Make sure to normalize the data. What is the best k? What does it mean?

b. Predict the MEDV for a tract with the following information, using the best k:

CRIM	ZN	INDUS	CHAS	NOX	RM	AGE	DIS	RAD	TAX	PTRATIO	LSTAT
0.2	0	7	0	0.538	6	62	4.7	4	307	21	10

c. If we used the above *k*-NN algorithm to score the training data, what would be the error of the training set?

d. If the purpose is to predict MEDV for several thousands of new tracts, what would be the disadvantage of using *k*-NN prediction? List the operations that the algorithm goes through to produce each prediction.

## CHAPTER 8

The Naive Bayes Classifier

In this chapter, we introduce the naive Bayes classifier, which can be applied to data with categorical predictors. We review the concept of conditional probabilities and then present the complete, or exact, Bayesian classifier. We next see how it is impractical in most cases and learn how to modify it and use instead the *naive Bayes* classifier, which is more generally applicable.

Naive Bayes in R

The main R function introduced in this chapter is *naiveBayes* in the `e1071` package.

8.1 INTRODUCTION

The naive Bayes method (and, indeed, an entire branch of statistics) is named after the Reverend Thomas Bayes (1702–1761). To understand the naive Bayes classifier, we first look at the complete, or exact, Bayesian classifier. The basic principle is simple. For each record to be classified:

1. Find all the other records with the same predictor profile (i.e., where the predictor values are the same).
2. Determine what classes the records belong to and which class is most prevalent.
3. Assign that class to the new record.

Alternatively (or in addition), it may be desirable to tweak the method so that it answers the question: "What is the propensity of belonging to the class of interest?" instead of "Which class is the most probable?" Obtaining class probabilities allows using a sliding threshold to classify a record as belonging to class

Machine Learning for Business Analytics: Concepts, Techniques, and Applications in R, Second Edition.
Galit Shmueli, Peter C. Bruce, Peter Gedeck, Inbal Yahav, and Nitin R. Patel.
© 2023 John Wiley & Sons, Inc. Published 2023 by John Wiley & Sons, Inc.

C_i, even if C_i is not the most probable class for that record. This approach is useful when there is a specific class of interest that we are interested in identifying, and we are willing to "overidentify" records as belonging to this class. (See Chapter 5 for more details on the use of thresholds for classification and on asymmetric misclassification costs.)

Threshold Probability Method

1. Establish a threshold probability for the class of interest above which we consider that a record belongs to that class.
2. Find all the training records with the same predictor profile as the new record (i.e., where the predictor values are the same).
3. Determine the probability that those records belong to the class of interest.
4. If that probability is above the threshold probability, assign the new record to the class of interest.

Conditional Probability

Both procedures incorporate the concept of *conditional probability* or the probability of event A given that event B has occurred [denoted $P(A|B)$]. In this case, we will be looking at the probability of the record belonging to class C_i given that its predictor values are $x_1, x_2, \ldots, x_p$. In general, for a response with m classes $C_1, C_2, \ldots, C_m$ and the predictor values $x_1, x_2, \ldots, x_p$, we want to compute

$$P(C_i|x_1, \ldots, x_p). \tag{8.1}$$

To classify a record, we compute its probability of belonging to each of the classes in this way and then classify the record to the class that has the highest probability or use the threshold probability to decide whether it should be assigned to the class of interest.

From this definition, we see that the Bayesian classifier works only with categorical predictors. If we use a set of numerical predictors, then it is highly unlikely that multiple records will have identical values on these numerical predictors. In that case, one option is to convert numerical predictors to categorical predictors by binning. Another option is to use a related method called *Gaussian naive Bayes classifier* that can incorporate numerical predictors and is discussed later in this chapter. For now, we will focus on categorical predictors only.

Example 1: Predicting Fraudulent Financial Reporting

An accounting firm has many large companies as customers. Each customer submits an annual financial report to the firm, which is then audited by the accounting firm. For simplicity, we will designate the outcome of the audit as "fraudulent" or "truthful," referring to the accounting firm's assessment of the customer's financial report. The accounting firm has a strong incentive to be accurate in identifying fraudulent reports—if it passes a fraudulent report as truthful, it would be in legal trouble.

The accounting firm notes that, in addition to all the financial records, it also has information on whether or not the customer has had prior legal trouble (criminal or civil charges of any nature filed against it). This information has not been used in previous audits, but the accounting firm is wondering whether it could be used in the future to identify reports that merit more intensive review. Specifically, it wants to know whether having had prior legal trouble is predictive of fraudulent reporting.

In this case, each customer is a record, and the outcome variable of interest, $Y = \{\text{fraudulent, truthful}\}$, has two classes into which a company can be classified: C_1 = fraudulent and C_2 = truthful. The predictor variable—"prior legal trouble"—has two values: 0 (no prior legal trouble) and 1 (prior legal trouble).

The accounting firm has data on 1500 companies that it has investigated in the past. For each company, it has information on whether the financial report was judged fraudulent or truthful and whether the company had prior legal trouble. The data were partitioned into a training set (1000 firms) and a holdout set (500 firms). Counts in the training set are shown in Table 8.1.

TABLE 8.1	PIVOT TABLE FOR FINANCIAL REPORTING EXAMPLE		
	Prior legal ($X = 1$)	No prior legal ($X = 0$)	Total
Fraudulent (C_1)	50	50	100
Truthful (C_2)	180	720	900
Total	230	770	1000

8.2 APPLYING THE FULL (EXACT) BAYESIAN CLASSIFIER

Now consider the financial report from a new company, which we wish to classify as either fraudulent or truthful by using these data. To do this, we compute the probabilities, as above, of belonging to each of the two classes.

If the new company had prior legal trouble, the probability of belonging to the fraudulent class would be $P(\text{fraudulent} \mid \text{prior legal}) = 50/230$ (of the 230 companies with prior legal trouble in the training set, 50 had fraudulent financial reports). The probability of belonging to the other class, "truthful," is, of course, the remainder = 180/230.

Using the "Assign to the Most Probable Class" Method

If a company had prior legal trouble, we assign it to the "truthful" class. Similar calculations for the case of no prior legal trouble are left as an exercise to the reader. In this example, using the rule "assign to the most probable class," all records are assigned to the "truthful" class. This is the same result as the naive rule of "assign all records to the majority class."

Using the Threshold Probability Method

In this example, we are more interested in identifying the fraudulent reports—those are the ones that can land the auditor in jail. We recognize that, to identify the fraudulent reports, some truthful reports will be misidentified as fraudulent, and the overall classification accuracy may decline. Our approach is, therefore, to establish a threshold value for the probability of being fraudulent and classify all records above that value as fraudulent. The Bayesian formula for the calculation of this probability that a record belongs to class C_i is as follows:

$$P(C_i|x_1,\ldots,x_p) = \frac{P(x_1,\ldots,x_p|C_i)P(C_i)}{P(x_1,\ldots,x_p|C_1)P(C_1) + \cdots + P(x_1,\ldots,x_p|C_m)P(C_m)}.$$

(8.2)

In this example (where frauds are rarer), if the threshold were established at 0.20, we would classify a prior legal trouble record as fraudulent because P(fraudulent | prior legal) = 50/230 = 0.22. The user can treat this threshold as a "slider" to be adjusted to optimize performance, like other parameters in any classification model.

Practical Difficulty with the Complete (Exact) Bayes Procedure

The approach outlined above amounts to finding all the records in the sample that are exactly like the new record to be classified in the sense that all the predictor values are all identical. This was easy in the small example presented above, where there was just one predictor.

When the number of predictors gets larger (even to a modest number like 20), many of the records to be classified will be without exact matches. This can be understood in the context of a model to predict voting on the basis of demographic variables. Even a sizable sample may not contain even a single match for a new record who is a male Hispanic with high income from the US Midwest who voted in the last election, did not vote in the prior election, has three daughters and one son, and is divorced. And this is just eight variables, a small number for most data mining exercises. The addition of just a single new variable with five equally frequent categories reduces the probability of a match by a factor of 5.

8.3 SOLUTION: NAIVE BAYES

In the naive Bayes solution, we no longer restrict the probability calculation to those records that match the record to be classified. Instead, we use the entire dataset.

Returning to our original basic classification procedure outlined at the beginning of the chapter, recall that the procedure for classifying a new record was as follows:

1. Find all the other records with the same predictor profile (i.e., where the predictor values are the same).

2. Determine what classes the records belong to and which class is most prevalent.

3. Assign that class to the new record.

The naive Bayes modification (for the basic classification procedure) is as follows:

1. For class C_1, estimate the individual conditional probabilities for each predictor $P(x_j|C_1)$—these are the probabilities that the predictor value in the record to be classified occurs in class C_1. For example, for X_1 this probability is estimated by the proportion of x_1 values among the C_1 records in the training set.

2. Multiply these probabilities by each other and then by the proportion of records belonging to class C_1.

3. Repeat Steps 1 and 2 for all the classes.

4. Estimate a probability for class C_i by taking the value calculated in Step 2 for class C_i and dividing it by the sum of such values for all classes.

5. Assign the record to the class with the highest probability for this set of predictor values.

The above steps lead to the naive Bayes formula for calculating the probability that a record with a given set of predictor values $x_1, \ldots, x_p$ belongs to class C_1 among m classes. The formula can be written as follows:

$$P_{nb}(C_1 \mid x_1, \ldots x_p) =$$

$$\frac{P(C_1)[P(x_1 \mid C_1)P(x_2 \mid C_1) \cdots P(x_p \mid C_1)]}{P(C_1)[P(x_1 \mid C_1)P(x_2 \mid C_1) \cdots P(x_p \mid C_1)] + \cdots + P(C_m)[P(x_1 \mid C_m)P(x_2 \mid C_m) \cdots P(x_p \mid C_m)]}.$$

$$(8.3)$$

This is a somewhat formidable formula; see Example 2 for a simpler numerical version. Note that all the needed quantities can be obtained from pivot tables of Y vs. each of the categorical predictors.

The Naive Bayes Assumption of Conditional Independence

In probability terms, we have made a simplifying assumption that the exact *conditional probability* of seeing a record with predictor profile $x_1, x_2, \ldots, x_p$ within a certain class, $P(x_1, x_2, \ldots, x_p | C_i)$, is well approximated by the product of the individual conditional probabilities $P(x_1 | C_i) \times P(x_2 | C_i) \cdots \times P(x_p | C_i)$. These two quantities are identical when the predictors are independent within each class.

For example, suppose that "lost money last year" is an additional variable in the accounting fraud example. The simplifying assumption we make with naive Bayes is that, within a given class, we no longer need to look for the records characterized both by "prior legal trouble" and "lost money last year." Rather, assuming that the two are independent, we can simply multiply the probability of "prior legal trouble" by the probability of "lost money last year." Of course, complete independence is unlikely in practice, where some correlation between predictors is expected.

In practice, despite the assumption violation, the procedure works quite well—primarily because what is usually needed is not a propensity for each record that is accurate in absolute terms but just a reasonably accurate *rank ordering* of propensities. Even when the assumption is violated, the rank ordering of the records' propensities is typically preserved.

Note that if all we are interested in is a rank ordering, and the denominator remains the same for all classes, it is sufficient to concentrate only on the numerator. The disadvantage of this approach is that the probability values it yields (the propensities), while ordered correctly, are not on the same scale as the exact values that the user would anticipate.

Using the Threshold Probability Method

The above procedure is for the basic case where we seek maximum classification accuracy for all classes. In the case of the *relatively rare class of special interest*, the procedure is as follows:

1. Establish a threshold probability for the class of interest above which we consider that a record belongs to that class.

2. For the class of interest, compute the probability that each individual predictor value in the record to be classified occurs in the training data.

3. Multiply these probabilities times each other and then times the proportion of records belonging to the class of interest.

4. Estimate the probability for the class of interest by taking the value calculated in Step 3 for the class of interest and dividing it by the sum of the similar values for all classes.

5. If this value falls above the threshold, assign the new record to the class of interest; otherwise not.

6. Adjust the threshold value as needed, as a parameter of the model.

Example 2: Predicting Fraudulent Financial Reports, Two Predictors

Let us expand the financial reports example to two predictors and, using a small subset of data, compare the complete (exact) Bayes calculations with the naive Bayes calculations.

Consider the 10 customers of the accounting firm listed in Table 8.2. For each customer, we have information on whether it had prior legal trouble, whether it is a small or large company, and whether the financial report was found to be fraudulent or truthful. Using this information, we will calculate the conditional probability of fraud, given each of the four possible combinations {y, small}, {y, large}, {n, small}, {n, large}.

TABLE 8.2   **INFORMATION ON 10 COMPANIES**

Company	Prior legal trouble	Company size	Status
1	Yes	Small	Truthful
2	No	Small	Truthful
3	No	Large	Truthful
4	No	Large	Truthful
5	No	Small	Truthful
6	No	Small	Truthful
7	Yes	Small	Fraudulent
8	Yes	Large	Fraudulent
9	No	Large	Fraudulent
10	Yes	Large	Fraudulent

Complete (Exact) Bayes Calculations: The probabilities are computed as

$P(\text{fraudulent}|\text{PriorLegal} = y, \text{Size} = \text{small}) = 1/2 = 0.5$

$P(\text{fraudulent}|\text{PriorLegal} = y, \text{Size} = \text{large}) = 2/2 = 1$

$P(\text{fraudulent}|\text{PriorLegal} = n, \text{Size} = \text{small}) = 0/3 = 0$

$P(\text{fraudulent}|\text{PriorLegal} = n, \text{Size} = \text{large}) = 1/3 = 0.33$

Naive Bayes Calculations: Now we compute the naive Bayes probabilities. For the conditional probability of fraudulent behaviors given {PriorLegal = y, Size = small}, the numerator is a multiplication of the proportion of {PriorLegal = y} instances among the fraudulent companies, times the proportion of {Size = small} instances among the fraudulent companies, times the proportion of fraudulent companies: $(3/4)(1/4)(4/10) = 0.075$. To get the actual probabilities, we must also compute the numerator for the conditional probability of truthful behaviors given {PriorLegal = y, Size = small}: $(1/6)(4/6)(6/10) =$ 0.067. The denominator is then the sum of these two conditional probabilities $(0.075 + 0.067 = 0.14)$. The conditional probability of fraudulent behaviors given {PriorLegal = y, Size = small} is therefore $0.075/0.14 = 0.53$. In a similar fashion, we compute all four conditional probabilities:

$$P_{nb}(\text{fraudulent}|\text{PriorLegal} = y, \text{Size} = \text{small}) = \frac{(3/4)(1/4)(4/10)}{(3/4)(1/4)(4/10) + (1/6)(4/6)(6/10)} = 0.53$$

$P_{nb}(\text{fraudulent}|\text{PriorLegal} = y, \text{Size} = \text{large}) = 0.87$

$P_{nb}(\text{fraudulent}|\text{PriorLegal} = n, \text{Size} = \text{small}) = 0.07$

$P_{nb}(\text{fraudulent}|\text{PriorLegal} = n, \text{Size} = \text{large}) = 0.31$

Note how close these naive Bayes probabilities are to the exact Bayes probabilities. Although they are not equal, both would lead to exactly the same classification for a threshold of 0.5 (and many other values). It is often the case that the rank ordering of probabilities is even closer to the exact Bayes method than the probabilities themselves, and for classification purposes it is the rank orderings that matter.

We now consider a larger numerical example, where information on flights is used to predict flight delays.

Example 3: Predicting Delayed Flights

Predicting flight delays can be useful to a variety of organizations: airport authorities, airlines, and aviation authorities. At times, joint task forces have been formed to address the problem. If such an organization were to provide ongoing real-time assistance with flight delays, it would benefit from some advance notice about flights that are likely to be delayed.

In this simplified illustration, we look at five predictors (see Table 8.3). The outcome of interest is whether or not the flight is delayed (*delayed* here means arrived more than 15 minutes late). Our data consist of all flights from the Washington, DC area into the New York City area during January 2004. A record is a particular flight. The percentage of delayed flights among these 2201 flights is 19.5%. The data were obtained from the Bureau of Transportation Statistics (available on the web at www.transtats.bts.gov). The goal is to accurately predict whether or not a new flight (not in this dataset) will be delayed. The outcome variable is whether the flight was delayed, and thus it has two classes (1 = delayed and 0 = on time). In addition, information is collected on the predictors listed in Table 8.3.

The data were first partitioned into training (60%) and holdout (40%) sets, and then a naive Bayes classifier was applied to the training set (we use package e1071).

TABLE 8.3	DESCRIPTION OF VARIABLES FOR FLIGHT DELAYS EXAMPLE
Day of Week	Coded as 1 = Monday, 2 = Tuesday, ..., 7 = Sunday
Sch. Dep. Time	Broken down into 18 intervals between 6:00 AM and 10:00 PM
Origin	Three airport codes: DCA (Reagan National), IAD (Dulles), and BWI (Baltimore–Washington Int'l)
Destination	Three airport codes: JFK (Kennedy), LGA (LaGuardia), and EWR (Newark)
Carrier	Eight airline codes: CO (Continental), DH (Atlantic Coast), DL (Delta), MQ (American Eagle), OH (Comair), RU (Continental Express), UA (United), and US (USAirways)

The first part of the output in Table 8.4 shows the ratios of delayed flights and on time flights in the training set (called a priori probabilities), followed by the conditional probabilities for each class, as a function of the predictor values. Note that the conditional probabilities in the naive Bayes output can be replicated simply by using pivot tables on the training data, looking at the proportion of records for each value relative to the entire class. This is illustrated in Table 8.5, which displays the proportion of delayed (or on time) flights by destination airport (each row adds up to 1).

Note that in this example, there are no predictor values that were not represented in the training data.

To classify a new flight, we compute the probability that it will be delayed and the probability that it will be on time. Recall that since both will have the same denominator, we can just compare the numerators. Each numerator is computed by multiplying all the conditional probabilities of the relevant predictor values and, finally, multiplying by the proportion of that class [in this case $\hat{P}$(delayed) = 0.195]. Let us use an example: to classify a Delta flight from DCA to LGA departing between 10:00 AM and 11:00 AM on a Sunday, we first compute the numerators:

$\hat{P}$(delayed|Carrier = DL, Day_Week = 7, Dep_Time = 10, Dest = LGA, Origin = DCA)
$\propto (0.105)(0.175)(0.027)(0.416)(0.486)(0.195) = 0.0000197$

$\hat{P}$(ontime|Carrier = DL, Day_Week = 7, Dep_Time = 10, Dest = LGA, Origin = DCA)
$\propto (0.183)(0.102)(0.056)(0.534)(0.641)(0.805) = 0.000292$

The symbol $\propto$ means "is proportional to," reflecting the fact that this calculation deals only with the numerator in the naive Bayes formula (8.3). Comparing the numerators, it is therefore more likely that the flight will be on time. Note that a record with such a combination of predictor values does not exist in the training set, and therefore we use the naive Bayes rather than the exact Bayes.

TABLE 8.4   NAIVE BAYES CLASSIFIER APPLIED TO FLIGHT DELAYS (TRAINING) DATA

R code for running naive Bayes

```
library(tidyverse)
library(caret)
library(e1071)
# load and preprocess dataset
delays.df <- mlba::FlightDelays %>%
  mutate(
    # change numerical variables to categorical
    DAY_WEEK = factor(DAY_WEEK),
    ORIGIN = factor(ORIGIN),
    DEST = factor(DEST),
    CARRIER = factor(CARRIER),
    Flight.Status = factor(Flight.Status),
    # create hourly bins for departure time
    CRS_DEP_TIME = factor(round(CRS_DEP_TIME / 100))
  ) %>%
  select(DAY_WEEK, CRS_DEP_TIME, ORIGIN, DEST, CARRIER, Flight.Status)

# create training and holdout sets
set.seed(1)
idx <- createDataPartition(delays.df$Flight.Status, p=0.6, list=FALSE)
train.df <- delays.df[idx, ]
holdout.df <- delays.df[-idx, ]

# run naive bayes
delays.nb <- naiveBayes(Flight.Status ~ ., data = train.df)
delays.nb
```

Partial Output

```
A-priori probabilities:
Y
delayed  ontime
  0.195    0.805

Conditional probabilities:
        DAY_WEEK
Y            1      2      3      4      5      6      7
  delayed 0.2101 0.1440 0.1284 0.1128 0.1790 0.0506 0.1751
  ontime  0.1241 0.1429 0.1532 0.1682 0.1805 0.1288 0.1024

        CRS_DEP_TIME
Y            6      7      8      9     10     11     12     13     14
  delayed 0.0350 0.0545 0.0545 0.0156 0.0272 0.0117 0.0623 0.0311 0.0350
  ontime  0.0573 0.0526 0.0705 0.0564 0.0536 0.0348 0.0677 0.0742 0.0677
        CRS_DEP_TIME
Y           15     16     17     18     19     20     21
  delayed 0.2179 0.0856 0.1751 0.0311 0.0661 0.0195 0.0778
  ontime  0.1316 0.0846 0.0996 0.0301 0.0432 0.0197 0.0564

        ORIGIN
Y          BWI    DCA    IAD
  delayed 0.105  0.486  0.409
  ontime  0.063  0.641  0.296

        DEST
Y          EWR    JFK    LGA
  delayed 0.374  0.210  0.416
  ontime  0.287  0.180  0.534

        CARRIER
Y           CO      DH      DL      MQ      OH      RU      UA      US
  delayed 0.05447 0.35019 0.10506 0.17899 0.00778 0.22568 0.01167 0.06615
  ontime  0.03853 0.23214 0.18327 0.12782 0.01786 0.18233 0.01692 0.20113
```

TABLE 8.5   PIVOT TABLE OF FLIGHT STATUS BY DESTINATION AIRPORT (TRAINING DATA)

```
# use prop.table() with margin = 1 to convert a count table to a proportions table,
# where each row sums up to 1 (use margin = 2 for column sums)
prop.table(table(train.df$Flight.Status, train.df$DEST), margin = 1)
```

Output

```
          EWR    JFK    LGA
delayed 0.374  0.210  0.416
ontime  0.287  0.180  0.534
```

To compute the actual probability, we divide each of the numerators by their sum:

$$\hat{P}(\text{delayed}|\text{Carrier}=\text{DL}, \text{Day\_Week}=7, \text{Dep\_Time}=10, \text{Dest}=\text{LGA}, \text{Origin}=\text{DCA})=$$
$$=\frac{0.0000197}{0.0000197+0.000292}=0.0632$$
$$\hat{P}(\text{on time}|\text{Carrier}=\text{DL}, \text{Day\_Week}=7, \text{Dep\_Time}=10, \text{Dest}=\text{LGA}, \text{Origin}=\text{DCA})=$$
$$=\frac{0.000292}{0.0000197+0.000292}=0.937$$

Of course, we rely on software to compute these probabilities for any records of interest (in the training set, the holdout set, or for scoring new data). Table 8.6 shows the estimated probability and class for the example flight.

Finally, to evaluate the performance of the naive Bayes classifier for our data, we use the confusion matrix, gains chart, and all the measures that were described in Chapter 5. For our example, the confusion matrices for the training and

TABLE 8.6   SCORING THE EXAMPLE FLIGHT (PROBABILITY AND CLASS)

 code for scoring data using naive Bayes

```
## predict probabilities
pred.prob <- predict(delays.nb, newdata=holdout.df, type="raw")
## predict class membership
pred.class <- predict(delays.nb, newdata=holdout.df)

df <- data.frame(actual=holdout.df$Flight.Status, predicted=pred.class, pred.prob)

df[holdout.df$CARRIER == "DL" & holdout.df$DAY_WEEK == 7
    & holdout.df$CRS_DEP_TIME == 10 & holdout.df$DEST == "LGA"
    & holdout.df$ORIGIN == "DCA",]
```

Output

```
   actual predicted delayed ontime
71 ontime    ontime  0.0665  0.934
```

holdout sets are shown in Table 8.7. We see that the overall accuracy level is around 80% for both the training and holdout data. In comparison, a naive rule that would classify all 880 flights in the holdout set as on time would have missed the 172 delayed flights, also resulting in a 80% accuracy. Thus, by a simple accuracy measure, the naive Bayes model does no better than the naive rule. However, examining the cumulative gains chart (Figure 8.1) shows the strength of the naive Bayes in capturing the delayed flights effectively, when the goal is ranking.

TABLE 8.7	CONFUSION MATRICES FOR FLIGHT DELAY USING A NAIVE BAYES CLASSIFIER

 code for confusion matrices

```
# training
confusionMatrix(predict(delays.nb, newdata=train.df), train.df$Flight.Status)

# holdout
confusionMatrix(predict(delays.nb, newdata=holdout.df), holdout.df$Flight.Status)
```

Partial Output

```
> # training
> confusionMatrix(predict(delays.nb, newdata=train.df), train.df$Flight.Status)
Confusion Matrix and Statistics

          Reference
Prediction delayed ontime
   delayed      46     47
   ontime      211   1017


          Accuracy : 0.805

> # holdout
> confusionMatrix(predict(delays.nb, newdata=holdout.df), holdout.df$Flight.Status)
Confusion Matrix and Statistics

          Reference
Prediction delayed ontime
   delayed      21     35
   ontime      150    674


          Accuracy : 0.79
```

Working with Continuous Predictors

Naive Bayes can be extended to numeric (continuous) predictor variables, most commonly by assuming a Gaussian (normal) distribution for these variables. This is useful when numeric predictors are present in the data and transforming them to categorical data types can lead to significant information loss. In applying the *Gaussian naive Bayes* method, each numeric predictor is summarized in the

R code for creating Figure 8.1

```
library(gains)
actual <- ifelse(holdout.df$Flight.Status == "delayed", 1, 0)
gain <- gains(actual, pred.prob[,"delayed"], groups=length(actual) - 2)

nactual <-sum(actual)
ggplot() +
  geom_line(aes(x=gain$cume.obs, y=gain$cume.pct.of.total * nactual)) +
  geom_line(aes(x=c(0, max(gain$cume.obs)), y=c(0, nactual)), color="darkgrey") +
  labs(x="# Cases", y="Cumulative")
```

FIGURE 8.1   LIFT CHART OF NAIVE BAYES CLASSIFIER APPLIED TO FLIGHT DELAYS DATA

form of its mean and standard deviation, for each target class. If we assume a normal (Gaussian) distribution for the numerical predictors, we can use the normal curve to "discretize" the numerical values. This is done by replacing μ and σ with the predictor mean and standard deviation in the Gaussian probability density function $f(x)$:

$$f(x) = \frac{1}{\sigma\sqrt{2\pi}} \exp\left(-\frac{1}{2}\left(\frac{x-\mu}{\sigma}\right)^2\right). \tag{8.4}$$

Using Equation (8.4), probability density values are computed by the software for each numeric predictor, for each outcome class. The idea is that the probability of any exact value is zero for a continuous predictor, but by using the probability density function, we are essentially considering a small range around the required exact value. Since this range is the same while computing the density values for each outcome class, it is possible to use the probability density values in a manner similar to the conditional probability values for categorical predictors in the naive Bayes probability computation. The *naiveBayes* from the e1071 package uses the Gaussian naive Bayes method for numerical variables. If the variables' distributions are very far from a normal curve, other packages, like e.g., `klaR`, provide extensions that can handle more complex distributions using *kernel* density estimates.

To illustrate how the naive Bayes computations work for continuous predictors, suppose DISTANCE were to be considered as the predictor for whether the flight was delayed or not. The mean and standard deviation of this variable for each outcome class are shown in Table 8.8. They can be used with Equation (8.4) to compute probability density values for any specific distance value.

TABLE 8.8	**MEANS AND STANDARD DEVIATIONS OF DISTANCE (A CONTINUOUS PREDICTOR) FOR EACH OUTCOME CLASS (ONTIME/DELAYED) IN FLIGHT DELAYS EXAMPLE**	
	Ontime	**Delayed**
Mean	211.99436	211.36215
Standard deviation	12.79	15.31

For example, for Distance = 213, we get

$$\hat{P}(\text{Distance} = 213 \mid \text{delayed}) = 0.0259089, \quad \text{and}$$
$$\hat{P}(\text{Distance} = 213 \mid \text{ontime}) = 0.0310955.$$

As before, we compute only the numerator in the naive Bayes formula (Equation (8.3)), indicated with the $\propto$ symbol, as follows:

$$\hat{P}(\text{delayed} \mid \text{Distance} = 213) \propto (0.0259089)(0.195) = 0.005052,$$
$$\hat{P}(\text{ontime} \mid \text{Distance} = 213) \propto (0.0310955)(0.805) = 0.025031.$$

By dividing each of the numerators by their sum, we obtain the actual probability values:

$$\hat{P}(\text{delayed} \mid \text{Distance} = 213) = \frac{0.005052}{0.005052 + 0.025031} = 0.168,$$
$$\hat{P}(\text{ontime} \mid \text{Distance} = 213) = \frac{0.025031}{0.005052 + 0.025031} = 0.832.$$

8.4 ADVANTAGES AND SHORTCOMINGS OF THE NAIVE BAYES CLASSIFIER

The naive Bayes classifier's beauty is in its simplicity, computational efficiency, good classification performance, and ability to handle categorical variables directly. In fact, it often outperforms more sophisticated classifiers even when the underlying assumption of independent predictors is far from true. This advantage is especially pronounced when the number of predictors is very large.

Three main issues should be kept in mind, however. First, the naive Bayes classifier requires a very large number of records to obtain good results.

Second, where a predictor category is not present in the training data, naive Bayes assumes that a new record with that category of the predictor has zero probability. This can be a problem if this rare predictor value is important. One example is the binary predictor *Weather* in the flights delay dataset, which we did not use for analysis and which denotes bad weather. When the weather was bad, all flights were delayed. Consider another example, where the outcome variable is *bought high-value life insurance* and a predictor category is *owns yacht*. If the training data have no records with *owns yacht* = 1, for any new records where *owns yacht* = 1, naive Bayes will assign a probability of 0 to the outcome variable *bought high-value life insurance*. With no training records with *owns yacht* = 1, of course, no data mining technique will be able to incorporate this potentially important variable into the classification model—it will be ignored. With naive Bayes, however, the absence of this predictor actively "outvotes" any other information in the record to assign a 0 to the outcome value (when, in this case, it has a relatively good chance of being a 1). The presence of a large training set (and judicious binning of continuous predictors, if required) helps mitigate this effect. A popular solution in such cases is to replace zero probabilities with non–zero values using a method called *smoothing* (e.g., Laplace smoothing can be applied by using argument *laplace* in function *naiveBayes()* with a value greater than zero).

Finally, good performance is obtained when the goal is *classification* or *ranking* of records according to their probability of belonging to a certain class. However, when the goal is to *estimate the probability of class membership (propensity)*, this method provides very biased results. For this reason, the naive Bayes method is rarely used in credit scoring (Larsen, 2005).

SPAM FILTERING

Filtering spam in e-mail has long been a widely familiar application of data mining. Spam filtering, which is based in large part on natural language vocabulary, is a natural fit for a naive Bayesian classifier, which uses exclusively categorical variables. Most spam filters are based on this method, which works as follows:

1. Humans review a large number of e-mails, classify them as "spam" or "not spam," and from these select an equal (also large) number of spam e-mails and non-spam e-mails. This is the training data.

2. These e-mails will contain thousands of words; for each word, compute the frequency with which it occurs in the spam dataset and the frequency with which it occurs in the non-spam dataset. Convert these frequencies into estimated probabilities (i.e., if the word "free" occurs in 500 out of 1000 spam e-mails, and only 100 out of 1000 non-spam e-mails, the probability that a spam e-mail will contain the word "free" is 0.5, and the probability that a non-spam e-mail will contain the word "free" is 0.1).

3. If the only word in a new message that needs to be classified as spam or not spam is "free," we would classify the message as spam, since the Bayesian posterior probability is 0.5/(0.5+01) or 5/6 that, given the appearance of "free," the message is spam.

4. Of course, we will have many more words to consider. For each such word, the probabilities described in Step 2 are calculated and multiplied together, and formula (8.3) is applied to determine the naive Bayes probability of belonging to the classes. In the simple version, class membership (spam or not spam) is determined by the higher probability.

5. In a more flexible interpretation, the ratio between the "spam" and "not spam" probabilities is treated as a score for which the operator can establish (and change) a threshold—anything above that level is classified as spam.

6. Users have the option of building a personalized training database by classifying incoming messages as spam or not spam and adding them to the training database. One person's spam may be another person's substance.

It is clear that, even with the "naive" simplification, this is an enormous computational burden. Spam filters now typically operate at two levels—at servers (intercepting some spam that never makes it to your computer) and on individual computers (where you have the option of reviewing it). Spammers have also found ways to "poison" the vocabulary-based Bayesian approach, by including sequences of randomly selected irrelevant words. Since these words are randomly selected, they are unlikely to be systematically more prevalent in spam than in non-spam, and they dilute the effect of key spam terms such as "Viagra" and "free." For this reason, sophisticated spam classifiers also include variables based on elements other than vocabulary, such as the number of links in the message, the vocabulary in the subject line, determination of whether the "From:" e-mail address is the real originator (anti-spoofing), use of HTML and images, and origination at a dynamic or static IP address (the latter are more expensive and cannot be set up quickly).

PROBLEMS

8.1 **Personal Loan Acceptance.** The dataset *mlba::UniversalBank* contains data on 5000 customers of Universal Bank. The data include customer demographic information (age, income, etc.), the customer's relationship with the bank (mortgage, securities account, etc.), and the customer response to the last personal loan campaign (Personal Loan). Among these 5000 customers, only 480 (= 9.6%) accepted the personal loan that was offered to them in the earlier campaign. In this exercise, we focus on two predictors: Online (whether or not the customer is an active user of online banking services) and Credit Card (abbreviated CC below) (does the customer hold a credit card issued by the bank) and the outcome Personal Loan (abbreviated Loan below).
   Partition the data into training (60%) and holdout (40%) sets.

a. Create a pivot table for the training data with Online as a column variable, CC as a row variable, and Loan as a secondary row variable. The values inside the table should convey the count. In R, use functions *melt()* and *cast()* or function *ftable()*.

b. Consider the task of classifying a customer who owns a bank credit card and is actively using online banking services. Looking at the pivot table, what is the probability that this customer will accept the loan offer? [This is the probability of loan acceptance (Loan = 1) conditional on having a bank credit card (CC = 1) and being an active user of online banking services (Online = 1)].

c. Create two separate pivot tables for the training data. One will have Loan (rows) as a function of Online (columns), and the other will have Loan (rows) as a function of CC.

d. Compute the following quantities [$P(A \mid B)$ means "the probability of A given B"]:
   i. $P(CC = 1 \mid Loan = 1)$ (the proportion of credit card holders among the loan acceptors)
   ii. $P(Online = 1 \mid Loan = 1)$
   iii. $P(Loan = 1)$ (the proportion of loan acceptors)
   iv. $P(CC = 1 \mid Loan = 0)$
   v. $P(Online = 1 \mid Loan = 0)$
   vi. $P(Loan = 0)$

e. Use the quantities computed above to compute the naive Bayes probability $P(Loan = 1 \mid CC = 1, Online = 1)$.

f. Compare this value with the one obtained from the pivot table in (b). Which is a more accurate estimate?

g. In R, run naive Bayes on the data. Examine the model output on the training data, and find an entry that corresponds to $P(Loan = 1 \mid CC = 1, Online = 1)$. Compare this with the number you obtained in (e).

8.2 **Automobile Accidents.** The dataset *mlba::AccidentsFull* contains information on 42,183 actual automobile accidents in 2001 in the United States that involved one of three levels of injury: NO INJURY, INJURY, or FATALITY. For each accident, additional information is recorded, such as day of week, weather conditions, and road type. A firm might be interested in developing a system for quickly classifying the severity of an accident based on initial reports and associated data in the system (some of which rely on GPS-assisted reporting).

Our goal here is to predict whether an accident just reported will involve an injury (MAX_SEV_IR = 1 or 2) or will not (MAX_SEV_IR = 0). For this purpose, create a dummy variable called INJURY that takes the value "yes" if MAX_SEV_IR = 1 or 2, and otherwise "no."

a. Using the information in this dataset, if an accident has just been reported and no further information is available, what should the prediction be? (INJURY = Yes or No?) Why?

b. Select the first 12 records in the dataset, and look only at the response (INJURY) and the two predictors WEATHER_R and TRAF_CON_R.

　i. Create a pivot table that examines INJURY as a function of the two predictors for these 12 records. Use all three variables in the pivot table as rows/columns.

　ii. Compute the exact Bayes conditional probabilities of an injury (INJURY = Yes) given the six possible combinations of the predictors.

　iii. Classify the 12 accidents using these probabilities and a threshold of 0.5.

　iv. Compute manually the naive Bayes conditional probability of an injury given WEATHER_R = 1 and TRAF_CON_R = 1.

　v. Run a naive Bayes classifier on the 12 records and two predictors using R. Check the model output to obtain probabilities and classifications for all 12 records. Compare this with the exact Bayes classification. Are the resulting classifications equivalent? Is the ranking (= ordering) of observations equivalent?

c. Let us now return to the entire dataset. Partition the data into training (60%) and holdout (40%).

　i. Assuming that no information or initial reports about the accident itself are available at the time of prediction (only location characteristics, weather conditions, etc.), which predictors can we include in the analysis?

　ii. Run a naive Bayes classifier on the complete training set with the relevant predictors (and INJURY as the response). Note that all predictors are categorical. Show the confusion matrix.

　iii. What is the overall error for the holdout set?

　iv. What is the percent improvement relative to the naive rule (using the holdout set)?

　v. Examine the conditional probabilities output. Why do we get a probability of zero (or close to zero) for P(INJURY = No | SPD_LIM = 5)?

## CHAPTER 9

Classification and Regression Trees

This chapter describes a flexible data-driven method that can be used for both classification (called *classification tree*) and prediction (called *regression tree*). Among the data-driven methods, trees (also known as *decision trees*) are the most transparent and easy to interpret. Trees are based on separating records into subgroups by creating splits on predictors. These splits create logical rules that are transparent and easily understandable, for example, "IF Age < 55 AND Education > 12 THEN class = 1." The resulting subgroups should be more homogeneous in terms of the outcome variable, thereby creating useful prediction or classification rules. We discuss the two key ideas underlying trees: *recursive partitioning* (for constructing the tree) and *pruning* (for cutting the tree back). In the context of tree construction, we also describe a few metrics of homogeneity that are popular in tree algorithms, for determining the homogeneity of the resulting subgroups of records. We explain that pruning is a useful strategy for avoiding overfitting and show how it is done. We also describe alternative strategies for avoiding overfitting and the use of cross-validation to improve stability. As with other data-driven methods, trees require large amounts of data. However, once constructed, they are computationally cheap to deploy even on large samples. They also have other advantages such as being highly automated, robust to outliers, and able to handle missing values. In addition to prediction and classification, we describe how trees can be used for dimension reduction. Finally, we introduce *random forests* and *boosted trees*, which combine results from multiple trees to improve predictive power.

Machine Learning for Business Analytics: Concepts, Techniques, and Applications in R, Second Edition.
Galit Shmueli, Peter C. Bruce, Peter Gedeck, Inbal Yahav, and Nitin R. Patel
© 2023 John Wiley & Sons, Inc. Published 2023 by John Wiley & Sons, Inc.

Classification and regression trees in R

In this chapter, we use the `rpart` and `rpart.plot` packages in R to build and visualize classification and regression trees. The packages `randomForest`, `xgboost`, and `adabag` are used to train ensemble models.

9.1 INTRODUCTION

If one had to choose a classification technique that performs well across a wide range of situations without requiring much effort from the analyst while being readily understandable by the consumer of the analysis, a strong contender would be the tree methodology developed by Breiman et al. (1984). Trees, also called *decision trees*, can be used for both classification and prediction. We discuss the classification procedure first, and then in later sections we show how the procedure can be extended to prediction of a numerical outcome. The program that Breiman et al. created to implement these procedures was called CART (Classification And Regression Trees). A related procedure is called C4.5.

What is a classification tree? Figure 9.1 shows a tree for classifying bank customers who receive a loan offer as either acceptors or nonacceptors, based on information such as their income, education level, and average credit card expenditure.

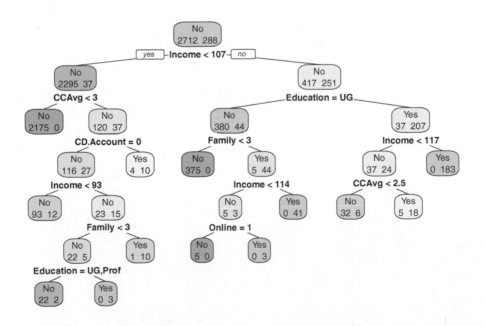

FIGURE 9.1   EXAMPLE OF A TREE FOR CLASSIFYING BANK CUSTOMERS AS LOAN ACCEPTORS OR NONACCEPTORS

Tree Structure

We have two types of nodes in a tree: decision (= splitting) nodes and leaf nodes. Nodes that have successors are called decision nodes because if we were to use a tree to classify a new record for which we knew only the values of the predictor, we would "drop" the record down the tree so that at each decision node, the appropriate branch is taken until we get to a node that has no successors. Such nodes are called the *leaf nodes* (or *terminal nodes* or *leaves* of the tree) and represent the partitioning of the data by predictors.

It is useful to note that the types of trees grown by R's *rpart()* function, also known as CART or *binary trees*, have the property that the number of leaf nodes is exactly one more than the number of decision nodes.

Decision Rules

One of the reasons that tree classifiers are very popular is that they provide easily understandable classification rules (at least if the trees are not too large). Consider the tree in the example. The *leaf nodes* are marked with "Yes" or "No" corresponding to an acceptor or nonacceptor. The values below the decision nodes give the predictor and splitting value (e.g., Income < 107). The values inside the decision nodes are the counts of the two classes in that node. This tree can easily be translated into a set of rules for classifying a bank customer. For example, the top-left leaf node under the "CCAvg < 3" decision node in this tree gives us the following rule:

IF(*Income* < 107) AND (*CCAvg* < 3)
THEN Class = No (nonacceptor).

Classifying a New Record

To classify a new record, it is "dropped" down the tree. When it has dropped all the way down to a leaf node, we can assign its class simply by taking a "vote" (or average, if the outcome is numerical) of all the training data that belonged to the leaf node when the tree was grown. The class with the highest vote is assigned to the new record. For instance, a new record reaching the rightmost leaf node in Figure 9.1, which has a majority of records that belong to the acceptor class, would be classified as "acceptor." Alternatively, we can convert the number of acceptor class records in the node to a proportion (propensity) and then compare the proportion to a user-specified threshold value. In a binary classification situation (typically, with a success class that is relatively rare and of particular interest), we can also establish a lower threshold to better capture those rare successes (at the cost of lumping in more failures as successes). With a lower threshold, the votes for the success class only need attain that lower threshold level for the entire leaf node to be classified as a success. The threshold therefore determines the proportion of votes needed for determining the leaf node class.

See Chapter 5 for further discussion of the use of a threshold value in classification for cases where a single class is of interest.

In the following, we show how trees are constructed and evaluated.

9.2 CLASSIFICATION TREES

Two key ideas underlie classification trees. The first is the idea of *recursive partitioning* of the space of the predictor variables. The second is the idea of *pruning* using holdout data. In the next few sections, we describe recursive partitioning and in subsequent sections explain the pruning methodology.

Recursive Partitioning

Let us denote the outcome variable by Y and the input (predictor) variables by $X_1, X_2, X_3, \ldots, X_p$. In classification, the outcome variable will be a categorical variable, sometimes called a class label. Recursive partitioning divides up the p-dimensional space of the X predictor variables into nonoverlapping multidimensional rectangles. The predictor variables here are considered to be continuous or categorical. This division is accomplished recursively (i.e., operating on the results of prior divisions). First, one of the predictor variables is selected, say X_i, and a value of X_i, say s_i, is chosen to split the p-dimensional space into two parts: one part that contains all the points with $X_i < s_i$ and the other with all the points with $X_i \geq s_i$. Then, one of these two parts is divided in a similar manner by again choosing a predictor variable (it could be X_i or another variable) and a split value for that variable. This results in three (multidimensional) rectangular regions. This process is continued so that we get smaller and smaller rectangular regions. The idea is to divide the entire X-space up into rectangles such that each rectangle is as homogeneous or "pure" as possible. By *pure*, we mean containing records that belong to just one class. (Of course, this is not always possible, as there may be records that belong to different classes but have exactly the same values for every one of the predictor variables.)

Let us illustrate recursive partitioning with an example.

Example 1: Riding Mowers

We again use the riding-mower example presented in Chapter 3. A riding-mower manufacturer would like to find a way of classifying families in a city into those likely to purchase a riding mower and those not likely to buy one. A pilot random sample of 12 owners and 12 nonowners in the city is undertaken. The data are shown and plotted in Table 9.1 and Figure 9.2.

If we apply the classification tree procedure to these data, the procedure will choose *Income* for the first split with a splitting value of 60. The (X_1, X_2) space

TABLE 9.1	LOT SIZE, INCOME, AND OWNERSHIP OF A RIDING MOWER FOR 24 HOUSEHOLDS		
Household number	Income ($000s)	Lot size (000s ft^2)	Ownership of riding mower
1	60.0	18.4	Owner
2	85.5	16.8	Owner
3	64.8	21.6	Owner
4	61.5	20.8	Owner
5	87.0	23.6	Owner
6	110.1	19.2	Owner
7	108.0	17.6	Owner
8	82.8	22.4	Owner
9	69.0	20.0	Owner
10	93.0	20.8	Owner
11	51.0	22.0	Owner
12	81.0	20.0	Owner
13	75.0	19.6	Nonowner
14	52.8	20.8	Nonowner
15	64.8	17.2	Nonowner
16	43.2	20.4	Nonowner
17	84.0	17.6	Nonowner
18	49.2	17.6	Nonowner
19	59.4	16.0	Nonowner
20	66.0	18.4	Nonowner
21	47.4	16.4	Nonowner
22	33.0	18.8	Nonowner
23	51.0	14.0	Nonowner
24	63.0	14.8	Nonowner

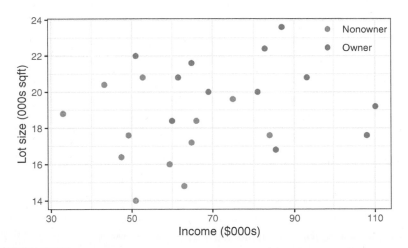

| FIGURE 9.2 | SCATTER PLOT OF LOT SIZE VS. INCOME FOR 24 OWNERS AND NONOWNERS OF RIDING MOWERS |

is now divided into two rectangles, one with Income < 60 and the other with Income ≥ 60. This is illustrated in Figure 9.3.

Notice how the split has created two rectangles, each of which is much more homogeneous than the rectangle before the split. The left rectangle contains

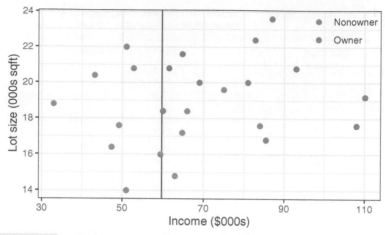

FIGURE 9.3   SPLITTING THE 24 RECORDS BY INCOME VALUE OF 60

points that are mostly nonowners (7 nonowners and 1 owner) and the right rectangle contains mostly owners (11 owners and 5 nonowners).

How was this particular split selected? The algorithm examined each predictor variable (in this case, Income and Lot Size) and all possible split values for each variable to find the best split. What are the possible split values for a variable? They are simply the values for each predictor. The possible split points for Income are $\{33.0, 43.2, 47.4, \ldots, 110.1\}$ and those for Lot Size are $\{14.0, 14.8, 16.0, \ldots, 23.6\}$. These split points are ranked according to how much they reduce impurity (heterogeneity) in the resulting rectangle. A pure rectangle is one that is composed of a single class (e.g., owners). The reduction in impurity is defined as overall impurity before the split minus the sum of the impurities for the two rectangles that result from a split.

Categorical Predictors   The previous description used numerical predictors; however, categorical predictors can also be used in the recursive partitioning context. To handle categorical predictors, the split choices for a categorical predictor are all ways in which the set of categories can be divided into two subsets. For example, a categorical variable with four categories, say $\{a, b, c, d\}$, can be split in seven ways into two subsets: $\{a\}$ and $\{b, c, d\}$; $\{b\}$ and $\{a, c, d\}$; $\{c\}$ and $\{a, b, d\}$; $\{d\}$ and $\{a, b, c\}$; $\{a, b\}$ and $\{c, d\}$; $\{a, c\}$ and $\{b, d\}$; and finally $\{a, d\}$ and $\{b, c\}$. When the number of categories is large, the number of splits becomes very large. As with k-nearest neighbors, a predictor with m categories ($m > 2$) should be factored into m dummies (not $m - 1$).

Normalization   Whether predictors are numerical or categorical, it does not make any difference if they are standardized (normalized) or not.

Measures of Impurity

There are a number of ways to measure impurity. The two most popular measures are the *Gini index* and an *entropy measure*. We describe both next. Denote the m classes of the response variable by $k = 1, 2, \ldots, m$.

The Gini impurity index for a rectangle A is defined by

$$I(A) = 1 - \sum_{k=1}^{m} p_k^2,$$

where p_k is the proportion of records in rectangle A that belong to class k. This measure takes values between 0 (when all the records belong to the same class) and $(m - 1)/m$ (when all m classes are equally represented). Figure 9.4 shows the values of the Gini index for a two-class case as a function of p_k. It can be seen that the impurity measure is at its peak when $p_k = 0.5$ (i.e., when the rectangle contains 50% of each of the two classes).

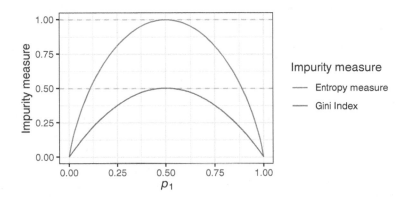

FIGURE 9.4   VALUES OF THE GINI INDEX AND ENTROPY MEASURE FOR A TWO-CLASS CASE AS A FUNCTION OF THE PROPORTION OF RECORDS IN CLASS 1 (p_1)

A second impurity measure is the entropy measure, also called *information index*. The entropy for a rectangle A is defined by

$$\text{entropy}(A) = - \sum_{k=1}^{m} p_k \log_2(p_k)$$

[to compute $\log_2(x)$ in R, use function *log2()*]. This measure ranges between 0 (most pure, all records belong to the same class) and $\log_2(m)$ (when all m classes are represented equally). As shown in Figure 9.4, in the two-class case, the entropy measure is maximized (like the Gini index) at $p_k = 0.5$.

Let us compute the impurity in the riding-mower example before and after the first split (using Income with the split value of 60). The unsplit dataset contains 12 owners and 12 nonowners. This is a two–class case with an equal number of records from each class. Both impurity measures are therefore at their maximum value: Gini $= 0.5$ and entropy $= \log_2(2) = 1$. After the split, the left rectangle contains seven nonowners and one owner. The impurity measures for this rectangle are:

$$\text{Gini\_left} = 1 - (7/8)^2 - (1/8)^2 = 0.219$$
$$\text{entropy\_left} = -(7/8)\log_2(7/8) - (1/8)\log_2(1/8) = 0.544$$

The right rectangle contains 11 owners and 5 nonowners. The impurity measures of the right rectangle are therefore

$$\text{Gini\_right} = 1 - (11/16)^2 - (5/16)^2 = 0.430$$
$$\text{entropy\_right} = -(11/16)\log_2(11/16) - (5/16)\log_2(5/16) = 0.896$$

The combined impurity of the two rectangles that were created by the split is a weighted average of the two impurity measures, weighted by the number of records in each:

$$\text{Gini} = (8/24)(0.219) + (16/24)(0.430) = 0.359$$
$$\text{entropy} = (8/24)(0.544) + (16/24)(0.896) = 0.779$$

Thus, the Gini impurity index decreased from 0.5 before the split to 0.359 after the split. Similarly, the entropy impurity measure decreased from 1 before the split to 0.779 after the split.

Aside from the Gini and entropy measures, a host of alternative criteria have been proposed and implemented in different software. Empirical research comparing these different criteria suggests that the choice of splitting criterion will not make much difference on the tree performance, and that each criterion might be superior in some cases but not in others (Rokach and Maimon, 2014).

By comparing the reduction in impurity across all possible splits in all possible predictors, the next split is chosen. If we continue splitting the mower data, the next split is on the Lot Size variable at the value 21. Figure 9.5 shows that once again the tree procedure has astutely chosen to split a rectangle to increase the purity of the resulting rectangles. The lower-left rectangle, which contains data points with Income < 60 and Lot Size < 21, has all points that are nonowners, whereas the upper-left rectangle, which contains data points with Income < 60 and Lot Size ≥ 21, consists exclusively of a single owner. In other words, the two left rectangles are now "pure." We can see how the recursive partitioning is refining the set of constituent rectangles to become purer as the algorithm proceeds. The final stage of the recursive partitioning is shown in

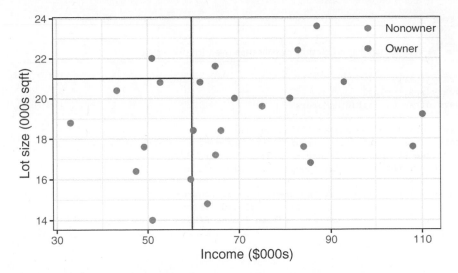

FIGURE 9.5   SPLITTING THE 24 RECORDS FIRST BY INCOME VALUE OF 60 AND THEN BY LOT SIZE VALUE OF 21

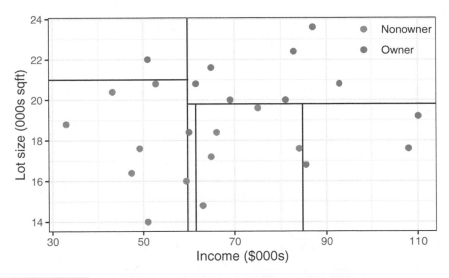

FIGURE 9.6   FINAL STAGE OF RECURSIVE PARTITIONING; EACH RECTANGLE CONSISTING OF A SINGLE CLASS (OWNERS OR NONOWNERS)

Figure 9.6. Notice that each rectangle is now pure: it contains data points from just one of the two classes.

The reason the method is called a *classification tree algorithm* is that each split can be depicted as a split of a node into two successor nodes. The first split is shown as a branching of the root node of a tree in Figure 9.7. The full-grown tree is shown in Figure 9.8.

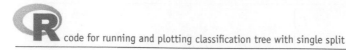 code for running and plotting classification tree with single split

```
library(rpart)
library(rpart.plot)
mowers.df <- mlba::RidingMowers

# use rpart() to run a classification tree.
# define rpart.control() in rpart() to determine the depth of the tree.
class.tree <- rpart(Ownership ~ ., data = mowers.df,
    control=rpart.control(maxdepth=2), method="class")
## plot tree
# use rpart.plot() to plot the tree. You can control plotting parameters such
# as color, shape, and information displayed (which and where).
rpart.plot(class.tree, extra=1, fallen.leaves=FALSE)
```

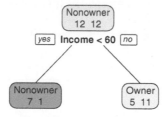

FIGURE 9.7   TREE REPRESENTATION OF FIRST SPLIT (CORRESPONDS TO FIGURE 9.3)

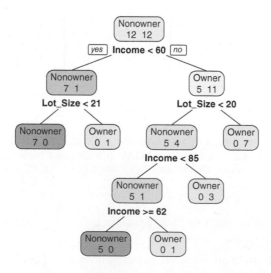

FIGURE 9.8   TREE REPRESENTATION AFTER ALL SPLITS (CORRESPONDS TO FIGURE 9.6). THIS IS THE FULL GROWN TREE

TREE STRUCTURE REPRESENTATION IN R

We can use the R function *rpart.plot()* from the rpart.plot package to create visual representations of the decision trees. Figures 9.7 and 9.8 show representations for the single split tree and the fully grown tree.

When using the R function *rpart.plot()* for plotting a tree, nodes are depicted by ovals with the color indicating the predicted class and the intensity of the color the purity of the node. The node is labeled with the name of the majority class and the two numbers below it give the counts of records in each class. For example, the green node in Figure 9.7 labeled *Owner* has 16 records, 5 of them are Nonowner and 11 Owner. The name of the variable chosen for splitting and its splitting value are below each decision node.

The arguments *type* and *extra* control the representation of the tree. The *rpart.plot()* function is convenient and offers a large variety of representations; however, if you want more control over the visualization, use the *prp()* function.

We can also get a textual representation of a decision tree. Below is the one for the fully grown tree. Line 2, for example, shows that the decision at the first split is Income < 59.7. There are eight records that match this condition. One record is labeled *Owner* and the majority of records are *Nonowner*. Finally, the two numbers in brackets give the propensity of the node: 0.875 for *Nonowner* and 0.125 for *Owner*.

```
> class.tree
n= 24

node), split, n, loss, yval, (yprob)
      * denotes terminal node

 1) root 24 12 Nonowner (0.5000000 0.5000000)
   2) Income< 59.7 8  1 Nonowner (0.8750000 0.1250000)
     4) Lot_Size< 21.4 7  0 Nonowner (1.0000000 0.0000000) *
     5) Lot_Size>=21.4 1  0 Owner (0.0000000 1.0000000) *
   3) Income>=59.7 16  5 Owner (0.3125000 0.6875000)
     6) Lot_Size< 19.8 9  4 Nonowner (0.5555556 0.4444444)
       12) Income< 84.75 6  1 Nonowner (0.8333333 0.1666667)
         24) Income>=61.5 5  0 Nonowner (1.0000000 0.0000000) *
         25) Income< 61.5 1  0 Owner (0.0000000 1.0000000) *
       13) Income>=84.75 3  0 Owner (0.0000000 1.0000000) *
     7) Lot_Size>=19.8 7  0 Owner (0.0000000 1.0000000) *
```

9.3 EVALUATING THE PERFORMANCE OF A CLASSIFICATION TREE

We have seen with previous methods that the modeling job is not completed by fitting a model to training data; we need out-of-sample data to assess and tune the model. This is particularly true with classification and regression trees, for two reasons:

- Tree structure can be quite unstable, shifting substantially depending on the sample chosen.
- A fully-fit tree will invariably lead to overfitting.

To visualize the first challenge, potential instability, imagine that we partition the data randomly into two samples, A and B, and we build a tree with each. If there are several predictors of roughly equal predictive power, you can see that it would be easy for samples A and B to select different predictors for the top level split, just based on which records ended up in which sample. And a different split at the top level would likely cascade down and yield completely different sets of rules. So we should view the results of a single tree with some caution.

To illustrate the second challenge, overfitting, let's examine another example.

Example 2: Acceptance of Personal Loan

Universal Bank is a relatively young bank that is growing rapidly in terms of overall customer acquisition. The majority of these customers are liability customers with varying sizes of relationship with the bank. The customer base of asset customers is quite small, and the bank is interested in growing this base rapidly to bring in more loan business. In particular, it wants to explore ways of converting its liability (deposit) customers to personal loan customers.

A campaign the bank ran for liability customers showed a healthy conversion rate of over 9% successes. This has encouraged the retail marketing department to devise smarter campaigns with better target marketing. The goal of our analysis is to model the previous campaign's customer behavior to analyze what combination of factors make a customer more likely to accept a personal loan. This will serve as the basis for the design of a new campaign.

Our predictive model will be a classification tree. To assess the accuracy of the tree in classifying new records, we start with the tools and criteria discussed in Chapter 5—partitioning the data into training and holdout sets, and later introduce the idea of *cross-validation*.

The bank's dataset includes data on 5000 customers. The data include customer demographic information (age, income, etc.), customer response to the last personal loan campaign (*Personal Loan*), and the customer's relationship with the bank (mortgage, securities account, etc.). Table 9.2 shows a sample of the bank's customer database for 20 customers, to illustrate the structure of the data. Among these 5000 customers, only 480 (= 9.6%) accepted the personal loan that was offered to them in the earlier campaign.

After randomly partitioning the data into training (3000 records) and holdout (2000 records), we use the training data to construct a tree. A tree with seven splits is shown in Figure 9.9 (this is the default tree produced by *rpart()* for this

TABLE 9.2   SAMPLE OF DATA FOR 20 CUSTOMERS OF UNIVERSAL BANK

ID	Age	Professional experience	Income	Family size	CC avg	Education	Mortgage	Personal loan	Securities account	CD account	Online banking	Credit card
1	25	1	49	4	1.60	UG	0	No	Yes	No	No	No
2	45	19	34	3	1.50	UG	0	No	Yes	No	No	No
3	39	15	11	1	1.00	UG	0	No	No	No	No	No
4	35	9	100	1	2.70	Grad	0	No	No	No	No	No
5	35	8	45	4	1.00	Grad	0	No	No	No	No	Yes
6	37	13	29	4	0.40	Grad	155	No	No	No	Yes	No
7	53	27	72	2	1.50	Grad	0	No	No	No	Yes	No
8	50	24	22	1	0.30	Prof	0	No	No	No	No	Yes
9	35	10	81	3	0.60	Grad	104	No	No	No	No	No
10	34	9	180	1	8.90	Prof	0	Yes	No	No	No	No
11	65	39	105	4	2.40	Prof	0	No	No	No	Yes	No
12	29	5	45	3	0.10	Grad	0	No	Yes	No	No	No
13	48	23	114	2	3.80	Prof	0	No	No	No	Yes	No
14	59	32	40	4	2.50	Grad	0	No	Yes	No	No	No
15	67	41	112	1	2.00	UG	0	No	No	No	Yes	Yes
16	60	30	22	1	1.50	Prof	0	No	No	No	No	No
17	38	14	130	4	4.70	Prof	134	Yes	No	No	No	No
18	42	18	81	4	2.40	UG	0	No	No	No	No	No
19	46	21	193	2	8.10	Prof	0	Yes	No	No	No	No
20	55	28	21	1	0.50	Grad	0	No	Yes	No	No	Yes

code for creating a default classification tree

```
library(tidyverse)
library(caret)

# Load and preprocess data
bank.df <- mlba::UniversalBank %>%
  # Drop ID and zip code columns.
  select(-c(ID, ZIP.Code)) %>%
  # convert Personal.Loan to a factor with labels Yes and No
  mutate(Personal.Loan = factor(Personal.Loan, levels=c(0, 1), labels=c("No", "Yes")),
         Education = factor(Education, levels=c(1, 2, 3), labels=c("UG", "Grad", "Prof")))

# partition
set.seed(1)
idx <- createDataPartition(bank.df$Personal.Loan, p=0.6, list=FALSE)
train.df <- bank.df[idx, ]
holdout.df <- bank.df[-idx, ]

# classification tree
default.ct <- rpart(Personal.Loan ~ ., data=train.df, method="class")
# plot tree
rpart.plot(default.ct, extra=1, fallen.leaves=FALSE)
```

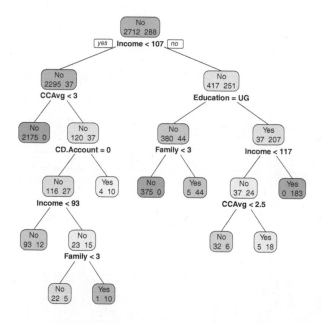

FIGURE 9.9   DEFAULT CLASSIFICATION TREE FOR THE LOAN ACCEPTANCE DATA USING THE
TRAINING SET (3000 RECORDS)

data). The top node refers to all the records in the training set, of which 2712 customers did not accept the loan and 288 customers accepted the loan. The "No" label in the top node represents the majority class ("did not accept"). The first split, which is on the income variable, generates left and right child nodes. To the left is the child node with customers who have income less than 107. Customers with income greater than or equal to 107 go to the right. The splitting process continues; where it stops depends on the parameter settings of the algorithm. The eventual classification of customer appears in the terminal nodes. Of the 10 terminal nodes, 5 lead to classification of "did not accept" and 5 lead to classification of "accept."

A full-grown tree is shown in Figure 9.10. Although it is difficult to see the exact splits, let us assess the performance of this tree with the holdout data and compare it to the smaller default tree. Each record in the holdout data is "dropped down" the tree and classified according to the terminal node it reaches. These predicted classes can then be compared to the actual memberships via a confusion matrix. When a particular class is of interest, a lift chart is useful for assessing the model's ability to capture those members.

Table 9.3 displays the confusion matrices for the training and holdout sets of the small default tree (top) and for the full tree (bottom). Comparing the two training matrices, we see that the full tree has higher accuracy: it is 100% accurate in classifying the training data, which means it has completely pure leaf nodes. In contrast, the confusion matrices for the holdout data show that the smaller tree is more accurate. The main reason is that the full-grown tree overfits the training data (to perfect accuracy!). This motivates the next section, where we describe ways to avoid overfitting either by stopping the growth of the tree before it is fully grown or by pruning the full-grown tree.

9.4 AVOIDING OVERFITTING

As the last example illustrated, using a full-grown tree (based on the training data) leads to complete overfitting of the data. As discussed in Chapter 5, overfitting will lead to poor performance on new data. If we look at the overall error at the various sizes of the tree, it is expected to decrease as the number of terminal nodes grows until the point of overfitting. Of course, for the training data the overall error decreases more and more until it is zero (or close to zero[1]) at the maximum depth of the tree. However, for new data, the overall error is expected to decrease until the point where the tree fully models the relationship between class and the predictors. After that, the tree starts to model the noise in the

---

[1]Non-zero leaf nodes can result if the training data contains records that have identical values for all predictors, but have different class labels.

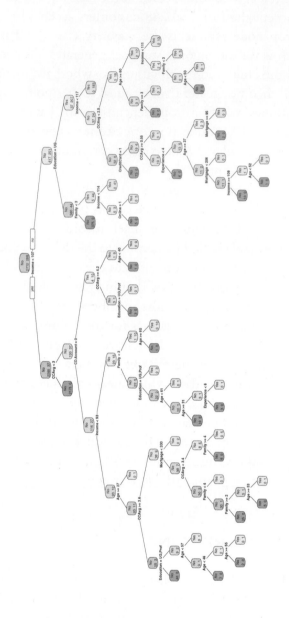

FIGURE 9.10   A FULL TREE FOR THE LOAN ACCEPTANCE DATA USING THE TRAINING SET (3000 RECORDS)

R code for creating a deeper classification tree

```
deeper.ct <- rpart(Personal.Loan ~ ., data=train.df, method="class", cp=0, minsplit=1)
# count number of leaves
sum(deeper.ct$frame$var == "<leaf>")
# plot tree
rpart.plot(deeper.ct, extra=1, fallen.leaves=FALSE)
```

TABLE 9.3   **CONFUSION MATRICES AND ACCURACY FOR THE DEFAULT (SMALL) AND DEEPER (FULL) CLASSIFICATION TREES, ON THE TRAINING AND HOLDOUT SETS OF THE PERSONAL LOAN DATA**

 code for classifying the holdout data using a tree and computing the confusion matrices and accuracy for the training and holdout data

```
# classify records in the holdout data.
# set argument type = "class" in predict() to generate predicted class membership.
default.ct.point.pred.train <- predict(default.ct,train.df,type = "class")
# generate confusion matrix for training data
confusionMatrix(default.ct.point.pred.train, train.df$Personal.Loan)
### repeat the code for the holdout set, and the deeper tree
```

Partial Output

```
> # default tree: training
> confusionMatrix(default.ct.point.pred.train, train.df$Personal.Loan)
Confusion Matrix and Statistics

          Reference
Prediction   No   Yes
       No  2697    23
       Yes   15   265


              Accuracy : 0.9873

> # default tree: holdout
> confusionMatrix(default.ct.point.pred.holdout, holdout.df$Personal.Loan)
Confusion Matrix and Statistics

          Reference
Prediction   No   Yes
       No  1795    17
       Yes   13   175


              Accuracy : 0.985

> # deeper tree: training
> confusionMatrix(deeper.ct.point.pred.train, train.df$Personal.Loan)
Confusion Matrix and Statistics

          Reference
Prediction   No   Yes
       No  2712     0
       Yes    0   288


              Accuracy : 1

> # deeper tree: holdout
> confusionMatrix(deeper.ct.point.pred.holdout, holdout.df$Personal.Loan)
Confusion Matrix and Statistics

          Reference
Prediction   No   Yes
       No  1795    17
       Yes   13   175


              Accuracy : 0.985
```

training set, and we expect the overall error for the holdout set to start increasing. This is depicted in Figure 9.11. One intuitive reason a large tree may overfit is that its final splits are based on very small numbers of records. In such cases, class difference is likely to be attributed to noise rather than predictor information.

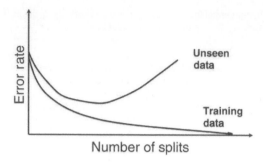

FIGURE 9.11   ERROR RATE AS A FUNCTION OF THE NUMBER OF SPLITS FOR TRAINING VS. HOLDOUT DATA: OVERFITTING

Stopping Tree Growth

One can think of different criteria for stopping the tree growth before it starts overfitting the data. Examples are tree depth (i.e., number of splits), minimum number of records in a terminal node, and minimum reduction in impurity. The problem is that it is not simple to determine what is a good stopping point using such rules.

Stopping Tree Growth: Grid Search for Parameter Tuning   As mentioned earlier, the challenge with using tree growth stopping rules such as maximum tree depth is that it is not simple to determine what is a good stopping point using such rules. One solution is to use grid search over combinations of different parameter values. For example, we might want to search for trees with eleven maximum depth values in the range of [5, 30], six minimum number of record values in leaf nodes between [5, 30], and eleven impurity criterion decrease values in the range [0.001, 0.01]. We can use an exhaustive grid search to find the combination that leads to the tree with smallest error (highest accuracy).

While it is in principle possible to implement and run an exhaustive grid search for all possible parameters in R, it can quickly become very time consuming. For example, the suggested grid search would require running $11 \times 6 \times 11 = 726$ combinations.

Stopping Tree Growth: Conditional Inference Trees   Previous methods developed were based on the idea of recursive partitioning, using rules to prevent the tree from growing excessively and overfitting the training data. One popular method called *CHAID* (chi-squared automatic interaction detection) is a recursive partitioning method that predates classification and regression tree (CART) procedures by several years and is widely used in database marketing applications to this day. It uses a well-known statistical test (the chi-square test for independence) to assess whether splitting a node improves the purity by a statistically significant amount. In particular, at each node, we split on the predictor with the strongest association with the outcome variable. The strength of association is measured by the p-value of a chi-squared test of independence. If for the best predictor the test does not show a significant improvement, the split is not carried out, and the tree is terminated. This method is more suitable for categorical predictors, but it can be adapted to continuous predictors by binning the continuous values into categorical bins.

A more general class of trees based on this idea is called *conditional inference trees* (see Hothorn et al., 2006). The R implementation is given in the `party` and `partykit` packages, and is suitable for both numerical and categorical outcome and predictor variables.

Pruning the Tree

An alternative popular solution that has proven to be more successful than stopping tree growth is pruning the full-grown tree. This is the basis of methods such as CART (developed by Breiman et al., implemented in multiple machine learning software packages such as R's `rpart` package, SAS Enterprise Miner, CART, and MARS) and C4.5 (developed by Quinlan and implemented in packages such as IBM SPSS Modeler, Weka, and in RapidMiner). In C4.5, the training data are used both for growing and pruning the tree. In CART, the innovation is to use the holdout data to prune back the tree that is grown from training data. CART and CART-like procedures use holdout data to prune back the tree that has deliberately been overgrown using the training data.

The idea behind pruning is to recognize that a very large tree is likely to overfit the training data, and that the weakest branches, which hardly reduce the error rate, should be removed. In the mower example, the last few splits resulted in rectangles with very few points (four rectangles in the full tree had a single record). We can see intuitively that these last splits are likely just capturing noise in the training set rather than reflecting patterns that would occur in future data, such as the holdout data. Pruning consists of successively selecting a decision node and redesignating it as a leaf node [lopping off the branches extending beyond that decision node (its *subtree*) and thereby reducing the size of the tree]. The pruning process trades off misclassification error in the holdout dataset against the number of decision nodes in the pruned tree to arrive at a tree that captures the patterns—but not the noise—in the training data.

Pruning the tree with the holdout data solves the problem of overfitting, but it does not address the problem of instability. Recall that the CART algorithm may be unstable in choosing one or another variable for the top level splits, and this effect then cascades down and produces highly variable rule sets. The solution is to avoid relying on just one partition of the data into training and holdout. Rather, we do so repeatedly using cross-validation and then pool the results. Of course, just accumulating a set of different trees with their different rules will not do much by itself. However, we can use the results from all those trees to learn how deep to grow the original tree. In this process, we introduce a parameter that can measure, and control, how deep we grow the tree. We will note this parameter value for each minimum-error tree in the cross-validation process, take an average, and then apply that average to limit tree growth to this optimal depth when working with new data.

The cost complexity (CC) of a tree is equal to its misclassification error (based on the training data) plus a penalty factor for the size of the tree. For a tree T that has $L(T)$ leaf nodes, the cost complexity can be written as

$$CC(T) = \mathrm{err}(T) + \alpha L(T),$$

where $\mathrm{err}(T)$ is the fraction of training records that are misclassified by tree T and α is a penalty factor ("complexity parameter," or cp, in R) for tree size. When $\alpha = 0$, there is no penalty for having too many nodes in a tree, and this yields a tree using the cost complexity criterion that is the full-grown unpruned tree. When we increase α to a very large value the penalty cost component swamps the misclassification error component of the cost complexity criterion, and the result is simply the tree with the fewest leaf nodes: namely, the tree with one node. So there is a range of trees, from tiny to large, corresponding to a range of α, from large to small.

Returning to the cross-validation process, we can now associate a value of α with the minimum error tree developed in each iteration of that process.

Here is a simple version of the algorithm:

1. Partition the data into training and validation sets.
2. Grow the tree with the training data.
3. Prune it successively, step by step, recording cp (using the *training* data) at each step.
4. Note the cp that corresponds to the minimum error on the *validation* data.
5. Repartition the data into training and validation, and repeat the growing, pruning, and cp recording process.
6. Do this again and again, and average the cp's that reflect minimum error for each tree.
7. Go back to the original data, or future data, and grow a tree, stopping at this optimum cp value.

Typically, cross-validation is done such that the partitions (also called "folds") used for validation are nonoverlapping. R automatically does this cross-validation process to select *cp* and build a default pruned tree, but the user can, instead, specify an alternate value of *cp* (e.g., if you wanted to see what a deeper tree looked like).

In Table 9.4, we see the complexity parameter table of cross-validation errors for eleven trees of increasing depth grown on the Universal Bank data. We can simply choose the tree with the lowest cross-validation error (*xerror*). In this case, the tree in row 7 has the lowest cross-validation error. Figure 9.12 displays the pruned tree with 15 leaf nodes. This tree was pruned back from the largest tree using the complexity parameter value $cp = 0.0046296$, which yielded the lowest cross-validation error in Table 9.4.

TABLE 9.4   TABLE OF COMPLEXITY PARAMETER (*cp*) VALUES AND ASSOCIATED TREE ERRORS

 code for tabulating tree error as a function of the complexity parameter (*cp*)

```
# argument xval refers to the number of folds to use in rpart's built-in
# cross-validation procedure
# argument cp sets the smallest value for the complexity parameter.
cv.ct <- rpart(Personal.Loan ~ ., data=train.df, method="class",
    cp=0.00001, minsplit=5, xval=5)
# use printcp() to print the table.
printcp(cv.ct)
```

Output

```
           CP nsplit rel error  xerror     xstd
1   0.2951389      0  1.000000 1.00000 0.056026
2   0.1354167      2  0.409722 0.43056 0.037858
3   0.0451389      3  0.274306 0.29514 0.031556
4   0.0104167      5  0.184028 0.19097 0.025514
5   0.0086806     10  0.121528 0.17361 0.024347
6   0.0069444     12  0.104167 0.15972 0.023369
7   0.0046296     14  0.090278 0.15625 0.023117
8   0.0034722     17  0.076389 0.17014 0.024106
9   0.0023148     22  0.059028 0.17014 0.024106
10  0.0017361     28  0.045139 0.19097 0.025514
11  0.0000100     30  0.041667 0.19444 0.025740
```

Best-Pruned Tree

A further enhancement, in the interest of model parsimony, is to incorporate the sampling error which might cause this minimum to vary if we had a different sample. The enhancement uses the estimated standard error of the cross-validation error (*xstd*) to prune the tree even further; we can add one standard error to the minimum *xerror*. This is sometimes called the *Best-Pruned Tree*. For example, *xstd* for the tree in row 7 is 0.023117. We can choose a smaller tree by

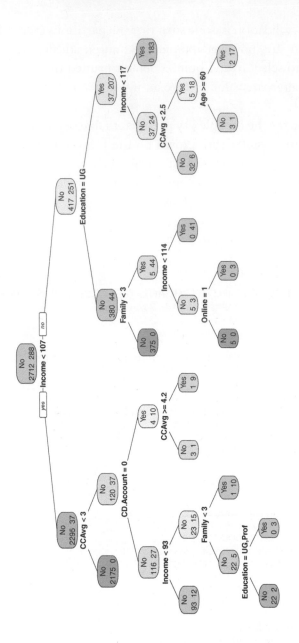

FIGURE 9.12   PRUNED CLASSIFICATION TREE FOR THE LOAN ACCEPTANCE DATA USING CP THAT YIELDED LOWEST XERROR IN TABLE 9.4

R code for pruning the tree

```
# prune by lower cp
pruned.ct <- prune(cv.ct,
    cp=cv.ct$cptable[which.min(cv.ct$cptable[,"xerror"]),"CP"])
sum(pruned.ct$frame$var == "<leaf>")
rpart.plot(pruned.ct, extra=1, fallen.leaves=FALSE)
```

going up to the row with a cross-validation error that is larger, but still within one standard error—that is, *xerror* plus *xstd* (0.1563 + 0.02312 = 0.17937). Here, the tree in row 5 is a smaller tree with the lowest *xerror* in this range. The best-pruned tree for the loan acceptance example is shown in Figure 9.13.

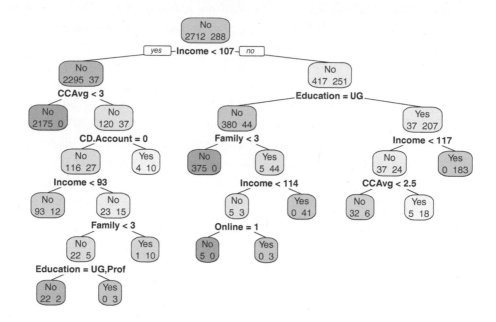

FIGURE 9.13   BEST-PRUNED TREE OBTAINED BY FITTING A FULL TREE TO THE TRAINING DATA, PRUNING IT USING THE CROSS-VALIDATION DATA, AND CHOOSING THE SMALLEST TREE WITHIN ONE STANDARD ERROR OF THE MINIMUM XERROR TREE

9.5 CLASSIFICATION RULES FROM TREES

As described in Section 9.1, classification trees provide easily understandable *classification rules* (if the trees are not too large). Each leaf node is equivalent to a classification rule. Returning to the example, the shallowest left-most leaf node in the best-pruned tree (Figure 9.13) gives us the rule

IF (*Income* < 107) AND (*CCAvg* < 3) THEN *Class* = No.

However, in many cases, the number of rules can be reduced by removing redundancies. For example, consider the rule from the second-from-bottom-left-most leaf node in Figure 9.13:

IF (*Income* < 107) AND (*CCAvg* ≥ 3) AND (*CD.Account* = 0)
AND (*Income* < 93)
THEN *Class* = No

This rule can be simplified to

IF (*Income* < 93) AND (*CCAvg* ≥ 3) AND (*CD.Account* = 0)
THEN *Class* = No

The `rpart.plot` package has the *rpart.rules()* function to extract rules from a tree. The resulting list of rules removes redundancies such as the one we described above. Table 9.5 shows the rules extracted from the best-pruned tree. The fourth rule coincides with our simplified rule above.

This transparency in the process and understandability of the algorithm that leads to classifying a record as belonging to a certain class is very advantageous in settings where the final classification is not the only thing of interest. Berry and Linoff (2000) give the example of health insurance underwriting, where the insurer is required to show that coverage denial is not based on discrimination. By showing rules that led to denial (e.g., income < $20K AND low credit history), the company can avoid law suits. Compared to the output of other classifiers, such as discriminant functions, tree-based classification rules are easily explained to managers and operating staff. Their logic is certainly far more transparent than that of weights in neural networks!

TABLE 9.5　　**EXTRACTING THE RULES FROM THE BEST-PRUNED TREE**

---

 code for extracting rules from a tree and the resulting rules for the best-pruned tree

---

```
> rpart.rules(best.ct)
Personal.Loan
     0.00 when Income <   107        & CCAvg <  3.0
     0.00 when Income >=  107        & Education is  UG & Family <  3
     0.08 when Income is  93 to 107  & CCAvg >= 3.0 & Education is UG or Prof
                                     & CD.Account is 0 & Family <  3
     0.11 when Income <   93         & CCAvg >= 3.0 & CD.Account is 0
     0.16 when Income is 107 to 117  & CCAvg <  2.5 & Education is Grad or Prof
     0.71 when Income <   107        & CCAvg >= 3.0 & CD.Account is 1
     0.78 when Income is 107 to 117  & CCAvg >= 2.5 & Education is Grad or Prof
     0.90 when Income >=  107        & Education is UG & Family >= 3
     0.91 when Income is  93 to 107  & CCAvg >= 3.0 & CD.Account is 0 & Family >= 3
     1.00 when Income is  93 to 107  & CCAvg >= 3.0 & Education is Grad
                                     & CD.Account is 0 & Family <  3
     1.00 when Income >=  117        & Education is Grad or Prof
```

9.6　CLASSIFICATION TREES FOR MORE THAN TWO CLASSES

Classification trees can be used with an outcome variable that has more than two classes. In terms of measuring impurity, the two measures presented earlier (the Gini impurity index and the entropy measure) were defined for m classes and hence can be used for any number of classes. The tree itself would have the same structure, except that its leaf nodes would take one of the m-class labels.

9.7 REGRESSION TREES

The tree method can also be used for a numerical outcome variable. Regression trees for prediction operate in much the same fashion as classification trees. The outcome variable (Y) is a numerical variable in this case, but both the principle and the procedure are the same: Many splits are attempted, and for each, we measure "impurity" in each branch of the resulting tree. The tree procedure then selects the split that minimizes the sum of such measures. To illustrate a regression tree, consider the example of predicting prices of Toyota Corolla automobiles (from Chapter 6). The dataset includes information on 1436 sold Toyota Corolla cars. (We use the first 1000 cars from the dataset *mlba::ToyotaCorolla*.) The goal is to find a predictive model of price as a function of 10 predictors (including mileage, horsepower, number of doors, etc.). A regression tree for these data was built using a training set of 600 records. The best-pruned tree is shown in Figure 9.14.

We see that from the 12 input variables (including dummies), only two predictors show up as useful for predicting price: the age of the car, its weight, and horsepower.

Three details differ between regression trees and classification trees: prediction, impurity measures, and evaluating performance. We describe these next.

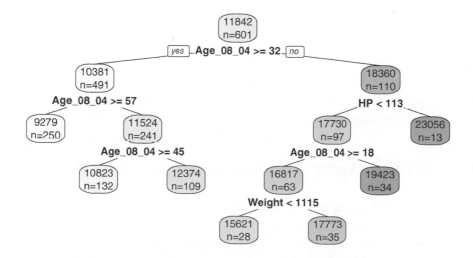

FIGURE 9.14   BEST-PRUNED REGRESSION TREE FOR TOYOTA COROLLA PRICES

Prediction

Predicting the outcome value for a record is performed in a fashion similar to the classification case: The predictor information is used for "dropping" the record down the tree until reaching a terminal node. For instance, to predict the price of a Toyota Corolla with Age = 60, Horse_Power = 100, and Weight = 1200, we drop it down the tree and reach the node that has the value $9279. This is the price prediction for this car according to the tree. In classification trees, the value of the terminal node (which is one of the categories) is determined by the "voting" of the training records that were in that terminal node. In regression trees, the value of the terminal node is determined by the average outcome value of the training records that were in that terminal node. In the example above, the value $9279 is the average of the 250 cars in the training set that fall in the category of Age $\geq$ 57.

Measuring Impurity

We described two types of impurity measures for nodes in classification trees: the Gini index and the entropy-based measure. In both cases, the index is a function of the *ratio* between the categories of the records in that node. In regression trees, a typical impurity measure is the sum of the squared deviations from the mean of the terminal node. This is equivalent to the sum of the squared errors, because the mean of the terminal node is exactly the prediction. In the example above, the impurity of the node with the value $9279 is computed by subtracting 9279 from the price of each of the 250 cars in the training set that fell in that terminal node and then squaring these deviations and summing them up. The lowest impurity possible is zero, when all values in the node are equal.

Evaluating Performance

As stated above, predictions are obtained by averaging the outcome values in the nodes. We therefore have the usual definition of predictions and errors. The predictive performance of regression trees can be measured in the same way that other predictive methods are evaluated (e.g., linear regression), using summary measures such as RMSE.

9.8 ADVANTAGES AND WEAKNESSES OF A TREE

Tree methods are good off-the-shelf classifiers and predictors. They are also useful for variable selection, with the most important predictors usually showing up at the top of the tree. Trees require relatively little effort from users in the following senses: First, there is no need for transformation of variables (any monotone transformation of the variables will give the same trees). Second, variable subset selection is automatic since it is part of the split selection. In the loan example, note that the best-pruned tree has automatically selected just 7 variables (Income, Education, CC.Avg, CD.Account, Online, Age, and Family) out of the set of 14 variables available.

Trees are also intrinsically robust to outliers, since the choice of a split depends on the *ordering* of values and not on the absolute *magnitudes* of these values. However, single trees are sensitive to changes in the data, and even a slight change can cause very different splits!

Unlike models that assume a particular relationship between the outcome and predictors (e.g., a linear relationship such as in linear regression and linear discriminant analysis), classification and regression trees are nonlinear and non-parametric. This allows for a wide range of relationships between the predictors and the outcome variable. However, this can also be a weakness: Since the splits are done on one predictor at a time, rather than on combinations of predictors, the tree is likely to miss relationships between predictors, in particular linear structures like those in linear or logistic regression models. Classification trees are useful classifiers in cases where horizontal and vertical splitting of the predictor space adequately divides the classes. But consider, for instance, a dataset with two predictors and two classes, where separation between the two classes is most obviously achieved by using a diagonal line (as shown in Figure 9.15). In such cases, a classification tree is expected to have lower performance than methods such as discriminant analysis. One way to improve performance is to create new predictors that are derived from existing predictors, which can capture hypothesized relationships between predictors (similar to interactions in regression models). Random forests and boosted trees (see next section) are popular ways to improve tree performance.

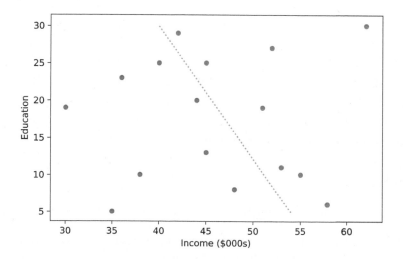

FIGURE 9.15   SCATTER PLOT DESCRIBING A TWO-PREDICTOR CASE WITH TWO CLASSES. THE BEST SEPARATION IS ACHIEVED WITH A DIAGONAL LINE, WHICH CLASSIFICATION TREES CANNOT DO

Another performance issue with classification trees is that they require a large dataset in order to construct a good classifier. From a computational aspect, trees can be relatively expensive to grow, because of the multiple sorting involved in computing all possible splits on every variable. Pruning the data using the holdout sets adds further computation time.

Although trees are useful for variable selection, one challenge is that they "favor" predictors with many potential split points. This includes categorical predictors with many categories and numerical predictors with many different values. Such predictors have a higher chance of appearing in a tree. One simplistic solution is to combine multiple categories into a smaller set and bin numerical predictors with many values. Alternatively, some special algorithms avoid this problem by using a two-step process: the first step chooses a predictor (e.g., via a statistical test) and the second step selects the splitting point on the chosen predictor. Examples include *conditional inference trees* in the R packages `party` and `partykit` (see Hothorn et al., 2006; Hothorn and Zeileis, 2015) and in QUEST classification trees (see Loh and Shih, 1997).

An appealing feature of trees is that they handle missing data without having to impute values or delete records with missing values. Finally, a very important practical advantage of trees is the transparent rules that they generate. Such transparency is often useful in managerial applications, though this advantage is lost in the ensemble versions of trees (random forests, boosted trees).

9.9 IMPROVING PREDICTION: RANDOM FORESTS AND BOOSTED TREES

Notwithstanding the transparency advantages of a single tree as described above, in a pure prediction application, where visualizing a set of rules does not matter, better performance is provided by several extensions to trees that combine results from multiple trees. These are examples of *ensembles* (see Chapter 13). One popular multitree approach is *random forests*, introduced by Breiman and Cutler.[2] Random forests are a special case of *bagging*, a method for improving predictive power by combining multiple classifiers or prediction algorithms. See Chapter 13 for further details on bagging.

Random Forests

The basic idea in random forests is to:

1. Draw multiple random samples, with replacement, from the data (this sampling approach is called the *bootstrap*).

---

[2]For further details on random forests, see www.stat.berkeley.edu/users/breiman/RandomForests/cc_home.htm.

2. Using a random subset of predictors at each stage, fit a classification (or regression) tree to each sample (and thus obtain a "forest").

3. Combine the predictions/classifications from the individual trees to obtain improved predictions. Use voting for classification and averaging for prediction.

The code and output in Figure 9.16 illustrate applying a random forest in R to the personal loan example. The accuracy of the random forest is slightly

 code for running a random forest, plotting variable importance plot, and computing accuracy

```
library(randomForest)
## random forest
rf <- randomForest(Personal.Loan ~ ., data=train.df, ntree=500,
    mtry=4, nodesize=5, importance=TRUE)

## variable importance plot
varImpPlot(rf, type=1)

## confusion matrix
rf.pred <- predict(rf, holdout.df)
confusionMatrix(rf.pred, holdout.df$Personal.Loan)
```

Partial Output

```
> confusionMatrix(rf.pred, holdout.df$Personal.Loan)
Confusion Matrix and Statistics

          Reference
Prediction   No   Yes
       No  1807    21
       Yes    1   171

              Accuracy : 0.989
```

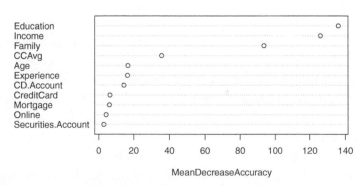

FIGURE 9.16   VARIABLE IMPORTANCE PLOT FROM RANDOM FOREST (PERSONAL LOAN EXAMPLE)

higher than the single default tree that we fit earlier (compare to the holdout performance in Table 9.3)

Unlike a single tree, results from a random forest cannot be displayed in a tree-like diagram, thereby losing the interpretability that a single tree provides. However, random forests can produce "variable importance" scores, which measure the relative contribution of the different predictors. The importance score for a particular predictor is computed by summing up the decrease in the Gini index for that predictor over all the trees in the forest. Figure 9.16 shows the variable importance plots generated from the random forest model for the personal loan example. We see that Income and Education have the highest scores, with Family being third. Importance scores for the other predictors are considerably lower.

Boosted Trees

The second type of multitree improvement is *boosted trees*. Here a sequence of trees is fitted, so that each tree concentrates on misclassified records from the previous tree.

1. Fit a single tree.
2. Draw a sample that gives higher selection probabilities to misclassified records.
3. Fit a tree to the new sample.
4. Repeat Steps 2 and 3 multiple times.
5. Use weighted voting to classify records, with heavier weight for later trees.

Figure 9.17 shows how to run a boosted tree on the loan acceptance example using the `xgboost` package with `caret`. The ROC curves compare the model performance against the best-pruned classification tree and the random forest. The ROC curves for the random forest and boosted tree show an improved overall performance compared to the single pruned tree. For high specificity levels (left side of ROC plot), the xgboost also has the highest sensitivity compared to the other two models, so is clearly superior. This reflects the ability of the boosted model to correctly classify *Yes*'s—the rare class of special interest. Where does boosting's special talent for finding *Yes*'s come from? When one class is dominant (*No*'s constitute over 90% of the data here), basic classifiers are tempted to classify cases as belonging to the dominant class, and the *Yes*'s in this case constitute most of the misclassifications with the single best-pruned tree. The boosting algorithm concentrates on the misclassifications (which are mostly *Yes*'s), so it is naturally going to do well in reducing the misclassification of *Yes*'s.

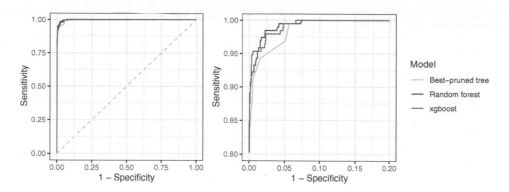

FIGURE 9.17   ROC CURVES COMPARING PERFORMANCE OF BOOSTED TREE, RANDOM FOREST, AND CLASSIFICATION TREE ON HOLDOUT SET (PERSONAL LOAN EXAMPLE). RIGHT PLOT ZOOMS IN TO HIGH SPECIFICITY VALUES.

 code for running boosted trees

```
library(caret)
library(xgboost)

xgb <- train(Personal.Loan ~ ., data=train.df, method="xgbTree", verbosity=0)

# compare ROC curves for classification tree, random forest, and boosted tree models
library(ROCR)
rocCurveData <- function(model, data) {
  prob <- predict(model, data, type="prob")[, "Yes"]
  predob <- prediction(prob, data$Personal.Loan)
  perf <- performance(predob, "tpr", "fpr")
  return (data.frame(tpr=perf@x.values[[1]], fpr=perf@y.values[[1]]))
}

performance.df <- rbind(
  cbind(rocCurveData(best.ct, holdout.df), model="Best-pruned tree"),
  cbind(rocCurveData(rf, holdout.df), model="Random forest"),
  cbind(rocCurveData(xgb, holdout.df), model="xgboost")
)
colors <- c("Best-pruned tree"="grey", "Random forest"="blue", "xgboost"="tomato")
ggplot(performance.df, aes(x=tpr, y=fpr, color=model)) +
  geom_line() +
  scale_color_manual(values=colors) +
  geom_segment(aes(x=0, y=0, xend=1, yend=1), color="grey", linetype="dashed") +
  labs(x="1 - Specificity", y="Sensitivity", color="Model")
```

We can tweak the boosted tree model even further by focusing the training of the model on the rarer *Yes* class. Figure 9.18 shows the effect of adding the *scale_pos_weight* argument on model performance. The ROC curve of the focused xgboost model shows an improved overall performance.

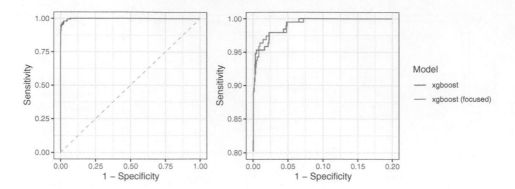

FIGURE 9.18   ROC CURVES OF BOOSTED TREE AND FOCUSED BOOSTED TREE (RIGHT PLOT
ZOOMS IN TO HIGH SPECIFICITY VALUES)

 code for running boosted trees with changed weight

```
xgb.focused <- train(Personal.Loan ~ ., data=train.df,
            method="xgbTree", verbosity=0,
            scale_pos_weight=10)

performance.df <- rbind(
cbind(rocCurveData(xgb, holdout.df), model="xgboost"),
cbind(rocCurveData(xgb.focused, holdout.df), model="xgboost (focused)")
)

colors <- c("xgboost"="tomato", "xgboost (focused)"="darkgreen")
ggplot(performance.df, aes(x=tpr, y=fpr, color=model)) +
  geom_line() +
  scale_color_manual(values=colors) +
  geom_segment(aes(x=0, y=0, xend=1, yend=1), color="grey", linetype="dashed") +
  labs(x="1 - Specificity", y="Sensitivity", color="Model")
```

PROBLEMS

9.1   **Competitive Auctions on eBay.com.** The dataset *mlba::eBayAuctions* contains information on 1972 auctions that transacted on eBay.com during May–June 2004. The goal is to use these data to build a model that will classify auctions as competitive or noncompetitive. A *competitive auction* is defined as an auction with at least two bids placed on the item auctioned. The data include variables that describe the item (auction category), the seller (his/her eBay rating), and the auction terms that the seller selected (auction duration, opening price, currency, day-of-week of auction close). In addition, we have the price at which the auction closed. The task is to predict whether or not the auction will be competitive.

Data Preprocessing. Convert variable *Duration* into a categorical variable. Split the data into training (60%) and holdout (40%) datasets.

a. Fit a classification tree using all predictors, using the best-pruned tree. To avoid overfitting, set the minimum number of records in a terminal node to 50 (in R: *minbucket=50*). Also, set the maximum number of levels to be displayed at seven (in R: *maxdepth=7*). Write down the results in terms of rules. (*Note*: If you had to slightly reduce the number of predictors due to software limitations, or for clarity of presentation, which would be a good variable to choose?)

b. Is this model practical for predicting the outcome of a new auction?

c. Describe the interesting and uninteresting information that these rules provide.

d. Fit another classification tree (using the best-pruned tree, with a minimum number of records per terminal node = 50 and maximum allowed number of displayed levels = 7), this time only with predictors that can be used for predicting the outcome of a new auction. Describe the resulting tree in terms of rules. Make sure to report the smallest set of rules required for classification.

e. Plot the resulting tree on a scatter plot: Use the two axes for the two best (quantitative) predictors. Each auction will appear as a point, with coordinates corresponding to its values on those two predictors. Use different colors or symbols to separate competitive and noncompetitive auctions. Draw lines (you can sketch these by hand or use R) at the values that create splits. Does this splitting seem reasonable with respect to the meaning of the two predictors? Does it seem to do a good job of separating the two classes?

f. Examine the lift chart and the confusion matrix for the tree. What can you say about the predictive performance of this model?

g. Based on this last tree, what can you conclude from these data about the chances of an auction obtaining at least two bids and its relationship to the auction settings set by the seller (duration, opening price, ending day, currency)? What would you recommend for a seller as the strategy that will most likely lead to a competitive auction?

9.2   **Predicting Delayed Flights.** The dataset *mlba::FlightDelays* contains information on all commercial flights departing the Washington, DC area and arriving at New York during January 2004. For each flight, there is information on the departure and arrival airports, the distance of the route, the scheduled time and date of the flight, and so on. The variable that we are trying to predict is whether or not a flight is delayed. A delay is defined as an arrival that is at least 15 minutes later than scheduled.

Data Preprocessing. Transform variable day of week (DAY_WEEK) info a categorical variable. Bin the scheduled departure time into eight bins (in R use function *cut()*). Use these and all other columns as predictors (excluding DAY_OF_MONTH, FL_DATE, FL_NUM, and TAIL_NUM). Partition the data into training (60%) and holdout (40%) sets.

a. Fit a classification tree to the flight delay variable using all the relevant predictors. Do not include DEP_TIME (actual departure time) in the model because it is unknown at the time of prediction (unless we are generating our predictions of delays after the plane takes off, which is unlikely). Explain why we excluded DAY_OF_MONTH, FL_DATE, FL_NUM, and TAIL_NUM as predictors in data preprocessing. Use a pruned tree with maximum of eight levels, setting *cp=0.001*. Express the resulting tree as a set of rules.

b. If you needed to fly between DCA and EWR on a Monday at 7:00 AM, would you be able to use this tree? What other information would you need? Is it available in practice? What information is redundant?

c. Fit the same tree as in (a), this time excluding the Weather predictor. Display both the pruned and unpruned tree. You will find that the pruned tree contains a single leaf node.

  i. How is the pruned tree used for classification? (What is the rule for classifying?)

  ii. To what is this rule equivalent?

  iii. Examine the unpruned tree. What are the top three predictors according to this tree?

  iv. Why, technically, does the pruned tree result in a single node?

  v. What is the disadvantage of using the top levels of the unpruned tree as opposed to the pruned tree?

  vi. Compare this general result to that from logistic regression in the example in Chapter 10. What are possible reasons for the classification tree's failure to find a good predictive model?

9.3 **Predicting Prices of Used Cars (Regression Trees).**   The dataset *mlba::ToyotaCorolla* contains the data on used cars (Toyota Corolla) on sale during late summer of 2004 in the Netherlands. It has 1436 records containing details on 38 variables, including Price, Age, Kilometers, HP, and other specifications. The goal is to predict the price of a used Toyota Corolla based on its specifications. (The example in Section 9.7 is a subset of this dataset.)

Data Preprocessing. Split the data into training (60%) and holdout (40%) datasets.

a. Run a regression tree (RT) with outcome variable Price and predictors Age_08_04, KM, Fuel_Type, HP, Automatic, Doors, Quarterly_Tax, Mfr_Guarantee, Guarantee_Period, Airco, Automatic_Airco, CD_Player, Powered_Windows, Sport_Model, and Tow_Bar. Keep the minimum number of records in a terminal node to 1, maximum number of tree levels to 30, and *cp* = 0.001, to make the run least restrictive.

  i. Which appear to be the three or four most important car specifications for predicting the car's price?

  ii. Compare the prediction errors of the training and holdout sets by examining their RMS error and by plotting the two boxplots. How does the predictive performance of the holdout set compare to the training set? Why does this occur?

   iii. How might we achieve better holdout predictive performance at the expense of training performance?

   iv. Create a smaller tree by leaving the arguments *cp*, *minbucket*, and *maxdepth* at their defaults. Compared to the deeper tree, what is the predictive performance on the holdout set?

b. Let us see the effect of turning the price variable into a categorical variable. First, create a new variable that categorizes price into 20 bins. Now repartition the data keeping Binned_Price instead of Price. Run a classification tree with the same set of input variables as in the RT, and with Binned_Price as the output variable. As in the less deep regression tree, leave the arguments *cp*, *minbucket*, and *maxdepth* at their defaults.

   i. Compare the smaller tree generated by the CT with the smaller tree generated by the RT. Are they different? (Look at structure, the top predictors, size of tree, etc.) Why?

   ii. Predict the price, using the smaller RT and the CT, of a used Toyota Corolla with the specifications listed in Table 9.6.

TABLE 9.6   **SPECIFICATIONS FOR A PARTICULAR TOYOTA COROLLA**

Variable	Value
Age_-08_-04	77
KM	117,000
Fuel_Type	Petrol
HP	110
Automatic	No
Doors	5
Quarterly_Tax	100
Mfg_Guarantee	No
Guarantee_Period	3
Airco	Yes
Automatic_Airco	No
CD_Player	No
Powered_Windows	No
Sport_Model	No
Tow_Bar	Yes

   iii. Compare the predictions in terms of the predictors that were used, the magnitude of the difference between the two predictions, and the advantages and disadvantages of the two methods.

## CHAPTER 10

Logistic Regression

In this chapter, we describe the highly popular and powerful classification method called logistic regression. Like linear regression, it relies on a specific model relating the predictors with the outcome. The user must specify the predictors to include as well as their form (e.g., including any interaction terms). This means that even small datasets can be used for building logistic regression classifiers and that, once the model is estimated, it is computationally fast and cheap to classify even large samples of new records. We describe the logistic regression model formulation and its estimation from data. We also explain the concepts of "logit," "odds," and "probability" of an event that arise in the logistic model context and the relations among the three. We discuss variable importance using coefficient and statistical significance and also mention variable selection algorithms for dimension reduction. Our presentation is strictly from a machine learning perspective, where classification is the goal and performance is evaluated on a separate holdout set.

Logistic Regression in R

The main R function introduced in this chapter is *glm* in the `caret` package. We also use package `glmnet` for variable selection.

10.1 INTRODUCTION

Logistic regression extends the ideas of linear regression to the situation where the outcome variable, Y, is categorical. We can think of a categorical variable as dividing the records into classes. For example, if Y denotes a recommendation on holding/selling/buying a stock, we have a categorical variable with three categories. We can think of each of the stocks in the dataset (the records) as

Machine Learning for Business Analytics: Concepts, Techniques, and Applications in R, Second Edition.
Galit Shmueli, Peter C. Bruce, Peter Gedeck, Inbal Yahav, and Nitin R. Patel
© 2023 John Wiley & Sons, Inc. Published 2023 by John Wiley & Sons, Inc.

belonging to one of three classes: the *hold* class, the *sell* class, and the *buy* class. Logistic regression can be used for classifying a new record, where its class is unknown, into one of the classes, based on the values of its predictor variables (called *classification*). It can also be used in data where the class is known, to find factors distinguishing between records in different classes in terms of their predictor variables, or "predictor profile" (called *profiling*). Logistic regression is used in applications such as the following:

1. Classifying customers as returning or nonreturning (classification).
2. Finding factors that differentiate between male and female top executives (profiling).
3. Predicting the approval or disapproval of a loan based on information such as credit scores (classification).

The logistic regression model is used in a variety of fields: whenever a structured model is needed to explain or predict categorical (in particular, binary) outcomes. One such application is in describing choice behavior in econometrics.

In this chapter, we focus on the use of logistic regression for classification. We deal only with a binary outcome variable having two possible classes. In Section 10.6, we show how the results can be extended to the case where Y assumes more than two possible classes. Popular examples of binary outcomes are success/failure, yes/no, buy/don't buy, default/don't default, and survive/die. For convenience, we often code the values of the binary outcome variable Y as 0 and 1.

Note that in some cases we may choose to convert a continuous outcome variable or an outcome variables with multiple classes into a binary outcome variable for purposes of simplification, reflecting the fact that decision-making may be binary (approve the loan/don't approve, make an offer/don't make an offer). As with multiple linear regression, the predictor variables $X_1, X_2, \ldots, X_k$ may be categorical variables, continuous variables, or a mixture of these two types. While in multiple linear regression the aim is to predict the value of the continuous Y for a new record, in logistic regression the goal is to predict which class a new record will belong to, or simply to *classify* the record into one of the classes. In the stock example, we would want to classify a new stock into one of the three recommendation classes: sell, hold, or buy. Or, we might want to compute for a new record its *propensity* (= the probability) to belong to each class and then possibly rank a set of new records from highest to lowest propensity in order to act on those with the highest propensity.

Potentially, one could use linear regression for classification, by training a linear regression on a 0/1 outcome (called a *Linear Probability Model*). The model is then used to generate numerical predictions which are converted into binary classifications using a threshold. However, linear probability models, despite their name, do not produce proper predicted probabilities. The numerical predictions they produce are useful for comparison with the classification threshold but are otherwise meaningless.

In logistic regression, we take two steps: the first step yields estimates of the *propensities* or *probabilities* of belonging to each class. In the binary case, we get an estimate of $p = P(Y = 1)$, the probability of belonging to class 1 (which also tells us the probability of belonging to class 0). In the next step, we use a cutoff value on these probabilities in order to classify each case into one of the classes. For example, in a binary case, a cutoff of 0.5 means that cases with an estimated probability of $P(Y = 1) \geq 0.5$ are classified as belonging to class 1, whereas cases with $P(Y = 1) < 0.5$ are classified as belonging to class 0. This cutoff does not need to be set at 0.5. When the event in question is a low probability but notable or important event (say, 1 = fraudulent transaction), a lower cutoff may be used to classify more cases as belonging to class 1.

10.2 THE LOGISTIC REGRESSION MODEL

The idea behind logistic regression is straightforward: instead of using Y directly as the outcome variable, we use a function of it, which is called the *logit*. The logit, it turns out, can be modeled as a linear function of the predictors. Once the logit has been predicted, it can be mapped back to a probability.

To understand the logit, we take several intermediate steps: first, we look at $p = P(Y = 1)$, the probability of belonging to class 1 (as opposed to class 0). In contrast to the binary variable Y, which only takes the values 0 and 1, p can take any value in the interval $[0, 1]$. However, if we express p as a linear function of the q predictors[1] in the form

$$p = \beta_0 + \beta_1 x_1 + \beta_2 x_2 + \cdots + \beta_q x_q, \tag{10.1}$$

it is not guaranteed that the right-hand side will lead to values within the interval $[0, 1]$. The solution is to use a nonlinear function of the predictors in the form

$$p = \frac{1}{1 + e^{-(\beta_0 + \beta_1 x_1 + \beta_2 x_2 + \cdots + \beta_q x_q)}}. \tag{10.2}$$

This is called the *logistic response function*. For any values $x_1, \ldots, x_q$, the right-hand side will always lead to values in the interval $[0, 1]$. Next, we look at a different measure of belonging to a certain class, known as *odds*. The odds of belonging to class 1 are defined as *the ratio of the probability of belonging to class 1*

---

[1] Unlike elsewhere in the book, where p denotes the number of predictors, in this chapter, we use q to avoid confusion with the probability p.

to the probability of belonging to class 0:

$$\text{Odds}(Y = 1) = \frac{p}{1 - p}. \tag{10.3}$$

This metric is very popular in horse races, sports, gambling, epidemiology, and other areas. Instead of talking about the *probability* of winning or contacting a disease, people talk about the *odds* of winning or contacting a disease. How are these two different? If, for example, the probability of winning is 0.5, the odds of winning are $0.5/0.5 = 1$. We can also perform the reverse calculation: given the odds of an event, we can compute its probability by manipulating equation (10.3):

$$p = \frac{\text{odds}}{1 + \text{odds}}. \tag{10.4}$$

Substituting (10.2) into (10.4), we can write the relationship between the odds and the predictors as

$$\text{Odds}(Y = 1) = e^{\beta_0 + \beta_1 x_1 + \beta_2 x_2 + \cdots + \beta_q x_q}. \tag{10.5}$$

This last equation describes a multiplicative (proportional) relationship between the predictors and the odds. Such a relationship is interpretable in terms of percentages, for example, a unit increase in predictor X_j is associated with an average increase of $e^{\beta_j} \times 100\%$ in the odds (holding all other predictors constant).

Now, if we take a natural logarithm[2] on both sides, we get the standard formulation of a logistic model:

$$\log(\text{odds}) = \beta_0 + \beta_1 x_1 + \beta_2 x_2 + \cdots + \beta_q x_q. \tag{10.6}$$

The log(odds), called the *logit*, takes values from $-\infty$ (very low odds) to ∞ (very high odds).[3] A logit of 0 corresponds to even odds of 1 (probability = 0.5). Thus, our final formulation of the relation between the outcome and the predictors uses the logit as the outcome variable and models it as a *linear function* of the q predictors.

To see the relationship between the probability, odds, and logit of belonging to class 1, look at Figure 10.1, which shows the odds (top) and logit (bottom) as a function of p. Notice that the odds can take any non-negative value and that the logit can take any real value.

10.3 EXAMPLE: ACCEPTANCE OF PERSONAL LOAN

Recall the example described in Chapter 9 of acceptance of a personal loan by Universal Bank. The bank's dataset includes data on 5000 customers. The data

---

[2]The natural logarithm function is typically denoted ln() or log(). In this book, we use log().
[3]We use the terms *odds* and *odds(Y = 1)* interchangeably.

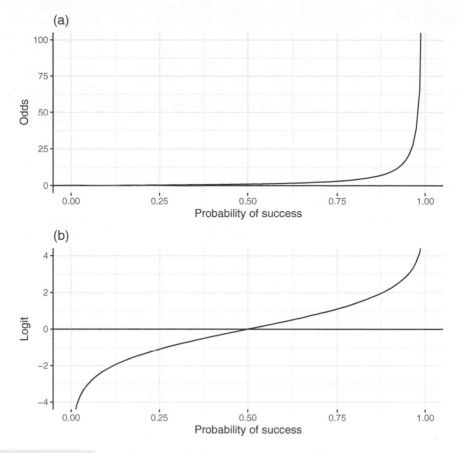

FIGURE 10.1   (a) ODDS AND (b) LOGIT AS A FUNCTION OF *p*

includes the customer's response to the last personal loan campaign (Personal Loan), as well as customer demographic information (Age, Income, etc.) and the customer's relationship with the bank (mortgage, securities account, etc.); see Table 10.1. Among these 5000 customers, only 480 (= 9.6%) accepted the personal loan offered to them in a previous campaign. The goal is to build a model that identifies customers who are most likely to accept the loan offer in future mailings.

Model with a Single Predictor

Consider first a simple logistic regression model with just one predictor. This is conceptually analogous to the simple linear regression model in which we fit a straight line to relate the outcome, Y, to a single predictor, X.

Let us construct a simple logistic regression model for classification of customers using the single predictor *Income*. The equation relating the outcome

TABLE 10.1   DESCRIPTION OF PREDICTORS FOR ACCEPTANCE OF PERSONAL LOAN EXAMPLE

Age	Customer's age in completed years
Experience	Number of years of professional experience
Income	Annual income of the customer ($000s)
Family Size	Family size of the customer
CCAvg	Average spending on credit cards per month ($000s)
Education	Education level: 1 = undergrad; 2 = graduate; 3 = advanced/professional
Mortgage	Value of house mortgage if any ($000s)
Securities Account	Coded as 1 if customer has securities account with bank
CD Account	Coded as 1 if customer has certificate of deposit (CD) account with bank
Online Banking	Coded as 1 if customer uses Internet banking facilities
Credit Card	Coded as 1 if customer uses credit card issued by Universal Bank

variable to the predictor in terms of probabilities is

$$P(\text{Personal Loan} = Yes \mid \text{Income} = x) = \frac{1}{1 + e^{-(\beta_0 + \beta_1 x)}},$$

or equivalently, in terms of odds,

$$\text{Odds}(\text{Personal Loan} = Yes \mid \text{Income} = x) = e^{\beta_0 + \beta_1 x}. \tag{10.7}$$

The estimated coefficients for the model are $\hat{\beta}_0 = -6.16715$ and $\hat{\beta}_1 = 0.03757$. So the fitted model is

$$P(\text{Personal Loan} = Yes \mid \text{Income} = x) = \frac{1}{1 + e^{6.16715 - 0.03757x}}. \tag{10.8}$$

Although logistic regression can be used for prediction in the sense that we predict the *probability* of a categorical outcome, it is most often used for classification. To see the difference between the two, consider predicting the probability of a customer accepting the loan offer as opposed to classifying the customer as an acceptor/nonacceptor. From Figure 10.2, it can be seen that the loan acceptance probabilities produced by the logistic regression model (the s-shaped curve in Figure 10.2) can yield values between 0 and 1. To end up with classifications into either 1 or 0 (e.g., a customer either accepts the loan offer or not), we need a threshold, or cutoff value (see section on "Propensities and Cutoff for Classification" in Chapter 5). This is true in the case of multiple predictor variables as well.

In the Universal Bank example, in order to classify a new customer as an acceptor/nonacceptor of the loan offer, we use the information on his/her income by plugging it into the fitted equation in (10.8). This yields an estimated probability of accepting the loan offer. We then compare it with the cutoff value.

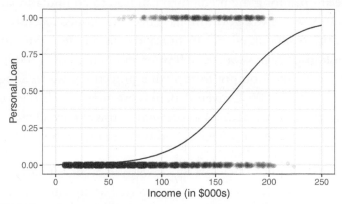

FIGURE 10.2   **PLOT OF DATA POINTS (PERSONAL LOAN AS A FUNCTION OF INCOME) AND THE FITTED LOGISTIC CURVE**

The customer is classified as an acceptor if the probability of his/her accepting the offer is above the cutoff.[4]

Estimating the Logistic Model from Data: Computing Parameter Estimates

In logistic regression, the relation between Y and the β parameters is nonlinear. For this reason, the β parameters are not estimated using the method of least squares (as in multiple linear regression). Instead, a method called *maximum likelihood* is used. The idea, in brief, is to find the estimates that maximize the chance of obtaining the data that we have. This requires iterations using a computer program.[5]

Algorithms to compute the coefficient estimates are less robust than algorithms for linear regression. Computed estimates are generally reliable for well-behaved datasets where the number of records with outcome variable values of both 0 and 1 is large; their ratio is "not too close" to either 0 or 1; and when the number of coefficients in the logistic regression model is small relative to the sample size (say, no more than 10%). As with linear regression, collinearity

---

[4]Here, we compared the probability with a cutoff c. If we prefer to look at *odds* of accepting rather than the probability, an equivalent method is to use the equation in (10.7) and compare the odds with $c/(1 - c)$. If the odds are higher than this number, the customer is classified as an acceptor. If it is lower, we classify the customer as a nonacceptor.

[5]The method of maximum likelihood ensures good asymptotic (large sample) properties for the estimates. Under very general conditions, maximum likelihood estimators are: (1) *Consistent*, meaning the probability of the estimator differing from the true value approaches zero with increasing sample size, (2) *Asymptotically efficient*, meaning the variance is the smallest possible among consistent estimators, and (3) *Asymptotically normally distributed*—This allows us to compute confidence intervals and perform statistical tests in a manner analogous to the analysis of multiple linear regression models, provided that the sample size is *large*.

(strong correlation among the predictors) can lead to computational difficulties. Computationally intensive algorithms have been developed recently that circumvent some of these difficulties. For technical details on the maximum likelihood estimation in logistic regression, see Hosmer and Lemeshow (2000).

To illustrate a typical output from such a procedure, we fit a logistic model to the training set of 3000 Universal Bank customers. The outcome variable is Personal Loan, with *Yes* defined as the *success* (this is equivalent to setting the outcome variable to 1 for an acceptor and 0 for a nonacceptor).

Data Preprocessing   We start by converting predictor variable Education into a factor variable. In the dataset, it is coded as an integer, taking on values 1, 2, or 3. To turn it into a factor variable, we use the R function *factor()*. Then when we include this predictor variable in R's logistic regression, it will automatically create two dummy variables from the factor's three levels. The logistic regression will only use two of the three levels because using all three would create a multicollinearity issue (see Chapter 6). In total, the logistic regression function in R will include $6 = 2 + 1 + 1 + 1 + 1$ dummy variables to describe the five categorical predictors from Table 10.1. Together with the six numerical predictors, we have a total of 12 predictors.

Next, we partition the data randomly into training (60%) and holdout (40%) sets. We use the training set to fit a logistic regression model and the holdout set to assess the model's performance.

Estimated Model   Table 10.2 presents the output from running a logistic regression using the 12 predictors on the training data.

Ignoring p-values for the coefficients, a model based on all 12 predictors has the estimated logistic equation

$$\text{Logit(Personal Loan = Yes)} = \tag{10.9}$$
$$-9.8329 - 0.1230\,\text{Age} + 0.1223\,\text{Experience}$$
$$+0.0594\,\text{Income} + 0.6264\,\text{Family} + 0.1325\,\text{CCAvg}$$
$$+3.9156\,\text{EducationGraduate} + 4.1670\,\text{EducationAdvanced/Professional}$$
$$+0.0010\,\text{Mortgage} - 0.7336\,\text{Securities.Account} + 4.2298\,\text{CD.Account}$$
$$+1.0064\,\text{Online} - 1.1630\,\text{Credit Card}$$

The positive coefficients for the dummy variables *EducationGraduate, EducationAdvanced/Professional, CD.Account*, and *Online* mean that holding a CD account, using online banking, and having graduate or professional education (all marked by 1 in the dummy variables) are associated with higher probabilities of accepting the loan offer. In contrast, having a securities account and owning a Universal Bank credit card are associated with lower acceptance rates. For the

TABLE 10.2   LOGISTIC REGRESSION MODEL FOR LOAN ACCEPTANCE (TRAINING DATA)

R code for fitting a logistic regression model

```
library(caret)
library(tidyverse)

# load and preprocess data
bank.df <- mlba::UniversalBank %>%
  select(-c(ID, ZIP.Code)) %>% # Drop ID and zip code columns.
  mutate(
    Education = factor(Education, levels=c(1:3),
                       labels=c("Undergrad", "Graduate", "Advanced/Professional")),
    Personal.Loan = factor(Personal.Loan, levels=c(0, 1),
                           labels=c("No", "Yes"))
  )

# partition data
set.seed(2)
idx <- caret::createDataPartition(bank.df$Personal.Loan, p=0.6, list=FALSE)
train.df <- bank.df[idx, ]
holdout.df <- bank.df[-idx, ]

# build model
trControl <- caret::trainControl(method="cv", number=5, allowParallel=TRUE)
logit.reg <- caret::train(Personal.Loan ~ ., data=train.df, trControl=trControl,
                    # fit logistic regression with a generalized linear model
                    method="glm", family="binomial")
logit.reg
summary(logit.reg$finalModel)
```

Output

	Estimate	Std. Error	z value	Pr(>|z|)	
(Intercept)	-9.832889	2.428319	-4.05	0.0000513803	***
Age	-0.123049	0.092475	-1.33	0.183	
Experience	0.122296	0.091723	1.33	0.182	
Income	0.059401	0.003939	15.08	< 0.0000000000000002	***
Family	0.626382	0.102863	6.09	0.0000000011	***
CCAvg	0.132459	0.056848	2.33	0.020	*
EducationGraduate	3.915627	0.352943	11.09	< 0.0000000000000002	***
`EducationAdvanced/Professional`	4.167042	0.350274	11.90	< 0.0000000000000002	***
Mortgage	0.001005	0.000765	1.31	0.189	
Securities.Account	-0.733557	0.376078	-1.95	0.051	.
CD.Account	4.229826	0.447329	9.46	< 0.0000000000000002	***
Online	-1.006379	0.220522	-4.56	0.0000050277	***
CreditCard	-1.162987	0.284661	-4.09	0.0000439778	***

```
---
Signif. codes:  0 '***' 0.001 '**' 0.01 '*' 0.05 '.' 0.1 ' ' 1

(Dispersion parameter for binomial family taken to be 1)

    Null deviance: 1897.22  on 2999  degrees of freedom
Residual deviance:  686.66  on 2987  degrees of freedom
AIC: 712.7

Number of Fisher Scoring iterations: 8
```

continuous predictors, positive coefficients indicate that a higher value on that predictor is associated with a higher probability of accepting the loan offer (e.g., Income: higher-income customers tend more to accept the offer). Similarly, negative coefficients indicate that a higher value on that predictor is associated with a lower probability of accepting the loan offer (e.g., Age: older customers are less likely to accept the offer).

Interpreting Results in Terms of Odds (for a Profiling Goal)

Logistic models, when they are appropriate for the data, can give useful information about the roles played by different predictor variables. For example, suppose we want to know how increasing family income by one unit will affect the probability of loan acceptance. This can be found straightforwardly if we consider not probabilities, but odds.

Recall that the odds are given by

$$\text{Odds} = e^{\beta_0 + \beta_1 x_1 + \beta_2 x_2 + \cdots + \beta_q x_q}.$$

At first, let us return to the single predictor example, where we model a customer's acceptance of a personal loan offer as a function of his/her income:

$$\text{Odds}(\text{Personal Loan} = \textit{Yes} \mid \text{Income}) = e^{\beta_0 + \beta_1 \text{Income}}.$$

We can think of the model as a multiplicative model of odds. The odds that a customer with income zero will accept the loan is estimated by $e^{-6.16715 + (0.03757)(0)} = 0.0021$. These are the *base case odds*. In this example, it is obviously economically meaningless to talk about a zero income; the value zero and the corresponding base-case odds could be meaningful, however, in the context of other predictors. The odds of accepting the loan with an income of \$100K will increase by a multiplicative factor of $e^{(0.03757)(100)} = 42.8$ over the base case, so the odds that such a customer will accept the offer are $e^{-6.16715 + (0.03757)(100)} = 0.0898$.

Suppose that the value of Income, or in general X_1, is increased by one unit from x_1 to $x_1 + 1$, while the other predictors are held at their current value $(x_2, \ldots, x_{12})$. We get the odds ratio

$$\frac{\text{odds}(x_1 + 1, x_2, \ldots, x_{12})}{\text{odds}(x_1, \ldots, x_{12})} = \frac{e^{\beta_0 + \beta_1(x_1 + 1) + \beta_2 x_2 + \cdots + \beta_{12} x_{12}}}{e^{\beta_0 + \beta_1 x_1 + \beta_2 x_2 + \cdots + \beta_{12} x_{12}}} = e^{\beta_1}.$$

This tells us that a single unit increase in X_1, holding $X_2, \ldots, X_{12}$ constant, is associated with an increase in the odds that a customer accepts the offer by a factor of e^{β_1}. In other words, e^{β_1} is the multiplicative factor by which the odds (of belonging to class 1) increase when the value of X_1 is increased by 1 unit, *holding all other predictors constant*. If $\beta_1 < 0$, an increase in X_1 is associated with a decrease in the odds of belonging to class 1, whereas a positive value of β_1 is associated with an increase in the odds.

When a predictor is a dummy variable, the interpretation is technically the same but has a different practical meaning. For instance, the coefficient for CD.Account was estimated from the data to be 4.023356. Recall that the reference group is customers not holding a CD account. We interpret this coefficient as follows: $e^{4.023356} = 55.9$ are the odds that a customer who has a CD account will accept the offer relative to a customer who does not have a CD account, holding all other variables constant. This means that customers who hold CD accounts at Universal Bank are more likely to accept the offer than customers without a CD account (holding all other variables constant).

The advantage of reporting results in odds as opposed to probabilities is that statements such as those above are true for any value of X_1. Unless X_1 is a dummy variable, we cannot apply such statements about the effect of increasing X_1 by a single unit to probabilities. This is because the result depends on the actual value of X_1. So if we increase X_1 from, say, 3 to 4, the effect on p, the probability of belonging to class 1, will be different than if we increase X_1 from 30 to 31. In short, the change in the probability, p, for a unit increase in a particular predictor variable, while holding all other predictors constant, is not a constant—it depends on the specific values of the predictor variables. We therefore talk about probabilities only in the context of specific records.

10.4 EVALUATING CLASSIFICATION PERFORMANCE

The general measures of performance that were described in Chapter 5 are used to assess the logistic model performance. Recall that there are several performance measures, the most popular being those based on the confusion matrix (accuracy alone or combined with costs) and the cumulative gains chart. As in other classification methods, the goal is to find a model that accurately classifies records to their class, using only the predictor information. A variant of this goal is *ranking* or finding a model that does a superior job of identifying the members of a particular class of interest for a set of new records (which might come at some cost to overall accuracy). Since the training data are used for selecting the model, we expect the model to perform quite well for those data and therefore prefer to test its performance on the holdout set. Recall that the data in the holdout set were not involved in the model building, and thus we can use them to test the model's ability to classify data that it has not "seen" before.

To obtain the confusion matrix from a logistic regression analysis, we use the estimated equation to predict the probability of class membership (the *propensities*) for each record in the holdout set and use the cutoff value to decide on the class assignment of these records. We then compare these classifications with the actual class memberships of these records. In the Universal Bank case, we use the estimated model in Equation (10.10) to predict the probability of offer acceptance in a holdout set that contains 2000 customers (these data were not used in the modeling step). Technically, this is done by predicting the logit using the estimated model in Equation (10.10) and then obtaining the probabilities p through the relation $p = e^{\text{logit}}/(1 + e^{\text{logit}})$. We then compare these probabilities with our chosen cutoff value in order to classify each of the 2000 holdout records as acceptors or nonacceptors.

Table 10.3 shows propensities for four records in the holdout set. Suppose that we use a cutoff of 0.5. We see that the first customer has a probability of accepting the offer, p1, that is lower than the cutoff of 0.5, and therefore he/she is classified as nonacceptor (0). And indeed, this customer was a nonacceptor (actual = 0). The second and third customers' probability of acceptance is estimated by the model to exceed 0.5, and they are therefore classified as acceptors (1). While the third customer was indeed an acceptor (actual = 1), our model misclassified the second customer as an acceptor, when in fact he/she was a nonacceptor (actual = 0). The fourth customer is also missclassified; this time as a nonacceptor while he/she was an acceptor.

Another set of useful tools for assessing model classification performance are the cumulative gains chart and decile-wise lift chart (see Chapter 5). Figure 10.3 illustrates the charts obtained for the personal loan offer logistic model using the

---

TABLE 10.3   **PROPENSITIES FOR THE FIRST FIVE CUSTOMERS IN HOLDOUT DATA**

---

 code for using logistic regression to generate predicted probabilities

---

```
# use predict() with type = "response" to compute predicted probabilities.
logit.reg.pred <- predict(logit.reg, holdout.df[, -8], type = "prob")

# display four different cases
interestingCases = c(1, 12, 32, 1333)
data.frame(
  actual = holdout.df$Personal.Loan[interestingCases],
  p0 = logit.reg.pred[interestingCases, 1],
  p1 = logit.reg.pred[interestingCases, 2],
  predicted = ifelse(logit.reg.pred[interestingCases, 2] > 0.5, 1, 0)
)
```

Output

---

	actual	p0	p1	predicted
1	0	1.000	0.000373	0
2	1	0.233	0.766630	1
3	1	0.298	0.701792	1
4	0	0.315	0.685438	1

---

code for creating cumulative gains chart and decile-wise lift chart

```
library(gains)
actual <- ifelse(holdout.df$Personal.Loan == "Yes", 1, 0)
gain <- gains(actual, logit.reg.pred[,2], groups=length(actual) - 2)

# plot gains chart
nactual <-sum(actual)
g1 <- ggplot() +
  geom_line(aes(x=gain$cume.obs, y=gain$cume.pct.of.total * nactual)) +
  geom_line(aes(x=c(0, max(gain$cume.obs)), y=c(0, nactual)), color="darkgrey") +
  labs(x="# Cases", y="Cumulative")

# plot decile-wise lift chart
gain10 <- gains(actual, logit.reg.pred[,2], groups=10)
g2 <- ggplot(mapping=aes(x=gain10$depth, y=gain10$lift / 100)) +
  geom_col(fill="steelblue") +
  geom_text(aes(label=round(gain10$lift / 100, 1)), vjust=-0.2, size=3) +
  ylim(0, 8) + labs(x="Percentile", y="Lift")
grid.arrange(g1, g2, ncol=2)
```

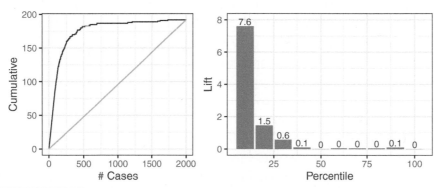

FIGURE 10.3   (LEFT) CUMULATIVE GAINS CHART AND (RIGHT) DECILE-WISE LIFT CHART FOR
THE HOLDOUT DATA FOR UNIVERSAL BANK LOAN OFFER

holdout set. In the cumulative gains chart, the "lift" over the base curve indicates for a given number of cases (read on the x-axis) the additional responders that you can identify by using the model beyond those you would get through random selection. The same information for percentiles is portrayed in the decile-wise lift chart: Taking the 10% of the records that are ranked by the model as "most probable 1's" yields 7.6 times as many 1's as would simply selecting 10% of the records at random.

10.5 VARIABLE SELECTION

The next step includes searching for alternative models. One option is to look for simpler models by trying to reduce the number of predictors used. We can also build more complex models that reflect interactions among predictors by creating and including new variables that are derived from the predictors. For example, if we hypothesize that there is an interactive effect between income and family size, we should add an interaction term of the form Income × Family. The choice among the set of alternative models is guided primarily by performance on the validation data. For models that perform roughly equally well, simpler models are generally preferred over more complex models. Note also that performance on validation data may be overly optimistic when it comes to predicting performance on data that have not been exposed to the model at all. This is because when the validation data are used to select a final model among a set of model, we are selecting based on how well the model performs with those data and therefore may be incorporating some of the random idiosyncrasies of the validation data into the judgment about the best model. The model still may be the best for the validation data among those considered, but it will probably not do as well with the unseen data. Therefore, it is useful to evaluate the chosen model on a new holdout set to get a sense of how well it will perform on new data. Alternatively, we can perform variable selection on the training set using cross-validation, and then evaluate the chosen model on the holdout set. In addition, one must consider practical issues such as costs of collecting variables, error-proneness, and model complexity in the selection of the final model.

As in linear regression, in logistic regression, we can use automated variable selection heuristics such as stepwise regression, forward selection, and backward elimination (see Section 6.4 in Chapter 6). For example, use method *glmStepAIC* and family *binomial* with **caret**'s *train* function. This selects predictors using the *MASS::stepAIC* method and the *AIC* criterion. If you are not using **caret**, use function *step()* in the **stats** package or function *stepAIC()* in the **MASS** package for stepwise, forward, and backward elimination. If the dataset is not too large, we can even try an exhaustive search over all possible models (use R function *glmulti()* in package **glmulti**, although it can be slow).

We can also control the complexity of the model using regularization by adding L1 or L2 penalties, as discussed in Section 6.4. In **caret**, we select the method *glmnet* with the additional argument *family="gaussian"* and the two parameters λ and α. When $\lambda = 0$, no regularization is applied (the α parameter is ignored), yielding ordinary logistic regression. We illustrate the use of regularized logistic regression in Section 10.7.

10.6 LOGISTIC REGRESSION FOR MULTI-CLASS CLASSIFICATION

The logistic model for a binary outcome can be extended for more than two classes. Suppose that there are m classes. Using a logistic regression model, for each record we would have m probabilities of belonging to each of the m classes. Since the m probabilities must add up to 1, we need to estimate only $m - 1$ probabilities.

Ordinal Classes

Ordinal classes are classes that have a meaningful order. For example, in stock recommendations, the three classes *buy*, *hold*, and *sell* can be treated as ordered. As a simple rule, if classes can be numbered in a meaningful way, we consider them ordinal. When the number of classes is large (typically, more than 5), we can treat the outcome variable as continuous and perform multiple linear regression. When $m = 2$, the logistic model described above is used. We therefore need an extension of the logistic regression for a small number of ordinal classes ($3 \leq m \leq 5$). There are several ways to extend the binary-class case. Here, we describe the *proportional odds* or *cumulative logit method*. For other methods, see Hosmer and Lemeshow (2000).

For simplicity of interpretation and computation, we look at *cumulative* probabilities of class membership. For example, in the stock recommendations, we have $m = 3$ classes. Let us denote them by $1 = buy$, $2 = hold$, and $3 = sell$. The probabilities estimated by the model are $P(Y \leq 1)$ (the probability of a *buy* recommendation) and $P(Y \leq 2)$ (the probability of a *buy* or *hold* recommendation). The three noncumulative probabilities of class membership can easily be recovered from the two cumulative probabilities:

$$
\begin{aligned}
P(Y = 1) &= P(Y \leq 1), \\
P(Y = 2) &= P(Y \leq 2) - P(Y \leq 1), \\
P(Y = 3) &= 1 - P(Y \leq 2).
\end{aligned}
$$

Next, we want to model each logit as a function of the predictors. Corresponding to each of the $m-1$ cumulative probabilities is a logit. In our example, we would have

$$
\text{logit}(buy) = \log \frac{P(Y \leq 1)}{1 - P(Y \leq 1)},
$$

$$
\text{logit}(buy \text{ or } hold) = \log \frac{P(Y \leq 2)}{1 - P(Y \leq 2)}.
$$

Each of the logits is then modeled as a linear function of the predictors (as in the two-class case). If in the stock recommendations we have a single predictor value x, we compute two logit values using two equations:

$$
\begin{aligned}
\text{logit}(buy) &= \alpha_0 + \beta_1 x, \\
\text{logit}(buy \text{ or } hold) &= \beta_0 + \beta_1 x.
\end{aligned}
$$

This means that both lines have the same slope (β_1) but different intercepts. Once the coefficients $\alpha_0, \beta_0, \beta_1$ are estimated, we can compute the class membership probabilities by rewriting the logit equations in terms of probabilities. For the three-class case, for example, we would have

$$P(Y = 1) \;=\; P(Y \le 1) = \frac{1}{1 + e^{-(a_0 + b_1 x)}},$$

$$P(Y = 2) \;=\; P(Y \le 2) - P(Y \le 1) = \frac{1}{1 + e^{-(b_0 + b_1 x)}} - \frac{1}{1 + e^{-(a_0 + b_1 x)}},$$

$$P(Y = 3) \;=\; 1 - P(Y \le 2) = 1 - \frac{1}{1 + e^{-(b_0 + b_1 x)}},$$

where a_0, b_0, and b_1 are the estimates obtained from the training set.

For each record, we now have the estimated probabilities that it belongs to each of the classes. In our example, each stock would have three probabilities: for a *buy* recommendation, a *hold* recommendation, and a *sell* recommendation. The last step is to classify the record into one of the classes. This is done by assigning it to the class with the highest membership probability. For example, if a stock had estimated probabilities $P(Y = 1) = 0.2$, $P(Y = 2) = 0.3$, and $P(Y = 3) = 0.5$, we would classify it as getting a *sell* recommendation.

Nominal Classes

When the classes cannot be ordered and are simply different from one another, we are in the case of nominal classes. An example is the choice between several brands of cereal. A simple way to verify that the classes are nominal is when it makes sense to tag them as $A, B, C, \ldots$, and the assignment of letters to classes does not matter. For simplicity, let us assume that there are $m = 3$ brands of cereal that consumers can choose from (assuming that each consumer chooses one). Then, we estimate the probabilities $P(Y = A)$, $P(Y = B)$, and $P(Y = C)$. As before, if we know two of the probabilities, the third probability is determined. We therefore use one of the classes as the reference class. Let us use C as the reference brand.

The goal, once again, is to model the class membership as a function of predictors. So in the cereals example, we might want to predict which cereal will be chosen if we know the cereal's price x.

Next, we form $m - 1$ pseudologit equations that are linear in the predictors. In our example, we would have

$$\mathrm{logit(A)} = \log \frac{P(Y = A)}{P(Y = C)} = \alpha_0 + \alpha_1 x,$$

$$\mathrm{logit(B)} = \log \frac{P(Y = B)}{P(Y = C)} = \beta_0 + \beta_1 x.$$

Once the four coefficients are estimated from the training set, we can estimate the class membership probabilities.[6]

$$P(Y = A) = \frac{e^{a_0+a_1x}}{1 + e^{a_0+a_1x} + e^{b_0+b_1x}},$$

$$P(Y = B) = \frac{e^{b_0+b_1x}}{1 + e^{a_0+a_1x} + e^{b_0+b_1x}},$$

$$P(Y = C) = 1 - P(Y = A) - P(Y = B),$$

where a_0, a_1, b_0, and b_1 are the coefficient estimates obtained from the training set. Finally, a record is assigned to the class that has the highest probability.

Table 10.4 presents the R code for ordinal and nominal multinomial regression.

10.7 EXAMPLE OF COMPLETE ANALYSIS: PREDICTING DELAYED FLIGHTS

Predicting flight delays can be useful to a variety of organizations: airport authorities, airlines, and aviation authorities. At times, joint task forces have been formed to address the problem. Such an organization, if it were to provide ongoing real-time assistance with flight delays, would benefit from some advance notice about flights likely to be delayed.

In this simplified illustration, we look at six predictors (see Table 10.5). The outcome of interest is whether the flight is delayed or not (*delayed* means more than 15 minutes late). Our data consist of all flights from the Washington, DC area into the New York City area during January 2004. The percent of delayed flights among these 2201 flights is 19.5%. The data were obtained from the Bureau of Transportation Statistics website (www.transtats.bts.gov).

The goal is to predict accurately whether a new flight, not in this dataset, will be delayed or not. The outcome variable is a variable called Flight Status, coded as *delayed* or *ontime*.

Other information available on the website, such as distance and arrival time, is irrelevant because we are looking at a certain route (distance, flight time, etc.

---

[6]From the two logit equations, we see that

$$P(Y = A) = P(Y = C)e^{\alpha_0+\alpha_1x} \qquad P(Y = B) = P(Y = C)e^{\beta_0+\beta_1x}$$

Since $P(Y = A) + P(Y = B) + P(Y = C) = 1$, we get

$$P(Y = C) = 1 - P(Y = C)e^{\alpha_0+\alpha_1x} - P(Y = C)e^{\beta_0+\beta_1x} = \frac{1}{e^{\alpha_0+\alpha_1x}+e^{\beta_0+\beta_1x}}.$$

By plugging this form into the two equations above it, we also obtain the membership probabilities in classes A and B.

TABLE 10.4   ORDINAL AND NOMINAL MULTINOMIAL REGRESSION IN R

---

 code for logistic regression with more than 2 classes

```
# simulate simple data
Y = rep(c("a", "b", "c"), 100)
x = rep(c(1, 2, 3), 100) +  rnorm(300, 0, 1)

# ordinal logistic regression
Y = factor(Y, ordered = T)
MASS::polr(Y ~ x)

# nominal logistic regression
Y = factor(Y, ordered = F)
nnet::multinom(Y ~ x)
```

Output

```
> MASS::polr(Y ~ x)
Call:
polr(formula = Y ~ x)

Coefficients:
       x
1.110152

Intercepts:
     a|b       b|c
1.328406 3.218809

Residual Deviance: 543.3761
AIC: 549.3761

> nnet::multinom(Y ~ x)
# weights:  9 (4 variable)
initial   value 329.583687
iter  10 value 268.610761
iter  10 value 268.610760
final   value 268.610760
converged
Call:
multinom(formula = Y ~ x)

Coefficients:
  (Intercept)        x
b   -1.715653 1.058281
c   -3.399917 1.738026

Residual Deviance: 537.2215
AIC: 545.2215
```

TABLE 10.5	DESCRIPTION OF PREDICTORS FOR FLIGHT DELAYS EXAMPLE

Day of Week	Coded as 1 = Monday, 2 = Tuesday,..., 7 = Sunday
Departure Time	Broken down into 18 intervals between 6:00 AM and 10:00 PM
Origin	Three airport codes: DCA (Reagan National), IAD (Dulles), and BWI (Baltimore–Washington Int'l)
Destination	Three airport codes: JFK (Kennedy), LGA (LaGuardia), and EWR (Newark)
Carrier	Eight airline codes: CO (Continental), DH (Atlantic Coast), DL (Delta), MQ (American Eagle), OH (Comair), RU (Continental Express), UA (United), and US (USAirways)
Weather	Coded as 1 if there was a weather-related delay

TABLE 10.6	SAMPLE OF 20 FLIGHTS

Flight status	Carrier	Day of week	Departure time	Destination	Origin	Weather
ontime	DL	2	728	LGA	DCA	0
delayed	US	3	1600	LGA	DCA	0
ontime	DH	5	1242	EWR	IAD	0
ontime	US	2	2057	LGA	DCA	0
ontime	DH	3	1603	JFK	IAD	0
ontime	CO	6	1252	EWR	DCA	0
ontime	RU	6	1728	EWR	DCA	0
ontime	DL	5	1031	LGA	DCA	0
ontime	RU	6	1722	EWR	IAD	0
delayed	US	1	627	LGA	DCA	0
delayed	DH	2	1756	JFK	IAD	0
ontime	MQ	6	1529	JFK	DCA	0
ontime	US	6	1259	LGA	DCA	0
ontime	DL	2	1329	LGA	DCA	0
ontime	RU	2	1453	EWR	BWI	0
ontime	RU	5	1356	EWR	DCA	0
delayed	DH	7	2244	LGA	IAD	0
ontime	US	7	1053	LGA	DCA	0
ontime	US	2	1057	LGA	DCA	0
ontime	US	4	632	LGA	DCA	0

should be approximately equal for all flights in the data). A sample of the data for 20 flights is shown in Table 10.6. Figures 10.4 and 10.5 show visualizations of the relationships between flight delays and different predictors or combinations of predictors. From Figure 10.4, we see that Sundays and Tuesdays saw the largest proportion of delays. Delay rates also seem to differ by carrier, by time of day,[7] as well as by origin and destination airports. For Weather, we see a strong distinction between delays when Weather = 1 (in that case there is always

---

[7]In the data, *CRS_DEP_TIME* is the scheduled departure time, and *DEP_TIME* is the actual departure time. Since we are interested in analyzing the effect of departure time, we use *CRS_DEP_TIME* and ignore the actual *DEP_TIME*.

code for generating bar charts of average delay vs. predictors

```
# code for generating top-left bar chart
# for other plots replace the aggregating variable in the group_by and ggplot commands
# adjust the x-label
library(tidyverse)

delays.df <- mlba::FlightDelays
averageDelay <- delays.df %>%
  group_by(DAY_WEEK) %>%
  summarize(mean=mean(Flight.Status == 'delayed'))

ggplot(averageDelay, aes(x=DAY_WEEK, y=mean)) +
  geom_col(fill='steelblue') +
  labs(x='Day of Week', y='Average delay')
```

FIGURE 10.4   PROPORTION OF DELAYED FLIGHTS BY EACH OF THE SIX PREDICTORS. TIME OF
DAY IS DIVIDED INTO HOURLY BINS

code for generating heatmap for exploring flight delays

```
# create matrix for plot
agg <- delays.df %>%
  mutate(isDelay=1 * (delays.df$Flight.Status == "delayed")) %>%
  group_by(DAY_WEEK, CARRIER, ORIGIN) %>%
  summarize(mean=mean(isDelay))

# plot with ggplot
# use facet_grid() with arguments scales = "free" and space = "free" to skip
# missing values.
ggplot(agg, aes(y=CARRIER, x=DAY_WEEK, fill=mean)) +
  geom_tile() +
  facet_grid(ORIGIN ~ ., scales="free", space="free") +
  scale_fill_gradient(low="white", high="steelblue")
```

FIGURE 10.5   PERCENT OF DELAYED FLIGHTS (DARKER = HIGHER %DELAYS) BY DAY OF WEEK, ORIGIN, AND CARRIER

a delay) and Weather = 0. The heatmap in Figure 10.5 reveals some specific combinations with high rates of delays, such as Sunday flights by carrier RU, departing from BWI, or Sunday flights by MQ departing from DCA. We can also see combinations with very low delay rates.

Our main goal is to find a model that can obtain accurate classifications of new flights based on their predictor information. An alternative goal is finding a certain percentage of flights that are most/least likely to get delayed (*ranking*).

And a third different goal is profiling flights: finding out which factors are associated with a delay (not only in this sample but also in the entire population of flights on this route), and for those factors we would like to quantify these effects. A logistic regression model can be used for all these goals, albeit in different ways.

Data Preprocessing

Create a binary outcome variable called isDelay that takes the value 1 if Flight Status = *delayed* and 0 otherwise. Transform day of week into a categorical variable, and bin and categorize the departure time into hourly intervals between 6:00 AM and 10:00 PM. Set reference categories for categorical variables: BWI for departure airport, EWR for arrival, CO for carrier, and Monday for day (see Figure 10.7 for R code). This yields a total of 34 dummies. In addition, we have a single dummy for Weather. While this is a large number of predictors, we start by using all of them, look at performance, and then explore reducing the dimension. We then partition the data into training set (60%) and holdout set (40%). We use the training set to fit a model. Cross-validation and the holdout set are used to assess the model's performance.

Model-Fitting and Estimation

The estimated model with 34 predictors is shown in Table 10.7. Note how negative coefficients in the logit model (the "Estimate" column) translate into odds coefficients lower than 1 and positive logit coefficients translate into odds coefficients larger than 1.

Model Interpretation

The coefficient for Arrival Airport JFK (DESTJFK) is estimated as -0.203. Note that the reference group is EWR. We interpret this coefficient as follows: $e^{-0.203} = 0.816$ are the odds of a flight arriving at JFK being delayed relative to a flight to EWR being delayed (= the base-case odds), holding all other variables constant. This means that flights to JFK are less likely to be delayed than those to EWR (holding everything else constant). If we consider statistical significance of the coefficients, we see that in general, the origin and destination airports are not associated with the chance of delays. For carriers, most carriers have negative coefficients with the exception of MQ which has odds of delay around 1, similar to the base carrier (CO). Weather has an enormous coefficient, which is not statistically significant. Flights leaving on Sunday or Monday have, on average, odds of 0.9–1 of delays relative to other days of the week (the other days have all odds lower than 0.78). Also, odds of delays appear to change over the course of the day, with the most noticeable difference from the reference category (6–7 AM) being 7–9 PM with over 3 times the odds of delay.

TABLE 10.7   ESTIMATED LOGISTIC REGRESSION MODEL FOR DELAYED FLIGHTS (BASED ON THE TRAINING SET)

 code for data preprocessing and running logistic regression

```
df <- mlba::FlightDelays %>%
  mutate(
    # transform variables and create bins
    DAY_WEEK = factor(DAY_WEEK, levels=c(1:7),
                      labels=c("Mon", "Tue", "Wed", "Thu", "Fri", "Sat", "Sun")),
    CRS_DEP_TIME = factor(round(CRS_DEP_TIME / 100)),
    Flight.Status = factor(Flight.Status, levels=c("ontime", "delayed")),
    # convert other variables to factors
    across(c(ORIGIN,DEST, CARRIER, DAY_WEEK), factor)
  ) %>%
  # select predictors and outcome variables
  select(DAY_WEEK, CRS_DEP_TIME, ORIGIN, DEST, CARRIER, Weather, Flight.Status)

# create training and holdout sets
set.seed(1)
idx <- caret::createDataPartition(df$Flight.Status, p=0.6, list=FALSE)
train.df <- df[idx, ]
holdout.df <- df[-idx, ]

# run logistic model, and show coefficients and odds
trControl <- caret::trainControl(method="cv", number=5, allowParallel=TRUE)
model <- caret::train(Flight.Status ~ ., data=train.df,
                      method="glm", family="binomial", trControl=trControl)
round(data.frame(summary(model$finalModel)$coefficients,
                 odds = exp(coef(model$finalModel))), 5)
```

```
              Estimate Std..Error z.value Pr...z..         odds
(Intercept)   -0.21384    0.69680 -0.30689  0.75892      0.80747
DAY_WEEKTue   -0.52429    0.27952 -1.87569  0.06070      0.59197
DAY_WEEKWed   -0.69392    0.27798 -2.49626  0.01255      0.49961
DAY_WEEKThu   -0.60191    0.27030 -2.22686  0.02596      0.54776
DAY_WEEKFri   -0.26015    0.25150 -1.03440  0.30095      0.77094
DAY_WEEKSat   -1.11520    0.33755 -3.30386  0.00095      0.32785
DAY_WEEKSun   -0.10445    0.28210 -0.37026  0.71119      0.90082
CRS_DEP_TIME7 -0.43838    0.54479 -0.80467  0.42101      0.64508
CRS_DEP_TIME8 -0.24910    0.48284 -0.51590  0.60593      0.77950
CRS_DEP_TIME9 -0.63715    0.58699 -1.08545  0.27772      0.52880
CRS_DEP_TIME10 -0.15908   0.51903 -0.30649  0.75923      0.85293
CRS_DEP_TIME11 -1.22648   0.81530 -1.50434  0.13249      0.29332
CRS_DEP_TIME12 -0.35617   0.49911 -0.71361  0.47547      0.70035
CRS_DEP_TIME13 -0.66094   0.53055 -1.24576  0.21285      0.51637
CRS_DEP_TIME14 -0.20777   0.51273 -0.40523  0.68531      0.81239
CRS_DEP_TIME15  0.82860   0.39011  2.12400  0.03367      2.29011
CRS_DEP_TIME16  0.25165   0.43368  0.58025  0.56174      1.28614
CRS_DEP_TIME17  0.65296   0.39735  1.64326  0.10033      1.92121
CRS_DEP_TIME18  0.12476   0.55253  0.22580  0.82136      1.13288
CRS_DEP_TIME19  1.13361   0.44727  2.53450  0.01126      3.10686
CRS_DEP_TIME20  1.17696   0.53655  2.19358  0.02827      3.24451
CRS_DEP_TIME21  0.72162   0.42745  1.68820  0.09137      2.05777
ORIGINDCA     -0.61459    0.43080 -1.42664  0.15368      0.54086
ORIGINIAD     -0.47502    0.42356 -1.12150  0.26208      0.62187
DESTJFK       -0.20290    0.34695 -0.58482  0.55867      0.81636
DESTLGA        0.14842    0.34988  0.42422  0.67141      1.16001
CARRIERDH     -0.35048    0.63475 -0.55216  0.58084      0.70435
CARRIERDL     -1.12127    0.53402 -2.09968  0.03576      0.32587
CARRIERMQ      0.01041    0.51025  0.02039  0.98373      1.01046
CARRIEROH     -1.69844    0.92132 -1.84349  0.06526      0.18297
CARRIERRU     -0.65571    0.45153 -1.45219  0.14645      0.51908
CARRIERUA     -0.48542    0.99757 -0.48660  0.62654      0.61544
CARRIERUS     -1.43210    0.54216 -2.64148  0.00825      0.23881
Weather       17.65528  520.28452  0.03393  0.97293 46514573.53201
```

Model Performance

How should we measure the performance of models? One possible measure is "percent of flights correctly classified." Accurate classification can be obtained from the confusion matrix for the holdout data. The confusion matrix gives a sense of the classification accuracy and what type of misclassification is more frequent. From the confusion matrix and error rates in Figure 10.6, it can be seen

 code for evaluating performance of all-predictor model

```
library(gains)
actual <- ifelse(holdout.df$Flight.Status == "delayed", 1, 0)
pred <- predict(model, holdout.df, type="prob")[, 2]
gain <- gains(actual, pred, groups=length(pred))

nactual <-sum(actual)
ggplot() +
  geom_line(aes(x=gain$cume.obs, y=gain$cume.pct.of.total * nactual)) +
  geom_line(aes(x=c(0, max(gain$cume.obs)), y=c(0, nactual)), color="darkgrey") +
  labs(x="# Cases", y="Cumulative")
```

Output

```
Confusion Matrix and Statistics

          Reference
Prediction ontime delayed
    ontime    704     155
    delayed     5      16

          Accuracy : 0.8182
```

FIGURE 10.6   CONFUSION MATRIX AND CUMULATIVE GAINS CHART FOR THE FLIGHT DELAY HOLDOUT DATA USING ALL PREDICTORS

that the model more accurately classifies nondelayed flights and is less accurate in classifying flights that were delayed. (*Note*: The same pattern appears in the confusion matrix for the training data, so it is not surprising to see it emerge for new data.) If there is an asymmetric cost structure so that one type of misclassification is more costly than the other, the cutoff value can be selected to minimize the cost. Of course, this tweaking should be carried out on the training data and assessed only using the holdout data.

In most conceivable situations, the purpose of the model would be to identify those flights most likely to be delayed among a set of flights so that resources can be directed toward either reducing the delay or mitigating its effects. Air traffic controllers might work to open up additional air routes or allocate more controllers to a specific area for a short time. Airlines might bring on personnel to rebook passengers and to activate standby flight crews and aircraft. Hotels might allocate space for stranded travelers. In all cases, the resources available are going to be limited and might vary over time and from organization to organization. In this situation, the most useful model would provide an ordering of flights by their probability of delay, letting the model users decide how far down that list to go in taking action. Therefore, model lift is a useful measure of performance—as you move down that list of flights, ordered by their delay probability, how much better does the model do in predicting delay than would a naive model which is simply the average delay rate for all flights? From the gains curve for the holdout data (Figure 10.6), we see that our model is superior to the baseline (simple random selection of flights).

Variable Selection

From the data exploration charts (Figures 10.4 and 10.5) and from the coefficient table for the flights delay model (Table 10.7), it appears that several of the predictors could be dropped or coded differently. Additionally, we look at the number of flights in different categories to identify categories with very few or no flights—such categories are candidates for removal or merger (see Table 10.8).

TABLE 10.8	NUMBER OF FLIGHTS BY CARRIER AND ORIGIN		
	BWI	DCA	IAD	Total
CO		94		94
DH		27	524	551
DL		388		388
MQ		295		295
OH	30			30
RU	115	162	131	408
UA			31	31
US		404		404
Total	145	1370	686	2201

First, we find that most carriers depart from a single airport (DCA): for those that depart from all three airports, the delay rates are similar regardless of airport. We therefore drop the departure airport distinction by excluding Origin dummies and find that the model performance and fit are not harmed. We also drop the destination airport for a practical reason: not all carriers fly to all airports. Our model would then be invalid for prediction in nonexistent combinations of carrier and destination airport. We also try grouping carriers, day of week, and hour of day into fewer categories that are more distinguishable with respect to delays. For example, Sundays and Mondays seem to have a similar rate of delays, which differs from the lower rate on Tuesday–Saturday. We therefore group the days of week into Sunday+Monday and Other, resulting in a single dummy variable.

Table 10.9 displays the estimated smaller model, with its training and hold-out confusion matrices and error rates. Figure 10.7 presents the gains chart on the holdout set. It can be seen that this model competes well with the larger model in terms of classification accuracy and gains chart while using much less information.

FIGURE 10.7   GAINS CHART FOR THE LOGISTIC REGRESSION MODEL WITH FEWER PREDICTORS (BLACK) AND THE LASSO LOGISTIC REGRESSION MODEL (RED) ON THE HOLDOUT SET. THE GAINS CHART OF THE FULL MODEL IS SHOWN IN GRAY FOR REFERENCE

Finally, we try an automated variable selection approach, by using regularization with L1 penalty (lasso). The code is shown in Table 10.10. The 5-fold cross-validation results in a model with 23 variables. It should be noted that the resulting model depends strongly on the splitting of the dataset.

We therefore conclude with a six-predictor model that requires only knowledge of the carrier, the day of week, the hour of the day, and whether it is likely that there will be a delay due to weather. However, this weather variable refers to actual weather at flight time, not a forecast, and is not known in advance! If the aim is to predict in advance whether a particular flight will be

TABLE 10.9   **LOGISTIC REGRESSION MODEL WITH FEWER PREDICTORS**

code for logistic regression with fewer predictors

```
# fewer predictors
reduced.df <- mlba::FlightDelays %>%
  mutate(
    HOUR = round(CRS_DEP_TIME / 100),
    SUN_MON = DAY_WEEK %in% c(1, 7),
    CARRIER_CO_MQ = CARRIER %in% c("CO", "MQ"),
    CARRIER_DL_US = CARRIER %in% c("DL", "US"),
    CRS_DEP_TIME15 = HOUR %in% c(15),
    EVENING = HOUR %in% c(19, 20, 21),
    Flight.Status = factor(Flight.Status, levels=c("ontime", "delayed"))
  ) %>%
  select(Weather, SUN_MON, CARRIER_CO_MQ, CARRIER_DL_US, CRS_DEP_TIME15, EVENING,
         Flight.Status)
# create training and holdout sets
set.seed(1)
idx <- caret::createDataPartition(reduced.df$Flight.Status, p=0.6, list=FALSE)
train.df <- reduced.df[idx, ]
holdout.df <- reduced.df[-idx, ]

# run logistic model, and show coefficients and odds
model <- caret::train(Flight.Status ~ ., data=train.df,
                      method="glm", family="binomial", trControl=trControl)
summary(model$finalModel)

# evaluate
pred <- predict(model, holdout.df)
confusionMatrix(pred, holdout.df$Flight.Status)
```

Output

```
> summary(model)

                    Estimate Std. Error z value        Pr(>|z|)
(Intercept)         -1.7872     0.1292  -13.831 < 0.0000000000000002 ***
Weather             17.8081   519.4979    0.034         0.97265
SUN_MONTRUE          0.5186     0.1625    3.190         0.00142 **
CARRIER_CO_MQTRUE    0.3501     0.1837    1.906         0.05667 .
CARRIER_DL_USTRUE   -0.7931     0.1857   -4.272         0.000019414 ***
CRS_DEP_TIME15TRUE   0.7798     0.1968    3.963         0.000073959 ***
EVENINGTRUE          1.0021     0.1923    5.210         0.000000189 ***
---
Signif. codes:  0 '***' 0.001 '**' 0.01 '*' 0.05 '.' 0.1 ' ' 1

> confusionMatrix(pred, holdout.df$Flight.Status)
          Reference
Prediction ontime delayed
    ontime    706     155
    delayed     3      16

                Accuracy : 0.8205
```

TABLE 10.10   REGULARIZED LOGISTIC REGRESSION MODEL FOR DELAYED FLIGHTS

 code for running regularized logistic regression

```
# recreate training and holdout sets
set.seed(1)
idx <- caret::createDataPartition(df$Flight.Status, p=0.6, list=FALSE)
train.df <- df[idx, ]
holdout.df <- df[-idx, ]

# run logistic model, and show coefficients and odds
trControl <- caret::trainControl(method="cv", number=5, allowParallel=TRUE)
tuneGrid <- expand.grid(lambda=10^seq(-1, -3, by=-0.1), alpha=1)
model <- caret::train(Flight.Status ~ ., data=train.df,
                  method="glmnet",  family="binomial",
                  tuneGrid=tuneGrid, trControl=trControl)
coefs <- coef(model$finalModel, s=model$bestTune$lambda)
coefs[which(as.matrix(coefs)!=0),]

confusionMatrix(predict(model, holdout.df), holdout.df$Flight.Status)

   (Intercept)    DAY_WEEKTue    DAY_WEEKWed  DAY_WEEKThu    DAY_WEEKSat    DAY_WEEKSun
      -1.47757       -0.14637       -0.32775    -0.25944       -0.74103        0.05774
 CRS_DEP_TIME7  CRS_DEP_TIME8  CRS_DEP_TIME9 CRS_DEP_TIME11 CRS_DEP_TIME12 CRS_DEP_TIME13
      -0.06598       -0.02352       -0.39623    -0.64285       -0.10597       -0.27250
CRS_DEP_TIME14 CRS_DEP_TIME15 CRS_DEP_TIME16 CRS_DEP_TIME17 CRS_DEP_TIME19 CRS_DEP_TIME20
      -0.01618        0.74212        0.10448     0.68014        1.08566        0.88910
CRS_DEP_TIME21       ORIGINDCA        DESTJFK    CARRIERDH      CARRIERDL      CARRIERMQ
       0.61381       -0.02787       -0.04498     0.09241       -0.48586        0.34602
     CARRIEROH       CARRIERUS        Weather
      -0.46270       -0.74293        4.34313

Confusion Matrix and Statistics

          Reference
Prediction ontime delayed
   ontime    709     159
   delayed     0      12

          Accuracy : 0.819
```

delayed, a model without Weather must be used. In contrast, if the goal is pro-filing delayed vs. ontime flights, we can keep Weather in the model to allow evaluating the impact of the other factors while holding weather constant [that is, (approximately) comparing days with weather delays to days without weather delays].

To conclude, based on the model built from January 2004 data, the highest chance of an ontime flight from DC to New York is on Tuesday–Saturday around noon, on Delta, Comair, United, or USAirways. And clearly, good weather is advantageous!

PROBLEMS

10.1 Financial Condition of Banks. The dataset *mlba::Banks* includes data on a sample of 20 banks. The "Financial Condition" column records the judgment of an expert on the financial condition of each bank. This outcome variable takes one of two possible values—*weak* or *strong*—according to the financial condition of the bank. The predictors are two ratios used in the financial analysis of banks: TotLns&Lses/Assets is the ratio of total loans and leases to total assets, and TotExp/Assets is the ratio of total expenses to total assets. The target is to use the two ratios for classifying the financial condition of a new bank.

    Run a logistic regression model (on the entire dataset) that models the status of a bank as a function of the two financial measures provided. The "Financial Condition" column encodes *weak* as 1 and *strong* as 0. Use the default threshold of 0.5.

a. Write the estimated equation that associates the financial condition of a bank with its two predictors in three formats:

    i. The logit as a function of the predictors.

    ii. The odds as a function of the predictors.

    iii. The probability as a function of the predictors.

b. Consider a new bank whose total loans and leases/assets ratio = 0.6 and total expenses/assets ratio = 0.11. From your logistic regression model, estimate the following four quantities for this bank (use R to do all the intermediate calculations; show your final answers to four decimal places): the logit, the odds, the probability of being financially weak, and the classification of the bank (use threshold = 0.5).

c. The threshold value of 0.5 is used in conjunction with the probability of being financially weak. Compute the threshold that should be used if we want to make a classification based on the odds of being financially weak and the threshold for the corresponding logit.

d. Interpret the estimated coefficient for the total loans & leases-to-total assets ratio (TotLns&Lses/Assets) in terms of the odds of being financially weak.

e. When a bank that is in poor financial condition is misclassified as financially strong, the misclassification cost is much higher than when a financially strong bank is misclassified as weak. To minimize the expected cost of misclassification, should the cutoff value for classification (which is currently at 0.5) be increased or decreased?

10.2 Identifying Good System Administrators. A management consultant is studying the roles played by experience and training in a system administrator's ability to complete a set of tasks in a specified amount of time. In particular, she is interested in discriminating between administrators who are able to complete given tasks within a specified time and those who are not. Data are collected on the performance of 75 randomly selected administrators. They are stored in the dataset *mlba::SystemAdministrators*.

    The variable Experience measures months of full-time system administrator experience, while Training measures the number of relevant training credits. The outcome variable Completed is either *Yes* or *No*, according to whether or not the administrator completed the tasks.

a. Create a scatter plot of Experience vs. Training using color or symbol to distinguish programmers who completed the task from those who did not complete it. Which predictor(s) appear(s) potentially useful for classifying task completion?

b. Run a logistic regression model with both predictors using the entire dataset as training data. Among those who completed the task, what is the percentage of programmers incorrectly classified as failing to complete the task?

c. To decrease the percentage in part (b), should the threshold probability be increased or decreased?

d. How much experience must be accumulated by a programmer with four years of training before his or her estimated probability of completing the task exceeds 0.5?

10.3 **Sales of Riding Mowers.** A company that manufactures riding mowers wants to identify the best sales prospects for an intensive sales campaign. In particular, the manufacturer is interested in classifying households as prospective owners or nonowners on the basis of Income (in \$1000s) and Lot Size (in 1000 ft^2). The marketing expert looked at a random sample of 24 households, given in the dataset *mlba::RidingMowers*. Use all the data to fit a logistic regression of ownership on the two predictors.

a. What percentage of households in the study were owners of a riding mower?

b. Create a scatter plot of Income vs. Lot Size using color or symbol to distinguish owners from nonowners. From the scatter plot, which class seems to have a higher average income, owners or nonowners?

c. Among nonowners, what is the percentage of households classified correctly?

d. To increase the percentage of correctly classified nonowners, should the threshold probability be increased or decreased?

e. What are the odds that a household with a \$60K income and a lot size of 20,000 ft^2 is an owner?

f. What is the classification of a household with a \$60K income and a lot size of 20,000 ft^2? Use threshold = 0.5.

g. What is the minimum income that a household with 16,000 ft^2 lot size should have before it is classified as an owner?

10.4 **Competitive Auctions on eBay.com.** The dataset *mlba::eBayAuctions* contains information on 1972 auctions transacted on eBay.com during May–June 2004. The goal is to use these data to build a model that will distinguish competitive auctions from noncompetitive ones. A competitive auction is defined as an auction with at least two bids placed on the item being auctioned. The data include variables that describe the item (auction category), the seller (his or her eBay rating), and the auction terms that the seller selected (auction duration, opening price, currency, day of week of auction close). In addition, we have the price at which the auction closed. The goal is to predict whether or not an auction of interest will be competitive.

Data Preprocessing. Create dummy variables for the categorical predictors. These include Category (18 categories), Currency (USD, GBP, Euro), EndDay (Monday–Sunday), and Duration (1, 3, 5, 7, or 10 days).

a. Create pivot tables for the mean of the binary outcome (Competitive?) as a function of the various categorical variables (use the original variables, not the dummies). Use the information in the tables to reduce the number of dummies that will be used in the model. For example, categories that appear most similar with respect to the distribution of competitive auctions could be combined.

b. Split the data into training (60%) and holdout (40%) datasets. Run a logistic model with all predictors with a threshold of 0.5.

c. If we want to predict at the start of an auction whether it will be competitive, we cannot use the information on the closing price. Run a logistic model with all predictors as above, excluding price. How does this model compare with the full model with respect to predictive accuracy?

d. Interpret the meaning of the coefficient for closing price. Does closing price have a practical significance? Is it statistically significant for predicting competitiveness of auctions? (Use a 10% significance level.)

e. Use stepwise regression (use method *glmStepAIC* in the `caret` package) to find the model with the best fit to the training data based on AIC. Which predictors are used?

f. Use stepwise regression to find the model with the lowest predictive error rate (use the holdout data). Which predictors are used?

g. What is the danger of using the best predictive model that you found?

h. Explain why the best-fitting model and the best predictive models are the same or different.

i. If the major objective is accurate classification, what cutoff value should be used?

j. Based on these data, what auction settings set by the seller (duration, opening price, ending day, currency) would you recommend as being most likely to lead to a competitive auction?

## CHAPTER 11

Neural Nets

In this chapter, we describe neural networks, a flexible data-driven method that can be used for classification or prediction. Although considered a "blackbox" in terms of interpretability, neural nets have been highly successful in terms of predictive accuracy. We discuss the concepts of "nodes" and "layers" (input layers, output layers, and hidden layers) and how they connect to form the structure of a network. We then explain how a neural network is fitted to data using a numerical example. Because overfitting is a major danger with neural nets, we present a strategy for avoiding it. We describe the different parameters that a user must specify and explain the effect of each on the process. Finally, we discuss the usefulness of neural nets and their limitations.

Neural Networks in R

The main R packages introduced in this chapter are **nnet** and `neuralnet`. For deep learning, we use the `keras` package.

11.1 INTRODUCTION

Neural networks, also called *artificial neural networks*, are models for classification and prediction. The neural network is based on a model of biological activity in the brain, where neurons are interconnected and learn from experience. Neural networks mimic the way that human experts learn. The learning and memory properties of neural networks resemble the properties of human learning and memory, and they also have a capacity to generalize from particulars.

Neural nets began to be applied successfully in the late 1990s in areas such as bankruptcy trading and detecting fraud in credit card and monetary transactions.

Machine Learning for Business Analytics: Concepts, Techniques, and Applications in R, Second Edition.
Galit Shmueli, Peter C. Bruce, Peter Gedeck, Inbal Yahav, and Nitin R. Patel
© 2023 John Wiley & Sons, Inc. Published 2023 by John Wiley & Sons, Inc.

They really took off in the early 2000s with the development of more complex networks and the growing power of computers. Often called "deep learning," these complex networks have been primarily responsible for a powerful revolution in machine learning. Indeed, much of what the public thinks of as "artificial intelligence" has at its heart deep (multilayer) neural networks. Text classification and image recognition are perhaps the most ubiquitous examples, but what has captured the public imagination the most is the promise of self-driving cars. It might surprise many machine learning practitioners today to learn that an application of neural nets from the 1980s was ALVINN, an autonomous vehicle driving application for normal speeds on highways. Using as input a 30×32 grid of pixel intensities from a fixed camera on the vehicle, the classifier provides the direction of steering. The target outcome is a categorical one with 30 classes, such as *sharp left*, *straight ahead*, and *bear right*.

The main strength of neural networks is their high predictive performance. Their structure supports capturing very complex relationships between predictors and an outcome variable, which is often not possible with other predictive models.

11.2 CONCEPT AND STRUCTURE OF A NEURAL NETWORK

The idea behind neural networks is to combine the predictor information in a very flexible way that captures complicated relationships among these variables and between them and the outcome variable. For instance, recall that in linear regression models, the form of the relationship between the outcome and the predictors is specified directly by the user (see Chapter 6). In many cases, the exact form of the relationship is very complicated or is generally unknown. In linear regression modeling we might try different transformations of the predictors, interactions between predictors, and so on, but the specified form of the relationship remains linear. In comparison, in neural networks, the user is not required to specify the correct form. Instead, the network tries to learn about such relationships from the data. In fact, linear regression and logistic regression can be thought of as special cases of very simple neural networks that have only input and output layers and no hidden layers.

Although researchers have studied numerous different neural network architectures, the most successful applications of neural networks in machine learning have been *multilayer feedforward networks*. These are networks in which there is an *input layer* consisting of nodes (sometimes called *neurons*) that simply accept the predictor values and successive layers of nodes that receive input from the previous layers. The outputs of nodes in each layer are inputs to nodes in the next layer. The last layer is called the *output layer*. Layers between the input and output layers are known as *hidden layers*. A feedforward network is a fully connected network with a one-way flow and no cycles. Figure 11.1 shows a diagram for this architecture, with two hidden layers and one node in the output layer representing the outcome value to be predicted. In a classification problem with m classes, there would be m output nodes (or $m - 1$ output nodes, depending on the software).

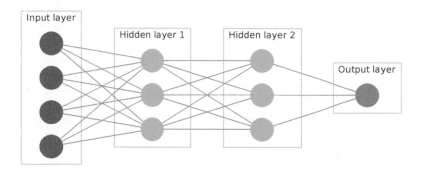

FIGURE 11.1   MULTILAYER FEEDFORWARD NEURAL NETWORK

11.3 FITTING A NETWORK TO DATA

To illustrate how a neural network is fitted to data, we start with a very small illustrative example. Although the method is by no means operational in such a small example, it is useful for explaining the main steps and operations, for showing how computations are done, and for integrating all the different aspects of neural network data fitting. We will later discuss a more realistic setting.

Example 1: Tiny Dataset

Consider the following very small dataset. Table 11.1 includes information on a tasting score for a certain processed cheese. The two predictors are scores for fat and salt, indicating the relative presence of fat and salt in the particular cheese sample (where 0 is the minimum amount possible in the manufacturing process, and 1 the maximum). The outcome variable is the cheese sample's consumer taste preference, where *like* or *dislike* indicates whether the consumer likes the cheese or not.

Figure 11.2 describes an example of a typical neural net that could be used for predicting cheese preference (*like/dislike*) by new consumers, based on these data.

We numbered the nodes in the example from 1 to 7. Nodes 1 and 2 belong to the input layer, nodes 3–5 belong to the hidden layer, and nodes 6 and 7

TABLE 11.1	TINY EXAMPLE ON TASTING SCORES FOR SIX CONSUMERS AND TWO PREDICTORS		
Consumer	Fat score	Salt score	Acceptance
1	0.2	0.9	like
2	0.1	0.1	dislike
3	0.2	0.4	dislike
4	0.2	0.5	dislike
5	0.4	0.5	like
6	0.3	0.8	like

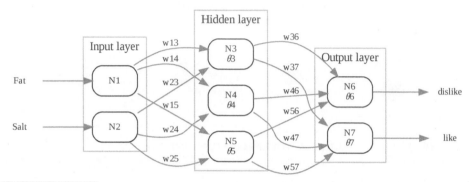

FIGURE 11.2   NEURAL NETWORK FOR THE TINY EXAMPLE. CIRCLES REPRESENT NODES ("NEURONS"), $W_{i,j}$ ON ARROWS ARE WEIGHTS, AND θ_j ARE NODE BIAS VALUES

belong to the output layer. The values on the connecting arrows are called *weights*, and the weight on the arrow from node i to node j is denoted by $w_{i,j}$. The additional *bias* nodes, denoted by θ_j, serve as an intercept for the output from node j. These are all explained in further detail below.

Computing Output of Nodes

We discuss the input and output of the nodes separately for each of the three types of layers (input, hidden, and output). The main difference is the function used to map from the input to the output of the node.

Input nodes take as input the values of the predictors. Their output is the same as the input. If we have p predictors, the input layer will usually include p nodes. In our example, there are two predictors, and therefore the input layer (shown in Figure 11.2) includes two nodes, each feeding into each node of the hidden layer. Consider the first record: the input into the input layer is Fat = 0.2 and Salt = 0.9, and the output of this layer is also $x_1 = 0.2$ and $x_2 = 0.9$.

Hidden layer nodes take as input the output values from the input layer. The hidden layer in this example consists of three nodes, each receiving input from all the input nodes. To compute the output of a hidden layer node, we compute a weighted sum of the inputs and apply a certain function to it. More formally, for a set of input values $x_1, x_2, \ldots, x_p$, we compute the output of node j by taking the weighted sum[1] $\theta_j + \sum_{i=1}^{p} w_{ij} x_i$, where $\theta_j, w_{1,j}, \ldots, w_{p,j}$ are weights that are initially set randomly and then adjusted as the network "learns." Note that θ_j, also called the *bias* of node j, is a constant that controls the level of contribution of node j. In the next step, we take a function g of this sum. The function g, also called a *transfer function* or *activation function*, is some monotone function. Examples include the linear function [$g(s) = bs$], an exponential function [$g(s) = \exp(bs)$], and a logistic/sigmoidal function [$g(s) = 1/1 + e^{-s}$]. This last function is by far the most popular one in neural networks. Its practical value arises from the fact that it has a squashing effect on very small or very large values but is almost linear in the range where the value of the function is between 0.1 and 0.9. Deep learning uses mostly the rectified linear unit (ReLU) activation function or variants of it. This function is identical to the linear function but set to zero for $s < 0$.

If we use a logistic activation function, we can write the output of node j in the hidden layer as

$$\text{Output}_j = g\left(\theta_j + \sum_{i=1}^{p} w_{ij} x_i\right) = \frac{1}{1 + e^{-(\theta_j + \sum_{i=1}^{p} w_{ij} x_i)}}. \qquad (11.1)$$

Initializing the Weights The values of θ_j and w_{ij} are initialized to small, usually random, numbers (typically, but not always, in the range 0.00 ± 0.05). Such values represent a state of no knowledge by the network, similar to a model with no predictors. The initial weights are used in the first round of training.

Returning to our example, suppose that the initial bias and weights for node 3 are $\theta_3 = -0.3$, $w_{1,3} = 0.05$, and $w_{2,3} = 0.01$ (as shown in Figure 11.3). Using the logistic function, we can compute the output of node N3 in the

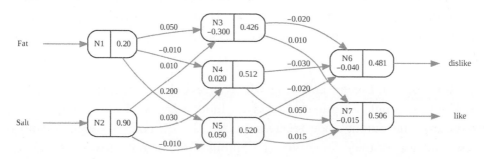

FIGURE 11.3 COMPUTING NODE OUTPUTS (ON THE RIGHT WITHIN EACH NODE) USING THE FIRST RECORD IN THE TINY EXAMPLE AND A LOGISTIC FUNCTION

---

[1] Other options exist for combining inputs, such as taking the maximum or minimum of the weighted inputs rather than their sum, but they are much less popular.

hidden layer (using the first record) as

$$\text{Output}_{N3} = \frac{1}{1 + e^{-[-0.3+(0.05)(0.2)+(0.01)(0.9)]}} = 0.43.$$

Figure 11.3 shows the initial weights, bias, inputs, and outputs for the first record in our tiny example. If there is more than one hidden layer, the same calculation applies, except that the input values for the second, third, and so on hidden layers would be the output of the preceding hidden layer. This means that the number of input values into a certain node is equal to the number of nodes in the preceding layer. (If there was an additional hidden layer in our example, its nodes would receive input from the three nodes in the first hidden layer.)

Finally, the output layer obtains input values from the (last) hidden layer. It applies the same function as above to create the output. In other words, it takes a weighted sum of its input values and then applies the function g. In our example, output nodes N6 and N7 receive input from the three hidden layer nodes. We can compute the output of these nodes by

$$\text{Output}_{N6} = \frac{1}{1 + e^{-[-0.04+(-0.02)(0.43)+(-0.03)(0.51)+(0.015)(0.52)]}} = 0.481$$

$$\text{Output}_{N7} = \frac{1}{1 + e^{-[-0.015+(0.01)(0.43)+(0.05)(0.51)+(0.015)(0.52)]}} = 0.506.$$

These two numbers are *almost* the propensities P(Y = *dislike* | Fat = 0.2, Salt = 0.9) and P(Y = *like* | Fat = 0.2. Salt = 0.9). The last step involves normalizing these two values so that they add up to 1. In other words,

$$P(Y = dislike) = \text{Output}_{N6}/(\text{Output}_{N6} + \text{Output}_{N7}) = 0.481/(0.481 + 0.506) = 0.49$$
$$P(Y = like) = 1 - P(Y = dislike) = 0.506/(0.481 + 0.506) = 0.51.$$

For classification, we use a threshold value (for a binary outcome) on the propensity. Using a threshold of 0.5, we would classify this record as *like*. For applications with more than two classes, we choose the output node with the largest value.

Relation to Linear and Logistic Regression   Consider a neural network with a single output node and no hidden layers. For a dataset with p predictors, the output node receives $x_1, x_2, \ldots, x_p$, takes a weighted sum of these, and applies the g function. The output of the neural network is therefore $g\left(\theta + \sum_{i=1}^{p} w_i x_i\right)$.

First, consider a numerical outcome variable Y. If g is the identity function $[g(s) = s]$, the output is simply

$$\hat{Y} = \theta + \sum_{i=1}^{p} w_i x_i.$$

This is exactly equivalent to the formulation of a multiple linear regression! This means that a neural network with no hidden layers, a single output node, and an identity function g searches only for linear relationships between the outcome and the predictors.

Now consider a binary output variable Y. If g is the logistic function, the output is simply

$$\hat{P}(Y = 1) = \frac{1}{1 + e^{-\left(\theta + \sum_{i=1}^{p} w_i x_i\right)}},$$

which is equivalent to the logistic regression formulation!

In both cases, although the formulation is equivalent to the linear and logistic regression models, the resulting estimates for the weights (*coefficients* in linear and logistic regression) can differ, because the estimation method is different. The neural net estimation method is different from *least squares*, the method used to calculate coefficients in linear regression, or the *maximum likelihood* method used in logistic regression. We explain below the method by which the neural network learns.

Preprocessing the Data

When using sigmoidal activation functions such as the logistic activation function (option *act.fct="logistic"* in R) or the hyperbolic tangent function (option *act.fct="tanh"*), neural networks perform best when the predictors and outcome variable are on a scale of [0,1] or [-1,1]. For this reason, all variables should be scaled to a [0,1] or a [-1,1] interval before training the network. For a numerical variable X that takes values in the range $[a, b]$ where $a < b$, we rescale the measurements to a [0,1] scale by subtracting a and dividing by $b - a$. The normalized measurement is then

$$X_{\text{norm}[0,1]} = \frac{X - a}{b - a}.$$

Note that if $[a, b]$ is within the [0,1] interval, the original scale will be stretched. Similarly, we can rescale the measurements to a [-1,1] scale by doubling the [0,1] scaled value and subtracting 1. The normalized [-1,1] measurement is then

$$X_{\text{norm}[-1,1]} = 2 \times \frac{X - a}{b - a} - 1.$$

If a and b are unknown, we can estimate them from the minimal and maximal values of X in the data. Even if new data exceed this range by a small amount (for example, scaled values are slighly larger than 1), yielding normalized values slightly lower than 0 or larger than 1, this will not affect the results much.

For binary variables, no adjustment is needed other than creating dummy variables. For categorical variables with m categories, if they are ordinal in nature, a choice of m fractions in [0,1] should reflect their perceived ordering. For example, if four ordinal categories are equally distant from each other, we can map them to [0,0.25,0.5,1]. If the categories are nominal, transforming into $m - 1$ dummies is a good solution.

Another operation that improves the performance of the network is to transform highly skewed predictors. In business applications, there tend to be many highly right-skewed variables (such as income). Taking a log transform of a right-skewed variable (before converting to a [0,1] scale) will usually spread out the values more symmetrically.

Training the Model

Training the model means estimating the weights θ_j and w_{ij} that lead to the best predictive results. The process that we described earlier (Section 11.1) for computing the neural network output for a record is repeated for all records in the training set. For each record, the model produces a prediction which is then compared with the actual outcome value. Their difference is the error for the output node. However, unlike least squares or maximum likelihood, where a global function of the errors (e.g., sum of squared errors) is used for estimating the coefficients, in neural networks, the estimation process uses the errors iteratively to update the estimated weights.

In particular, the error for the output node is distributed across all the hidden nodes that led to it so that each node is assigned "responsibility" for part of the error. Each of these node-specific errors is then used for updating the weights.

Back Propagation of Error   The most popular method for using model errors to update weights ("learning") is an algorithm called *back propagation*. As the name implies, errors are computed from the last layer (the output layer) back to the hidden layers.

Let us denote by $\hat{y}_k$ the output from output node k. y_k is 1 or 0 depending on whether the actual class of the observation coincides with node k's label or not (for example, in Figure 11.3, for a person with output class "like" we have $y_6 = 0$ and $y_7 = 1$). The error associated with output node k is computed by

$$\text{err}_k = \hat{y}_k(1 - \hat{y}_k)(y_k - \hat{y}_k).$$

Notice that this is similar to the ordinary definition of an error $(y_k - \hat{y}_k)$ multiplied by a correction factor. The weights are then updated as follows:

$$\begin{aligned} \theta_j^{\text{new}} &= \theta_j^{\text{old}} + l \times \text{err}_j, \\ w_{i,j}^{\text{new}} &= w_{i,j}^{\text{old}} + l \times \text{err}_j, \end{aligned} \tag{11.2}$$

where l is a *learning rate* or *weight decay* parameter, a constant ranging typically between 0 and 1, which controls the amount of change in weights from one iteration to the next.

In our example, the error associated with output node 7 for the first record is $(0.506)(1 - 0.506)(1 - 0.506) = 0.123$. For output node 6, the error is

$0.481(1-0.481)(0-0.481) = -0.120$. These errors are then used to compute the errors associated with the hidden layer nodes, and those weights are updated accordingly using a formula similar to (11.2).

Two methods for updating the weights are *case updating* and *batch updating*. In case updating, the weights are updated after each record is run through the network (called a *trial*). For example, if we used case updating in the tiny example, the weights would first be updated after running record 1 as follows: using a learning rate of 0.5, the weights θ_7, $w_{3,7}$, $w_{4,7}$, and $w_{5,7}$ are updated to

$$
\begin{aligned}
\theta_7 &= -0.015 + (0.5)(0.123) = 0.047 \\
w_{3,7} &= 0.01 + (0.5)(0.123) = 0.072 \\
w_{4,7} &= 0.05 + (0.5)(0.123) = 0.112 \\
w_{5,7} &= 0.015 + (0.5)(0.123) = 0.077
\end{aligned}
$$

Similarly, we obtain updated weights $\theta_6 = 0.025$, $w_{3,6} = 0.045$, $w_{4,6} = 0.035$, and $w_{5,6} = 0.045$. These new weights are next updated after the second record is run through the network, the third, and so on, until all records are used. This is called one *epoch*, *sweep*, *iteration*, or *training cycle* through the data. Typically, there are many iterations.

In batch updating, the entire training set is run through the network before each updating of weights takes place. In that case, the error err_k in the updating equation is the sum of the errors from all records. In practice, case updating tends to yield more accurate results than batch updating but requires a longer run time. This is a serious consideration, since even in batch updating, hundreds or even thousands of sweeps through the training data are executed.

When does the updating stop? The most common conditions are one of the following:

1. When the new weights are only incrementally different from those of the preceding iteration.

2. When the misclassification rate reaches a required threshold or if there is no improvement in the misclassification rate over the prior epochs (also called *early stopping strategy*).

3. When the limit on the number of iterations is reached.

Let us examine the output from running a neural network on the tiny data. Following Figures 11.2 and 11.3, we used a single hidden layer with three nodes.

R has several packages for neural nets, the most common ones are **nnet** and **neuralnet**. We note that package **nnet** does not enable multilayer networks and has no plotting option. We used **neuralnet** in this example. The weights and model output are shown in Table 11.2. Figure 11.4 shows these weights in a format similar to that of our previous diagrams.

TABLE 11.2   NEURAL NETWORK WITH A SINGLE HIDDEN LAYER (THREE NODES) FOR THE TINY
DATA EXAMPLE

R code for running a neural network

```
nn <- neuralnet(Like + Dislike ~ Salt + Fat, data = df, linear.output = F, hidden = 3)

# display weights
nn$weights

# display predictions
prediction(nn)

# plot network
plot(nn, rep="best")
```

Output

```
> nn$weights
[[1]]
[[1]][[1]]
            [,1]        [,2]        [,3]
[1,]  -1.061144   3.057022   3.337952
[2,]   2.326024  -3.408663  -4.293214
[3,]   4.106435  -6.525668  -5.929419

[[1]][[2]]
            [,1]        [,2]
[1,]  -0.3495333  -1.677856
[2,]   5.8777146  -3.606625
[3,]  -5.3529201   5.620330
[4,]  -6.1115039   6.696287

> prediction(nn)
Data Error:        0;
$rep1
  Salt Fat        Like      Dislike
1  0.1 0.1 0.0002415536 0.99965512
2  0.4 0.2 0.0344215787 0.96556788
3  0.5 0.2 0.1248666748 0.87816828
4  0.9 0.2 0.9349452648 0.07022732
5  0.8 0.3 0.9591361793 0.04505631
6  0.5 0.4 0.8841904620 0.12672438
```

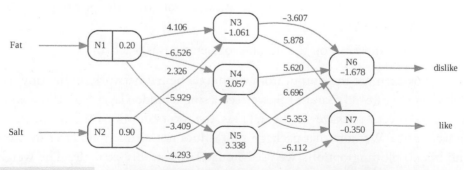

FIGURE 11.4   NEURAL NETWORK FOR THE TINY EXAMPLE WITH FINAL WEIGHTS FROM R
OUTPUT. VALUES ON THE FIVE DOWNWARDS ARROWS DENOTE THE BIAS

The first 3×3 table shows the weights that connect the input layer and the hidden layer. The *Bias nodes* (first row of the weights table) are the weights θ_3, θ_4, and θ_5. The weights in this table are used to compute the output of the hidden layer nodes. They were computed iteratively after choosing a random initial set of weights (like the set we chose in Figure 11.3). We use the weights in the way we described earlier to compute the hidden layer's output. For instance, for the first record, the output of our previous node 3 is:

$$\text{Output}_{N3} = \frac{1}{1 + e^{-[-1.06+(2.33)(0.9)+(4.11)(0.2)]}} = 0.86.$$

Similarly, we can compute the output from the two other hidden nodes for the same record and get $\text{Output}_4 = 0.21$ and $\text{Output}_5 = 0.15$. The second 4×2 table gives the weights connecting the hidden and output layer nodes. To compute the probability (= propensity) for the *dislike* output node for the first record, we use the outputs from the hidden layer that we computed above and get

$$\text{Output}_{dislike} = \frac{1}{1 + e^{-[-1.68+(-3.61)(0.86)+(5.62)(0.21)+(6.70)(0.15)]}} = 0.07.$$

Similarly, we can compute the probability for the *like* output node, obtaining the value $\text{Output}_{like} = 0.93$.

The probabilities for the other five records are computed in the same manner, replacing the input value in the computation of the hidden layer outputs and then plugging these outputs into the computation for the output layer. The confusion matrix based on these probabilities, using a threshold of 0.5, is given in Table 11.3. We can see that the network correctly classifies all six records.

TABLE 11.3   CONFUSION MATRIX FOR THE TINY EXAMPLE

 code for the confusion matrix

```
library(caret)
predict <- compute(nn, data.frame(df$Salt, df$Fat))
predicted.class=apply(predict$net.result,1,which.max)-1
confusionMatrix(factor(ifelse(predicted.class=="1", "dislike", "like")),
                factor(df$Acceptance))
```

Output

```
> confusionMatrix(as.factor(ifelse(predicted.class=="1", "dislike", "like")),
+ df$Acceptance)
Confusion Matrix and Statistics

          Reference
Prediction dislike like
   dislike       3    0
   like          0    3

              Accuracy : 1
```

Example 2: Classifying Accident Severity

Let's apply the network training process to some real data: US automobile accidents that have been classified by their level of severity as *no injury*, *injury*, or *fatality*. A firm might be interested in developing a system for quickly classifying the severity of an accident, based on initial reports and associated data in the system (some of which rely on GPS-assisted reporting). Such a system could be used to assign emergency response team priorities. Table 11.4 shows a small extract (10 records, 4 predictor variables) from a US government database.

TABLE 11.4   SUBSET FROM THE ACCIDENTS DATA, FOR A HIGH-FATALITY REGION

Obs.	ALCHL_I	PROFIL_I_R	SUR_COND	VEH_INVL	MAX_SEV_IR
1	1	1	1	1	1
2	2	1	1	1	0
3	2	1	1	1	1
4	1	1	1	1	0
5	2	1	1	1	2
6	2	0	1	1	1
7	2	0	1	3	1
8	2	0	1	4	1
9	2	0	1	2	0
10	2	0	1	2	0

The explanation of the four predictor variables and outcome variable is given in Table 11.5. For the analysis, we convert ALCHL_I to a 0/1 dummy variable (1 = presence of alcohol) and create four dummies for SUR_COND. This gives us a total of seven predictors.

TABLE 11.5   DESCRIPTION OF VARIABLES FOR AUTOMOBILE ACCIDENT EXAMPLE

ALCHL_I	Presence (1) or absence (2) of alcohol
PROFIL_I_R	Profile of the roadway: level (1), other (0)
SUR_COND	Surface condition of the road: dry (1), wet (2), snow/slush (3), ice (4), unknown (9)
VEH_INVL	Number of vehicles involved
MAX_SEV_IR	Presence of injuries/fatalities: no injuries (0), injury (1), fatality (2)

With the exception of alcohol involvement and a few other variables in the larger database, most of the variables are ones that we might reasonably expect to be available at the time of the initial accident report, before accident details and severity have been determined by first responders. A machine learning model that could predict accident severity on the basis of these initial reports would have value in allocating first responder resources.

To use a neural net architecture for this classification problem, we use seven nodes in the input layer, one for each of the seven predictors, and three neurons (one for each class) in the output layer. We use a single hidden layer and experiment with the number of nodes. If we increase the number of nodes from one to five and examine the resulting confusion matrices, we find that two nodes gives a good balance between improving the predictive performance on the training set without deteriorating the performance on the holdout set. (Networks with more than two nodes in the hidden layer performed as well as the two-node network, but add undesirable complexity.) Table 11.6 shows the R code and output for the accidents data.

Our results can depend on how we set the different parameters, and there are a few pitfalls to avoid. We discuss these next.

Avoiding Overfitting

A weakness of the neural network is that it can easily overfit the data, causing the error rate on holdout data (and most important, on new data) to be too large. It is therefore important to limit the number of training iterations and not to overtrain on the data (e.g., in R's *neuralnet()* function you can control the number of iterations using argument *stepmax*). As in classification and regression trees, overfitting can be detected by examining the performance on the validation set, or better, on a cross-validation set, and seeing when it starts deteriorating, while the training set performance is still improving. This approach is used in some algorithms to limit the number of training iterations. The validation error decreases in the early iterations of the training, but after a while, it begins to increase. The point of minimum validation error is a good indicator of the best number of iterations for training, and the weights at that stage are likely to provide the best error rate in new data.

Using the Output for Prediction and Classification

When the neural network is used for predicting a numerical outcome variable, the resulting output needs to be scaled back to the original units of that outcome variable. Recall that numerical variables (both predictor and outcome variables) are usually rescaled to a $[0,1]$ interval before being used by the network. The output will therefore also be on a $[0,1]$ scale. To transform the prediction back to the original y units, which were in the range $[a, b]$, we multiply the network output by $b - a$ and add a.

In the case of a binary outcome ($m = 2$), we use two output nodes with a threshold value to map a predicted probability to one of the two classes.

TABLE 11.6   A NEURAL NETWORK WITH TWO NODES IN THE HIDDEN LAYER (ACCIDENTS DATA)

 code for running and evaluating a neural net on the accidents data

```
library(tidyverse)
library(fastDummies)

# convert SUR_COND and ALCHL_I to dummy variables (remove firest dummy)
# convert outcome MAX_SEV_IR to dummy variables keeping all
accidents.df <- mlba::AccidentsNN %>%
  dummy_cols(select_columns=c("ALCHL_I", "SUR_COND"),
             remove_selected_columns=TRUE, remove_first_dummy=TRUE) %>%
  dummy_cols(select_columns=c("MAX_SEV_IR"),
             remove_selected_columns=TRUE)

# partition the data
set.seed(1)
idx <- createDataPartition(mlba::AccidentsNN$MAX_SEV_IR, p=0.6, list=FALSE)
train.df <- accidents.df[idx, ]
holdout.df <- accidents.df[-idx, ]
train.actual <- mlba::AccidentsNN[idx, ]$MAX_SEV_IR
holdout.actual <- mlba::AccidentsNN[-idx, ]$MAX_SEV_IR

nn <- neuralnet(MAX_SEV_IR_0 + MAX_SEV_IR_1 + MAX_SEV_IR_2 ~ .,
                data=train.df, hidden=2)

# predict the three outcome variables and assign class using maximum score
pred.train <- predict(nn, train.df)
class.train <- apply(pred.train, 1, which.max)-1
confusionMatrix(factor(class.train), factor(train.actual))

pred.holdout <- predict(nn, holdout.df)
class.holdout <- apply(pred.holdout, 1, which.max)-1
confusionMatrix(factor(class.holdout), factor(holdout.actual))
```

Partial Output

```
>   confusionMatrix(factor(class.train), factor(train.actual))
Confusion Matrix and Statistics

          Reference
Prediction   0   1   2
         0 329   0  33
         1   0 173  36
         2   0   8  21

Overall Statistics

              Accuracy : 0.8717


>   confusionMatrix(factor(class.holdout), factor(holdout.actual))
Confusion Matrix and Statistics

          Reference
Prediction   0   1   2
         0 220   0  21
         1   0 115  26
         2   2   3  12

Overall Statistics

              Accuracy : 0.8697
```

Although we typically use a threshold of 0.5 with other classifiers, in neural networks there is a tendency for values to cluster around 0.5 (from above and below). An alternative is to use the validation set to determine a threshold that produces reasonable predictive performance.

For multi-class classification, where we have a categorical outcome with m classes, we will obtain an output from each of the m output nodes (or $m - 1$ output nodes depending on the software).[2] How do we translate these m outputs into a classification rule? Usually, the output node with the largest value determines the net's classification.

11.4 REQUIRED USER INPUT

One of the time-consuming and complex aspects of training a model using back propagation is that we first need to decide on a network architecture. This means specifying the number of hidden layers and the number of nodes in each layer. The usual procedure is to make intelligent guesses using past experience and to do several trial-and-error runs on different architectures. Algorithms exist that grow the number of nodes selectively during training or trim them in a manner analogous to what is done in classification and regression trees (see Chapter 9). Research continues on such methods. As of now, no automatic method seems clearly superior to the trial-and-error approach. A few general guidelines for choosing an architecture follow:

Number of hidden layers. The most popular choice for the number of hidden layers is one. A single hidden layer is usually sufficient to capture even very complex relationships between the predictors.

Size of hidden layer. The number of nodes in the hidden layer also determines the level of complexity of the relationship between the predictors that the network captures. The trade-off is between under- and overfitting. On the one hand, using too few nodes might not be sufficient to capture complex relationships (recall the special cases of a linear relationship such as in linear and logistic regression, in the extreme case of zero nodes or no hidden layer). On the other hand, too many nodes might lead to overfitting. A rule of thumb is to start with p (number of predictors) nodes and gradually decrease or increase while checking for overfitting. The number of hidden layers and the size of each hidden layer can be specified in R's *neuralnet()* function using argument *hidden*.

---

[2]Function *neuralnet()* by default generates $m - 1$ output nodes for an outcome with m classes. To get m output nodes, specify each class on the left-hand side of the formula—see Table 11.2.

Number of output nodes. For a categorical outcome with m classes, the number of nodes should equal m or $m - 1$. For a numerical outcome, typically a single output node is used unless we are interested in predicting more than one function.

In addition to the choice of architecture, the user should pay attention to the *choice of predictors*. Since neural networks are highly dependent on the quality of their input, the choice of predictors should be done carefully, using domain knowledge, feature selection, and dimension reduction techniques before using the network. We return to this point in the discussion of advantages and weaknesses.

A key parameter that the user can control is the *learning rate* (also called *weight decay*), l, which is used primarily to avoid overfitting, by down-weighting new information. This helps to tone down the effect of outliers on the weights and avoids getting stuck in local optima. This parameter typically takes a value in the range [0,1]. Berry and Linoff (2000) suggest starting with a large value (moving away from the random initial weights, thereby "learning quickly" from the data) and then slowly decreasing it as the iterations progress and as the weights are more reliable. Han and Kamber (2001) suggest the more concrete rule of thumb of setting $l = 1/$(current number of iterations). This means that at the start, $l = 1$, during the second iteration it is $l = 0.5$, and then it keeps decaying toward $l = 0$. In R, you can set the learning rate in function *neuralnet()* using argument *learningrate*.

11.5 EXPLORING THE RELATIONSHIP BETWEEN PREDICTORS AND OUTCOME

Neural networks are known to be "blackboxes" in the sense that their output does not shed light on the patterns in the data that it models (like our brains). In fact, that is one of the biggest criticisms of the method. However, in some cases, it is possible to learn more about the relationships that the network captures by conducting a sensitivity analysis on the holdout set. This is done by setting all predictor values to their mean and obtaining the network's prediction. Then, the process is repeated by setting each predictor sequentially to its minimum, and then maximum, value. By comparing the predictions from different levels of the predictors, we can get a sense of which predictors affect predictions more and in what way.

11.6 DEEP LEARNING[3]

Neural nets had their greatest impact in the period from 2006 onward, with a paper published by AI researcher Geoffrey Hinton, and the rapidly growing popularity of what came to be called *deep learning*. Deep learning involves complex networks with many layers, incorporating processes for dimension reduction and feature discovery.

The data we have dealt with so far in this book are structured data, typically from organizational databases. The predictor variables, or features, that we think might be meaningful in predicting an outcome of interest already exist in our data. In predicting possible bank failure, for example, we would guess that certain financial ratios (return on assets, return on equity, etc.) might have predictive value. In predicting insurance fraud, we might guess that policy age would be predictive. We are not limited, of course, to variables that we know are predictive; sometimes a useful predictor emerges in an unexpected way.

With tasks like voice and image recognition, structured high-level predictor information like this is not available. All we have are individual "low-level" sound wave frequency and amplitude or pixel values indicating intensity and color. You'd like to be able to tell the computer "just look for two eyes" and then provide further detail on how an eye appears—a small solid circle (pupil), surrounded by a ring (iris), surrounded by a white area. However, again, all the computer has are columns of (low-level) pixel values—you'd need to do a lot of extra work to define all the different (higher-level) pixel patterns that correspond to eyes. That's where deep learning comes in—it can "learn" how to identify these higher level features by itself.

Deep learning is a rapidly growing and evolving field, with many aspects that distinguish it from simpler predictive models. A full examination of the field of deep learning is beyond the scope of this book, but let us consider one key innovation in the area of algorithmic design that is associated with deep learning and extends the ability of simple neural networks to perform the tasks of supervised and unsupervised learning that we have been discussing. This innovation is "convolution." Convolutional neural networks are used in many different applications and fields and have enabled major advances in voice recognition and the extraction of meaning from text via natural language processing (see Section 21.3 and the discussion of latent semantic indexing in Section 21.4 for a brief discussion of this topic). The basic idea of convolution is illustrated well in the context of image recognition.

---

[3]This section copyright © 2019 Datastats, LLC, Galit Shmueli, and Peter Gedeck. Used by permission.

Convolutional Neural Networks (CNNs)

In a standard neural network, each predictor gets its own weight at each layer of the network. A convolution, by contrast, selects a subset of predictors (pixels) and applies the same operation to the entire subset. It is this grouping that fosters the automated discovery of features. Recall that the data in image recognition tasks consist of a large number of pixel values, which, in a black and white image, range from 0 (black) to 255 (white). Since we are interested in detecting the black lines and shadings, we will reverse this to 255 for black and 0 for white.

Consider the line drawing in Figure 11.5, from a 1893 Funk and Wagnalls publication. Before the computer can begin to identify complex features like eyes, ears, noses, and heads, it needs to master very simple features like lines and borders. For example, the line of the man's chin (Figure 11.6). In a typical convolution, the algorithm considers a small area at a time, say, 3 pixels × 3 pixels. Figure 11.7 illustrates such a case. The line at the chin might look like the Figure 11.7a; the matrix in Figure 11.7b might be our pixel values. In

FIGURE 11.5   LINE DRAWING, FROM A 1893 FUNK AND WAGNALLS PUBLICATION

FIGURE 11.6   FOCUSING ON THE LINE OF THE MAN'S CHIN

(a)   (b)   (c)

25	200	25
25	225	25
25	225	25

0	1	0
0	1	0
0	1	0

FIGURE 11.7   3 × 3 PIXEL REPRESENTATION OF LINE ON MAN'S CHIN USING SHADING (a) AND VALUES (b). THE FILTER (c) IDENTIFIES VERTICAL LINES

its first convolution operation, the network could apply a filter operation by multiplying the pixel values by a 3×3 matrix of values that happens to be good at identifying vertical lines, such as the matrix in Figure 11.7c. The sum of the individual cell multiplications is $[0 + 0 + 0 + 200 + 225 + 225 + 0 + 0 + 0] = 650$. This is a relatively high value, compared with what another arrangement of the filter matrix might produce, because both the image section and the filter have high values in the center column and low values elsewhere. (A little experimentation with other 3×3 arrangements of three 1's and six 0's will reveal why this particular matrix is good at identifying vertical lines.) So, for this initial filter action, we can say that the filter has detected a vertical line, and thus we can consolidate the initial nine values of the image section into a single value (say, a value between 0 and 1 to indicate the absence or presence of a vertical line).

Local Feature Map

The "vertical line detector" filter moves across and down the original image matrix, recalculating and producing a single output each time. We end up with a smaller matrix; how much smaller depends on whether the filter moves one pixel at a time, two, or more (called the *stride*). While the original image values were simply individual pixel values, the new, smaller matrix is a map of features, answering the question, "is there a vertical line in this section?"

The fact that the frame for the convolution is relatively small means that the overall operation can identify features that are local in character. We could imagine other local filters to discover horizontal lines, diagonal lines, curves, boundaries, etc. Further layers of different convolutional operations, taking these local feature maps as inputs, can then successively build up higher-level features (corners, rectangles, circles, etc.).

A Hierarchy of Features

The first feature map is of vertical lines; we could repeat the process to identify horizontal lines and diagonal lines. We could also imagine filters to identify boundaries between light and dark areas. Then, having produced a set of initial low-level feature maps, the process could repeat, except this time working with these feature maps instead of the original pixel values. This iterative process continues, building up multidimensional matrix maps, or tensors, of higher and higher level features. As the process proceeds, the matrix representation of higher-level features becomes somewhat abstract, so it is not necessarily possible to peer into a deep network and identify, for example, an eye.

In this process, the information is progressively compressed (simplified) as the higher-level features emerge, as illustrated in Figure 11.8.

FIGURE 11.8   CONVOLUTION NETWORK PROCESS, SUPERVISED LEARNING: THE REPEATED FILTERING IN THE NETWORK CONVOLUTION PROCESS PRODUCES HIGH-LEVEL FEATURES THAT FACILITATE THE APPLICATION OF CLASS LABELS, WHICH ARE COMPARED WITH ACTUAL CLASSES TO TRAIN THE NETWORK

The Learning Process

How does the net know which convolutional operations to do? To put it simply, it retains the ones that lead to successful classifications. In a basic neural net, the individual weights are what get adjusted in the iterative learning process. In a convolutional network, the net also learns which convolutions to do.

In a supervised learning setting, the network keeps building up features up to the highest level, which might be the goal of the learning task. Consider the task of deciding whether an image contains a face. You have a training set of labeled images with faces and images without faces. The training process yields convolutions that identify hierarchies of features (e.g., edges > circles > eyes) that lead to success in the classification process. Other hierarchies that the net might conceivably encounter (e.g., edges > rectangles > houses) get dropped because they do not contribute to success in the identification of faces. Sometimes it is the case that the output of a single node in the network is an effective classifier, an indication that this node codes for the feature you are focusing on.

Unsupervised Learning

The most magical-seeming accomplishment of deep learning is its ability to identify features and, hence, objects in an unsupervised setting. Famous examples include identifying images with faces and identifying dogs and cats in images (see, e.g., Le et al., 2012). How is this done?

One method is to use a so-called autoencoder network. These networks are trained to reproduce the input that is fed into them, by first creating a lower-dimensional representation of the data and then using the created representation to reproduce the original data. The network is trained to retain the features that facilitate accurate reproduction of the input.

Viewed in the context of our image example, autoencoders have the high-level architecture shown in Figure 11.9.

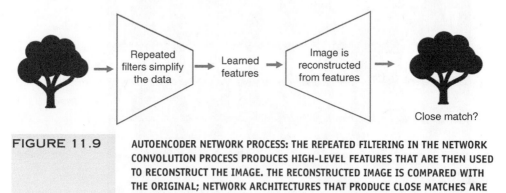

FIGURE 11.9   AUTOENCODER NETWORK PROCESS: THE REPEATED FILTERING IN THE NETWORK CONVOLUTION PROCESS PRODUCES HIGH-LEVEL FEATURES THAT ARE THEN USED TO RECONSTRUCT THE IMAGE. THE RECONSTRUCTED IMAGE IS COMPARED WITH THE ORIGINAL; NETWORK ARCHITECTURES THAT PRODUCE CLOSE MATCHES ARE SAVED AS THE NETWORK IS "TRAINED" WITHOUT BENEFIT OF LABELED DATA

Up to the learned features point (the bottleneck in the image), the network is similar to the supervised network. Once it has developed the learned features, which are a low-dimensional representation of the data, it expands those features into an image by a reverse process. The output image is compared with the input image, and if they are not similar, the network keeps working (using the same backpropagation method we discussed earlier). Once the network reliably produces output images that are similar to the inputs, the process stops.

This internal representation at the bottleneck now has useful information about the general domain (here, images) on which the network was trained. It turns out that the learned features (outputs of nodes at the bottleneck) that emerge in this process are often useful. Since the features can be considered a low-dimensional representation of the original data (similar in spirit to principal components in PCA—see Chapter 4), they can be used, for example, for building a supervised predictive model or for unsupervised clustering.

Example: Classification of Fashion Images

This example demonstrates using a deep learning architecture with CNN for a classification task—to classify fashion images of different types of clothing and footwear. The open source *Fashion MNIST* data made available by Zalando[4] consists of a training set of 60,000 images and a holdout set of 10,000 images.

---

[4]https://github.com/zalandoresearch/fashion-mnist

Each image is a 28×28 pixel grayscale image, associated with a label from one of 10 classes. The *keras::dataset_fashion_mnist* is provided with the **keras** package in a format suitable for model building. A small sample of 10 images from each class is shown in Figure 11.10.

Class 0: T-shirt/top

Class 1: Trouser

Class 2: Pullover

Class 3: Dress

Class 4: Coat

Class 5: Sandal

Class 6: Shirt

Class 7: Sneaker

Class 8: Bag

Class 9: Ankle boot

FIGURE 11.10   FASHION MNIST DATA: SAMPLE OF 10 IMAGES FROM EACH CLASS

Data Preprocessing   While the data in *keras::dataset_fashion_mnist* are already in a numerical format, we still require a few preprocessing steps. Table 11.7 lists the required steps. The **Keras** package requires the input data to be in the form of a *tensor*. A tensor is a generalized and computationally efficient representation of matrix data in higher dimension.[5] Here, the first tensor dimension identifies the individual image (image ID), the next two dimensions correspond to the row and column of the image. The final dimension describes the properties of the pixel. As we have greyscale images, a pixel is described by a

---

[5]You are already familiar with three special types of tensors: a scalar is a rank 0 tensor, a vector is a rank 1 tensor, and a matrix is a rank 2 tensor.

TABLE 11.7   DATA PREPROCESSING OF FASHION MNIST FOR DEEP LEARNING

 code for preprocessing data and converting into matrices of required dimensions

```
# load required packages
# Keras and TensorFlow require a Python conda environment with these packages installed
library(reticulate)
use_condaenv('mlba-r')
library(keras)
library(tensorflow)

# load the data and split into training and validation sets
fashion_mnist <- keras::dataset_fashion_mnist()
x_train <- fashion_mnist$train$x
y_train <- fashion_mnist$train$y
x_valid <- fashion_mnist$test$x
y_valid <- fashion_mnist$test$y

# pixel values need to be scaled to range [0, 1]
x_train <- x_train / 255
x_valid <- x_valid / 255

# input require an additional dimension to describe pixel values
# dimensions are (samples, row, column, pixel)
x_train <- array_reshape(x_train, c(dim(x_train), 1))
x_valid <- array_reshape(x_valid, c(dim(x_valid), 1))

# output values need to be converted into a matrix with one-hot-encoding of classes
# dimensions are (samples, classes)
y_train <- to_categorical(y_train, 10)
y_valid <- to_categorical(y_valid, 10)
dim(x_train)
dim(y_train)
```

single value (vector of length 1), measuring its intensity on the scale of 0 (black) to 255 (white).

Prior to training and tuning the network, the image pixel values must be normalized, aligned with our earlier discussion on preprocessing the data for neural network models. The pixel value, a number between 0 and 255, is rescaled to the range [0,1] by dividing by 255.

We can now define and train the convolutional network. The required steps are shown in Table 11.8. The network consists of a sequence of layers. The first two layers are *convolutional layers* (*layer_conv_2d*) converting the 28×28 images into 24×24×32 and 22×22×64 feature maps using trainable filters (*kernels*) of size 5 and 3, respectively. In addition to the size of the filter (*kernel_size*, k), we can define a *padding*[6] (*p*, default no padding) and a stride (*strides*, *s*, default 1). As

---

[6]Padding adds empty pixels around the edges of an image. This is done to allow full convolutions on the edge pixels when applying a convolutional filter while preserving the original size of an image.

TABLE 11.8   **MODEL DEFINITION AND TRAINING OF FASHION MNIST CONVOLUTIONAL NETWORK**

 code for defining and training a convolutional neural network

```
# Model definition (architecture taken from
# https://keras.rstudio.com/articles/examples/mnist_cnn.html
input_shape = dim(x_train)[2:4]
num_classes <- 10

model <- keras_model_sequential()
model %>%
  layer_conv_2d(filters=32, kernel_size=c(5,5), activation='relu',
                input_shape=input_shape) %>%
  layer_conv_2d(filters=64, kernel_size=c(3,3), activation='relu') %>%
  layer_max_pooling_2d(pool_size=c(2,2)) %>%
  layer_dropout(rate=0.25) %>%
  layer_flatten() %>%
  layer_dense(units = 128, activation = 'relu') %>%
  layer_dropout(rate = 0.5) %>%
  layer_dense(units = num_classes, activation = 'softmax')

model

# compile model
model %>% compile(
  loss = loss_categorical_crossentropy,
  optimizer = optimizer_adadelta(),
  metrics = c('accuracy')
)

# train and evaluate
model %>% fit(
  x_train, y_train,
  batch_size = 128,
  epochs = 20,
  verbose = 1,
  validation_data = list(x_valid, y_valid)
)
```

Partial Output

```
> model
Model: "sequential_3"
--------------------------------------------------------------------------
Layer (type)                     Output Shape              Param #
==========================================================================
conv2d_7 (Conv2D)                (None, 24, 24, 32)        832
conv2d_6 (Conv2D)                (None, 22, 22, 64)        18496
max_pooling2d_3 (MaxPooling2D)   (None, 11, 11, 64)        0
dropout_7 (Dropout)              (None, 11, 11, 64)        0
flatten_3 (Flatten)              (None, 7744)              0
dense_7 (Dense)                  (None, 128)               991360
dropout_6 (Dropout)              (None, 128)               0
dense_6 (Dense)                  (None, 10)                1290
==========================================================================
Total params: 1,011,978
Trainable params: 1,011,978
Non-trainable params: 0

> model %>% fit(...)
Epoch 1/20
469/469 [==============================] - 42s 87ms/step -
      loss: 0.5934 - accuracy: 0.7860 - val_loss: 0.3676 - val_accuracy: 0.8652
Epoch 2/20
469/469 [==============================] - 39s 82ms/step -
      loss: 0.3717 - accuracy: 0.8690 - val_loss: 0.3202 - val_accuracy: 0.8845
Epoch 3/20
389/469 [=====================>......] - ETA: 5s -
      loss: 0.3207 - accuracy: 0.8864
```

discussed earlier, the filter moves across and down each image, recalculating and producing a new feature map. These convolutions are designed to identify basic image features like edges.[7] The ReLU activation function is used to produce the output of each feature map in both layers.

The images are classified into one of 10 different classes. This multi-class classification problem requires *one-hot encoding* of the class label. This is achieved here using the `keras` function *to_categorical*.

The preprocessing steps result in two tensors. The training tensor object represents 60,000 images, each with 28×28 dimension. The validation tensor object represents 10,000 images, each with 28×28 dimension.

DEEP LEARNING IN R

The TensorFlow and Keras implementations in R require a Python environment with both installed. Find up to date installation instructions at https://tensorflow.rstudio.com. Building deep learning models requires the following three packages:

`reticulate` Interface to 'Python' modules, classes, and functions.

`tensorflow` R interface to 'TensorFlow' (https://www.tensorflow.org), an open source software library for numerical computation using data flow graphs.

`keras` R interface to 'Keras' (https://keras.io), a high-level neural networks API.

Training a Deep Learning Network   Next, we want to highlight the most dominant feature in an image using the iterative process described earlier in "A Hierarchy of Features." To do this, we use the convolutional layer output as the input for the max pooling layer (*layer_max_pooling_2d*). Here, we set the pool size to 2×2 with default values for strides and padding (*strides=2, padding=0*).[8] Often, we experiment with multiple combinations of convolutional and max pooling layers to determine which configuration is best at identifying different high-level features in the images.

To reduce the chance of overfitting and to make the network more resilient, we randomly drop nodes during training. This is done using a *drop out layer* (*layer_dropout*), which we use to randomly drop 25% of the nodes from the network (*rate=0.25*). The *layer_flatten* function converts any tensor (here a rank-3

---

[7]With an image of input dimension $n = n_{\text{width}} = n_{\text{height}} = 28$, the output dimension for each feature map is given by $(n + 2p - k)/s + 1 = (28 - 5)/1 + 1 = 24$. That is, a 24×24 matrix.

[8]Considering the previous layer's feature maps as input, the output dimension of each feature map is now $(n + 2p - k)/s + 1 = (22 + 2 \times 0 - 2)/2 + 1 = 11$. That is, an 11×11 matrix.

tensor) to a vector without changing its values.[9] Each image is now described by a vector of length 7744.

Following this, we add two fully-connected layers (*layer_dense*) using the ReLU activation function to learn nonlinear combinations of features learned from the previous convolutional and pooling layers. The first dense layer reduces the tensor of length 7744 to a much shorter tensor of length 128. After an additional dropout layer, we finally map the 128-dimensional tensor to our final output. The last layer uses the Softmax activation function. Like the sigmoid activation function, Softmax results in values in the range [0,1]. For this multiclass classification task, we have 10 output nodes corresponding to the 10 class labels.

The model summary in Table 11.8 shows the final architecture [Layer (type)], the dimensionality of the individual layers (Output Shape), and the number of tunable parameters (Param #). Our model has more than 1,000,000 parameters.

The deep learning network is trained on the training partition, and its performance is measured on the validation partition after each epoch. The training uses the multiclass cross-entropy loss on the outcome (*loss_categorical_crossentropy*.) The parameters are optimized using a stochastic gradient descent method called Adadelta (*optimizer_adadelta*) that uses an adaptive learning rate per dimension. In Figure 11.11, we see the change in loss (error) over training for 50 epochs. The training set loss decreases continuously. However, the validation set loss shows an increase starting around epoch 17. Monitoring the validation set loss would allow early stopping if there is no improvement in the validation set performance for a defined number of consecutive epochs (use *callback_early_stopping* with argument *patience*; see package documentation). When using early stopping, the epoch at which the best validation performance was recorded would be used.

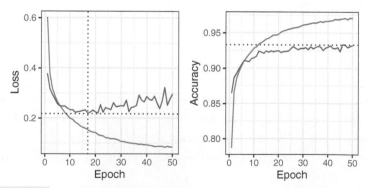

FIGURE 11.11   **LEARNING CURVE FOR THE DEEP LEARNING NETWORK: TRAINING SET (BLUE LINE), VALIDATION SET (RED LINE)**

---

[9]Converting the tensor to a vector assures the next layers, added by *layer_dense*, are applied to the correct information.

Applying the Predictive Model   We now use the convolutional network model that was trained for 20 epochs, to study the performance using the validation set. Table 11.9 shows propensities for a sample of five images from the validation set, their predicted class and the confusion matrix. The network was able to achieve an accuracy of 92.7%. From the confusion matrix, we can see that the model does well in identifying most classes. The worst performance is for class 7 (Shirts), that is often confused with classes 1 (t-shirt/tops), 3 (pullovers),

---

TABLE 11.9   PREDICTING IMAGES

```
propensities <- predict(model, x_valid)
propensities[1:5, ]

# convert to class using winner takes all
predClass <- apply(propensities, 1, which.max)
predClass[1:5]

# confusion matrix
caret::confusionMatrix(factor(predClass), factor(fashion_mnist$test$y + 1))

> propensities[1:5, ]
              [,1]          [,2]          [,3]          [,4]          [,5]
[1,] 1.629392e-13 7.208416e-12 4.222819e-12 4.366966e-12 2.184462e-11
[2,] 6.799936e-06 1.282430e-13 9.999745e-01 2.178376e-10 1.849656e-05
[3,] 5.244245e-11 1.000000e+00 2.762271e-13 8.370839e-11 2.392724e-12
[4,] 2.019367e-10 1.000000e+00 3.580798e-14 1.162730e-10 1.932113e-13
[5,] 2.356437e-02 9.984149e-08 5.419953e-04 6.728077e-06 2.430152e-04
              [,6]          [,7]          [,8]          [,9]         [,10]
[1,] 3.777349e-06 1.063734e-13 7.376956e-07 6.681040e-12 9.999955e-01
[2,] 8.402717e-14 2.519680e-07 3.140332e-11 2.043337e-10 8.708465e-13
[3,] 5.575455e-12 4.551109e-12 7.231787e-13 1.257118e-13 1.763203e-13
[4,] 9.197171e-13 4.528943e-11 1.610595e-13 7.811785e-15 2.414051e-14
[5,] 4.504887e-09 9.756437e-01 2.593327e-09 6.526992e-08 4.971027e-08

> predClass[1:5]
[1] 10  3  2  2  7


> # confusion matrix
> caret::confusionMatrix(factor(predClass), factor(fashion_mnist$test$y + 1))
Confusion Matrix and Statistics

          Reference
Prediction   1    2    3    4    5    6    7    8    9   10
        1  891    1   15    5    0    0   91    0    2    0
        2    1  983    0    2    0    0    0    0    1    0
        3   18    1  889    7   45    0   53    0    3    0
        4   12   12    9  943   24    0   29    0    2    0
        5    3    1   46   23  890    0   61    0    4    0
        6    1    0    0    0    0  988    0   10    2    7
        7   71    0   41   20   41    0  763    0    2    0
        8    0    0    0    0    0    9    0  983    2   37
        9    3    2    0    0    0    0    3    0  982    0
       10    0    0    0    0    0    3    0    7    0  956

Overall Statistics

               Accuracy : 0.9268
```

4 (dresses), and 5 (coats). The achieved accuracy is in line with what has been reported for similar CNN architectures.[10]

Conclusion

The key to convolutional networks' success is their ability to build, through iteration, multidimensional feature maps of great complexity (requiring substantial computing power and capacity), leading to the development of learned features that form a lower-dimensional representation of the data. You can see that different convolutional architectures (e.g., types of filtering operations) would be suitable for different tasks. The AI community shares pre-trained networks that allow analysts to short-circuit the lengthy and complex training process that is required, as well as datasets that allow training and benchmarking to certain tasks (e.g., datasets of generic images in many different classes, images specifically of faces, satellite imagery, text data, voice data, etc.).

Finally, you may have heard of other types of deep learning. At the time of writing, Recurrent Neural Networks (RNN) are very popular. They are usually implemented with either Long Short-Term Memory (LSTM) or Gated Recurrent Unit (GRU) building blocks. These networks are especially useful for data that are sequential in nature or have temporal behavior, such as time series, music, text, and speech (where the order of words in a sentence matters), and user or robot behavior (e.g., clickstream data, where the order of a user's actions can be important). These networks' memory helps them capture such sequences. R's integration of TensorFlow, Keras, or similar packages supports building a variety of complex deep learning architectures. We illustrated the use of CNN in this chapter. We discuss the use of LSTM for time series forecasting in Chapter 19 and a special application of LSTM for text processing called word embedding in Chapter 21. Various deep learning architectures can be composed by using the different types of layers as building blocks. A thorough discussion of the possibilities is beyond the scope of this book. In deciding whether to use such methods in a given business analytics application, a key consideration is their performance relative to other methods and their required resources (in terms of data and computing).

11.7 ADVANTAGES AND WEAKNESSES OF NEURAL NETWORKS

The most prominent advantage of neural networks is their good predictive performance. They are known to have high tolerance to noisy data and the ability

---

[10]Similar CNN architectures with the complete training data have reported 90–95% accuracy. See https://github.com/zalandoresearch/fashion-mnist

to capture highly complicated relationships between the predictors and an outcome variable. Their weakest point is in providing insight into the structure of the relationship, hence their blackbox reputation.

Several considerations and dangers should be kept in mind when using neural networks. First, although they are capable of generalizing from a set of examples, extrapolation is still a serious danger. If the network sees only records in a certain range, its predictions outside this range can be completely invalid.

Second, the extreme flexibility of the neural network relies heavily on having sufficient data for training purposes. A related issue is that in classification problems, the network requires sufficient records of the minority class in order to learn it. This is achieved by oversampling, as explained in Chapter 2.

Finally, a practical consideration that can determine the usefulness of a neural network is the computation time. Neural networks are relatively heavy on computation time, requiring a longer runtime than other classifiers. This runtime grows greatly when the number of predictors is increased (as there will be many more weights to compute). In applications where real-time or near-real-time prediction is required, runtime should be measured to make sure that it does not cause unacceptable delay in the decision-making.

PROBLEMS

11.1 Credit Card Use. Consider the hypothetical bank data in Table 11.10 on consumers' use of credit card credit facilities. Create a small worksheet in Excel to illustrate one pass through a simple neural network.

TABLE 11.10 DATA FOR CREDIT CARD EXAMPLE AND VARIABLE DESCRIPTIONS

Years	Salary	Used credit
4	43	0
18	65	1
1	53	0
3	95	0
15	88	1
6	112	1

Years: number of years the customer has been with the bank
Salary: customer's salary (in thousands of dollars)
Used credit: 1 = customer has left an unpaid credit card balance at the end of at least one month in the prior year, 0 = balance was paid off at the end of each month

11.2 Neural Net Evolution. A neural net typically starts out with random coefficients; hence, it produces essentially random predictions when presented with its first case. What is the key ingredient by which the net evolves to produce a more accurate prediction?

11.3 Car Sales. Consider the data on used cars (*mlba::ToyotaCorolla*) with 1436 records and details on 38 variables, including Price, Age, KM, HP, and other specifications. The goal is to predict the price of a used Toyota Corolla based on its specifications.

- Fit a neural network model to the data. Use a single hidden layer with two nodes.

- Use predictors Age_08_04, KM, Fuel_Type, HP, Automatic, Doors, Quarterly_Tax, Mfr_Guarantee, Guarantee_Period, Airco, Automatic_airco, CD_Player, Powered_Windows, Sport_Model, and Tow_Bar.

- Remember to first scale the numerical predictor and outcome variables to a 0–1 scale, and convert categorical predictors to dummies.

- Record the RMS error for the training data and the holdout data. Repeat the process, changing the number of hidden layers and nodes to {single layer with 5 nodes} and {two layers, 5 nodes in each layer}.

  a. What happens to the RMS error for the training data as the number of layers and nodes increases?

  b. What happens to the RMS error for the holdout data?

  c. Comment on the appropriate number of layers and nodes for this application.

11.4 Direct Mailing to Airline Customers. East-West Airlines has entered into a partnership with the wireless phone company Telcon to sell the latter's service via direct mail. The dataset *mlba::EastWestAirlinesNN* contains a subset of a data sample of who has already received a test offer. About 13% accepted.

You are asked to develop a model to classify East–West customers as to whether they purchase a wireless phone service contract (outcome variable Phone_Sale). This model will be used to classify additional customers.

a. Run a neural net model on these data, using a single hidden layer with five nodes. Remember to first convert categorical variables into dummies, and scale numerical predictor variables to a 0–1. Generate a decile-wise lift chart for the training and holdout sets. Interpret the meaning (in business terms) of the leftmost bar of the holdout decile-wise lift chart.

b. Comment on the difference between the training and holdout lift charts.

c. Run a second neural net model on the data, this time setting the number of hidden nodes to 1. Comment now on the difference between this model and the model you ran earlier, and how overfitting might have affected results.

d. What sort of information, if any, is provided about the effects of the various predictor variables?

## CHAPTER 12

Discriminant Analysis

In this chapter, we describe the method of discriminant analysis, which is a model-based approach to classification. We discuss the main principle, where classification is based on the distance of a record from each of the class means. We explain the underlying measure of "statistical distance," which takes into account the correlation between predictors. The output of a discriminant analysis procedure generates estimated "classification functions," which are then used to produce classification scores that can be translated into classifications or propensities (probabilities of class membership). One can also directly integrate misclassification costs into the discriminant analysis setup, and we explain how this is achieved. Finally, we discuss the underlying model assumptions, the practical robustness to some assumption violations, and the advantages of discriminant analysis when the assumptions are reasonably met (for example, the sufficiency of a small training sample).

Discriminant Analysis in R

The main R packages introduced in this chapter are `DiscriMiner` and `MASS` (function *lda*), for performing discriminant analysis.

12.1 INTRODUCTION

Discriminant analysis is a classification method. Like logistic regression, it is a classical statistical technique that can be used for classification and profiling. It uses sets of measurements on different classes of records to classify new records into one of those classes (*classification*). Common uses of the method have been in classifying organisms into species and subspecies; classifying applications for loans, credit cards, and insurance into low- and high-risk categories;

Machine Learning for Business Analytics: Concepts, Techniques, and Applications in R, Second Edition.
Galit Shmueli, Peter C. Bruce, Peter Gedeck, Inbal Yahav, and Nitin R. Patel
© 2023 John Wiley & Sons, Inc. Published 2023 by John Wiley & Sons, Inc.

classifying customers of new products into early adopters, early majority, late majority, and laggards; classifying bonds into bond rating categories; classifying skulls of human fossils; as well as in research studies involving disputed authorship, decisions on college admission, medical studies involving alcoholics and nonalcoholics, and methods to identify human fingerprints. Discriminant analysis can also be used to highlight aspects that distinguish the classes (*profiling*).

We return to two examples that were described in earlier chapters, the Riding Mowers and Personal Loan Acceptance examples. In each of these, the outcome variable has two classes. We close with a third example involving more than two classes.

Example 1: Riding Mowers

We return to the example from Chapter 7, where a riding-mower manufacturer would like to find a way of classifying families in a city into those likely to purchase a riding mower and those not likely to purchase one. A pilot random sample of 12 owners and 12 nonowners in the city is undertaken. The data are given in Chapter 7 (Table 7.1), and a scatter plot is shown in Figure 12.1. We can think of a linear classification rule as a line that separates the two-dimensional region into two parts, with most of the owners in one half-plane and most nonowners in the complementary half-plane. A good classification rule would separate the data so that the fewest points are misclassified: the line shown in Figure 12.1 seems to do a good job in discriminating between the two classes as it makes four misclassifications out of 24 points. Can we do better?

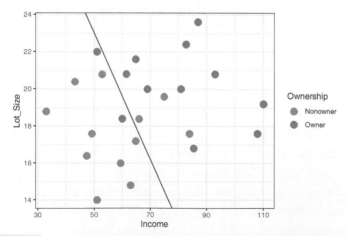

FIGURE 12.1   SCATTER PLOT OF LOT SIZE VS. INCOME FOR 24 OWNERS AND NONOWNERS OF RIDING MOWERS. THE (AD HOC) LINE TRIES TO SEPARATE OWNERS FROM NONOWNERS

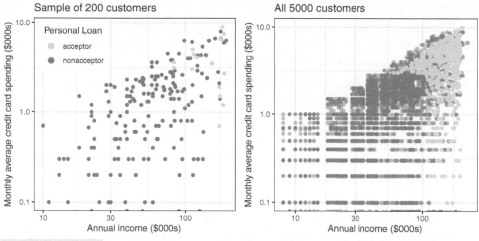

FIGURE 12.2   PERSONAL LOAN ACCEPTANCE AS A FUNCTION OF INCOME AND CREDIT CARD SPENDING FOR 5000 CUSTOMERS OF THE UNIVERSAL BANK AND A RANDOM SAMPLE OF 200 CUSTOMERS

Example 2: Personal Loan Acceptance

The riding-mowers example is a classic example and is useful in describing the concept and goal of discriminant analysis. However, in today's business applications, the number of records is much larger, and their separation into classes is much less distinct. To illustrate this, we return to the Universal Bank example described in Chapter 9, where the bank's goal is to identify new customers most likely to accept a personal loan. For simplicity, we will consider only two predictor variables: the customer's annual income (Income, in $000s) and the average monthly credit card spending (CCAvg, in $000s). The left plot of Figure 12.2 shows the acceptance of a personal loan by a subset of 200 customers from the bank's database as a function of Income and CCAvg. We use a logarithmic scale on both axes to enhance visibility because there are many points condensed in the low-income, low-CC spending area. Even for this small subset, the separation is not clear. The right plot shows all 5000 customers and the added complexity of dealing with large numbers of records.

12.2 DISTANCE OF A RECORD FROM A CLASS

Finding the best separation between records involves measuring their distance from their class. The general idea is to classify a record to the class to which it is closest. Suppose that we are required to classify a new customer of Universal Bank as being an *acceptor* or a *nonacceptor* of their personal loan offer, based on an income of x. From the bank's database we find that the mean income for loan acceptors was $144.75K and for nonacceptors $66.24K. We can use Income as a predictor of loan acceptance via a simple *Euclidean distance rule*: if x is closer to the mean income of the acceptor class than to the mean income of the nonacceptor class, classify the customer as an *acceptor*; otherwise, classify the customer as a *nonacceptor*. In other words, if $|x - 144.75| < |x - 66.24|$, then classification = *acceptor*; otherwise, *nonacceptor*. Moving from a single predictor variable (income) to two or more predictor variables, the equivalent of the mean of a class is the *centroid* of a class. This is simply the vector of means $\overline{\mathbf{x}} = [\overline{x}_1, \ldots, \overline{x}_p]$. The Euclidean distance between a record with p measurements $\mathbf{x} = [x_1, \ldots, x_p]$ and the centroid $\overline{\mathbf{x}}$ is defined as the square root of the sum of the squared differences between the individual values and the means:

$$D_{\text{Euclidean}}(\mathbf{x}, \overline{\mathbf{x}}) = \sqrt{(x_1 - \overline{x}_1)^2 + \cdots + (x_p - \overline{x}_p)^2}. \tag{12.1}$$

Using the Euclidean distance has three drawbacks. First, the distance depends on the units we choose to measure the predictor variables. We will get different answers if we decide to measure income in dollars, for instance, rather than in thousands of dollars.

Second, Euclidean distance does not take into account the variability of the variables. For example, if we compare the variability in income in the two classes, we find that for acceptors, the standard deviation is lower than for nonacceptors ($\$31.6$K vs. $\$40.6$K). Therefore, the income of a new customer might be closer to the acceptors' mean income in dollars, but because of the large variability in income for nonacceptors, this customer is just as likely to be a nonacceptor. We therefore want the distance measure to take into account the variance of the different variables and measure a distance in standard deviations rather than in the original units. This is equivalent to z-scores.

Third, Euclidean distance ignores the correlation between the variables. This is often a very important consideration, especially when we are using many predictor variables to separate classes. In this case, there will often be variables, which by themselves are useful discriminators between classes, but in the presence of other predictor variables are practically redundant, as they capture the same effects as the other variables.

A solution to these drawbacks is to use a measure called *statistical distance* (or *Mahalanobis distance*). Let us denote by S the covariance matrix between the p variables. The definition of a statistical distance is

$$D_{\text{Statistical}}(\mathbf{x}, \overline{\mathbf{x}}) = \sqrt{[\mathbf{x} - \overline{\mathbf{x}}]' S^{-1} [\mathbf{x} - \overline{\mathbf{x}}]}$$

$$= \sqrt{[(x_1 - \overline{x}_1), (x_2 - \overline{x}_2), \ldots, (x_p - \overline{x}_p)] S^{-1} \begin{bmatrix} x_1 - \overline{x}_1 \\ x_2 - \overline{x}_2 \\ \vdots \\ x_p - \overline{x}_p \end{bmatrix}} \tag{12.2}$$

(the notation $'$, which represents *transpose operation*, simply turns the column vector into a row vector). S^{-1} is the inverse matrix of S, which is the p-dimension extension to division. When there is a single predictor ($p = 1$), this formula reduces to a (squared) z-score calculation, since we subtract the mean and divide by the standard deviation. The statistical distance takes into account not only the predictor means, but also the spread of the predictor values and the correlations between the different predictors. To compute a statistical distance between a record and a class, we must compute the predictor means (the centroid) and the covariances between each pair of predictors. These are used to construct the distances. The method of discriminant analysis uses statistical distance as the basis for finding a separating line (or, if there are more than two variables, a separating hyperplane) that is equally distant from the different class means.[1] It is based on measuring the statistical distances of a record to each of the classes and allocating it to the closest class. This is done through *classification functions*, which are explained next.

12.3 FISHER'S LINEAR CLASSIFICATION FUNCTIONS

Linear classification functions were proposed in 1936 by the noted statistician R. A. Fisher as the basis for improved separation of records into classes. The idea is to find linear functions of the measurements that maximize the ratio of between-class variability to within-class variability. In other words, we would obtain classes that are very homogeneous and differ the most from each other. For each record, these functions are used to compute scores that measure the proximity of that record to each of the classes. A record is classified as belonging to the class for which it has the highest classification score (equivalent to the smallest statistical distance).

USING CLASSIFICATION FUNCTION SCORES TO CLASSIFY RECORDS

For each record, we calculate the value of the classification function (one for each class); whichever class's function has the highest value (= score) is the class assigned to that record.

The classification functions are estimated using software. In R, we can obtain the estimated classification functions using function *linDA()* in the DiscriMiner

---

[1]An alternative approach finds a separating line or hyperplane that is "best" at separating the different clouds of points. In the case of two classes, the two methods coincide.

TABLE 12.1	DISCRIMINANT ANALYSIS FOR RIDING-MOWER DATA, DISPLAYING THE ESTIMATED CLASSIFICATION FUNCTIONS

 code for linear discriminant analysis

```
library(caret)
mowers.df <- mlba::RidingMowers
trControl <- caret::trainControl(method='none')
model <- train(Ownership ~ Income + Lot_Size, data=mowers.df,
               method='lda', trControl=trControl)
model$finalModel  # access the wrapped LDA model

# DiscriMiner exposes the Fisher's linear classification function
library(DiscriMiner)
mowers.df <- mlba::RidingMowers
da.mower <- linDA(mowers.df[,1:2], mowers.df[,3])
da.mower$functions
```

Output

```
> model$finalModel
Call:
lda(x, grouping = y)

Prior probabilities of groups:
Nonowner   Owner
    0.5     0.5

Group means:
        Income Lot_Size
Nonowner 57.400 17.63333
Owner    79.475 20.26667

Coefficients of linear discriminants:
             LD1
Income   0.0484468
Lot_Size 0.3795228

> da.mower$functions
              Nonowner         Owner
constant -51.4214499777 -73.1602116488
Income     0.3293554091   0.4295857129
Lot_Size   4.6815655074   5.4667502174
```

package.[2] For example, Table 12.1 shows the classification functions obtained from running discriminant analysis on the riding-mowers data, using two predictors. Note that the number of classification functions is equal to the number of classes (in this case, two: *owner/nonowner*).

To classify a family into the class of *owners* or *nonowners*, we use the classification functions to compute the family's classification scores: a family is

___

[2]An alternative is the function *lda()* in the caret package, but it does not provide the estimated classification functions. However, we will use it later as it provides simpler training and scoring. We also note that *lda()* generates *coefficients of linear discriminants* with a single coefficient for each predictor. This is called the *decision function*, which differs from the *classification functions*.

classified into the class of *owners* if the owner function score is higher than the nonowner function score and into *nonowners* if the reverse is the case. These functions are specified in a way that can be easily generalized to more than two classes. The values given for the functions are simply the weights to be associated with each variable in the linear function in a manner analogous to multiple linear regression. For instance, the first household has an income of \$60K and a lot size of 18.4K ft^2. Their *owner* score is therefore $-73.16 + (0.43)(60) + (5.47)(18.4) = 53.20$, and their *nonowner* score is $-51.42 + (0.33)(60) + (4.68)(18.4) = 54.48$. Since the second score is higher, the household is (mis)classified by the model as a nonowner. Such calculations are done by the software and do not need to be done manually. For example, the scores and classifications for all 24 households—produced by R's *linDA()* function—are given in Table 12.2.

An alternative way for classifying a record into one of the classes is to compute the probability of belonging to each of the classes and assigning the record to the most likely class. If we have two classes, we need only compute a single probability for each record (of belonging to *owners*, for example). Using a threshold of 0.5 is equivalent to assigning the record to the class with the highest classification score. The advantage of this approach is that we obtain propensities, which can be used for goals such as ranking: we sort the records in order of descending probabilities and generate lift curves.

Let us assume that there are m classes. To compute the probability of belonging to a certain class k, for a certain record i, we need to compute all the classification scores $c_1(i), c_2(i), \ldots, c_m(i)$ and combine them using the following formula:

$$P[\text{record } i \text{ (with measurements } x_1, x_2, \ldots, x_p) \text{ belongs to class } k]$$
$$= \frac{e^{c_k(i)}}{e^{c_1(i)} + e^{c_2(i)} + \cdots + e^{c_m(i)}}.$$

These probabilities and their computation for the riding-mower data are given in Table 12.2. In R, function *linDA()* in package `DiscriMiner` provides scores and classifications, but does not directly provide propensities, so we need to use the above formula to compute probabilities from the scores (see R code in Table 12.2). Alternatively, use function *lda* in package `MASS` or through `caret` to automatically compute probabilities.

We now have three misclassifications, compared to four in our original (ad hoc) classification. This can be seen in Figure 12.3, which includes the line resulting from the discriminant model.[3]

---

[3]The slope of the line is given by $-a_1/a_2$ and the intercept is $a_1/a_2 \, \bar{x}_1 + \bar{x}_2$, where a_i is the difference between the ith classification function coefficients of owners and nonowners (e.g., here $a_{\text{income}} = 0.43 - 0.33$).

TABLE 12.2   CLASSIFICATION SCORES, PREDICTED CLASSES, AND PROBABILITIES FOR RIDING-MOWER DATA

R code for obtaining classification scores, predicted classes, and probabilities

```
da.mower <- linDA(mowers.df[,1:2], mowers.df[,3])
# compute propensities manually (below); or, use lda() in package MASS or caret with predict()
propensity.owner <- exp(da.mower$scores[,2])/(exp(da.mower$scores[,1])+exp(da.mower$scores[,2]))
data.frame(Actual=mowers.df$Ownership, Predicted=da.mower$classification,
           da.mower$scores, propensity.owner=propensity.owner)
```

Output

	Actual	Predicted	Nonowner	Owner	propensity.owner
1	Owner	Nonowner	54.48067990	53.20313512	0.21796844638
2	Owner	Owner	55.38873802	55.41077045	0.50550788510
3	Owner	Owner	71.04259549	72.75874724	0.84763249334
4	Owner	Owner	66.21047023	66.96771421	0.68075507343
5	Owner	Owner	87.71741659	93.22905050	0.99597675014
6	Owner	Owner	74.72663830	79.09877951	0.98753320250
7	Owner	Owner	66.54448713	69.44984917	0.94811086581
8	Owner	Owner	80.71624526	84.86469025	0.98445646665
9	Owner	Owner	64.93538340	65.81620689	0.70699283969
10	Owner	Owner	76.58516562	80.49966417	0.98043968864
11	Owner	Owner	68.37011705	69.01716449	0.65634480272
12	Owner	Owner	68.88764830	70.97123544	0.88929767077
13	Nonowner	Owner	65.03888965	66.20702108	0.76280709688
14	Nonowner	Nonowner	63.34507817	63.23031851	0.47134152980
15	Nonowner	Nonowner	50.44370726	48.70504628	0.14948309577
16	Nonowner	Nonowner	58.31064004	56.91959558	0.19924106677
17	Nonowner	Owner	58.63995731	59.13979206	0.62242049465
18	Nonowner	Nonowner	47.17838908	44.19020925	0.04796273478
19	Nonowner	Nonowner	43.04730944	39.82518317	0.03834151004
20	Nonowner	Nonowner	56.45681236	55.78064940	0.33711822839
21	Nonowner	Nonowner	40.96767073	36.85685471	0.01612995010
22	Nonowner	Nonowner	47.46071006	43.79102096	0.02485107730
23	Nonowner	Nonowner	30.91759299	25.28316275	0.00355999342
24	Nonowner	Nonowner	38.61511030	34.81159148	0.02180608595

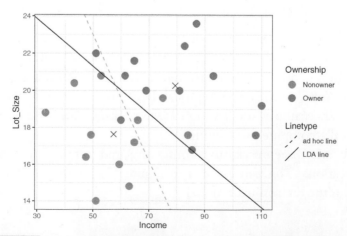

FIGURE 12.3   CLASS SEPARATION OBTAINED FROM THE DISCRIMINANT MODEL COMPARED TO AD HOC LINE FROM FIGURE 12.1 (CROSSES INDICATE THE CLASS MEANS)

12.4 CLASSIFICATION PERFORMANCE OF DISCRIMINANT ANALYSIS

The discriminant analysis method relies on two main assumptions to arrive at classification scores: first, it assumes that the predictor measurements in all classes come from a multivariate normal distribution. When this assumption is reasonably met, discriminant analysis is a more powerful tool than other classification methods, such as logistic regression. In fact, Efron (1975) showed that discriminant analysis is 30% more efficient than logistic regression if the data are multivariate normal, in the sense that we require 30% less records to arrive at the same results. In practice, it has been shown that this method is relatively robust to departures from normality in the sense that predictors can be non–normal and even dummy variables. This is true as long as the smallest class is sufficiently large (approximately more than 20 records). This method is also known to be sensitive to outliers in both the univariate space of single predictors and in the multivariate space. Exploratory analysis should therefore be used to locate extreme cases and determine whether they can be eliminated.

The second assumption behind discriminant analysis is that the correlation structure between the different predictors within a class is the same across classes. This can be roughly checked by computing the correlation matrix between the predictors separately for each class and comparing matrices. If the correlations differ substantially across classes, the classifier will tend to classify records into the class with the largest variability. When the correlation structure differs significantly and the dataset is very large, an alternative is to use quadratic discriminant analysis.[4]

Notwithstanding the caveats embodied in these statistical assumptions, recall that in a predictive modeling environment, the ultimate test is whether the model works effectively. A reasonable approach is to conduct some exploratory analysis with respect to normality and correlation, train and evaluate a model, and then, depending on classification accuracy and what you learned from the initial exploration, circle back and explore further whether outliers should be examined or choice of predictor variables revisited.

With respect to the evaluation of classification accuracy, we once again use the general measures of performance that were described in Chapter 5 (judging the performance of a classifier), with the principal ones based on the confusion

---

[4]In practice, quadratic discriminant analysis has not been found useful except when the difference in the correlation matrices is large and the number of records available for training and testing is large. The reason is that the quadratic model requires estimating many more parameters that are all subject to error [for m classes and p variables, the total number of parameters to be estimated for all the different correlation matrices is $mp(p+1)/2$].

matrix (accuracy alone or combined with costs) for classification and the lift and gains chart for ranking. The same argument for using the holdout set for evaluating performance still holds. For example, in the riding-mowers example, families 1, 13, and 17 are misclassified. This means that the model yields an error rate of 12.5% for these data. However, this rate is a biased estimate—it is overly optimistic, because we have used the same data for fitting the classification functions and for estimating the error. Therefore, as with all other models, we test performance on a holdout set that includes data that were not involved in estimating the classification functions.

To obtain the confusion matrix from a discriminant analysis, we either use the classification scores directly or the propensities (probabilities of class membership) that are computed from the classification scores. In both cases, we decide on the class assignment of each record based on the highest score or probability. We then compare these classifications to the actual class memberships of these records. This yields the confusion matrix.

12.5 PRIOR PROBABILITIES

So far we have assumed that our objective is to minimize the classification error. The method presented above assumes that the chances of encountering a record from either class are the same as the proportion of the classes in the training set. If the probability of encountering a record for classification in the future is not equal for the different classes, we should modify our functions to reduce our expected (long-run average) error rate. This can easily be done in function *lda()* by setting the prior probabilities using the *prior* argument.

To illustrate this, suppose that the percentage of riding-mower owners in the population is 15%, compared to 50% in the sample. This means that the model should classify fewer households as *owners*. As shown in Table 12.3, we add *prior=c(0.85, 0.15)* to the training step. To see how this can affect classifications, consider family 13, which was misclassified as an owner in the case involving equal probability of class membership. When we account for the lower probability of owning a mower in the population, family 13 is classified properly as a nonowner (its *owner* classification score is below the *nonowner* score).

12.6 UNEQUAL MISCLASSIFICATION COSTS

A second practical modification is needed when misclassification costs are not symmetrical. If the cost of misclassifying a class 1 record is very different from the cost of misclassifying a class 2 record, we may want to minimize the expected

| TABLE 12.3 | DISCRIMINANT ANALYSIS FOR RIDING-MOWER DATA WITH MODIFIED PRIOR PROBABILITIES |

 code for linear discriminant analysis

```
trControl <- caret::trainControl(method='none')
model <- train(Ownership ~ Income + Lot_Size, data=mowers.df,
               method='lda', trControl=trControl)
model.prior <- train(Ownership ~ Income + Lot_Size, data=mowers.df,
               method='lda', prior=c(0.85, 0.15),
               trControl=trControl)

family.13 <- mowers.df[13,]
predict(model, family.13)
predict(model.prior, family.13)
```

Output

```
> predict(model, family.13)
[1] Owner
Levels: Nonowner Owner
> predict(model.prior, family.13)
[1] Nonowner
Levels: Nonowner Owner
```

cost of misclassification rather than the simple error rate (which does not account for unequal misclassification costs). In the two-class case, it is easy to manipulate the classification functions to account for differing misclassification costs (in addition to prior probabilities). We denote by q_1 the cost of misclassifying a class 1 member (into class 2). Similarly, q_2 denotes the cost of misclassifying a class 2 member (into class 1). To incorporate both prior probabilities (p_1, p_2) and misclassification costs (q_1, q_2), we calculate their pairwise product $(p_1 q_1, p_2 q_2)$ and then divide by their sum:

$$p_1^* = \frac{p_1 q_1}{p_1 q_1 + p_2 q_2}$$
$$p_2^* = \frac{p_2 q_2}{p_1 q_1 + p_2 q_2}$$

We use p_1^* and p_2^* in the *prior* argument for the *lda()* function, as described in the previous section.

In practice, it is not always simple to come up with misclassification costs q_1 and q_2 for each class. It is usually much easier to estimate the *ratio of costs* q_2/q_1 (e.g., if credit nondefaulter is class 1 and credit defaulter is class 2, the cost of misclassifying a credit defaulter is 10 times more expensive than that of misclassifying a nondefaulter). Luckily, the relationship between the classification functions depends only on this ratio. Therefore, we can set $q_1 = 1$ and $q_2 = ratio$ and adjust the priors using:

$$p_1^* = \frac{p_1}{p_1 + p_2 \times ratio}$$

$$p_2^* = \frac{p_2 \times ratio}{p_1 + p_2 \times ratio}$$

12.7 CLASSIFYING MORE THAN TWO CLASSES

Example 3: Medical Dispatch to Accident Scenes

Ideally, every automobile accident call to the emergency number 911 results in the immediate dispatch of an ambulance to the accident scene. However, in some cases the dispatch might be delayed (e.g., at peak accident hours or in some resource-strapped towns or shifts). In such cases, the 911 dispatchers must make decisions about which units to send based on sketchy information. It is useful to augment the limited information provided in the initial call with additional information in order to classify the accident as minor injury, serious injury, or death. For this purpose, we can use data that were collected on automobile accidents in the United States in 2001 that involved some type of injury. For each accident, additional information is recorded, such as day of week, weather conditions, and road type. Table 12.4 shows a small sample of records with 11 measurements of interest.

TABLE 12.4   SAMPLE OF 20 AUTOMOBILE ACCIDENTS FROM THE 2001 DEPARTMENT OF TRANSPORTATION DATABASE

Accident	RushHour	WRK_ZONE	WKDY	INT_HWY	LGTCON	LEVEL	SPD_LIM	SUR_COND	TRAF_WAY	WEATHER	MAX_SEV
1	1	0	1	1	dark_light	1	70	ice	one_way	adverse	no-injury
2	1	0	1	0	dark_light	0	70	ice	divided	adverse	no-injury
3	1	0	1	0	dark_light	0	65	ice	divided	adverse	non-fatal
4	1	0	1	0	dark_light	0	55	ice	two_way	not_adverse	non-fatal
5	1	0	0	0	dark_light	0	35	snow	one_way	adverse	no-injury
6	1	0	1	0	dark_light	1	35	wet	divided	adverse	no-injury
7	0	0	1	1	dark_light	1	70	wet	divided	adverse	non-fatal
8	0	0	1	0	dark_light	1	35	wet	two_way	adverse	no-injury
9	1	0	1	0	dark_light	0	25	wet	one_way	adverse	non-fatal
10	1	0	1	0	dark_light	0	35	wet	divided	adverse	non-fatal
11	1	0	1	0	dark_light	0	30	wet	divided	adverse	non-fatal
12	1	0	1	0	dark_light	0	60	wet	divided	not_adverse	no-injury
13	1	0	1	0	dark_light	0	40	wet	two_way	not_adverse	no-injury
14	0	0	1	0	day	1	65	dry	two_way	not_adverse	fatal
15	1	0	0	0	day	0	55	dry	two_way	not_adverse	fatal
16	1	0	1	0	day	0	55	dry	two_way	not_adverse	non-fatal
17	1	0	0	0	day	0	55	dry	two_way	not_adverse	non-fatal
18	0	0	1	0	dark	0	55	ice	two_way	not_adverse	no-injury
19	0	0	0	0	dark	0	50	ice	two_way	adverse	no-injury
20	0	0	0	0	dark	1	55	snow	divided	adverse	no-injury

Each accident is classified as one of three injury types (no-injury, non-fatal, or fatal), and has 10 more measurements (extracted from a larger set of measurements).

The goal is to see how well the predictors can be used to classify injury type correctly. To evaluate this, a reduced sample of 1000 records was drawn (with categories combined so that most predictors are binary) and partitioned into training and holdout sets, and a discriminant analysis was performed on the training data containing 600 records. The training set is available as *mlba::Accidents*. The output structure is very similar to that for the two-class case. The only difference is that each record now has three classification functions (one for each injury type), and the confusion and error matrices are of size 3×3 to account for all the combinations of correct and incorrect classifications (see Table 12.5).

The rule for classification is still to classify a record to the class that has the highest corresponding classification score. The classification scores are

TABLE 12.5   DISCRIMINANT ANALYSIS FOR THE THREE-CLASS INJURY EXAMPLE: CLASSIFICATION FUNCTIONS AND CONFUSION MATRIX FOR TRAINING SET

 code for running linear discriminant analysis on the accidents data

```
library(DiscriMiner)
library(caret)

accidents.df <- mlba::Accidents
lda.model <- linDA(accidents.df[,1:10], accidents.df[,11])
lda.model$functions
confusionMatrix(as.factor(lda.model$classification), as.factor(accidents.df$MAX_SEV))
```

Output

```
> lda.model$functions
                      fatal      no-injury       non-fatal
constant       -25.5958095610 -24.514323034 -24.2336221574
RushHour         0.9225623509   1.952403425   1.9031991672
WRK_ZONE         0.5178609440   1.195060274   0.7705682214
WKDY             4.7801494470   6.417633787   6.1165223679
INT_HWY         -1.8418782656  -2.673037935  -2.5366224810
LGTCON_day       3.7070124215   3.666075602   3.7276207831
LEVEL            2.6268937732   1.567550702   1.7138656960
SPD_LIM          0.5051317221   0.461479676   0.4520847732
SUR_COND_dry     9.9988600752  15.833794528  16.2565639740
TRAF_two_way     7.1079766143   6.342147286   6.3549435330
WEATHER_adverse  9.6880211017  16.363876853  16.3172755675

> confusionMatrix(as.factor(lda.model$classification), as.factor(accidents.df$MAX_SEV))
Confusion Matrix and Statistics

           Reference
Prediction  fatal no-injury non-fatal
  fatal         1         6         6
  no-injury     1       114        95
  non-fatal     3       172       202

Overall Statistics

              Accuracy : 0.5283333
```

computed, as before, using the classification function coefficients. This can be seen in Table 12.6. For instance, the *no-injury* classification score for the first accident in the training set is $-24.51 + (1.95)(1) + (1.19)(0) + \cdots + (16.36)(1) = 31.42$.

TABLE 12.6   CLASSIFICATION SCORES, MEMBERSHIP PROBABILITIES, AND CLASSIFICATIONS FOR THE THREE-CLASS INJURY TRAINING DATASET

R code for producing linear discriminant analysis scores and propensities

```
propensity <- exp(lda.model$scores[,1:3])/
    (exp(lda.model$scores[,1])+exp(lda.model$scores[,2])+exp(lda.model$scores[,3]))

res <- data.frame(Actual = accidents.df$MAX_SEV,
            Classification = lda.model$classification,
            Score = round(lda.model$scores,2),
            Propensity = round(propensity,2))
head(res)
```

Output

```
  Actual Classification Score.fatal Score.no.injury Score.non.fatal
1 no-injury      no-injury       25.94           31.42           30.93
2 non-fatal      no-injury       15.00           15.58           15.01
3 no-injury      no-injury        2.69            9.95            9.81
4 no-injury      no-injury       10.10           17.94           17.64
5 non-fatal      no-injury        2.42           11.76           11.41
6 non-fatal      no-injury        7.47           16.37           15.93
  Propensity.fatal Propensity.no.injury Propensity.non.fatal
1             0.00                 0.62                 0.38
2             0.26                 0.47                 0.27
3             0.00                 0.54                 0.46
4             0.00                 0.57                 0.43
5             0.00                 0.59                 0.41
6             0.00                 0.61                 0.39
```

We can also compute for each accident, the propensities (estimated probabilities) of belonging to each of the three classes using the same relationship between classification scores and probabilities as in the two-class case. For instance, the probability of the above accident involving non-fatal injuries is estimated by the model as

$$\frac{e^{30.93}}{e^{31.42} + e^{30.93} + e^{25.94}} = 0.38. \tag{12.3}$$

The probabilities of an accident involving no injuries or fatal injuries are computed in a similar manner. For the first accident in the training set, the highest probability is that of involving no injuries, and therefore it is classified as a *no-injury* accident.

We illustrated the above approach using the **discriMiner** package that produces classification scores. If you only want predictions, class membership or propensities, you can also use **caret** and *MASS::lda()*. Table 12.7 shows how this can be done.

TABLE 12.7   **CLASSIFICATION AND MEMBERSHIP PROBABILITIES**

code for producing classification and propensities using linear discriminant analysis with `caret` and *lda()*

```
library(tidyverse)
accidents.df <-  mlba::Accidents %>%
  mutate(MAX_SEV = factor(MAX_SEV))
da.model <- train(MAX_SEV ~ ., data=accidents.df, method='lda')
res <- data.frame(Actual=accidents.df$MAX_SEV,
          Classification=predict(da.model),
          Propensity=predict(da.model, type='prob') %>% round(2))
head(res)
```

Output

```
    Actual Classification Propensity.fatal Propensity.no.injury Propensity.non.fatal
1 no-injury      no-injury           0.00                 0.62                 0.38
2 non-fatal      no-injury           0.26                 0.47                 0.27
3 no-injury      no-injury           0.00                 0.54                 0.46
4 no-injury      no-injury           0.00                 0.57                 0.43
5 non-fatal      no-injury           0.00                 0.59                 0.41
6 non-fatal      no-injury           0.00                 0.61                 0.39
```

12.8 ADVANTAGES AND WEAKNESSES

Discriminant analysis is typically considered more of a statistical classification method than a data mining method. This is reflected in its absence or short mention in many machine learning resources. However, it is very popular in social sciences and has shown good performance. The use and performance of discriminant analysis are similar to those of multiple linear regression. The two methods therefore share several advantages and weaknesses.

Like linear regression, discriminant analysis searches for the optimal weighting of predictors. In linear regression, weighting is with relation to the numerical outcome variable, whereas in discriminant analysis, it is with relation to separating the classes. Both use least squares for estimation, and the resulting estimates are robust to local optima.

In both methods, an underlying assumption is normality. In discriminant analysis, we assume that the predictors are approximately from a multivariate normal distribution. Although this assumption is violated in many practical situations (such as with commonly used binary predictors), the method is surprisingly robust. According to Hastie et al. (2001), the reason might be that data can usually support only simple separation boundaries, such as linear boundaries. However, for continuous variables that are found to be very skewed (as can be seen through a histogram), transformations such as the log transform can improve performance. In addition, the method's sensitivity to outliers commands exploring the data for extreme values and removing those records from the analysis.

An advantage of discriminant analysis as a classifier (like logistic regression in this respect) is that it provides estimates of single-predictor contributions.[5] This is useful for obtaining a ranking of predictor importance and for variable selection.

Finally, the method is computationally simple, parsimonious, and especially useful for small datasets. With its parametric form, discriminant analysis makes the most out of the data and is therefore especially useful with small samples (as explained in Section 12.4).

---

[5]Comparing predictor contribution requires normalizing all the predictors before running discriminant analysis. Then, compare each coefficient across the two classification functions: coefficients with large differences indicate a predictor with high separation power.

PROBLEMS

12.1 **Personal Loan Acceptance.** Universal Bank is a relatively young bank growing rapidly in terms of overall customer acquisition. The majority of these customers are liability customers with varying sizes of relationship with the bank. The customer base of asset customers is quite small, and the bank is interested in expanding this base rapidly to bring in more loan business. In particular, it wants to explore ways of converting its liability customers to personal loan customers.

A campaign the bank ran for liability customers last year showed a healthy conversion rate of over 9% successes. This has encouraged the retail marketing department to devise smarter campaigns with better target marketing. The goal of our analysis is to model the previous campaign's customer behavior to analyze what combination of factors makes a customer more likely to accept a personal loan. This will serve as the basis for the design of a new campaign.

The dataset *mlba::UniversalBank* contains data on 5000 customers. The data include customer demographic information (e.g., age, income), the customer's relationship with the bank (e.g., mortgage, securities account), and the customer response to the last personal loan campaign (Personal Loan). Among these 5000 customers, only 480 (= 9.6%) accepted the personal loan that was offered to them in the previous campaign.

Partition the data (60% training and 40% holdout), and then perform a discriminant analysis that models Personal Loan as a function of the remaining predictors (excluding zip code). Remember to turn categorical predictors with more than two categories into dummy variables first if you use `DiscriMiner`. If you use `caret` or *MASS::lda*, categorical predictors will be automatically expanded into dummy variables. Specify the success class as 1 (personal loan acceptance), and use the default cutoff value of 0.5.

a. Compute summary statistics for the predictors separately for loan acceptors and nonacceptors. For continuous predictors, compute the mean and standard deviation. For categorical predictors, compute the percentages. Are there predictors where the two classes differ substantially?

b. Examine the model performance on the holdout set.
   i. What is the accuracy rate?
   ii. Is one type of misclassification more likely than the other?
   iii. Select three customers who were misclassified as *acceptors* and three who were misclassified as *nonacceptors*. The goal is to determine why they are misclassified. First, examine their probability of being classified as acceptors: is it close to the threshold of 0.5? If not, compare their predictor values to the summary statistics of the two classes to determine why they were misclassified.

c. As in many marketing campaigns, it is more important to identify customers who will accept the offer rather than customers who will not accept it. Therefore, a good model should be especially accurate at detecting acceptors. Examine the cumulative gains chart and lift curve for the holdout set, and interpret them in light of this ranking goal.

d. Compare the results from the discriminant analysis with those from a logistic regression (both with cutoff 0.5 and the same predictors). Examine the confusion matrices, and the cumulative gains chart and lift curve. Which method performs better on your holdout set in detecting the acceptors?

e. The bank is planning to continue its campaign by sending its offer to 1000 additional customers. Suppose that the cost of sending the offer is $1 and the profit from an accepted offer is $50. What is the expected profitability of this campaign?

f. The cost of misclassifying a loan acceptor customer as a nonacceptor is much higher than the opposite misclassification cost. To minimize the expected cost of misclassification, should the cutoff value for classification (which is currently at 0.5) be increased or decreased?

12.2 **Identifying Good System Administrators.** A management consultant is studying the roles played by experience and training in a system administrator's ability to complete a set of tasks in a specified amount of time. In particular, she is interested in discriminating between administrators who are able to complete given tasks within a specified time and those who are not. Data are collected on the performance of 75 randomly selected administrators. They are stored in the dataset *mlba::SystemAdministrators*.

Using these data, the consultant performs a discriminant analysis. The variable Experience measures months of full-time system administrator experience, while Training measures number of relevant training credits. The dependent variable Completed is either *Yes* or *No*, according to whether or not the administrator completed the tasks.

a. Create a scatter plot of Experience vs. Training using color or symbol to differentiate administrators who completed the tasks from those who did not complete them. See if you can identify a line that separates the two classes with minimum misclassification.

b. Run a discriminant analysis with both predictors using the entire dataset as training data. Among those who completed the tasks, what is the percentage of administrators who are classified incorrectly as failing to complete the tasks?

c. Compute the two classification scores for an administrator with 4 months of experience and six credits of training. Based on these, how would you classify this administrator?

d. How much experience must be accumulated by an administrator with four training credits before his or her estimated probability of completing the tasks exceeds 0.5?

e. Compare the classification accuracy of this model to that resulting from a logistic regression with cutoff 0.5.

12.3 **Detecting Spam Email (from the UCI Machine Learning Repository).** A team at Hewlett–Packard collected data on a large number of email messages from their postmaster and personal email for the purpose of finding a classifier that can separate email messages that are *spam* vs. *nonspam* (a.k.a. "ham"). The spam concept is diverse: it includes advertisements for products or websites, "make money fast" schemes, chain letters, pornography, and so on. The definition used here is "unsolicited commercial email." The dataset *mlba::Spambase* contains information on 4601 e-mail messages, among which 1813 are tagged "spam." The predictors include 57 variables; most of them are the average number of times a certain word (e.g., mail, George) or symbol (e.g., #, !) appears in the email. A few predictors are related to the number and length of capitalized words.

a. To reduce the number of predictors to a manageable size, examine how each predictor differs between the *spam* and *nonspam* emails by comparing the spam-class average and nonspam-class average. Which are the 11 predictors that appear to vary the most between *spam* and *nonspam* emails? From these 11, which words or signs occur more often in spam?

b. Partition the data into training and holdout sets and then perform a discriminant analysis on the training data using only the 11 predictors.

c. If we are interested mainly in detecting spam messages, is this model useful? Use the confusion matrix, cumulative gains chart, and lift curve for the holdout set for the evaluation.

d. In the sample, almost 40% of the email messages were tagged as spam. However, suppose that the actual proportion of spam messages in these email accounts is 10%. Adjust the constants to reflect the actual proportions, and discuss the effect on model performance.

e. A spam filter that is based on your model is used, so that only messages that are classified as *nonspam* are delivered, while messages that are classified as *spam* are quarantined. In this case, misclassifying a nonspam email (as spam) has much heftier results. Suppose that the cost of quarantining a nonspam email is 20 times that of not detecting a spam message. Adjust the constants to reflect the actual proportions, and discuss the effect on model performance.

## CHAPTER 13

Generating, Comparing, and Combining Multiple Models

The previous chapters in this part of the book introduced different supervised methods for prediction and classification. Earlier, in Chapter 5, we learned about evaluating predictive performance, which can be used to compare several models and choose the best one. In this chapter, we look at collections of supervised models. First, we look at an approach for handling multiple models called *ensembles*, which combines multiple supervised models into a "super-model." Instead of choosing a single predictive model, we can combine several models to achieve improved predictive accuracy. We explain the underlying logic of why ensembles can improve predictive accuracy and introduce popular approaches for combining models, including simple averaging, bagging, boosting, and stacking. Secondly, we introduce the idea of *automated machine learning*, or *AutoML*, which allows us to automatically train many supervised models and see their resulting performance. While in previous chapters we have shown how to manually tune parameters for each supervised method, AutoML automates the full pipeline from data loading to generating a rank-ordered list of candidate models with automatic parameter tuning. We illustrate this process and its results using R's h2o package and highlight some of its key features. Finally, we discuss how model predictions can be understood by analyzing explanations of predictions and simulating different scenarios for variable values.

Machine Learning for Business Analytics: Concepts, Techniques, and Applications in R, Second Edition.
Galit Shmueli, Peter C. Bruce, Peter Gedeck, Inbal Yahav, and Nitin R. Patel
© 2023 John Wiley & Sons, Inc. Published 2023 by John Wiley & Sons, Inc.

13.1 ENSEMBLES[1]

Ensembles played a major role in the million-dollar Netflix Prize contest that started in 2006. At the time, Netflix, the largest DVD rental service in the United States, wanted to improve their movie recommendation system (from www.netflixprize.com):

> Netflix is all about connecting people to the movies they love. To help customers find those movies, we've developed our world-class movie recommendation system: Cinematch[SM] . . . And while Cinematch is doing pretty well, it can always be made better.

In a bold move, the company decided to share a large amount of data on movie ratings by their users and set up a contest, open to the public, aimed at improving their recommendation system:

> We provide you with a lot of anonymous rating data, and a prediction accuracy bar that is 10% better than what Cinematch can do on the same training data set.

During the contest, an active leader-board showed the results of the competing teams. An interesting behavior started appearing: different teams joined forces to create combined, or *ensemble* predictions, which proved more accurate than the individual predictions. The winning team, called "BellKor's Pragmatic Chaos," combined results from the "BellKor" and "Big Chaos" teams alongside additional members. In a 2010 article in *Chance* magazine, the Netflix Prize winners described the power of their ensemble approach:

> An early lesson of the competition was the value of combining sets of predictions from multiple models or algorithms. If two prediction sets achieved similar RMSEs, it was quicker and more effective to simply average the two sets than to try to develop a new model that incorporated the best of each method. Even if the RMSE for one set was much worse than the other, there was almost certainly a linear combination that improved on the better set.

Why Ensembles Can Improve Predictive Power

The principle of combining methods is popular for reducing risk. For example, in finance, portfolios are created for reducing investment risk. The return from a portfolio is typically less risky, because the variation is smaller than each of the individual components.

---

[1]This and subsequent sections in this chapter copyright © 2023 Datastats, LLC, and Galit Shmueli. Used by permission.

THE WISDOM OF CROWDS

In his book *The Wisdom of Crowds*, James Surowiecki recounts how Francis Galton, a prominent statistician from the 19th century, watched a contest at a county fair in England. The contest's objective was to guess the weight of an ox. Individual contest entries were highly variable, but the mean of all the estimates was surprisingly accurate—within 1% of the true weight of the ox. On balance, the errors from multiple guesses tended to cancel one another out. You can think of the output of a predictive model as a more informed version of these guesses. Averaging together multiple guesses will yield a more precise answer than the vast majority of the individual guesses. Note that in Galton's story, there were a few (lucky) individuals who scored better than the average. An ensemble estimate will not always be more accurate than all the individual estimates in all cases, but it will be more accurate most of the time.

In predictive modeling, "risk" is equivalent to variation in prediction error. The more our prediction errors vary, the more volatile our predictive model. Consider predictions from two different models for a set of n records. $e_{1,i}$ is the prediction error for the ith record by method 1, and $e_{2,i}$ is the prediction error for the same record by method 2.

Suppose that each model produces prediction errors that are, on average, zero (for some records the model over-predicts and for some it under-predicts, but on average the error is zero):

$$E(e_{1,i}) = E(e_{2,i}) = 0.$$

If, for each record, we take an average of the two predictions: $\bar{y}_i = \frac{\hat{y}_{1,i} + \hat{y}_{2,i}}{2}$, then the expected mean error will also be zero:

$$
\begin{aligned}
E(y_i - \bar{y}_i) &= E\left(y_i - \frac{\hat{y}_{1,i} + \hat{y}_{2,i}}{2}\right) \quad\quad (13.1)\\
&= E\left(\frac{y_i - \hat{y}_{1,i}}{2} + \frac{y_i - \hat{y}_{2,i}}{2}\right) = E\left(\frac{e_{1,i} + e_{2,i}}{2}\right) = 0.
\end{aligned}
$$

This means that the ensemble has the same mean error as the individual models. Now let us examine the variance of the ensemble's prediction errors:

$$\text{Var}\left(\frac{e_{1,i} + e_{2,i}}{2}\right) = \frac{1}{4}\left(\text{Var}(e_{1,i}) + \text{Var}(e_{2,i})\right) + \frac{1}{4} \times 2\text{Cov}(e_{1,i}, e_{2,i}). \quad (13.2)$$

This variance can be lower than each of the individual variances $\text{Var}(e_{1,i})$ and $\text{Var}(e_{2,i})$ under some circumstances. A key component is the covariance (or equivalently, correlation) between the two prediction errors. The case of no correlation leaves us with a quantity that can be smaller than each of the individual variances. The variance of the average prediction error will be even smaller when the two prediction errors are negatively correlated.

In summary, using an average of two predictions can potentially lead to smaller error variance and therefore better predictive power. These results generalize to more than two methods; you can combine results from multiple prediction methods or classifiers.

Simple Averaging or Voting

The simplest approach for creating an ensemble is to combine the predictions, classifications, or propensities from multiple models. For example, we might have a linear regression model, a regression tree, and a k-NN algorithm. We use each of the three methods to score, say, a test set. We then combine the three sets of results.

The three models can also be variations that use the same algorithm. For example, we might have three linear regression models, each using a different set of predictors.

Combining Predictions   In prediction tasks, where the outcome variable is numerical, we can combine the predictions from the different methods simply by taking an average. In the above example, for each record in the test set, we have three predictions (one from each model). The ensemble prediction is then the average of the three values.

One alternative to a simple average is taking the median prediction, which would be less affected by extreme predictions. Another possibility is computing a weighted average, where weights are proportional to a quantity of interest. For instance, weights can be proportional to the accuracy of the model, or if different data sources are used, the weights can be proportional to the quality of the data.

Ensembles for prediction are useful not only in cross-sectional prediction, but also in time series forecasting (see Chapters 17–19). In forecasting, the same approach of combining future forecasts from multiple methods can lead to more precise predictions. One example is the weather forecasting application mobile app Dark Sky (formerly Forecast.io, www.darksky.net/app), which described their algorithm as follows:

> Forecast.io is backed by a wide range of data sources, which are aggregated together statistically to provide the most accurate forecast possible for a given location.

Combining Classifications   In the case of classification, combining the results from multiple classifiers can be done using "voting": for each record, we have multiple classifications. A simple rule would be to choose the most popular class among these classifications. For example, we might use a classification tree, a naive Bayes classifier, and discriminant analysis for classifying a binary outcome.

For each record, we then generate three predicted classes. Simple voting would choose the most common class among the three.

As in prediction, we can assign heavier weights to scores from some models, based on considerations such as model accuracy or data quality. This would be done by setting a "majority rule" that is different from 50%.

Combining Propensities   Similar to predictions, propensities can be combined by taking a simple (or weighted) average. Recall that some algorithms, such as naive Bayes (see Chapter 8), produce biased propensities and should therefore not be simply averaged with propensities from other methods.

Bagging

Another form of ensembles is based on averaging across multiple random data samples. *Bagging*, short for "bootstrap aggregating," comprises two steps:

1. Generating multiple random samples (by sampling with replacement from the original data)—this method is called "bootstrap sampling."
2. Running an algorithm on each sample and producing scores.

Bagging improves the performance stability of a model and helps avoid overfitting by separately modeling different data samples and then combining the results. It is therefore especially useful for algorithms such as trees and neural networks.

Boosting

Boosting is a slightly different approach to creating ensembles that sequentially builds better models by leveraging the prediction errors from the previous model. Here, the goal is to directly improve areas in the data where our model makes errors, by forcing the model to pay more attention to those records. The steps in boosting are as follows:

1. Fit a model to the data.
2. Draw a sample from the data so that misclassified records (or records with large prediction errors) have higher probabilities of selection.
3. Fit the model to the new sample.
4. Repeat Steps 2–3 multiple times.

Bagging and Boosting in R

Although bagging and boosting can be applied to any supervised machine learning method, most applications are for trees, where they have proved extremely effective. In Chapter 9, we described random forests, an ensemble based on bagged trees, and boosted trees, in which the model focuses on misclassified records. We illustrated both a random forest implementation and a boosted tree for the personal loan example. The `adabag`, `randomForest`, and `xgboost` packages in R can be used to generate bagged and boosted trees. Table 13.1 shows the R code to train bagged and boosted trees for the personal loan data. Figure 13.1 compares the ROC curves of the different models using the holdout dataset. The bagged and boosted tree models using the `adabag` package show a clear improvement over the single tree model. The performance is further improved with parameter tuning as seen for the `randomForest` and `xgboost` models.

Stacking

Yet another form of ensembles is based on the idea of taking heterogeneous "base learners," that is, different model algorithms, and then using their predictions as

TABLE 13.1   **EXAMPLE OF BAGGING AND BOOSTING CLASSIFICATION TREES ON THE PERSONAL LOAN DATA: R CODE**

 code for bagging and boosing trees

```
library(tidyverse)
library(adabag)
library(rpart)
library(caret)

set.seed(1)
# load and preprocess the data
bank.df <- mlba::UniversalBank %>%
    select(-c(ID, ZIP.Code)) %>%
    mutate(
      Personal.Loan = factor(Personal.Loan, levels=c(0, 1), labels=c("No", "Yes"))
    )

# partition the data
train.index <- sample(c(1:dim(bank.df)[1]), dim(bank.df)[1]*0.6)
train.df <- bank.df[train.index, ]
holdout.df <- bank.df[-train.index, ]

# single tree (rpart)
tr <- rpart(Personal.Loan ~ ., data=train.df)

# bagging and boosting using adabag
bag <- bagging(Personal.Loan ~ ., data=train.df)
boost <- boosting(Personal.Loan ~ ., data=train.df)

# bagging and boosting using randomForest and xgboost with parameter tuning
bag.rf <- train(Personal.Loan ~ ., data=train.df, method="rf")
boost.xgb <- train(Personal.Loan ~ ., data=train.df, method="xgbTree", verbosity=0)
```

FIGURE 13.1 EXAMPLE OF BAGGING AND BOOSTING CLASSIFICATION TREES ON THE PERSONAL LOAN DATA: ROC CURVES FOR ADABAG (LEFT) AND RANDOMFOREST/XGBOOST MODELS (RIGHT)

predictors for training a meta-learner model. This is called *stacking*, short for "stacked generalization." The steps in stacking are as follows:

1. Fit different models to the data; these are called "base learners."

2. Create a new dataset containing just the predictions from each model and the target outcome (i.e., omitting the original predictors).

3. Fit a new meta-model called a "stacking model learner," to the new dataset.

R's `tidymodels` and `h2o` packages implement stacking.

Advantages and Weaknesses of Ensembles

Combining scores from multiple models is aimed at generating more precise predictions (lowering the prediction error variance). The ensemble approach is most useful when the combined models generate prediction errors that are negatively associated, but it can also be useful when the correlation is low. Ensembles can use simple averaging, weighted averaging, voting, medians, etc. Models can be based on the same algorithm or on different algorithms, using the same sample or different samples. Ensembles have become a major strategy for participants in machine learning contests (e.g., Kaggle), where the goal is to optimize some predictive measure. In that sense, ensembles also provide an operational way to obtain solutions with high predictive power in a fast way, by engaging multiple teams of "data crunchers" working in parallel and combining their results.

Ensembles that are based on different data samples help avoid overfitting. However, remember that you can also overfit the data with an ensemble if you tweak it (e.g., choosing the "best" weights when using a weighted average).

The major disadvantage of an ensemble is the resources that it requires: computationally, as well as in terms of software availability and the analyst's skill and time investment. Ensembles that combine results from different algorithms require developing each of the models and evaluating them. Boosting-type ensembles and bagging-type ensembles do not require such effort, but they do have a computational cost (although boosting can be parallelized easily). Ensembles that rely on multiple data sources require collecting and maintaining multiple data sources. And finally, ensembles are "blackbox" methods, in that the relationship between the predictors and the outcome variable usually becomes nontransparent.

13.2   AUTOMATED MACHINE LEARNING (AUTOML)

Machine learning platforms have now started incorporating features for automating the machine learning workflow from data loading to generating a rank-ordered list of candidate models with automatic parameter tuning. This is called *automated machine learning* or *AutoML*. As we have seen in previous chapters, `caret` provides a consistent interface to a large variety of machine learning models and with some basic R programming experience it is straightforward to train a variety of models and rank them based on their performance. However, there are several packages for R with a complete *AutoML* implementation. Here, we will use the open source `h2o` package to demonstrate *automated machine learning*.[2] The steps in this example follow the general machine learning steps shown earlier in Figure 2.1 and are discussed next in the context of the personal loan example.

AutoML: Explore and Clean Data

Once the data relevant to the business purpose is imported and loaded, machine learning platforms vary in terms of the integration of data preparation steps as part of the AutoML process. Most platforms support some elementary tasks related to data transformation and feature selection; however, since these steps rightly require domain knowledge application, they are handled separately or in a semi-automatic manner.

Table 13.2 shows loading and preprocessing of the *mlba::UniversalBank* dataset as well as its splitting into training and holdout set. The `h2o` package moves data processing and model building into a separate server. This allows the use of specialized hardware like clusters or dedicated machines with large GPUs. Here, we start a local cluster using the *h2o.init()* function. The final step is to make the datasets available on this cluster using the *as.h2o()* function.

---

[2]The open-source package is developed by the company *h2o.ai*. While it is currently open source, this may change in the future.

TABLE 13.2   **DATA PREPROCESSING AND MAKING AVAILABLE IN H2O.AI**

 code for data preprocessing

```
library(tidyverse)

# load and preprocess the data
bank.df <- mlba::UniversalBank %>%
  # Drop ID and zip code columns.
  select(-c(ID, ZIP.Code)) %>%
  # convert Personal.Loan to a factor with labels Yes and No
  mutate(Personal.Loan = factor(Personal.Loan, levels=c(0, 1), labels=c("No", "Yes")))

# partition the data
set.seed(1)
idx <- caret::createDataPartition(bank.df$Personal.Loan, p=0.6, list=FALSE)
train.df <- bank.df[idx, ]
holdout.df <- bank.df[-idx, ]
```

 code for initializing *h2o.ai* and preparing data for use in *h2o.ai*

```
library(h2o)

# Start the H2O cluster (locally)
h2o.init()

train.h2o <- as.h2o(train.df)
holdout.h2o <- as.h2o(holdout.df)
```

AutoML: Determine Machine Learning Task

The *h2o.automl()* function supports classification (including binary and multi-class classification) and prediction of a numerical outcome. The specific task is selected based on the type of the outcome variable. Similar to *caret::train()*, if the outcome is a factor the function will train a classification model, and otherwise, it will train a numerical prediction model. As can be seen in Table 13.2, we converted the *Personal.Loan* outcome to a factor, so *h2o.automl()* will train classification models.

If one class has many more records than the other, we call the dataset *imbalanced*. For imbalanced datasets, *h2o.automl()* can be told to oversample the minority class by setting the *balance_classes* to *TRUE* (see Chapter 12.4 for handling imbalanced data). In our case, 90% of the records belong to the *No* class, and only 10% belong to the *Yes* class. We will therefore try to build models with and without balancing during training.

AutoML: Choose Features and Machine Learning Methods

At this step, we select the features to be used as predictors in the supervised model. As is the case when fitting individual models, the decision should be guided by considerations of data quality and regulatory/ethical requirements (in some applications some variables are forbidden, such as using gender in loan applications in the United States). We also select the machine learning algorithms we'd like to run. Considerations include potential runtime (for example, some algorithms might take much longer to train and/or to score) and the suitability of the algorithm to the type and size of our data and our goal. For example, the k-nearest neighbors algorithm requires a large training sample; simple classification and regression trees are not stable and can result in different trees for slightly different data; linear and logistic regression without regularization have trouble with highly correlated predictors.

Table 13.3 shows the steps required to train the *AutoML* models using h2o. *h2o.automl()* requires specifying the predictor names (x), the outcome name (y), and the training data (*training_frame*). In addition, we set the maximum number of models (*max_models*) and a random seed for reproducibility (*seed*). All other model parameters are automatically tuned.

By default, the model-building phase explores generalized linear models (GLM) that include linear and logistic regression, random forest, extremely randomized trees,[3] the tree boosting implementations xgboost and gbm, and deep learning models. We exclude the deep learning models in this example using *exclude_algos=c("DeepLearning")* as it will lead to non-reproducible results. The argument *max_models=20* specifies that the search for models is stopped once 20 models were explored. In addition to these models, *h2o.automl()* adds stacked ensemble models, one using all models and the other one using the best model for each model type, leading to a total of 22 models.

AutoML: Evaluate Model Performance

The result of the AutoML procedures *h2o.automl()* shows the performance of each trained model based on cross-validation (the default is 5-fold cross-validation; see Table 13.3). In the example shown in Table 13.3, the best performing model (called *leader*) was the stacked ensemble model trained on the imbalanced data. The fifth-best model is the gradient boosting using (gbm) applied to the balanced training data. This model performed best on the balanced training data.

---

[3]Extremely randomized trees are a modification of the random forest that only explores a random subset of all possible splits in the tree construction. The performance of this method is comparable to random forest but is faster to train.

TABLE 13.3   TRAINING AND COMPARING AUTOML MODELS

code for data preprocessing

```
# identify outcome and predictors
y <- "Personal.Loan"
x <- setdiff(names(train.df), y)

# run AutoML for 20 base models
aml <- h2o.automl(x=x, y=y, training_frame=train.h2o,
                  max_models=20, exclude_algos=c("DeepLearning"),
                  seed=1)
aml.balanced <- h2o.automl(x=x, y=y, training_frame=train.h2o,
                  max_models=20, exclude_algos=c("DeepLearning"),
                  balance_classes=TRUE,
                  seed=1)

aml

> aml
AutoML Details
==============
Project Name: AutoML_11_20220423_111446
Leader Model ID: StackedEnsemble_AllModels_1_AutoML_11_20220423_111446
Algorithm: stackedensemble

Total Number of Models Trained: 22
Start Time: 2022-04-23 11:14:46 UTC
End Time: 2022-04-23 11:15:38 UTC
Duration: 52 s

Leaderboard
===========
                                                     model_id       auc    logloss     aucpr
1     StackedEnsemble_AllModels_1_AutoML_11_20220423_111446 0.9979003 0.03369809 0.9837530
2 StackedEnsemble_BestOfFamily_1_AutoML_11_20220423_111446 0.9978529 0.03371447 0.9836039
3                         GBM_5_AutoML_11_20220423_111446 0.9978292 0.03988919 0.9842069
4                         GBM_3_AutoML_11_20220423_111446 0.9975533 0.03994164 0.9814398
5              GBM_grid_1_AutoML_11_20220423_111446_model_2 0.9969048 0.04140080 0.9767822
6                         GBM_2_AutoML_11_20220423_111446 0.9967550 0.04117947 0.9785292
7                         DRF_1_AutoML_11_20220423_111446 0.9965982 0.04989680 0.9752261
8                         GBM_4_AutoML_11_20220423_111446 0.9963959 0.04383481 0.9765449
9          XGBoost_grid_1_AutoML_11_20220423_111446_model_3 0.9960797 0.04341706 0.9740565
10             GBM_grid_1_AutoML_11_20220423_111446_model_3 0.9960259 0.04355292 0.9767514
   mean_per_class_error       rmse        mse
1            0.03785644 0.09990381 0.009980771
2            0.04114430 0.09991297 0.009982601
3            0.04424779 0.10474681 0.010971893
4            0.04845747 0.10735949 0.011526061
5            0.07018191 0.10917959 0.011920182
6            0.06515794 0.10623055 0.011284930
7            0.06589540 0.11541087 0.013319668
8            0.07036627 0.11024840 0.012154710
9            0.04280359 0.10958549 0.012008979
10           0.06031834 0.10812285 0.011690550

[22 rows x 7 columns]
```

In addition to comparing the performance of all the models, we can evaluate the performance of the best performers (*leaders*) on the holdout set. (Note that using the holdout data like this to evaluate multiple models is different from how we have generally been using it to this point—i.e., to estimate performance with new data. For that purpose, we would need a second holdout set that is not used at all in comparing models.) The results for above best-performing models on imbalanced and balanced training data are shown in Table 13.4. Balancing the classes leads to a slight improvement. Two points are important to note about the *h2o.automl()* output which are slightly different from what we saw earlier. First, the confusion matrix is transposed compared to `caret`, which means the actual classes are in rows and the predicted classes are in columns. Second, the confusion matrix is calculated using a threshold that maximizes the F1 score (the harmonic mean of precision and recall).

TABLE 13.4   **OVERVIEW OF AUTO MODEL RESULTS: COMPARING ACCURACY AND RUN TIME OF CANDIDATE MODELS (PERSONAL LOAN DATA)**

 evaluting the performance of the two best performing h2o models using the holdout set

```
> h2o.confusionMatrix(aml@leader, holdout.h2o)
Confusion Matrix (vertical: actual; across: predicted)
                            for max f1 @ threshold = 0.647088545186049:
          No Yes   Error     Rate
No      1803    5 0.002765  =5/1808
Yes       17  175 0.088542  =17/192
Totals  1820  180 0.011000  =22/2000

> h2o.confusionMatrix(aml.balanced@leader, holdout.h2o)
Confusion Matrix (vertical: actual; across: predicted)
                            for max f1 @ threshold = 0.263295844576429:
          No Yes   Error     Rate
No      1803    5 0.002765  =5/1808
Yes       16  176 0.083333  =16/192
Totals  1819  181 0.010500  =21/2000
```

AutoML: Model Deployment

There are various ways to deploy the chosen model. In all cases, it is important to make sure that the R environment is defined to ensure long-term use. This means the versions of used packages should be fixed. It is also advisable to add tests that compare model predictions to the expected outcome after changes to the R environment.

It is important to remember that data preprocessing steps are an integral part of the model. New data must be treated in exactly the same way as the training data. It is therefore advisable to define preprocessing steps using R code. For example, if data are standardized, the z-transformation learned from the training data must be applied to new data.

While for small datasets it is often sufficient to use files, large datasets are often stored in databases. Packages such as `RMySQL` and `RSQLite` allow accessing data from a database. The `dbplyr` package offers a consistent interface to a wide variety of databases. Once datasets get very large or when the machine learning operations are extremely computationally intensive, it may be necessary to consider using parallelization or clusters. The necessary solutions are beyond the scope of this book.

When the machine learning model should be made available to a wide audience, consider a web application or web service. Using a package such as `shiny`, the model can be wrapped into a web application and made available either on *shinyapps.io* or on self-hosted servers. There are also commercial offerings, from companies such as Microsoft and h2o.ai, that provide a more integrated model development and deployment environment. In general, full deployment solutions usually require tailored solutions with engineering considerations (see Section 2.8 in Chapter 2).

Advantages and Weaknesses of Automated Machine Learning

Automated machine learning functionality, such as *h2o.ai*'s implementation, can be a valuable tool for beginners and advanced data scientists. For beginners, it can provide a useful starting point for quickly experimenting with a dataset for a business problem by building predictive models that can then be used for further understanding and learning. For advanced users, it can save time in creating common machine learning workflows by relying on automated model selection and tuning for getting quick insights into a business problem before spending extensive efforts on fine-tuning models.

Automated machine learning has the additional advantage of providing transparency in modeling. By analyzing the final model resulting from the AutoML process, the data scientist can spend more efforts in data understanding, preparation, feature generation, and so on. Also, the data scientist can focus on further fine tuning the models of interest. For example, consider an AutoML implementation that optimizes a decision tree by only changing the *maximal depth* parameter. What would be the effect of changing other parameters such as *minimal leaf size*? While automated machine learning speeds up the general model tuning process by considering important model parameters, depending on the problem context or the nature of the data, the data scientist would need to consider further model tuning.

The major disadvantage of automated machine learning is its deceptive ability to hide attention to key business-related details and questions. Since the AutoML process lends itself to importing and loading data and generating results fairly quickly, data scientists may not spend adequate time in understanding the nuances of data, exploring and preparing it for the modeling phase, which can lead to garbage-in, garbage-out outcomes, and thoughtless models.

13.3 EXPLAINING MODEL PREDICTIONS

When comparing predictive models, an important aspect is how different predictor variables affect the predicted values. This is especially important in applications where predicted values must be justified, such as in loan and judicial decisions. Uncovering the effect of predictors on the predicted values is called *explainability*. "Explaining" predictions provides insight on (1) how the predicted score (e.g., predicted value, class, or probability) is affected by the values of the predictor variables, and (2) how changes to the values of predictor variables might change the predicted score. The first is a descriptive question, while the second is a causal question. There are different "explainability" methods, each with its strengths and weaknesses. In the following, we briefly describe two approaches for explaining individual record predictions: LIME and counterfactual explanations. Chapter 22 describes additional approaches, with an emphasis on global explanations that cover the entire dataset.

Explaining Model Predictions: LIME

Given a predicted score for a certain record, the data scientist, decision maker, or even the person being scored might ask "What predictor variables contributed to this record's predicted score?" The originators of the LIME (Local Interpretable Model-agnostic Explanations) approach described their goal of explaining a prediction as "presenting textual or visual artifacts that provide qualitative understanding of the relationship between the [features ...] and the model's prediction" (Ribeiro et al., 2016). The LIME algorithm generates additional training data around the record to be explained, then generates predicted values for these synthetic data, and subsequently builds a linear regression model on the newly created dataset. Because the linear regression model is trained only on the record and its created "neighbors," it is called a *local* model. We note that even if the overall global relationship between the variables and the predictions is nonlinear, the *local* linear relationship is useful when the objective is to explain the predictions.

The R package `lime` implements the LIME approach. The explanations are computed as follows:

1. Copy a record, and randomly perturb (slightly change) each variable value in the copy, thus creating a neighboring record.

2. Use the predictive model to compute a prediction, or a propensity for a class, for the neighboring record.

3. Repeat the above steps to create a set of neighboring records and predictions.

4. Within this set of neighboring records, calculate the correlation between each variable and the predicted values (or propensities for classification). These are called "local correlations." These local correlations tell you how much individual predictors contribute to the prediction for a given record.

5. Repeat this process for all the records. Note that the local correlations, and thus the information about variable importance, will differ from record to record.

It may seem counter-intuitive that useful information can be derived from synthetically generated data. Think of the model as a blackbox, and you are making small changes to the inputs, observing the output, and drawing conclusions about how the inputs are correlated to the output.

Figure 13.2 uses the `lime` package to explain the predictions of the AutoML model for four different cases. Cases 3055 and 2 are predicted *Yes* and *No*, respectively, with a high propensity. In both cases, income, education, and average credit card spending give strong support to the model's classification. The predictions for cases 3358 and 1178 on the other hand have propensities of around 0.6. In this case, it can be useful to change some of the predictor values to understand when the classification reverses. For example, reducing the income of case 3358 from 112K to 108K changes the classification from *Yes* to *No*. The same happens if the average credit card spending is reduced from 2.7K to 2.4K. For case 1178, an increase of the income from 71K to 80K would have changed the decision to *Yes*. Such granular prediction explanations can be a valuable tool for conveying model predictions to stakeholders and building their trust in predictive models, particularly in the case of "blackbox" models like deep learning. We note that the record-level interpretability measures are most important for nonlinear and complex relationships, where, say, having a CD account may be very important as a predictor for some customers, but unimportant for others. In contrast, the feature importance measures (see Chapter 22 and Figure 9.16) capture the overall

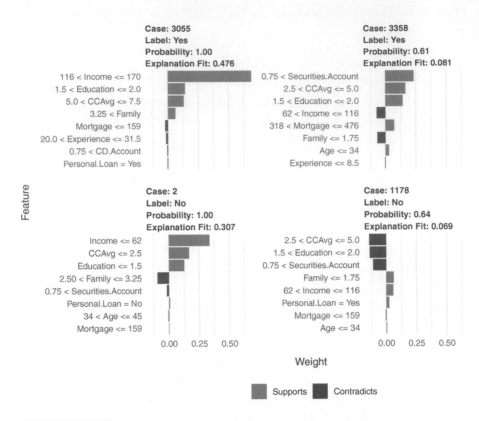

FIGURE 13.2   EXPLAINING DECISIONS USING LIME. TOP: TWO CASES WHERE THE MODEL PREDICTS APPROVAL. BOTTOM: TWO NON-APPROVED CASES

```
cases <- c('3055', '3358', # predicted Yes
           '2', '1178')    # predicted No
explainer <- lime::lime(train.df, aml@leader, bin_continuous=TRUE, quantile_bins=FALSE)
explanations <- lime::explain(holdout.df[cases,], explainer, n_labels=1, n_features=8)

lime::plot_features(explanations, ncol=2)
```

importance of predictors for a specific model when considered in the context of a given validation set.

13.4 SUMMARY

In practice, the methods discussed earlier in this book are often used not in isolation, but as building blocks in an analytic process whose goal is always to inform and provide insight.

In this chapter, we looked at two ways that multiple models are deployed, and at ways in which predicted values can be investigated. In ensembles, multiple models are weighted and combined to produce improved predictions. Through automated machine learning, the machine learning process of selecting, applying, and tuning different models for better model performance can be made more efficient, while focusing on evaluating the results and comparing the models. As models and the modeling process become more complex and less transparent, decision makers and data scientists need tools for understanding individual predicted scores and how they relate to predictor values. We described one such popular approach, called LIME, for explaining predicted scores.

PROBLEMS

13.1 **Acceptance of Consumer Loan.** Universal Bank has begun a program to encourage its existing customers to borrow via a consumer loan program. The bank has promoted the loan to 5000 customers, of whom 480 accepted the offer. The data are available in dataset *mlba::UniversalBank*. The bank now wants to develop a model to predict which customers have the greatest probability of accepting the loan, to reduce promotion costs and send the offer only to a subset of its customers.

We will develop several models and then combine them in an ensemble. The models we will use are (1) logistic regression, (2) k-nearest neighbors with $k = 3$, and (3) classification trees. Preprocess the data as follows:

- Zip code can be ignored.

- Partition the data: 60% training and 40% validation.

  a. Fit models to the data for (1) logistic regression, (2) k-nearest neighbors with $k = 3$, and (3) classification trees. Use Personal Loan as the outcome variable. Report the validation confusion matrix for each of the three models.

  b. Create a data frame with the actual outcome, predicted outcome, and each of the three models. Report the first 10 rows of this data frame.

  c. Add two columns to this data frame for (1) a majority vote of predicted outcomes and (2) the average of the predicted probabilities. Using the classifications generated by these two methods derive a confusion matrix for each method and report the overall accuracy.

  d. Compare the error rates for the three individual methods and the two ensemble methods.

13.2 **eBay Auctions—Boosting and Bagging.** Using the eBay auction data (file *mlba::eBayAuctions*) with variable Competitive as the outcome variable, partition the data into training (60%) and validation (40%).

  a. Run a classification tree, using the default controls of *rpart()*. Looking at the validation set, what is the overall accuracy? What is the lift on the first decile?

  b. Run a boosted tree with the same predictors (use function *boosting()* in the **adabag** package). For the validation set, what is the overall accuracy? What is the lift on the first decile?

  c. Run a bagged tree with the same predictors (use function *bagging()* in the **adabag** package). For the validation set, what is the overall accuracy? What is the lift on the first decile?

  d. Run a random forest (use function *randomForest()* in package **randomForest** with argument *mtry=4*). Compare the bagged tree to the random forest in terms of validation accuracy and lift on first decile. How are the two methods conceptually different?

13.3 **Predicting Delayed Flights (Boosting).** The dataset *mlba::FlightDelays* contains information on all commercial flights departing the Washington, DC area and arriving at New York during January 2004. For each flight, there is information on the departure and arrival airports, the distance of the route, the scheduled time and date of the flight, and so on. The variable that we are trying to predict is whether or not a flight is delayed. A delay is defined as an arrival that is at least 15 minutes later than scheduled.

Data Preprocessing. Transform variable day of week info a categorical variable. Bin the scheduled departure time into eight bins (in R use function *cut()*). Partition the data into training (60%) and validation (40%).

Run a boosted classification tree for delay. Leave the default number of weak learners, and select resampling. Set maximum levels to display at 6, and minimum number of records in a terminal node to 1.

a. Compared with the single tree, how does the boosted tree behave in terms of overall accuracy?

b. Compared with the single tree, how does the boosted tree behave in terms of accuracy in identifying delayed flights?

c. Explain why this model might have the best performance over the other models you fit.

## PART V

Intervention and User Feedback

## CHAPTER 14

Interventions: Experiments, Uplift Models, and Reinforcement Learning

In this chapter, we describe a third paradigm of machine learning, different from supervised and unsupervised learning, that deals with interventions and feedback. Data used in supervised and unsupervised learning are typically *observational data*, being passively collected about the entities of interest (customers, households, transactions, flights, etc.). In contrast, in this chapter, we discuss *experimental* data, resulting from applying interventions to the entities of interest and measuring the outcomes of those interventions. We start with the simplest form of intervention—the A/B test, which is a randomized experiment for testing the causal effect of a treatment or intervention on outcomes of interest. A/B tests are routinely used by Internet platforms such as Google, Microsoft, and Uber for testing new features. We then describe *uplift modeling*, a method that combines A/B testing with supervised learning for providing customized targeting. Uplift modeling is commonly used in direct marketing and in political analytics. Finally, we describe *reinforcement learning*, a general machine learning methodology used in personalization, where the algorithm (or *agent*) learns the best treatment assignment policy by interacting with experimental units through dynamic treatment assignment and gathering their feedback.

Uplift and Reinforcement Learning in R

The main R package introduced in this chapter is `contextual` for simulation and analysis of multi-arm bandit policies.

Machine Learning for Business Analytics: Concepts, Techniques, and Applications in R, Second Edition.
Galit Shmueli, Peter C. Bruce, Peter Gedeck, Inbal Yahav, and Nitin R. Patel
© 2023 John Wiley & Sons, Inc. Published 2023 by John Wiley & Sons, Inc.

14.1   A/B Testing

A/B testing is the marketing industry's term for a standard scientific experiment in which results can be tracked for each individual experimental unit (subject). The idea is to test one treatment against another, or a treatment against a control. "Treatment" is simply the term for the intervention you are testing. In a medical trial, it is typically a drug, device, vaccine, or other therapy; in marketing, it is typically an offering to a consumer—for example, an email, online ad, push notification, or a webpage shown to a consumer. A display ad in a magazine would not generally qualify, unless it had a specific call to action that allowed the marketer to trace the action (e.g., purchase) to a given ad, plus the ability to split the magazine distribution randomly and provide a different offer to each segment of consumers.

A/B testing has become extremely popular online. Amazon, Microsoft, Facebook, Google, and similar companies conduct thousands to tens of thousands of A/B tests each year, on millions of users, testing user interface changes, enhancements to algorithms (search, ads, personalization, recommendation, etc.), changes to apps, content management system, and more.[1] A/B testing on an Internet or mobile platform involves randomizing user traffic to one of two experiences (current version and new version), computing the difference in relevant outcome metrics between the two groups, and performing statistical tests to rule out differences that are likely due to noise.

In an A/B test, a "subject" can be an individual customer, a user, an online user session, or any unit of interest.

An important element of A/B testing is random allocation—the treatments are assigned or delivered to subjects randomly. That way, any difference between treatment A and treatment B can be attributed to the treatment (unless it is due to chance). For this reason, A/B tests are extremely popular in online advertising, where it is relatively easy to randomly serve different ad designs or content ("treatments") to different users and where user reactions are automatically recorded. A/B tests are also routinely used by Internet platforms and website owners for evaluating new small intended improvements to the user interface design, such as changing the color of a submit button or adding a new navigation link. For example, Optimizely describes a case study showing how Electronic Arts, the maker of the popular SimCity franchise, created and tested several different versions of their preorder webpage. They hypothesized that placing a call to action higher on the webpage by changing the way the promotional offer was displayed could drive more purchases and increase revenue generated from Sim-City.com. Using A/B testing, they found that, contrary to their hypothesis, the

---

[1] See *Trustworthy online controlled experiments: A practical guide to A/B testing* by Kohavi et al. (2020).

TABLE 14.1	EXAMPLE OF RAW DATA RESULTING FROM A/B TEST	
User ID	Treatment	Outcome
1234	A	Click
1235	A	No click
1236	B	No click
...	...	...

version *without* a special promotion offer across the top of the page performed 43% better than the other variation.[2]

In an A/B test, only two measurements are needed for each subject: which treatment it received (A or B) and the outcome. For example, in an online advertising A/B test that compares a new ad design with an existing one, for each user, we would record which ad they were served (*Treat*={old,new}) and what was the outcome, such as whether they clicked the ad or not (Y={click,no-click}). Table 14.1 shows a schematic sample of such data. In practice, we do not need to keep all individual outcome values for each subject (unless the results will be used beyond the A/B test, such as in uplift modeling). For a binary outcome (e.g., click/no-click), we only need the proportion of clicks in each treatment group. In the ad example, that means the proportion of clicks among users who viewed the old ad ($\hat{p}_A$) and the proportion of clicks among users who viewed the new ad ($\hat{p}_B$). For a numerical outcome (e.g., engagement time), we need only the average and standard deviation of the outcome in each treatment group ($\overline{y}_A, \hat{\sigma}_A$ and $\overline{y}_B, \hat{\sigma}_B$).

Example: Testing a New Feature in a Photo Sharing App

PhoToTo, a fictitious photo sharing app, is interested in testing a new feature that allows users to make uploaded photos disappear after 24 hours. Their goal is to gauge their customers' interest in this feature, with the purpose of increasing user activity and converting users from the free version to the advanced paid version. PhoToTo deploys an A/B test to 2000 of its users who use the free version: 1000 of these users are randomly assigned to an interface with the new feature, while the other 1000 remain with the existing functionality. The experiment is run for a week. For each of the 2000 users, two performance metrics are measured at the end of the experimental week: the total number of uploaded photos and whether the user upgraded to the paid version of PhoToTo. The results of the experiment are shown in Table 14.2. We can see that the average number of photo uploads and the conversion to paid users are both higher in the treatment group where the new feature was introduced. But can we infer the difference

---

[2]https://www.optimizely.com/insights/blog/ea_simcity_optimizely_casestudy/

between the two groups will generalize when deployed to the larger population of users, or is this a "fluke sample"?

TABLE 14.2	RESULTS FROM A/B TEST AT PhoToTo, EVALUATING THE EFFECT OF A NEW FEATURE	
Metric	Existing interface (A)	New feature available (B)
Average number of photo uploads	50	60
Standard deviation of photo uploads	50	100
Proportion of conversion to paid users	0.02	0.04

Success is measured by the number of photo uploads and user conversion

The Statistical Test for Comparing Two Groups (T-Test)

The A/B test is a statistical test comparing the average outcome of a treatment group with that of a control group (or, in general, of two groups A and B). Suppose group A receives the existing ad, and group B receives the new design. Suppose the outcome of interest is whether users click on the ad. What if 5% of users shown the new ad clicked and 4% of those shown the existing ad clicked? In many cases, we would now be ready to go with the treatment that did best. This is especially so if we are starting fresh with two new treatments—say, sending our prospects email version A or email version B to promote a new product or testing a new web landing page with a blue banner at the top or an orange banner.

In other cases, there may be a substantial cost difference between the treatments, or we may be testing a new treatment against an existing "standard." In such a case, we may worry about fluke results in an A/B test, particularly if based on a small sample. If random chance produced a result in favor of the costlier or the new treatment, we might not want to switch away from the cheaper or the tried and true standard treatment. Doing so regularly would mean chasing after inconsequential results and losing a firm base of information. In such a case, we can use a statistical test to determine how "unusual" our result is compared with what chance might produce. If our result is very unusual (say, it might not occur more often than 5% of the time in a chance model), we would be prepared to abandon our existing standard in favor of the new treatment. If, on the other hand, our new treatment produced an outcome that occurs 35% of the time by chance anyway, we might stick with the standard treatment. In this way, we minimize our chance of being fooled by chance.

Such a statistical test is termed a *significance test*. The metric "percent of time a chance model produces an outcome at least as unusual as the experiment" is termed a *p-value*. We could calculate p-values by constituting a chance model and simulating results. For example, in a test of engagement times, we could put all the engagement times from both treatments into a hat, shuffle the hat, and then repeatedly draw out pairs of samples like the original samples. Do those pairs rarely yield a difference in mean engagement times across the two re-samples as great as we saw in our actual experiment? If so, we conclude that the difference we saw in the experiment was unlikely to happen by chance: it is "statistically significant." A formula-based equivalent of this procedure is the *t-test for independent samples* (see box) and is included in most statistical software and in some platforms for automating marketing experiments.

T-TEST FOR COMPARING TWO INDEPENDENT GROUPS

All basic statistics courses and textbooks cover the t-test for testing the difference between two group means (or proportions). Here is a quick reminder of the basics for the case relevant for A/B testing. For testing whether the difference between two group means (or proportions) is significantly in favor of group B (e.g., the new ad design) or not—that is, whether there's evidence that the difference between the population means $\mu_B - \mu_A > 0$—we compute the t-statistic:

$$T = \frac{\overline{y}_B - \overline{y}_A}{StandardError(\overline{y}_B - \overline{y}_A)}.$$

When the outcome metric of interest is binary (e.g., buy/not-buy), a similar formula is used, replacing averages ($\overline{y}$) with proportions ($\hat{p}$).

The denominator of the t-statistic (the standard error of the difference in means or proportions) has the following formulas.[3] For a numerical measure:

$$StandardError(\overline{y}_B - \overline{y}_A) = \sqrt{s_A^2/n_A + s_B^2/n_B},$$

and for a binary measure:

$$StandardError(\hat{p}_B - \hat{p}_A) = \sqrt{\frac{\hat{p}_A(1 - \hat{p}_A)}{n_A} + \frac{\hat{p}_B(1 - \hat{p}_B)}{n_B}}.$$

The statistical significance of the t-value (its p-value) is computed by software. Comparing the p-value with a user-determined threshold will then yield a result. For example, if the threshold is 5%, then a p-value below 5% will indicate the click-through rate (CTR) on the new design is statistically higher than on the existing design. The results of such tests are subject to two potential errors: false discovery (called Type I error) and missed discovery (Type II error). The choice of threshold value is determined by the false discovery risk level we are prepared to take.

Critically, one must carefully consider the magnitude of the difference and its practical meaning, especially since A/B tests are typically conducted on very large samples of users (tens and even hundreds of thousands of users). Statistical significance is strongly affected by the sample size: the larger the groups, the more likely even a very small difference that is practically meaningless will appear statistically significant. For example, with sufficiently large groups, a CTR of 5.000001% will appear significantly (statistically) higher than 5%.

Returning to our earlier example of the photo sharing app PhoToTo, we can compute the t-statistics for each of the two metrics of interest: the number of uploaded photos and the conversion rate to paid users:

$$T_{\text{photo uploads}} = \frac{60 - 50}{\sqrt{(50^2/1000 + 100^2/1000)}} = 2.828$$

$$T_{\text{paid users}} = \frac{0.04 - 0.02}{\sqrt{(0.04)(0.96)/1000 + (0.02)(0.98)/1000}} = 2.626$$

The corresponding two p-values are as follows: for the increase[4] in average photo uploads, p-value = 0.0024; for increase in paid users, p-value = 0.0044. Table 14.3 shows the code and result for computing the above two p-values using R function *pt()*.

TABLE 14.3   COMPUTING P-VALUES FOR T-TESTS IN R

```
> pt(q=2.828, df=1998, lower.tail=FALSE)
[1] 0.002365339
> pt(q=2.626, df=1998, lower.tail=FALSE)
[1] 0.004352719
```

Both p-values are very small, thereby indicating that the effect of the new feature on number of uploads and conversion to paid users will generalize to the larger population of users. Note that with much smaller sample sizes, the same outcome values in Table 14.2 could yield statistical insignificance. For example, for $n_A = n_B = 100$, we get p-values of 0.186 and 0.204, respectively.

Multiple Treatment Groups: A/B/n Tests

A/B testing can be extended from two groups (treatment and control, or two groups) to multiple groups. In A/B/n testing, we have n groups. For example, testing three new ad designs against an existing design would use an A/B/4 test. The procedure is very similar to A/B testing, with the difference being the replacement of the t-test with analysis of variance (ANOVA) for a numerical outcome or a chi-square test for comparing proportions. For more on these tests, consult a statistics textbook such as Anderson et al. (2021).

Multiple A/B Tests and the Danger of Multiple Testing

As we mentioned earlier, digital platforms and their business customers (e.g., advertisers and marketers) often perform routine and frequent A/B tests, resulting in thousands of tests. Large companies such as Microsoft have their

---

[4]We use a *one-sided test*, because we are testing whether the average number of uploads *increases* with the new feature. When the direction of the effect is unknown, we'd use a two-sided test.

internal experimentation infrastructure. However, even small companies can perform such testing using services by third parties: Optimizely (https://www.optimizely.com/) is one commercial service that provides online tools for routine A/B testing for online advertisers.

When deploying many A/B tests, there is a high risk of false discoveries: mistakenly concluding that a treatment effect is real, where it is just due to chance. While each statistical t-test carries with it a small probability of false discovery, a combination of many A/B tests dramatically increases the overall false discovery probability. This phenomenon is known as *multiple testing*. Multiple testing can arise from testing multiple metrics (click-through rate, views, purchases, etc.), running the test for multiple use subgroups (countries, zip codes, device type, etc.), and repeating the same A/B test many times. Kohavi et al. (2020) describe a case of multiple testing that arose in early versions of Optimizely, which allowed those running an A/B test to "peek" at the p-values before the experimental period has been completed. For example, if the A/B test was supposed to run for a week, the tester could peek at test results throughout the week. This peeking was effectively multiple testing, leading to false discoveries of apparent effects. The problem was later detected and eliminated.

Solutions to false discoveries due to multiple testing are based on adjusting the threshold on each p-value, or adjusting the p-values themselves, by considering the total number of tests.[5] However, beyond technical solutions, it is good practice to carefully consider which tests are essential, set the experimental period in advance, disallow "peeking," and select treatments that have reasonable justification (although sometimes new ideas are hard to justify but turn out to be successes).

14.2 UPLIFT (PERSUASION) MODELING

Long before the advent of the Internet, sending messages directly to individuals (i.e., direct mail) held a big share of the advertising market. Direct marketing affords the marketer the ability to invite and monitor direct responses from consumers. This, in turn, allows the marketer to learn whether the messaging is paying off. A message can be tested with a small section of a large list, and, if it pays off, the message can be rolled out to the entire list. With predictive modeling, we have seen that the rollout can be targeted to that portion of the list that is most likely to respond or behave in a certain way. None of this was possible with traditional media advertising (television, radio, newspaper, magazine).

---

[5]One common method is the "False Discovery Rate" (FDR), which is the expected number of false discoveries among all discoveries. Using the FDR entails sorting the p-values from low to high and assigning different thresholds.

Direct response also made it possible to test one message against another and find out which does better.

An A/B test tells you which treatment does better on average but says nothing about which treatment does better for which individual. A classic example is in political campaigns. Consider the following scenario: the campaign director for Smith, a Democratic Congressional candidate, would like to know which voters should be called to encourage to support Smith. Voters that tend to vote Democratic but are not activists might be more inclined to vote for Smith if they got a call. Active Democrats are probably already supportive of him, and therefore a call to them would be wasted. Calls to Republicans are not only wasteful, but they could be harmful.

Campaigns now maintain extensive data on voters to help guide decisions about outreach to individual voters. Prior to the 2008 Obama campaign, the practice was to make rule-based decisions based on expert political judgment. Since 2008, it has increasingly been recognized that, rather than relying on judgment or supposition to determine whether an individual should be called, it is best to use the data to develop a model that can predict whether a voter will respond positively to outreach.

Gathering the Data

US states maintain publicly available files of voters, as part of the transparent oversight process for elections. The voter file contains data such as name, address, and date of birth. Political parties have "poll-watchers" at elections to record who votes, so they have additional data on which elections voters voted in. Census data for neighborhoods can be appended, based on voter address. Finally, commercial demographic data can be purchased and matched to the voter data. Table 14.4 shows a small extract of data derived from the voter file for the US state of Delaware.[6] The actual data used in this problem are in the dataset *mlba::VoterPersuasion* and contain 10,000 records and many additional variables beyond those shown in Table 14.4.

First, the campaign director conducts a survey of 10,000 voters to determine their inclination to vote Democratic. Then, she conducts an experiment, randomly splitting the sample of 10,000 voters in half and mailing a message promoting Smith to half the list (treatment A) and nothing to the other half (treatment B). The control group that gets no message is essential, since other campaigns or news events might cause a shift in opinion. The goal is to measure the change in opinion after the message is sent out, relative to the no-message control group.

---

[6]Thanks to Ken Strasma, founder of the microtargeting firm HaystaqDNA and director of targeting for the 2004 Kerry campaign and the 2008 Obama campaign, for these data.

TABLE 14.4   DATA ON VOTERS (SMALL SUBSET OF VARIABLES AND RECORDS) AND
              DATA DICTIONARY

Voter	Age	NH_White	Comm_PT	H_F1	Reg_Days	PR_Pelig	E_Elig	Political_C
1	28	70	0	0	3997	0	20	1
2	23	67	3	0	300	0	0	1
3	57	64	4	0	2967	0	0	0
4	70	53	2	1	16,620	100	90	1
5	37	76	2	0	3786	0	20	0

Data dictionary

Age	Voter age in years
NH_White	Neighborhood average of % non-Hispanic white in household
Comm_PT	Neighborhood % of workers who take public transit
H_F1	Single female household (1 = yes)
Reg_Days	Days since voter registered at current address
PR_Pelig	Voted in what % of non-presidential primaries
E_Pelig	Voted in what % of any primaries
Political_C	Is there a political contributor in the home? (1 = yes)

The next step is conducting a post-message survey of the same sample of 10,000 voters, to measure whether each voter's opinion of Smith has shifted in a positive direction. A binary variable, Moved_AD, will be added to the above data, indicating whether opinion has moved in a Democratic direction (1) or not (0).

Table 14.5 summarizes the results of the survey, by comparing the movement in a Democratic direction for each of the treatments. Overall, the message (Message = 1) is modestly effective.

TABLE 14.5   RESULTS OF SENDING A PRO-DEMOCRATIC
              MESSAGE TO VOTERS

	#Voters	# Moved Dem.	% Moved Dem.
Message = 1 (message sent)	5000	2012	40.2
Message = 0 (no message sent)	5000	1722	34.4

Movement in a Democratic direction among those who got no message is 34.4%. This probably reflects the approach of the election, the heightening campaign activity, and the reduction in the "no opinion" category. It also illustrates the need for a control group. Among those who did get the message, the movement in a Democratic direction is 40.2%. So, overall, the lift from the message is 5.8%.

We can now append two variables to the voter data shown earlier in Table 14.4: *message* [whether they received the message (1) or not (0)] and *Moved_AD* [whether they moved in a Democratic direction (1) or not (0)]. The augmented data are shown in Table 14.6.

TABLE 14.6	OUTCOME VARIABLE (MOVED_AD) AND TREATMENT VARIABLE (MESSAGE) ADDED TO VOTER DATA

Voter	Age	NH_White	Comm_PT	H_F1	Reg_Days	PR_Pelig	E_Elig	Political_C	Message	Moved_AD
1	28	70	0	0	3997	0	20	1	0	1
2	23	67	3	0	300	0	0	1	1	1
3	57	64	4	0	2967	0	0	0	0	0
4	70	53	2	1	16620	100	90	1	0	0
5	37	76	2	0	3786	0	20	0	1	0

A Simple Model

We can develop a predictive model with Moved_AD as the outcome variable and various predictor variables, *including the treatment Message*. Any classification method can be used; Table 14.7 shows the first few lines from the output of some predictive model used to predict Moved_AD.

TABLE 14.7	CLASSIFICATIONS AND PROPENSITIES FROM PREDICTIVE MODEL (SMALL EXTRACT)

Voter	Message	Actual Moved_AD	Predicted Moved_AD	Predicted Prob.
1	0	1	1	0.5975
2	1	1	1	0.5005
3	0	0	0	0.2235
4	0	0	0	0.3052
5	1	0	0	0.4140

However, our interest is not just how the message did overall, nor is it whether we can predict the probability that a voter's opinion will move in a favorable direction. Rather our goal is to predict how much (positive) impact the message will have on a specific voter. That way the campaign can direct its limited resources toward the voters who are the most persuadable—those for whom sending the message will have the greatest positive effect.

Modeling Individual Uplift

To answer the question about the message's impact on each voter, we need to model the effect of the message at the individual voter level. For each voter, uplift is defined as follows:

Uplift = increase in propensity of favorable opinion after receiving message

To build an uplift model, we follow the following steps to estimate the change in probability of "success" (propensity) that comes from receiving the treatment (the message):

1. Randomly split a data sample into treatment and control groups, conduct an A/B test, and record the outcome (in our example: Moved_AD).

2. Recombining the data sample, partition it into training and holdout sets; build a predictive model with this outcome variable, and include a predictor variable that denotes treatment status (in our example: Message). If logistic regression is used, additional interaction terms between treatment status and other predictors can be added as predictors to allow the treatment effect to vary across records (in data-driven methods such as trees and KNN this happens automatically).

3. Score this predictive model to a partition of the data; you can use the holdout partition. This will yield, for each holdout record, its propensity of success given its treatment.

4. Reverse the value of the treatment variable, and re-score the same model to that partition. This will yield for each holdout record its propensity of success had it received the other treatment.

5. Uplift is estimated for each individual by $P(\text{Success} \mid \text{Treatment} = 1) - P(\text{Success} \mid \text{Treatment} = 0)$.

6. For new data where no experiment has been performed, simply add a synthetic predictor variable for treatment and assign first a "1," score the model, then assign a "0," and score the model again. Estimate uplift for the new record(s) as above.

Continuing with the small voter example, the results from Step 3 were shown in Table 14.7—the right column shows the propensities from the model. Next, we retrain the predictive model, but with the values of the treatment variable Message reversed for each row. Table 14.8 shows the propensities with variable Message reversed (you can see the reversed values in column Message). Finally, in Step 5, we calculate the uplift for each voter.

TABLE 14.8 CLASSIFICATIONS AND PROPENSITIES FROM PREDICTIVE MODEL (SMALL EXTRACT) WITH MESSAGE VALUES REVERSED

Voter	Message	Actual Moved_AD	Predicted Moved_AD	Predicted Prob.
1	1	1	1	0.6908
2	0	1	1	0.3996
3	1	0	0	0.3022
4	1	0	0	0.3980
5	0	0	0	0.3194

Table 14.9 shows the uplift for each voter—the success (Moved_AD = 1) propensity given Message = 1 minus the success propensity given Message = 0.

TABLE 14.9	UPLIFT: CHANGE IN PROPENSITIES FROM SENDING MESSAGE VS. NOT SENDING MESSAGE		
Voter	Prob. if Message = 1	Prob. if Message = 0	Uplift
1	0.6908	0.5975	0.0933
2	0.5005	0.3996	0.1009
3	0.3022	0.2235	0.0787
4	0.3980	0.3052	0.0928
5	0.4140	0.3194	0.0946

Computing Uplift with R

This entire process that we showed manually can be done using R. One difference to our manual computation is that we used a logistic regression, whereas here we will use a random forest classifier. Table 14.10 shows the result of implementing the uplift analysis in R using a random forest. The output shows the two conditional probabilities, $P(\text{Success}|\text{Treatment} = 1)$ and $P(\text{Success}|\text{Treatment} = 0)$, estimated for each record. The difference between the values in Tables 14.9 and 14.10 is due to the use of two different predictive algorithms (logistic regression vs. random forests).

Using the Results of an Uplift Model

Once we have estimated the uplift for each individual, the results can be ordered by uplift. The message could then be sent to all those voters with a positive uplift, or, if resources are limited, only to a subset—those with the greatest uplift.

Uplift modeling is used mainly in marketing and, more recently, in political campaigns. It has two main purposes:

- To determine whether to send someone a persuasion message or just leave them alone.

- When a message is definitely going to be sent, to determine which message, among several possibilities, to send.

Technically this amounts to the same thing—"send no message" is simply another category of treatment, and an experiment can be constructed with multiple treatments, for example, no message, message A, and message B. However, practitioners tend to think of the two purposes as distinct and tend to focus on the first. Marketers want to avoid sending discount offers to customers who would make a purchase anyway, or renew a subscription anyway. Political campaigns, likewise, want to avoid calling voters who would vote for their candidate in any case. And both parties especially want to avoid sending messages or offers where the effect might be antagonistic—where the uplift is negative.

TABLE 14.10   **UPLIFT IN R APPLIED TO THE VOTERS DATA**

 code for uplift

```
library(tidyverse)
# load and preprocess the data
predictors <- c("AGE", "NH_WHITE", "COMM_PT", "H_F1", "REG_DAYS",
                "PR_PELIG", "E_PELIG", "POLITICALC", "MESSAGE_A")
outcome <- "MOVED_AD"
voter.df <- mlba::VoterPersuasion %>%
  select(all_of(c(predictors, outcome)))


set.seed(1)
nrows <- dim(voter.df)[1]
train.index <- sample(1:nrows, nrows * 0.6)
train.df <- voter.df[train.index, ]
holdout.df <- voter.df[-train.index, ]

# build a random forest model using caret
train_control <- caret::trainControl(method="none")
model <- caret::train(MOVED_AD ~ ., data=train.df,
                      trControl=train_control,
                      method="rf")

# calculating the uplift
uplift_df <- data.frame(holdout.df)
uplift_df$MESSAGE_A <- 1
predTreatment <- predict(model, newdata=uplift_df, type="prob")
uplift_df$MESSAGE_A <- 0
predControl <- predict(model, newdata=uplift_df, type="prob")
upliftResult <- data.frame(
  probMessage = predTreatment[, 1],
  probNoMessage = predControl[, 1]
)
upliftResult$uplift <- upliftResult$probMessage - upliftResult$probNoMessage
head(upliftResult)
```

Output

```
> head(upliftResult)
  probMessage probNoMessage uplift
1      0.704         0.708 -0.004
2      0.648         0.754 -0.106
3      0.472         0.190  0.282
4      0.650         0.750 -0.100
5      0.808         0.848 -0.040
6      0.644         0.618  0.026
```

14.3 REINFORCEMENT LEARNING

A/B testing derives causal knowledge about an intervention of interest by actively assigning experimental units (customers, website users, etc.) to treatment/intervention groups, measuring the outcome(s) of interest, and drawing a conclusion about the effectiveness of the intervention. We can think of this process as "learning by interacting" with the experimental units. The notion of *learning by interaction* is what separates supervised and unsupervised learning methods from interventional methods such as A/B testing and reinforcement learning. For example, in recommendation algorithms such as collaborative filtering, we might generate a recommended item (or set of items) for a user. However, unless we actually display the recommendation to the user and measure the outcome, it is impossible to know what the user would have done given the recommendation.

We've seen that interventional methods such as uplift modeling are intended to answer the personalized "what if" question: what would be the user's outcome if s/he were served (or not) a certain recommendation or offer? We now turn to a family of methods called *reinforcement learning*, which are computational algorithms (or *agents*) that "learn by interacting" with experimental units, through dynamic treatment assignment. In both supervised learning and reinforcement learning, the goal is to "learn" a predictive model of the outcome Y as a function of predictors $X_1, X_2, \ldots$. But whereas in supervised learning we train the model on preexisting data, in reinforcement learning we start without data, and the algorithm decides which X (treatment) information to deploy that would generate outcome Y data most useful for learning the optimal treatment–outcome model. In the recommendation example above, a reinforcement learning approach would choose which items to recommend in order to collect user feedback useful for learning the optimal input–output model.

We describe two popular frameworks: multi-armed bandits and Markov Decision Processes. In both cases the challenge is identifying the best treatment assignment policy in the presence of a plethora of potential interventions (e.g., which news item to display on a user's social media feed, which song to recommend in a music streaming service, and which of many coupons to offer a customer on an e-commerce website).

Explore-Exploit: Multi-armed Bandits

The name *multi-armed bandit* (MAB, or simply "bandit") derives from a gambler playing multiple slot machines, each with a different unknown payoff rate. The gambler's goal is to figure out which machine has the highest payoff rate.

In an A/B test, after learning which treatment did best, you deploy that treatment, and the other treatment(s) get left behind. A multi-armed bandit uses sequential assignment of experimental units to treatment groups, dynamically updating treatment assignments to new units as the experiment progresses. The idea is to increase the proportion of assignments to the treatment group that shows the best performance (the best slot machine). This is especially useful when there are multiple treatments (e.g., multiple ad designs). For example, if we initially display 10 new ad designs to mobile app users, each with equal probability, then if initial experimental results indicate the new ad #3 leads to the best outcomes, for the next set of users we might increase the probability of displaying ad #3 compared to all other designs. However, we do not increase this probability to 100% because there is still uncertainty regarding the superiority of this ad design—perhaps with more data, a different ad design will turn out to be the best one. We therefore still want to continue testing the value of the other nine ad designs. A multi-armed bandit tries to achieve a dual goal: improving the outcome by increasing the chance of assignment to the "winning" treatment (called *exploit*) while continuing to evaluate the potential of the "losing" treatment(s) (called *Explore*).

There are different multi-armed bandit parameters and implementations, which differ in terms of determining how and when to update the treatment assignment probabilities. For example, an *Epsilon First* strategy explores randomly for some period of time and then exploits the treatment with the highest estimated outcome (if one treatment is clearly better than the others, it assigns all new subjects to this treatment). Another approach, the *Epsilon–Greedy* approach, explores ϵ% of the time and exploits $1-\epsilon$% of the time. A variation of the *Epsilon–Greedy* strategy adjusts the ϵ parameter over time, exploring sub-optimal treatments less frequently.

The multi-armed bandit scenario assumes the intervention effects remain constant from one assignment to the next. However, in some cases the best intervention will depend on a changing context. For example, in music recommendation, it is likely that song preference changes for the same user over different times of the day (waking up, while commuting to work, in the evening, etc.) or across devices (mobile phone, TV, etc.). In such cases, we'd want the algorithm to take into account the context. *Contextual multi-armed bandits*, also known as *contextual bandits*, do exactly this: they search for the best context-specific intervention, thereby combining trial-and-error treatment assignment search with estimating the association between treatment assignment and context variables.

Bandits and contextual bandits are implemented in the R package `contextual`. This package allows simulation and evaluation of ordinary and contextual bandits. Evaluation uses preexisting data (*offline* evaluation).

MULTI-ARMED BANDIT: SIMPLE EXAMPLE

Let's consider the scenario of selecting the best online ad to display among 10 different designs, by running a 7-day experiment. Suppose that each day we have a large number of customers accessing the webpage where the ad will be displayed. A 10-armed bandit algorithm that uses an Epsilon-first strategy would take the following steps:

- **Day 1 Initialization:** Each ad i has probability $p_i = 0.1$ to be displayed. In other words, each customer is randomly assigned to view one of the 10 ads.
- **Day 1 Evaluation and Update:** At the end of Day 1, compute the *reward* metric of interest r_i (e.g., click-through rate (CTR), or average ad revenues per ad view), resulting from each of the 10 ads.
- **Day 2 Deployment:** All customers assigned to view the best performing Day 1 ad.
- **Day 2 Evaluation and Update:** At the end of Day 2, compute the average daily *reward* for the displayed ad.
- **Days 3, 5, 7 Deployment:** Each customer is randomly assigned to view one of the 10 ads (as in Day 1).
- **Day 3, 5, 7 Evaluation and Update:** At the end of the day, compute the average daily *reward* for each of the 10 ads (accumulated across the days thus far).
- **Days 4, 6 Deployment:** All customers assigned to view the best performing ad thus far.
- **Day 4, 6 Evaluation and Update:** At the end of the day, compute the average daily *reward* for each of the 10 ads (accumulated across the days thus far).
- **Day 7 Experiment Conclusion:** The ad with the highest average 7-day reward is selected and will be displayed in the future.

Note that on odd days, where customers are randomized across all 10 ads, the scenario is similar to A/B/10 testing in terms of treatment assignment strategy. The difference is that we do not carry out a statistical test at the end of an odd day to conclude about the best ad. Instead, we accumulate the rewards since Day 1 and reach a conclusion only after the multi-day experiment is complete.

The above example treats each day separately. An alternative is to consider batches of customers visiting the webpage (for example, replacing a day with 10,000 customer visits).

Example of Using a Contextual Multi-Arm Bandit for Movie Recommendations

To illustrate reinforcement learning using a contextual multi-armed bandit, we use the MovieLens dataset from Section 15.10 in Chapter 15. The dataset contains 100,836 ratings provided by 610 users for 9742 movies. Our goal here is to develop a recommender system that suggests to a user one of the top-50 most rated movies, while taking the user's previous preferences of movie genres into account.

The code required to use the **contextual** package is shown in Table 14.11 and Figure 14.1.[7] Table 14.11 describes the preparation of the three data structures required for the simulation. Each movie is categorized as belonging to one or more genres. For example, the 1995 movie *Toy Story* is characterized as *Adventure*, *Animation*, *Children*, *Comedy*, and *Fantasy*. This genre profile is used to characterize the top-50 most rated movies which form the 50 arms of the multi-armed bandit (*arm_features*).

The movie genres are also used to characterize individual users by looking at their viewing profile across the movies they've rated. In order to create a user profile that is not dominated by the top-rated movies, we only use movies that are not in the top-50. The counts of ratings in each category are tabulated, and this count vector is normalized by dividing by the total count. This profile is used to provide the *context* for each user (*user_features*).

The final dataset includes the reactions of the users to the top-50 movies. The data are in the form of a table that contains *userId*, *movieId* (choice), and the *reward* (1 if the user gave the movie a 5-star rating). A few more columns are required for the simulation.

The simulation is described in Figure 14.1. The agents are trained in an offline learning scenario (where we use preexisting data instead of interacting with live users). *OfflineLookupReplayEvaluatorBandit* creates "realistic" data by sampling users with their profiles, choices, and ratings (rewards). For each record, the user's choice is compared with the agent's recommendation, and the agent's model is updated based on the resulting reward.

In this simulation, we analyze the performance of the disjoint LinUCB policy (*LinUCBDisjointOptimizedPolicy*) relative to random recommendations (*RandomPolicy*). The disjoint LinUCB uses separate ridge regression models for each arm, using the user profile as the context (the predictor variables) and the rating (5-star or not) as the outcome. The rating is assumed to be the user's reaction to the treatment. It then chooses the arm based on the individual predictions. We can clearly see in Figure 14.1 that using the disjoint LinUCB policy gives a higher reward than random recommendations.

Markov Decision Process (MDP)

In contrast to A/B tests, in bandit algorithms, the allocation of treatments to users is a multistage process, in which the allocation at one stage might depend on what happened in the previous stage. Bandit algorithms are actually a special case of a more general staged process, termed a Markov Decision Process (MDP).

---

[7] At the time of writing **contextual** could not be installed from CRAN. Should this still be the case, install the package using *devtools::install_github('Nth-iteration-labs/contextual')*

TABLE 14.11   USING A CONTEXTUAL MULTI-ARMED BANDIT (DATA PREPARATION)

 code for preparing the data for use with the `contextual` package

```
library(tidyverse)
library(mlba)
library(contextual)
library(data.table)
library(splitstackshape)

# preprocess movies data to create indicator variables for the different genres
movies_dat <- as.data.table(mlba::MovieLensMovies)
movies_dat <- splitstackshape::cSplit_e(movies_dat, "genres", sep="|", type="character",
                              fill=0, drop=TRUE)
movies_dat[[3]] <- NULL  # deletes the third column

ratings_dat <- as.data.table(mlba::MovieLensRatings)
all_movies <- ratings_dat[movies_dat, on=c(movieId="movieId")]
all_movies <- na.omit(all_movies, cols=c("movieId", "userId"))
# renumber userId to sequential numbers starting at 1
all_movies[, userId := as.numeric(as.factor(userId))]

# find the top-50 most frequently rated movies
top_50 <- all_movies %>%
  count(movieId) %>%
  slice_max(n, n=50) %>%
  pull(movieId)
top_50_movies    <- all_movies[movieId %in% top_50]
# renumber movieId to sequential numbers starting at 1
top_50_movies[, movieId    := as.numeric(as.factor(movieId))]

# create profile of genres for each movie in the top-50 (arm_features)
arm_features <- top_50_movies %>%
  select(-c(userId, rating, timestamp, title)) %>%
  # select one row for each movieId
  group_by(movieId) %>% slice(1) %>% ungroup()

# for each user, create their profile of genre preferences based on
# their viewed movies that are not in the top-50 (user_features)
user_features <- all_movies %>%
  filter(! movieId %in% top_50) %>%   # restrict to movies not in the top-50
  select(-c(movieId, rating, timestamp, title)) %>%
  # for each user, sum
  group_by(userId) %>%
  summarise_all(sum) %>%
  # normalize user profile
  group_by(userId) %>%
  mutate(
    total = sum(c_across(genres_Action:genres_Western)),
    across(genres_Action:genres_Western, ~ ./total)
  ) %>%
  select(-c(total)) %>%
  as.data.table()


# add users who only rated top-50 movies
# their genre preference profile is set to 0 for all genres
all_users <- as.data.table(unique(all_movies$userId))
user_features <- user_features[all_users, on=c(userId="V1")]
user_features[is.na(user_features)] <- 0
setorder(user_features, userId)
```

FIGURE 14.1 **REINFORCEMENT LEARNING USING A CONTEXTUAL MULTI-ARM BANDIT (SIMULATION)**

 code for simulating different strategies (policies) using the `contextual` package

```
# prepare the data for use with the contextual package
top_50_movies[, t := .I]
top_50_movies[, sim := 1]
top_50_movies[, agent := "Offline"]
top_50_movies[, choice := movieId]
top_50_movies[, reward := ifelse(rating <= 4, 0, 1)]
setorder(top_50_movies,timestamp, title)

# the bandit samples users with their genre preferences (user_features),
# movie choices (choice), and ratings.
# each movie is characterized by the genre profile (arm_features)
# these data are used to train the agent
environment <- OfflineLookupReplayEvaluatorBandit$new(
    top_50_movies,
    k = 50,
    unique_col = "userId",
    unique_lookup = user_features,
    shared_lookup = arm_features)

# define list of strategies to evaluate
agents <-list(
    Agent$new(RandomPolicy$new(), environment, "Random"),
    Agent$new(LinUCBDisjointUptimizedPolicy$new(2.1), environment, "LinUCB Dis"))

# setup and run simulation
simulation  <- Simulator$new(
    agents = agents,
    simulations = 20,
    horizon = 10000L,
    save_interval = 1)
results  <- simulation$run()

plot(results, type="cumulative", regret=FALSE, rate=TRUE,
     legend_position="topleft", disp="sd")
```

MDPs can allow the algorithm to learn a longer-term relationship between interventions (treatments) and outcomes—for example, a movie recommendation might lead to higher long-term user satisfaction even if the user's immediate reaction is not the most profitable. Hence, MDPs are especially useful in digital environments where long-term goals, such as user satisfaction or brand recognition, are of interest.

An MDP represents the problem of learning the optimal intervention policy through *states* and *rewards*. Consider a music streaming service that provides a recommendation system to its users. Suppose the business goal is to increase overall user engagement with the service (by providing useful recommendations), where engagement is measured by the number of songs played by the user. The algorithm (agent) must discover which song recommendations (interventions) yield the best outcome overall by trying them and recording the user's reactions. To achieve this, we define for the agent an intermediate "reward" such as whether the recommended song was played for at least 30 seconds. The agent's objective is to maximize the total reward over the long run. With such a longer-term optimization, we might recommend an item with a low immediate reward (e.g., low-profit item), but that is likely to lead to profitable rewards in the future. Another advantage of the MDP formulation is that the reward can represent the business value of a particular recommendation so that we might recommend high-profit items even if they have a low probability of purchase.

In addition to the rewards, the MDP records the *state* at each time of treatment assignment. The state includes all the information available to the algorithm about the user, the context, and the items. In the music streaming example, the state might be the user's profile (age, gender, etc.), behavior on the platform (app use frequency, songs played, sharing with friends, etc.), context (time of day, location, device, etc.), and song features (singer, genre, etc.).

The agent's actions (e.g., recommendation or ad displayed) might affect not only the reward but also the next state (e.g., the user's time on app, songs played), thereby affecting future rewards.[8] To capture this, the MDP has a *value function* (specified by the data scientist) that assigns to each state a value corresponding to the expected long-term overall rewards when starting from that state and using a specific treatment assignment policy.

Figure 14.2 shows a schematic of an MDP and how the agent interacts with the user by assigning an intervention (action) and recording the user's reaction (reward) and new state. The terms "agent" and "environment," sometimes called "controller" and "controlled system," reflect the origins of reinforcement

---

[8]An multi-armed bandit is a simplified type of reinforcement learning where the assignment to intervention (action) affects only the immediate reward.

FIGURE 14.2   SCHEMATIC OF REINFORCEMENT LEARNING, WHERE THE SOFTWARE AGENT "LEARNS" THE HUMAN USER BY PROVIDING ACTIONS, RECORDING THE USER'S NEW STATE, AND RECEIVING A REWARD BASED ON THE USER'S REACTION.

learning in engineering applications (such as thermostats for regulating the temperature in a room) and more recently in games such as chess and Go where the algorithm searches for the best next move.

The term "Markov" in MDP implies that we think of rewards, states, and treatment assignments (actions) in discrete time (periods $t = 1, 2, 3, \ldots$) and that the sequence of rewards, states, and actions form a *Markov chain*—this is a sequence of possible events in which the probability of each event depends only on the state attained in the previous event. In other words, to determine its next action (a_{t+1}), the agent only uses information on the most recent state (s_t), reward (r_t), and action (a_t).

For an item recommendation scenario, a generic MDP strategy might look like this:

1. *Initialization:* Using a predictive model, predict what item user u will select next given their user data (state).[9] (This model is based on data without recommendations.)

2. *Action (a_t):* Recommend to user u an item based on the user's data, context, and the item's features (state s_{t_1}). (The item is the result of Step 1 for the initial run and then of Step 4 thereafter.)

3. *Reward (r_t):* Collect the user's feedback to the recommendation (e.g., purchase, clicks)

4. *Model Update:* Using the pre-recommendation user/context/item data (state s_{t-1}), the recommendation (action a_t), and the user's feedback (reward r_t), the agent updates its predictive model linking the outcome (next step's state and reward) to the input (current step's state and action) $P(s_{t+1}, r_{t+1}|s_t, a_t)$. The agent then computes the value function (the expected long-term overall reward) to choose the next best action.

5. *Repeat* Steps 2–4.

---

[9]This means estimating the initial *state transition function* that includes the probabilities of moving from each state to each of the other states.

There exist a variety of ways to implement MDPs and reinforcement learning algorithms in practice, as well as variations and extensions, some including deep neural networks for the model updating step. The interested reader can learn more in the classic book *Reinforcement Learning* by Sutton and Barto (2018).

MDPs can be implemented in R using the `ReinforcementLearning` package. The package uses preexisting (offline) data in the form of sample sequences consisting of states, actions, and rewards. Based on such training data, the package allows a reinforcement learning agent to learn an optimal policy that defines the best possible action in each state.

As a final note about reinforcement learning, it is important to realize that while in this AI technique the data scientist determines the rewards, value function, the set of states, and set of possible actions, this does not guarantee that the agent will arrive at an optimal solution. In his book *Human Compatible*, AI expert Stewart Russell describes how agents designed to achieve a human-designed goal ended up reaching the goal by unacceptable solutions: the ECHO smart home controller was designed to reduce energy consumption by learning from the household behavior. However, inhabitants at Washington State university "often had to sit in the dark if their visitors stayed later than the usual bedtime." The agent has not fully "understood" the human objective, because the goals and rules have not been, and perhaps cannot be, fully specified. By contrast, in games like Go or chess, the ends are easy to define, and the rules can be comprehensively specified. In such games, highly creative solutions may result. The solution path may seem outlandish to a human in its initial stages, but the agent does not care and has been able to determine that it will be ultimately successful.

Reinforcement learning algorithms were designed for tasks that are fully observable, involve short time horizons, and have a small number of states and simple, predictable rules. Stewart Russell (2019) concludes: "Relaxing any of these conditions means that the standard methods will fail."

14.4 SUMMARY

In this chapter, we looked at the use of randomized experiments and user feedback for determining the best intervention. These methods differ from supervised learning and unsupervised learning and involve interaction with the units of interest (customers, website users, etc.). We described A/B testing, uplift modeling, and reinforcement learning.

A/B testing is used to test the effect of an intervention on an outcome of interest. This is done by randomly assigning units to an intervention group or a control (non-intervention) group and comparing the two groups' outcomes. A/B/n testing extends the idea to more than two groups.

In uplift modeling, the results of A/B testing are folded into the predictive modeling process as a predictor variable to guide choices not only about whether to send an offer or persuasion message, but also as to who to send it to.

Reinforcement learning uses computational algorithms for identifying best intervention assignments. This is especially useful when there are many possible interventions (such as in recommendation systems) and in environments that allow user–algorithm interaction. The algorithm learns the best intervention policy by trial and error, balancing between exploration (trying different treatment assignments) and exploitation (assigning the best-so-far treatment). Two popular reinforcement learning formulations are multi-armed bandits and Markov decision processes.

PROBLEMS

14.1 **Marketing Message—A/B Testing.** Which is a more effective marketing message—a plain text email or an email with images and design elements? Statistics.com conducted an A/B test in June 2012, sending an email to a list of potential customers that was randomly split into two groups. The measure of success was whether the email was opened by the receiver or not. For some reason, the email service used by Statistics.com did not produce an even split. The results for each of the 426 sent emails are in the dataset *mlba::EmailABtest*.

a. Before conducting such a test, would you have an opinion as to which would do better: a message with or without images?

b. What were the results in terms of open rates? Which message did better? (*Hint:* you can use pivot tables to get this summary.)

c. We would like to know whether this difference could be due to chance, and so will conduct a statistical test. Conduct a t-test to determine whether the difference is statistically significant and report the p-value.

d. Summarize your conclusion from the A/B test.

14.2 **Hair Care Product—Uplift Modeling.** This problem uses the dataset in *mlba::HairCareProduct*, courtesy of SAS. In this hypothetical case, a promotion for a hair care product was sent to some members of a buyers club. Purchases were then recorded for both the members who got the promotion and those who did not.

a. What is the purchase propensity:

i. Among those who received the promotion?

ii. Among those who did not receive the promotion?

b. Partition the data into training (60%) and holdout (40%) and fit:

i. Uplift using a random forest.

ii. Uplift using k-NN.

c. Report the two models' recommendations for the first three members.

Mining Relationships Among Records

## CHAPTER 15

Association Rules and Collaborative Filtering

In this chapter, we describe the unsupervised learning methods of association rules (also called "affinity analysis" and "market basket analysis") and collaborative filtering. Both methods are popular in marketing for cross-selling products associated with an item that a consumer is considering.

In association rules, the goal is to identify item clusters in transaction-type databases. Association rule discovery in marketing is termed "market basket analysis" and is aimed at discovering which groups of products tend to be purchased together. These items can then be displayed together, offered in post-transaction coupons, or recommended in online shopping. We describe the two-stage process of rule generation and then assessment of rule strength to choose a subset. We look at the popular rule-generating Apriori algorithm and then criteria for judging the strength of rules.

In collaborative filtering, the goal is to provide personalized recommendations that leverage user-level information. User-based collaborative filtering starts with a user and then finds users who have purchased a similar set of items or ranked items in a similar fashion and makes a recommendation to the initial user based on what the similar users purchased or liked. Item-based collaborative filtering starts with an item being considered by a user and then locates other items that tend to be co-purchased with that first item. We explain the technique and the requirements for applying it in practice.

Association Rules and Collaborative Filtering in R

The main R packages introduced in this chapter are `arules` for association rules and `recommenderlab` for collaborative filtering.

Machine Learning for Business Analytics: Concepts, Techniques, and Applications in R, Second Edition.
Galit Shmueli, Peter C. Bruce, Peter Gedeck, Inbal Yahav, and Nitin R. Patel
© 2023 John Wiley & Sons, Inc. Published 2023 by John Wiley & Sons, Inc.

15.1 ASSOCIATION RULES

Put simply, association rules, or *affinity analysis*, constitute a study of "what goes with what." This method is also called *market basket analysis* because it originated with the study of customer transactions databases to determine dependencies between purchases of different items. Association rules are heavily used in retail for learning about items that are purchased together, but they are also useful in other fields. For example, a medical researcher might want to learn what symptoms appear together. In law, word combinations that appear too often might indicate plagiarism.

Discovering Association Rules in Transaction Databases

The availability of detailed information on customer transactions has led to the development of techniques that automatically look for associations between items that are stored in the database. An example is data collected using barcode scanners in supermarkets. Such *market basket databases* consist of a large number of transaction records. Each record lists all items bought by a customer on a single-purchase transaction. Managers are interested to know if certain groups of items are consistently purchased together. They could use such information for making decisions on store layouts and item placement, for cross-selling, for promotions, for catalog design, and for identifying customer segments based on buying patterns. Association rules provide information of this type in the form of "if–then" statements. These rules are computed from the data; unlike the if–then rules of logic, association rules are probabilistic in nature.

Association rules are commonly encountered in online *recommendation systems* (or *recommender systems*), where customers examining an item or items for possible purchase are shown other items that are often purchased in conjunction with the first item(s). The display from Amazon.com's online shopping system illustrates the application of rules like this under "Frequently bought together." In the example shown in Figure 15.1, a user browsing a Samsung Galaxy S21 cell phone is shown a case and a screen protector that are often purchased along with this phone.

We introduce a simple artificial example and use it throughout the chapter to demonstrate the concepts, computations, and steps of association rules. We end by applying association rules to a more realistic example of book purchases.

Example 1: Synthetic Data on Purchases of Phone Faceplates

A store that sells accessories for cellular phones runs a promotion on faceplates. Customers who purchase multiple faceplates from a choice of six different colors get a discount. The store managers who would like to know what colors of

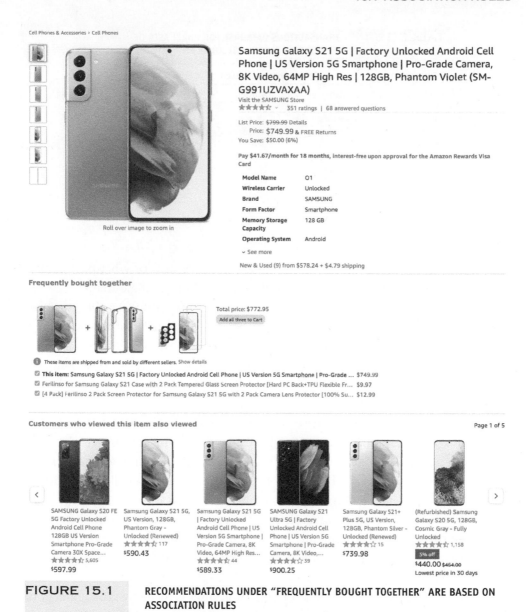

FIGURE 15.1   RECOMMENDATIONS UNDER "FREQUENTLY BOUGHT TOGETHER" ARE BASED ON ASSOCIATION RULES

faceplates customers are likely to purchase together, collected the transaction database as shown in Table 15.1.

Generating Candidate Rules

The idea behind association rules is to examine all possible rules between items in an if–then format and select only those that are most likely to be indicators of true dependence. We use the term *antecedent* to describe the IF part and *consequent* to describe the THEN part. In association analysis, the antecedent and consequent are sets of items (called *itemsets*) that are disjoint (do not have

| TABLE 15.1 | TRANSACTIONS DATABASE FOR PURCHASES OF DIFFERENT-COLORED CELLULAR PHONE FACEPLATES | | |

Transaction	Faceplate colors purchased			
1	red	white	green	
2	white	orange		
3	white	blue		
4	red	white	orange	
5	red	blue		
6	white	blue		
7	red	blue		
8	red	white	blue	green
9	red	white	blue	
10	yellow			

any items in common). Note that itemsets are not records of what people buy; they are simply possible combinations of items, including single items.

Returning to the phone faceplate purchase example, one example of a possible rule is "if red, then white," meaning that if a red faceplate is purchased, a white one is, too. Here, the antecedent is *red* and the consequent is *white*. The antecedent and consequent each contain a single item in this case. Another possible rule is "if red and white, then green." Here, the antecedent includes the itemset {*red, white*}, and the consequent is {*green*}.

The first step in association rules is to generate all the rules that would be candidates for indicating associations between items. Ideally, we might want to look at all possible combinations of items in a database with p distinct items (in the phone faceplate example, $p = 6$). This means finding all combinations of single items, pairs of items, triplets of items, and so on, in the transactions database. However, generating all these combinations requires a long computation time that grows exponentially[1] in p. A practical solution is to consider only combinations that occur with higher frequency in the database. These are called *frequent itemsets*.

Determining what qualifies as a frequent itemset is related to the concept of *support*. The support of a rule is simply the number of transactions that include both the antecedent and consequent itemsets. It is called a support because it measures the degree to which the data "support" the validity of the rule. The support is sometimes expressed as a percentage of the total number of records in the database. For example, the support for the itemset {red, white} in the phone faceplate example is 4 (or, $100 \times \frac{4}{10} = 40\%$).

---

[1]The number of rules that one can generate for p items is $3^p - 2^{p+1} + 1$. Computation time therefore grows by a factor for each additional item. For six items we have 602 rules, while for seven items the number of rules grows to 1932.

What constitutes a frequent itemset is therefore defined as an itemset that has a support that exceeds a selected minimum support, determined by the user.

The Apriori Algorithm

Several algorithms have been proposed for generating frequent itemsets, but the classic algorithm is the *Apriori algorithm* of Agrawal et al. (1993). The key idea of the algorithm is to begin by generating frequent itemsets with just one item (one-itemsets) and to recursively generate frequent itemsets with two items, then with three items, and so on, until we have generated frequent itemsets of all sizes.

It is easy to generate frequent one-itemsets. All we need to do is to count, for each item, how many transactions in the database include the item. These transaction counts are the supports for the one-itemsets. We drop one-itemsets that have support below the desired minimum support to create a list of the frequent one-itemsets.

To generate frequent two-itemsets, we use the frequent one-itemsets. The reasoning is that if a certain one-itemset did not exceed the minimum support, any larger size itemset that includes it will not exceed the minimum support. In general, generating k-itemsets uses the frequent $(k-1)$-itemsets that were generated in the preceding step. Each step requires a single run through the database, and therefore the Apriori algorithm is very fast even for a large number of unique items in a database.

Selecting Strong Rules

From the abundance of rules generated, the goal is to find only the rules that indicate a strong dependence between the antecedent and consequent itemsets. To measure the strength of association implied by a rule, we use the measures of *confidence* and *lift*, as described below.

Support and Confidence   In addition to support, which we described earlier, there is another measure that expresses the degree of uncertainty about the if–then rule. This is known as the *confidence*[2] of the rule. This measure compares the co-occurrence of the antecedent and consequent itemsets in the database with the occurrence of the antecedent itemsets. Confidence is defined as the ratio of the number of transactions that include all antecedent and consequent itemsets (namely, the support) to the number of transactions that include

---

[2]The concept of confidence is different from and unrelated to the ideas of confidence intervals and confidence levels used in statistical inference.

all the antecedent itemsets:

$$\text{Confidence} = \frac{\text{No. transactions with both antecedent and consequent itemsets}}{\text{No. transactions with antecedent itemset}}.$$

For example, suppose that a supermarket database has 100,000 point-of-sale transactions. Of these transactions, 2000 include both orange juice and (over-the-counter) flu medication, and 800 of these include soup purchases. The association rule "IF orange juice and flu medication are purchased THEN soup is purchased on the same trip" has a support of 800 transactions (alternatively, 0.8% = 800/100,000) and a confidence of 40% (= 800/2000).

To see the relationship between support and confidence, let us think about what each is measuring (estimating). One way to think of support is that it is the (estimated) probability that a transaction selected randomly from the database will contain all items in the antecedent and the consequent:

$$\text{Support} = \hat{P}(\text{antecedent AND consequent}).$$

In comparison, the confidence is the (estimated) *conditional probability* that a transaction selected randomly will include all the items in the consequent *given* that the transaction includes all the items in the antecedent:

$$\text{Confidence} = \frac{\hat{P}(\text{antecedent AND consequent})}{\hat{P}(\text{antecedent})} = \hat{P}(\text{consequent} \mid \text{antecedent}).$$

A high value of confidence suggests a strong association rule (in which we are highly confident). However, this can be deceptive because if the antecedent and/or the consequent has a high level of support, we can have a high value for confidence even when the antecedent and consequent are independent! For example, if nearly all customers buy bananas and nearly all customers buy ice cream, the confidence level of a rule such as "IF bananas THEN ice-cream" will be high regardless of whether there is an association between the items.

Coverage   Coverage (also called *cover* or *LHS-support*) is the support of the left-hand side of the rule.

$$\text{Coverage} = \hat{P}(\text{antecedent}).$$

It will tell you how often the rule can be applied.

Lift   A better way to judge the strength of an association rule is to compare the confidence of the rule with a benchmark value, where we assume that the occurrence of the consequent itemset in a transaction is independent of the occurrence of the antecedent for each rule. In other words, if the antecedent and consequent itemsets are independent, what confidence values would we expect to see? Under independence, the support would be

$$P(\text{antecedent AND consequent}) = P(\text{antecedent}) \times P(\text{consequent}),$$

and the benchmark confidence would be

$$\frac{P(\text{antecedent}) \times P(\text{consequent})}{P(\text{antecedent})} = P(\text{consequent}).$$

The estimate of this benchmark from the data, called the *benchmark confidence value* for a rule, is computed by

$$\text{Benchmark confidence} = \frac{\text{No. transactions with consequent itemset}}{\text{No. transactions in database}}.$$

We compare the confidence with the benchmark confidence by looking at their ratio: this is called the *lift* (or *lift ratio*) of a rule. The lift is the confidence of the rule divided by the benchmark confidence, assuming independence of consequent from antecedent:

$$\text{Lift} = \frac{\text{Confidence}}{\text{Benchmark confidence}}.$$

A lift greater than 1.0 suggests that there is some usefulness to the rule. In other words, the level of association between the antecedent and consequent itemsets is higher than would be expected if they were independent. The larger the lift value, the greater the strength of the association.

To illustrate the computation of support, confidence, and lift for the cellular phone faceplate example, we introduce an alternative presentation of the data that is better suited to this purpose.

Data Format

Transaction data are usually displayed in one of two formats: a transactions database (with each row representing a list of items purchased in a single transaction) or a binary incidence matrix in which columns are items, rows again represent transactions, and each cell has either a 1 or a 0, indicating the presence or absence of an item in the transaction. For example, Table 15.1 displays the data for the cellular faceplate purchases in a transactions database. We translate these into binary incidence matrix format in Table 15.2.

Now suppose that we want association rules between items for this database that have a support count of at least 2 (equivalent to a percentage support of $2/10 = 20\%$): In other words, these are rules based on items that were purchased together in at least 20% of the transactions. By enumeration, we can see that only the itemsets listed in Table 15.3 have a count of at least 2.

TABLE 15.2   PHONE FACEPLATE DATA IN BINARY INCIDENCE MATRIX FORMAT

Transaction	Red	White	Blue	Orange	Green	Yellow
1	1	1	0	0	1	0
2	0	1	0	1	0	0
3	0	1	1	0	0	0
4	1	1	0	1	0	0
5	1	0	1	0	0	0
6	0	1	1	0	0	0
7	1	0	1	0	0	0
8	1	1	1	0	1	0
9	1	1	1	0	0	0
10	0	0	0	0	0	1

TABLE 15.3   ITEMSETS WITH SUPPORT COUNT OF AT LEAST TWO

Itemset	Support (count)
{red}	6
{white}	7
{blue}	6
{orange}	2
{green}	2
{red, white}	4
{red, blue}	4
{red, green}	2
{white, blue}	4
{white, orange}	2
{white, green}	2
{red, white, blue}	2
{red, white, green}	2

The first itemset {red} has a support of 6, because six of the transactions included a red faceplate. Similarly, the last itemset {red, white, green} has a support of 2, because only two transactions included red, white, and green faceplates.

> In R, the user will input data using the package `arules` in the transactions database format. The package only creates rules with one item as the consequent. It calls the consequent the *right-hand side (RHS)* of the rule, and the antecedent the *left-hand side (LHS)* of the rule.

The Process of Rule Selection

The process of selecting strong rules is based on generating all association rules that meet stipulated support and confidence requirements. This is done in two stages. The first stage, described earlier, consists of finding all "frequent" itemsets, those itemsets that have a requisite support. In the second stage, we generate, from the frequent itemsets, association rules that meet a confidence requirement. The first step is aimed at removing item combinations that are rare in the database. The second stage then filters the remaining rules and selects only those with high confidence. For most association analysis data, the computational challenge is the first stage, as described in the discussion of the Apriori algorithm.

The computation of confidence in the second stage is simple. Since any subset (e.g., {red} in the phone faceplate example) must occur at least as frequently as the set it belongs to (e.g., {red, white}), each subset will also be in the list. It is then straightforward to compute the confidence as the ratio of the support for the itemset to the support for each subset of the itemset. We retain the corresponding association rule only if it exceeds the desired cutoff value for confidence. For example, from the itemset {red, white, green} in the phone faceplate purchases, we get the following single-consequent association rules, confidence values, and lift values:

Rule	Confidence	Lift
{red, white} $\Rightarrow$ {green}	$\dfrac{\text{Support of } \{red, white, green\}}{\text{Support of } \{red, white\}} = \dfrac{2}{4} = 50\%$	$\dfrac{\text{Confidence of rule}}{\text{Benchmark confidence}} = \dfrac{50\%}{20\%} = 2.5$
{green} $\Rightarrow$ {red}	$\dfrac{\text{Support of } \{green, red\}}{\text{Support of } \{green\}} = \dfrac{2}{2} = 100\%$	$\dfrac{\text{Confidence of rule}}{\text{Benchmark confidence}} = \dfrac{100\%}{60\%} = 1.67$
{white, green} $\Rightarrow$ {red}	$\dfrac{\text{Support of } \{white, green, red\}}{\text{Support of } \{white, green\}} = \dfrac{2}{2} = 100\%$	$\dfrac{\text{Confidence of rule}}{\text{Benchmark confidence}} = \dfrac{100\%}{60\%} = 1.67$

If the desired minimum confidence is 70%, we would report only the second and third rules.

We can generate association rules in R by converting the binary incidence matrix in Table 15.2 into a transaction database like in Table 15.1. We specify the minimum support (20%) and minimum confidence level percentage (50%). Table 15.4 shows the code and output. The output includes information on each rule and its support, confidence, and lift. (Note that here we consider all possible itemsets, not just {red, white, green} as above.)

Interpreting the Results

We can translate each of the rules from Table 15.4 into an understandable sentence that provides information about performance. For example, we can read rule [4] as follows:

> If orange is purchased, then with confidence 100% white will also be purchased. This rule has a lift of 1.43.

In interpreting results, it is useful to look at the various measures. The support for the rule indicates its impact in terms of overall size: how many

TABLE 15.4   BINARY INCIDENCE MATRIX, TRANSACTIONS DATABASE, AND RULES FOR
FACEPLATE EXAMPLE

 code for running the Apriori algorithm

```
library(arules)
fp.df <- mlba::Faceplate

# remove first column and convert to matrix
fp.mat <- as.matrix(fp.df[, -1])

# convert the binary incidence matrix into a transactions database
fp.trans <- as(fp.mat, "transactions")
inspect(fp.trans)

## get rules
# when running apriori(), include the minimum support, minimum confidence, and target
# as arguments.
rules <- apriori(fp.trans, parameter = list(supp = 0.2, conf = 0.5, target = "rules"))

# inspect the first six rules, sorted by their lift
inspect(head(sort(rules, by = "lift"), n = 6))
```

Output

```
> fp.mat
      Red White Blue Orange Green Yellow
 [1,]  1    1    0    0      1     0
 [2,]  0    1    0    1      0     0
 [3,]  0    1    1    0      0     0
 [4,]  1    1    0    1      0     0
 [5,]  1    0    1    0      0     0
 [6,]  0    1    1    0      0     0
 [7,]  1    0    1    0      0     0
 [8,]  1    1    1    0      1     0
 [9,]  1    1    1    0      0     0
[10,]  0    0    0    0      0     1

> inspect(fp.trans)
     items
[1]  {Red,White,Green}
[2]  {White,Orange}
[3]  {White,Blue}
[4]  {Red,White,Orange}
[5]  {Red,Blue}
[6]  {White,Blue}
[7]  {Red,Blue}
[8]  {Red,White,Blue,Green}
[9]  {Red,White,Blue}
[10] {Yellow}

> inspect(head(sort(rules, by = "lift"), n = 6))
    lhs              rhs        support confidence coverage lift     count
[1] {Red,White}   => {Green} 0.2      0.5        0.4      2.500000 2
[2] {Green}       => {Red}   0.2      1.0        0.2      1.666667 2
[3] {White,Green} => {Red}   0.2      1.0        0.2      1.666667 2
[4] {Orange}      => {White} 0.2      1.0        0.2      1.428571 2
[5] {Green}       => {White} 0.2      1.0        0.2      1.428571 2
[6] {Red,Green}   => {White} 0.2      1.0        0.2      1.428571 2
```

transactions are affected? If only a small number of transactions are affected, the rule may be of little use (unless the consequent is very valuable and/or the rule is very efficient in finding it).

The lift indicates how efficient the rule is in finding consequents compared with random selection. A very efficient rule is preferred to an inefficient rule, but we must still consider support: a very efficient rule that has very low support may not be as desirable as a less efficient rule with much greater support.

The confidence tells us at what rate consequents will be found and is useful in determining the business or operational usefulness of a rule: a rule with low confidence may find consequents at too low a rate to be worth the cost of (say) promoting the consequent in all the transactions that involve the antecedent.

Rules and Chance

What about confidence in the nontechnical sense? How sure can we be that the rules we develop are meaningful? Considering the matter from a statistical perspective, we can ask: Are we finding associations that are really just chance occurrences?

Let us examine the output from an application of this algorithm to a small database of 50 transactions, where each of the nine items is assigned randomly to each transaction. The data are shown in Table 15.5, and the association rules generated are shown in Table 15.6. In looking at these tables, remember that "lhs" and "rhs" refer to itemsets, not records.

TABLE 15.5   FIFTY TRANSACTIONS OF RANDOMLY ASSIGNED ITEMS

Transaction	Items					Transaction	Items					Transaction	Items			
1	8					18	8					35	3	4	6	8
2	3	4	8			19						36	1	4	8	
3	8					20	9					37	4	7	8	
4	3	9				21	2	5	6	8		38	8	9		
5	9					22	4	6	9			39	4	5	7	9
6	1	8				23	4	9				40	2	8	9	
7	6	9				24	8	9				41	2	5	9	
8	3	5	7	9		25	6	8				42	1	2	7	9
9	8					26	1	6	8			43	5	8		
10						27	5	8				44	1	7	8	
11	1	7	9			28	4	8	9			45	8			
12	1	4	5	8	9	29	9					46	2	7	9	
13	5	7	9			30	8					47	4	6	9	
14	6	7	8			31	1	5	8			48	9			
15	3	7	9			32	3	6	9			49	9			
16	1	4	9			33	7	9				50	6	7	8	
17	6	7	8			34	7	8	9							

TABLE 15.6   ASSOCIATION RULES OUTPUT FOR RANDOM DATA

Min. Support: 2 = 4%
Min. Conf. % :   70

```
> rules.tbl[rules.tbl$support >= 0.04 & rules.tbl$confidence >= 0.7,]
                lhs            rhs support confidence    lift
[18]          {item.2} => {item.9}    0.08        0.8 1.481481
[89]   {item.2,item.7} => {item.9}    0.04        1.0 1.851852
[104]  {item.3,item.4} => {item.8}    0.04        1.0 1.851852
[105]  {item.3,item.8} => {item.4}    0.04        1.0 5.000000
[113]  {item.3,item.7} => {item.9}    0.04        1.0 1.851852
[119]  {item.1,item.5} => {item.8}    0.04        1.0 1.851852
[149]  {item.4,item.5} => {item.9}    0.04        1.0 1.851852
[155]  {item.5,item.7} => {item.9}    0.06        1.0 1.851852
[176]  {item.6,item.7} => {item.8}    0.06        1.0 1.851852
```

R code is provided in the next example

In this example, the lift values highlight Rule [105] as most interesting, as it suggests that purchase of item 4 is almost five times as likely when items 3 and 8 are purchased than if item 4 was not associated with the itemset {3, 8}. Yet we know there is no fundamental association underlying these data—they were generated randomly.

Two principles can guide us in assessing rules for possible spuriousness due to chance effects:

1. The more records the rule is based on, the more solid the conclusion.

2. The more distinct rules we consider seriously (perhaps consolidating multiple rules that deal with the same items), the more likely it is that at least some will be based on chance sampling results. For one person to toss a coin 10 times and get 10 heads would be quite surprising. If 1000 people toss a coin 10 times each, it would not be nearly so surprising to have one get 10 heads. Formal adjustment of "statistical significance" when multiple comparisons are made is a complex subject in its own right and beyond the scope of this book. A reasonable approach is to consider rules from the top-down in terms of business or operational applicability and not consider more than what can reasonably be incorporated in a human decision-making process. This will impose a rough constraint on the dangers that arise from an automated review of hundreds or thousands of rules in search of "something interesting."

We now consider a more realistic example, using a larger database and real transactional data.

Example 2: Rules for Similar Book Purchases

The following example (drawn from the Charles Book Club case; see Chapter 23) examines associations among transactions involving various types of books. The database includes 4000 transactions, and there are 11 different types of books. The data, in binary incidence matrix form, are shown in Table 15.7.

TABLE 15.7   SUBSET OF BOOK PURCHASE TRANSACTIONS IN BINARY MATRIX FORMAT

ChildBks	YouthBks	CookBks	DoItYBks	RefBks	ArtBks	GeogBks	ItalCook	ItalAtlas	ItalArt	Florence
0	1	0	1	0	0	1	0	0	0	0
1	0	0	0	0	0	0	0	0	0	0
0	0	0	0	0	0	0	0	0	0	0
1	1	1	0	1	0	1	0	0	0	0
0	0	1	0	0	0	1	0	0	0	0
1	0	0	0	0	1	0	0	0	0	1
0	1	0	0	0	0	0	0	0	0	0
0	1	0	0	1	0	0	0	0	0	0
1	0	0	1	0	0	0	0	0	0	0
1	1	1	0	0	0	1	0	0	0	0
0	0	0	0	0	0	0	0	0	0	0

For instance, the first transaction included *YouthBks* (youth books), *DoItYBks* (do-it-yourself books), and *GeogBks* (geography books). Table 15.8 shows some of the rules generated for these data using function *apriori()* in the **arules** package, given that we specified a minimal support of 200 transactions (out of 4000 transactions) and a minimal confidence of 50%. This resulted in 72 rules (the 30 rules with the highest lift are shown in Table 15.8).

In reviewing these rules, we see that the information can be compressed. *ChildBks* is included in almost every rule. Including children books in the analysis is probably meaningless, as the purchase of children books is not associated with individual preferences of the customer. In this case, one could consider removing this item from the analysis or filtering the rules to those that do not include *ChildBks*.

Another rule is {ItalCook} => {CookBks} (not shown) which has high confidence, but is probably meaningless. It says: "If Italian cooking books have been purchased, then cookbooks are purchased." It seems likely that Italian cooking books are simply a subset of cookbooks.

Rules 3, 18, and 29 involve the same trio of books, with different antecedents and consequents. The same is true of rules 10 and 12. (Pairs and groups like this are easy to track down by looking for rows that share the same support.) This does not mean that the rules are not useful. On the contrary, it can reduce the number of itemsets to be considered for possible action from a business perspective.

TABLE 15.8   **RULES FOR BOOK PURCHASE TRANSACTIONS**

R code for running the Apriori algorithm

```
all.books.df <- mlba::CharlesBookClub

# create a binary incidence matrix
count.books.df <- all.books.df[, 8:18]
incid.books.mat <- as.matrix(count.books.df > 0)

#  convert the binary incidence matrix into a transactions database
books.trans <- as(incid.books.mat, "transactions")
inspect(books.trans[1:10])

# plot data
itemFrequencyPlot(books.trans)

# run apriori function
rules <- apriori(books.trans,
    parameter = list(supp= 200/4000, conf = 0.5, target = "rules"))

# inspect top-30 rules sorted by lift
inspect(head(sort(rules, by = "lift"), n=30))
```

Output

```
> inspect(head(sort(rules, by = "lift"), n=30))
     lhs                              rhs           support confidence coverage lift     count
[1]  {ChildBks,CookBks,GeogBks}    => {YouthBks} 0.06325 0.5776256  0.10950  2.424452 253
[2]  {ChildBks,CookBks,RefBks}     => {DoItYBks} 0.06125 0.5917874  0.10350  2.323013 245
[3]  {DoItYBks,GeogBks}            => {YouthBks} 0.05450 0.5396040  0.10100  2.264864 218
[4]  {ChildBks,CookBks,RefBks}     => {YouthBks} 0.05525 0.5338164  0.10350  2.240573 221
[5]  {ChildBks,CookBks,DoItYBks}   => {YouthBks} 0.06700 0.5244618  0.12775  2.201309 268
[6]  {ChildBks,YouthBks,CookBks}   => {DoItYBks} 0.06700 0.5583333  0.12000  2.191691 268
[7]  {ChildBks,RefBks}             => {DoItYBks} 0.07100 0.5536062  0.12825  2.173135 284
[8]  {ChildBks,CookBks,GeogBks}    => {DoItYBks} 0.06050 0.5525114  0.10950  2.168838 242
[9]  {ChildBks,GeogBks}            => {YouthBks} 0.07550 0.5162393  0.14625  2.166797 302
[10] {CookBks,GeogBks}             => {YouthBks} 0.08025 0.5136000  0.15625  2.155719 321
[11] {ChildBks,YouthBks,RefBks}    => {CookBks}  0.05525 0.8911290  0.06200  2.144715 221
[12] {ChildBks,YouthBks}           => {DoItYBks} 0.08025 0.5440678  0.14750  2.135693 321
[13] {CookBks,RefBks}              => {DoItYBks} 0.07450 0.5330948  0.13975  2.092619 298
[14] {CookBks,DoItYBks,RefBks}     => {ChildBks} 0.06125 0.8221477  0.07450  2.086669 245
[15] {ChildBks,DoItYBks,RefBks}    => {CookBks}  0.06125 0.8626761  0.07100  2.076236 245
[16] {ChildBks,CookBks}            => {DoItYBks} 0.12775 0.5278926  0.24200  2.072198 511
[17] {YouthBks,CookBks,RefBks}     => {ChildBks} 0.05525 0.8095238  0.06825  2.054629 221
[18] {YouthBks,GeogBks}            => {DoItYBks} 0.05450 0.5215311  0.10450  2.047227 218
[19] {YouthBks,CookBks}            => {DoItYBks} 0.08375 0.5201863  0.16100  2.041948 335
[20] {ChildBks,RefBks,GeogBks}     => {CookBks}  0.05025 0.8481013  0.05925  2.041158 201
[21] {YouthBks,CookBks,DoItYBks}   => {ChildBks} 0.06700 0.8000000  0.08375  2.030457 268
[22] {YouthBks,RefBks}             => {CookBks}  0.06825 0.8400000  0.08125  2.021661 273
[23] {ChildBks,YouthBks,GeogBks}   => {CookBks}  0.06325 0.8377483  0.07550  2.016242 253
[24] {ChildBks,YouthBks,DoItYBks}  => {CookBks}  0.06700 0.8348910  0.08025  2.009365 268
[25] {ChildBks,ArtBks}             => {DoItYBks} 0.05375 0.5106888  0.10525  2.004667 215
[26] {YouthBks,CookBks,GeogBks}    => {ChildBks} 0.06325 0.7881620  0.08025  2.000411 253
[27] {CookBks,DoItYBks,GeogBks}    => {ChildBks} 0.06050 0.7806452  0.07750  1.981333 242
[28] {ChildBks,GeogBks}            => {DoItYBks} 0.07375 0.5042735  0.14625  1.979484 295
[29] {YouthBks,DoItYBks}           => {GeogBks}  0.05450 0.5278450  0.10325  1.978801 218
[30] {CookBks,RefBks,GeogBks}      => {ChildBks} 0.05025 0.7790698  0.06450  1.977334 201
```

15.2 COLLABORATIVE FILTERING[3]

Recommendation systems are a critically important part of websites that offer a large variety of products or services. Examples come readily to mind: Amazon.com offers millions of different products, Netflix has thousands of movies for rental, Google searches over huge numbers of webpages, Internet radio websites such as Spotify and Pandora include a large variety of music albums by various artists, travel websites offer many destinations and hotels, and social network websites have many groups. The recommender engine provides personalized recommendations to a user based on the user's information and on similar users' information. Information means behaviors indicative of preference, such as purchase, ratings, and clicking.

The value that recommendation systems provide to users helps online companies convert browsers into buyers, increase cross-selling, and build loyalty.

Collaborative filtering is a popular technique used by such recommendation systems. The term *collaborative filtering* is based on the notions of identifying relevant items for a specific user from the very large set of items ("filtering") by considering preferences of many users ("collaboration").

The Fortune.com article "Amazon's Recommendation Secret" (June 30, 2012) describes the company's use of collaborative filtering not only for providing personalized product recommendations but also for customizing the entire website interface for each user:

> At root, the retail giant's recommendation system is based on a number of simple elements: what a user has bought in the past, which items they have in their virtual shopping cart, items they've rated and liked, and what other customers have viewed and purchased. Amazon calls this homegrown math "item-to-item collaborative filtering," and it's used this algorithm to heavily customize the browsing experience for returning customers.

Data Type and Format

Collaborative filtering requires availability of all item–user information. Specifically, for each item–user combination, we should have some measure of the user's preference for that item. Preference can be a numerical rating or a binary behavior such as a purchase, a "like," or a click.

For n users $(u_1, u_2, \ldots, u_n)$ and p items $(i_1, i_2, \ldots i_p)$, we can think of the data as an $n \times p$ matrix of n rows (users) by p columns (items). Each cell includes the rating or the binary event corresponding to the user's preference of the item (see schematic in Table 15.9). Typically not every user purchases or rates every item, and therefore a purchase matrix will have many zeros (it is sparse), and a rating matrix will have many missing values. Such missing values sometimes convey "uninterested" (as opposed to non-missing values that convey interest).

TABLE 15.9 SCHEMATIC OF MATRIX FORMAT WITH RATING DATA

User ID	Item ID			
	I_1	I_2	$\cdots$	I_p
U_1	$r_{1,1}$	$r_{1,2}$	$\cdots$	$r_{1,p}$
U_2	$r_{2,1}$	$r_{2,2}$	$\cdots$	$r_{2,p}$
$\vdots$				
U_n	$r_{n,1}$	$r_{n,2}$	$\cdots$	$r_{n,p}$

When both n and p are large, it is not practical to store the preferences data $(r_{u,i})$ in an $n \times p$ table. Instead, the data can be stored in many rows of triplets of the form $(U_u, I_i, r_{u,i})$, where each triplet contains the user ID, the item ID, and the preference information.

Example 3: Netflix Prize Contest

We have been considering both association rules and collaborative filtering as unsupervised techniques, but it is possible to judge how well they do by looking at holdout data to see what users purchase and how they rate items. The famous Netflix contest, mentioned in Chapter 13, did just this and provides a useful example to illustrate collaborative filtering, though the extension into training and validation is beyond the scope of this book.

In 2006, Netflix, the largest movie rental service in North America, announced a one million USD contest (www.netflixprize.com) for the purpose of improving its recommendation system called *Cinematch*. Participants were provided with a number of datasets, one for each movie. Each dataset included all the customer ratings for that movie (and the timestamp). We can think of one large combined dataset of the form [customer ID, movie ID, rating, date] where each record includes the rating given by a certain customer to a certain movie on a certain date. Ratings were on a 1–5 star scale. Contestants were asked to develop a recommendation algorithm that would improve over the existing Netflix system. Table 15.10 shows a small sample from the contest data, organized in matrix format. Rows indicate customers and columns are different movies.

It is interesting to note that the winning team was able to improve their system by considering not just the ratings for a movie but also *whether* a movie was rated by a particular customer or not. In other words, the information on which movies a customer decided to rate turned out to be critically informative of customers' preferences, more than simply considering the 1–5 rating information[4]:

---

[4]Bell, R. M., Koren, Y., and Volinsky, C., "The BellKor 2008 Solution to the Netflix Prize," https://api.semanticscholar.org/CorpusID:11877045

TABLE 15.10 SAMPLE OF RECORDS FROM THE NETFLIX PRIZE CONTEST, FOR A SUBSET OF 10 CUSTOMERS AND 9 MOVIES

Customer ID	1	5	8	17	18	28	30	44	48
30878	4	1			3	3	4	5	
124105	4								
822109	5								
823519	3		1	4		4	5		
885013	4	5							
893988	3						4	4	
1248029	3					2	4		3
1503895	4								
1842128	4						3		
2238063	3								

Collaborative filtering methods address the sparse set of rating values. However, much accuracy is obtained by also looking at other features of the data. First is the information on which movies each user chose to rate, regardless of specific rating value ("the binary view"). This played a decisive role in our 2007 solution, and reflects the fact that the movies to be rated are selected deliberately by the user, and are not a random sample.

This is an example where converting the rating information into a binary matrix of rated/unrated proved to be useful.

User-Based Collaborative Filtering: "People Like You"

One approach to generating personalized recommendations for a user using collaborative filtering is based on finding users with similar preferences and recommending items that they liked but the user hasn't purchased. The algorithm has two steps:

1. Find users who are most similar to the user of interest (neighbors). This is done by comparing the preference of our user with the preferences of other users.

2. Considering only the items that the user has *not* yet purchased, recommend the ones that are most preferred by the user's neighbors.

This is the approach behind Amazon's "Customers Who Viewed This Item Also Viewed..." (see Figure 15.1). It is also used in a Google search for generating the "Similar pages" link shown near each search result.

Step 1 requires choosing a distance (or proximity) metric to measure the distance between our user and the other users. Once the distances are computed, we can use a threshold on the distance or on the number of required neighbors to determine the nearest neighbors to be used in Step 2. This approach is called "user-based top-N recommendation."

A nearest-neighbors approach measures the distance of our user to each of the other users in the database, similar to the k-nearest-neighbors algorithm (see Chapter 7). The Euclidean distance measure we discussed in that chapter does not perform as well for collaborative filtering as some other measures. A popular proximity measure between two users is the Pearson correlation between their ratings. We denote the ratings of items $I_1, \ldots, I_p$ by user U_1 as $r_{1,1}, r_{1,2}, \ldots, r_{1,p}$ and their average by $\bar{r}_1$. Similarly, the ratings by user U_2 are $r_{2,1}, r_{2,2}, \ldots, r_{2,p}$, with average $\bar{r}_2$. The correlation proximity between the two users is defined by

$$\text{Corr}(U_1, U_2) = \frac{\sum (r_{1,i} - \bar{r}_1)(r_{2,i} - \bar{r}_2)}{\sqrt{\sum (r_{1,i} - \bar{r}_1)^2} \sqrt{\sum (r_{2,i} - \bar{r}_2)^2}}, \tag{15.1}$$

where the summations are only over the items co-rated by both users.

To illustrate this, let us compute the correlation between customer 30878 and customer 823519 in the small Netflix sample in Table 15.10. We'll assume that the data shown in the table is the entire information. First, we compute the average rating by each of these users:

$$\bar{r}_{30878} = (4 + 1 + 3 + 3 + 4 + 5)/6 = 3.333$$

$$\bar{r}_{823519} = (3 + 1 + 4 + 4 + 5)/5 = 3.4$$

Note that the average is computed over a different number of movies for each of these customers, because they each rated a different set of movies. The average for a customer is computed over *all* the movies that a customer rated. The calculations for the correlation involve the departures from the average, but *only for the items that they co-rated.* In this case the co-rated movie IDs are 1, 28, and 30:

$\text{Corr}(U_{30878}, U_{823519}) =$

$$\frac{(4 - 3.333)(3 - 3.4) + (3 - 3.333)(4 - 3.4) + (4 - 3.333)(5 - 3.4)}{\sqrt{(4 - 3.333)^2 + (3 - 3.333)^2 + (4 - 3.333)^2} \sqrt{(3 - 3.4)^2 + (4 - 3.4)^2 + (5 - 3.4)^2}}$$

$$= 0.6/1.75 = 0.34$$

The same approach can be used when the data are in the form of a binary matrix (e.g., purchased or didn't purchase.)

Another popular measure is a variant of the Pearson correlation called *cosine similarity*. It differs from the correlation formula by not subtracting the means. Subtracting the mean in the correlation formula adjusts for users' different overall approaches to rating—for example, a customer who always rates highly vs. one who tends to give low ratings.[5]

---

[5]Correlation and cosine similarity are popular in collaborative filtering because they are computationally fast for high-dimensional sparse data, and they account for both the rating values and the number of rated items.

For example, the cosine similarity between the two Netflix customers is

$$\text{Cos Sim}(U_{30878}, U_{823519}) = \frac{4 \times 3 + 3 \times 4 + 4 \times 5}{\sqrt{4^2 + 3^2 + 4^2}\sqrt{3^2 + 1^2 + 5^2}}$$

$$= 44/45.277 = 0.972$$

Note that when the data are in the form of a binary matrix, say, for purchase or no-purchase, the cosine similarity must be calculated over all items that either user has purchased; it cannot be limited to just the items that were co-purchased.

> Collaborative filtering suffers from what is called a *cold start*: it cannot be used as is to create recommendations for new users or new items. For a user who rated a single item, the correlation coefficient between this and other users (in user-generated collaborative filtering) will have a denominator of zero, and the cosine proximity will be 1 regardless of the rating. In a similar vein, users with just one item, and items with just one user, do not qualify as candidates for nearby neighbors.

For a user of interest, we compute his/her similarity to each of the users in our database using a correlation, cosine similarity, or another measure. Then, in Step 2, we look only at the k nearest users, and among all the other items that they rated/purchased, we choose the best one and recommend it to our user. What is the best one? For binary purchase data, it is the item most purchased. For rating data, it could be the highest rated, most rated, or a weighting of the two.

The nearest-neighbors approach can be computationally expensive when we have a large database of users. One solution is to use clustering methods (see Chapter 16) to group users into homogeneous clusters in terms of their preferences and then to measure the distance of our user to each of the clusters. This approach places the computational load on the clustering step that can take place earlier and offline; it is then cheaper (and faster) to compare our user to each of the clusters in real time. The price of clustering is less accurate recommendations, because not all the members of the closest cluster are the most similar to our user.

Item-Based Collaborative Filtering

When the number of users is much larger than the number of items, it is computationally cheaper (and faster) to find similar items rather than similar users. Specifically, when a user expresses interest in a particular item, the item-based collaborative filtering algorithm has two steps:

1. Find the items that were co-rated, or co-purchased, (by any user) with the item of interest.
2. Recommend the most popular or correlated item(s) among the similar items.

Similarity is now computed between items, instead of users. For example, in our small Netflix sample (Table 15.10), the correlation between movie 1 (with average $\bar{r}_1 = 3.7$) and movie 5 (with average $\bar{r}_5 = 3$) is

$$\text{Corr}(I_1, I_5) = \frac{(4 - 3.7)(1 - 3) + (4 - 3.7)(5 - 3)}{\sqrt{(4 - 3.7)^2 + (4 - 3.7)^2}\sqrt{(1 - 3)^2 + (5 - 3)^2}} = 0$$

The zero correlation is due to the two opposite ratings of movie 5 by the users who also rated 1. One user rated it 5 stars and the other gave it a 1 star.

In like fashion, we can compute similarity between all the movies. This can be done offline. In real time, for a user who rates a certain movie highly, we can look up the movie correlation table and recommend the movie with the highest positive correlation to the user's newly rated movie.

According to an industry report[6] by researchers who developed the Amazon item-to-item recommendation system:

> [The item-based] algorithm produces recommendations in real time, scales to massive data sets, and generates high-quality recommendations.

The disadvantage of item-based recommendations is that there is less diversity between items (compared to users' taste), and therefore, the recommendations are often obvious.

Evaluating Performance

Collaborative filtering can be considered an unsupervised learning method, because data are not typically organized for analysis in the form "X was recommended, user did Y." We do, however, have data on what has been purchased or rated by a user without regard to any recommendations. We can "hide" some items in the user–item matrix (this constitutes the holdout set), and use collaborative filtering to make recommendations for the hidden items. This is effectively the same thing as predicting the hidden user rating, or whether the user purchases the item. We can then un-hide the actual user action and see how the recommendations compare to the actual.

Two types of offline learning evaluations are *predictive performance* and *ranking performance*—each measures a different aspect of the recommender system. Predictive performance assesses how close the recommendation is to the actual user's behavior. We have already encountered many such metrics in Chapter 5. In contrast, ranking evaluation considers only performance on the top set of recommended items ("Top-N") produced by the recommender algorithm. This approach is useful in many applications where the a user is shown a set of the "best" recommended items for him/her (such as the results of a Google search). Ranking metrics therefore focus on the accuracy of only the top-ranked items.

---

[6]Linden, G., Smith, B., and York J., "Amazon.com Recommendations: Item-to-Item Collaborative Filtering," *IEEE Internet Computing*, vol. 7, no. 1, pp. 76–80, 2003.

Common performance metrics include the following:

Predictive performance for numerical predictions (e.g., ratings):
Metrics such as holdout RMSE and MAE are commonly used. Note
that these metrics are strongly influenced by long-tail items: a rare item
that is incorrectly predicted can mask excellent performance on common
items. One solution is to weight items within these metrics so that more
important/profitable items have higher weights.

**Predictive performance for categorical predictions (e.g., click or
no-click):** Metrics based on the holdout confusion matrix such as accuracy,
recall and precision, and ROC curves are common.

Ranking performance for numerical predictions (e.g., ratings): A
common ranking performance metric is the correlation between the *ordering*
of the true ratings and the *ordering* of the predicted ratings. This is known
as the Spearman coefficient.

Ranking performance for categorical classifications: Common metrics include Top-N precision and Top-N recall, which are the precision and
recall computed only on the top-N recommendation sets and which measure
the fraction of relevant items in the recommendation list and the fraction of
relevant items that are missed by the list.

There also exist specialized metrics for other important properties of a recommendation algorithm, beyond accuracy, such as novelty, trust, coverage, and
serendipity. To learn more about these, see Aggarwal (2016).

Lastly, we note that partitioning the data into training, validation, and holdout sets is done a bit differently than in supervised learning: rather than sampling
users, for collaborative filtering evaluation, the sampling is done on *matrix entries*
(e.g., $r_{u,i}$ in Table 15.9): these are the user–item combinations in the user–item
matrix.

Example 4: Predicting Movie Ratings with MovieLens Data

In this example, we analyze movie ratings data from MovieLens,[7] a website that
recommends movies for people to watch. The goal is to predict ratings for
movies that users have not watched thus far and then use the movies with the
highest prediction ratings as top-k recommendations for the user. We use the
100K latest dataset[8] that contains 100,836 ratings provided by 610 users for 9742
movies. The datasets are available in the **mlba** package as *mlba::MovieLensRatings*

---

[7]MovieLens (https://movielens.org) website is managed by the GroupLens research lab at the University of Minnesota.
[8]Source: https://grouplens.org/datasets/movielens/ (Dataset creation date: September 26, 2018); see
Harper and Konstan (2015).

and *mlba::MovieLensMovies* and through the book website as *ratings.csv* and *movies.csv* files containing ratings data and movies data, respectively. A description of each variable is given in Table 15.11. Additional movie attributes (e.g., actors) can be retrieved through movie databases such as IMDB.

TABLE 15.11   DESCRIPTION OF VARIABLES IN MOVIELENS DATASET

Ratings data

userId	Anonymized MovieLens user ID. Each user has rated at least 20 movies.
movieId	Movie ID consistent with that used on the MovieLens website (e.g., information for movie id 1 is available at https://movielens.org/movies/1).
rating	Movie rating provided by user on a 5-star scale, with half-star increments (0.5 star - 5 stars)
timestamp	Timestamp when rating was recorded. Time is in seconds since midnight Coordinated Universal Time (UTC) of January 1, 1970.

Movies data

movieId	Same as ratings data
title	Movie titles, including the year of release in parentheses
genres	Pipe-separated list of genres for corresponding movie title

Table 15.12 shows the data preprocessing steps, starting with loading the data. The ratings information is then converted into a rating matrix suitable for the **recommenderlab** package.

TABLE 15.12   DATA PREPROCESSING FOR THE MOVIELENS DATA

 code for downloading data and converting ratings data into a rating matrix

```
library(recommenderlab)

# download MovieLens data
ratings <- mlba::MovieLensRatings
movies <- mlba::MovieLensMovies

# convert ratings to rating matrix
idxUserId <- sort(unique(ratings$userId))
idxMovieId <- sort(unique(ratings$movieId))
m <- matrix(NA, nrow=length(idxUserId), ncol=length(idxMovieId),
            dimnames=list(
              user=paste("u", 1:length(idxUserId), sep=''),
              item=movies$title[match(idxMovieId, movies$movieId)]
            ))
for (i in 1:nrow(ratings)) {
  rating <- ratings[i,]
  irow <- match(rating$userId, idxUserId)
  icol <- match(rating$movieId, idxMovieId)
  m[irow, icol] <- rating$rating
}
ratingMatrix <- as(m, "realRatingMatrix")
```

Table 15.13 shows the code for building user-based collaborative filtering (UBCF) and item-based collaborative filtering (IBCF) models. The models are used to recommend the top 10 movies to user 1 based on sorted prediction ratings for the movie titles. The recommendations for user 1 based on their similarity to other users contain a few well-known movies like *The Maltese Falcon*, *Michael Clayton*, and *Enemy at the Gates*. The top 10 movies that would be recommended to user 1 based on item-based rating similarity are also shown in Table 15.13.

The recommended movies are different from UBCF with one exception, the Brazilian-American comedy *Bossa Nova*.

The `recommenderlab` package also allows estimating and comparing the predictive performance of different approaches. Table 15.14 compares

---

TABLE 15.13   TRAIN RECOMMENDERLAB MODELS AND PREDICT NEW USERS

R code for building UBCF and IBCF recommender models and creating recommendations for user 1

```
# UBCF model and prediction
recommender <- Recommender(ratingMatrix[-1], method="UBCF")
pred <- predict(recommender, ratingMatrix[1])
as(pred, 'list')

# IBCF model and prediction
recommender <- Recommender(ratingMatrix[-1], method="IBCF")
pred <- predict(recommender, ratingMatrix[1])
as(pred, 'list')
```

Output

```
$u1
 [1] "Bossa Nova (2000)"
 [2] "Maltese Falcon, The (1941)"
 [3] "Michael Clayton (2007)"
 [4] "3-Iron (Bin-jip) (2004)"
 [5] "Battlestar Galactica (2003)"
 [6] "Enemy at the Gates (2001)"
 [7] "Watchmen (2009)"
 [8] "Walk to Remember, A (2002)"
 [9] "Tristan & Isolde (2006)"
[10] "Atonement (2007)"

$u1
 [1] "Sunset Park (1996)"
 [2] "Bossa Nova (2000)"
 [3] "Galaxy of Terror (Quest) (1981)"
 [4] "Looker (1981)"
 [5] "Alien Contamination (1980)"
 [6] "Master of the Flying Guillotine (Du bi quan wang da po xue di zi) (1975)"
 [7] "Dancemaker (1998)"
 [8] "Trippin' (1999)"
 [9] "Love Jones (1997)"
[10] "Secret Policeman's Other Ball, The (1982)"
```

TABLE 15.14 **EVALUATE PERFORMANCE OF RECOMMENDERLAB MODELS**

 code for evaluating UBCF and IBCF recommender models

```
set.seed(1)
e <- evaluationScheme(ratingMatrix, method="split", train=0.9, given=10)

r1 <- Recommender(getData(e, "train"), "UBCF")
r2 <- Recommender(getData(e, "train"), "IBCF")
r3 <- Recommender(getData(e, "train"), "RANDOM")

p1 <- predict(r1, getData(e, "known"), type="ratings")
p2 <- predict(r2, getData(e, "known"), type="ratings")
p3 <- predict(r3, getData(e, "known"), type="ratings")
error <- rbind(
  UBCF = calcPredictionAccuracy(p1, getData(e, "unknown")),
  IBCF = calcPredictionAccuracy(p2, getData(e, "unknown")),
  RANDOM = calcPredictionAccuracy(p3, getData(e, "unknown"))
)
error
```

Output

```
> error
       RMSE MSE   MAE
UBCF   1.10 1.21 0.848
IBCF   1.33 1.77 1.043
RANDOM 1.33 1.76 1.029
```

the performance of the two methods. As a baseline, we also estimate the performance of a recommender that makes random suggestions. The function *evaluationScheme* prepares the dataset for performance evaluation. The *train* argument defines the fraction of the dataset used for training (here 90%). The function *getData* returns this subset. The predictive performance is estimated with the other 10% of the dataset. Each record is split into a *known* subset of ratings of size *given* (here 10), and the predictions from this subset are compared with the remaining other *unknown* ratings. The result of the comparison in this case shows that user-based collaborative filtering gives better performance. The estimated performance of the item-based filtering recommender is similar to random.

Advantages and Weaknesses of Collaborative Filtering

Collaborative filtering relies on the availability of subjective information regarding users' preferences. It provides useful recommendations, even for "long-tail" items, if our database contains sufficient similar users (not necessarily many, but at least a few per user), so that each user can find other users with similar tastes. Similarly, the data should include sufficient per-item ratings or purchases. One limitation of collaborative filtering is therefore that it cannot generate recommendations for new users, nor for new items. There are various approaches for tackling this challenge.

User-based collaborative filtering looks for similarity in terms of highly rated or preferred items. However, it is blind to data on low-rated or unwanted items. We can therefore not expect to use it as is for detecting unwanted items.

User-based collaborative filtering helps leverage similarities between people's tastes for providing personalized recommendations. However, when the number of users becomes very large, collaborative filtering becomes computationally difficult. Solutions include item-based algorithms, clustering of users, and dimension reduction. The most popular dimension reduction method used in such cases is singular value decomposition (SVD), a computationally superior form of principal component analysis (see Chapter 4).

Although the term "prediction" is often used to describe the output of collaborative filtering, this method is unsupervised by nature. It can be used to generate predicted ratings or purchase indication for a user, but usually we do not have the true outcome value in practice. Evaluating performance is therefore challenging and treats the user's actual behavior as if it were their response to the recommendation. One important way to improve recommendations generated by collaborative filtering is by getting actual user feedback. Once a recommendation is generated, the user can indicate whether the recommendation was adequate or not. For this reason, many recommender systems entice users to provide feedback on their recommendations. When user reactions are measured with respect to the presented recommendations, this is called *online learning*. This is in contrast to *offline learning*, where such "online" feedback information is not used. Lastly, using online learning, many companies now measure the direct impact of a recommender system in terms of a business-relevant metric, such as conversion rate. In Chapter 14, we describe approaches that obtain user feedback that are useful for evaluating recommender systems and other interventions.

Collaborative Filtering vs. Association Rules

While collaborative filtering and association rules are both unsupervised methods used for generating recommendations, they differ in several ways.

Frequent Itemsets vs. Personalized Recommendations Association rules look for frequent item combinations and will provide recommendations only for those items. In contrast, collaborative filtering provides personalized recommendations for every item, thereby catering to users with unusual taste. In this sense, collaborative filtering is useful for capturing the "long tail" of user preferences, while association rules look for the "head." This difference has implications for the data needed: association rules require data on a very large number of "baskets" (transactions) to find a sufficient number of baskets that contain certain combinations of items. In contrast, collaborative filtering does not require many "baskets," but does require data on as many items as possible for many users. Also, association rules operate at the basket level (our database can include multiple transactions for each user), while collaborative filtering operates at the user level.

Because association rules produce generic, impersonal rules (association-based recommendations such as Amazon's "Frequently Bought Together" display the same recommendations to all users searching for a specific item), they can be used for setting common strategies such as product placement in a store or sequencing of diagnostic tests in hospitals. In contrast, collaborative filtering generates user-specific recommendations (e.g., Amazon's "Customers Who Viewed This Item Also Viewed...") and is therefore a tool designed for personalization.

Transactional Data vs. User Data Association rules provide recommendations of items based on their co-purchase with other items in *many transactions/baskets*. In contrast, collaborative filtering provides recommendations of items based on their co-purchase or co-rating by even a small number of other *users*. Considering distinct baskets is useful when the same items are purchased over and over again (e.g., in grocery shopping). Considering distinct users is useful when each item is typically purchased/rated once (e.g., purchases of books, music, and movies).

Binary Data and Ratings Data Association rules treat items as binary data (1 = purchase, 0 = nonpurchase), whereas collaborative filtering can operate on either binary data or on numerical ratings.

Two or More Items In association rules, the antecedent and consequent can each include one or more items (e.g., IF milk THEN cookies and cornflakes). Hence, a recommendation might be a bundle of the item of interest with multiple items ("buy milk, cookies, and cornflakes and receive 10% discount"). In contrast, in collaborative filtering, similarity is measured between *pairs* of items or pairs of users. A recommendation will therefore be either for a single item (the most popular item purchased by people like you, which you haven't purchased) or for multiple single items which do not necessarily relate to each other (the top two most popular items purchased by people like you, which you haven't purchased).

These distinctions are sharper for purchases and recommendations of non-popular items, especially when comparing association rules with user-based collaborative filtering. When considering what to recommend to a user who purchased a popular item, then association rules and item-based collaborative filtering might yield the same recommendation for a single item. However, a user-based recommendation will likely differ. Consider a customer who purchases milk every week, as well as gluten-free products (which are rarely purchased by other customers). Suppose that using association rules on the transactions database, we identify the rule "IF milk THEN cookies." Then, the next time our customer purchases milk, s/he will receive a recommendation (e.g., a coupon) to purchase cookies, whether or not s/he purchased cookies and irrespective of his/her gluten-free item purchases. In item-based collaborative filtering, we would look at all items co-purchased with milk across all users and recommend the most popular item among them (which was not purchased by our customer). This might also lead to a recommendation of cookies, because this item was not purchased by our customer.[9] Now consider user-based collaborative filtering. User-based collaborative filtering searches for similar customers—those who purchased the same set of items—and then recommends the item most commonly purchased by these neighbors, which *was not purchased by our customer*. The user-based recommendation is therefore unlikely to recommend cookies and more likely to recommend popular gluten-free items that the customer has not purchased.

15.3 SUMMARY

Association rules (also called market basket analysis) and collaborative filtering are unsupervised methods for deducing associations between purchased items from databases of transactions. Association rules search for generic rules about items that are purchased together. The main advantage of this method is that it generates clear, simple rules of the form "IF X is purchased, THEN Y is also likely to be purchased." The method is very transparent and easy to understand.

The process of creating association rules is two-staged. First, a set of candidate rules based on frequent itemsets is generated (the Apriori algorithm being the most popular rule-generating algorithm). Then from these candidate rules, the rules that indicate the strongest association between items are selected. We use the measures of support and confidence to evaluate the uncertainty in a rule. The user also specifies minimal support and confidence values to be used in the rule generation and selection process. A third measure, the lift, compares the efficiency of the rule to detect a real association with a random combination.

One shortcoming of association rules is the profusion of rules that are generated. There is therefore a need for ways to reduce these to a small set of useful and strong rules. An important nonautomated method to condense the information involves examining the rules for uninformative and trivial rules and for rules that share the same support. Another issue that needs to be kept in mind is that rare combinations tend to be ignored, because they do not meet the minimum

---

[9]If the rule is "IF milk, THEN cookies and cornflakes," then the association rules would recommend cookies and cornflakes to a milk purchaser, while item-based collaborative filtering would recommend the most popular single item purchased with milk.

support requirement. For this reason, it is better to have items that are approximately equally frequent in the data. This can be achieved by using higher-level hierarchies as the items. An example is to use types of books rather than titles of individual books in deriving association rules from a database of bookstore transactions.

Collaborative filtering is a popular technique used in online recommendation systems. It is based on the relationship between items formed by users who acted similarly on an item, such as purchasing or rating an item highly. User-based collaborative filtering operates on data on item–user combinations, calculates the similarities between users, and provides personalized recommendations to users. An important component for the success of collaborative filtering is that users provide feedback about the recommendations provided and have sufficient information on each item. One disadvantage of collaborative filtering methods is that they cannot generate recommendations for new users or new items. Also, with a huge number of users, user-based collaborative filtering becomes computationally challenging, and alternatives such as item-based methods or dimension reduction are popularly used.

PROBLEMS

15.1 **Satellite Radio Customers.** An analyst at a subscription-based satellite radio company has been given a sample of data from their customer database, with the goal of finding groups of customers who are associated with one another. The data consist of company data, together with purchased demographic data that are mapped to the company data (see Table 15.15). The analyst decides to apply association rules to learn more about the associations between customers. Comment on this approach.

TABLE 15.15   SAMPLE OF DATA ON SATELLITE RADIO CUSTOMERS

Row ID	zipconvert_2	zipconvert_3	zipconvert_4	zipconvert_5	homeowner dummy	NUMCHLD	INCOME	gender	WEALTH dummy
17	0	1	0	0	1	1	5	1	9
25	1	0	0	0	1	1	1	0	7
29	0	0	0	1	0	2	5	1	8
38	0	0	0	1	1	1	3	0	4
40	0	1	0	0	1	1	4	0	8
53	0	1	0	0	1	1	4	1	8
58	0	0	0	1	1	1	4	1	8
61	1	0	0	0	1	1	1	0	7
71	0	0	1	0	1	1	4	0	5
87	1	0	0	0	1	1	4	1	8
100	0	0	0	1	1	1	4	1	8
104	1	0	0	0	1	1	1	1	5
121	0	0	1	0	1	1	4	1	5
142	1	0	0	0	0	1	5	0	8

15.2 **Identifying Course Combinations.** The Institute for Statistics Education at Statistics.com offers online courses in statistics and analytics and is seeking information that will help in packaging and sequencing courses. Consider the dataset *mlba::CourseTopics*, the first few rows of which are shown in Table 15.16. These data are for purchases of online statistics courses at Statistics.com. Each row represents the courses attended by a single customer. The firm wishes to assess alternative sequencings and bundling of courses. Use association rules to analyze these data, and interpret several of the resulting rules.

TABLE 15.16   DATA ON PURCHASES OF ONLINE STATISTICS COURSES

Intro	DataMining	Survey	CatData	Regression	Forecast	DOE	SW
1	1	0	0	0	0	0	0
0	0	1	0	0	0	0	0
0	1	0	1	1	0	0	1
1	0	0	0	0	0	0	0
1	1	0	0	0	0	0	0
0	1	0	0	0	0	0	0
1	0	0	0	0	0	0	0
0	0	0	1	0	1	1	1
1	0	0	0	0	0	0	0
0	0	0	1	0	0	0	0
1	0	0	0	0	0	0	0

15.3 Recommending Courses. We again consider the data in *mlba::CourseTopics* describing course purchases at Statistics.com (see Problem 15.2 and data sample in Table 15.16). We want to provide a course recommendation to a student who purchased the Regression and Forecast courses. Apply user-based collaborative filtering to the data. You will get a Null matrix. Explain why this happens.

15.4 Cosmetics Purchases. The data shown in Table 15.17 and the output in Table 15.18 are based on a subset of a dataset on cosmetic purchases (*mlba::Cosmetics*) at a large chain drugstore. The store wants to analyze associations among purchases of these items for purposes of point-of-sale display, guidance to sales personnel in promoting cross-sales, and guidance for piloting an eventual time-of-purchase electronic recommender system to boost cross-sales. Consider first only the data shown in Table 15.17, given in binary matrix form.

TABLE 15.17   EXCERPT FROM DATA ON COSMETICS PURCHASES IN BINARY MATRIX FORM

Trans	Bag	Blush	Nail Polish	Brushes	Concealer	Eyebrow Pencils	Bronzer
1	0	1	1	1	1	0	1
2	0	0	1	0	1	0	1
3	0	1	0	0	1	1	1
4	0	0	1	1	1	0	1
5	0	1	0	0	1	0	1
6	0	0	0	0	1	0	0
7	0	1	1	1	1	0	1
8	0	0	1	1	0	0	1
9	0	0	0	0	1	0	0
10	1	1	1	1	0	0	0
11	0	0	1	0	0	0	1
12	0	0	1	1	1	0	1

a. Select several values in the matrix and explain their meaning.

b. Consider the results of the association rules analysis shown in Table 15.18.

   i. For the first row, explain the "confidence" output and how it is calculated.

   ii. For the first row, explain the "support" output and how it is calculated.

   iii. For the first row, explain the "lift" and how it is calculated.

   iv. For the first row, explain the rule that is represented there in words.

c. Now, use the complete dataset on the cosmetics purchases (in the dataset *mlba::Cosmetics*). Using R, apply association rules to these data (use the default parameters).

   i. Interpret the first three rules in the output in words.

   ii. Reviewing the first couple of dozen rules, comment on their redundancy and how you would assess their utility.

TABLE 15.18   ASSOCIATION RULES FOR COSMETICS PURCHASES DATA

```
    lhs                 rhs             support   confidence      lift
1 {Blush,
   Concealer,
   Mascara,
   Eye.shadow,
   Lipstick}   => {Eyebrow.Pencils}   0.013   0.3023255814   7.198228128
2 {Trans.,
   Blush,
   Concealer,
   Mascara,
   Eye.shadow,
   Lipstick}   => {Eyebrow.Pencils}   0.013   0.3023255814   7.198228128
3 {Blush,
   Concealer,
   Mascara,
   Lipstick}   => {Eyebrow.Pencils}   0.013   0.2888888889   6.878306878
4 {Trans.,
   Blush,
   Concealer,
   Mascara,
   Lipstick}   => {Eyebrow.Pencils}   0.013   0.2888888889   6.878306878
5 {Blush,
   Concealer,
   Eye.shadow,
   Lipstick}   => {Eyebrow.Pencils}   0.013   0.2826086957   6.728778468
6 {Trans.,
   Blush,
   Concealer,
   Eye.shadow,
   Lipstick}   => {Eyebrow.Pencils}   0.013   0.2826086957   6.728778468
```

15.5 **Course Ratings.** The Institute for Statistics Education at Statistics.com asks students to rate a variety of aspects of a course as soon as the student completes it. The Institute is contemplating instituting a recommendation system that would provide students with recommendations for additional courses as soon as they submit their rating for a completed course. Consider the excerpt from student ratings of online statistics courses shown in Table 15.19 and the problem of what to recommend to student E.N.

TABLE 15.19   RATINGS OF ONLINE STATISTICS COURSES: 4 = BEST, 1 = WORST, BLANK = NOT TAKEN

	SQL	Spatial	PA 1	DM in R	Python	Forecast	R Prog	Hadoop	Regression
L N	4				3	2	4		2
M H	3	4			4				
J H	2	2							
E N	**4**		**4**				**4**		**3**
D U	4	4							
F L		4							
G L		4							
A H		3							
S A			4						
R W			2					4	
B A			4						
M G			4			4			
A F			4						
K G			3						
D S	4			2			4		

a. First consider a user-based collaborative filter. This requires computing correlations between all student pairs. For which students, is it possible to compute correlations with E.N.? Compute them.

b. Based on the single nearest student to E.N., which single course should we recommend to E.N.? Explain why.

c. Use R (function *similarity()* in `recommenderlab`) to compute the cosine similarity between users.

d. Based on the cosine similarities of the nearest students to E.N., which course should be recommended to E.N.?

e. What is the conceptual difference between using the correlation as opposed to cosine similarities? (*Hint*: how are the missing values in the matrix handled in each case?)

f. With large datasets, it is computationally difficult to compute user-based recommendations in real time, and an item-based approach is used instead. Returning to the rating data (not the binary matrix), let's now take that approach.

    i. If the goal is still to find a recommendation for E.N., for which course pairs is it possible and useful to calculate correlations?

    ii. Just looking at the data, and without yet calculating course pair correlations, which course would you recommend to E.N., relying on item-based filtering? Calculate two course pair correlations involving your guess, and report the results.

g. Apply item-based collaborative filtering to this dataset (using R) and based on the results, recommend a course to E.N.

15.6 Movie Ratings. Consider the MovieLens data (*mlba::MovieLensMovies* and *mlba::MovieLensRatings*) discussed in this chapter. After merging the two datasets, split the data into training (60%) and holdout (40%).

a. Perform user-based collaborative filtering with different nn values (5, 10, 20, and 40), and apply the model on the holdout data. For each value of nn, record the top 5 movies for the first user in the holdout set. Compare the extent of overlap. What role does nn play in this model? Use the following command to train a model for $nn = 5$

```
model <- Recommender(train, method = "UBCF", parameter=list(nn=5))
```

b. Perform item-based collaborative filtering with different k values (5, 10, 20, and 40), and conduct the same analysis as in part (a).

```
model <- Recommender(train, method = "UBCF", parameter=list(k=5))
```

c. What is the key difference between user-based collaborative filtering and item-based collaborative filtering? Find and briefly discuss two business applications of each of these recommendation techniques.

d. Based on your experience in solving (a) and (b), identify a practical difficulty a business may face when setting up a recommendation engine using collaborative filtering techniques. What are one or more ways to address this challenge?

## CHAPTER 16

Cluster Analysis

This chapter is about the popular unsupervised learning task of clustering, where the goal is to segment the data into a set of homogeneous clusters of records for the purpose of generating insight. Separating a dataset into clusters of homogeneous records is also useful for improving performance of supervised methods, by modeling each cluster separately rather than the entire, heterogeneous dataset. Clustering is used in a vast variety of business applications, from customized marketing to industry analysis. We describe two popular clustering approaches: *hierarchical clustering* and *k-means clustering*. In hierarchical clustering, records are sequentially grouped to create clusters, based on distances between records and distances between clusters. We describe how the algorithm works in terms of the clustering process and mention several common distance metrics used. Hierarchical clustering also produces a useful graphical display of the clustering process and results, called a dendrogram. We present dendrograms and illustrate their usefulness. *k*-means clustering is widely used in large dataset applications. In *k*-means clustering, records are allocated to one of a prespecified set of clusters, according to their distance from each cluster. We describe the *k*-means clustering algorithm and its computational advantages. Finally, we present techniques that assist in generating insight from clustering results.

Clustering in R

The main R functions introduced in this chapter are *hclust* and *kmeans* in the `stats` package. We also use package `ggdendro` for visualizing the results of hierarchical clustering.

Machine Learning for Business Analytics: Concepts, Techniques, and Applications in R, Second Edition.
Galit Shmueli, Peter C. Bruce, Peter Gedeck, Inbal Yahav, and Nitin R. Patel
© 2023 John Wiley & Sons, Inc. Published 2023 by John Wiley & Sons, Inc.

16.1　INTRODUCTION

Cluster analysis is used to form groups or clusters of similar records based on several measurements made on these records. The key idea is to characterize the clusters in ways that would be useful for the aims of the analysis. This idea has been applied in many areas, including astronomy, archaeology, medicine, chemistry, education, psychology, linguistics, and sociology. Biologists, for example, have made extensive use of classes and subclasses to organize species. A spectacular success of the clustering idea in chemistry was Mendeleev's periodic table of the elements.

One popular use of cluster analysis in marketing is for *market segmentation:* customers are segmented based on demographic and transaction history information, and a marketing strategy is tailored for each segment. In countries such as India, where customer diversity is extremely location-sensitive, chain stores often perform market segmentation at the store level, rather than chain-wide (called "micro-segmentation"). Another use is for *market structure analysis:* identifying groups of similar products according to competitive measures of similarity. In marketing and political forecasting, clustering of neighborhoods using US postal zip codes has been used successfully to group neighborhoods by lifestyles. Claritas, a company that pioneered this approach, grouped neighborhoods into 40 clusters using various measures of consumer expenditure and demographics. Examining the clusters enabled Claritas to come up with evocative names, such as "Bohemian Mix," "Furs and Station Wagons," and "Money and Brains," for the groups that captured the dominant lifestyles. Knowledge of lifestyles can be used to estimate the potential demand for products (such as sports utility vehicles) and services (such as pleasure cruises). Similarly, sales organizations will derive customer segments and give them names—"personas"—to focus sales efforts.

In finance, cluster analysis can be used for creating *balanced portfolios:* given data on a variety of investment opportunities (e.g., stocks), one may find clusters based on financial performance variables such as return (daily, weekly, or monthly), volatility, beta, and other characteristics, such as industry and market capitalization. Selecting securities from different clusters can help create a balanced portfolio. Another application of cluster analysis in finance is for *industry analysis:* for a given industry, we are interested in finding groups of similar firms based on measures such as growth rate, profitability, market size, product range, and the presence in various international markets. These groups can then be analyzed to understand industry structure and to determine, for instance, who is a competitor.

An interesting and unusual application of cluster analysis, described in Berry and Linoff (1997), is the design of a new set of sizes for army uniforms for women in the US Army. The study came up with a new clothing size system with only 20 sizes, where different sizes fit different body types. The 20 sizes are combinations of five measurements: chest, neck, and shoulder circumference, sleeve outseam, and neck-to-buttock length (for further details, see McCullugh et al., 1998). This example is important because it shows how a completely new insightful view can be gained by examining clusters of records.

Cluster analysis can be applied to huge amounts of data. For instance, Internet search engines use clustering techniques to cluster queries that users submit. These can then be used for improving search algorithms. The objective of this chapter is to describe the key ideas underlying the most commonly used techniques for cluster analysis and to lay out their strengths and weaknesses.

Typically, the basic data used to form clusters are a table of measurements on several numerical variables, where each column represents a variable and a row represents a record. Our goal is to form groups of records so that similar records are in the same group. The number of clusters may be prespecified or determined from the data.

Example: Public Utilities

Table 16.1 gives corporate data on 22 public utilities in the United States (the variable definitions are given in the table footnote). We are interested in forming groups of similar utilities. The records to be clustered are the utilities, and the clustering will be based on the eight measurements on each utility. An example where clustering would be useful is a study to predict the cost impact of deregulation. To do the requisite analysis, economists would need to build a detailed cost model of the various utilities. It would save a considerable amount of time and effort if we could cluster similar types of utilities and build detailed cost models for just one "typical" utility in each cluster and then scale up from these models to estimate results for all utilities.

For simplicity, let us consider only two of the measurements: Sales and Fuel Cost. Figure 16.1 shows a scatter plot of these two variables, with labels marking each company. At first glance, there appear to be two or three clusters of utilities: one with utilities that have high fuel costs, a second with utilities that have lower fuel costs and relatively low sales, and a third with utilities with low fuel costs but high sales.

We can therefore think of cluster analysis as a more formal algorithm that measures the distance between records and, according to these distances (here, two-dimensional distances), forms clusters.

Two general types of clustering algorithms for a dataset of n records are hierarchical and non-hierarchical clustering:

Hierarchical methods can be either *agglomerative* or *divisive*. Agglomerative methods begin with n clusters and sequentially merge similar clusters until a single cluster is obtained. Divisive methods work in the opposite

TABLE 16.1   DATA ON 22 PUBLIC UTILITIES

Company	Fixed	RoR	Cost	Load	Demand	Sales	Nuclear	Fuel Cost
Arizona Public Service	1.06	9.2	151	54.4	1.6	9077	0.0	0.628
Boston Edison Co.	0.89	10.3	202	57.9	2.2	5088	25.3	1.555
Central Louisiana Co.	1.43	15.4	113	53.0	3.4	9212	0.0	1.058
Commonwealth Edison Co.	1.02	11.2	168	56.0	0.3	6423	34.3	0.700
Consolidated Edison Co. (NY)	1.49	8.8	192	51.2	1.0	3300	15.6	2.044
Florida Power & Light Co.	1.32	13.5	111	60.0	−2.2	11127	22.5	1.241
Hawaiian Electric Co.	1.22	12.2	175	67.6	2.2	7642	0.0	1.652
daho Power Co.	1.10	9.2	245	57.0	3.3	13082	0.0	0.309
Kentucky Utilities Co.	1.34	13.0	168	60.4	7.2	8406	0.0	0.862
Madison Gas & Electric Co.	1.12	12.4	197	53.0	2.7	6455	39.2	0.623
Nevada Power Co.	0.75	7.5	173	51.5	6.5	17441	0.0	0.768
New England Electric Co.	1.13	10.9	178	62.0	3.7	6154	0.0	1.897
Northern States Power Co.	1.15	12.7	199	53.7	6.4	7179	50.2	0.527
Oklahoma Gas & Electric Co.	1.09	12.0	96	49.8	1.4	9673	0.0	0.588
Pacific Gas & Electric Co.	0.96	7.6	164	62.2	−0.1	6468	0.9	1.400
Puget Sound Power & Light Co.	1.16	9.9	252	56.0	9.2	15991	0.0	0.620
San Diego Gas & Electric Co.	0.76	6.4	136	61.9	9.0	5714	8.3	1.920
The Southern Co.	1.05	12.6	150	56.7	2.7	10140	0.0	1.108
Texas Utilities Co.	1.16	11.7	104	54.0	−2.1	13507	0.0	0.636
Wisconsin Electric Power Co.	1.20	11.8	148	59.9	3.5	7287	41.1	0.702
United Illuminating Co.	1.04	8.6	204	61.0	3.5	6650	0.0	2.116
Virginia Electric & Power Co.	1.07	9.3	174	54.3	5.9	10093	26.6	1.306

Fixed = fixed-charge covering ratio (income/debt); RoR = rate of return on capital
Cost = cost per kilowatt capacity in place; Load = annual load factor
Demand = peak kilowatt-hour demand growth from 1974 to 1975
Sales = sales (kilowatt-hour use per year)
Nuclear = percent nuclear
Fuel Cost = total fuel costs (cents per kilowatthour)

direction, starting with one cluster that includes all records. Hierarchical methods are especially useful when the goal is to arrange the clusters into a natural hierarchy.

Non-hierarchical methods such as k-means. Using a prespecified number of clusters, the method assigns records to each cluster. These methods are generally less computationally intensive and are therefore preferred with very large datasets.

We concentrate here on the two most popular methods: hierarchical agglomerative clustering and k-means clustering. In both cases, we need to define two types of distances: distance between two records and distance between two clusters. In both cases, there is a variety of metrics that can be used.

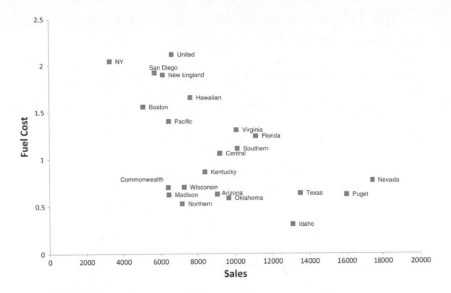

FIGURE 16.1   **SCATTER PLOT OF FUEL COST VS. SALES FOR THE 22 UTILITIES**

16.2 MEASURING DISTANCE BETWEEN TWO RECORDS

We denote by d_{ij} a *distance metric*, or *dissimilarity measure*, between records i and j. For record i we have the vector of p measurements $(x_{i1}, x_{i2}, \ldots, x_{ip})$, while for record j we have the vector of measurements $(x_{j1}, x_{j2}, \ldots, x_{jp})$. For example, we can write the measurement vector for Arizona Public Service as $[1.06, 9.2, 151, 54.4, 1.6, 9077, 0, 0.628]$.

Distances can be defined in multiple ways, but in general, the following properties are required:

Non-negative: $d_{ij} \geq 0$

Self-proximity: $d_{ii} = 0$ (the distance from a record to itself is zero)

Symmetry: $d_{ij} = d_{ji}$

Triangle inequality: $d_{ij} \leq d_{ik} + d_{kj}$ (the distance between any pair cannot exceed the sum of distances between the other two pairs)

Euclidean Distance

The most popular distance measure is the *Euclidean distance*, d_{ij}, which between two records, i and j, is defined by

$$d_{ij} = \sqrt{(x_{i1} - x_{j1})^2 + (x_{i2} - x_{j2})^2 + \cdots + (x_{ip} - x_{jp})^2}.$$

For instance, the Euclidean distance between Arizona Public Service and Boston Edison Co. can be computed from the raw data by

$$d_{12} = \sqrt{(1.06 - 0.89)^2 + (9.2 - 10.3)^2 + (151 - 202)^2 + \cdots + (0.628 - 1.555)^2}$$
$$= 3989.408.$$

To compute Euclidean distance in R, see Table 16.2.

TABLE 16.2	DISTANCE MATRIX BETWEEN PAIRS OF UTILITIES, USING EUCLIDEAN DISTANCE (SHOWING FIRST FIVE UTILITIES)

 code for computing distance between records

```
library(tidyverse)
# load data and use Company column as row names
utilities.df <- mlba::Utilities %>%
  column_to_rownames("Company")

# compute Euclidean distance
# (to compute other distance measures, change the value in the method argument)
d <- dist(utilities.df, method = "euclidean")
```

Output (showing first five pairs only)

```
> d
                Arizona      Boston    Central  Commonwealth          NY
Boston       3989.40808
Central       140.40286  4125.04413
Commonwealth 2654.27763  1335.46650  2789.75967
NY           5777.16767  1788.06803  5912.55291    3123.15322
Florida      2050.52944  6039.68908  1915.15515    4704.36310  7827.42921
```

Normalizing Numerical Variables

The measure computed above is highly influenced by the scale of each variable so that variables with larger scales (e.g., Sales) have a much greater influence over the total distance. It is therefore customary to *normalize* continuous measurements before computing the Euclidean distance. This converts all measurements to the same scale. Normalizing a measurement means subtracting the average and dividing by the standard deviation (normalized values are also called *z-scores*). For instance, the average sales amount across the 22 utilities is 8914.045, and the standard deviation is 3549.984. The normalized sales for Arizona Public Service is therefore $(9077 - 8914.045)/3549.984 = 0.046$.

Returning to the simplified utilities data with only two measurements (Sales and Fuel Cost), we first normalize the measurements using R's *scale()* function (see Table 16.3) and then compute the Euclidean distance between each pair. Table 16.4 gives these pairwise distances for the first five utilities. A similar table can be constructed for all 22 utilities.

TABLE 16.3   ORIGINAL AND NORMALIZED MEASUREMENTS FOR SALES AND FUEL COST

Company	Sales	Fuel Cost	NormSales	NormFuel
Arizona Public Service	9077	0.628	0.0459	−0.8537
Boston Edison Co.	5088	1.555	−1.0778	0.8133
Central Louisiana Co.	9212	1.058	0.0839	−0.0804
Commonwealth Edison Co.	6423	0.7	−0.7017	−0.7242
Consolidated Edison Co. (NY)	3300	2.044	−1.5814	1.6926
Florida Power & Light Co.	11127	1.241	0.6234	0.2486
Hawaiian Electric Co.	7642	1.652	−0.3583	0.9877
Idaho Power Co.	13082	0.309	1.1741	−1.4273
Kentucky Utilities Co.	8406	0.862	−0.1431	−0.4329
Madison Gas & Electric Co.	6455	0.623	−0.6927	−0.8627
Nevada Power Co.	17441	0.768	2.4020	−0.6019
New England Electric Co.	6154	1.897	−0.7775	1.4283
Northern States Power Co.	7179	0.527	−0.4887	−1.0353
Oklahoma Gas & Electric Co.	9673	0.588	0.2138	−0.9256
Pacific Gas & Electric Co.	6468	1.4	−0.6890	0.5346
Puget Sound Power & Light Co.	15991	0.62	1.9935	−0.8681
San Diego Gas & Electric Co.	5714	1.92	−0.9014	1.4697
The Southern Co.	10140	1.108	0.3453	0.0095
Texas Utilities Co.	13507	0.636	1.2938	−0.8393
Wisconsin Electric Power Co.	7287	0.702	−0.4583	−0.7206
United Illuminating Co.	6650	2.116	−0.6378	1.8221
Virginia Electric & Power Co.	10093	1.306	0.3321	0.3655
Mean	8914.05	1.10	0.00	0.00
Standard deviation	3549.98	0.56	1.00	1.00

TABLE 16.4   DISTANCE MATRIX BETWEEN PAIRS OF UTILITIES, USING EUCLIDEAN DISTANCE
AND NORMALIZED VARIABLES (SHOWING FIRST SIX UTILITIES)

    code for normalizing data and computing distance

```
# normalize input variables
utilities.df.norm <- scale(utilities.df)

# compute normalized distance based on Sales and Fuel Cost
d.norm <- dist(utilities.df.norm[,c("Sales","Fuel_Cost")], method="euclidean")
```

Output (showing first five pairs only)

```
> d.norm
              Arizona    Boston    Central Commonwealth        NY
Boston      2.0103293
Central     0.7741795 1.4657027
Commonwealth 0.7587375 1.5828208 1.0157104
NY          3.0219066 1.0133700 2.4325285    2.5719693
Florida     1.2444219 1.7923968 0.6318918    1.6438566 2.6355728
```

Other Distance Measures for Numerical Data

It is important to note that the choice of the distance measure plays a major role in cluster analysis. The main guideline is domain dependent: What exactly is being measured? How are the different variables related? What scale should each variable be treated as (numerical, ordinal, or nominal)? Are there outliers? Finally, depending on the goal of the analysis, should the clusters be distinguished mostly by a small set of variables, or should they be separated by multiple variables that weight moderately?

Although Euclidean distance is the most widely used distance, it has three main features that need to be kept in mind. First, as mentioned earlier, it is highly scale dependent. Changing the units of one variable (e.g., from cents to dollars) can have a huge influence on the results. Normalizing is therefore a common solution. However, unequal weighting should be considered if we want the clusters to depend more on certain variables and less on others. The second feature of Euclidean distance is that it completely ignores the relationship between the variables. Thus, if the variables are in fact strongly correlated, a different distance (such as the statistical distance, described later) is likely to be a better choice. The third is that Euclidean distance is sensitive to outliers. If the data are believed to contain outliers and careful removal is not a choice, the use of more robust distances (such as the Manhattan distance, described later) is preferred.

Additional popular distance metrics often used (for reasons such as the ones above) are as follows:

Correlation-based similarity: Sometimes it is more natural or convenient to work with a similarity measure between records rather than distance, which measures dissimilarity. A popular similarity measure is the square of the Pearson correlation coefficient, r_{ij}^2, where the correlation coefficient is defined by

$$r_{ij} = \frac{\sum_{m=1}^{p}(x_{im} - \overline{x}_m)(x_{jm} - \overline{x}_m)}{\sqrt{\sum_{m=1}^{p}(x_{im} - \overline{x}_m)^2 \sum_{m=1}^{p}(x_{jm} - \overline{x}_m)^2}}. \tag{16.1}$$

Such measures can always be converted to distance measures. In the example above, we could define a distance measure $d_{ij} = 1 - r_{ij}^2$.

Statistical distance (also called *Mahalanobis distance*): This metric has an advantage over the other metrics mentioned in that it takes into account the correlation between variables. With this metric, variables that are highly correlated with other variables do not contribute as much as those that are uncorrelated or mildly correlated. The statistical distance between records i

and j is defined as

$$d_{i,j} = \sqrt{(\mathbf{x}_i - \mathbf{x}_j)' S^{-1} (\mathbf{x}_i - \mathbf{x}_j)},$$

where $\mathbf{x}_i$ and $\mathbf{x}_j$ are p-dimensional vectors of the variables' values for records i and j, respectively, and S is the covariance matrix for these vectors ($'$, a transpose operation, simply turns a column vector into a row vector). S^{-1} is the inverse matrix of S, which is the p-dimensional extension to division. For further information on statistical distance, see Chapter 12.

Manhattan distance ("city block"): This distance looks at the absolute differences rather than squared differences and is defined by

$$d_{i,j} = \sum_{m=1}^{p} \mid x_{im} - x_{jm} \mid.$$

Maximum coordinate distance: This distance looks only at the measurement on which records i and j deviate most. It is defined by

$$d_{i,j} = \max_{m=1,2,\ldots,p} \mid x_{im} - x_{jm} \mid.$$

Distance Measures for Categorical Data

In the case of variables with binary values, it is more intuitively appealing to use similarity measures than distance measures. Suppose that we have binary values for all the p variables and, for records i and j, we have the following 2×2 table:

		Record j		
		0	1	
Record i	0	a	b	$a+b$
	1	c	d	$c+d$
		$a+c$	$b+d$	p

where a denotes the number of variables for which records i and j each have value 0 for that variable (measurement absent), d is the number of variables for which the two records each have a value 1 for that variable (measurement present), and so on. The most useful similarity measures in this situation are:

Matching coefficient: $(a + d)/p$.

Jaccard's coefficient: $d/(b+c+d)$. This coefficient ignores zero matches. This is desirable when we do not want to consider two people to be similar simply because a large number of characteristics are absent in both. For example, if *owns a Corvette* is one of the variables, a matching "yes" would be evidence of similarity, but a matching "no" tells us little about whether the two people are similar.

Distance Measures for Mixed Data

When the variables are mixed (some continuous and some binary), a similarity coefficient suggested by Gower is very useful. *Gower's similarity measure* is a weighted average of the distances computed for each variable, after scaling each variable to a [0, 1] scale. It is defined as

$$
s_{ij} = \frac{\sum\limits_{m=1}^{p} w_{ijm} s_{ijm}}{\sum\limits_{m=1}^{p} w_{ijm}},
$$

where s_{ijm} is the similarity between records i and j on variable m, and w_{ijm} is a binary weight given to the corresponding distance.

The similarity measures s_{ijm} and weights w_{ijm} are computed as follows:

1. For continuous variables, $s_{ijm} = 1 - \frac{|x_{im} - x_{jm}|}{\max(x_m) - \min(x_m)}$ and $w_{ijm} = 1$ unless the value for variable m is unknown for one or both of the records, in which case $w_{ijm} = 0$.

2. For binary variables, $s_{ijm} = 1$ if $x_{im} = x_{jm} = 1$ and 0 otherwise. $w_{ijm} = 1$ unless $x_{im} = x_{jm} = 0$.

3. For nonbinary categorical variables, $s_{ijm} = 1$ if both records are in the same category, and otherwise $s_{ijm} = 0$. As in continuous variables, $w_{ijm} = 1$ unless the category for variable m is unknown for one or both of the records, in which case $w_{ijm} = 0$.

16.3   MEASURING DISTANCE BETWEEN TWO CLUSTERS

We define a cluster as a set of one or more records. How do we measure distance between clusters? The idea is to extend measures of *distance between records* into *distances between clusters*. Consider cluster A, which includes the m records $A_1, A_2, \ldots, A_m$, and cluster B, which includes n records $B_1, B_2, \ldots, B_n$. The most widely used measures of distance between clusters are as follows:

Minimum Distance

The distance between the pair of records A_i and B_j that are closest:

$$
\min(\text{distance}(A_i, B_j)), \quad i = 1, 2, \ldots, m; \quad j = 1, 2, \ldots, n.
$$

Maximum Distance

The distance between the pair of records A_i and B_j that are farthest:

$$\max(\text{distance}(A_i, B_j)), \quad i = 1, 2, \ldots, m; \quad j = 1, 2, \ldots, n.$$

Average Distance

The average distance of all possible distances between records in one cluster and records in the other cluster:

$$\text{Average}(\text{distance}(A_i, B_j)), \quad i = 1, 2, \ldots, m; \quad j = 1, 2, \ldots, n.$$

Centroid Distance

The distance between the two cluster centroids. A *cluster centroid* is the vector of variable averages across all the records in that cluster. For cluster A, this is the vector $\overline{x}_A = [(1/m \sum_{i=1}^{m} x_{1i}, \ldots, 1/m \sum_{i=1}^{m} x_{pi})]$. The centroid distance between clusters A and B is

$$\text{distance}(\overline{x}_A, \overline{x}_B).$$

Minimum distance, maximum distance, and centroid distance are illustrated visually for two dimensions with a map of Portugal and France in Figure 16.2.

FIGURE 16.2   TWO-DIMENSIONAL REPRESENTATION OF SEVERAL DIFFERENT DISTANCE MEASURES BETWEEN PORTUGAL AND FRANCE

For instance, consider the first two utilities (Arizona, Boston) as cluster A and the next three utilities (Central, Commonwealth, Consolidated) as cluster B. Using the normalized scores in Table 16.3 and the distance matrix in Table 16.4, we can compute each of the distances described above. Using Euclidean distance for each distance calculation, we get the following:

- The closest pair is Arizona and Commonwealth, and therefore the minimum distance between clusters A and B is 0.76.

- The farthest pair is Arizona and Consolidated, and therefore the maximum distance between clusters A and B is 3.02.

- The average distance is $(0.77 + 0.76 + 3.02 + 1.47 + 1.58 + 1.01)/6 = 1.44$.

- The centroid of cluster A is

$$\left[\frac{0.0459 - 1.0778}{2}, \frac{-0.8537 + 0.8133}{2}\right] = [-0.516, -0.020],$$

and the centroid of cluster B is

$$\left[\frac{0.0839 - 0.7017 - 1.5814}{3}, \frac{-0.0804 - 0.7242 + 1.6926}{3}\right] = [-0.733, 0.296].$$

The distance between the two centroids is then

$$\sqrt{(-0.516 + 0.733)^2 + (-0.020 - 0.296)^2} = 0.38.$$

In deciding among clustering methods, domain knowledge is key. If you have good reason to believe that the clusters might be chain- or sausage-like, minimum distance would be a good choice. This method does not require that cluster members all be close to one another, only that the new members being added be close to one of the existing members. An example of an application where this might be the case would be characteristics of crops planted in long rows or disease outbreaks along navigable waterways that are the main areas of settlement in a region. Another example is laying and finding mines (land or marine). Minimum distance is also fairly robust to small deviations in the distances. However, adding or removing data can influence it greatly.

Maximum and average distance are better choices if you know that the clusters are more likely to be spherical (e.g., customers clustered on the basis of numerous variables). If you do not know the probable nature of the cluster, these are good default choices, since most clusters tend to be spherical in nature.

We now move to a more detailed description of the two major types of clustering algorithms: hierarchical (agglomerative) and non-hierarchical.

16.4 HIERARCHICAL (AGGLOMERATIVE) CLUSTERING

The idea behind hierarchical agglomerative clustering is to start with each cluster comprising exactly one record and then progressively agglomerating (combining) the two nearest clusters until there is just one cluster left at the end, which consists of all the records.

Returning to the small example of five utilities and two measures (Sales and Fuel Cost) and using the distance matrix (Table 16.4), the first step in the hierarchical clustering would join Arizona and Commonwealth, which are the closest (using normalized variables and Euclidean distance). Next, we would recalculate a 4×4 distance matrix that would have the distances between these four clusters: {Arizona, Commonwealth}, {Boston}, {Central}, and {Consolidated}. At this point, we use a measure of distance between clusters such as the ones described in Section 16.3. Each of these distances (minimum, maximum, average, and centroid distance) can be implemented in the hierarchical scheme as described below.

HIERARCHICAL AGGLOMERATIVE CLUSTERING ALGORITHM

1. Start with n clusters (each record = cluster).

2. The two closest records are merged into one cluster.

3. At every step, the two clusters with the smallest distance are merged. This means that either single records are added to existing clusters or two existing clusters are combined.

Single Linkage

In *single linkage clustering*, the distance measure that we use is the minimum distance (the distance between the nearest pair of records in the two clusters, one record in each cluster). In our utilities example, we would compute the distances between each of {Boston}, {Central}, and {Consolidated} with {Arizona, Commonwealth} to create the 4×4 distance matrix shown in Table 16.5.

TABLE 16.5 DISTANCE MATRIX AFTER ARIZONA AND COMMONWEALTH CONSOLIDATION CLUSTER TOGETHER, USING SINGLE LINKAGE

	Arizona–Commonwealth	Boston	Central	Consolidated
Arizona–Commonwealth	0			
Boston	min(2.01,1.58)	0		
Central	min(0.77,1.02)	1.47	0	
Consolidated	min(3.02,2.57)	1.01	2.43	0

The next step would consolidate {Central} with {Arizona, Commonwealth} because these two clusters are closest. The distance matrix will again be recomputed (this time it will be 3×3), and so on.

This method has a tendency to cluster together at an early stage records that are distant from each other because of a chain of intermediate records in the same cluster. Such clusters have elongated sausage-like shapes when visualized as objects in space.

Complete Linkage

In *complete linkage clustering*, the distance between two clusters is the maximum distance (between the farthest pair of records). If we used complete linkage with the five-utilities example, the recomputed distance matrix would be equivalent to Table 16.5, except that the "min" function would be replaced with a "max."

This method tends to produce clusters at the early stages with records that are within a narrow range of distances from each other. If we visualize them as objects in space, the records in such clusters would have roughly spherical shapes.

Average Linkage

Average linkage clustering is based on the average distance between clusters (between all possible pairs of records). If we used average linkage with the five-utilities example, the recomputed distance matrix would be equivalent to Table 16.5, except that the "min" function would be replaced with "average." This method is also called *Unweighted Pair-Group Method using Averages* (UPGMA).

Note that unlike average linkage, the results of the single and complete linkage methods depend only on the ordering of the inter-record distances. Linear transformations of the distances (and other transformations that do not change the ordering) do not affect the results.

Centroid Linkage

Centroid linkage clustering is based on centroid distance, where clusters are represented by their mean values for each variable, which forms a vector of means. The distance between two clusters is the distance between these two vectors. In average linkage, each pairwise distance is calculated, and the average of all such distances is calculated. In contrast, in centroid distance clustering, just one distance is calculated: the distance between group means. This method is also called *Unweighted Pair-Group Method using Centroids* (UPGMC).

Ward's Method

Ward's method is also agglomerative, in that it joins records and clusters together progressively to produce larger and larger clusters, but operates slightly differently from the general approach described above. Ward's method considers the "loss of information" that occurs when records are clustered together. When each cluster has one record, there is no loss of information, and all individual values remain available. When records are joined together and represented in clusters, information about an individual record is replaced by the information for the cluster to which it belongs. To measure loss of information, Ward's method employs "error sum of squares" (ESS) that measures the difference between individual records and a group mean.

This is easiest to see in univariate data. For example, consider the values (2, 6, 5, 6, 2, 2, 2, 2, 0, 0, 0) with a mean of 2.5. Their ESS is equal to

$$(2 - 2.5)^2 + (6 - 2.5)^2 + (5 - 2.5)^2 + \cdots + (0 - 2.5)^2 = 50.5.$$

The loss of information associated with grouping the values into a single group is therefore 50.5. Now group the records into four groups: (0, 0, 0), (2, 2, 2, 2), (5), (6, 6). The loss of information is the sum of the ESS's for each group, which is 0 (each record in each group is equal to the mean for that group, so the ESS for each group is 0). Thus, clustering the 10 records into 4 clusters results in no loss of information, and this would be the first step in Ward's method. In moving to a smaller number of clusters, Ward's method would choose the configuration that results in the smallest incremental loss of information.

Ward's method tends to result in convex clusters that are of roughly equal size, which can be an important consideration in some applications (e.g., in establishing meaningful customer segments).

Dendrograms: Displaying Clustering Process and Results

A *dendrogram* is a treelike diagram that summarizes the process of clustering. On the x-axis are the records. Similar records are joined by lines whose vertical length reflects the distance between the records. Figure 16.3 shows the dendrograms that results from clustering the 22 utilities using the 8 normalized variables, Euclidean distance, once with single linkage (top), and once with average linkage (bottom).

By choosing a cutoff distance on the y-axis, a set of clusters is created. Visually, this means drawing a horizontal line on a dendrogram (we added such lines manually in Figure 16.3). Records with connections below the horizontal line (that is, their distance is smaller than the cutoff distance) belong to the same cluster. For example, setting the cutoff distance to 2.7 on the single linkage dendrogram in Figure 16.3 (top) results in six clusters. The six clusters are (from left to right on the dendrogram):

{NY}, {Nevada}, {San Diego}, {Idaho, Puget}, {Central}, {Others}.

If we want six clusters using average linkage, we can choose a cutoff distance of 3.5. The resulting six clusters are slightly different.

R code for running hierarchical clustering and generating a dendrogram. Horizontal red lines added manually.

```
library(ggplot2)
library(ggdendro)
d.norm <- dist(utilities.df.norm, method="euclidean")

# in hclust() set argument method {to}
# "ward.D", "single", "complete", "average", "median", or "centroid"
hc1 <- hclust(d.norm, method="single")
plot(hc1, hang=-1, ann=FALSE)  # use baseR
ggdendrogram(hc1)      # use ggdendro package (shown in figure below)
hc2 <- hclust(d.norm, method="average")
plot(hc2, hang=-1, ann=FALSE)
ggdendrogram(hc2)
```

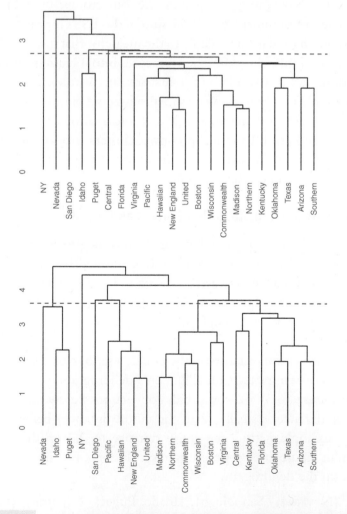

FIGURE 16.3   **DENDROGRAM: SINGLE LINKAGE (TOP) AND AVERAGE LINKAGE (BOTTOM) FOR ALL 22 UTILITIES, USING ALL EIGHT MEASUREMENTS**

The six (or other number of) clusters can be computed in R by applying the function *cutree()* to the dendrogram object. Table 16.6 shows the results for the single linkage and the average linkage clustering with six clusters. Each record is assigned a cluster number. While some records remain in the same cluster in both methods (e.g., Arizona, Florida, Kentucky, Oklamona, Texas), others change.

Note that if we wanted five clusters, they would be identical to the six above, with the exception that two of the clusters would be merged into a single cluster. For example, in the single linkage case, the two right-most clusters in the dendrogram would be merged into one cluster. In general, all hierarchical methods have clusters that are nested within each other as we decrease the number of clusters. This is a valuable property for interpreting clusters and is essential in certain applications, such as taxonomy of varieties of living organisms.

TABLE 16.6   COMPUTING CLUSTER MEMBERSHIP BY "CUTTING" THE DENDROGRAM

Single Linkage

```
> memb <- cutree(hc1, k = 6)
> memb
     Arizona        Boston    Central  Commonwealth           NY
           1             1          2             1            3
     Florida      Hawaiian      Idaho      Kentucky      Madison
           1             1          4             1            1
      Nevada  New England   Northern      Oklahoma      Pacific
           5             1          1             1            1
       Puget    San Diego   Southern         Texas    Wisconsin
           4             6          1             1            1
      United     Virginia
           1             1
```

Average Linkage

```
> memb <- cutree(hc2, k = 6)
> memb
     Arizona        Boston    Central  Commonwealth           NY
           1             2          1             2            3
     Florida      Hawaiian      Idaho      Kentucky      Madison
           1             4          5             1            2
      Nevada  New England   Northern      Oklahoma      Pacific
           5             4          2             1            4
       Puget    San Diego   Southern         Texas    Wisconsin
           5             6          1             1            2
      United     Virginia
           4             2
```

Validating Clusters

One important goal of cluster analysis is to come up with *meaningful clusters*. Since there are many variations that can be chosen, it is important to make sure that the resulting clusters are valid, in the sense that they really generate some insight. To see whether the cluster analysis is useful, consider each of the following aspects:

1. *Cluster interpretability.* Is the interpretation of the resulting clusters reasonable? To interpret the clusters, explore the characteristics of each cluster by:

    a. Obtaining summary statistics (e.g., average, min, max) from each cluster on each variable that was used in the cluster analysis.

    b. Examining the clusters for separation along some common feature (variable) that was not used in the cluster analysis.

    c. Labeling the clusters: based on the interpretation, trying to assign a name or label to each cluster.

2. *Cluster stability.* Do cluster assignments change significantly if some of the inputs are altered slightly? Another way to check stability is to partition the data and see how well clusters formed based on one part apply to the other part. To do this:

    a. Cluster partition A.

    b. Use the cluster centroids from A to assign each record in partition B (each record is assigned to the cluster with the closest centroid).

    c. Assess how consistent the cluster assignments are compared with the assignments based on all the data.

3. *Cluster separation.* Examine the ratio of between-cluster variation to within-cluster variation to see whether the separation is reasonable. There exist statistical tests for this task (an F-ratio), but their usefulness is somewhat controversial.

4. *Number of clusters.* The number of resulting clusters must be useful, given the purpose of the analysis. For example, suppose the goal of the clustering is to identify categories of customers and assign labels to them for market segmentation purposes. If the marketing department can only manage to sustain three different marketing presentations, it would probably not make sense to identify more than three clusters.

Returning to the utilities example, we notice that both methods (single and average linkage) identify {NY} and {San Diego} as singleton clusters. Also, both dendrograms imply that a reasonable number of clusters in this dataset is four. One insight that can be derived from the average linkage clustering is that clusters tend to group geographically. The four non-singleton clusters form (approximately) a southern group, a northern group, an east/west seaboard group, and a west group.

We can further characterize each of the clusters by examining the summary statistics of their variables or visually looking at a heatmap of their individual variables. Figure 16.4 shows a heatmap of the four clusters and two singletons,

R code for creating heatmap

```
# set labels as cluster membership and utility name
row.names(utilities.df.norm) <- paste(memb, ": ", row.names(utilities.df), sep = "")

# plot heatmap
heatmap(utilities.df.norm, Colv=NA, hclustfun=hclust)
```

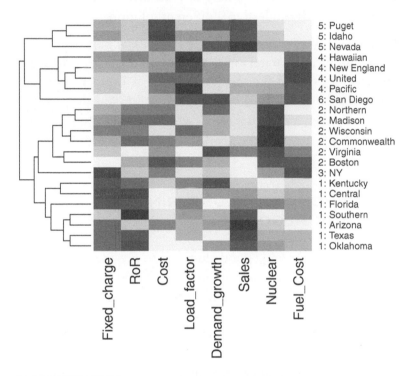

FIGURE 16.4   HEATMAP FOR THE 22 UTILITIES (IN ROWS). ROWS ARE SORTED BY THE SIX CLUSTERS FROM AVERAGE LINKAGE CLUSTERING. DARKER CELLS DENOTE HIGHER VALUES WITHIN A COLUMN

highlighting the different profile that each cluster has in terms of the eight variables. We see, for instance, that cluster 2 is characterized by utilities with a high percent of nuclear power, cluster 1 is characterized by high fixed charge and RoR, and cluster 4 has high fuel costs.

Limitations of Hierarchical Clustering

Hierarchical clustering is very appealing in that it does not require specification of the number of clusters and in that sense is purely data-driven. The ability to represent the clustering process and results through dendrograms is also an advantage of this method, as it is easier to understand and interpret. There are, however, a few limitations to consider:

1. Hierarchical clustering requires the computation and storage of an $n \times n$ distance matrix. For very large datasets, this can be expensive and slow.

2. The hierarchical algorithm makes only one pass through the data. This means that records that are allocated incorrectly early in the process cannot be reallocated subsequently.

3. Hierarchical clustering also tends to have low stability. Reordering data or dropping a few records can lead to a different solution.

4. With respect to the choice of distance between clusters, single and complete linkage are robust to changes in the distance metric (e.g., Euclidean, statistical distance) as long as the relative ordering is kept. In contrast, average linkage is more influenced by the choice of distance metric and might lead to completely different clusters when the metric is changed.

5. Hierarchical clustering is sensitive to outliers.

16.5 NON-HIERARCHICAL CLUSTERING: THE k-MEANS ALGORITHM

A non-hierarchical approach to forming good clusters is to pre-specify a desired number of clusters, k, and assign each case to one of the k clusters so as to minimize a measure of dispersion within the clusters. In other words, the goal is to divide the sample into a predetermined number k of non-overlapping clusters so that clusters are as homogeneous as possible with respect to the variables used.

A common measure of within-cluster dispersion is the sum of distances (or sum of squared Euclidean distances) of records from their cluster centroid. The problem can be set up as an optimization problem involving integer programming, but because solving integer programs with a large number of variables is time-consuming, clusters are often computed using a fast, heuristic method that produces good (although not necessarily optimal) solutions. The k-means algorithm is one such method.

The k-means algorithm starts with an initial partition of the records into k clusters. Subsequent steps modify the partition to reduce the sum of the distances of each record from its cluster centroid. The modification consists of allocating each record to the nearest of the k centroids of the previous partition. This leads to a new partition for which the sum of distances is smaller than before. The means of the new clusters are computed, and the improvement step is repeated until the improvement is very small.

---

k-MEANS CLUSTERING ALGORITHM

1. Start with k initial clusters (user chooses k).

2. At every step, each record is reassigned to the cluster with the "closest" centroid.

3. Recompute the centroids of clusters that lost or gained a record, and repeat Step 2.

4. Stop when moving any more records between clusters increases cluster dispersion.

Returning to the example with the five utilities and two variables, let us assume that $k = 2$ and that the initial clusters are A = {Arizona, Boston} and B = {Central, Commonwealth, Consolidated}. The cluster centroids were computed in Section 16.3:

$$\overline{x}_A = [-0.516, -0.020] \text{ and } \overline{x}_B = [-0.733, 0.296].$$

The distance of each record from each of these two centroids is shown in Table 16.7.

TABLE 16.7   DISTANCE OF EACH RECORD FROM EACH CENTROID

	Distance from Centroid A	Distance from Centroid B
Arizona	1.0052	1.3887
Boston	1.0052	0.6216
Central	0.6029	0.8995
Commonwealth	0.7281	1.0207
Consolidated	2.0172	1.6341

We see that Boston is closer to cluster B and that Central and Commonwealth are each closer to cluster A. We therefore move each of these records to the other cluster and obtain A = {Arizona, Central, Commonwealth} and B = {Consolidated, Boston}. Recalculating the centroids gives

$$\overline{x}_A = [-0.191, -0.553] \text{ and } \overline{x}_B = [-1.33, 1.253].$$

The distance of each record from each of the newly calculated centroids is given in Table 16.8. At this point we stop, because each record is allocated to its closest cluster.

Choosing the Number of Clusters (k)

The choice of the number of clusters can either be driven by external considerations (e.g., previous knowledge, practical constraints, etc.), or we can try a few

TABLE 16.8   DISTANCE OF EACH RECORD FROM EACH NEWLY CALCULATED CENTROID

	Distance from Centroid A	Distance from Centroid B
Arizona	0.3827	2.5159
Boston	1.6289	0.5067
Central	0.5463	1.9432
Commonwealth	0.5391	2.0745
Consolidated	2.6412	0.5067

different values for k and compare the resulting clusters. After choosing k, the n records are partitioned into these initial clusters. If there is external reasoning that suggests a certain partitioning, this information should be used. Alternatively, if there exists external information on the centroids of the k clusters, this can be used to initially allocate the records.

In many cases, there is no information to be used for the initial partition. In these cases, the algorithm can be rerun with different randomly generated starting partitions to reduce chances of the heuristic producing a poor solution. The number of clusters in the data is generally not known, so it is a good idea to run the algorithm with different values for k that are near the number of clusters that one expects from the data, to see how the sum of distances reduces with increasing values of k. Note that the clusters obtained using different values of k will not be nested (unlike those obtained by hierarchical methods).

The results of running the k-means algorithm using function *kmeans()* for all 22 utilities and 8 measurements with $k = 6$ are shown in Table 16.9. As in the results from the hierarchical clustering, we see once again that {New Yort} is a singleton cluster. Two more clusters (cluster 5 = {Commonwealth, Madison, Northern, Virginia, Wisconsin} and cluster 6 = {Idaho, Nevada, Puget}) are nearly identical to those that emerged in the hierarchical clustering with average linkage.

To characterize the resulting clusters, we examine the cluster centroids [numerically in Table 16.10 and in the line chart ("profile plot") in Figure 16.5]. We see, for instance, that cluster 6 is characterized by especially low Fixed–charge and RoR, and high Sales. We can also see which variables do the best job of separating the clusters. For example, the spread of clusters for Sales and Fixed–charge is quite high and not so high for the other variables.

| **TABLE 16.9** | *k*-MEANS CLUSTERING OF 22 UTILITIES INTO $k = 6$ CLUSTERS (SORTED BY CLUSTER ID |

 code for *k*-means clustering

```
set.seed(123) # set random seed for reproducability
# load and preprocess data
utilities.df <- mlba::Utilities %>%
  column_to_rownames("Company")

# normalized distance:
utilities.df.norm <- scale(utilities.df)

# run kmeans algorithm
km <- kmeans(utilities.df.norm, 6)

# show cluster membership
sort(km$cluster)
```

Output

```
> sort(km$cluster)
    Boston      Hawaiian   New England      Pacific    San Diego      United
         1             1             1            1            1           1
   Central       Florida      Oklahoma        Texas      Arizona    Kentucky
         2             2             2            2            3           3
  Southern      Virginia    NY Commonwealth   Madison     Northern
         3             3             4            5            5           5
 Wisconsin         Idaho        Nevada        Puget
         5             6             6            6
```

We can also inspect the information on the within–cluster dispersion. From Table 16.10, we see that cluster 1, with six records, has the largest within–cluster sum of squared distances. In comparison, cluster 6, with three records, has a smaller within–cluster sum of squared distances. This means that cluster 6 is more homogeneous than cluster 3 (although it is also has fewer records).

When the number of clusters is not predetermined by domain requirements, we can use a graphical approach to evaluate different numbers of clusters. An "elbow chart" is a line chart depicting the decline in cluster heterogeneity as we add more clusters. Figure 16.6 shows the overall average within–cluster squared distance (normalized) for different choices of k. Moving from 1 to 2 tightens clusters considerably (reflected by the large reduction in within–cluster squared distance), and so does moving from 2 to 3 and even to 4. Adding more clusters beyond 4 brings less improvement to cluster homogeneity.

TABLE 16.10	CLUSTER CENTROIDS AND SQUARED DISTANCES FOR k-MEANS WITH $k = 6$

```
> # centroids
> km$centers
   Fixed_charge         RoR        Cost Load_factor Demand_growth
1   -0.61834147 -0.6252226  0.2019400   1.1482980   0.056364166
2    0.73659004  1.0755719 -1.5095844  -0.6225467  -0.999249196
3    0.08622291  0.1286230 -0.1804218  -0.1181922   0.355677321
4    2.03732429 -0.8628882  0.5782326  -1.2950193  -0.718643112
5    0.04557497  0.5742460  0.2383554  -0.2975182  -0.005101929
6   -0.60027572 -0.8331800  1.3389101  -0.4805802   0.991717777
        Sales    Nuclear  Fuel_Cost
1  -0.7402978 -0.3722028  1.1759426
2   0.5537221 -0.3796469 -0.3991693
3   0.1450583 -0.3186056 -0.2278866
4  -1.5814284  0.2143888  1.6926380
5  -0.5853676  1.7389316 -0.8356930
6   1.8565214 -0.7146294 -0.9657660

> # within-cluster sum of squares
> km$withinss
[1]   21.187976 12.200433 10.773938  0.000000  5.830596  9.533522

> # cluster size
> km$size
[1] 6 4 4 1 4 3
```

 code for plotting profile plot of centroids

```
library(GGally)
centroids <- data.frame(km$centers)
centroids['Cluster'] = paste('Cluster', seq(1, 6))

ggparcoord(centroids, columns=1:8, groupColumn='Cluster', showPoints=TRUE) +
    scale_color_viridis_d() + labs(x='Variable', y='Value')
```

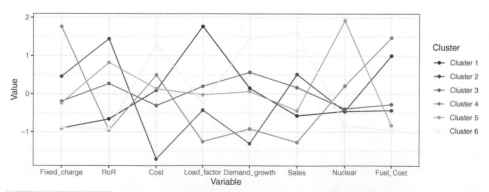

FIGURE 16.5	VISUAL PRESENTATION (PROFILE PLOT) OF CLUSTER CENTROIDS

FIGURE 16.6 COMPARING DIFFERENT CHOICES OF k IN TERMS OF OVERALL AVERAGE WITHIN-CLUSTER DISTANCE

From the distances between clusters, measured by Euclidean distance between the centroids (see Table 16.11), we can learn about the separation of the different clusters. For instance, we see that clusters 3 and 4 are the closest to one another, and clusters 5 and 6 are the farthest from one another. Cluster 6 is farthest from the other clusters, overall, but no cluster is a striking outlier.

TABLE 16.11 EUCLIDEAN DISTANCE BETWEEN CLUSTER CENTROIDS

```
> dist(km$centers)
         1        2        3        4        5
2 4.038817
3 2.379484 2.805529
4 4.007941 4.433858 2.318757
5 3.535897 4.078732 2.382086 3.294624
6 3.890969 5.556508 3.854580 4.430223 4.166643
```

Finally, we can use the information on the distance between the final clusters to evaluate the cluster validity. The ratio of the sum of within–cluster squared distances to cluster means for a given k to the sum of squared distances to the mean of all the records (in other words, $k = 1$) can measure the usefulness of the clustering. If the ratio is near 1.0, the clustering has not been very effective, whereas if it is small, we have well-separated groups.

PROBLEMS

16.1 University Rankings. The dataset *mlba::Universities* on American College and University Rankings contains information on 1302 American colleges and universities offering an undergraduate program. For each university, there are 17 measurements, including continuous variables (such as tuition and graduation rate) and categorical variables (such as location by state and whether it is a private or public school).

Note that many records are missing some measurements. Our first goal is to estimate these missing values from "similar" records. This will be done by clustering the complete records and then finding the closest cluster for each of the partial records. The missing values will be imputed from the information in that cluster.

a. Remove all records with missing measurements from the dataset.

b. For all the continuous variables, run hierarchical clustering using complete linkage and Euclidean distance. Make sure to normalize the variables. From the dendrogram: how many clusters seem reasonable for describing these data?

c. Compare the summary statistics for each cluster, and describe each cluster in this context (e.g., "Universities with high tuition, low acceptance rate..."). *Hint*: To obtain cluster statistics for hierarchical clustering, use the *aggregate()* function.

d. Use the categorical variables that were not used in the analysis (State and Private/Public) to characterize the different clusters. Is there any relationship between the clusters and the categorical information?

e. What other external information can explain the contents of some or all of these clusters?

f. Consider Tufts University, which is missing some information. Compute the Euclidean distance of this record from each of the clusters that you found above (using only the variables that you have). Which cluster is it closest to? Impute the missing values for Tufts by taking the average of the cluster on those variables.

16.2 Pharmaceutical Industry. An equities analyst is studying the pharmaceutical industry and would like your help in exploring and understanding the financial data collected by her firm. Her main objective is to understand the structure of the pharmaceutical industry using some basic financial measures.

Financial data gathered on 21 firms in the pharmaceutical industry are available in the dataset *mlba::Pharmaceuticals*. For each firm, the following variables are recorded:

1. Market capitalization (in billions of dollars)
2. Beta
3. Price/earnings ratio
4. Return on equity
5. Return on assets
6. Asset turnover
7. Leverage
8. Estimated revenue growth
9. Net profit margin
10. Median recommendation (across major brokerages)
11. Location of firm's headquarters
12. Stock exchange on which the firm is listed

Use cluster analysis to explore and analyze the given dataset as follows:

a. Use only the numerical variables (1–9) to cluster the 21 firms. Justify the various choices made in conducting the cluster analysis, such as weights for different variables, the specific clustering algorithm(s) used, the number of clusters formed, and so on.

b. Interpret the clusters with respect to the numerical variables used in forming the clusters.

c. Is there a pattern in the clusters with respect to the categorical variables (10–12) (those not used in forming the clusters)?

d. Provide an appropriate name for each cluster using any or all of the variables in the dataset.

16.3 Customer Rating of Breakfast Cereals. The dataset *mlba::Cereals* includes nutritional information, store display, and consumer ratings for 77 breakfast cereals.

Data Preprocessing. Remove all cereals with missing values.

a. Apply hierarchical clustering to the data using Euclidean distance to the normalized variables. Compare the dendrograms from single linkage and complete linkage, and look at cluster centroids. Comment on the structure of the clusters and on their stability. (*Hint*: To obtain cluster centroids for hierarchical clustering, compute the average values of each cluster members, using the *aggregate()* function.)

b. Which method leads to the most insightful or meaningful clusters?

c. Choose one of the methods. How many clusters would you use? What distance is used for this cutoff? (Look at the dendrogram.)

d. The elementary public schools would like to choose a set of cereals to include in their daily cafeterias. Every day a different cereal is offered, but all cereals should support a healthy diet. For this goal, you are requested to find a cluster of "healthy cereals." Should the data be normalized? If not, how should they be used in the cluster analysis?

16.4 Marketing to Frequent Fliers. The dataset *mlba::EastWestAirlinesCluster* contains information on 3999 passengers who belong to an airline's frequent flier program. For each passenger, the data include information on their mileage history and on different ways they accrued or spent miles in the last year. The goal is to try to identify clusters of passengers that have similar characteristics for the purpose of targeting different segments for different types of mileage offers.

a. Apply hierarchical clustering with Euclidean distance and Ward's method. Make sure to normalize the data first. How many clusters appear?

b. What would happen if the data were not normalized?

c. Compare the cluster centroid to characterize the different clusters, and try to give each cluster a label.

d. To check the stability of the clusters, remove a random 5% of the data (by taking a random sample of 95% of the records), and repeat the analysis. Does the same picture emerge?

e. Use k-means clustering with the number of clusters that you found above. Does the same picture emerge?

f. Which clusters would you target for offers, and what types of offers would you target to customers in that cluster?

## PART VII

Forecasting Time Series

## CHAPTER 17

Handling Time Series

In this chapter, we describe the context of business time series forecasting and introduce the main approaches that are detailed in the next chapters and, in particular, regression-based forecasting and smoothing-based methods. Our focus is on forecasting future values of a single time series. These three chapters are meant as an introduction to the general forecasting approach and methods.

We discuss the difference between the predictive nature of time series forecasting vs. the descriptive or explanatory task of time series analysis. A general discussion of combining forecasting methods or results for added precision follows. Next, we present a time series in terms of four components (level, trend, seasonality, and noise) and methods for visualizing the different components and exploring time series data. We close with a discussion of data partitioning (creating training and holdout sets), which is performed differently from cross-sectional data partitioning.

Forecasting in R

In this and the next two chapters, we use the `forecast` package, which offers a wide range of operations and forecasting models suitable for time series.

17.1 INTRODUCTION[1]

Time series forecasting is performed in nearly every organization that works with quantifiable data. Retail stores use it to forecast sales. Energy companies use it to forecast reserves, production, demand, and prices. Educational institutions use

---

[1]This and subsequent sections in this chapter, copyright © 2023 Datastats, LLC, and Galit Shmueli. Used by permission.

---

it to forecast enrollment. Governments use it to forecast tax receipts and spending. International financial organizations like the World Bank and International Monetary Fund use it to forecast inflation and economic activity. Transportation companies use time series forecasting to forecast future travel. Banks and lending institutions use it (sometimes badly!) to forecast new home purchases. Also, venture capital firms use it to forecast market potential and to evaluate business plans.

Previous chapters in this book deal with classifying and predicting data where time is not a factor, in the sense that it is not treated differently from other variables and where the sequence of measurements over time does not matter. These are typically called cross-sectional data. In contrast, this chapter deals with a different type of data: time series.

With today's technology, many time series are recorded on very frequent time scales. Stock data are available at ticker level. Purchases at online and offline stores are recorded in real time. The Internet of Things (IoT) generates huge numbers of time series, produced by sensors and other measurements devices. Although data might be available at a very frequent scale, for the purpose of forecasting, it is not always preferable to use this time scale. In considering the choice of time scale, one must consider the scale of the required forecasts and the level of noise in the data. For example, if the goal is to forecast next-day sales at a grocery store, using minute-by-minute sales data is likely to be less useful for forecasting than using daily aggregates. The minute-by-minute series will contain many sources of noise (e.g., variation by peak and non-peak shopping hours) that degrade its forecasting power, and these noise errors, when the data are aggregated to a cruder level, are likely to average out.

The focus in this part of the book is on forecasting a single time series. In some cases, multiple time series are to be forecasted (e.g., the monthly sales of multiple products). Even when multiple series are being forecasted, the most popular forecasting practice is to forecast each series individually. The advantage of single-series forecasting is its simplicity. The disadvantage is that it does not take into account possible relationships between series. The statistics literature contains models for multivariate time series which directly model the cross-correlations between series. Such methods tend to make restrictive assumptions about the data and the cross-series structure. They also require statistical expertise for estimation and maintenance. Econometric models often include information from one or more series as inputs into another series. However, such models are based on assumptions of causality that are based on theoretical models. An alternative approach is to capture the associations between the series of interest and external information more heuristically. An example is using the sales of lipstick to forecast some measure of the economy, based on the observation by Ronald Lauder, chairman of Estee Lauder, that lipstick sales tend to increase before tough economic times (a phenomenon called the "leading lipstick indicator").

17.2 Descriptive vs. Predictive Modeling

As with cross-sectional data, modeling time series data is done for either descriptive or predictive purposes. In descriptive modeling, or *time series analysis*, a time series is modeled to determine its components in terms of seasonal patterns, trends, relation to external factors, etc. These can then be used for decision-making and policy formulation. In contrast, *time series forecasting* uses the information in a time series (and perhaps other information) to forecast future values of that series. The difference between the goals of time series analysis and time series forecasting leads to differences in the type of methods used and in the modeling process itself. For example, in selecting a method for describing a time series, priority is given to methods that produce understandable results (rather than "blackbox" methods) and sometimes to models based on causal arguments (explanatory models). Furthermore, describing can be done in retrospect, while forecasting is *prospective* in nature. This means that descriptive models might use "future" information (e.g., averaging the values of yesterday, today, and tomorrow to obtain a smooth representation of today's value), whereas forecasting models cannot.

The focus in this chapter is on time series forecasting, where the goal is to predict future values of a time series. For information on time series analysis, see Chatfield (2003).

17.3 Popular Forecasting Methods in Business

In this part of the book, we focus on two main types of forecasting methods that are popular in business applications. Both are versatile and powerful yet relatively simple to understand and deploy. One type of forecasting tool is multiple linear regression, where the user specifies a certain model and then estimates it from the time series. The other includes more data-driven methods, such as smoothing and deep learning, where the method learns patterns from the data. Each of the two types of tools has advantages and disadvantages, as detailed in Chapters 18 and 19. We also note that machine learning methods such as neural networks and others that are intended for cross-sectional data are also sometimes used for time series forecasting, especially for incorporating external information into the forecasts (see Shmueli & Lichtendahl, 2016).

Combining Methods

Before a discussion of specific forecasting methods in the following two chapters, it should be noted that a popular approach for improving predictive performance is to combine forecasting methods. This is similar to the ensembles approach described in Chapter 13. Combining forecasting methods can be done via two-level (or multi-level) forecasters, where the first method uses the original time series to generate forecasts of future values and the second method uses the residuals from the first model to generate forecasts of future forecast errors, thereby "correcting" the first-level forecasts. We describe two-level forecasting in Chapter 18 (Section 18.6). Another combination approach is via "ensembles," where multiple methods are applied to the time series, and their resulting forecasts are averaged in some way to produce the final forecast. Combining methods can take advantage of the strengths of different forecasting methods to capture different aspects of the time series (also true in cross-sectional data). The averaging across multiple methods can lead to forecasts that are more robust and of higher precision.

17.4   TIME SERIES COMPONENTS

In both types of forecasting methods, regression models and smoothing, and in general, it is customary to dissect a time series into four components: *level*, *trend*, *seasonality*, and *noise*. The first three components are assumed to be invisible, as they characterize the underlying series, which we only observe with added noise. Level describes the average value of the series, trend is the change in the series from one period to the next, and seasonality describes a short-term cyclical behavior of the series which can be observed several times within the given series. Finally, noise is the random variation that results from measurement error or other causes not accounted for. It is always present in a time series to some degree.

> Don't get confused by the standard conversational meaning of "season" (winter, spring, etc.). The statistical meaning of "season" refers to any time period that repeats itself in cycles within the larger time series. Also, note that the term "period" in forecasting means simply a span of time, and not the specific meaning that it has in physics, of the distance between two equivalent points in a cycle.

To identify the components of a time series, the first step is to examine a time plot. In its simplest form, a time plot is a line chart of the series values over time, with temporal labels (e.g., calendar date) on the horizontal axis. To illustrate this, consider the following example.

Example: Ridership on Amtrak Trains

Amtrak, a US railway company, routinely collects data on ridership. Here we focus on forecasting future ridership using the series of monthly ridership between January 1991 and March 2004. These data are publicly available at www.forecastingprinciples.com.[2]

A time plot for the monthly Amtrak ridership series is shown in Figure 17.1. Note that the values are in thousands of riders.

code for creating a time series plot

```
library(forecast)
library(ggplot2)
Amtrak.data <- mlba::Amtrak

# create time series object using ts()
# ts() takes three arguments: start, end, and freq.
# with monthly data, the frequency of periods per cycle is 12 (per year).
# arguments start and end are (cycle [=year] number, seasonal period [=month] number) pairs.
# here start is Jan 1991: start = c(1991, 1); end is Mar 2004: end = c(2004, 3).
ridership.ts <- ts(Amtrak.data$Ridership,
    start = c(1991, 1), end = c(2004, 3), freq = 12)

# plot the series using the autoplot function to make use of ggplot
autoplot(ridership.ts, xlab="Time", ylab="Ridership (in 000s)") +
  scale_y_continuous(limits=c(1300, 2300))
```

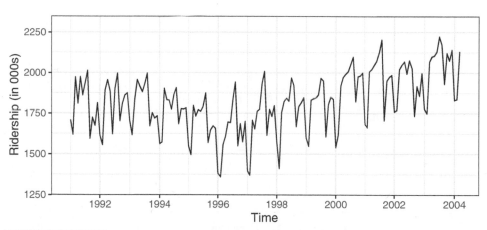

FIGURE 17.1 **MONTHLY RIDERSHIP ON AMTRAK TRAINS (IN THOUSANDS) FROM JANUARY 1991 TO MARCH 2004**

Looking at the time plot reveals the nature of the series components: the overall level is around 1,800,000 passengers per month. A slight U-shaped trend

[2]To get this series: click on Data. Under T-Competition Data, click "time-series data" (the direct URL to the data file is www.forecastingprinciples.com/files/MHcomp1.xls as of July 2015). This file contains many time series. In the Monthly worksheet, column AI contains series M034.

is discernible during this period, with pronounced annual seasonality, with peak travel during summer (July and August).

A second step in visualizing a time series is to examine it more carefully. A few tools are useful:

Zoom in: Zooming in to a shorter period within the series can reveal patterns that are hidden when viewing the entire series. This is especially important when the time series is long. Consider a series of the daily number of vehicles passing through the Baregg tunnel in Switzerland (data are available in the same location as the Amtrak Ridership data; series D028). The series from November 1, 2003 to November 16, 2005 is shown in Figure 17.2 (top). Zooming in to a 4-month period (Figure 17.2, bottom) reveals a strong day-of-week pattern that is not visible in the time plot of the complete time series.

Change scale of series: In order to better identify the shape of a trend, it is useful to change the scale of the series. One simple option, to check for an exponential trend, is to change the vertical scale to a logarithmic scale (use $log="y"$). If the trend on the new scale appears more linear, then the trend in the original series is closer to an exponential trend.

Add trend lines: Another possibility for better discerning the shape of the trend is to add a trend line. By trying different trend lines, one can see

FIGURE 17.2   TIME PLOTS OF THE DAILY NUMBER OF VEHICLES PASSING THROUGH THE BAREGG TUNNEL, SWITZERLAND. THE BOTTOM PANEL ZOOMS IN TO A 4-MONTH PERIOD, REVEALING A DAY-OF-WEEK PATTERN

what type of trend (e.g., linear, exponential, quadratic) best approximates the data.

Suppress seasonality: It is often easier to see trends in the data when seasonality is suppressed. Suppressing seasonality patterns can be done by plotting the series at a cruder time scale (e.g., aggregating monthly data into years) or creating separate lines or time plots for each season (e.g., separate lines for each day of week). Another popular option is to use moving average charts. We will discuss these in Section 19.2.

Continuing our example of Amtrak ridership, the charts in Figure 17.3 help make the series' components more visible.

Some forecasting methods directly model these components by making assumptions about their structure. For example, a popular assumption about trend is that it is linear or exponential over the given time period or part of it. Another common assumption is about the noise structure: many statistical methods assume that the noise follows a normal distribution. The advantage of methods that rely on such assumptions is that when the assumptions are reasonably met, the resulting forecasts will be more robust and the models more understandable. Other forecasting methods, which are data–adaptive, make fewer assumptions about the structure of these components and instead try to estimate them only from the data. Data-adaptive methods are advantageous when such assumptions are likely to be violated or when the structure of the time series changes over time. Another advantage of many data-adaptive methods is their simplicity and computational efficiency.

A key criterion for deciding between model-driven and data-driven forecasting methods is the nature of the series in terms of global vs. local patterns. A global pattern is one that is relatively constant throughout the series. An example is a linear trend throughout the entire series. In contrast, a local pattern is one that occurs only in a short period of the data and then changes, for example, a trend that is approximately linear within four neighboring time points, but the trend size (slope) changes slowly over time.

Model-driven methods are generally preferable for forecasting series with global patterns as they use all the data to estimate the global pattern. For a local pattern, a model-driven model would require specifying how and when the patterns change, which is usually impractical and often unknown. Therefore, data-driven methods are preferable for local patterns. Such methods "learn" patterns from the data, and their memory length can be set to best adapt to the rate of change in the series. Patterns that change quickly warrant a "short memory," whereas patterns that change slowly warrant a "long memory." In conclusion, the time plot should be used to identify not only the time series component but also the global/local nature of the trend and seasonality.

code for creating Figure 17.3

```
library(gridExtra)

# to zoom in to a certain period, use window() to create a new, shorter time series
# we create a new, 3-year time series of ridership.ts from Jan 1997 to Dec 1999
ridership.ts.3yrs <- window(ridership.ts, start = c(1997, 1), end = c(1999, 12))
g1 <- autoplot(ridership.ts.3yrs, xlab="Time", ylab="Ridership (in 000s)") +
  scale_y_continuous(limits=c(1300, 2300))

# fit a trend line to the time series
g2 <- autoplot(ridership.ts, xlab="Time", ylab="Ridership (in 000s)") +
  scale_y_continuous(limits=c(1300, 2300)) +
  geom_smooth(method="lm", formula=y~poly(x, 2))

grid.arrange(g1, g2, nrow=2)
```

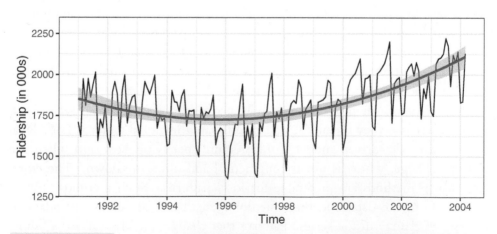

FIGURE 17.3   PLOTS THAT ENHANCE THE DIFFERENT COMPONENTS OF THE TIME SERIES. TOP: ZOOM IN TO 3 YEARS OF DATA AND BOTTOM: ORIGINAL SERIES WITH OVERLAID QUADRATIC TRENDLINE

17.5 DATA PARTITIONING AND PERFORMANCE EVALUATION

As in the case of cross-sectional data, to avoid overfitting and to be able to assess the predictive performance of the model on new data, we first partition the data into a training set and a holdout (test) set. However, there is one important difference between data partitioning in cross-sectional and time series data. In cross-sectional data, the partitioning is usually done randomly, with a random set of records designated as training data and the remainder as holdout data. However, in time series, a random partition would create two time series with "holes." Most standard forecasting methods cannot handle time series with missing values. Therefore, we partition a time series into training and holdout sets differently. The series is trimmed into two periods; the earlier period is set as the training data, and the later period as the holdout data. Methods are then trained on the earlier training period, and their predictive performance is assessed on the later holdout period. This approach also has the advantage of mimicking how the forecasting model will be used in practice: trained on existing data to forecast future values. R's forecast package uses the term *test* for the holdout period. We will use the terms interchangeably in the time series chapters.

Evaluation measures typically use the same metrics as in cross-sectional evaluation (see Chapter 5) with *MAE*, *MAPE*, and *RMSE* being the most popular metrics in practice. In evaluating and comparing forecasting methods, another important tool is visualization: examining time plots of the actual and predicted series can shed light on performance and hint toward possible improvements.

Benchmark Performance: Naive Forecasts

While it is tempting to apply "sophisticated" forecasting methods, we must evaluate their value added compared with a very simple approach: the *naive forecast*. A naive forecast is simply the most recent value of the series. In other words, at time t, our forecast for any future period $t + k$ is simply the value of the series at time t. While simple, naive forecasts are sometimes surprisingly difficult to outperform with more sophisticated models. It is therefore important to benchmark against results from a naive-forecasting approach.

When a time series has seasonality, a *seasonal naive forecast* can be generated. It is simply the value on the most recent similar season. For example, to forecast April 2001 for Amtrak ridership, we use the ridership from the most recent April, April 2000. Similarly, to forecast April 2002, we also use April 2000 ridership. In Figure 17.4, we show naive (horizontal line) and seasonal naive forecasts, as well as actual values (dotted line), in a 3-year training set from April 2001 to March 2004. We used functions *naive* and *snaive* in the `forecast` package to generate these forecasts (see Figure 17.4).

R partial code for creating Figure 17.4 (see accompanying source code for full instructions)

```
nTest <- 36
nTrain <- length(ridership.ts) - nTest

# partition the data
train.ts <- window(ridership.ts, start = c(1991, 1), end = c(1991, nTrain))
test.ts <- window(ridership.ts, start = c(1991, nTrain + 1),
                                end = c(1991, nTrain + nTest))

# generate the naive and seasonal naive forecasts
naive.pred <- naive(train.ts, h=nTest)
snaive.pred <- snaive(train.ts, h=nTest)

# compare the actual values and forecasts for both methods
colData <- "steelblue"; colModel <- "tomato"
autoplot(train.ts, xlab="Time", ylab="Ridership (in 000s$)", color=colData) +
  autolayer(test.ts, linetype=2, color=colData) +
  autolayer(naive.pred, PI=FALSE, color=colModel, size=0.75) +
  autolayer(snaive.pred, PI=FALSE, color=colModel, size=0.75)
```

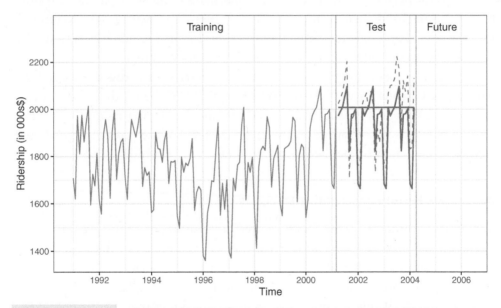

FIGURE 17.4   **NAIVE AND SEASONAL NAIVE FORECASTS IN A 3-YEAR TEST SET FOR AMTRAK RIDERSHIP**

Performance on the holdout (test) set is more indicative of how the models will perform in the future. Table 17.1 compares the accuracies of these two naive forecasts. Because Amtrak ridership has monthly seasonality, the seasonal naive forecast is the clear winner on both training and test sets and on all popular measures. In choosing between the two models, the accuracy on the test set is more relevant than the accuracy on the training set.

TABLE 17.1	PREDICTIVE ACCURACY OF NAIVE AND SEASONAL NAIVE FORECASTS IN THE TEST SET FOR AMTRAK RIDERSHIP

```
> accuracy(naive.pred, test.ts)
                  ME      RMSE      MAE        MPE      MAPE
Training set   2.45091  168.1470  125.2975  -0.3460027  7.271393
Test set     -14.71772  142.7551  115.9234  -1.2749992  6.021396
> accuracy(snaive.pred, test.ts)
                  ME      RMSE      MAE       MPE      MAPE
Training set  13.93991  99.26557  82.49196  0.5850656  4.715251
Test set      54.72961  95.62433  84.09406  2.6527928  4.247656
```

Generating Future Forecasts

Another important difference between cross-sectional and time series partition-ing occurs when creating the actual forecasts. Before attempting to forecast future values of the series, the training and test sets are recombined into one long series, and the chosen method/model is rerun on the complete data. This final model is then used to forecast future values. The three advantages in recom-bining are the following:

1. The test set, which is the most recent period, usually contains the most valuable information in terms of being the closest in time to the forecast period.

2. With more data (the complete time series compared to only the training set), some models can be estimated more accurately.

3. If only the training set is used to generate forecasts, then it will require forecasting farther into the future (e.g., if the test set contains four time points, forecasting the next period will require a 5-step-ahead forecast from the training set).

PROBLEMS

17.1 Impact of September 11 on Air Travel in the United States. The Research and Innovative Technology Administration's Bureau of Transportation Statistics conducted a study to evaluate the impact of the September 11, 2001 terrorist attack on US transportation. The 2006 study report and the data can be found at bts.gov/archive/publications/estimated_impacts_of_9_11_on_us_travel/index. The goal of the study was stated as follows:

> The purpose of this study is to provide a greater understanding of the passenger travel behavior patterns of persons making long distance trips before and after 9/11.

The report analyzes monthly passenger movement data between January 1990 and May 2004. Data on three monthly time series are given in the dataset *mlba::Sept11Travel* for this period:

(1) Actual airline revenue passenger miles (Air)

(2) Rail passenger miles (Rail)

(3) Vehicle miles traveled (Car)

To assess the impact of September 11, the Bureau of Transportation Statistics took the following approach: using data before September 11, they forecasted future data (under the assumption of no terrorist attack). Then, they compared the forecasted series with the actual data to assess the impact of the event. Our first step, therefore, is to split each of the time series into two parts: pre- and post-September 11. We now concentrate only on the earlier time series.

a. Is the goal of this study descriptive or predictive?

b. Plot each of the three pre-event time series (Air, Rail, Car).

   i. What time series components appear from the plot?

   ii. What type of trend appears? Change the scale of the series, add trendlines, and suppress seasonality to better visualize the trend pattern.

17.2 Performance on Training and Test Data. Two different models were fit to the same time series. The first 100 time periods were used for the training set, and the last 12 periods were treated as a test (holdout) set. Assume that both models make sense practically and fit the data pretty well. Below are the RMSE values for each of the models:

	Training set	Test set
Model A	543	690
Model B	669	675

a. Which model appears more useful for explaining the different components of this time series? Why?

b. Which model appears to be more useful for forecasting purposes? Why?

17.3 Forecasting Department Store Sales. The dataset *mlba::DepartmentStoreSales* contains data on the quarterly sales for a department store over a 6-year period (data courtesy of Chris Albright).

a. Create a well-formatted time plot of the data.

b. Which of the four components (level, trend, seasonality, noise) seems to be present in this series?

17.4 Shipments of Household Appliances. The dataset *mlba::ApplianceShipments* contains the series of quarterly shipments (in million $) of US household appliances between 1985 and 1989 (data courtesy of Ken Black).

a. Create a well-formatted time plot of the data.

b. Which of the four components (level, trend, seasonality, noise) seems to be present in this series?

17.5 Canadian Manufacturing Workers Workhours. The time plot in Figure 17.5 describes the average annual number of weekly hours spent by Canadian manufacturing workers (data are available in *mlba::CanadianWorkHours*—thanks to Ken Black for the data).

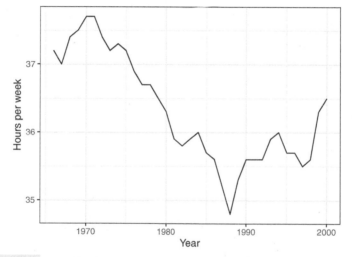

FIGURE 17.5   AVERAGE ANNUAL WEEKLY HOURS SPENT BY CANADIAN MANUFACTURING WORKERS

a. Reproduce the time plot.

b. Which of the four components (level, trend, seasonality, noise) seems to be present in this series?

17.6 Souvenir Sales. The dataset *mlba::SouvenirSales* contains monthly sales for a souvenir shop at a beach resort town in Queensland, Australia, between 1995 and 2001. [Source: Hyndman and Yang (2018).]

Back in 2001, the store wanted to use the data to forecast sales for the next 12 months (year 2002). They hired an analyst to generate forecasts. The analyst first partitioned the data into training and test sets, with the test set containing the last

12 months of data (year 2001). She then fit a regression model to sales, using the training set.

a. Create a well-formatted time plot of the data.

b. Change the scale on the x-axis or on the y-axis, or on both, to logarithmic scale to achieve a linear relationship. Select the time plot that seems most linear.

c. Comparing the two time plots, what can be said about the type of trend in the data?

d. Why were the data partitioned? Partition the data into the training and test sets as explained above.

17.7 **Shampoo Sales.** The dataset *mlba::ShampooSales* contains data on the monthly sales of a certain shampoo over a 3-year period. [Source: Hyndman and Yang (2018).]

a. Create a well-formatted time plot of the data.

b. Which of the four components (level, trend, seasonality, noise) seem to be present in this series?

c. Do you expect to see seasonality in sales of shampoo? Why?

d. If the goal is forecasting sales in future months, which of the following steps should be taken?

- Partition the data into training and test sets.
- Tweak the model parameters to obtain good fit to the test data.
- Look at MAPE and RMSE values for the training set.
- Look at MAPE and RMSE values for the test set.

## CHAPTER 18

Regression-Based Forecasting

A popular forecasting tool is based on multiple linear regression models, using suitable predictors to capture trend and/or seasonality. In this chapter, we show how a linear regression model can be set up to capture a time series with a trend and/or seasonality. The model, which is estimated from the data, can then produce future forecasts by inserting the relevant predictor information into the estimated regression equation. We describe different types of common trends (linear, exponential, polynomial) and two types of seasonality (additive and multiplicative). Next, we show how a regression model can be used to quantify the correlation between neighboring values in a time series (called autocorrelation). This type of model, called an autoregressive (AR) model, is useful for improving forecast precision by making use of the information contained in the autocorrelation (beyond trend and seasonality). It is also useful for evaluating the predictability of a series, by evaluating whether the series is a "random walk." The various steps of fitting linear regression and autoregressive models, using them to generate forecasts, and assessing their predictive accuracy, are illustrated using the Amtrak ridership series.

18.1 A MODEL WITH TREND[1]

Linear Trend

To create a linear regression model that captures a time series with a global linear trend, the outcome variable (Y) is set as the time series values or some function of it, and the predictor (X) is set as a time index. Let us consider a simple example:

---

[1]This and subsequent sections in this chapter copyright © 2019 Datastats, LLC, and Galit Shmueli. Used by permission.

Machine Learning for Business Analytics: Concepts, Techniques, and Applications in R, Second Edition.
Galit Shmueli, Peter C. Bruce, Peter Gedeck, Inbal Yahav, and Nitin R. Patel
© 2023 John Wiley & Sons, Inc. Published 2023 by John Wiley & Sons, Inc.

fitting a linear trend to the Amtrak ridership data described in Chapter 17. This type of trend is shown in Figure 18.1.

From the time plot, it is obvious that the global trend is not linear. However, we use this example to illustrate how a linear trend is fitted, and later we consider more appropriate models for this series.

To obtain a linear relationship between Ridership and Time, we set the output variable Y as the Amtrak ridership and create a new variable that is a time index $t = 1, 2, 3, \ldots$ This time index is then used as a single predictor in the regression model:

$$Y_t = \beta_0 + \beta_1 t + \epsilon,$$

where Y_t is the ridership at period t and ϵ is the standard noise term in a linear regression. Thus, we are modeling three of the four time series components:

 code for creating Figure 18.1

```
library(forecast)
library(ggplot2)
Amtrak.data <- mlba::Amtrak

# create time series
ridership.ts <- ts(Amtrak.data$Ridership,
                   start=c(1991, 1), end=c(2004, 3), freq=12)

# produce linear trend model
ridership.lm <- tslm(ridership.ts ~ trend)

# plot the series using the autoplot function to make use of ggplot
autoplot(ridership.ts, xlab="Time", ylab="Ridership (in 000s)", color="steelblue") +
  autolayer(ridership.lm$fitted.values, color="tomato", size=0.75) +
  scale_y_continuous(limits=c(1300, 2300))
```

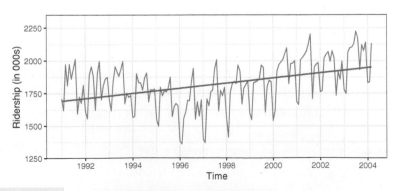

FIGURE 18.1   A LINEAR TREND FIT TO AMTRAK RIDERSHIP

TABLE 18.1	OUTCOME VARIABLE (MIDDLE) AND PREDICTOR VARIABLE (RIGHT) USED TO FIT A LINEAR TREND

Month	Ridership (Y_t)	t
Jan 91	1709	1
Feb 91	1621	2
Mar 91	1973	3
Apr 91	1812	4
May 91	1975	5
Jun 91	1862	6
Jul 91	1940	7
Aug 91	2013	8
Sep 91	1596	9
Oct 91	1725	10
Nov 91	1676	11
Dec 91	1814	12
Jan 92	1615	13
Feb 92	1557	14

level (β_0), trend (β_1), and noise (ϵ). Seasonality is not modeled. A snapshot of the two corresponding columns (Y and t) is shown in Table 18.1.

After partitioning the data into training and test (holdout) sets, the next step is to fit a linear regression model to the training set, with t as the single predictor (function *tslm()* relies on *ts()* which automatically creates t and calls it *trend*). Applying this to the Amtrak ridership data (with a test set consisting of the last 36 months) results in the estimated model shown in Figure 18.2. The actual and fitted values and the residuals (or forecast errors) are shown in the two time plots.

Table 18.2 contains a report of the estimated coefficients. Note that examining only the estimated coefficients and their statistical significance can be misleading! In this example, the statistically insignificant trend coefficient might indicate "no trend," although it is obvious from the plot that a trend does exist, albeit a quadratic one. The training RMSE is 158.9 and the test RMSE is 239.5. This discrepancy is indicative of an inadequate trend shape. However, an inadequate trend shape is easiest to detect by examining the time plot of the residuals (Figure 18.2).

LINEAR REGRESSION FOR TIME SERIES IN R

Fitting a regression model to time series (and using it to generate forecasts) can be done in R using the function *tslm()* in the forecast package.

code for creating Figure 18.2

```
# fit linear trend model to training set
train.lm <- tslm(train.ts ~ trend)
train.lm.pred <- forecast(train.lm, h=length(test.ts), level=0)

# define functions to create consistent plots of models
library(gridExtra)
colData <- "steelblue"; colModel <- "tomato"
plotForecast <- function(model, train.ts, test.ts) {
  model.pred <- forecast(model, h=length(test.ts), level=0)
  g <- autoplot(train.ts, xlab="Time", ylab="Ridership (in 000s)", color=colData) +
    autolayer(test.ts, color=colData) +
    autolayer(model$fitted.values, color=colModel, size=0.75) +
    autolayer(model.pred$mean, color=colModel, size=0.75)
  return (g)
}
plotResiduals <- function(model, test.ts) {
  model.pred <- forecast(model, h=length(test.ts), level=0)
  g <- autoplot(model$residuals, xlab="Time", ylab="Forecast errors", color=colModel, size=0.75) +
    autolayer(test.ts - model.pred$mean, color=colModel, size=0.75) +
    geom_hline(yintercept=0, color="darkgrey") +
    coord_cartesian(ylim=c(-410, 410))
  return (g)
}
g1 <- plotForecast(train.lm, train.ts, test.ts)
g2 <- plotResiduals(train.lm, test.ts)
grid.arrange(g1, g2, nrow=2)
```

Code for data partition is given in Figure 17.4

FIGURE 18.2   A LINEAR TREND FIT TO AMTRAK RIDERSHIP IN THE TRAINING PERIOD AND
FORECASTED IN THE TEST PERIOD. (TOP) AND FORECAST ERRORS (BOTTOM)

TABLE 18.2   SUMMARY OF OUTPUT FROM A LINEAR REGRESSION MODEL APPLIED TO THE AMTRAK RIDERSHIP DATA IN THE TRAINING PERIOD

```
> summary(train.lm)

Call: lm(formula = formula, data = "train.ts", na.action = na.exclude)

Residuals:
    Min      1Q  Median      3Q     Max
-411.29 -114.02   16.06  129.28  306.35

Coefficients:
            Estimate Std. Error t value Pr(>|t|)
(Intercept) 1750.3595    29.0729  60.206   <2e-16 ***
trend          0.3514     0.4069   0.864     0.39
---
Signif. codes:  0 *** 0.001 ** 0.01 * 0.05 . 0.1   1

Residual standard error: 160.2 on 121 degrees of freedom
Multiple R-squared:  0.006125,  Adjusted R-squared:  -0.002089
F-statistic: 0.7456 on 1 and 121 DF,  p-value: 0.3896

> accuracy(train.lm.pred, test.ts)
                     ME     RMSE      MAE       MPE       MAPE
Training set 3.720601e-15 158.9269 129.6778 -0.853984  7.535999
Test set     1.931316e+02 239.4863 209.4371  9.209919 10.147732
```

Exponential Trend

Several alternative trend shapes are useful and easy to fit via a linear regression model. One such shape is an exponential trend. An exponential trend implies a multiplicative increase/decrease of the series over time ($Y_t = ce^{\beta_1 t + \epsilon}$). To fit an exponential trend, simply replace the outcome variable Y with $\log Y$ (where log is the natural logarithm), and fit a linear regression ($\log Y_t = \beta_0 + \beta_1 t + \epsilon$). In the Amtrak example, for instance, we would fit a linear regression of log(Ridership) on the index variable t. Exponential trends are popular in sales data, where they reflect percentage growth. In R, fitting exponential trend is done by setting argument *lambda=0* in function *tslm()* .[2]

Note: As in the general case of linear regression, when comparing the predictive accuracy of models that have a different output variable, such as a linear trend model (with Y) and an exponential trend model (with $\log Y$), it is essential to compare forecasts or forecast errors on the same scale. In R, when using an exponential trend model, the forecasts of $\log Y$ are made and then automatically converted back to the original scale. An example is shown in Figure 18.3, where an exponential trend is fit to the Amtrak ridership data, overlaid with our previously fitted linear trend.

---

[2]Argument *lambda* is used to apply the Box-Cox transformation to the values of the time series: $(y^\lambda - 1)/\lambda$ if $\lambda \neq 0$. When $\lambda = 0$, the transformation is defined as $\log(y)$. When $\lambda = 1$, the series is not transformed (except for the subtraction of 1 from each value), so the model has a linear trend.

code for creating Figure 18.3

```
# fit exponential trend using tslm() with argument lambda = 0
train.lm.expo.trend <- tslm(train.ts ~ trend, lambda=0)
train.lm.expo.trend.pred <- forecast(train.lm.expo.trend, h=nTest, level=0)

# fit linear trend using tslm() with argument lambda = 1 (no transform of y)
train.lm.linear.trend <- tslm(train.ts ~ trend, lambda=1)
train.lm.linear.trend.pred <- forecast(train.lm.linear.trend, h=nTest, level=0)

plotForecast(train.lm.expo.trend, train.ts, test.ts) +
  autolayer(train.lm.linear.trend$fitted.values, color="forestgreen", size=0.75) +
  autolayer(train.lm.linear.trend.pred, color="forestgreen", size=0.75)
```

FIGURE 18.3   **EXPONENTIAL (AND LINEAR) TREND USED TO FORECAST AMTRAK RIDERSHIP**

Polynomial Trend

Another nonlinear trend shape that is easy to fit via linear regression is a polynomial trend and, in particular, a quadratic relationship of the form $Y_t = \beta_0 + \beta_1 t + \beta_2 t^2 + \epsilon$. This is done by creating an additional predictor t^2 (the square of t) and fitting a multiple linear regression with the two predictors t and t^2. In R, we fit a quadratic trend using function $I()$, which treats an object "as is" (Figure 18.4). For the Amtrak ridership data, we have already seen a U-shaped trend in the data. We therefore fit a quadratic model. The fitted and residual charts are shown in Figure 18.4. We conclude from these plots that this shape adequately captures the trend during the training period. The training forecast errors are now devoid of trend and exhibit only seasonality. The forecasts now overshoot for the test period, indicating that the quadratic trend that seemed to fit the training data well may not be useful for future data.

In general, any type of trend shape can be fit as long as it has a mathematical representation. However, the underlying assumption is that this shape is

code for creating Figure 18.4

```
# fit quadratic trend using function I(), which treats an object "as is".
train.lm.poly <- tslm(train.ts ~ trend + I(trend^2))
summary(train.lm.poly)

g1 <- plotForecast(train.lm.poly, train.ts, test.ts)
g2 <- plotResiduals(train.lm.poly, test.ts)
grid.arrange(g1, g2, nrow=2)
```

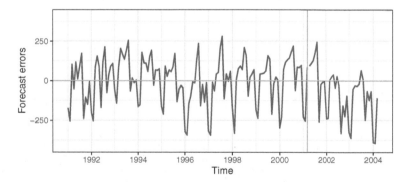

FIGURE 18.4   QUADRATIC TREND MODEL USED TO FORECAST AMTRAK RIDERSHIP. PLOTS OF FITTED, FORECASTED, AND ACTUAL VALUES (TOP) AND FORECAST ERRORS (BOTTOM)

applicable throughout the period of data that we have and also during the period that we are going to forecast. Do not choose an overly complex shape. Although it will fit the training data well, it will in fact be overfitting them. To avoid overfitting, always examine the test performance, and refrain from choosing overly complex trend patterns.

18.2   A MODEL WITH SEASONALITY

A seasonal pattern in a time series means that observations that fall in some seasons have consistently higher or lower values than those that fall in other seasons. Examples are day-of-week patterns, monthly patterns, and quarterly patterns. The Amtrak ridership monthly time series, as can be seen in the time plot, exhibits strong monthly seasonality (with highest traffic during summer months).

Seasonality is captured in a regression model by creating a new categorical variable that denotes the season for each value. This categorical variable is then turned into dummies, which in turn are included as predictors in the regression model. To illustrate this, we created a new "Season" column for the Amtrak data, as shown in Table 18.3.

TABLE 18.3	NEW CATEGORICAL VARIABLE (RIGHT) TO BE USED (VIA DUMMIES) AS PREDICTOR(S) IN A LINEAR REGRESSION MODEL (FIRST 17 MONTHS SHOWN)	
Month	**Ridership**	**Season**
Jan 91	1709	Jan
Feb 91	1621	Feb
Mar 91	1973	Mar
Apr 91	1812	Apr
May 91	1975	May
Jun 91	1862	Jun
Jul 91	1940	Jul
Aug 91	2013	Aug
Sep 91	1596	Sep
Oct 91	1725	Oct
Nov 91	1676	Nov
Dec 91	1814	Dec
Jan 92	1615	Jan
Feb 92	1557	Feb
Mar 92	1891	Mar
Apr 92	1956	Apr
May 92	1885	May

Then, to include the Season categorical variable as a predictor in a regression model for Y (Ridership), we turn it into dummies (for $m = 12$ seasons, we create 11 dummies, which are binary variables that take on the value 1 if the record falls in that particular season and 0 otherwise[3]).

In R, function *tslm()* uses *ts()* which automatically creates the categorical Season column (called *season*) and converts it into dummy variables.

After partitioning the data into training and test sets (see Section 17.5), we fit the regression model to the training data. The fitted series and the

---

[3]We use only $m - 1$ dummies because information about the $m - 1$ seasons is sufficient. If all $m - 1$ variables are zero, then the season must be the mth season. Including the mth dummy causes redundant information and multicollinearity.

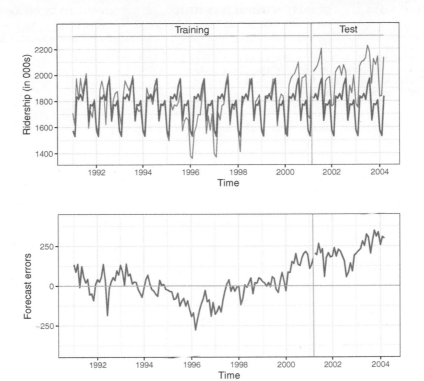

FIGURE 18.5   REGRESSION MODEL WITH SEASONALITY APPLIED TO THE AMTRAK RIDERSHIP (TOP) AND ITS FORECAST ERRORS (BOTTOM)

residuals from this model are shown in Figure 18.5. The model appears to capture the seasonality in the data. However, since we have not included a trend component in the model (as shown in Section 18.1), the fitted values do not capture the existing trend. Therefore, the residuals, which are the difference between the actual and the fitted values, clearly display the remaining U-shaped trend.

Additive vs. Multiplicative Seasonality

When seasonality is added as described above (create categorical seasonal variable, then create dummies from it and then regress on Y), it captures *additive seasonality*. This means that the average value of Y in a certain season is a fixed amount more or less than that in another season. For example, consider the regression coefficients in Table 18.4 for the model with additive seasonality that we just fitted. The coefficient for season8 (396.66) indicates that the average number of passengers in August is higher by 396.66 thousand passengers than the average in January (the reference category).

TABLE 18.4	SUMMARY OF OUTPUT FROM FITTING ADDITIVE SEASONALITY TO THE AMTRAK RIDERSHIP DATA IN THE TRAINING PERIOD

```
> # include season as a predictor in tslm(). Here it creates 11 dummies,
> # one for each month except for the first season, January.
> train.lm.season <- tslm(train.ts ~ season)
> summary(train.lm.season)

Call:
lm(formula = formula, data = "train.ts", na.action = na.exclude)

Residuals:
     Min      1Q   Median      3Q      Max
 -276.165  -52.934    5.868   54.544  215.081

Coefficients:
            Estimate Std. Error t value Pr(>|t|)
(Intercept)  1573.97      30.58  51.475  < 2e-16 ***
season2       -42.93      43.24  -0.993   0.3230
season3       260.77      43.24   6.030 2.19e-08 ***
season4       245.09      44.31   5.531 2.14e-07 ***
season5       278.22      44.31   6.279 6.81e-09 ***
season6       233.46      44.31   5.269 6.82e-07 ***
season7       345.33      44.31   7.793 3.79e-12 ***
season8       396.66      44.31   8.952 9.19e-15 ***
season9        75.76      44.31   1.710   0.0901 .
season10      200.61      44.31   4.527 1.51e-05 ***
season11      192.36      44.31   4.341 3.14e-05 ***
season12      230.42      44.31   5.200 9.18e-07 ***
---
Signif. codes:  0 *** 0.001 ** 0.01 * 0.05 . 0.1   1

Residual standard error: 101.4 on 111 degrees of freedom
Multiple R-squared:  0.6348,  Adjusted R-squared:  0.5986
F-statistic: 17.54 on 11 and 111 DF,  p-value: < 2.2e-16
```

Using regression models, we can also capture *multiplicative seasonality*, where values in a certain season are on average, higher or lower by a percentage amount compared to another season. To fit multiplicative seasonality, we use the same model as above, except that we use $\log(Y)$ as the outcome variable. In R, this is achieved by setting *lambda=0* in the *tslm()* function.

18.3 A MODEL WITH TREND AND SEASONALITY

Finally, we can create models that capture both trend and seasonality by including predictors of both types. For example, from our exploration of the Amtrak ridership data, it appears that a quadratic trend and monthly seasonality are both warranted. We therefore fit a model to the training data with 13 predictors: 11 dummies for month and t and t^2 for trend. The fit and output from this final model are shown in Figure 18.6 and Table 18.5. If we are satisfied with this model after evaluating its predictive performance on the test data and comparing it against alternatives, we would re-fit it to the entire un-partitioned series. This

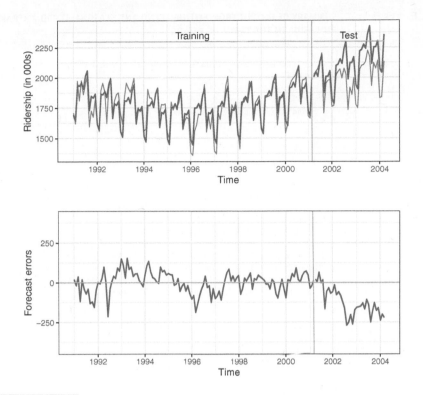

REGRESSION MODEL WITH TREND AND SEASONALITY APPLIED TO AMTRAK RIDERSHIP (TOP) AND ITS FORECAST ERRORS (BOTTOM)

re-fitted model can then be used to generate k-step-ahead forecasts (denoted by F_{t+k}) by plugging in the appropriate month and index terms. However, the forecasts on the test data are still missing the mark, indicating that the trend we have identified may not be so global, after all. More on this in the next chapter, where we allow a local trend component.

18.4 AUTOCORRELATION AND ARIMA MODELS

When we use linear regression for time series forecasting, we are able to account for patterns such as trend and seasonality. However, ordinary regression models do not account for dependence between values in different periods, which in cross-sectional data is assumed to be absent. Yet, in the time series context, values in neighboring periods tend to be correlated. Such correlation, called *autocorrelation*, is informative and can help in improving forecasts. If we know that a high value tends to be followed by high values (positive autocorrelation), then we can use that to adjust forecasts. We will now discuss how to compute the autocorrelation of a series and how best to utilize the information for improving forecasts.

TABLE 18.5	SUMMARY OF OUTPUT FROM FITTING TREND AND SEASONALITY TO AMTRAK RIDERSHIP IN THE TRAINING PERIOD

```
> train.lm.trend.season <- tslm(train.ts ~ trend + I(trend^2) + season)
> summary(train.lm.trend.season)

Call:
tslm(formula = train.ts ~ trend + I(trend^2) + season)

Residuals:
    Min     1Q  Median     3Q     Max
-213.77  -39.36    9.71  42.42  152.19

Coefficients:
             Estimate Std. Error t value         Pr(>|t|)
(Intercept) 1696.9794    27.6752   61.32 < 0.0000000000000002 ***
trend         -7.1559     0.7293   -9.81 < 0.0000000000000002 ***
I(trend^2)     0.0607     0.0057   10.66 < 0.0000000000000002 ***
season2      -43.2458    30.2407   -1.43            0.1556
season3      260.0149    30.2423    8.60  0.00000000000006604 ***
season4      260.6175    31.0210    8.40  0.00000000000018264 ***
season5      293.7966    31.0202    9.47  0.00000000000000069 ***
season6      248.9615    31.0199    8.03  0.00000000000126033 ***
season7      360.6340    31.0202   11.63 < 0.0000000000000002 ***
season8      411.6513    31.0209   13.27 < 0.0000000000000002 ***
season9       90.3162    31.0223    2.91            0.0044 **
season10     214.6037    31.0241    6.92  0.00000000032920793 ***
season11     205.6711    31.0265    6.63  0.00000000133918009 ***
season12     242.9294    31.0295    7.83  0.00000000000344281 ***
---
Signif. codes:  0 *** 0.001 ** 0.01 * 0.05 . 0.1   1

Residual standard error: 70.9 on 109 degrees of freedom
Multiple R-squared:  0.825,  Adjusted R-squared:  0.804
F-statistic: 39.4 on 13 and 109 DF,  p-value: <0.0000000000000002
```

Computing Autocorrelation

Correlation between values of a time series in neighboring periods is called *auto-correlation*, because it describes a relationship between the series and itself. To compute autocorrelation, we compute the correlation between the series and a lagged version of the series. A *lagged series* is a "copy" of the original series which is moved forward one or more time periods. A lagged series with lag-1 is the original series moved forward one time period, a lagged series with lag-2 is the original series moved forward two time periods, etc. Table 18.6 shows the first 24 months of the Amtrak ridership series, the lag-1 series, and the lag-2 series.

Next, to compute the lag-1 autocorrelation, which measures the linear relationship between values in consecutive time periods, we compute the correlation between the original series and the lag-1 series (e.g., via the function *cor()*) to be 0.08. Note that although the original series in Table 18.6 has 24 time periods, the lag-1 autocorrelation will only be based on 23 pairs (because the lag-1 series does not have a value for January 1991). Similarly, the lag-2 autocorrelation, measuring the relationship between values that are two time periods apart, is the correlation between the original series and the lag-2 series (yielding −0.15).

TABLE 18.6	FIRST 24 MONTHS OF AMTRAK RIDERSHIP SERIES WITH LAG-1 AND LAG-2 SERIES		
Month	Ridership	Lag-1 series	Lag-2 series
Jan 91	1709		
Feb 91	1621	1709	
Mar 91	1973	1621	1709
Apr 91	1812	1973	1621
May 91	1975	1812	1973
Jun 91	1862	1975	1812
Jul 91	1940	1862	1975
Aug 91	2013	1940	1862
Sep 91	1596	2013	1940
Oct 91	1725	1596	2013
Nov 91	1676	1725	1596
Dec 91	1814	1676	1725
Jan 92	1615	1814	1676
Feb 92	1557	1615	1814
Mar 92	1891	1557	1615
Apr 92	1956	1891	1557
May 92	1885	1956	1891
Jun 92	1623	1885	1956
Jul 92	1903	1623	1885
Aug 92	1997	1903	1623
Sep 92	1704	1997	1903
Oct 92	1810	1704	1997
Nov 92	1862	1810	1704
Dec 92	1875	1862	1810

We can use R's *Acf()* function in the **forecast** package to directly compute and plot the autocorrelation of a series at different lags. For example, the output for the 24-month ridership is shown in Figure 18.7.

 code for creating Figure 18.7

```
ridership.24.ts <- window(train.ts, start=c(1991, 1), end=c(1991, 24))
Acf(ridership.24.ts, lag.max=12, main="")
```

FIGURE 18.7   AUTOCORRELATION PLOT FOR LAGS 1–12 (FOR FIRST 24 MONTHS OF AMTRAK RIDERSHIP)

A few typical autocorrelation behaviors that are useful to explore are the following:

Strong autocorrelation (positive or negative) at a lag k larger than 1 and its multiples $(2k, 3k, \ldots)$ typically reflects a cyclical pattern. For example, strong positive lag-12 autocorrelation in monthly data will reflect an annual seasonality (where values during a given month each year are positively correlated).

Positive lag-1 autocorrelation (called "stickiness") describes a series where consecutive values move generally in the same direction. In the presence of a strong linear trend, we would expect to see a strong and positive lag-1 autocorrelation.

Negative lag-1 autocorrelation reflects swings in the series, where high values are immediately followed by low values and vice versa.

Examining the autocorrelation of a series can therefore help to detect seasonality patterns. In Figure 18.7, for example, we see that the strongest autocorrelation is at lag-6 and is negative. This indicates a bi-annual pattern in ridership, with 6-month switches from high to low ridership. A look at the time plot confirms the high-summer low-winter pattern.

In addition to looking at the autocorrelation of the raw series, it is very useful to look at the autocorrelation of the *residual series* (that is, the forecast errors series). For example, after fitting a regression model (or using any other forecasting method), we can examine the autocorrelation of the series of residuals. If we have adequately modeled the seasonal pattern, then the residual series should show no autocorrelation at the season's lag. Figure 18.8 displays the autocorrelations for the residuals from the regression model with seasonality and quadratic trend shown in Figure 18.6. It is clear that the 6-month (and 12-month) cyclical behavior no longer dominates the series of residuals, indicating that the regression model captured them adequately. However, we can also see a strong positive

FIGURE 18.8   AUTOCORRELATION PLOT OF FORECAST ERRORS SERIES FROM FIGURE 18.6

autocorrelation from lag-1 on, indicating a positive relationship between neighboring residuals. This is valuable information, which can be used to improve forecasts.

Improving Forecasts by Integrating Autocorrelation Information

In general, there are two approaches to taking advantage of autocorrelation. One is by directly building the autocorrelation into the regression model, and the other is by constructing a second-level forecasting model on the residual series.

Among regression-type models that directly account for autocorrelation are *autoregressive* (AR) models, or the more general class of models called ARIMA (Autoregressive Integrated Moving Average) models. AR models are similar to linear regression models, except that the predictors are the past values of the series. For example, an autoregressive model of order 2, denoted AR(2), can be written as

$$Y_t = \beta_0 + \beta_1 Y_{t-1} + \beta_2 Y_{t-2} + \epsilon \tag{18.1}$$

Estimating such models is roughly equivalent to fitting a linear regression model with the series as the outcome variable and the two lagged series (at lag-1 and 2 in this example) as the predictors. However, it is better to use designated ARIMA estimation methods (e.g., those available in R's `forecast` package) over ordinary linear regression estimation, to produce more accurate results.[4] Although moving from AR to ARIMA models creates a larger set of more flexible forecasting models, it also requires much more statistical expertise. Even with the simpler AR models, fitting them to raw time series that contain patterns such as trends and seasonality requires the user to perform several initial data transformations and to choose the order of the model. These are not straightforward tasks. Because ARIMA modeling is less robust and requires more experience and statistical expertise than other methods, we do not discuss it here and direct the interested reader to classic time series textbooks (e.g., see chapter 4 in Chatfield, 2003).

However, we do discuss one particular use of AR models that is straightforward to apply in the context of forecasting, which can provide a significant improvement to short-term forecasts. This relates to the second approach for utilizing autocorrelation, which requires constructing a second-level forecasting model for the residuals, as follows:

1. Generate a k-step-ahead forecast of the series (F_{t+k}), using any forecasting method

2. Generate a k-step-ahead forecast of the forecast error (residual) (E_{t+k}), using an AR (or other) model

---

[4] ARIMA model estimation differs from ordinary regression estimation by accounting for the dependence between records.

3. Improve the initial k-step-ahead forecast of the series by adjusting it according to its forecasted error: *Improved* $F^*_{t+k} = F_{t+k} + E_{t+k}$.

In particular, we can fit low-order AR models to series of residuals (or *forecast errors*) which can then be used to forecast future forecast errors. By fitting the series of residuals, rather than the raw series, we avoid the need for initial data transformations (because the residual series is not expected to contain any trends or cyclical behavior besides autocorrelation).

To fit an AR model to the series of residuals, we first examine the autocorrelations of the residual series. We then choose the order of the AR model according to the lags in which autocorrelation appears. Often, when autocorrelation exists at lag-1 and higher, it is sufficient to fit an AR(1) model of the form

$$E_t = \beta_0 + \beta_1 E_{t-1} + \epsilon \tag{18.2}$$

where E_t denotes the residual (or *forecast error*) at time t. For example, although the autocorrelations in Figure 18.8 appear large from lags 1 to 10 or so, it is likely that an AR(1) would capture all of these relationships. The reason is that if immediate neighboring values are correlated, then the relationship propagates to values that are two periods away, then three periods away, etc.[5]

The result of fitting an AR(1) model to the Amtrak ridership residual series is shown in Table 18.7. The AR(1) coefficient (0.5998) is close to the lag-1 autocorrelation (0.6041) that we found earlier (Figure 18.8). The forecasted residual for April 2001 is computed by plugging in the most recent residual from March 2001 (equal to 12.108) into the AR(1) model[6]:

$$0.3728491 + (0.5997814)(12.108 - 0.3728491) = 7.411.$$

You can obtain this number directly by using the *forecast()* function (see output in Table 18.7). The positive value tells us that the regression model will produce a ridership forecast for April 2001 that is too low and that we should adjust it up by adding 7411 riders. In this particular example, the regression model (with quadratic trend and seasonality) produced a forecast of 2,004,271 riders, and the improved two-stage model [regression + AR(1) correction] corrected it by increasing it to 2,011,906 riders. The actual value for April 2001 turned out to be 2,023,792 riders—much closer to the improved forecast.

From the plot of the actual vs. forecasted residual series (Figure 18.9), we can see that the AR(1) model fits the residual series quite well. Note, however, that

---

[5] *Partial autocorrelations* (use function *Pacf()*) measure the contribution of each lag series *over and above* smaller lags. For example, the lag-2 partial autocorrelation is the contribution of lag-2 beyond that of lag-1.

[6] The *mean* in the Coefficients table resulting from function *Arima()* is the estimated mean of the series. To get a forecast, we must subtract this mean from our value. In this case, we have $F_{t+1} = \text{mean} + \text{slope } (y_t - \text{mean})$.

TABLE 18.7   OUTPUT FOR AR(1) MODEL ON RIDERSHIP RESIDUALS

 code for running AR(1) model on residuals

```
# fit linear regression with quadratic trend and seasonality to Ridership
train.lm.trend.season <- tslm(train.ts ~ trend + I(trend^2) + season)

# fit AR(1) model to training residuals
# use Arima() in the forecast package to fit an ARIMA model
# (that includes AR models); order = c(1,0,0) gives an AR(1).
train.res.arima <- Arima(train.lm.trend.season$residuals, order = c(1,0,0))
test.res.arima.pred <- forecast(train.res.arima, h = 1)
```

Output

```
> summary(train.res.arima)
Series: train.lm.trend.season$residuals
ARIMA(1,0,0) with non-zero mean

Coefficients:
         ar1      mean
      0.5998    0.3728
s.e.  0.0712   11.8408

sigma^2 = 2876:  log likelihood = -663.54
AIC=1333.08   AICc=1333.29   BIC=1341.52

Training set error measures:
                       ME     RMSE     MAE       MPE      MAPE      MASE        ACF1
Training set -0.1223159 53.19141 39.8277 103.3885 175.2219 0.5721356 -0.07509305

> test.res.arima.pred
         Point Forecast   Lo 80    Hi 80      Lo 95     Hi 95
Apr 2001        7.41111 -61.31748 76.1397  -97.70019 112.5224
```

the plot is based on the training data (until March 2001). To evaluate predictive performance of the two-level model [regression + AR(1)], we would have to examine performance (e.g., via MAPE or RMSE metrics) on the test data, in a fashion similar to the calculation that we performed for April 2001.

Finally, to examine whether we have indeed accounted for the autocorrelation in the series and that no more information remains in the series, we examine the autocorrelations of the series of residuals-of-residuals (the residuals obtained after the AR(1), which was applied to the regression residuals). This is seen in Figure 18.10. It is clear that no more autocorrelation remains and that the addition of the AR(1) model has captured the autocorrelation information adequately.

We mentioned earlier that improving forecasts via an additional AR layer is useful for short-term forecasting. The reason is that an AR model of order k will usually only provide useful forecasts for the next k periods, and after that

code for creating Figure 18.9

```
autoplot(train.lm.trend.season$residuals, xlab="Time", ylab="Residuals", color=colData) +
    autolayer(test.res.arima.pred$fitted, color=colModel, size=0.75)
```

FIGURE 18.9   FITTING AN AR(1) MODEL TO THE RESIDUAL SERIES FROM FIGURE 18.6

FIGURE 18.10   AUTOCORRELATIONS OF RESIDUALS-OF-RESIDUALS SERIES

forecasts will rely on earlier forecasts rather than on actual data. For example, to forecast the residual of May 2001 when the time of prediction is March 2001, we would need the residual for April 2001. However, because that value is not available, it would be replaced by its forecast. Hence, the forecast for May 2001 would be based on the forecast for April 2001.

Evaluating Predictability

Before attempting to forecast a time series, it is important to determine whether it is predictable, in the sense that its past can be used to predict its future beyond the naive forecast. One useful way to assess predictability is to test whether the series is a *random walk*. A random walk is a series in which changes from one time period to the next are random. According to the efficient market hypothesis in economics, asset prices are random walks, and therefore predicting stock prices is a game of chance.[7]

A random walk is a special case of an AR(1) model, where the slope coefficient is equal to 1:

$$Y_t = \beta_0 + Y_{t-1} + \epsilon_t. \tag{18.3}$$

We can also write this as

$$Y_t - Y_{t-1} = \beta_0 + \epsilon_t. \tag{18.4}$$

We see from the last equation that the difference between the values at periods $t-1$ and t is random, hence the term "random walk." Forecasts from such a model are basically equal to the most recent observed value (the naive forecast), reflecting the lack of any other information.

Testing whether a series is a random walk is equivalent to testing whether the lag-1 differenced series $Y_t - Y_{t-1}$ ($t = 2, 3, \ldots$) behaves like a random series. The latter can be done by examining the autocorrelations of the differenced series: if all autocorrelation values are close to zero, then the original series is likely a random walk.

As an example, consider the series of S&P500 monthly closing prices between May 1995 and August 2003 shown in Figure 18.11 (dataset *mlba::SP500*). The autocorrelation plot of the lag-1 differenced closing prices series is shown in Table 18.8. We see that all autocorrelation values are practically zero, indicating that the closing prices series is a random walk.

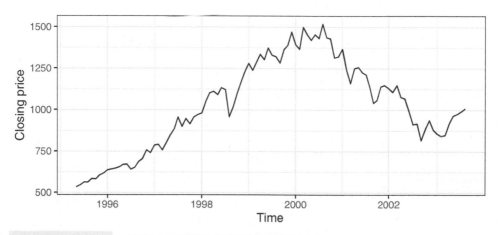

FIGURE 18.11   **S&P500 MONTHLY CLOSING PRICES SERIES**

---

[7]There is some controversy surrounding the efficient market hypothesis, with claims that there is slight autocorrelation in asset prices, which does make them predictable to some extent. However, transaction costs and bid–ask spreads tend to offset any prediction benefits.

TABLE 18.8	COMPUTING AUTOCORRELATIONS OF LAG-1 DIFFERENCED S&P500 MONTHLY CLOSING PRICES

 code for calculating autocorrelations of a lag-1 differenced time series

```
sp500.df <- mlba::SP500
sp500.ts <- ts(sp500.df$Close, start = c(1995, 5), end = c(2003, 8), freq = 12)
delta <- sp500.ts[2:length(sp500.ts)] - sp500.ts[1:length(sp500.ts)-1]
ggAcf(delta, lag.max=12, main="")
```

Another approach for evaluating whether the above S&P series is a random walk is to use an AR(1) model. The AR(1) model fitted to the series of S&P500 monthly closing prices is shown in Table 18.9. Here the slope coefficient is 0.9833, with a standard error of 0.0145. The coefficient is sufficiently close to 1 (around one standard error away), indicating—as we found by looking at the differenced series' ACF—that this is a random walk. Forecasting this series using any of the methods described earlier (aside from the naive forecast) is therefore futile.

TABLE 18.9	OUTPUT FOR AR(1) MODEL ON S&P500 MONTHLY CLOSING PRICES

```
> sp500.df <- mlba::SP500
> sp500.ts <- ts(sp500.df$Close, start = c(1995, 5), end = c(2003, 8), freq = 12)
> sp500.arima <- Arima(sp500.ts, order = c(1,0,0))
> sp500.arima
Series: sp500.ts
ARIMA(1,0,0) with non-zero mean

Coefficients:
         ar1      mean
      0.9833  890.0707
s.e.  0.0145  221.0280

sigma^2 = 2833:  log likelihood = -540.05
AIC=1086.1   AICc=1086.35   BIC=1093.92
```

PROBLEMS

18.1 **Impact of September 11 on Air Travel in the United States.** The Research and Innovative Technology Administration's Bureau of Transportation Statistics conducted a study to evaluate the impact of the September 11, 2001 terrorist attack on US transportation. The 2006 study report and the data can be found at bts.gov/archive/publications/estimated_impacts_of_9_11_on_us_travel/index. The goal of the study was stated as follows:

> The purpose of this study is to provide a greater understanding of the passenger travel behavior patterns of persons making long distance trips before and after 9/11.

The report analyzes monthly passenger movement data between January 1990 and May 2004. Data on three monthly time series are given in dataset *mlba::Sept11Travel* for this period: (1) actual airline revenue passenger miles (Air), (2) rail passenger miles (Rail), and (3) vehicle miles traveled (Car).

To assess the impact of September 11, the Bureau of Transportation Statistics took the following approach: using data before September 11, they forecasted future data (under the assumption of no terrorist attack). Then, they compared the forecasted series with the actual data to assess the impact of the event. Our first step, therefore, is to split each of the time series into two parts: pre- and post-September 11. We now concentrate only on the earlier time series.

a. Plot the pre-event AIR time series. What time series components appear?

b. Figure 18.12 shows a time plot of the **seasonally adjusted** pre–September-11 AIR series. Which of the following methods would be adequate for forecasting the series shown in the figure?

- Linear regression model seasonality
- Linear regression model with trend
- Linear regression model with trend and seasonality

c. Specify a linear regression model for the AIR series that would produce a seasonally adjusted series similar to the one shown in Figure 18.12, with multiplicative seasonality. What is the outcome variable? What are the predictors?

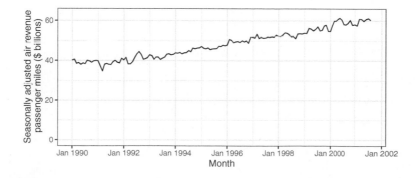

FIGURE 18.12   SEASONALLY ADJUSTED PRE-SEPTEMBER-11 AIR SERIES

d. Run the regression model from (c). Remember to use only pre-event data.

   i. What can we learn from the statistical insignificance of the coefficients for October and September?

   ii. The actual value of AIR (air revenue passenger miles) in January 1990 was 35.153577 billion. What is the residual for this month, using the regression model? Report the residual in terms of air revenue passenger miles.

e. Create an ACF (autocorrelation) plot of the regression residuals.

   i. What does the ACF plot tell us about the regression model's forecasts?

   ii. How can this information be used to improve the model?

f. Fit linear regression models to Air, Rail, and Auto with additive seasonality and an appropriate trend. For Air and Rail, fit a linear trend. For Rail, use a quadratic trend. Remember to use only pre-event data. Once the models are estimated, use them to forecast each of the three post-event series.

   i. For each series (Air, Rail, Auto), plot the complete pre-event and post-event actual series overlaid with the predicted series.

   ii. What can be said about the effect of the September 11 terrorist attack on the three modes of transportation? Discuss the magnitude of the effect, its time span, and any other relevant aspects.

18.2 **Analysis of Canadian Manufacturing Workers, Workhours.** The time plot in Figure 18.13 describes the average annual number of weekly hours spent by Canadian manufacturing workers (data are available in the dataset *mlba::CanadianWorkHours*, data courtesy of Ken Black).

a. Which of the following regression models would fit the series best? (Choose one.)

- Linear trend model
- Linear trend model with seasonality
- Quadratic trend model
- Quadratic trend model with seasonality

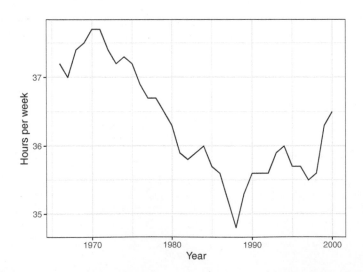

FIGURE 18.13   AVERAGE ANNUAL WEEKLY HOURS SPENT BY CANADIAN MANUFACTURING WORKERS

b. If we computed the autocorrelation of this series, would the lag-1 autocorrelation exhibit negative, positive, or no autocorrelation? How can you see this from the plot?

c. Compute the autocorrelation of the series and produce an ACF plot. Verify your answer to the previous question.

18.3 Toys "R" Us Revenues. Figure 18.14 is a time plot of the quarterly revenues of Toys "R" Us between 1992 and 1995 (thanks to Chris Albright for suggesting the use of these data, which are available in the dataset *mlba::ToysRUsRevenues*).

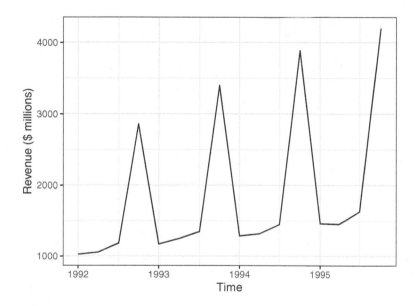

FIGURE 18.14   QUARTERLY REVENUES OF TOYS "R" US, 1992–1995

a. Fit a regression model with a linear trend and additive seasonality. Use the entire series (excluding the last two quarters) as the training set.

b. A partial output of the regression model is shown in Table 18.10 (where *season2* is the Quarter 2 dummy). Use this output to answer the following questions:

   i. Which two statistics (and their values) measure how well this model fits the training data?

   ii. Which two statistics (and their values) measure the predictive accuracy of this model?

   iii. After adjusting for trend, what is the average difference between sales in Q3 and sales in Q1?

   iv. After adjusting for seasonality, which quarter (Q_1, Q_2, Q_3, or Q_4) has the highest average sales?

TABLE 18.10	REGRESSION MODEL FITTED TO TOYS "R" US TIME SERIES AND ITS PREDICTIVE PERFORMANCE IN TRAINING AND TEST PERIODS

```
Coefficients:
            Estimate Std. Error t value Pr(>|t|)
(Intercept)   906.75     115.35   7.861 2.55e-05 ***
trend          47.11      11.26   4.185  0.00236 **
season2       -15.11     119.66  -0.126  0.90231
season3        89.17     128.67   0.693  0.50582
season4      2101.73     129.17  16.272 5.55e-08 ***
---
Signif. codes:  0 *** 0.001 ** 0.01 * 0.05 .

                  ME     RMSE      MAE       MPE     MAPE      MASE
Training set  0.0000 135.0795 92.53061 0.1614994 5.006914 0.4342122
Test set    183.1429 313.6820 254.66667 3.0193814 7.404655 1.1950571
```

18.4 **Walmart Stock.** Figure 18.15 shows the series of Walmart daily closing prices between February 2001 and February 2002 (Thanks to Chris Albright for suggesting the use of these data, which are publicly available, for example, at http://finance.yahoo.com and are in the dataset *mlba::WalMartStock*).

a. Compute a lag-1 differenced series of the closing prices. Create a time plot of the differenced series. Note your observations by visually inspecting the differenced series.

b. Fit an AR(1) model to the close price series. Report the coefficient table.

FIGURE 18.15   DAILY CLOSE PRICE OF WALMART STOCK, FEBRUARY 2001–2002

c. Which of the following is/are relevant for testing whether this stock is a random walk?

- The autocorrelations of the close prices series
- The autocorrelations of the lag-1 differenced close prices series
- The AR(1) slope coefficient
- The AR(1) constant coefficient

d. Use the relevant information from Figure 18.16 to decide whether this is a random walk. Explain how you reached your conclusion and based on which statistics and/or plots.

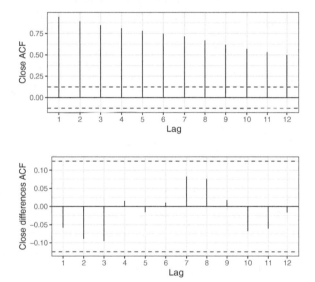

FIGURE 18.16   (TOP) AUTOCORRELATIONS OF WALMART STOCK PRICES AND (BOTTOM) AUTOCORRELATIONS OF LAG-1 DIFFERENCED WALMART STOCK PRICES

e. Does the AR model indicate that this is a random walk? Explain how you reached your conclusion.

f. What are the implications of finding that a time series is a random walk? Choose the correct statement(s) below.

- It is impossible to obtain forecasts that are more accurate than naive forecasts for the series.
- The series is random.
- The changes in the series from one period to the next are random.

18.5 Department Store Sales. The time plot in Figure 18.17 describes actual quarterly sales for a department store over a 6-year period (data are available in dataset *mlba::DepartmentStoreSales*, data courtesy of Chris Albright).

a. The forecaster decided that there is an exponential trend in the series. In order to fit a regression-based model that accounts for this trend, which of the following operations must be performed?

FIGURE 18.17   DEPARTMENT STORE QUARTERLY SALES SERIES

- Take log of quarter index.
- Take log of sales.
- Take an exponent of sales.
- Take an exponent of quarter index.

b. Fit a regression model with an exponential trend and seasonality, using the first 20 quarters as the training data (remember to first partition the series into training and test series).

c. A partial output is shown in Table 18.11. From the output, after adjusting for trend, are Q2 average sales higher, lower, or approximately equal to the average Q1 sales?

TABLE 18.11   OUTPUT FROM REGRESSION MODEL FIT TO DEPARTMENT STORE SALES IN THE TRAINING PERIOD

```
> summary(tslm(sales.ts ~ trend + season, lambda=0))

Coefficients:
            Estimate Std. Error t value Pr(>|t|)
(Intercept) 10.748945   0.018725 574.057  < 2e-16 ***
trend        0.011088   0.001295   8.561 3.70e-07 ***
season2      0.024956   0.020764   1.202    0.248
season3      0.165343   0.020884   7.917 9.79e-07 ***
season4      0.433746   0.021084  20.572 2.10e-12 ***
---
Signif. codes:  0 *** 0.001 ** 0.01 * 0.05 .
```

d. Use this model to forecast sales in Q21 and Q22.

e. The plots in Figure 18.18 describe the fit (top) and forecast errors (bottom) from this regression model.

   i. Recreate these plots.

   ii. Based on these plots, what can you say about your forecasts for Q21 and Q22? Are they likely to over-forecast, under-forecast, or be reasonably close to the real sales values?

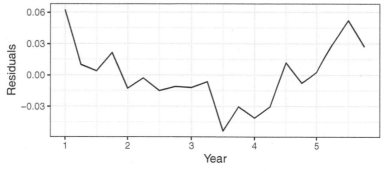

FIGURE 18.18   **FIT OF REGRESSION MODEL FOR DEPARTMENT STORE SALES**

f. From the forecast errors plot, which of the following statements appear true?

- Seasonality is not captured well

- The regression model fits the data well

- The trend in the data is not captured well by the model

g. Which of the following solutions is adequate *and* a parsimonious solution for improving model fit?

- Fit a quadratic trend model to the residuals (with Quarter and Quarter^2).

- Fit an AR model to the residuals.

- Fit a quadratic trend model to Sales (with Quarter and Quarter^2).

18.6   Souvenir Sales. Figure 18.19 shows a time plot of monthly sales for a souvenir shop at a beach resort town in Queensland, Australia, between 1995 and 2001. [Data are available in *mlba::SouvenirSales*, Source: Hyndman and Yang (2018).] The series is presented twice, in Australian dollars and in log scale. Back in 2001, the store wanted to use the data to forecast sales for the next 12 months (year 2002). They hired an analyst to generate forecasts. The analyst first partitioned the data into training and test sets, with the test set containing the last 12 months of data (year 2001). She then fit a regression model to sales, using the training set.

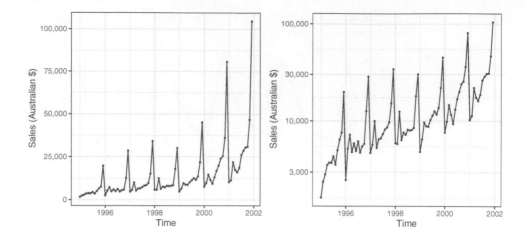

FIGURE 18.19   **MONTHLY SALES AT AUSTRALIAN SOUVENIR SHOP IN DOLLARS (TOP) AND IN LOG SCALE (BOTTOM)**

a. Based on the two time plots, which predictors should be included in the regression model? What is the total number of predictors in the model?

b. Run a regression model with Sales (in Australian dollars) as the outcome variable and with a linear trend and monthly seasonality. Remember to fit only the training data. Call this model A.

    i. Examine the estimated coefficients: which month tends to have the highest average sales during the year? Why is this reasonable?

    ii. The estimated trend coefficient in model A is 245.36. What does this mean?

c. Run a regression model with an exponential trend and multiplicative seasonality. Remember to fit only the training data. Call this model B.

    i. Fitting a model to log(Sales) with a linear trend is equivalent to fitting a model to Sales (in dollars) with what type of trend?

    ii. The estimated trend coefficient in model B is 0.02. What does this mean?

    iii. Use this model to forecast the sales in February 2002.

d. Compare the two regression models (A and B) in terms of forecast performance. Which model is preferable for forecasting? Mention at least two reasons based on the information in the outputs.

e. Continuing with model B, create an ACF plot until lag-15 for the full series of forecast errors (without partitioning into training/test). Now fit an AR model with lag-2 [ARIMA(2,0,0)] to this series of forecast errors. We will use this model to improve the forecast for January 2002.

    i. Examining the ACF plot and the estimated coefficients of the AR(2) model (and their statistical significance), what can we learn about the forecasts that result from model B?

    ii. Use the autocorrelation information to compute an improved forecast for January 2002, using model B and the AR(2) model above.

f. How would you model these data differently if the goal was to understand the different components of sales in the souvenir shop between 1995 and 2001? Mention two differences.

18.7 **Shipments of Household Appliances.** The time plot in Figure 18.20 shows the series of quarterly shipments (in million dollars) of US household appliances between 1985 and 1989 (data are available in *mlba::ApplianceShipments*, data courtesy of Ken Black). If we compute the autocorrelation of the series, which lag (> 0) is most likely to have the largest coefficient (in absolute value)? Create an ACF plot and compare with your answer.

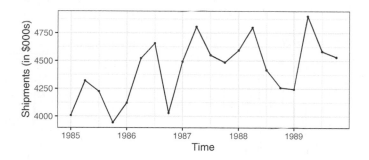

FIGURE 18.20   QUARTERLY SHIPMENTS OF US HOUSEHOLD APPLIANCES OVER 5 YEARS

18.8 **Australian Wine Sales.** Figure 18.21 shows time plots of monthly sales of six types of Australian wines (red, rose, sweet white, dry white, sparkling, and fortified) for 1980–1994. [Data are available in *mlba::AustralianWines*, Source: Hyndman and Yang (2018).] The units are thousands of litres. You are hired to obtain short term forecasts (2–3 months ahead) for each of the six series, and this task will be repeated every month.

a. Which forecasting method would you choose if you had to choose the same method for all series? Why?

b. Fortified wine has the largest market share of the above six types of wine. You are asked to focus on fortified wine sales alone and produce as accurate as possible forecasts for the next 2 months.

 • First partition the data: use the period until December 1993 as the training set.

 • Fit a regression model to sales with a linear trend and additive seasonality.

   i. Create the "actual vs. forecast" plot. What can you say about the model fit?

   ii. Use the regression model to forecast sales in January and February 1994.

c. Create an ACF plot for the training residuals from the above model until lag-12. Examining this plot (only), which of the following statements are reasonable conclusions?

 • Decembers (month 12) are not captured well by the model.

 • There is a strong correlation between sales on the same calendar month.

 • The model does not capture the seasonality well.

 • We should try to fit an AR model with lag-12 to the residuals.

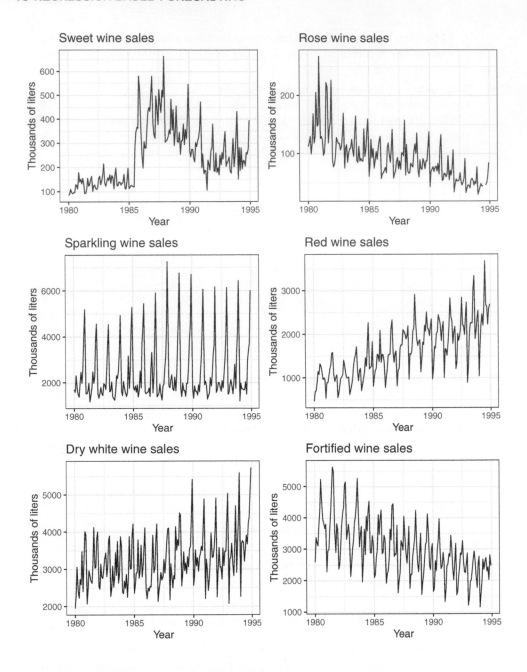

FIGURE 18.21   **MONTHLY SALES OF SIX TYPES OF AUSTRALIAN WINES BETWEEN 1980 AND 1994**

## CHAPTER 19

Smoothing and Deep Learning Methods for Forecasting

In this chapter, we describe a set of popular and flexible methods for forecasting time series that rely on *smoothing*. Smoothing is based on averaging over multiple periods in order to reduce the noise. We start with two simple smoothers, the *moving average* and *simple exponential smoother*, which are suitable for forecasting series that contain no trend or seasonality. In both cases, forecasts are averages of previous values of the series (the length of the series history considered and the weights used in the averaging differ between the methods). We also show how a moving average can be used, with a slight adaptation, for data visualization. We then proceed to describe smoothing methods suitable for forecasting series with a trend and/or seasonality. Smoothing methods are data-driven and are able to adapt to changes in the series over time. Although highly automated, the user must specify *smoothing constants* that determine how fast the method adapts to new data. We discuss the choice of such constants and their meaning. We then describe basic deep learning methods suitable for forecasting time series: recurrent neural networks (RNN) and Long Short-Term Memory (LSTM) networks. The different methods are illustrated using the Amtrak ridership series.

Smoothing and Deep Learning Methods in R

In this chapter, we use the `forecast` package for the smoothing methods. For the deep learning methods, we use the `keras` package.

19.1 SMOOTHING METHODS: INTRODUCTION[1]

A second class of methods for time series forecasting is *smoothing methods*. Unlike regression models, which rely on an underlying theoretical model for the components of a time series (e.g., linear or quadratic trend), smoothing methods are data-driven, in the sense that they estimate time series components directly from the data without assuming a predetermined structure. Data-driven methods are especially useful in series where patterns change over time. Smoothing methods "smooth" out the noise in a series in an attempt to uncover the patterns. Smoothing is done by averaging the series over multiple periods, where different smoothers differ by the number of periods averaged, how the average is computed, how many times averaging is performed, and so on. We now describe two types of smoothing methods that are popular in business applications due to their simplicity and adaptability. These are the moving average method and exponential smoothing.

19.2 MOVING AVERAGE

The moving average is a simple smoother: it consists of averaging values across a window of consecutive periods, thereby generating a series of averages. A moving average with window width w means averaging across each set of w consecutive values, where w is determined by the user.

In general, there are two types of moving averages: a *centered moving average* and a *trailing moving average*. Centered moving averages are powerful for visualizing trends, because the averaging operation can suppress seasonality and noise, thereby making the trend more visible. In contrast, trailing moving averages are useful for forecasting. The difference between the two is in terms of the window's location on the time series.

Centered Moving Average for Visualization

In a centered moving average, the value of the moving average at time t (MA_t) is computed by centering the window around time t and averaging across the w values within the window:

$$\mathrm{MA}_t = \left(Y_{t-(w-1)/2} + \cdots + Y_{t-1} + Y_t + Y_{t+1} + \cdots + Y_{t+(w-1)/2}\right)/w.$$
(19.1)

For example, with a window of width $w = 5$, the moving average at time point $t = 3$ means averaging the values of the series at time points $1, 2, 3, 4, 5$; at

---

[1]This and subsequent sections in this chapter copyright © 2019 Datastats, LLC, and Galit Shmueli. Used by permission.

Centered window ($w = 5$)

$t - 2 \quad t - 1 \quad t \quad t + 1 \quad t + 2$

Trailing window ($w = 5$)

$t - 4 \quad t - 3 \quad t - 2 \quad t - 1 \quad t$

FIGURE 19.1   SCHEMATIC OF CENTERED MOVING AVERAGE (TOP) AND TRAILING MOVING AVERAGE (BOTTOM), BOTH WITH WINDOW WIDTH $w = 5$

time point $t = 4$, the moving average is the average of the series at time points $2, 3, 4, 5, 6$, and so on.[2] This is illustrated in the top panel of Figure 19.1.

Choosing the window width in a seasonal series is straightforward: because the goal is to suppress seasonality for better visualizing the trend, the default choice should be the length of a seasonal cycle. Returning to the Amtrak ridership data, the annual seasonality indicates a choice of $w = 12$. Figure 19.2 shows a centered moving average line (green line) overlaid on the original series. We can see a global U shape, but unlike the regression model that fits a strict U-shape, the moving average shows some deviation, such as the slight dip during the last year.

Trailing Moving Average for Forecasting

Centered moving averages are computed by averaging across data in the past and the future of a given time point. In that sense, they cannot be used for forecasting because at the time of forecasting, the future is typically unknown. Hence, for purposes of forecasting, we use *trailing moving averages*, where the window of width w is set on the most recent available w values of the series. The k-step-ahead forecast F_{t+k} ($k = 1, 2, 3, \ldots$) is then the average of these w values (see also bottom plot in Figure 19.1):

$$F_{t+k} = \left(Y_t + Y_{t-1} + \cdots + Y_{t-w+1} \right) / w.$$

For example, in the Amtrak ridership series, to forecast ridership in February 1992 or later months, given information until January 1992 and using a moving average with window width $w = 12$, we would take the average ridership during the most recent 12 months (February 1991 to January 1992). Figure 19.2 (orange line) shows a trailing moving average line overlaid on the original series.

Next, we illustrate a 12-month moving average forecaster for the Amtrak ridership. We partition the Amtrak ridership time series, leaving the last 36

---

[2]For an even window width, for example, $w = 4$, we can obtain the moving average at time point $t = 3$ by averaging across two windows: across time points $1, 2, 3, 4$ and across time points $2, 3, 4, 5$. The average of the two averages is the final moving average.

code for creating Figure 19.2

```
library(zoo)
library(forecast)

# centered moving average with window order = 12
ma.centered <- ma(ridership.ts, order = 12)

# trailing moving average with window k = 12
# in rollmean(), use argument align = right to calculate a trailing moving average.
ma.trailing <- rollmean(ridership.ts, k = 12, align = "right")

# generate a plot
colData <- "steelblue"; colModel <- "tomato"
autoplot(ridership.ts, ylab="Ridership", color=colData) +
  autolayer(ma.centered, series="Centered", size=1.1) +
  autolayer(ma.trailing, series="Trailing", size=1.1) +
  scale_color_manual(name="Moving average", values=c("forestgreen", colModel))
```

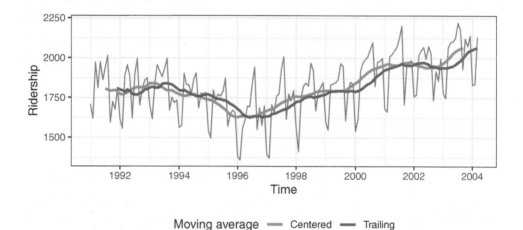

FIGURE 19.2   CENTERED MOVING AVERAGE (GREEN LINE) AND TRAILING MOVING AVERAGE (ORANGE LINE) WITH WINDOW $w = 12$, OVERLAID ON AMTRAK RIDERSHIP SERIES

months as the test (holdout) period. Applying a moving average forecaster with window $w = 12$, we obtained the output shown in Figure 19.3. Note that for the first 12 records of the training period, there is no forecast (because there are less than 12 past values to average). Also, note that the forecasts for all months in the test period are identical (1938.481) because the method assumes that information is known only until March 2001.

In this example, it is clear that the moving average forecaster is inadequate for generating monthly forecasts because it does not capture the seasonality in the data. Seasons with high ridership are under-forecasted, and seasons with

code for creating Figure 19.3

```
# Code for data partitioning is given in Figure 17.4

# moving average on training with window of size 12
ma.trailing <- rollmean(train.ts, k=12, align="right")

# obtain the last moving average in the training period
last.ma <- tail(ma.trailing, 1)

# create forecast based on last MA
ma.trailing.pred <- ts(rep(last.ma, nTest), start=c(1991, nTrain + 1),
    end=c(1991, nTrain + nTest), freq=12)

# plot the series
autoplot(train.ts, ylab="Ridership", color=colData) +
  autolayer(test.ts, color=colData, linetype=2) +
  autolayer(ma.trailing, color=colModel, size=0.75) +
  autolayer(ma.trailing.pred, color=colModel, size=0.75)
```

FIGURE 19.3   TRAILING MOVING AVERAGE FORECASTER WITH $w = 12$ APPLIED TO AMTRAK RIDERSHIP SERIES

low ridership are over-forecasted. A similar issue arises when forecasting a series with a trend: the moving average "lags behind," thereby under-forecasting in the presence of an increasing trend and over-forecasting in the presence of a decreasing trend. This "lagging behind" of the trailing moving average can also be seen in Figure 19.2.

In general, the moving average should be used for forecasting *only in series that lack seasonality and trend.* Such a limitation might seem impractical. However, there are a few popular methods for removing trends (de-trending) and removing seasonality (de-seasonalizing) from a series, such as regression models. The moving average can then be used to forecast such de-trended and de-seasonalized series, and then the trend and seasonality can be added back to the forecast. For example, consider the regression model shown in Figure 18.6 in Chapter 18, which yields residuals devoid of seasonality and trend (see bottom chart). We can apply a moving average forecaster to that series of residuals (also called forecast errors), thereby creating a forecast for the next *forecast error*. For example, to forecast ridership in April 2001 (the first period in the test set), assuming that we have information until March 2001, we use the regression model in Table 18.5 to generate a forecast for April 2001 (which yields 2004.271 thousand riders). We then use a 12-month moving average (using the period April 2000 to March 2001) to forecast the *forecast error* for April 2001, which yields 30.781 (manually, or using R, as shown in Table 19.1). The positive value implies that the regression model's forecast for April 2001 is too low, and therefore we should adjust it by adding approximately 31 thousand riders to the regression model's forecast of 2004.271 thousand riders.

TABLE 19.1	APPLYING MA TO THE RESIDUALS FROM THE REGRESSION MODEL (WHICH LACK TREND AND SEASONALITY), TO FORECAST THE APRIL 2001 RESIDUAL

 code for applying moving average to residuals

```
# fit regression model with trend and seasonality
train.lm.trend.season <- tslm(train.ts ~ trend + I(trend^2) + season)

# create single-point forecast
train.lm.trend.season.pred <- forecast(train.lm.trend.season, h = 1, level = 0)

# apply MA to residuals
ma.trailing <- rollmean(train.lm.trend.season$residuals, k = 12, align = "right")
last.ma <- tail(ma.trailing, 1)
```

Output

```
> train.lm.trend.season.pred
         Point Forecast    Lo 0     Hi 0
Apr 2001      2004.271 2004.271 2004.271
> last.ma
[1] 30.78068
```

Choosing Window Width (w)

With moving average forecasting or visualization, the only choice that the user must make is the width of the window (w). As with other methods such as k-nearest neighbors, the choice of the smoothing parameter is a balance between under-smoothing and over-smoothing. For visualization (using a centered window), wider windows will expose more global trends, while narrow windows will reveal local trends. Hence, examining several window widths is useful for exploring trends of differing local/global nature. For forecasting (using a trailing window), the choice should incorporate domain knowledge in terms of relevance of past values and how fast the series changes. Empirical predictive evaluation can also be done by experimenting with different values of w and comparing performance. However, care should be taken not to overfit!

19.3 SIMPLE EXPONENTIAL SMOOTHING

A popular forecasting method in business is exponential smoothing. Its popularity derives from its flexibility, ease of automation, cheap computation, and good performance. Simple exponential smoothing is similar to forecasting with a moving average, except that instead of taking a simple average over the w most recent values, we take a *weighted average* of *all* past values, such that the weights decrease exponentially into the past. The idea is to give more weight to recent information, yet not to completely ignore older information.

Like the moving average, simple exponential smoothing should only be used for forecasting *series that have no trend or seasonality*. As mentioned earlier, such series can be obtained by removing trend and/or seasonality from raw series and then applying exponential smoothing to the series of residuals (which are assumed to contain no trend or seasonality).

The exponential smoother generates a forecast at time $t+1$ (F_{t+1}) as follows:

$$F_{t+1} = \alpha Y_t + \alpha(1-\alpha)Y_{t-1} + \alpha(1-\alpha)^2 Y_{t-2} + \cdots, \qquad (19.2)$$

where α is a constant between 0 and 1 called the *smoothing parameter*. The above formulation displays the exponential smoother as a weighted average of all past observations, with exponentially decaying weights.

It turns out that we can write the exponential forecaster in another way, which is very useful in practice:

$$F_{t+1} = F_t + \alpha E_t, \qquad (19.3)$$

where E_t is the forecast error at time t. This formulation presents the exponential forecaster as an "active learner": it looks at the previous forecast (F_t) and how far it was from the actual value (E_t) and then corrects the next forecast based on that information. If in one period the forecast was too high, the next period is adjusted down. The amount of correction depends on the value of the smoothing parameter α. The formulation in (19.3) is also advantageous in terms of data storage and computation time: it means that we need to store and use only the forecast and forecast error from the most recent period, rather than the entire series. In applications where real-time forecasting is done, or many series are being forecasted in parallel and continuously, such savings are critical.

Note that forecasting further into the future yields the same forecast as a one-step-ahead forecast. Because the series is assumed to lack trend and seasonality, forecasts into the future rely only on information until the time of prediction. Hence, the k-step-ahead forecast is equal to

$$F_{t+k} = F_{t+1}.$$

Choosing Smoothing Parameter α

The smoothing parameter α, which is set by the user, determines the rate of learning. A value close to 1 indicates fast learning (that is, only the most recent values have influence on forecasts), whereas a value close to 0 indicates slow learning (past values have a large influence on forecasts). This can be seen by plugging 0 or 1 into Equation (19.2) or (19.3). Hence, the choice of α depends on the required amount of smoothing and on how relevant the history is for generating forecasts. Default values that have been shown to work well are around 0.1–0.2. Some trial and error can also help in the choice of α: examine the time plot of the actual and predicted series, as well as the predictive accuracy (e.g., MAPE or RMSE of the test set). Finding the α value that optimizes predictive accuracy on the test set can be used to determine the degree of local vs. global nature of the trend. However, beware of choosing the "'best α" for forecasting purposes, as this will most likely lead to model overfitting and low predictive accuracy on future data.

To illustrate forecasting with simple exponential smoothing, we return to the residuals from the regression model, which are assumed to contain no trend or seasonality. To forecast the residual on April 2001, we apply exponential smoothing to the entire period until March 2001 and use the default $\alpha = 0.2$ value. The forecasts of this model are shown in Figure 19.4. The forecast for the residual (the horizontal broken line) is 14.143 (in thousands of riders), implying that we should adjust the regression's forecast by adding 14,143 riders to that forecast.

Relation Between Moving Average and Simple Exponential Smoothing

In both smoothing methods, the user must specify a single parameter: in moving averages, the window width (w) must be set; in exponential smoothing, the smoothing parameter (α) must be set. In both cases, the parameter determines the importance of fresh information over older information. In fact, the two smoothers are approximately equal if the window width of the moving average is equal to $w = 2/\alpha - 1$.

code for creating Figure 19.4

```
# get residuals
residuals.ts <- train.lm.trend.season$residuals

# run simple exponential smoothing
# use ets() with model = "ANN" (additive error (A), no trend (N), no seasonality (N))
# and alpha = 0.2 to fit simple exponential smoothing.
ses <- ets(residuals.ts, model="ANN", alpha=0.2)
ses.pred <- forecast(ses, h=nTest, level=0)

autoplot(residuals.ts, ylab="Residuals", color=colData) +
  autolayer(ses$fitted, color=colModel, size=0.75) +
  autolayer(ses.pred$mean, color=colModel, size=0.75)
```

FIGURE 19.4   OUTPUT FOR SIMPLE EXPONENTIAL SMOOTHING FORECASTER WITH α = 0.2, APPLIED TO THE SERIES OF RESIDUALS FROM THE REGRESSION MODEL (WHICH LACK TREND AND SEASONALITY). THE FORECAST VALUE IS 14.143.

19.4 ADVANCED EXPONENTIAL SMOOTHING

As mentioned earlier, both the moving average and simple exponential smoothing should only be used for forecasting series with no trend or seasonality, series that have only a level and noise. One solution for forecasting series with trend and/or seasonality is first to remove those components (e.g., via regression models). Another solution is to use a more sophisticated version of exponential smoothing, which can capture trend and/or seasonality. In the following, we describe an extension of exponential smoothing that can capture a trend and/or seasonality. These different methods are all available in R's forecast package.

Series with a Trend

For series that contain a trend, we can use Holt's exponential smoothing (or "double exponential smoothing"). Unlike in regression models, the trend shape is not assumed to be global, but rather, it can change over time. In Holt's exponential smoothing, the local trend is estimated from the data and is updated as more data arrive. Similar to simple exponential smoothing, the level of the series is also estimated from the data and is updated as more data arrive. The k-step-ahead forecast is given by combining the level estimate at time t (L_t) and the trend estimate at time t (T_t):

$$F_{t+k} = L_t + kT_t \qquad (19.4)$$

Note that in the presence of a trend, one-, two-, three-step-ahead (etc.), forecasts are no longer identical. The level and trend are updated through a pair of updating equations:

$$L_t = \alpha Y_t + (1 - \alpha)(L_{t-1} + T_{t-1}) \qquad (19.5)$$

$$T_t = \beta (L_t - L_{t-1}) + (1 - \beta)T_{t-1}. \qquad (19.6)$$

The first equation means that the level at time t is a weighted average of the actual value at time t and the level in the previous period, adjusted for trend (in the presence of a trend, moving from one period to the next requires factoring in the trend). The second equation means that the trend at time t is a weighted average of the trend in the previous period and the more recent information on the change in level.[3] Here, there are two smoothing parameters, α and β, which determine the rate of learning. As in simple exponential smoothing, they are both constants in the range [0,1], set by the user, with higher values leading to faster learning (more weight to most recent information).

Series with a Trend and Seasonality

For series that contain both trend and seasonality, the "Holt–Winters exponentials smoothing" method can be used. This is a further extension of double exponential smoothing, where the k-step-ahead forecast also takes into account the seasonality at period $t + k$. Assuming seasonality with M seasons (e.g., for weekly seasonality $M = 7$), the forecast is given by

$$F_{t+k} = (L_t + kT_t) S_{t+k-M} \qquad (19.7)$$

(Note that by the time of forecasting t, the series must have included at least one full cycle of seasons in order to produce forecasts using this formula, that is, $t > M$.)

Being an adaptive method, Holt–Winters exponential smoothing allows the level, trend, and seasonality patterns to change over time. These three

---

[3]There are various ways to estimate the initial values L_1 and T_1, but the differences among these ways usually disappear after a few periods.

components are estimated and updated as more information arrives. The three updating equations are given by

$$L_t \;=\; \alpha Y_t / S_{t-M} + (1-\alpha)(L_{t-1} + T_{t-1}) \qquad (19.8)$$

$$T_t \;=\; \beta\,(L_t - L_{t-1}) + (1-\beta)T_{t-1} \qquad (19.9)$$

$$S_t \;=\; \gamma Y_t / L_t + (1-\gamma)S_{t-M}. \qquad (19.10)$$

The first equation is similar to that in double exponential smoothing, except that it uses the seasonally-adjusted value at time t rather than the raw value. This is done by dividing Y_t by its seasonal index, as estimated in the last cycle. The second equation is identical to double exponential smoothing. The third equation means that the seasonal index is updated by taking a weighted average of the seasonal index from the previous cycle and the current trend-adjusted value. Note that this formulation describes a multiplicative seasonal relationship, where values on different seasons differ by percentage amounts. There is also an additive seasonality version of Holt–Winters exponential smoothing, where seasons differ by a constant amount (for more detail, see Shmueli and Lichtendahl, 2016).

To illustrate forecasting a series with the Holt–Winters method, consider the raw Amtrak ridership data. As we observed earlier, the data contain both a trend and monthly seasonality. Figure 19.5 depicts the fitted and forecasted values. Table 19.2 presents a summary of the model, showing the smoothing parameters; the initial values for the level, trend, and seasonality; and the model performance.

Series with Seasonality (No Trend)

Finally, for series that contain seasonality but no trend, we can use a Holt–Winters exponential smoothing formulation that lacks a trend term, by deleting the trend term in the forecasting equation and updating equations.

EXPONENTIAL SMOOTHING USING ets() IN R

In R, forecasting using exponential smoothing can be done via the *ets()* function in the forecast package. The three letters in *ets* stand for *error*, *trend*, and *seasonality*. Applying this function to a time series will yield forecasts and residuals for both the training and test periods. You can use the default values for the smoothing parameters, set them to other values, or choose to find the optimal values (which optimize AIC—see Chapter 5). We also choose the type of trend, seasonality, and error. The three choices are made in the *method=* argument in the form of a three-letter combination (e.g., "MAA"). The first letter denotes the error type (A, M, or Z); the second letter denotes the trend type (N, A, M, or Z); and the third letter denotes the season type (N, A, M, or Z). In all cases, N = none, A = additive, M = multiplicative, and Z = automatically selected. For example, *method="MAA"* indicates a multiplicative error, additive trend, and additive seasonality.

R code for creating Figure 19.5

```
# run Holt-Winters exponential smoothing
# use ets() with option model = "MAA" to fit Holt-Winters exponential smoothing
# with multiplicative error, additive trend, and additive seasonality.
hwin <- ets(train.ts, model="MAA")
hwin.pred <- forecast(hwin, h=nTest, level=0)

# plot the series
autoplot(train.ts, ylab="Ridership", color=colData) +
  autolayer(test.ts, color=colData, linetype=2) +
  autolayer(hwin$fitted, color=colModel, size=0.75) +
  autolayer(hwin.pred$mean, color=colModel, size=0.75)
```

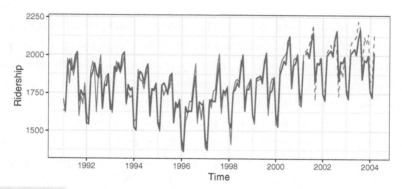

FIGURE 19.5   OUTPUT FOR HOLT–WINTERS EXPONENTIAL SMOOTHING APPLIED TO AMTRAK
RIDERSHIP SERIES

TABLE 19.2   SUMMARY OF HOLT–WINTERS EXPONENTIAL SMOOTHING APPLIED TO THE
AMTRAK RIDERSHIP DATA

```
> hwin
ETS(M,A,A)

Call:
 ets(y = train.ts, model = "MAA")

  Smoothing parameters:
    alpha = 0.5518
    beta  = 1e-04
    gamma = 1e-04

  Initial states:
    l = 1838.577
    b = 0.8081
    s = 28.4454 -11.2187 -0.5337 -124.2766 200.1969 146.8103
          36.5908 76.044 60.153 44.1791 -249.4682 -206.9221

  sigma:  0.0342

     AIC     AICc     BIC
1617.596 1623.424 1665.403

> accuracy(hwin.pred$mean, ridership.ts)
                ME     RMSE      MAE      MPE     MAPE     ACF1 Theil's U
Test set 33.66844 76.65107 62.16977 1.581526 3.122042 0.6165553 0.4430438
```

19.5 DEEP LEARNING FOR FORECASTING

While smoothing-based methods have been successfully used for decades, the data-driven toolkit for forecasting time series has recently been supplemented with deep learning methods. Recurrent neural networks (RNN) are a type of deep learning method suited for temporal data such as time series or other sequential data such as music, text, and speech. Compared with the multi-layer feed-forward network shown in Figure 11.1 in Chapter 11, the RNN has an additional arrow within each hidden layer, as shown in Figure 19.6. This allows the network to "remember" the information it learned in the previous epoch (iteration through the data). In other words, RNNs incorporate a looping mechanism that allows information to flow from one epoch to the next. Here, an epoch means a pass through one subsequence of the series (see below).

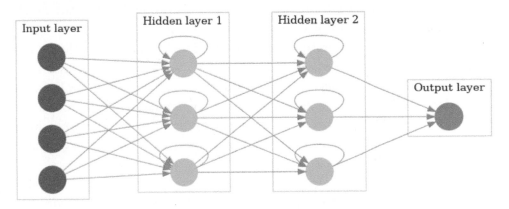

FIGURE 19.6 SCHEMATIC OF RECURRENT NEURAL NETWORK (RNN)

Training an RNN on a time series requires partitioning the training series into a sequence of "rolling windows" (sub-series) of width w. Each sub-series serves as the predictor series and has an associated future period that serves as the label (output variable). For example, for one-step-ahead forecasts, we convert the training series $y_1, y_2, \ldots, y_t$ into the set shown in Table 19.3. These sub-series are then fed into the RNN sequentially (into the input layer in Figure 19.6). The arrow from each hidden node to itself then "remembers" the information learned from the previous sub-series.

A simple RNN, however, suffers from "short-term memory" in the sense that it remembers information from very recent periods, but not from longer

TABLE 19.3	CONVERTING A TIME SERIES OF LENGTH T INTO A SEQUENCE OF SUB-SERIES AND ASSOCIATED ONE-STEP-AHEAD LABELS

Predictor series	Label
$y_1, y_2, \ldots, y_w$	y_{w+1}
$y_2, y_3, \ldots, y_{w+1}$	y_{w+2}
$\vdots$	$\vdots$
$y_{t-w}, \ldots, y_{t-1}$	y_t

history. This results from the so-called vanishing gradient problem. Gradients are values computed to update the neural network weights during backpropagation. The vanishing gradient problem occurs since the gradient updates become small over time, and the earlier layers that receive a small gradient update stop learning. Because these layers don't learn, a simple RNN can forget what it saw much earlier in the sequence, thus having a short-term memory.

To overcome the short-term memory issue, a variant of RNN called Long Short-Term Memory (LSTM) was developed. LSTM adds to each hidden node special mechanisms called *gates* that can regulate the information flow by learning which data in a sequence is important to keep (remember) or throw away (forget). Through this process, it can relay relevant information down the long chain of sequences to make predictions. We set the gate to remember a greater or lesser portion of the old information.

To illustrate forecasting a series with LSTM, consider the Amtrak ridership data. Table 19.4 shows the preparation of the sequence of sub-series with the associated multi-step-ahead labels. This is achieved in a few steps. First, the training data is normalized to 0–1 scale. We define two functions here, one to normalize the time series and the other to transform the data back (de-normalize). The next step is to create the subsequences of length 24 (12 predictor values and one outcome value). This results in 111 subsequences of length 12 as input and associated subsequences of length 1 as output.

Next, we define the architecture and set the parameters for an LSTM model. Table 19.5 shows this process. The architecture consists of a sequence of two LSTM layers followed by a dense linear layer. The first LSTM layers expand the input data to a 12×50 tensor, which is passed into the second LSTM layer. The output of the second LSTM layer is first flattened and then mapped onto a single output value using a dense linear layer. Dropout is used to reduce the risk of overfitting. The model is trained for 400 epochs using mean absolute error

TABLE 19.4   PREPARATION OF TRAINING DATA FOR FORECASTING A SERIES WITH LSTM

 code for preprocessing

```
# define function for normalization of training set and it's inverse
minmax <- range(train.ts)
normalize_ts <- function(x) (x - minmax[1]) / (minmax[2] - minmax[1])
inv_normalize_ts <- function(x) (minmax[2] - minmax[1]) * x + minmax[1]
norm_train.ts <- normalize_ts(train.ts)

# convert timeseries into sequence of subseries of length (ninput + noutput)
ninput <- 12
noutput <- 1
nSubsequences <- length(norm_train.ts) - (ninput + noutput) + 1
getSubsequence <- function(i) norm_train.ts[i:(i - 1 + ninput+noutput)]
subsequences <- t(sapply(1:nSubsequences, getSubsequence))

# split subsequences into input (x) and output (y) and convert both to arrays
x.train <- subsequences[, 1:ninput]
y.train <- subsequences[, (ninput+1):(ninput+noutput)]
x.train <- array(data=x.train, dim=c(nrow(x.train), ninput, 1))
y.train <- array(data=y.train, dim=c(nrow(x.train), noutput, 1))
dim(x.train); dim(y.train)
```

Output

```
#> [1] 111  12   1
#> [1] 111   1   1
```

(MAE) as the loss. (See Chapter 11 for a discussion of the concepts of flattening and dropout.)

Figure 19.7 shows the result of applying the LSTM to the Amtrak data and summarizes the predictive performance of the resulting model. Because we can only use the training period to generate forecasts for the test period, we use a rolling window approach: we start by using a window of the last 12 months of the training set to forecast the first month in the test set. This forecast is then added to the window, and the earliest value in the window discarded. The new window is then used to forecast the second month. This is repeated until we have forecasts for the 36–month period of the test set.

Note that the RMSE of the LSTM model is dramatically worse for the test period (193) compared with the training period (31). This difference indicates potential overfitting. The test RMSE is also much worse than the Holt–Winters RMSE (76). Interestingly, we can see in the plot that performance during the first few test months is quite good, while for longer-term forecasts (more than one year ahead), predictive performance degrades quickly. This means that the LSTM model might be more suitable for applications where the model can be updated month by month.

TABLE 19.5   DEFINING AN LSTM MODEL FOR FORECASTING A SERIES

 code for model definition

```
# load required packages
# Keras and TensorFlow require a Python conda environment with these packages installed
library(reticulate)
use_condaenv('mlba-r')
library(keras)
library(tensorflow)

lstm_model <- keras_model_sequential() %>%
  layer_lstm(units = 50, # size of the layer
             batch_input_shape = c(1, ninput, 1), # batch size, timesteps, features
             dropout = 0.01,
             recurrent_dropout = 0.01,
             return_sequences = TRUE,
             stateful = TRUE) %>%
  layer_lstm(units = 50,
             dropout = 0.01,
             recurrent_dropout = 0.01,
             return_sequences = TRUE,
             stateful = TRUE) %>%
  layer_flatten() %>%
  layer_dense(units = 1)
summary(lstm_model)

lstm_model %>%
  compile(loss = 'mae', optimizer = 'adam', metrics = 'mse')

lstm_model %>% fit(
  x = x.train,
  y = y.train,
  batch_size = 1,
  epochs = 400,
  verbose = 1,
  shuffle = TRUE
)
```

Output

```
Model: "sequential"

--------------------------------------------------------------------------------
 Layer (type)                    Output Shape                 Param #
================================================================================
 lstm_1 (LSTM)                   (1, 12, 50)                  10400
 lstm (LSTM)                     (1, 12, 50)                  20200
 flatten_7 (Flatten)             (1, 600)                     0
 dense_11 (Dense)                (1, 1)                       601
================================================================================
Total params: 31,201
Trainable params: 31,201
Non-trainable params: 0

--------------------------------------------------------------------------------

> lstm_model %>% fit(...)
Epoch 1/400
111/111 [==============================] - 5s 16ms/step - loss: 0.1983 - mse: 0.0583
Epoch 2/400
111/111 [==============================] - 1s 12ms/step - loss: 0.1946 - mse: 0.0604
...
Epoch 400/400
111/111 [==============================] - 1s 11ms/step - loss: 0.0393 - mse: 0.0025
```

code for model prediction

```
# code for forecasting one month ahead with sliding window
forecast.ts <- c()
window <- norm_train.ts[(nTrain-12):nTrain]
for (i in 1:36) {
  x <- array(data=window, dim=c(1, ninput, 1))
  pred <- predict(lstm_model, x, batch_size=1)
  window <- c(window[2:length(window)], pred[1])
  forecast.ts <- c(forecast.ts, pred[1])
}

forecast.ts <- inv_normalize_ts(forecast.ts)
forecast.ts <- ts(forecast.ts, start=c(1991, 1 + nTrain), freq=12)

fitted <- predict(lstm_model, x.train, batch_size=1)
fitted.ts <- ts(inv_normalize_ts(fitted), start=c(1991, 1 + ninput), freq=12)

autoplot(train.ts, xlab="Time", ylab="Ridership (in 000s)", color=colData) +
  autolayer(test.ts, color=colData, linetype=2) +
  autolayer(fitted.ts, color=colModel, size=0.75) +
  autolayer(forecast.ts, color=colModel, size=0.75)

accuracy(fitted.ts, ridership.ts)
accuracy(forecast.ts, ridership.ts)
```

Output

```
> accuracy(fitted.ts, ridership.ts)
                    ME      RMSE      MAE        MPE     MAPE      ACF1 Theil's U
Training set -9.766977 30.78878 24.25096 -0.6015371 1.392375 0.3157792 0.1850095
> accuracy(forecast.ts, ridership.ts)
               ME      RMSE      MAE       MPE     MAPE      ACF1 Theil's U
Test set 14.88605 193.2634 152.5417 0.1910492 7.851184 0.1495465  1.149939
```

FIGURE 19.7   **ACTUAL AND FORECASTED VALUES USING THE DEEP LEARNING LSTM MODEL FOR AMTRAK RIDERSHIP SERIES**

PROBLEMS

19.1   **Impact of September 11 on Air Travel in the United States.** The Research and Innovative Technology Administration's Bureau of Transportation Statistics conducted a study to evaluate the impact of the September 11, 2001 terrorist attack on US transportation. The 2006 study report and the data can be found at bts.gov/archive/publications/estimated_impacts_of_9_11_on_us_travel/index. The goal of the study was stated as follows:

> The purpose of this study is to provide a greater understanding of the passenger travel behavior patterns of persons making long distance trips before and after 9/11.

The report analyzes monthly passenger movement data between January 1990 and May 2004. Data on three monthly time series are given in dataset *mlba::Sept11Travel* for this period: (1) actual airline revenue passenger miles (Air), (2) rail passenger miles (Rail), and (3) vehicle miles traveled (Car).

To assess the impact of September 11, the Bureau of Transportation Statistics took the following approach: using data before September 11, they forecasted future data (under the assumption of no terrorist attack). Then, they compared the forecasted series with the actual data to assess the impact of the event. Our first step, therefore, is to split each of the time series into two parts: pre- and post-September 11. We now concentrate only on the earlier time series.

a. Create a time plot for the pre-event AIR time series. What time series components appear from the plot?

b. Figure 19.8 shows a time plot of the **seasonally adjusted** pre-September-11 AIR series. Which of the following smoothing methods would be adequate for forecasting this series?

- Moving average (with what window width?)

- Simple exponential smoothing

- Holt's exponential smoothing

- Holt–Winters exponential smoothing

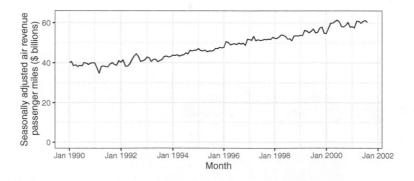

FIGURE 19.8   **SEASONALLY ADJUSTED PRE-SEPTEMBER-11 AIR SERIES**

19.2 Relation Between Moving Average and Exponential Smoothing. Assume that we apply a moving average to a series, using a very short window span. If we wanted to achieve an equivalent result using simple exponential smoothing, what value should the smoothing coefficient take?

19.3 Forecasting with a Moving Average. For a given time series of sales, the training set consists of 50 months. The first 5 months' data are shown below:

Month	Sales
Sept 98	27
Oct 98	31
Nov 98	58
Dec 98	63
Jan 99	59

a. Compute the sales forecast for January 1999 based on a moving average with $w = 4$.

b. Compute the forecast error for the above forecast.

19.4 Optimizing Holt–Winters Exponential Smoothing. The table below shows the optimal smoothing constants from applying exponential smoothing to data, using automated model selection:

Level	1.000
Trend	0.000
Seasonality	0.246

a. The value of zero that is obtained for the trend smoothing constant means that (choose one of the following):

- There is no trend.
- The trend is estimated only from the first two periods.
- The trend is updated throughout the data.
- The trend is statistically insignificant.

b. What is the danger of using the optimal smoothing constant values?

19.5 Department Store Sales. The time plot in Figure 19.9 describes actual quarterly sales for a department store over a 6-year period (data are available in *mlba::DepartmentStoreSales*, data courtesy of Chris Albright).

a. Which of the following methods would **not** be suitable for forecasting this series?

- Moving average of raw series
- Moving average of deseasonalized series
- Simple exponential smoothing of the raw series
- Holt's exponential smoothing of the raw series
- Holt–Winters exponential smoothing of the raw series

FIGURE 19.9   **DEPARTMENT STORE QUARTERLY SALES SERIES**

b. The forecaster was tasked to generate forecasts for four quarters ahead. He therefore partitioned the data such that the last four quarters were designated as the test period. The forecaster approached the forecasting task by using multiplicative Holt–Winters exponential smoothing. The smoothing parameters used were $\alpha = 0.2, \beta = 0.15,$ and $\gamma = 0.05.$

   i. Run this method on the data.

   ii. The forecasts for the test set are given in Table 19.3. Compute the MAPE values for the forecasts of Q21 and Q22.

TABLE 19.3   **FORECASTS FOR TEST SERIES USING EXPONENTIAL SMOOTHING**

Quarter	Actual	Forecast	Error
21	60800	62453.26	1653.26
22	64900	65877.39	977.39
23	76997	77900.25	903.25
24	103337	104384.22	1047.22

c. The fit and residuals from the exponential smoothing are shown in Figure 19.10. Using all the information thus far, is this model suitable for forecasting Q21 and Q22?

19.6 **Shipments of Household Appliances.** The time plot in Figure 19.11 shows the series of quarterly shipments (in million dollars) of US household appliances between 1985 and 1989 (data are available in *mlba::ApplianceShipments*, data courtesy of Ken Black).

   a. Which of the following methods would be suitable for forecasting this series if applied to the raw data?

     • Moving average

     • Simple exponential smoothing

     • Holt's exponential smoothing

     • Holt–Winters exponential smoothing

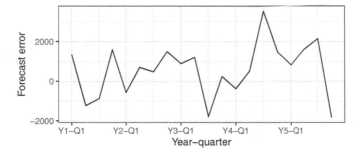

FIGURE 19.10   FORECASTS AND ACTUALS (TOP) AND FORECAST ERRORS (BOTTOM) USING
EXPONENTIAL SMOOTHING

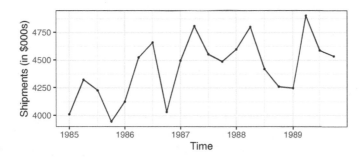

FIGURE 19.11   QUARTERLY SHIPMENTS OF US HOUSEHOLD APPLIANCES OVER 5 YEARS

b. Apply a moving average with window span $w = 4$ to the data. Use all but the last
year as the training set. Create a time plot of the moving average series.

    i. What does the MA(4) chart reveal?

   ii. Use the MA(4) model to forecast appliance sales in Q1-1990.

  iii. Use the MA(4) model to forecast appliance sales in Q1-1991.

  iv. Is the forecast for Q1-1990 most likely to underestimate, overestimate, or
accurately estimate the actual sales on Q1-1990? Explain.

   v. Management feels most comfortable with moving averages. The analyst therefore plans to use this method for forecasting future quarters. What else should

be considered before using the MA(4) to forecast future quarterly shipments of household appliances?

c. We now focus on forecasting beyond 1989. In the following, continue to use all but the last year as the training set and the last four quarters as the test set. First, fit a regression model to sales with a linear trend and quarterly seasonality to the training data. Next, apply Holt–Winters exponential smoothing (with the default smoothing values) to the training data. Choose an adequate "season length."

   i. Compute the MAPE for the test period using the regression model.

   ii. Compute the MAPE for the test period using Holt–Winters exponential smoothing.

   iii. Which model would you prefer to use for forecasting Q1-1990? Give three reasons.

   iv. If we optimize the smoothing parameters in the Holt–Winters method, are the optimal parameters likely to get values that are close to zero? Why or why not?

19.7 Shampoo Sales. The time plot in Figure 19.12 describes monthly sales of a certain shampoo over a 3-year period [Data are available in *mlba::ShampooSales*, Source: Hyndman and Yang (2018)].

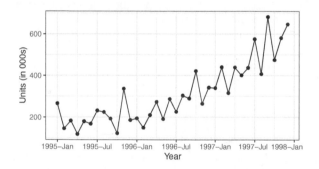

FIGURE 19.12   **MONTHLY SALES OF A CERTAIN SHAMPOO**

Which of the following methods would be suitable for forecasting this series if applied to the raw data?

- Moving average

- Simple exponential smoothing

- Holt's exponential smoothing

- Holt–Winters exponential smoothing

19.8 Natural Gas Sales. Figure 19.13 is a time plot of quarterly natural gas sales (in billions of BTU) of a certain company, over a period of 4 years (data is available in *mlba::NaturalGasSales*, courtesy of George McCabe). The company's analyst is asked to use a moving average to forecast sales in Winter 2005.

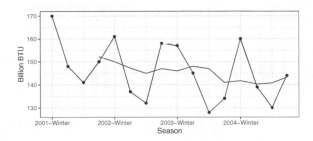

FIGURE 19.13   QUARTERLY SALES OF NATURAL GAS OVER 4 YEARS

a. Reproduce the time plot with the overlaying MA(4) line.

b. What can we learn about the series from the MA line?

c. Run a moving average forecaster with adequate season length. Are forecasts generated by this method expected to over-forecast, under-forecast, or accurately forecast actual sales? Why?

19.9 **Australian Wine Sales.** Figure 19.14 shows time plots of monthly sales of six types of Australian wines (red, rose, sweet white, dry white, sparkling, and fortified) for 1980–1994 [Data are available in *mlba::AustralianWines*, Source: Hyndman and Yang (2018)]. The units are thousands of liters. You are hired to obtain short term forecasts (2–3 months ahead) for each of the six series, and this task will be repeated every month.

a. Which forecasting method would you choose if you had to choose the same method for all series? Why?

b. Fortified wine has the largest market share of the above six types of wine. You are asked to focus on fortified wine sales alone and produce as accurate as possible forecasts for the next 2 months.

- Start by partitioning the data using the period until December 1993 as the training set.

- Apply Holt–Winters exponential smoothing to sales with an appropriate season length (use the default values for the smoothing constants).

c. Create an ACF plot for the training residuals from the Holt–Winters exponential smoothing until lag 12.

i. Examining this plot, which of the following statements are reasonable conclusions?

- Decembers (month 12) are not captured well by the model.

- There is a strong correlation between sales on the same calendar month.

- The model does not capture the seasonality well.

- We should try to fit an autoregressive model with lag 12 to the residuals.

- We should first deseasonalize the data and then apply Holt–Winters exponential smoothing.

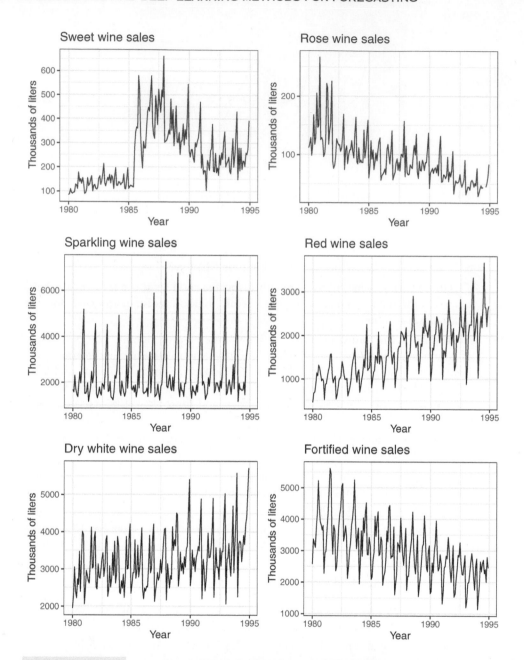

FIGURE 19.14   MONTHLY SALES OF SIX TYPES OF AUSTRALIAN WINES BETWEEN 1980 AND 1994

    ii. How can you handle the above effect without adding another layer to your model?

  d. Use the LSTM deep learning technique to forecast the fortified wine series. As before, use the period until December 1993 as the training period and the rest as the test period.

   i. Report the RMSE and MAPE for the test period.

  ii. Change the deep learning network architecture by replacing the LSTM layer with an RNN layer (*keras::layer_simple_rnn()*) while keeping the preprocessing steps as is. Report the RMSE and MAPE for the test period.

 iii. Which of the two models would you select for forecasting future values? Why?

## PART VIII

Data Analytics

## CHAPTER 20

Social Network Analytics[1]

In this chapter, we examine the basic ways to visualize and describe social networks, measure linkages, and analyze the network with both supervised and unsupervised techniques. The methods we use long predate the Internet but gained widespread use with the explosion in social media data. Twitter, for example, makes its feed available for public analysis, and some other social media firms make some of their data available to programmers and developers via an application programming interface (API).

Social Network Analysis in R

In this chapter, we use the `igraph` package to create, analyze, and visualize networks. Using the `twitteR` package, we briefly demonstrate how information from the Twitter social network can be retrieved.

20.1 INTRODUCTION[2]

The use of social media began its rapid growth in the early 2000s with the advent of Friendster and MySpace and, in 2004, Facebook. LinkedIn, catering to professionals, soon followed, as did Twitter, Tumblr, Instagram, Yelp, TripAdvisor, and others. These information-based companies quickly began generating a deluge of data—especially data concerning links among people (friends, followers, connections, etc.).

For some companies, like Facebook, Twitter, and LinkedIn, nearly the entire value of the company lies in the analytic and predictive value of this data from

---

[1] The organization of ideas in this chapter owes much to Jennifer Golbeck and her *Analyzing the Social Web*. The contribution of Marc Smith, developer and shepherd of NodeXL, is also acknowledged.
[2] This and the subsequent sections in this chapter copyright © 2023 Datastats, LLC, and Galit Shmueli. Used by permission.

Machine Learning for Business Analytics: Concepts, Techniques, and Applications in R, Second Edition.
Galit Shmueli, Peter C. Bruce, Peter Gedeck, Inbal Yahav, and Nitin R. Patel
© 2023 John Wiley & Sons, Inc. Published 2023 by John Wiley & Sons, Inc.

their social networks. As of this writing (March 2022), Facebook was worth more than double General Motors and Ford combined. Other companies, like Amazon and Spotify, use social network data as important components of predictive engines aimed at selling products and services.

Social networks are basically entities (e.g., people) and the connections among them. Let's look at the building blocks for describing, depicting, and analyzing networks. The basic elements of a network are:

- Nodes (also called vertices or vertexes)
- Edges (connections or links between nodes)

A very simple LinkedIn network might be depicted as shown in Figure 20.1. This network has six nodes depicting members, with edges connecting some, but not all, of the pairs of nodes.

 code for plotting hypothetical LinkedIn network

```
library(igraph)

# define links in data
edges <- rbind(
  c("Dave", "Jenny"), c("Peter", "Jenny"), c("John", "Jenny"),
  c("Dave", "Peter"), c("Dave", "John"), c("Peter", "Sam"),
  c("Sam", "Albert"), c("Peter", "John")
)

# generate and plot network
# set argument directed = FALSE in graph.edgelist() to plot an undirected network.
g <- graph.edgelist(edges, directed = FALSE)
plot(g, vertex.size = 5, vertex.label.dist = 2)
```

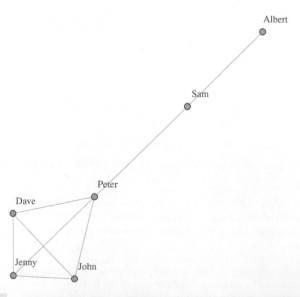

FIGURE 20.1   **TINY HYPOTHETICAL LINKEDIN NETWORK; THE EDGES REPRESENT CONNECTIONS AMONG THE MEMBERS**

20.2 DIRECTED VS. UNDIRECTED NETWORKS

In the plot shown in Figure 20.1, edges are bidirectional or undirected, meaning that if John is connected to Peter, then Peter must also be connected to John, and there is no difference in the nature of these connections. You can see from this plot that there is a group of well-connected members (Peter, John, Dave, and Jenny), plus two less-connected members (Sam and Albert).

Connections might also be directional, or directed. For example, on Twitter, Dave might follow Peter, but Peter might not follow Dave. A simple Twitter network (using the same members and connections) might be depicted using edges with arrows as shown in Figure 20.2.

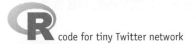

R code for tiny Twitter network

```
# generate and plot network
# set argument directed = TRUE in graph.edgelist() to plot a directed network.
g <- graph.edgelist(edges, directed = TRUE)
plot(g, vertex.size = 5, vertex.label.dist = 2)
```

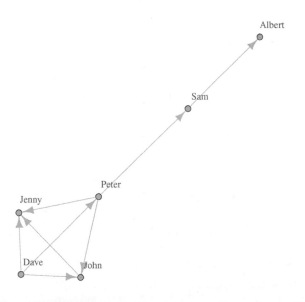

FIGURE 20.2 **TINY HYPOTHETICAL TWITTER NETWORK WITH DIRECTED EDGES (ARROWS) SHOWING WHO FOLLOWS WHOM**

Edges can also be weighted to reflect attributes of the connection. For example, the thickness of the edge might represent the level of email traffic between two members in a network or the bandwidth capacity between two nodes in a digital network (as illustrated in Figure 20.3). The length of an edge can also be used to represent attributes such as physical distance between two points on a map.

FIGURE 20.3   EDGE WEIGHTS REPRESENTED BY LINE THICKNESS.

20.3 VISUALIZING AND ANALYZING NETWORKS

You have probably seen network plots[3] used as a tool for visualizing and exploring networks; they are used widely in the news media. Jason Buch and Guillermo Contreras, reporters for the *San Antonio Express News*,[4] pored over law enforcement records and produced the network diagram shown in Figure 20.4 to understand and illustrate the connections used to launder drug money.[5] You can see that there is a well-connected central node; it is the address of an expensive residence in the gated Dominion community in San Antonio, owned by accused launderers Mauricio and Alejandro Sanchez Garza. There are several entities in the lower left connected only to themselves and one singleton. Nodes are sized according to how central they are to the network (specifically, in proportion to their *eigenvector centrality*, which is discussed in Section 20.4).

Plot Layout

It is important to note that x, y coordinates usually carry no meaning in network plots; the meaning is conveyed in other elements such as node size, edge width, labels, and directional arrows. Consequently, the same network may be depicted by two very different looking plots. For example, Figure 20.5 presents two different layouts of the hypothetical LinkedIn network.

As a result, visualization tools face innumerable choices in plot layout. The first step in making a choice is to establish what principles should govern the

---

[3]In the field of network analysis, the term *graph* refers to the data structure of networks (i.e., lists of edges and nodes). In a more general sense, and in other areas of statistics, the term is used synonymously with "chart" or "plot." Here, to avoid confusion, we will use the term *plot* or *network plot* to refer to the visualization and *network data* to refer to the data itself.

[4]*San Antonio Express News*, May 23, 2012, accessed May 3, 2022.

[5]The original visualization can be seen at https://www.slideshare.net/borderzine/immigration-reporting-data-tools-and, accessed May 3, 2022.

code for plotting the drug money laundries network

```
library(igraph)
drug.df <- mlba::Drug

# convert edges to edge list matrix
edges <- as.matrix(drug.df[, c(1,2)])
g <- graph.edgelist(edges,directed=FALSE)

# plot network
# nodes' size is proportional to their eigenvector centrality
plot(g, vertex.label = NA, vertex.size = eigen_centrality(g)$vector * 20)
```

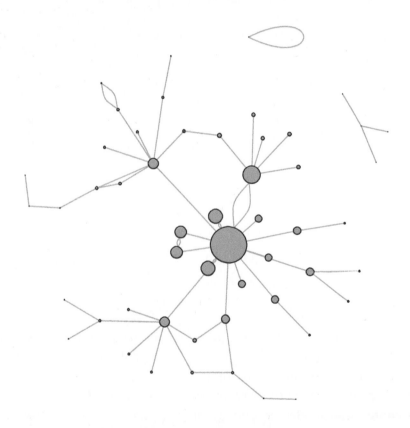

FIGURE 20.4   DRUG LAUNDRY NETWORK IN SAN ANTONIO, TX

code for plotting different layouts

```
# Building on the code presented in Figure 19.1
plot(g, layout = layout_in_circle, vertex.size = 5, vertex.label.dist = 2)
plot(g, layout = layout_on_grid, vertex.size = 5, vertex.label.dist = 2)
```

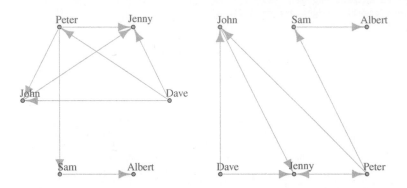

FIGURE 20.5   **TWO DIFFERENT LAYOUTS OF THE TINY LINKEDIN NETWORK PRESENTED IN FIGURE 20.1**

layout. Dunne and Shneiderman (2009, cited in Golbeck, 2013) list these four plot readability principles:

1. Every node should be visible.
2. For every node, you should be able to count its degree (explained below).
3. For every link, you should be able to follow it from source to destination.
4. Clusters and outliers should be identifiable.

These general principles are then translated into readability metrics by which plots can be judged. Two simple layouts are *circular* (all nodes lie in a circle) and *grid* (all nodes lie at the intersection of grid lines in a rectangular grid).

You can probably think of alternate layouts that more clearly reveal structures such as clusters and singletons, and so can computers using a variety of algorithms. These algorithms typically use a combination of fixed arbitrary starting structures, random tweaking, analogs to physical properties (e.g., springs connecting nodes), and a sequence of iteration and measurement against the readability principles. A detailed discussion of layout algorithms is beyond the scope of this chapter; see Golbeck (2013, chapter 4) for an introduction to layout issues, including algorithms, the use of size, shape and color, scaling issues, and labeling.

Edge List

A network plot such as the one in Figure 20.4 (drug laundry network) is always tied to a data table called an *edge list* or an *adjacency list*. Table 20.1 shows an excerpt from the data table used to generate Figure 20.4. All the entities in both columns are nodes, and each row represents a link between the two nodes. If the network is directional, the link is usually structured from the left column to the right column.

TABLE 20.1	EDGE LIST EXCERPT CORRESPONDING TO THE DRUG-LAUNDERING NETWORK IN FIGURE 20.4
6451 Babcock Road	Q & M LLC
Q & M LLC	10 Kings Heath
Maurico Sanchez	Q & M LLC
Hilda Riebeling	Q & M LLC
Ponte Vedra Apartments	Q & M LLC
O S F STEAK HOUSE, LLC	Mauricio Sanchez
Arturo Madrigal	O S F STEAK HOUSE
HARBARD BAR, LLC	Arturo Madrigal
10223 Sahara Street	O S F STEAK HOUSE
HARBARD BAR, LLC	Maurico Sanchez
9510 Tioga Drive, Suite 206	Mauricio Sanchez
FDA FIBER, INC	Arturo Madrigal
10223 Sahara Street	O S F STEAK HOUSE
A G Q FULL SERVICE, LLC	Alvaro Garcia de Quevedo
19510 Gran Roble	Arturo Madrigal
Lorenza Madrigal Cristan	19519 Gran Roble
Laredo National Bank	19519 Gran Roble

In a typical network visualization tool, you can select a row from the data table and see its node and connections highlighted in the network plot. Likewise, in the plot, you can click on a node and see it highlighted in the data table.

Adjacency Matrix

The same relationships can be presented in a matrix. The adjacency matrix for the small directed network for Twitter in Figure 20.2 is shown in Table 20.2.

TABLE 20.2	ADJACENCY MATRIX EXCERPT CORRESPONDING TO THE TWITTER DATA IN FIGURE 20.2				
	Dave	Peter	Jenny	Sam	John	Albert
Dave	0	1	1	0	1	0
Peter	0	0	1	1	1	0
Jenny	0	0	0	0	0	0
Sam	0	0	0	0	0	1
John	0	1	1	0	0	0
Albert	0	0	0	0	0	0

Each cell in the matrix indicates an edge, with the originating node in the left header column and the destination node in the top row of headers. Reading the first row, we see that Dave is following three people—Peter, Jenny, and John.

Using Network Data in Classification and Prediction

In our discussion of classification and prediction, as well as clustering and data reduction, we were dealing mostly with highly structured data in the form of a data frame—columns were variables (features), and rows were records. We saw how to use R to sample from relational databases to bring data into the form of a data frame.

Highly structured data can be used for network analysis, but network data often start out in a more unstructured or semi-structured format. Twitter provides a public feed of a portion of its voluminous stream of tweets, which has captured researchers' attention and accelerated interest in the application of network analytics to social media data. Network analysis can take this unstructured data and turn it into structured data with usable metrics.

We now turn our attention to those metrics. These metrics can be used not only to describe the attributes of networks but also as inputs to more traditional data mining methods.

20.4 SOCIAL DATA METRICS AND TAXONOMY

Several popular network metrics are used in network analysis. Before introducing them, we introduce some basic network terminology used for constructing the metrics:

Edge weight measures the strength of the relationship between the two connected nodes. For example, in an e-mail network, there might be an edge weight that reflects the number of e-mails exchanged between two individuals linked by that edge.

Path and **path length** are important for measuring distance between nodes. A path is the route of nodes needed to go from node A to node B; path length is the number of edges in that route. Typically these terms refer to the shortest route. In a weighted network, the shortest path does not necessarily reflect the path with the fewest edges, but rather the path with the least weight. For example, if the weights reflect a cost factor, the shortest path would reflect the minimal cost.

Connected network is a network where each node in the network has a path, of any length, to all other nodes. A network may be unconnected in its entirety but consist of segments that are connected within themselves.

In the money laundering visualization (Figure 20.4), the network as a whole is unconnected—the nodes are not all connected to one another. You can see one large connected segment and, in the lower left, a small connected segment and a singleton.

A clique is a network in which each node is directly connected by an edge to every other node. The connections must all be single edges—a connection via a multi-node path does not count.

A singleton is an unconnected node. It might arise when an individual signs up for a social network service (e.g., to read reviews) and does not participate in any networking activities.

Node-Level Centrality Metrics

Often we may be interested in the importance or influence of a particular individual or node, which is reflected in how central that node is in the network.

The most common way to calculate this is by degree—how many edges are connected to the node. Nodes with many connections are more central. In Figure 20.1, the Albert node is of degree 1, Sam of degree 2, and Jenny of degree 3. In a directed network, we are interested in both indegree and outdegree—the number of incoming and outgoing connections of a node. In Figure 20.2, Peter has indegree of 2 and outdegree of 1.

Another metric for a node's centrality is *closeness*—how close the node is to the other nodes in the network. This is measured by finding the shortest path from that node to each of the other nodes and then taking the reciprocal of the sum of these path lengths. In the Figure 20.1 example, Albert's closeness is $1/(1 + 2 + 3 + 3 + 3) = 0.0833$.

Still another metric is *betweenness*—the extent to which a given node lies on the shortest path between pairs of nodes. The calculation starts with the given node, say, node A, and two other nodes, say, B and C, out of perhaps many nodes in a network. The shortest paths between B and C are listed, and the proportion of paths that include A is recorded. This proportion is recorded also for all other nodal pairs, and betweenness is the average proportion.

An aphorism relevant for social media networks is "it's not what you know, but who you know." A more accurate rendition would qualify it further—"it's who you know and who they know." A link to a member that has many other connections can be more valuable than a link to a member with few connections. A metric that measures this connectivity aspect is *eigenvector centrality*, which factors in both the number of links from a node and the number of onward connections from those links. The details of the calculation is not discussed here, but the result always lies between 0 (not central) and 1 (maximum centrality). The larger the value for a given node, the more central it is.

Centrality can be depicted on a network plot by the size of a node—the more central the node, the larger it is.

Code for computing centrality measures in R for the small undirected LinkedIn data is given in Table 20.3.

TABLE 20.3   COMPUTING CENTRALITY IN R

```
> degree(g)
  Dave  Jenny  Peter   John    Sam Albert
     3      3      4      3      2      1
> betweenness(g)
  Dave  Jenny  Peter   John    Sam Albert
     0      0      6      0      4      0
> betweenness(g)/sum(betweenness(g))
  Dave  Jenny  Peter   John    Sam Albert
   0.0    0.0    0.6    0.0    0.4    0.0
> closeness(g)
      Dave      Jenny      Peter       John        Sam      Albert
0.12500000 0.12500000 0.16666667 0.12500000 0.12500000 0.08333333
> eigen_centrality(g)
$vector
      Dave      Jenny      Peter       John        Sam      Albert
 0.9119867  0.9119867  1.0000000  0.9119867  0.3605471  0.1164367
```

Egocentric Network

It is often important to gain information that comes only from the analysis of individuals and their connections. For example, an executive recruiting firm may be interested in individuals with certain job titles and the people those individuals are connected to.

An egocentric network is the network of connections centered around an individual node. A degree 1 egocentric network consists of all the edges connected to the individual node, plus their connections. A degree 2 egocentric network is the network of all those nodes and edges, plus the edges and nodes connected to them. The degree 1 and degree 2 egocentric network for Peter in the LinkedIn network are shown in Figure 20.6. Note that the degree 2 egocentric network for Peter is the entire network shown in Figure 20.1.

Network Metrics

To this point, we have discussed metrics and terms that apply to nodes and edges. We can also measure attributes of the network as a whole. Two main network metrics are *degree distribution* and *density*.

Degree distribution describes the range of *connectedness* of the nodes—how many nodes have (for example) five connections, how many have four connections, how many have three, etc. In the tiny LinkedIn network

code for computing egocentric network

```
# get Peter's 1-level ego network
# for a 2-level ego network set argument order = 2 in make_ego_graph().
peter.ego <- make_ego_graph(g, order = 1, nodes = "Peter")
plot(peter.ego[[1]], vertex.size = 1, vertex.label.dist = 0.5)
```

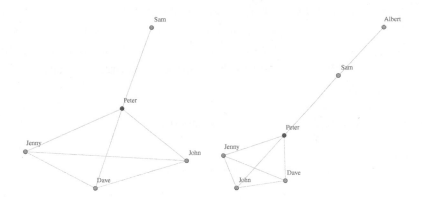

FIGURE 20.6   THE DEGREE 1 (LEFT) AND DEGREE 2 (RIGHT) EGOCENTRIC NETWORKS FOR PETER, FROM THE LINKEDIN NETWORK IN FIGURE 20.1

(Figure 20.1), we see that Peter, Jenny, and Dave have three connections, John and Sam have two connections, and Albert has one. A table of this degree distribution is shown in Table 20.4.

TABLE 20.4   DEGREE DISTRIBUTION OF TINY LINKEDIN NETWORK

Degree	Frequency
Degree 0	0
Degree 1	1
Degree 2	1
Degree 3	3
Degree 4	1

Density is another way to describe the overall connectedness of network data which focuses on the edges, not the nodes. The metric looks at the ratio of the actual number of edges to the maximum number of potential edges (i.e., if every node were connected to every other node) in a network with a fixed number of nodes. For a directed network with n nodes, there can be a maximum of $n(n-1)$ edges. For an undirected network, the number is $n(n-1)/2$. More formally, density calculations for directed and undirected networks are as follows:

$$\text{Density (directed)} \quad = \quad \frac{e}{n(n-1)} \tag{20.1}$$

$$\text{Density (undirected)} \quad = \quad \frac{e}{n(n-1)/2} \tag{20.2}$$

where e is the number of edges and n is the number of nodes. This metric ranges between just above 0 (not dense at all) and 1 (as dense as possible). Code for computing network measures in R for the small LinkedIn data is given in Table 20.5. Figures 20.7 and 20.8 illustrate a sparse and dense network, respectively.

TABLE 20.5   COMPUTING NETWORK MEASURES IN R

```
> degree.distribution(g) # normalized
[1] 0.0000000 0.1666667 0.1666667 0.5000000 0.1666667

> edge_density(g)
[1] 0.2666667
```

20.5 USING NETWORK METRICS IN PREDICTION AND CLASSIFICATION

Network attributes can be used along with other predictors in standard classification and prediction procedures. The most common applications involve the concept of *matching*. Online dating services, for example, will predict for their members which other members might be potentially compatible. Their algorithms typically involve calculation of a distance measure between a member seeking a relationship and candidate matches. It might also go beyond the members' self-reported features and incorporate information about links between the member and candidate matches. A link might represent the action "viewed candidate profile."

Link Prediction

Social networks such as Facebook and LinkedIn use network information to recommend new connections. The translation of this goal into an analytics problem is:

"If presented with a network, can you predict the next link to form?"

Prediction algorithms list all possible node pairs and then assign a score to each pair that reflects the similarity of the two nodes. The pair that scores as most

FIGURE 20.7   A RELATIVELY SPARSE NETWORK

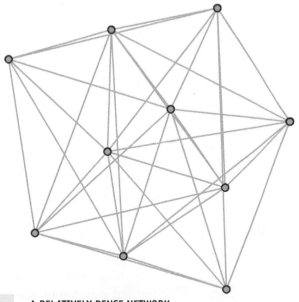

FIGURE 20.8   A RELATIVELY DENSE NETWORK

similar (closest) is the next link predicted to form, if it does not already exist. See Chapter 16 for a discussion of such distance measures. Some variables used in calculating similarity measures are the same as those based on non–network information (e.g., years of education, age, sex, location). Other metrics used in link prediction apply specifically to network data:

- Shortest path
- Number of common neighbors
- Edge weight

Link prediction is also used in targeting intelligence surveillance. "Collecting everything" may be technically, politically, or legally unfeasible, and an agency must therefore identify a priori a smaller set of individuals requiring surveillance. The agency will often start with known targets and then use link prediction to identify additional targets and prioritize collection efforts.

Entity Resolution

Governments use network analysis to track terrorist networks, and a key part of that effort is identification of individuals. The same individual may appear multiple times from different data sources, and the agencies want to know, for example, whether individual A identified by French surveillance in Tunisia is the same as individual AA identified by Israeli intelligence in Lebanon and individual AAA identified by US intelligence in Pakistan.

One way to evaluate whether an individual appears in multiple databases is to measure distances and use them in a similar fashion to nearest neighbors or clustering. In Chapter 16, we looked in particular at Euclidean distance and discussed this metric not in terms of the network an individual belongs to, but rather in terms of the profile (predictor values) of the individual. When basing entity resolution on these variables, it is useful to bring domain knowledge into the picture to weight the importance of each variable. For example, two variables in an individual's record might be street address and zip code. A match on street address is more definitive than a match on zip code, so we would probably want to give street address more weight in the scoring algorithm. For a more detailed discussion of automated weight calculation and assignment, see p. 137 in Golbeck (2013).

In addition to measuring distance based on individual profiles, we can bring network attributes into the picture. Consider the simple networks for each individual in Figure 20.9, showing connections to known individuals: based on network connections, you would conclude that A and AA are likely the same person, while AAA is probably a different person. The metrics that can formalize this search and be used in automated fashion where human-intermediated visualization is not practical are the same ones that are used in link prediction.

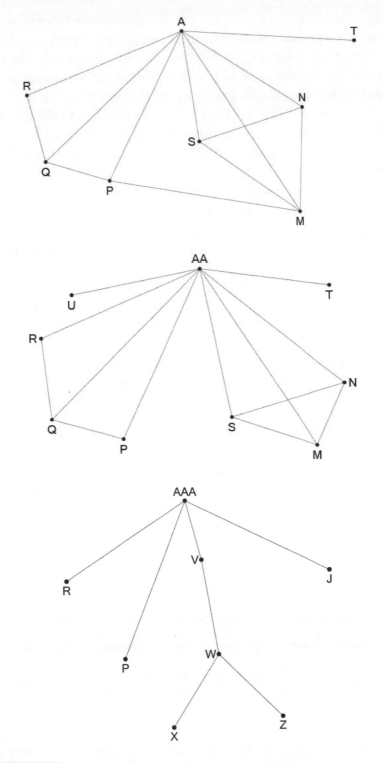

FIGURE 20.9   THE NETWORKS FOR SUSPECT A (TOP), SUSPECT AA (MIDDLE), AND SUSPECT AAA (BOTTOM)

Entity resolution is also used extensively in customer record management and search. For example, a customer might contact a company inquiring about a product or service, triggering the creation of a customer record. The same customer might later inquire again or purchase something. The customer database system should flag the second interaction as belonging to the first customer. Ideally, the customer will enter his or her information exactly the same way in each interaction, facilitating the match, but this does not necessarily happen. Failing an exact match, other customers may be proposed as matches based on proximity.

Another area where entity resolution is used is fraud detection. For example, a large telecom used link resolution to detect customers who "disappeared" after accumulating debt but then reappeared by opening a new account. The network of phone calls to and from such people tends to remain stable, assisting the company to identify them.

In traditional business operations, the match may be based on variables such as name, address, and postal code. In social media products, matches may also be calculated on the basis of network similarity.

Collaborative Filtering

We saw in Chapter 15 that collaborative filtering uses similarity metrics to identify similar individuals and thereby develop recommendations for a particular individual. Companies that have a social media component to their business can use information about network connections to augment other data in measuring similarity.

For example, in a company where Internet advertising revenue is important, a key question is what ads to show consumers.

Consider the following small illustration for a company whose business is centered around online users: user A has just logged on and is to be compared with users B–D. Table 20.6 shows some demographic and user data for each of the users.

TABLE 20.6   FOUR MEASUREMENTS FOR USERS A, B, C, AND D

User	Months as customer	Age	Spending	Education
A	7	23	0	3
B	3	45	0	2
C	5	29	100	3
D	11	59	0	3

Our initial step is to compute distances based on these values, to determine which user is closest to user A. First, we convert the raw data to normalized values to place all the measurements on the same scale (for Education, 1 = high school, 2 = college, and 3 = post-college degree). Normalizing means subtracting the mean and dividing by the standard deviation. The normalized data are shown in Table 20.7.

TABLE 20.7   NORMALIZED MEASUREMENTS FOR USERS A, B, C, AND D

User	Months as customer	Age	Spending	Education
A	0.17	−1.14	−0.58	0.58
B	−1.18	0.43	−0.58	−1.73
C	−0.51	−0.71	1.73	0.58
D	1.52	1.42	−0.58	0.58

Next, we calculate the Euclidean distance between A and each of the other users (see Table 20.8). Based on these calculations, which only take into account the demographic and user data, user C is the closest one to the new user A.

TABLE 20.8   EUCLIDEAN DISTANCE BETWEEN EACH PAIR OF USERS

Pair	Months as customer	Age	Spending	Education	Euclidean distance
A–B	1.83	2.44	0	5.33	3.1
A–C	0.46	0.18	5.33	0	2.44
A–D	1.83	6.55	0	0	2.89

Let's now bring in network metrics, and suppose that the inter-user distances in terms of shortest path are A–B = 2, A–C = 4, and A–D = 3 (Table 20.9).

TABLE 20.9   NETWORK METRICS

Pair	Shortest path
A–B	2
A–C	4
A–D	3

Finally, we can combine this network metric with the other user measurement distances calculated earlier. There is no need to calculate and normalize differences, as we did with the other user measurements, since the shortest-path metric itself already measures distance between records. We therefore take a weighted average of the network and non-network metrics, using weights that reflect the relative importance we want to attach to each. Using equal weights (Table 20.10), user B is scored as the closest to A and could be recommended as a link for user A (in a social environment) or could be used as a source for product and service recommendations. With different weights, it is possible to obtain different results. Choosing weights is not a scientific process; rather, it depends on the business judgment about the relative importance of the network metrics vs. the non-network user measurements.

In addition to recommending social media connections and providing data for recommendations, network analysis has been used for identifying clusters

TABLE 20.10   COMBINING THE NETWORK AND NON-NETWORK METRICS

Pair	Shortest path	Weight	Non-network	Weight	Mean
A–B	2	0.5	3.1	0.5	2.55
A–C	4	0.5	2.44	0.5	3.22
A–D	3	0.5	2.89	0.5	2.95

of similar individuals based on network data (e.g., for marketing purposes), identifying influential individuals (e.g., to target with promotions or outreach), and understanding—in some cases, controlling—the propagation of disease and information.

USING SOCIAL NETWORK DATA

The primary users of social network data are the social networks themselves, those who develop applications (apps) for the networks, and their advertisers. Facebook, Twitter, other networks, and associated app developers use the network data to customize each user's individual experience and increase engagement (that is, encourage more and longer use).

Social network data are also a powerful advertising tool. Facebook generates roughly $50 billion in advertising revenue annually, Twitter $2 billion, and LinkedIn about $5 billion, at this writing. Unlike traditional media, Internet social media platforms offer highly specific microtargeting of ads, the ability to experiment with different ads on a continuous basis to optimize performance, and the ability to measure response and charge advertisers only for the ads that people click on. Facebook gains its advantage from its large user base and the rich information portfolio it has on its regular users (including the identity of a user's connection and information on those connected users).

Perhaps the most well-known example of this advantage was Donald Trump's 2016 campaign for President. Although Trump is most often associated with Twitter, Brad Parscale, Digital Director of the 2016 campaign, gives credit for the victory to Facebook, due to its ability to microtarget ads. He put it this way in a 2018 *60 Minutes* television interview:

> "Facebook now lets you get to places ... that you would never go with TV ads. Now, I can find, you know, 15 people in the Florida Panhandle that I would never buy a TV commercial for."

Parscale explained that he was able to generate 50,000–60,000 different ads per day, combining both microtargeting and continuous massive experimentation to see what ads worked best with what individuals. Although Trump lost the popular vote by 2.8 million votes overall, he was able to win the Electoral College by a razor thin margin of 77,744 votes in three key states—Pennsylvania, Wisconsin, and Michigan. The ability to surgically target voters where they would be most effective was crucial, and Facebook was instrumental in this effort. Facebook experts were embedded with the Trump campaign to implement the complex job, and Parscale credited the company with a key role in Trump's victory: "Donald Trump won, but I think Facebook was the method."

Facebook and Twitter have in the past made data publicly available via Application Programming Interfaces (APIs). Controversial use of Facebook data via third-party apps has resulted in changes to Facebook procedures and significant limitations. Twitter requires that you register as an app developer to gain access to its API. Twitter data is especially popular with researchers for more than just its network data—it is used for analysis of social trends, political opinions, and consumer sentiment. Social media APIs are updated on a regular basis, as are the limits on what you can do with the data. See www.dataminingbook.com for updated references on social media API documentation.

As ethical issues in data science have come to the fore, social media has come in for increased scrutiny. Companies' command of huge amounts of detailed user data raises privacy concerns, heightened by the use of algorithms to microtarget advertising. Rapid sharing of user activity and opinion, coupled with powerful recommender systems, has the effect of magnifying and speeding up malignant social movements. These topics are covered in greater detail in Chapter 22.

20.6 Collecting Social Network Data with R

In this section, we briefly show how to collect data from one of the most used social networks: Twitter. An interface to this social network is provided in R via the package TwitteR. It requires pre-registration as a developer to obtain an application authorization code. Before crawling for Twitter data, create a new Twitter application and obtain a consumer key, consumer secret code, access token, and access secret from https://developer.twitter.com. For more information on the Twitter interface in R, see https://cran.r-project.org/web/packages/twitteR/twitteR.pdf

Table 20.11 provides a simple example for the TwitteR package. The code collects data on 25 recent tweets that contain the words "text mining." The output shows the content of the resulting first two tweets.

20.7 Advantages and Disadvantages

The key value of social network data to businesses is the information it provides about individuals and their needs, desires, and tastes. This information can be used to improve target advertising—and perfectly targeted advertising is the holy grail of the advertising business. People often disdain or ignore traditional "broad spectrum" advertising, whereas they pay close attention when presented with information about something specific that they are interested in. The power of network data is that they allow capturing information on individual needs and tastes without measuring or collecting such data directly. Moreover, network data are often user-provided rather than actively collected.

TABLE 20.11   **TWITTER INTERFACE IN R**

code for Twitter interface

```
library(twitteR)
# replace key and secret number with those you obtained from Twitter
setup_twitter_oauth(consumer_key = "XXX", consumer_secret = "XXX",
                    access_token = "XXX", access_secret = "XXX")

# get recent tweets
recent.25.tweets <- searchTwitter("text mining", resultType="recent", n = 25)
```

Output

```
> recent.25.tweets
[[1]]
[1] "B6UwcAWgHRTeaTv: RT @Harithkhadhoori: Text Data Mining\ncan be described
as the process of extracting essential data from standard language text. Text mining…"

[[2]]
[1] "piyushrathee: RT @lamba_manika: Finally, my book on "Text Mining for Information
Professional" is available online https://t.co/q8Tm8IDUYO. #librarytwit…"
```

To see the power of social network data, one need look no further than the data-based social media giants of the 21st century—Facebook, LinkedIn, Twitter, Yelp, and others. They have built enormous value based almost exclusively on the information contained in their social data—they manufacture no products and sell no services (in the traditional sense) to their users. The main value they generate is the ability to generate real-time information at the level of the individual to better target ads.

It is important to distinguish between social network *engagement* and the use of social network *analytics*. Many organizations have social media policies and use social media as part of their communications and advertising strategies; however, this does not mean they have access to detailed social network data that they can use for analysis. Abrams Research, an Internet marketing agency, cited the edgy online retailer Zappos in 2009 for the best use of social media, but Zappos' orientation was engagement—use of social media for product support and customer service—rather than analytics.

Reliance on social network analytics comes with hazards and challenges. One major hazard is the dynamic, faddish, and somewhat ephemeral nature of social media use. In part this is because social media involvement is relatively new, and the landscape is changing with the arrival of new players and new technologies. It also stems from the essential nature of social media. People use social media not to provide essential needs like food and shelter, but as a voluntary avocation to provide entertainment and interaction with others. Tastes change, and what's in and out of fashion shifts rapidly in these spheres.

Facebook was a pioneer, and its initial appeal was to the college crowd and later to young adults. Eight years later, nearly half its users were of age 45 years or older, significantly higher than in the rest of the social media industry. These users spend more time per visit and are wealthier than college students, so Facebook may be benefiting from this demographic trend. However, this rapid shift shows how fast the essentials of their business model can shift.

Other challenges lie in the public and personal nature of the data involved. Although individuals nearly always engage with social media voluntarily, this does not mean they do so responsibly or with knowledge of the potential consequences. Information posted on Facebook became evidence in 33% of US divorce cases, and numerous cases have been cited of individuals being fired because of information they posted on Facebook.

One enterprising programmer created the website pleaserobme.com (since removed) that listed the real-time location of people who had "checked in" via FourSquare to a cafe or restaurant, thus letting the world know that they were not at home. FourSquare was not making this information easily available to hackers, but the check-ins were auto-posted to Twitter, where they could be harvested via an API. Thus, information collected for the purpose of enriching the "targetability" of advertising to users ended up creating a liability for both FourSquare and Twitter. Twitter's liability came about indirectly, and it would have been easy for Twitter to overlook this risk in setting up their connection with FourSquare.

In summary, despite the potential for abuse and exposure to risk, the value provided by social network analytics seems large enough to ensure that the analytics methods outlined in this chapter will continue to be in demand.

PROBLEMS

20.1 **Describing a Network.** Consider an undirected network for individuals A, B, C, D, and E. A is connected to B and C. B is connected to A and C. C is connected to A, B, and D. D is connected to C and E. E is connected to D.

    a. Produce a network plot for this network.

    b. What node(s) would need to be removed from the network for the remaining nodes to constitute a clique?

    c. What is the degree for node A?

    d. Which node(s) have the lowest degree?

    e. Tabulate the degree distribution for this network.

    f. Is this network connected?

    g. Calculate the betweenness centrality for nodes A and C.

    h. Calculate the density of the network.

20.2 **Network Density and Size.** Imagine that two new nodes are added to the undirected network in the previous exercise.

    a. By what percent has the number of nodes increased?

    b. By what percent has the number of possible edges increased?

    c. Suppose the new node has a typical (median) number of connections. What will happen to network density?

    d. Comment on comparing densities in networks of different sizes.

    e. Tabulate the degree distribution for this network.

20.3 **Link Prediction.** Consider the network shown in Figure 20.10.

    a. Using the number of common neighbors score, predict the next link to form (that is, suggest which new link has the best chance of success).

    b. Using the shortest path score, identify the link that is least likely to form.

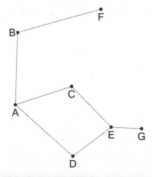

FIGURE 20.10   **NETWORK FOR LINK PREDICTION EXERCISE**

## CHAPTER 21

Text Mining

In this chapter, we introduce text as a form of data. First we discuss a tabular representation of text data in which each column is a word, each row is a document, and each cell is a 0 or 1, indicating whether that column's word is present in that row's document. Then, we consider how to move from unstructured documents to this structured matrix. Finally, we illustrate how to integrate this process into the standard machine learning procedures covered in earlier parts of the book.

Text Mining in R

In this chapter, we use the `tm`, `lsa`, `SnowballC` and `text2vec` packages to represent and preprocess text data, extract "concepts," and perform text mining operations.

21.1 INTRODUCTION[1]

Up to this point, and in machine learning in general, we have been primarily dealing with three types of data:

- Numerical
- Binary (yes/no, true/false)
- Multicategory

In some common predictive analytics applications, though, data come in text form. An Internet service provider, for example, might want to use an

---

[1] This and the subsequent sections in this chapter copyright © 2023 Datastats, LLC, and Galit Shmueli. Used by permission.

Machine Learning for Business Analytics: Concepts, Techniques, and Applications in R, Second Edition.
Galit Shmueli, Peter C. Bruce, Peter Gedeck, Inbal Yahav, and Nitin R. Patel
© 2023 John Wiley & Sons, Inc. Published 2023 by John Wiley & Sons, Inc.

automated algorithm to classify support tickets as urgent or routine so that the urgent ones can receive immediate human review. A law firm facing a massive discovery process (review of large numbers of documents) would benefit from a document review algorithm that could classify documents as relevant or irrelevant. In both of these cases, the predictor variables (features) are embedded as text in documents.

Text mining methods have gotten a boost from the availability of social media data—the Twitter feed, for example, as well as blogs, online forums, review sites, and news articles. The public availability of web-based text has provided a huge repository of data on which researchers can hone text mining methods. One area of growth has been the application of text mining methods to notes and transcripts from contact centers and service centers.

21.2 THE TABULAR REPRESENTATION OF TEXT: TERM–DOCUMENT MATRIX AND "BAG-OF-WORDS"

Consider the following three sentences:

```
S1. this is the first sentence.
S2. this is a second sentence.
S3. the third sentence is here.
```

We can represent the words (called *terms*) in these three sentences (called *documents*) in a *term–document matrix*, where each row is a word and each column is a sentence. In R, converting a set of documents into a term–document matrix can be done by first combining the documents into a collection (using function *corpus*) and then using function *tdm()* in the `tm` package. Table 21.1 illustrates this process for the three-sentence example.

Note that all the words in all three sentences (except "is," which is removed by R's *TermDocumentMatrix* function) are represented in the matrix and each word has exactly one row. Order is not important, and the number in the cell indicates the frequency of that term in that sentence. This is the *bag-of-words* approach, where the document is treated simply as a collection of words in which order, grammar, and syntax do not matter.

The three sentences have now been transformed into a tabular data format just like those we have seen to this point. In a simple world, this binary matrix could be used in clustering or, with the appending of an outcome variable, for classification or prediction. However, the text mining world is not a simple one. Even confining our analysis to the bag-of-words approach, considerable thinking and preprocessing may be required. Some human review of the documents, beyond simply classifying them for training purposes, may be indispensable.

TABLE 21.1   **TERM–DOCUMENT MATRIX REPRESENTATION OF WORDS IN SENTENCES S1–S3**

R code for term frequency

```
library(tm)

# define vector of sentences ("docs")
text <- c("this is the first sentence",
          "this is a second sentence",
          "the third sentence is here")

# convert sentences into a corpus
corp <- Corpus(VectorSource(text))

# compute term frequency
tdm <- TermDocumentMatrix(corp)
inspect(tdm)
```

Output

```
> inspect(tdm)
<<TermDocumentMatrix (terms: 7, documents: 3)>>
Non-/sparse entries: 11/10
Sparsity          : 40%
Maximal term length: 8
Weighting         : term frequency (tf)
Sample            :
         Docs
Terms     1 2 3
  first   1 0 0
  here    0 0 1
  second  0 1 0
  sentence 1 1 1
  the     1 0 1
  third   0 0 1
  this    1 1 0
```

21.3 BAG-OF-WORDS VS. MEANING EXTRACTION AT DOCUMENT LEVEL

We can distinguish between two undertakings in text mining:

- Label a document as belonging to a class or cluster similar documents
- Extract more detailed meaning from a document

The first goal requires a sizable collection of documents, or a *corpus*,[2] the ability to extract predictor variables from documents, and, for the classification task, lots

---

[2]The term "corpus" is often used to refer to a large, fixed standard set of documents that can be used by text preprocessing algorithms, often to train algorithms for a specific type of text or to compare the results of different algorithms. A specific text mining setting may rely on algorithms trained on a corpus specially suited to that task. One early general-purpose standard corpus was the Brown corpus of 500 English language documents of varying types (named Brown because it was compiled at Brown University in the early 1960s). These days many corpora rely on web-based sources such as Wikipedia and Twitter, which provide huge amounts of documents.

of pre-labeled documents to train a model. The models that are used, though, are the standard statistical and machine learning predictive models that we have already dealt with for numerical and categorical data.

The second goal might involve a single document, and is much more ambitious. The computer must learn at least some version of the complex "algorithms" that make up human language comprehension: grammar, syntax, punctuation, etc. In other words, it must undertake the processing of a natural (that is, noncomputer) language to *understand* documents in that language. Understanding the meaning of one document on its own is a far more formidable task than probabilistically assigning a class to a document based on rules derived from hundreds or thousands of similar documents.

For one thing, text comprehension requires maintenance and consideration of word order. "San Francisco beat Boston in last night's baseball game" is very different from "Boston beat San Francisco in last night's baseball game."

Even identical words in the same order can carry different meanings, depending on the cultural and social context: "Hitchcock shot The Birds in Bodega Bay," to an avid outdoors person indifferent to capitalization and unfamiliar with Alfred Hitchcock's films, might be about bird hunting. Ambiguity resolution is a major challenge in text comprehension—does "bot" mean "bought," or does it refer to robots?

Our focus will remain with the overall focus of the book and the easier goal—probabilistically assigning a class to a document or clustering similar documents. The second goal—deriving understanding from a single document—is the subject of the field of natural language processing (NLP).

21.4 PREPROCESSING THE TEXT

The simple example we presented had ordinary words separated by spaces and a period to denote the end of the each sentence. A fairly simple algorithm could break the sentences up into the word matrix with a few rules about spaces and periods. It should be evident that the rules required to parse data from real-world sources will need to be more complex. It should also be evident that the preparation of data for text mining is a more involved undertaking than the preparation of numerical or categorical data for predictive models. For example, consider the modified example in Table 21.2, based on the following sentences:

```
S1.  this is the first    sentence!!
S2.  this is a second Sentence :)
S3.  the third sentence, is here
S4.  forth of all sentences
```

TABLE 21.2   TERM–DOCUMENT MATRIX REPRESENTATION OF WORDS IN SENTENCES S1–S4

 code for term frequency of second example

```
text <- c("this is the first     sentence!!",
          "this is a second Sentence :)",
          "the third sentence, is here",
          "forth of all sentences")
corp <- Corpus(VectorSource(text))
tdm <- TermDocumentMatrix(corp)
inspect(tdm)
```

Output

```
> inspect(tdm)
<<TermDocumentMatrix (terms: 12, documents: 4)>>
Non-/sparse entries: 14/34
Sparsity           : 71%
Maximal term length: 10
Weighting          : term frequency (tf)

            Docs
Terms        1 2 3 4
  all        0 0 0 1
  first      1 0 0 0
  forth      0 0 0 1
  here       0 0 1 0
  second     0 1 0 0
  sentence   0 1 0 0
  sentence!! 1 0 0 0
  sentence,  0 0 1 0
  sentences  0 0 0 1
  the        1 0 1 0
  third      0 0 1 0
  this       1 1 0 0
```

This set of sentences has extra spaces, non-alpha characters, incorrect capitalization, and a misspelling of "fourth."

Tokenization

Our first simple data set was composed entirely of words found in the dictionary. A real set of documents will have more variety—it will contain numbers, alphanumeric strings like date stamps or part numbers, web and email addresses, abbreviations, slang, proper nouns, misspellings, and more.

Tokenization is the process of taking a text and, in an automated fashion, dividing it into separate "tokens" or terms. A token (term) is the basic unit of analysis. A word separated by spaces is a token. 2+3 would need to be separated into three tokens, while 23 would remain as one token. Punctuation might also stand as its own token (e.g., the @ symbol). These tokens become the row headers in the data matrix. Each text mining software program will have its own list of delimiters (spaces, commas, colons, etc.) that it uses to divide up the text into tokens. In Table 21.3, we use R's *tm_map()* to remove white space and punctuation marks from the four sentences shown in Table 21.2.

For a sizeable corpus, tokenization will result in a huge number of variables—the English language has over a million words, let alone the non-word terms that will be encountered in typical documents. Anything that can be done in the preprocessing stage to reduce the number of terms will aid in the analysis. The initial focus is on eliminating terms that simply add bulk and noise.

Some of the terms that result from the initial parsing of the corpus might not be useful in further analyses and can be eliminated in the preprocessing stage. For example, in a legal discovery case, one corpus of documents might be emails, all of which have company information and some boilerplate as part of the signature. These terms might be added to a *stopword list* of terms that are to be automatically eliminated in the preprocessing stage.

TABLE 21.3   TOKENIZATION OF S1–S4 EXAMPLE

 code for tokenization

```
# tokenization
corp <- tm_map(corp, stripWhitespace)
corp <- tm_map(corp, removePunctuation)
tdm <- TermDocumentMatrix(corp)
inspect(tdm)
```

Output

```
> inspect(tdm)
<<TermDocumentMatrix (terms: 10, documents: 4)>>
Non-/sparse entries: 14/26
Sparsity           : 65%
Maximal term length: 9
Weighting          : term frequency (tf)

          Docs
Terms      1 2 3 4
  all       0 0 0 1
  first     1 0 0 0
  forth     0 0 0 1
  here      0 0 1 0
  second    0 1 0 0
  sentence  1 1 1 0
  sentences 0 0 0 1
  the       1 0 1 0
  third     0 0 1 0
  this      1 1 0 0
```

Text Reduction

Most text-processing software (the `tm` package in R included) come with a generic *stopword* list of frequently occurring terms to be removed. If you review R's stopword list during preprocessing stages, you will see that it contains a large number of terms to be removed (Table 21.4 shows the first 174 stopwords). You can add additional terms or remove existing terms from the generic list.

Additional techniques to reduce the volume of text ("vocabulary reduction") and to focus on the most meaningful text include the following:

- *Stemming* is a linguistic method that reduces different variants of words to a common core.

- Frequency filters can be used to eliminate either terms that occur in a great majority of documents or very rare terms. Frequencty filters can also be used to limit the vocabulary to the *n* most frequent terms.

- Synonyms or synonymous phrases may be consolidated.

- Letter case (uppercase/lowercase) can be ignored.

TABLE 21.4   **STOPWORDS IN R**

```
> stopwords("english")
  [1] "i"          "me"         "my"         "myself"     "we"           "our"
  [7] "ours"       "ourselves"  "you"        "your"       "yours"        "yourself"
 [13] "yourselves" "he"         "him"        "his"        "himself"      "she"
 [19] "her"        "hers"       "herself"    "it"         "its"          "itself"
 [25] "they"       "them"       "their"      "theirs"     "themselves"   "what"
 [31] "which"      "who"        "whom"       "this"       "that"         "these"
 [37] "those"      "am"         "is"         "are"        "was"          "were"
 [43] "be"         "been"       "being"      "have"       "has"          "had"
 [49] "having"     "do"         "does"       "did"        "doing"        "would"
 [55] "should"     "could"      "ought"      "i'm"        "you're"       "he's"
 [61] "she's"      "it's"       "we're"      "they're"    "i've"         "you've"
 [67] "we've"      "they've"    "i'd"        "you'd"      "he'd"         "she'd"
 [73] "we'd"       "they'd"     "i'll"       "you'll"     "he'll"        "she'll"
 [79] "we'll"      "they'll"    "isn't"      "aren't"     "wasn't"       "weren't"
 [85] "hasn't"     "haven't"    "hadn't"     "doesn't"    "don't"        "didn't"
 [91] "won't"      "wouldn't"   "shan't"     "shouldn't"  "can't"        "cannot"
 [97] "couldn't"   "mustn't"    "let's"      "that's"     "who's"        "what's"
[103] "here's"     "there's"    "when's"     "where's"    "why's"        "how's"
[109] "a"          "an"         "the"        "and"        "but"          "if"
[115] "or"         "because"    "as"         "until"      "while"        "of"
[121] "at"         "by"         "for"        "with"       "about"        "against"
[127] "between"    "into"       "through"    "during"     "before"       "after"
[133] "above"      "below"      "to"         "from"       "up"           "down"
[139] "in"         "out"        "on"         "off"        "over"         "under"
[145] "again"      "further"    "then"       "once"       "here"         "there"
[151] "when"       "where"      "why"        "how"        "all"          "any"
[157] "both"       "each"       "few"        "more"       "most"         "other"
[163] "some"       "such"       "no"         "nor"        "not"          "only"
[169] "own"        "same"       "so"         "than"       "too"          "very"
```

- A variety of specific terms in a category can be replaced with the category name. This is called *normalization*. For example, different email addresses or different numbers might all be replaced with "emailtoken" or "numbertoken."

Table 21.5 presents the text reduction step applied to the four sentences example, after tokenization. We can see the number of terms has been reduced to five.

TABLE 21.5   **TEXT REDUCTION OF S1–S4 (AFTER TOKENIZATION)**

code for text reduction

```
# stopwords
library(SnowballC)
corp <- tm_map(corp, removeWords, stopwords("english"))

# stemming
corp <- tm_map(corp, stemDocument)

tdm <- TermDocumentMatrix(corp)
inspect(tdm)
```

Output

```
> inspect(tdm)
<<TermDocumentMatrix (terms: 5, documents: 4)>>
Non-/sparse entries: 8/12
Sparsity           : 60%
Maximal term length: 7
Weighting          : term frequency (tf)

        Docs
Terms    1 2 3 4
  first  1 0 0 0
  forth  0 0 0 1
  second 0 1 0 0
  sentenc 1 1 1 1
  third  0 0 1 0
```

Presence/Absence vs. Frequency

The bag-of-words approach can be implemented in terms of either *frequency* of terms or *presence/absence* of terms. The latter might be appropriate in some circumstances—in a forensic accounting classification model, for example, the presence or absence of a particular vendor name might be a key predictor variable, without regard to how often it appears in a given document. *Frequency* can be important in other circumstances, however. For example, in processing support tickets, a single mention of "IP address" might be non-meaningful—all support tickets might involve a user's IP address as part of the submission.

Repetition of the phrase multiple times, however, might provide useful information that IP address is part of the problem (e.g., DNS resolution). *Note:* The `tm` package in R only implements the frequency option. To implement the presence/absence option, you would need to convert the frequency data to a binary matrix (i.e., convert all non-zero counts to 1's).

Term Frequency–Inverse Document Frequency (TF-IDF)

There are additional popular options that factor in both the frequency of a term in a document and the frequency of documents with that term. One such popular option, which measures the importance of a term to a document, is *Term Frequency–Inverse Document Frequency* (TF-IDF). For a given document d and term t, the term frequency is the number of times term t appears in document d:

$$\text{TF}(d, t) = \# \text{ times term } t \text{ appears in document } d.$$

To account for terms that appear frequently in the domain of interest, we compute the *Inverse Document Frequency* of term t, calculated over the entire corpus and defined as[3]

$$\text{IDF}(t) = \log \left(\frac{\text{total number of documents}}{\# \text{ documents containing term } t} \right).$$

TF-IDF(t, d) for a specific term–document pair is the product of term frequency TF(t, d) and inverse document frequency IDF(t):

$$\text{TF-IDF}(t, d) = \text{TF}(t, d) \times \text{IDF}(t). \tag{21.1}$$

The TF-IDF matrix contains the value for each term–document combination. The above definition of TF-IDF is a common one; however there are multiple ways to define and weight both TF and IDF, so there are a variety of possible definitions of TF-IDF. For example, Table 21.6 shows the TF-IDF matrix for the four-sentence example (after tokenization and text reduction). The function *weightTfIdf()* uses a base 2 logarithm for the computation of IDF and normalizes the numerator by dividing by the total number of terms in document d. For example, the TF-IDF value for the term "first" in document 1 is computed by

$$\text{TF-IDF}(\textit{first}, 1) = \frac{1}{2} \times \log_2 \left(\frac{4}{1} \right) = 1.$$

As can be seen in Table 21.6, the term *sentenc*, which occurs in all documents, now has TF-IDF values of 0.

The general idea of TF-IDF is that it identifies documents with frequent occurrences of rare terms. TF-IDF yields high values for documents with a relatively high frequency for terms that are relatively rare overall and near–zero values for terms that are absent from a document or present in most documents.

---

[3]IDF(t) is actually just the fraction, without the logarithm, although using a logarithm is very common.

TABLE 21.6	TF-IDF MATRIX FOR S1–S4 EXAMPLE (AFTER TOKENIZATION AND TEXT REDUCTION)

```
> tfidf <- weightTfIdf(tdm)
> inspect(tfidf)
<<TermDocumentMatrix (terms: 5, documents: 4)>>
Non-/sparse entries: 4/16
Sparsity           : 80%
Maximal term length: 7
Weighting          : term frequency - inverse document frequency (normalized) (tf-idf)

        Docs
Terms    1 2 3 4
  first  1 0 0 0
  forth  0 0 0 1
  second 0 1 0 0
  sentenc 0 0 0 0
  third  0 0 1 0
```

From Terms to Concepts: Latent Semantic Indexing

In Chapter 4, we showed how numerous numeric variables can be reduced to a small number of "principal components" that explain most of the variation in a set of variables. The principal components are linear combinations of the original (typically correlated) variables, and a subset of them serve as new variables to replace the numerous original variables.

An analogous dimension reduction method—*latent semantic indexing* [or *latent semantic analysis* (LSA)]—can be applied to text data. The mathematics of the algorithm are beyond the scope of this chapter,[4] but a good intuitive explanation comes from the user guide for Analytic Solver Data Mining software[5]:

> For example, if we inspected our document collection, we might find that each time the term "alternator" appeared in an automobile document, the document also included the terms "battery" and "headlights." Or each time the term "brake" appeared in an automobile document, the terms "pads" and "squeaky" also appeared. However, there is no detectable pattern regarding the use of the terms "alternator" and "brake" together. Documents including "alternator" might or might not include "brake" and documents including "brake" might or might not include "alternator." Our four terms, battery, headlights, pads, and squeaky describe two different automobile repair issues: failing brakes and a bad alternator.

So, in this case, latent semantic indexing would reduce the four terms to two concepts:

- Brake failure

- Alternator failure

---

[4] Generally, in PCA, the dimension is reduced by replacing the covariance matrix by a smaller one; in LSA, dimension is reduced by replacing the term-document matrix by a smaller one.

[5] https://www.solver.com/text-mining-example

We illustrate latent semantic indexing using R in the example in Section 21.6.

Extracting Meaning

In the simple latent semantic indexing example, the concepts to which the terms map (failing brakes, bad alternator) are clear and understandable. In many cases, unfortunately, this will not be true—the concepts to which the terms map will not be obvious. In such cases, latent semantic indexing will greatly enhance the manageability of the text for purposes of building predictive models and sharpen predictive power by reducing noise, but it will turn the model into a blackbox device for prediction, not so useful for understanding the roles that terms and concepts play. This is OK for our purposes—as noted earlier, we are focusing on text mining to classify or cluster new documents, not to extract meaning.

From Terms to High-Dimensional Word Vectors: Word2Vec or GloVe

Word embedding is a form of text representation technique in which each word is represented in the form of a multidimensional vector (called *word vector*) so that words that are closer to one another in this vector space would also be similar in meaning. Latent semantic indexing discussed earlier was one such word embedding that considers occurrences of terms at a document level. Yet another form of word embedding approaches is Word2Vec[6] which considers occurrences of terms at a context level and uses prediction-based models to arrive at the word vector representations.

The Word2Vec technique uses a neural network model and trains words against other words in its neighborhood within the corpus. The technique has two variants based on how the model is trained: *continuous bag of words* (CBOW) and *skip-gram*. In both variants, a window of specified length (context) is moved along the text in the training corpus, and in each iteration the network is trained using only the words inside the window. The CBOW model is trained to predict the word in the center of the window (focus word) based on the surrounding words (context words). The skip-gram model is trained to predict the context words based on the focus word. After the training is complete, the hidden layer with its learned weights is used as the word vector representation.

Google has published pretrained Word2Vec word vectors trained with CBOW on a Google News dataset (about 100 billion words) that contain 300-dimensional vectors for 3 million words and phrases. Interestingly, these high-dimensional word vectors support vector operations that often make semantic sense. For example, the mathematical operation vector(Paris) − vector(France) + vector(Italy) is found to be very similar to vector(Rome), thus implicitly capturing the notion of countries and their capitals.

---

[6]https://code.google.com/archive/p/word2vec/

GloVe is an alternative to Word2Vec that generates word vectors using global word-word co-occurrences within a corpus of documents. (Two words co-occur if they both occur in a document within a specified window, say within three words of one another.) Unusually high or low levels of co-occurrence are informative. GloVe has similar properties to Word2Vec. We illustrate an application of GloVe using R in Section 21.7.

21.5   IMPLEMENTING MACHINE LEARNING METHODS

After the text has gone through the preprocessing stage, it is then in a numeric matrix format, and you can apply the various machine learning methods discussed earlier in this book. Clustering methods can be used to identify clusters of documents—for example, large numbers of medical reports can be mined to identify clusters of symptoms. Prediction methods can be used with tech support tickets to predict how long it will take to resolve an issue. Perhaps the most popular application of text mining is for classification—also termed *labeling*—of documents.

21.6   EXAMPLE: ONLINE DISCUSSIONS ON AUTOS AND ELECTRONICS

This example[7] illustrates a classification task—to classify Internet discussion posts as either auto-related or electronics-related. One post looks like this:

> From: smith@logos.asd.sgi.com (Tom Smith) Subject: Ford Explorer 4WD - do I need performance axle?
> We're considering getting a Ford Explorer XLT with 4WD and we have the following questions (All we would do is go skiing - no off-roading):
> 1. With 4WD, do we need the "performance axle" - (limited slip axle). Its purpose is to allow the tires to act independently when the tires are on different terrain.
> 2. Do we need the all-terrain tires (P235/75X15) or will the all-season (P225/70X15) be good enough for us at Lake Tahoe?
> Thanks,
> Tom
> _
>
> ==
>
> Tom Smith Silicon Graphics smith@asd.sgi.com 2011 N. Shoreline Rd. MS 8U-815 415-962-0494 (fax) Mountain View, CA 94043
> ==

---

[7]The dataset is taken from www.cs.cmu.edu/afs/cs/project/theo-20/www/data/news20.html, with minor modifications.

The posts are taken from Internet groups devoted to autos and electronics, so are pre-labeled. This one, clearly, is auto-related. A related organizational scenario might involve messages received by a medical office that must be classified as medical or non-medical (the messages in such a real scenario would probably have to be labeled by humans as part of the preprocessing).

The posts are in the form a zipped file that contains two folders: *auto posts* and *electronics posts*, each contains a set of 1000 posts organized in small files. In the following, we describe the main steps from preprocessing to building a classification model on the data. Table 21.7 provides R code for the text processing step for this example. We describe each step separately next.

Importing and Labeling the Records

Package `tm` in R contains multiple load functions for different document formats. In our example, we use function *ZipSource()* to load the zipped file from *mlba::AutosElectronics*[8] and read it. Other options include reading an entire directory, reading PDF or XML files, and more. We additionally create a label array that corresponds to the order of the documents—we will use "1" for autos and "0" for electronics. The first 1000 documents should be classified as "1" and the remaining 1000 documents "0" (see Step 1 in Table 21.7).

Text Preprocessing in R

The first preprocessing step is *tokenization*, which includes the removal of white space, punctuations, and numbers. The next step is removing *stopwords*. The last preprocessing step is *stemming*, or the consolidation of multiple forms of a word into a single core. For example, "road" and "Rd." might stem to "road." These two operations are shown in Step 2 in Table 21.7.

Producing a Concept Matrix

The preprocessing step will produce a "clean" corpus and term–document matrix that can be used to compute the TF-IDF term–document matrix described earlier. The TF-IDF matrix incorporates both the frequency of a term and the frequency with which documents containing that term appear in the overall corpus.

The resulting matrix is probably too large to efficiently analyze in a predictive model (specifically, the number of predictors in the example is 21,789), so we use latent semantic indexing to extract a reduced space, termed "concepts." For manageability, we will limit the number of concepts to 20. Table 21.7 shows the

---

[8]The file *AutosElectronics.zip* is provided with the `mlba` package. The variable *mlba::AutosElectronics* contains the location of the installed file on your computer.

TABLE 21.7	IMPORTING AND LABELING THE RECORDS, PREPROCESSING TEXT, AND PRODUCING CONCEPT MATRIX

 code for importing and labeling records, preprocessing text, and producing concept matrix

```
library(tm)
# step 1: import and label records
# read zip file into a corpus
corp <- Corpus(ZipSource(mlba::AutosElectronics, recursive = T))

# create an array of records labels
label <- c(rep(1, 1000), rep(0, 1000))

# step 2: text preprocessing
# tokenization
corp <- tm_map(corp, stripWhitespace)
corp <- tm_map(corp, removePunctuation)
corp <- tm_map(corp, removeNumbers)

# stopwords
corp <- tm_map(corp, removeWords, stopwords("english"))

# stemming
corp <- tm_map(corp, stemDocument)

# step 3: TF-IDF and latent semantic analysis
# compute TF-IDF
tdm <- TermDocumentMatrix(corp)
tfidf <- weightTfIdf(tdm)

# extract (20) concepts
library(lsa)
lsa.tfidf <- lsa(tfidf, dim = 20)

# convert to data frame
words.df <- as.data.frame(as.matrix(lsa.tfidf$dk))
```

R code for applying these two operations—creating a TF-IDF matrix and latent semantic indexing—to the example.[9]

Finally, we can use this reduced set of concepts to facilitate the building of a predictive model. We will not attempt to interpret the concepts for meaning.

Fitting a Predictive Model

At this point, we have transformed the original text data into a familiar form needed for predictive modeling—a single target variable (1 = autos, 0 = electronics) and 20 predictor variables (the concepts).

We can now partition the data (60% training and 40% holdout) and try applying several classification models. Table 21.8 shows the performance of a logistic

---

[9]The **topicmodels** package is also commonly used for latent semantic analysis.

TABLE 21.8 FITTING A PREDICTIVE MODEL TO THE AUTOS AND ELECTRONICS DISCUSSION DATA

 code for fitting and evaluating a logistic regression predictive model

```
library(caret)

# prepare training and holdout sets
set.seed(1)
df <- cbind(label=factor(label), words.df)
idx <- caret::createDataPartition(df$label, p=0.6, list=FALSE)
train.df <- df[idx, ]
holdout.df <- df[-idx, ]

# fit logistic regression
logit.reg <- train(label ~ ., data=train.df,
                    trControl=trainControl(method="none"),
                    method="glm", family="binomial")

# compute accuracy on holdout set
pred <- predict(logit.reg, newdata=holdout.df)
confusionMatrix(pred, holdout.df$label)
```

Output

```
> confusionMatrix(ifelse(pred>0.5, 1, 0), label[-training])
Confusion Matrix and Statistics

          Reference
Prediction   0    1
         0 385    7
         1  15  393

              Accuracy : 0.9725
```

regression, with "class" as the outcome variable and the 20 concept variables as the predictors.

The confusion matrix (Table 21.8) shows reasonably high accuracy in separating the two classes of documents—an accuracy of 97.25%. The decile-wise lift chart (Figure 21.1) confirms the high separability of the classes and the usefulness of this model for a ranking goal. For a two class dataset with a nearly 50/50 split between the classes, the maximum lift per decile is 2, and the lift shown here is just under 2 for the first 50 % of the cases and close to 0 for the last 40%. In a decision-making process, human review could be concentrated on the middle ranked 20% where the classification error is most likely to occur.

Next, we would also try other models to see how they compare; this is left as an exercise.

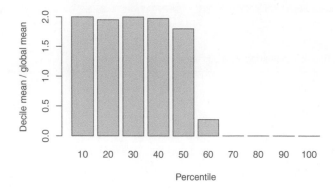

FIGURE 21.1   DECILE-WISE LIFT CHART FOR AUTOS-ELECTRONICS DOCUMENT CLASSIFICATION

 code for creating a decile lift chart

```
library(gains)

prob <- predict(logit.reg, newdata=holdout.df, type="prob")[,2]
actual <- ifelse(holdout.df$label == 1, 1, 0)
gain <- gains(actual, prob)
barplot(gain$mean.resp/mean(actual), names.arg=seq(10, 100, by=10),
        xlab="Percentile", ylab="Decile mean / global mean")
```

Prediction

The most prevalent application of text mining is classification ("labeling"), but it can also be used for prediction of numerical values. For example, maintenance or support tickets could be used to predict length or cost of repair. The only step that would be different in the above process is the label that is applied after the preprocessing, which would be a numeric value rather than a class.

21.7 EXAMPLE: SENTIMENT ANALYSIS OF MOVIE REVIEWS

This example demonstrates using word embeddings for a classification task—to classify the sentiment of movie reviews as either positive or negative. The dataset *mlba::IMDBdataset10K* contains 5000 positive and 5000 negative movie reviews collected from the Internet Movie Database (IMDB) (Maas et al., 2011).[10]

A snippet of a positive review looks like this:

> It is so gratifying to see one great piece of art converted into another without distortion or contrivance. I had no guess as to how such an extraordinary piece of literature could be recreated as a film worth seeing. …So now my favorite book and movie have the same title.

On the other hand, a snippet of a negative review looks like this:

> I did not expect much from this film, but boy-o-boy, I did not expect the movie to be this bad. …This is a very bad film! I gave it three out of ten because of few smiles it gave me, but I did never laugh!

Data Loading, Preparation, and Partitioning

In the following, we describe the key steps from preprocessing to building a classification model on the data. Table 21.9 shows the steps to prepare the dataset for training the GloVe word embeddings. After splitting the dataset into training and holdout, we tokenize the reviews and build the term-co-occurence matrix required for GloVe using the `text2vec` package.[11]

Generating and Applying the GloVe Model

The term–co–occurence matrix is processed with the *GlobalVector* class from `text2vec` (see Table 21.10). The *GlobalVectors$fit_transform()* function returns the embedded word vectors. These are numerical representations for each word. Each vector is a 100-dimensional word embedding model. A given word occurring in different documents has the same values for all dimensions. For example, the word "love" has the same dimension values for any movie review it appears in.

At this point, each review consists of 100 values for each of its words. To transform the data into the familiar tabular format with each record corresponding to a movie review, an aggregate value for each of the 100 values is required. We can do this in several different ways. Here, we compute the weighted dimension value for each movie review, which are available in the trained GloVe model. The result of this process is a description of each review using 100 predictors.

---

[10]The original large movie dataset is published at http://ai.stanford.edu/~amaas/data/sentiment/ and contains 25K positive and 25K negative movie reviews collected from the Internet Movie Database (IMDB). A stratified sample of 10K records from this dataset is used in this example.

[11]Glove word embeddings can also be created with `keras` (https://keras.io/examples/nlp/)

TABLE 21.9   PREPARE DATA FOR SENTIMENT ANALYSIS OF MOVIE REVIEWS DATA

code for loading and preprocessing data for sentiment analysis

```
library(tidyverse)
library(text2vec)

# load and split data into training and holdout set
data <- mlba::IMDBdataset10K %>%
  mutate(
    id = row_number(),
    sentiment = as.factor(sentiment)
  )

set.seed(1)
trainIndex <- createDataPartition(data$sentiment, p=0.8, list=FALSE)
data_train <- data[trainIndex, ]
data_holdout <- data[-trainIndex, ]
```

Tokenize reviews and create term-cooccurence matrix (TCM)

```
prep_fun <- tolower
tok_fun <- word_tokenizer

it_train <- itoken(data_train$review, ids=data_train$id,
                   preprocessor=prep_fun, tokenizer=tok_fun)
it_holdout <- itoken(data_holdout$review, ids=data_holdout$id,
                     preprocessor=prep_fun, tokenizer=tok_fun)

vocab <- create_vocabulary(it_train)
vocab <- prune_vocabulary(vocab, term_count_min = 5L)
vectorizer <- vocab_vectorizer(vocab)
tcm_train <- create_tcm(it_train, vectorizer, skip_grams_window = 5L)
```

The holdout data is processed in the same way. The only difference is that the GloVe model trained earlier is now used for the holdout data as well.

Fitting a Predictive Model

The data is now ready for predictive modeling with a single outcome "sentiment" (class labels: positive and negative) and 100 predictors (the averaged word embedding dimensions). Different classification models may be applied to this data. Table 21.11 shows the code to train a logistic regression model. The confusion matrix shows a moderately high accuracy in separating reviews with positive and negative sentiments—an accuracy of 78.1%. This is confirmed by the ROC curve in Figure 21.2.

TABLE 21.10   CREATE WORD AND SENTENCE VECTORS USING GLOVE

 code for loading and preprocessing data for sentiment analysis

```
# determine word vectors
glove <- GlobalVectors$new(rank=100, x_max=10)
wv_main <- glove$fit_transform(tcm_train, n_iter=10, convergence_tol=0.01, n_threads=8)
wv_context <- glove$components
word_vectors <- wv_main + t(wv_context)
```

Combine word vectors for documents to obtain numerical description of reviews

```
dtm_train <- create_dtm(it_train, vectorizer)
common_terms <- intersect(colnames(dtm_train), rownames(word_vectors) )
dtm_averaged <-  normalize(dtm_train[, common_terms], "l1")
sentence_vectors_train <- dtm_averaged %*% word_vectors[common_terms, ]

dtm_holdout <- create_dtm(it_holdout, vectorizer)
common_terms <- intersect(colnames(dtm_holdout), rownames(word_vectors) )
dtm_averaged <-  normalize(dtm_holdout[, common_terms], "l1")
sentence_vectors_holdout <- dtm_averaged %*% word_vectors[common_terms, ]
```

TABLE 21.11   TRAIN SENTIMENT ANALYSIS MODEL

code for training logistic regression model using sentence vectors

```
train.df <- as.data.frame(as.matrix(sentence_vectors_train))
train.df$sentiment <- data_train$sentiment

trControl <- caret::trainControl(method="cv", number=5, allowParallel=TRUE)
logit.reg <- caret::train(sentiment ~ ., data=train.df, trControl=trControl,
                    # fit logistic regression with a generalized linear model
                    method="glm", family="binomial")

holdout.df <- as.data.frame(as.matrix(sentence_vectors_holdout))
holdout.df$sentiment <- data_holdout$sentiment

caret::confusionMatrix(predict(logit.reg, holdout.df), holdout.df$sentiment)
```

Output

```
Confusion Matrix and Statistics

          Reference
Prediction negative positive
  negative      772      210
  positive      228      790

          Accuracy : 0.781
```

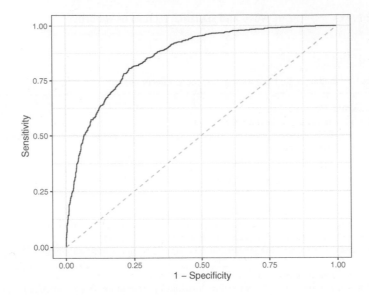

FIGURE 21.2   ROC CURVE FOR THE SENTIMENT ANALYSIS MODEL TRAINED USING GLOVE WORD EMBEDDINGS

```
library(ROCR)
prob <- predict(logit.reg, newdata=holdout.df, type="prob")$positive

predob <- prediction(prob, holdout.df$sentiment)
perf <- performance(predob, "tpr", "fpr")
perf.df <- data.frame(
  tpr=perf@x.values[[1]],
  fpr=perf@y.values[[1]]
)
ggplot(perf.df, aes(x=tpr, y=fpr)) +
  geom_line() +
  geom_segment(aes(x=0, y=0, xend=1, yend=1), color="grey", linetype="dashed") +
  labs(x="1 - Specificity", y="Sensitivity")
```

21.8 SUMMARY

In this chapter, we drew a distinction between text processing for the purpose of extracting meaning from a single document (natural language processing—NLP) and classifying or labeling numerous documents in probabilistic fashion (text mining). We concentrated on the latter and examined the preprocessing steps that need to occur before text can be mined. Those steps are more varied and involved than those involved in preparing numerical data. The ultimate goal is to produce a matrix in which rows are terms and columns are documents. The nature of language is such that the number of terms is excessive for effective model-building, so the preprocessing steps include vocabulary reduction. A final major reduction takes place if we use, instead of the terms, a limited set of concepts that represents most of the variation in the documents, in the same way that principal components capture most of the variation in numerical data. Finally, we end up with a quantitative matrix in which the cells represent the frequency or presence of terms and the columns represent documents. To this, we append document labels (classes), and then we are ready to use this matrix for classifying documents using classification methods.

PROBLEMS

21.1 **Tokenization.** Consider the following text version of a post to an online learning forum in a statistics course:

```
Thanks John!<br /><br /><font size="3">
&quot;Illustrations and demos will be
provided for students to work through on
their own&quot;</font>.
Do we need that to finish project? If yes,
where to find the illustration and demos?
Thanks for your help.\<img title="smile"
alt="smile" src="\url{http://lms.statistics.
com/pix/smartpix.php/statistics_com_1/s/smil
ey.gif}" \><br /> <br />
```

a. Identify 10 non-word tokens in the passage.

b. Suppose this passage constitutes a document to be classified, but you are not certain of the business goal of the classification task. Identify material (at least 20% of the terms) that, in your judgment, could be discarded fairly safely without knowing that goal.

c. Suppose the classification task is to predict whether this post requires the attention of the instructor or whether a teaching assistant might suffice. Identify the 20% of the terms that you think might be most helpful in that task.

d. What aspect of the passage is most problematic from the standpoint of simply using a bag-of-words approach, as opposed to an approach in which meaning is extracted?

21.2 **Classifying Internet Discussion Posts.** In this problem, you will use the data and scenario described in this chapter's example, in which the task is to develop a model to classify documents as either auto-related or electronics-related.

a. Load the zipped file into R and create a label vector.

b. Following the example in this chapter, preprocess the documents. Explain what would be different if you did not perform the "stemming" step.

c. Use the `lsa` package to create 10 concepts. Explain what is different about the concept matrix, as opposed to the TF-IDF matrix.

d. Using this matrix, fit a predictive model (different from the model presented in the chapter illustration) to classify documents as autos or electronics. Compare its performance with that of the model presented in the chapter illustration.

21.3 **Classifying Classified Ads Submitted Online.** Consider the case of a website that caters to the needs of a specific farming community and carries classified ads intended for that community. Anyone, including robots, can post an ad via a web interface, and the site owners have problems with ads that are fraudulent, spam, or simply not relevant to the community. They have provided a dataset with 4143 ads, each ad in a row, and each ad labeled as either −1 (not relevant) or 1 (relevant). The goal is to develop a predictive model that can classify ads automatically.

- Open the dataset *mlba::FarmAds*, and briefly review some of the relevant and non-relevant ads to get a flavor for their contents.

- Following the example in the chapter, preprocess the data in R, and create a term–document matrix, and a concept matrix. Limit the number of concepts to 20.

  a. Examine the term–document matrix.

     i. Is it sparse or dense?

     ii. Find two non-zero entries and briefly interpret their meaning, in words (you do not need to derive their calculation)

  b. Briefly explain the difference between the term–document matrix and the concept–document matrix. Relate the latter to what you learned in the principal components chapter (Chapter 4).

  c. Using logistic regression, partition the data (60% training, 40% holdout), and develop a model to classify the documents as "relevant" or "non-relevant." Comment on its efficacy.

  d. Why use the concept–document matrix, and not the term-document matrix, to provide the predictor variables?

21.4 Clustering Auto Posts. In this problem, you will use the data and scenario described in this chapter's example. The task is to cluster the auto posts.

  a. Following the example in this chapter, preprocess the documents, except do not create a label vector.

  b. Use the `lsa` package to create 10 concepts.

  c. Before doing the clustering, state how many natural clusters you expect to find.

  d. Perform hierarchical clustering, and inspect the dendrogram.

    i. From the dendrogram, how many natural clusters appear?

    ii. Examining the dendrogram as it branches beyond the number of main clusters, select a subcluster and assess its characteristics.

  e. Perform k-means clustering for two clusters, and report how distant and separated they are (using between-cluster distance and within-cluster dispersion).

## CHAPTER 22

Responsible Data Science[1]

In this chapter, we go beyond technical considerations of model fitting, selection, and performance and discuss the potentially harmful effects of machine learning. The catalog of harms is now extensive, including a host of cases where AI has deliberately been put to ill purposes in service of big brother surveillance and state suppression of minorities. Our focus, however, is on cases where the intentions of the model developer are good, and the resulting bias or unfairness has been unintentional. We review the principles of responsible data science (RDS) and discuss a concrete framework that can govern data science work to put those principles into practice. We also discuss some key elements of that framework: datasheets, model cards, and model audits.

Responsible data science in R

The main R package introduced in this chapter is `iml` which provides multiple approaches that help to analyze complex models and understand their predictions.

22.1 INTRODUCTION[2]

Machine learning and AI bring the promise of seemingly unlimited good. After all, the ability to ingest any set of arbitrarily sized, minimally structured data and produce predictions or explanations for these data is applicable to almost every domain. Our societal attention often focuses on the revolutionary future applications of this potential: cars that drive themselves, computers that can

---

[1] This chapter draws on material from *Responsible Data Science*, Wiley 2021, by Grant Fleming and Peter Bruce, used by permission.

[2] This chapter copyright ©2021 Datastats, LLC. and Galit Shmueli. Used by permission

---

Machine Learning for Business Analytics: Concepts, Techniques, and Applications in R, Second Edition.
Galit Shmueli, Peter C. Bruce, Peter Gedeck, Inbal Yahav, and Nitin R. Patel
© 2023 John Wiley & Sons, Inc. Published 2023 by John Wiley & Sons, Inc.

hold natural conversations with humans, precision medications tailored to our specific genomes, cameras that can instantly recognize any object, and software that can automatically generate new images or videos. Conversations about these benefits, though, too often ignore the harms that machine learning models can cause.

Example: Predicting Recidivism

Decisions about criminal defendants in the US justice system are based on the weight of probabilistic evidence at multiple stages: whether to arrest, whether to go to trial, arrival at a verdict, and sentencing. At the sentencing phase, judges determine the length and terms of sentences, in part, by assessing the likelihood that a convicted defendant will commit another crime (recidivate). Courts have started relying increasingly on machine learning recidivism algorithms to inform decisions on sentencing. The COMPAS algorithm,[3] sold by Northpointe, Inc., is among the most prominent of these, and critics have charged that it is biased against African–Americans. The algorithm is not public and involves more than 170 predictors. Its advocates retort that COMPAS has good overall predictive performance and that its accuracy, as measured by the area under the ROC curve (Receiver Operating Characteristics curve), is similar for African–American and White defendants. The trouble is that the errors made are quite different:

- African–American defendants are over-predicted to re-offend (leading to tougher sentences).

- White defendants are under-predicted to re-offend (leading to lighter sentences).

The over-prediction errors (penalizing African–Americans) balance out the under-prediction errors (favoring Whites), so the overall error rate is the same for both. A single-minded focus on one overall accuracy metric obscures this bias against African–Americans. We will work through this example in greater detail below.

22.2 UNINTENTIONAL HARM

The COMPAS algorithm did not set out to penalize African–Americans. Its goal was to make sentencing decisions overall more consistent and "scientific." The bias against African–Americans was unintended and unwanted.

---

[3]COMPAS stands for "Correctional Offender Management Profiling for Alternative Sanctions"; a good summary by the public interest group ProPublica can be found here: https://www.propublica.org/article/how-we-analyzed-the-compas-recidivism-algorithm

Another stark example of unintentional harm was the Optum healthcare algorithm. In 2001, the healthcare company Optum launched Impact-Pro, a predictive modeling tool that purported to predict patients' future need for followup care and assign a risk score, based on a variety of predictor inputs. The result would be better healthcare for patients, as follow-up interventions could be better timed and calibrated. Hospitals could use the tool to better manage resources, and insurers could use it to better set insurance rates. Unfortunately, experience proved that the algorithm was biased against African–Americans: a research team led by Ziad Obermeyer studied these algorithms and found that, for any given risk score, African–American patients consistently experienced more chronic health conditions than did White patients.

It turned out that a key predictor for "future health care need" is "prior healthcare spending." African–American spending on healthcare was, on average, less than that for Whites, but not because of better health. Rather, it was due to lower income levels and less access to health insurance and costly medical facilities. Hence, an African–American individual would be predicted to need less follow-up care than a White individual with similar health.

There are numerous other examples of well-intentioned algorithms going wrong.[4] The algorithms that power social media and Internet ads foster connections among people and with things they are interested in, "bringing the world closer together" in Facebook's words. Those same algorithms can also nurture communities of hate and facilitate the spread of false news and conspiracy theories.

INTENDED HARM

Not all damage from machine learning algorithms is unintentional. In some cases, bad actors "weaponize" algorithms for purposes that are malicious. In other cases, seemingly legitimate law enforcement practices creep into the realm of "big brother":

- Facial recognition and identification technology, combined with the widespread presence of security cameras, enable police departments to track down criminal suspects who would have gone undetected in the pre-technology age. This is a good thing!

- Those same technologies, though, have enabled US immigration authorities to track down and deport undocumented individuals who may have been living and working peacefully for years or decades. This is not so clearly a good thing—the technology empowered bureaucrats (not legislators) to shift the terms of a highly contentious political debate that was broadly agreed on only one thing:

---

[4]The popular author Cathy O'Neil coined the catchphrase "Weapons of Math Destruction" in recounting such examples in her book of the same name (O'Neil, 2016).

> authorities should not be sweeping the country to round up and deport long-term residents who are undocumented.
>
> - These technologies have also aided Chinese police authorities in their surveillance and suppression of Uighur and Tibetan communities, a bad thing by the standards of most pluralistic societies that honor the rule of law.
>
> Some might also consider that knowing about damage caused by algorithms and proceeding anyway ("turning a blind eye") constitutes intentional harm. In late 2021, a disaffected employee at Facebook released a trove of internal Facebook research showing that ML-enabled algorithms harmed teenagers (for teen girls with mental health and body-image issues, Instagram exacerbated those issues) and fostered civil discord (2018 algorithm changes for the Facebook newsfeed boosted angry and contentious content). Top executives knew about the internal research but were reluctant to make significant changes in highly profitable platforms.
>
> The framework and process we discuss in this chapter will do little to counter the individual or entity that is determined to develop or repurpose algorithms for harmful purposes. However, the framework outlined below does have an important message for data scientists involved in developing algorithms: anticipate and be mindful of potentially harmful uses to which their work might be put.

22.3 LEGAL CONSIDERATIONS

Many treatments of the ethical aspects of data science focus on legal issues. This is understandable, as avoiding legal jeopardy is a strong motivator. Legal compliance is ultimately a matter for attorneys more than data scientists. The latter may contribute best by pursuing a general framework for responsible data science, so our legal discussion will be brief and focused on two points: the European Union's GDPR and the concept of "protected groups."

The General Data Protection Regulation (GDPR)

The most recognized legal environment for machine learning is the General Data Protection Regulation (GDPR) of the European Union (EU), which went into effect in August 2018. The GDPR provides sweeping protections to those in the EU (whether citizens of EU countries or not) including a "right to be forgotten" (a requirement that technology companies provide mechanisms by which individuals can have their data removed from online platforms), as well as the right to data portability and the right to object to automated decision-making and profiling. The GDPR's focus is strongly on empowering the individual, educated citizen with greater leverage to enforce the privacy of their data. Because the GDPR was the first comprehensive regulatory framework for big data services, it set the pattern for other legal initiatives that followed, including the

California Consumer Protection Act (CCPA) and Canada's Personal Information Protection and Electronic Documents Act (PIPEDA). Given the size of the EU market and the global nature of internet activity, the GDPR has become, in effect, a global regulatory regime.

Protected Groups

Regulations and laws that address not simply consumer privacy, but also issues of algorithmic discrimination and bias, are less well developed. However, one guiding principle is that laws that restrict behavior by individuals or corporations do not disappear merely because the decisions are made by algorithms. Decisions or actions that are illegal for a human in a company (discrimination in lending based on gender or age, for example) are also illegal for an algorithm to do in automated fashion. In US law (and in other countries as well), there are various "protected groups" where such restrictions apply. Protected groups may be identified on the basis of race, gender, age, sexual orientation, medical disability, or other factors. Although there may be no AI-specific or big data-specific laws in this area, there is ample and long-standing legal history that must be considered in the deployment of algorithms.

To evaluate fairness and calculate fairness metrics, a "privileged group" is designated. Often this reflects actual societal advantage enjoyed by the group (terminology coinciding with the social justice movement), but it is also a technical requirement. Fairness metrics must be calculated relative to some base group, so the term by itself does not imply privilege in the lay meaning.

22.4 PRINCIPLES OF RESPONSIBLE DATA SCIENCE

Legal statutes and regulations are typically lengthy, detailed, and difficult to understand. Moreover, legal compliance alone is not sufficient to avoid some of the harm caused by machine learning. The potential for reputational harm may be just as great as that for legal jeopardy. In late 2021, Facebook began conducting "reputational reviews" of its services and products. The publicly-stated purpose was to avoid harm to children, but news stories also cited Facebook's desire to anticipate how its algorithms might be criticized. A significant movement has arisen in the data science community to focus greater attention on this potential for harm and how to avoid it. A number of commentators have suggested that data scientists should adhere to a framework for responsible data science: a set of best practices. Common to most suggested frameworks are five principles:

- Non-maleficence (avoiding harm)
- Fairness

- Transparency
- Accountability
- Privacy

Non-maleficence

Non-maleficence covers concepts associated with causing or avoiding harm. At a high level, following this principle requires that data scientists ensure that their models do not cause foreseeable harms or harms of negligence. While unforeseen harms are sometimes unavoidable, they should be accounted for as much as reasonably possible. Harms that ought to be avoided include risks of physical harm, legal risks, reductions in future opportunities, privacy violations, emotional distress, facilitating illegal activities, and other results which could negatively impact individuals.

Non-maleficence is the hardest principle to guarantee in practice, and we recommend thinking of it as more of a goal to strive for than a necessary box to check for every data science project. A model can be fair, transparent, accountable to users, and respecting of privacy yet still make predictions that advantage some people while causing harm for others. Medical triaging algorithms for prioritizing scarce medical resources necessarily place some individuals further back in the queue or out of the queue entirely. Credit scoring algorithms make life difficult for those receiving low credit scores. In such cases, non-maleficence must be considered in the context of other principles.

Fairness

Fairness covers concepts associated with equal representation, non-discrimination, dignity, and just outcomes. Dimensions of interest for fairness evaluations typically involve human-specific factors like ethnicity, gender, sexual orientation, age, socioeconomic status, education, disability status, presence of preexisting conditions (healthcare), and history of adverse events. Model fairness is primarily a function of whether the model produces fair outcomes, with input factors (how the model uses certain features, how the features were created, etc.) being less relevant. Like non-maleficence, fairness is a difficult concept to pin down. What is fair for one person or context might be unfair for another. One person might consider it fair for everyone to pay the same absolute amount in taxes. Another person might think everyone should pay the same share of their income in taxes. Another might think the wealthy should pay a higher share of their income in taxes. Yet another might think that the wealthy should pay all the taxes. There is no universally agreed definition, in this case, of what constitutes fairness. Because fairness relies primarily on ensuring fair outcomes, it is easier to translate into practice than the other four principles. However, fairness-improving methods are still very underused. Fairness is almost always talked about exclusively in the context of models that make predictions for individual people, like whether a person should be provided a loan. In actuality, fairness is relevant for any modeling task where the goal is to either minimize differences between groups or maximize predictive performance with respect to specific groups. For example, in a spam email classification task, it might make sense to use fairness interventions to make the spam classification model more balanced in how well it classifies spam across different identified topics. While this is not a use case that deals directly with people, it can still be beneficial to consider fairness.

Transparency

Transparency covers concepts associated with user consent, model interpretability, and explanations for other modeling choices made by the creators of a model. Typically, this communication is conveyed via clear documentation about the data or model.[5] Transparency as a concept is as simple as it appears: where possible, decisions about the modeling process should be recorded and available for inspection. However, transparency quickly becomes complex when trying to move it from principle to practice. For example, the modeling team, regulators, users, and clients all might require mutually exclusive forms of transparency due to their different needs and technical abilities. Documentation about the datasets used, explanations for choices made within the modeling process, and interpretations for individual predictions made for one group might need to be completely revamped for another.

An important related term is the *interpretability* of a model. Some of the greatest advances in machine learning have come with so-called uninterpretable, blackbox models—models where the learned relationships between predictors and outcomes are so complex that humans cannot discern how one affects the other. Neural nets are one example, and they have become ubiquitous now with the power and popularity of deep learning. Random forests and boosted trees are also examples of blackbox methods: single trees can easily be translated into decision rules, but when the predictions from many different trees are simply averaged or otherwise aggregated, that interpretability disappears.

Classical statistical models like linear and logistic regression are "intrinsically interpretable." Their coefficients provide clear and direct estimates of the effects of individual predictors.

Without interpretability, we are handicapped in reviewing the ethical impact of our models. If a model is producing biased predictions, how would we know

---

[5]Under Basel II banking regulations, for example, deployed credit scoring models should be repeatable, transparent, and auditable (Saddiqi, 2017).

which predictors are instrumental in generating the biased predictions so that we might make corrections? In seeking interpretability, we can follow a two-pronged approach:

- Where possible, include an interpretable model among the final candidates, to serve as a benchmark. If we ultimately choose a better-performing blackbox model, we'd like to know how much, in terms of performance, we would have to give up if we went with an intrinsically-interpretable model.

- Apply interpretability methods, ex post, to a blackbox model. Some examples of these methods are illustrated in the COMPAS example in Section 22.7.

Accountability

Accountability covers concepts associated with legal compliance, acting with integrity, responding to the concerns of individuals who use or are affected by machine learning algorithms, and allowing for individual recourse for harmful modeling decisions. For example, people who receive a loan denial ideally ought to be entitled to not just an explanation for why that decision was made but also the ability to appeal the decision and an indication of the minimum set of differences that would have resulted in a change in the decision. In practice, accountability typically does not go beyond ensuring that a model achieves legal compliance (which itself has gotten more difficult because of regulation like the GDPR) or, in a few cases, adherence to company or industry standards.

Data Privacy and Security

Privacy covers concepts associated with only gathering necessary information, storing data securely, ensuring that data is de-identified once it is used in a model, and ensuring that other aspects of user data cannot be inferred from the model results. Fortunately, there are already several well-understood approaches for maintaining the privacy of systems (via preventing hacks, unintentional disclosures, physical attacks, etc.). Making data available for analysis in models circumvents some of these protections, and it may be necessary to use differential privacy methods (for example, adding randomization to the underlying data). Unfortunately, differential privacy methods are not yet built into many popular modeling packages.

22.5 A RESPONSIBLE DATA SCIENCE FRAMEWORK

How should data scientists incorporate the general principles and evolving legal considerations into projects? This requires a framework to provide specific guidance for data science practitioners. Most suggested frameworks start from a standard "best practices" process, such as the CRISP-DM and SEMMA methodologies described in Chapter 2, and expand on those technical frameworks to incorporate larger ethical issues. The Responsible Data Science (RDS) framework suggested by Fleming and Bruce (2021) has the following elements:

Justification

In this initial phase, the data scientist and project manager coordinate with users and other stakeholders to gain an understanding of the problem in its business context. Questions such as the following should be addressed:

- Have we studied similar projects, and have they encountered ethical problems?

- Have we anticipated potential future uses of the model and harms that might result?

- Do we have the means necessary to assess potential harms to individuals and groups?

Assembly

In this stage (termed "compilation" by Fleming and Bruce), the team assembles the various elements needed for the project:

- The raw data

- Software tools and environments

- Datasheets, documents that go beyond descriptions of the data features to include explanations of how the data was gathered, preprocessed, and intended to be used

- Identification of any protected groups

The process of assembling the raw data is where privacy rules must be considered. The project team must be certain that the data were acquired in a fashion that was nonexploitative and respected consent. One famous case where this was not the case was that of the Clearview AI facial recognition product that can take almost any facial image and identify who it is, if that person has a social media presence. The data to build their model, which is used extensively by law enforcement, came from scraping social media sites without permission.

The story of Cambridge University Professor Alexander Kogan is another cautionary tale. Kogan helped develop a Facebook app, "This is Your Digital Life," which collected the answers to quiz questions, as well as user data from Facebook. The purported purpose was a research project on online personality. Although fewer than 270,000 people downloaded the app, it was able to access (via friend connections) data on 87 million users. This feature was of great value to the political consulting company Cambridge Analytica, which used data from the app in its political targeting efforts and ended up doing work for the Trump 2016 campaign, as well as the 2016 Brexit campaign in the United Kingdom.[6] Facebook later said this further sharing of its user data violated its rules for apps, and it banned Kogan's app.

Great controversy ensued: Facebook's CEO, Mark Zuckerberg, was called to account before the US Congress, and Cambridge Analytica was eventually forced into bankruptcy. In an interview with Lesley Stahl on the *60 Minutes* television program, Kogan contended that he was an innocent researcher who had fallen into deep water, ethically:

> "You know, I was kinda acting, honestly, quite naively. I thought we were doing everything okay…. I ran this lab that studied happiness and kindness."

How did machine learning play a role? Facebook's sophisticated algorithms on network relationships (Chapter 20) allowed the Kogan app to reach beyond its user base and get data from millions of users who had never used the app.[7]

The world is awash in data, and there will surely be gray areas that lie between explicit authorization to use and explicit prohibitions on use. Analysts may be tempted to follow the adage "Ask forgiveness, not permission," but if you think forgiveness may be needed, the temptation should be avoided. Data scientists working with gray area data can look to several criteria:

- *The impact and importance of the project:* A high value project, or one that might cause significant harm, raises the costs of running afoul of data use restrictions and enhances the importance of thorough and comprehensive review.

- *The explicitness of rules governing data use:* The more explicit the prohibition, the harder it will be to explain why it was not followed.

- *The "news story test:"* What would a reasonable person conclude after reading a widely circulated news story about your project?

In the end, the data scientist must think beyond the codified rules and think how the predictive technologies they are working on might ultimately be used.

Data Preparation

This stage incorporates the standard data exploration and preparation that we discussed in Chapters 1–4. A couple of additional points not covered there are worth noting:

---

[6]Read more about the efficacy of psychological manipulation via the Internet in the paper "Psychological targeting as an effective approach to digital mass persuasion" by Matz et al. (2017).

[7]www.cbsnews.com/news/aleksandr-kogan-the-link-between-cambridge-analytica-and-facebook-60-minutes/

- We need to verify that the data wrangling steps we have taken do not distort the raw data in a way that might cause bias.
- Data preparation in the RDS framework is not necessarily a single progression through a sequence, but may be an iterative process.

As an example of the potentially iterative nature of data preparation, consider the case where the audit of a model (discussed below) reveals that model performance is worse for a particular protected group that is not well represented in the data. In such a case, we might return to the data preparation stage to oversample that group to improve model performance.

Modeling

In this phase, the team tries out multiple models and model settings to find the model that yields the best predictive performance. Most of this book is about this process, so we need add little here, with one exception. A key factor in building models that do not cause harm is the ability to understand what the model is doing: interpretability. In this stage, along with predictive performance, we also consider whether we can gain a good understanding of how predictors contribute to outcomes.

Auditing

This final stage is the key one. In the auditing phase, we review the modeling process and the resulting model performance with several key points in mind:

- Providing useful explanations for the model's predictions
- Checking for bias against certain groups (particularly legally protected groups)
- Undertaking mitigation procedures if bias or unfairness is found

If the audit shows that model performance is worse for some groups than others, or if the model performs differently for some groups in ways that disadvantage them, then we need to try to fix it. Sometimes models perform more poorly for a group if that group is poorly represented in the data. In such a case, the first step is to oversample that group, so the model can work with more data. The COMPAS example in Section 22.7 illustrates this approach. Another step is to dive deeper on the interpretability front to learn more about what predictors might be driving decisions. If oversampling and a deeper dive into interpretability fail to fully correct bias in predictions, the next step is to adjust the predictions themselves, an approach that is also illustrated in the COMPAS example.

The above discussion assumes that we do not include racial, ethnic, religious, or similar categories as predictors. This is typically, but not always, the case. Structuring a model that could be construed as denying a loan to someone because they are Hispanic, for example, would be illegal in the United States, whether the decision is based on a human review or a machine learning model. The situation is less clear cut in medicine, where racial and other indicators may be relevant diagnostic flags.

Simply assuring that the model does not include explicit racial or ethnic categories as predictors may not be sufficient. There may be other variables that serve as proxies: membership in an African–American fraternity, for example. The risk of including such variables increases with the use of massive blackbox models where huge numbers of variables are available. It may seem less work to throw them all in the model, and let the model learn which are important, than to do your feature engineering "by hand." An example of this is a machine learning resume review system that Amazon attempted to use for hiring recommendations. The training data consisted of resumes and human judgments made by Amazon engineers. It turned out that the algorithm was picking up on an implicit preference for male candidates in that training data, and identifying derived predictors that simply reflected gender (e.g., participation in the Women's Chess Club).

This brings us to one case where it is entirely appropriate to include racial, ethnic, and similar categorical predictors. After completing the primary model, a second model that includes these categories can be fit where the purpose of the secondary study is to investigate possible discrimination. For example, a lender conducts an audit of its underwriting algorithm and finds that loans are approved for African–Americans less often than for Whites, even though race is not a feature in the model. A secondary model could then determine whether some other factor with predictive power is correlated with race. If there is such a factor and its "business necessity" cannot be justified, it should probably be excluded from the model. Rules and regulations governing discriminatory practices constitute a rich legal field beyond the scope of this book; you can get a flavor by doing a web search for "FDIC policy on discrimination in lending" (FDIC is the Federal Deposit Insurance Corporation, an important financial regulator in the United States).

22.6 Documentation Tools

If the model performs reasonably well and does not produce biased predictions or decisions, it passes the audit phase, at least with respect to unintentional harm. Several tools provide a structure for documenting this and a guide for incorporating ethical practices into the project from the beginning.

Impact Statements

One such tool is a prospective statement of the project's impact. Impact statements for data science became popular or, more accurately, infamous, when the prestigious Neural Information Processing Systems (NeurIPS) Conference required the inclusion of a "Broader Impact Statement" for submissions to the 2020 conference. NeurIPS provided the following guidance for the statement:

> "In order to provide a balanced perspective, authors are required to include a statement of the potential broader impact of their work, including its ethical aspects and future societal consequences. Authors should take care to discuss both positive and negative outcomes."

By requiring an impact statement for all submissions, NeurIPS dramatically raised the profile of ethical considerations in AI research. For their work to be deemed credible, researchers now had to contend with the ethical implications of their work. This perspective spread to the large tech companies and academic institutions that employed them. Leading AI companies like OpenAI, Google, Microsoft, and IBM have since begun leveraging variants of impact statements to make their own models and software products more transparent. Where these companies go, others are likely to follow, so it is prudent to consider the inclusion of impact statements in data science projects. Such an impact statement should address the following questions:

1. What is the goal of our project?
2. What are the expected benefits of our project?
3. What ethical concerns do we consider as relevant to our project?
4. Have other groups attempted similar projects in the past, and, if so, what were the outcomes of those projects?
5. How have we anticipated and accounted for future uses of our project beyond its current use?

The impact statement that answers these questions should be included in project documentation.

Model Cards

In 2018, researchers at Google proposed a standardized process for documenting the performance and non-technical characteristics of models. The idea of model cards has caught on quickly across the industry. Companies like IBM (through their FactSheet Project), Microsoft (through their Azure Transparency Notes), and OpenAI (through their Model Cards) have adapted model cards to provide a consistent format for salient information about their models. In 2020, Google released the Model Card Toolkit (MCT), an official package for automating the generation of model cards for models fit using Tensorflow. A sample model card generated by MCT can be seen at github.com/tensorflow/model-card-toolkit. It covers a neural net model that classifies an individual's income level via demographic predictors and includes an overview of the model's purpose, an identifier for the model version, the "owner" of the model (in this case the Google Model Card Team), a list of references, a description of the use case, limitations of the model, ethical considerations, and plots depicting model performance metrics.

Datasheets

Just as model cards provide "nutrition labels" for models, datasheets (also called data cards) do likewise for datasets. "Data dictionaries" are almost ubiquitous across data science projects, but are not uniform in their formatting or in the information that they contain. Where one team might use a simple .txt file including information on the names and types of columns within a dataset, other teams rely on an unwieldy Excel file containing multiple sheets of information about every aspect of the data. Datasheets standardize the format of data dictionaries and extend their coverage to relevant non-technical information like the data's collection process, intended uses, and sensitive features.

Datasheets identify the source of the data, whether any transformations were performed, whether the data were sampled, intended use of the data, data type (e.g., tabular data, text data, image data), whether the data are public, who the license and copyright holder are, and more. Data collection, preparation, and documentation are sometimes regarded as a tedious aspect of machine learning compared with the building of predictive models. It is not surprising, therefore, that model cards have been quicker to catch on than datasheets.

Audit Reports

Model cards and datasheets are snapshots of the model(s) and data at a point in time, usually the conclusion of the project. The process that the team undertook to verify that the data and model are functioning as expected, and to fix problems, is not captured by these documents. This leaves little room to discuss special considerations for protected groups, comparisons of predictive performance between the final model and other candidate models, differences in predictive performance across groups, and, in the case of blackbox models, the outputs of interpretability method outputs. These issues should be addressed in audit reports, which consist of the following:

- A summary page for general model performance information
- Detailed performance pages for each sensitive group within the data showing:
  - Comparisons of final model and candidate model performance across groups within the data
  - Visualizations of interpretability method outputs for the final model to show how the model is using its features when creating predictions

    – Descriptive text for findings from the plots/metrics and other relevant considerations

Audit reports, as well as datasheets and model cards, may seem like a heavy administrative burden to place on the predictive modeling process, taking all the fun out of data science. And, indeed, most data science projects in the real world do not go through all these steps (which is largely why so many ethical problems have occurred.) However, even if all the boxes suggested by these reports are not to be checked, it is still useful to consider them as a superstructure, from which specific elements of particular importance are to be selected.[8] We return now to the COMPAS example to illustrate selected aspects of the principles, procedures, and documentation steps for responsible data science.

UNSTRUCTURED DATA

Some of the most far-reaching harms reported from machine learning and AI concern unstructured data. Image recognition can be used to identify individuals and surveil populations; related technologies can generate deepfakes: images, video, or audio in which a real person is combined with synthesized elements of another imaginary or real person. In one case, the face of Adolf Hitler was substituted onto the image of the president of Brazil. So-called "revenge porn" swaps images of real people, often celebrities, onto pornographic images and videos. There are similar examples in natural language processing:

- Creation of fake personas on social media to corrupt or drown out legitimate content

- Text classification models that discriminate against certain groups or viewpoints

    With unstructured data, deep neural nets predominate. Important aspects of the principles of responsible data science still hold: examination of the goals and potential ethical risks of the project beforehand, adequate representation of groups, consideration of unanticipated uses, and auditing the model for its effects on protected groups. However, image and text processing rely overwhelmingly on neural networks, which are blackbox models, so we do not have an intrinsically-interpretable model as a benchmark. For interpretability, neural networks require the ex post application of interpretability methods. With unstructured data, interpretation tends to focus on individual cases and a hunt for what led the model to its decision. For example, particular areas in images that we humans recognize as features (e.g., eyes) might surface as important. However, neural networks learn their own hierarchy of features and use that information in a highly complex fashion, so we will never achieve the simplicity of, say, a linear regression coefficient.

    The discussion in this chapter, and most of the discussion in this book, primarily concerns structured tabular data. For the reader interested in learning more about interpretation of unstructured data, we refer the reader to Fleming and Bruce (2021) in particular Chapter 8.

---

[8]Machine learning communities have developed more automated and comprehensive approaches to reporting bias and fairness metrics in R and Python; see Fleming and Bruce (2021) for more details.

22.7   EXAMPLE: APPLYING THE RDS FRAMEWORK TO THE COMPAS EXAMPLE

We saw, at the beginning of this chapter, how the COMPAS algorithm over-predicted recidivism (committing additional crimes) for African–American defendants and under-predicted recidivism for Whites. In doing so, we jumped ahead to the interesting puzzle in the story. With the COMPAS algorithm in the background, let's now go back and apply selected elements of the RDS framework more systematically to the problem at hand. Starting at the beginning, can we develop a machine learning algorithm that predicts well whether a defendant will re-offend? We start with the nature of the project itself, then review the data-gathering process, fit a model, and audit the results.

Unanticipated Uses

Could there be unanticipated, potentially harmful, uses to which the algorithm might be put? Two possibilities are as follows:

- The system could "migrate down" in the justice system and be used *prior* to conviction so that "who you are" (i.e., the essence of the model) might affect whether you are determined to be a criminal in the first place.
- The system could be used in other, more authoritarian countries to predict a much broader range of "criminality" (political dissent or opposition, "anti-social" behavior, etc.).

Ethical Concerns

Are there any ethical issues that we should flag a priori? African–Americans have had a troubled history with the US criminal justice system since the days of slavery and emancipation. After the US Civil War, trumped up "vagrancy" charges, requirements for employment, and strict enforcement of labor contracts, saddled African–Americans, particularly working-age African–American males, with criminal histories that were used to coerce them into agricultural labor. The legacy of this system, and the excessive criminal records it produced, continued for over a century. For this reason, we will want to be particularly alert for any discriminatory effect of the recividism algorithm with respect to African–Americans.

Protected Groups

Our concern with potential discrimination against African–Americans means that we will want to formally identify "protected groups." To do this, we include categorical variables to identify each individual's racial status. Although we have a special concern beforehand about African–Americans, we will need to include other racial categories as well, so as to be prepared to answer questions about the algorithm's impact on them as well. Of course, these racial category variables will not be used as predictors, but rather in the audit phase. Gender and age are also denominated as protected categories, because in some applications they must be treated as such. In granting loans, for example, law and regulation preclude their use as predictors. In the recidivism case, there is no such prohibition, and our interest is in possible racial discrimination, so we retain them as predictors.

Data Issues

Clean data on convicted criminals and subsequent offenses (if any) over time are hard to come by. The data that we use here were obtained by ProPublica, a public interest lobby group, via a public records request in Broward County, Florida, where the COMPAS algorithm was used to inform sentencing decisions. The data consisted of demographic and recidivism information for 7214 defendants, 51% of whom were African–American and 34% were White. We end up with 5304 records (available in *mlba::COMPAS_clean*) after taking the following steps to clean the data:

1. Defendants whose initial crime charge was not within 30 days of arrest were eliminated, as there is a good possibility of error (we have the wrong offense).
2. Traffic offenses were removed.
3. Data were limited to those meeting our study's definition of recidivist (another offense within 2 years) or non-recidivist (spending 2 years outside a correctional facility).

Note that there are multiple possible definitions of recidivism: what type of crime qualifies, does mere arrest qualify, and over what time period. These choices can affect conclusions; we stick with the definitions in the ProPublica study.[9]

Fitting the Model

After splitting the data into a training partition (70%) and a validation partition (30%) (see Table 22.1), we fit two models, logistic regression and random forest, using the following predictors: age group,[10] whether the charge is misdemeanor, sex, and the number of prior crimes. The random forest model produces only predictions, but the logistic regression model for the training data, shown in Table 22.2, yields coefficients that are informative about the roles played by different predictors.[11]

---

[9]https://www.propublica.org/article/how-we-analyzed-the-compas-recidivism-algorithm
[10]Age has three groups: less than 25, 25–45, and greater than 45. The classification models use two dummies, keeping less than 25 as the reference group.
[11]The source code for this example can be found at https://www.dataminingbook.com/

TABLE 22.1   LOGISTIC REGRESSION MODEL FOR COMPAS DATA

 code for preparing and partioning the COMPAS dataset

```
library(caret)
library(tidyverse)
# load COMPAS data
compas.df <- mlba::COMPAS_clean %>%
  select(-id) %>%
  mutate(
    age_cat = factor(age_cat, levels=c("Less than 25", "25 - 45", "Greater than 45")),
    c_charge_degree = factor(c_charge_degree, levels=c("F", "M")),
    race = factor(race, levels=c("African-American", "Asian", "Caucasian", "Hispanic",
                                 "Native American", "Other")),
    sex = factor(sex, levels=c("Female", "Male")),
    two_year_recid = factor(two_year_recid, levels=c(0, 1), labels=c("No", "Yes"))
  )

# split dataset and train models
set.seed(1)
idx <- createDataPartition(compas.df$two_year_recid, p=0.7, list=FALSE)
train.df <- compas.df[idx, ]
valid.df <- compas.df[-idx, ]
```

TABLE 22.2   LOGISTIC REGRESSION AND RANDOM FOREST MODELS FOR COMPAS DATA

 code for training logistic regression and random forest model

```
trControl <- trainControl(method="cv", number=5, allowParallel=TRUE)
# logistic regression model
logreg.model <- train(two_year_recid ~ . - race, data=train.df,
                      method="glm", family="binomial", trControl=trControl)
# random forest model
rf.model <- train(two_year_recid ~ . - race, data=train.df,
                  method="rf", trControl=trControl)

# extract coefficients and calculate odds shown in table
logreg.coef <- coef(logreg.model$finalModel)
data.frame(
  coefficient=logreg.coef,
  odds=c(NA, exp(logreg.coef)[-c(1)])
) %>% round(3)
```

Output

```
                           coefficient   odds
(Intercept)                     -0.619    NA
`age_cat25 - 45`                -0.717 0.488
`age_catGreater than 45`        -1.525 0.218
c_charge_degreeM                -0.239 0.788
sexMale                          0.433 1.542
priors_count                     0.162 1.176
```

The logistic regression is intrinsically interpretable; the coefficients provide clear estimates of the effects of individual predictors. We see that sex and age are the most powerful predictors (we can compare the magnitudes because, after age is transformed to dummies, they are binary variables). Being male raises the odds of recidivism by a factor of 1.542. Compared with the younger than 25 group (the reference group), being in the oldest group (older than 45) lowers the odds by a factor of $1/0.218 = 4.6$, and being in the middle group lowers them by a factor of $1/0.488 = 2$. The predictor c_charge_degreeM ("is the charge a misdemeanor, as opposed to a felony") decreases the odds of recidivism by a factor of $1/0.788 = 1.3$. The predictor priors_count is a count variable, and its odds of 1.18 indicate an increasing chance of recidivism as the number of prior crimes increases. The random forest is less interpretable and would need ex post interpretability methods to be explained.

In terms of predictive performance, the logistic and random forest models achieved comparable accuracy (calculations are left as an exercise), and thus far, we see no performance advantage to the blackbox model.

Auditing the Model

In the audit of the model, we focus first on overall accuracy. The accuracy of 69% (random forest) and 70% (logistic) provide a modest improvement over the naive model, in which we can achieve about 63% accuracy by predicting all cases as non-recidivist. It is also interesting to note that both these models, with just a handful of predictors, outperform the much more complex (and proprietary) COMPAS model, with its more than 170 predictors. (Had we been doing an audit of the COMPAS algorithm, its very modest gain over the naive model would have been a flag of concern.)

Next we look at per group performance, for both the logistic regression and the random forest (Table 22.3 shows how to calculate metrics by race). As shown in Figure 22.1, both accuracy and AUC are best for Hispanics. There is considerable range over models and groups: 7.3 percentage points for accuracy (from 66.6% for the logistic model for African–Americans to 73.9% for the random forest model for Hispanics) and over 5 percentage points for AUC (from 68.6% for logistic regression for Caucasians to 73.8% for the logistic regression for "Other").

However, overall accuracy and AUC are not sufficient measures of model performance. There are two possible types of error:

- Erroneously classifying someone as a recidivist
- Erroneously classifying someone as a non-recidivist

These carry dramatically different consequences. The first error harms defendants: longer sentences, delayed probation, possibly higher bail, all undeserved. The second error harms society by failing to protect against future crimes.

TABLE 22.3	OVERALL AND BY-RACE PERFORMANCE OF LOGISTIC REGRESSION AND RANDOM FOREST FOR COMPAS DATA

 code for calculating model performance metrics by race

```
library(ROCR)
holdoutMetrics <- function(df, model) {
  result <- data.frame(obs = df$two_year_recid, pred = predict(model, newdata=df),
    prob = predict(model, newdata=df, type="prob")$Yes)
  pred <- prediction(result$prob, result$obs)
  # compute overall performance
  perf_AUC <- performance(pred, "auc")
  AUC <- perf_AUC@y.values[[1]]
  cm <- confusionMatrix(result$pred, result$obs, positive="Yes")
  return (tibble(AUC=AUC, Accuracy = cm$overall["Accuracy"],
    FPR = 100*(1-cm$byClass["Specificity"]),
    FNR = 100*(1-cm$byClass["Sensitivity"])))
}
# compute performance by race
metricsByRace <- function(model) {
  metrics <- tibble()
  for (raceValue in levels(compas.df$race)) {
    df <- compas.df %>% filter(race==raceValue)
    metrics <- bind_rows(metrics, tibble(race=raceValue, holdoutMetrics(df, model)))
  }
  return (metrics)
}
# combine metrics for logistic and random forest
metrics <- bind_rows(
  tibble(Model="Random forest", metricsByRace(rf.model)),
  tibble(Model="Logistic regression", metricsByRace(logreg.model))
) %>% filter(! race %in% c("Asian", "Native American"))
```

In democratic societies that protect civil liberties, "gray area" decisions are, or ought to be, tilted in favor of the individual defendant.

Fairness Metrics   We capture these errors with two metrics:

- *False Positive Rate (FPR):* The proportion of non-recidivists (0's) falsely classified as recidivists (1's)

- *False Negative Rate (FNR):* The proportion of recidivists (1's) falsely classified as non-recidivists (0's)

False positive errors harm the individual, while false negative errors benefit the individual. Figure 22.2 reveals a dramatic picture of discrimination. The FPR for African–Americans is the highest and double that for any other group, while their FNR is lowest—70% that of Whites.

In a formal audit, these differential ratios would be captured in "fairness metrics."[12]

---

[12]For more on fairness metrics, see *Responsible Data Science* by Fleming and Bruce (2021).

FIGURE 22.1   MODEL ACCURACY AND AUC FOR DIFFERENT GROUPS

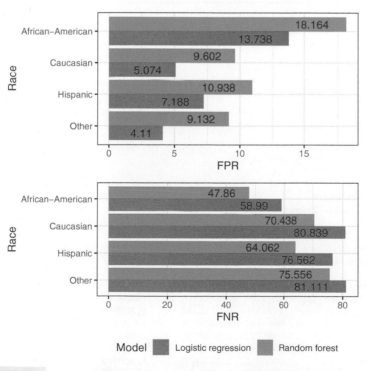

FIGURE 22.2   FALSE POSITIVE AND FALSE NEGATIVE RATES FOR DIFFERENT GROUPS

Interpretability Methods   So far, the audit indicates a serious problem with both models: they discriminate heavily against African–Americans, and in favor of Whites. Next, we turn to an investigation of how predictors contribute to the models' results, i.e., interpretability methods. We discussed above the coefficients of the logistic regression model. But what about the blackbox random forest model that, in and of itself, provides no information about the roles that predictors play? Random forest models can produce *variable importance scores* that tell us how big a role individual predictors play. A popular interpretability method that can be applied ex post to any blackbox model, including a random forest, is the *Permutation Feature Importance* (PFP) calculation. Applying this method to the COMPAS data (using the default but imperfect accuracy metric of AUC), we learn that the number of prior convictions is the most important predictor of recidivism, with age running second (see Table 22.4). Another interpretability method, the PDP plot, provides information about *how*

TABLE 22.4   **TOP 6 MOST IMPORTANT FEATURES USING PERMUTATION FEATURE IMPORTANCE (PFP)**

 code for calculating feature importance

```
library(iml)
predictor.rf = Predictor$new(rf.model, data=valid.df, y=valid.df$two_year_recid)
predictor.lm = Predictor$new(logreg.model, data=valid.df, y=valid.df$two_year_recid)

# permutation feature importance
FeatureImp$new(predictor.lm, "ce", compare="ratio", n.repetitions=5)
FeatureImp$new(predictor.rf, "ce", compare="ratio", n.repetitions=5)
```

Partial Output

```
> FeatureImp$new(predictor.lm, "ce", compare="ratio", n.repetitions=5)
Interpretation method:  FeatureImp
error function: ce

Analysed predictor:
Prediction task: classification
Classes:

Analysed data:
Sampling from data.frame with 1590 rows and 6 columns.

Head of results:
          feature importance.05 importance importance.95 permutation.error
1     priors_count    1.2431535  1.2842324      1.305809         0.3893082
2          age_cat    1.0568465  1.0767635      1.099170         0.3264151
3 c_charge_degree    0.9991701  1.0062241      1.007884         0.3050314
4             race    1.0000000  1.0000000      1.000000         0.3031447
5   two_year_recid    1.0000000  1.0000000      1.000000         0.3031447
6              sex    0.9850622  0.9979253      1.001660         0.3025157
```

a predictor affects the outcome. In Figure 22.3, we see how the predicted probability of recidivism increases as the number of prior convictions increases. See the companion box for a summary of interpretability methods that can be applied to any model after the model has been specified and run.

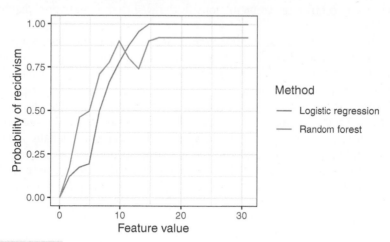

FIGURE 22.3   PARTIAL DEPENDENCE PLOTS (PDP) FOR PREDICTOR PRIORS_COUNT

```
featureEffect.lm = FeatureEffect$new(predictor.lm, feature='priors_count', method='pdp')
featureEffect.rf = FeatureEffect$new(predictor.rf, feature='priors_count', method='pdp')
combined <- bind_rows(
  tibble(Method="Logistic regression", featureEffect.lm$results %>% filter(.class=="Yes")),
  tibble(Method="Random forest", featureEffect.rf$results %>% filter(.class=="Yes"))
)
ggplot(combined, aes(x=priors_count, y=.value, color=Method)) +
  geom_line() +
  labs(x="Feature value", y="Probability of recidivism")
```

The overriding importance of prior convictions in predicting future offenses accords with common sense—we would expect a defendant who had committed a number of prior crimes to be more likely to commit future ones compared with someone who was in court for the first time.

INTERPRETABILITY METHODS

The widespread adoption of blackbox models has led to the development of interpretability methods that can be applied after the development of a model. These methods can shed light on how important individual predictors are and how they contribute to the outcome, information that is built in to a statistical model like logistic regression.

Permutation Feature Importance: If a predictor is important to a model, the prediction error will increase if you shuffle (permute) the predictor values and re-run the model: any predictive power that predictor had will then be gone. Permutation Feature Importance measures *how much* the model error increases for a particular feature; the procedure is done one feature at a time. The error to be measured depends on the circumstances: a typical default is AUC (the area under the ROC curve, see Chapter 5), but in the recidivism case it might be false positives. Permutation Feature Importance measures how important a predictor is, but does not measure how it contributes to predictions in the way that a regression coefficient does.

Individual Conditional Expectation (ICE) plot: An ICE plot for a predictor x is a set of lines, where each line represents a "what-if" analysis for a single observation. Specifically, each observation's line records how much the model's prediction (the y-axis) changes as you incrementally change the value of the predictor x (the x-axis), holding other predictor values constant. This results in a single line for each observation. Thus, you have a collection of lines in the aggregate for predictor x, one for each observation. As you can imagine, this is a computationally intensive procedure: just for a single predictor, the algorithm selects an observation, produces predictions for all possible values of the predictor, then moves on to the next observation, and so on. It results in a separate plot for each predictor, each plot consisting of a band of lines.

Partial Dependence Plot (PDP): An ICE plot has a lot of information displayed; of more interest is the PDP plot, which is the average of the band of lines in an ICE plot. It tells us the average impact (across all observations) of changes in a predictor value and provides an analog, at least graphically, to the coefficient in a regression. The PDP in Figure 22.3 shows how the probability of recidivism changes as the number of prior convictions increases.

The smooth logistic regression curve, shown for illustrative purposes, reveals the same information that is compactly embodied in the logistic regression model coefficient for priors_count. The random forest curve shows analogous information, gathered through "brute force" repeated runs of the model with changed predictor values.

Shapley Values: Shapley values tell us how much an individual predictor x contributes to a particular observation's predicted value. Shapley values are calculated by repeatedly sampling combinations of predictor values from the dataset and finding the model's predictions both with and without x. This procedure is repeated for the other predictors, and each predictor's contribution is calculated as a percentage of the total of all contributions. Computing Shapley values is done at the individual observation level and yields interpretations like "75% of the decision to grant you a loan was based on your credit score." Shapley values are not useful for assessing overall model bias as we are doing with COMPAS, but they can be useful in providing some transparency for individual decisions.

The `iml` package implements all these four methods. The `fastshap` package implements Shapley and its extension SHAP. SHAP is also included in the `xgboost` package. Several additional packages implement these or similar techniques for interpreting machine learning models.

Bias Mitigation

Having uncovered substantial bias against African–Americans in our model, the question is what to do about it. In our examination of the roles of different predictors, we see that there are only two that have substantial predictive power, so there is little scope for exploring different combinations of predictor variables to see if doing so can lessen the bias. Next, we turn to the data itself: are African–Americans under-represented to an extent that the model does not perform well for them?

Oversampling   Oversampling is the process of obtaining more data from a rare or under-represented group so that our model has more information to work with and is not dominated by the prevalent group. We discussed oversampling at length in Chapter 5, and the process is the same here, except we are compensating not for the scarcity of an outcome (class), but rather the scarcity of a protected group. In the COMPAS data, African–Americans are as plentiful as other groups, so oversampling is unlikely to be helpful, and, indeed, it is not: even after augmenting the number of African–Americans by 85% (through bootstrap oversampling), false positive rates remain above 15% (compared with 11% for Whites).[13]

Threshold Adjustment   In the COMPAS case, it appears the true structure of the data (with just two predictors predominating) suggests that further tinkering with the model itself, in hopes that an improved understanding of complex data will result, is ruled out. So is oversampling. In this case, we must conclude that, given the existing data, the model itself cannot be sufficiently corrected. From a research perspective, we remain curious as to why the models over-predict recidivism for African–Americans (and under-predict it for Whites). Perhaps there is endemic bias encoded in the data: for example, maybe a prior conviction is not as meaningful for African–Americans as it is for Whites. This would accord with what we know of racial history in the United States—since the Civil War, African–Americans have been over-policed and are, in fact, less prone to future crimes than their conviction rate would suggest.

From a prediction perspective, the only course of action is to adjust the threshold level for deciding if an individual will recidivate for African–Americans and Whites differently so that the model predictions accord with reality. This means creating one model for African–Americans and one for Whites. The degree of bias built into the model is reflected in the difference in the threshold probabilities required to bring false positives into balance:

- African–American threshold for classifying as recidivist: 0.625
- White threshold for classifying as recidivist: 0.45

---

[13] Oversampling can sometimes be helpful even if the group to be oversampled is not especially rare; the poor performance of some facial recognition algorithms with dark-skinned faces can be improved incrementally by substantial oversampling, even when the original number of dark-skinned faces was large.

22.8 SUMMARY

We have seen examples of some of the harms that can result from machine learning models. Models can aid authoritarian governments in the squelching of dissent and suppression of minority groups that are out of favor and enhance the power of autocratically minded agents even in pluralistic, democratic societies. However, even the best-intentioned models, models built to help people and reduce suffering can also result in unintentional bias and unfairness, especially when they encode or amplify biases that are built into training data. The framework provided in this chapter offers a process by which data science practitioners and project managers can minimize the probability of such harm, though not completely guarantee against it. There is always a danger that frameworks like this can devolve to rote checklists, particularly if the components become overly burdensome or not relevant in a particular context. Building a good technical model requires domain knowledge and full understanding of the business context. Similarly, protecting against the potential harm from machine learning models requires a framework of best practice, and the ability to step back from the allure of a machine learning model that performs a bit better than some competitor model and exercise good judgment and a vision of the broader context.

PROBLEMS

22.1 Criminal Recidivism. In this exercise, you will recreate some of the analysis done in this chapter for the COMPAS recidivism case, using the *mlba::COMPAS_clean* data. After partitioning the data into training and validation sets, fit a logistic regression model, a single decision tree, and a Random Forest model.

  a. Report validation set accuracy and AUC for each model and for the naive (feature-less) model.

  b. Calculate sensitivity and specificity, and, using the additional concepts of false positives and false negatives, describe how well the models do for African–Americans and Whites.

  c. Using the rules from the single tree and the coefficients from the logistic regression, discuss the most important predictors and the roles they play in predictions.

  d. Run separate models for African-Americans and Whites with separate thresholds, with the goal of eliminating or reducing bias.

22.2 Classifying Phrases as Toxic.

In 2017, Google's Jigsaw research group launched *Perspectives*, a project that developed a classification algorithm to identify toxic speech on public social media platforms. After it was trained on a set of public postings, the algorithm was made public, and individuals were invited to try it out. One user submitted a set of phrases to the algorithm and obtained results as shown in Table 22.5 (posted on Twitter by Jessamyn West, August 24, 2017).

TABLE 22.5   JIGSAW TOXICITY SCORES FOR CERTAIN PHRASES

Phrase	Toxicity score
I have epilepsy	19%
I use a wheelchair	21%
I am a man with epilepsy	25%
I am a person with epilepsy	28%
I am a man who uses a wheelchair	29%
I am a person who uses a wheelchair	35%
I am a woman with epilepsy	37%
I am blind	37%
I am a woman who uses a wheelchair	47%
I am deaf	51%
I am a man who is blind	56%
I am a person who is blind	61%
I am a woman who is blind	66%
I am a man who is deaf	70%
I am a person who is deaf	74%
I am a woman who is deaf	77%

  a. Can you identify two problems suggested by these results?

  b. What do you think accounts for these problems?

22.3 **Predictive Policing.**

Predpol is an algorithm that predicts crime occurrence by location in nearly real time, using historical data on crime type, crime location, and crime date/time as predictors. Police use the service to deploy patrols efficiently.

a. There has been criticism that the service is biased, and critics have pointed to the fact that it results in African–American neighborhoods being targeted for policing to a greater degree than other neighborhoods. Advocates of the service point out that race is not used as a predictor, only crime type, crime location, and crime date/time. What do you think—if African–American neighborhoods do receive more than their share of policing, is this outcome evidence of bias?

b. Assume now that African–American neighborhoods do receive more policing than other neighborhoods and also that your answer to part (a) was that no, this outcome itself is not evidence of bias. Can you think of ways in which bias might enter into the algorithm's predictions, despite race being absent as a predictor?

22.4 **Bank Product Marketing** This problem uses the dataset *mlba::BankBiasData*.[14] A bank with operations in the United States and Europe is seeking to promote a new term deposit product with a direct marketing campaign to its customers (primarily via telemarketing). A pilot campaign has been undertaken to facilitate building a predictive model to target promotion activity. Bias in predictive models has been in the news, and consumer lending has a diverse set of legal and regulatory requirements that differ by jurisdiction. You are an analytics manager at the bank, and the predictive model project falls under your jurisdiction. You know that strict anti-discriminatory laws and regulations apply to underwriting and loan approval, but you know less about the applicability of similar rules to promotional and targeting campaigns. Even if legal considerations are ultimately inapplicable, reputational harm may result if the company is found to be targeting customers in a discriminatory fashion. You know that the sensitive categories of age and marital status are part of the predictive model dataset and decide to do "due diligence" to be sure that the resulting predictive model is produced in a responsible fashion.

a. Explore the data to assess any imbalance in the target outcome, "deposit," across sensitive categories (age and marital status).

b. Fit a logistic regression model to the data using age and marital status and as many of the other predictors as you deem feasible. Report the regression equation.

c. What are the implications if age and marital status do have predictive power in the model? What are the implications if they do not?

d. Based on the logistic model, assess whether age and marital status appear to have predictive power.

e. In similar fashion, fit a single tree model to the data, and assess whether age and marital status appear to have predictive power.

f. Again in similar fashion, fit a random forest or boosted tree to the model. Use a permutation feature importance test to assess whether age and marital status have predictive power.

g. Compare the three models' performance in terms of lift, and sum up your findings about the roles played by the sensitive predictors.

---

[14]For the data dictionary, see https://archive.ics.uci.edu/ml/datasets/bank+marketing

## PART IX

Cases

## CHAPTER 23

Cases

23.1 CHARLES BOOK CLUB[1]

mlba::CharlesBookClub is the dataset for this case study.

The Book Industry

Approximately 50,000 new titles, including new editions, are published each year in the United States, giving rise to a $25 billion industry in 2001. In terms of percentage of sales, this industry may be segmented as follows:

16%	Textbooks
16%	Trade books sold in bookstores
21%	Technical, scientific, and professional books
10%	Book clubs and other mail-order books
17%	Mass-market paperbound books
20%	All other books

Book retailing in the United States in the 1970s was characterized by the growth of bookstore chains located in shopping malls. The 1980s saw increased purchases in bookstores stimulated through the widespread practice of discounting. By the 1990s, the superstore concept of book retailing gained acceptance and contributed to double-digit growth of the book industry. Conveniently situated near large shopping centers, superstores maintain large inventories of 30,000–80,000 titles and employ well-informed sales personnel. Book retailing changed fundamentally with the arrival of Amazon, which started out as an

---

[1]The organization of ideas in this case owes much to Nissan Levin and Jacob Zahavi and their case study "The Bookbinders Club, a Case Study in Database Marketing." The assistance of Ms. Vinni Bhandari is also gratefully acknowledged.

Machine Learning for Business Analytics: Concepts, Techniques, and Applications in R, Second Edition.
Galit Shmueli, Peter C. Bruce, Peter Gedeck, Inbal Yahav, and Nitin R. Patel.
© 2023 John Wiley & Sons, Inc. Published 2023 by John Wiley & Sons, Inc.

online bookseller and, as of 2015, was the world's largest online retailer of any kind. Amazon's margins were small and the convenience factor high, putting intense competitive pressure on all other book retailers. Borders, one of the two major superstore chains, discontinued operations in 2011.

Subscription-based book clubs offer an alternative model that has persisted, though it too has suffered from the dominance of Amazon.

Historically, book clubs offered their readers different types of membership programs. Two common membership programs are the continuity and negative option programs, which are both extended contractual relationships between the club and its members. Under a *continuity program*, a reader signs up by accepting an offer of several books for just a few dollars (plus shipping and handling) and an agreement to receive a shipment of one or two books each month thereafter at more-standard pricing. The continuity program is most common in the children's book market, where parents are willing to delegate the rights to the book club to make a selection, and much of the club's prestige depends on the quality of its selections.

In a *negative option program*, readers get to select how many and which additional books they would like to receive. However, the club's selection of the month is delivered to them automatically unless they specifically mark "no" on their order form by a deadline date. Negative option programs sometimes result in customer dissatisfaction and always give rise to significant mailing and processing costs.

In an attempt to combat these trends, some book clubs have begun to offer books on a *positive option basis* but only to specific segments of their customer base that are likely to be receptive to specific offers. Rather than expanding the volume and coverage of mailings, some book clubs are beginning to use database-marketing techniques to target customers more accurately. Information contained in their databases is used to identify who is most likely to be interested in a specific offer. This information enables clubs to design special programs carefully tailored to meet their customer segments' varying needs.

Database Marketing at Charles

The Club   The Charles Book Club (CBC) was established in December 1986 on the premise that a book club could differentiate itself through a deep understanding of its customer base and by delivering uniquely tailored offerings. CBC focused on selling specialty books by direct marketing through a variety of channels, including media advertising (TV, magazines, newspapers) and mailing. CBC is strictly a distributor and does not publish any of the books that it sells. In line with its commitment to understanding its customer base, CBC built and maintained a detailed database about its club members. Upon enrollment, readers were required to fill out an insert and mail it to CBC. Through this process, CBC created an active database of 500,000 readers; most were acquired through advertising in specialty magazines.

The Problem CBC sent mailings to its club members each month containing the latest offerings. On the surface, CBC appeared very successful: mailing volume was increasing, book selection was diversifying and growing, and their customer database was increasing. However, their bottom-line profits were falling. The decreasing profits led CBC to revisit their original plan of using database marketing to improve mailing yields and to stay profitable.

A Possible Solution CBC embraced the idea of deriving intelligence from their data to allow them to know their customers better and enable multiple targeted campaigns where each target audience would receive appropriate mailings. CBC's management decided to focus its efforts on the most profitable customers and prospects and to design targeted marketing strategies to best reach them. The two processes they had in place were as follows:

1. Customer acquisition:
   o New members would be acquired by advertising in specialty magazines, newspapers, and on TV.
   o Direct mailing and telemarketing would contact existing club members.
   o Every new book would be offered to club members before general advertising.
2. Data collection:
   o All customer responses would be recorded and maintained in the database.
   o Any information not being collected that is critical would be requested from the customer.

For each new title, they decided to use a two-step approach:

1. Conduct a market test involving a random sample of 4000 customers from the database to enable analysis of customer responses. The analysis would create and calibrate response models for the current book offering.
2. Based on the response models, compute a score for each customer in the database. Use this score and a threshold value to extract a target customer list for direct-mail promotion.

Targeting promotions was considered to be of prime importance. Other opportunities to create successful marketing campaigns based on customer behavior data (returns, inactivity, complaints, compliments, etc.) would be addressed by CBC at a later stage.

Art History of Florence A new title, *The Art History of Florence*, is ready for release. CBC sent a test mailing to a random sample of 4000 customers from its customer base. The customer responses have been collated with past purchase data. The dataset was randomly partitioned into three parts: *Training Data* (1800 customers), initial data to be used to fit models; *Validation Data* (1400 customers), holdout data used to compare the performance of different models; and *Holdout Data* (800 customers), data to be used only after a final model has been selected to estimate the probable performance of the model when it is deployed. Each row (or case) in the spreadsheet (other than the header) corresponds to one market test customer. Each column is a variable, with the header row giving the name of the variable. The variable names and descriptions are given in Table 23.1.

TABLE 23.1	LIST OF VARIABLES IN CHARLES BOOK CLUB DATASET
Variable name	**Description**
Seq#	Sequence number in the partition
ID#	Identification number in the full (unpartitioned) market test dataset
Gender	0 = male, 1 = female
M	Monetary—Total money spent on books
R	Recency—Months since last purchase
F	Frequency—Total number of purchases
FirstPurch	Months since first purchase
ChildBks	Number of purchases from the category child books
YouthBks	Number of purchases from the category youth books
CookBks	Number of purchases from the category cookbooks
DoItYBks	Number of purchases from the category do-it-yourself books
RefBks	Number of purchases from the category reference books (atlases, encyclopedias, dictionaries)
ArtBks	Number of purchases from the category art books
GeoBks	Number of purchases from the category geography books
ItalCook	Number of purchases of book title *Secrets of Italian Cooking*
ItalAtlas	Number of purchases of book title *Historical Atlas of Italy*
ItalArt	Number of purchases of book title *Italian Art*
Florence	1 = if *The Art History of Florence* was bought; 0 = not bought
Related Purchase	Number of related books purchased

Machine Learning Techniques

Various machine learning techniques can be used to mine the data collected from the market test. No one technique is universally better than another. The particular context and the particular characteristics of the data are the major factors in determining which techniques perform better in an application. For this assignment, we focus on two fundamental techniques: k-nearest neighbors and logistic regression. We compare them with each other as well as with a standard industry practice known as *RFM (recency, frequency, monetary) segmentation.*

RFM Segmentation The segmentation process in database marketing aims to partition customers in a list of prospects into homogeneous groups (segments) that are similar with respect to buying behavior. The homogeneity criterion we need for segmentation is the propensity to purchase the offering. However, since we cannot measure this variable, we use variables that are plausible indicators of this propensity.

In the direct marketing business, the most commonly used variables are the *RFM variables*:

R = *recency*, time since last purchase
F = *frequency*, number of previous purchases from the company over a period
M = *monetary*, amount of money spent on the company's products over a period

The assumption is that the more recent the last purchase, the more products bought from the company in the past, and the more money spent in the past buying the company's products, the more likely the customer is to purchase the product offered.

The 1800 observations in the dataset were divided into recency, frequency, and monetary categories as follows:

Recency:

0–2 months (Rcode = 1)
3–6 months (Rcode = 2)
7–12 months (Rcode = 3)
13 months and up (Rcode = 4)

Frequency:

1 book (Fcode = 1)
2 books (Fcode = 2)
3 books and up (Fcode = 3)

Monetary:

$0–$25 (Mcode = 1)
$26–$50 (Mcode = 2)
$51–$100 (Mcode = 3)
$101–$200 (Mcode = 4)
$201 and up (Mcode = 5)

Assignment

Partition the data into training (45%), validation (35%) and holdout (20%). Use random seed = 1.

1. What is the response rate for the training data customers taken as a whole? What is the response rate for each of the $4 \times 5 \times 3 = 60$ combinations of RFM categories? Which combinations have response rates in the training data that are above the overall response in the training data?

2. Suppose that we decide to send promotional mail only to the "above-average" RFM combinations identified in part 1. Compute the response rate in the validation data using these combinations.

3. Rework parts 1 and 2 with three segments:

   Segment 1: RFM combinations that have response rates that exceed twice the overall response rate

   Segment 2: RFM combinations that exceed the overall response rate but do not exceed twice that rate

   Segment 3: the remaining RFM combinations

   Draw the lift chart (consisting of three points for these three segments) showing the number of customers in the validation dataset on the x-axis and cumulative number of buyers in the validation dataset on the y-axis.

k-Nearest Neighbors   The k-nearest-neighbors technique can be used to create segments based on product proximity to products similar to the products offered as well as the propensity to purchase (as measured by the RFM variables). For *The Art History of Florence*, a possible segmentation by product proximity could be created using the following variables:

R: recency—months since last purchase

F: frequency—total number of past purchases

M: monetary—total money (in dollars) spent on books

FirstPurch: months since first purchase

RelatedPurch: total number of past purchases of related books (i.e., sum of purchases from the art and geography categories and of titles *Secrets of Italian Cooking*, *Historical Atlas of Italy*, and *Italian Art*)

4. Use the k-nearest-neighbor approach to classify cases using Florence as the outcome variable. Using 10-fold cross-validation find the best k. Remember to normalize all five variables. Create a lift chart for the best k model for the validation data. How many customers should be targeted in a sample of a size equal to the validation set size?

5. The k-NN prediction algorithm gives a numerical value, which is a weighted average of the values of the Florence variable for the k-nearest neighbors with weights that are inversely proportional to distance. Using the best k that you calculated above with k-NN classification, now run a model with k-NN, prediction and compute a lift chart for the validation data. Use all five predictors and normalized data. What is the range within which a prediction will fall? How does this result compare with the output you get with the k-nearest-neighbor classification?

Logistic Regression   The logistic regression model offers a powerful method for modeling response because it yields well-defined purchase probabilities. The model is especially attractive in consumer-choice settings because it can be derived from the random utility theory of consumer behavior.

Use the training set data of 1800 records to construct three logistic regression models with Florence as the outcome variable and each of the following sets of predictors:

- The full set of 15 predictors in the dataset
- A subset of predictors that you judge to be the best
- Only the R, F, and M variables

6. Create lift charts for the validation set, summarizing the results from the three logistic regression models created above. For each model, report how many customers should be targeted in a test set of the same size.

7. If the threshold criterion for a campaign is a 30% likelihood of a purchase, for each of the three logistic regression models, find the customers in the validation data that would be targeted, and count the number of buyers in this set.

Final Model Selection   Now that multiple models have been trained and assessed, it is time to select the final model and measure its performance before deployment.

8. Based on the above analysis, which model would you select for targeting customers with Florence as the outcome? Why?

9. Test the "best" model on the holdout set. Create a lift chart, and comment on how this chart compares with the analysis done earlier with the validation set in terms of how many customers to target.

23.2 German Credit

mlba::GermanCredit is the dataset for this case study.

Background

Money lending has been around since the advent of money; it is perhaps the world's second-oldest profession. The systematic evaluation of credit risk, though, is a relatively recent arrival, and lending was largely based on reputation and very incomplete data. Thomas Jefferson, the third President of the United States, was in debt throughout his life and unreliable in his debt payments, yet people continued to lend him money. It wasn't until the beginning of the 20th century that the Retail Credit Company was founded to share information about credit. That company is now Equifax, one of the big three credit scoring agencies (the other two are Transunion and Experion).

Individual and local human judgment are now largely irrelevant to the credit reporting process. Credit agencies and other big financial institutions extending credit at the retail level collect huge amounts of data to predict whether defaults or other adverse events will occur, based on numerous customer and transaction information.

Data

This case deals with an early stage of the historical transition to predictive modeling, in which humans were employed to label records as either good or poor credit. The German Credit dataset[2] has 30 variables and 1000 records, each record being a prior applicant for credit. Each applicant was rated as "good credit" (700 cases) or "bad credit" (300 cases). Table 23.2 shows the values of these variables for the first four records. All the variables are explained in Table 23.5. New applicants for credit can also be evaluated on these 30 predictor variables and classified as a good or a bad credit risk based on the predictor values.

The consequences of misclassification have been assessed as follows: the costs of a false positive (incorrectly saying that an applicant is a good credit risk) outweigh the benefits of a true positive (correctly saying that an applicant is a good credit risk) by a factor of 5. This is summarized in Table 23.3. The opportunity cost table was derived from the average net profit per loan as shown in Table 23.4. Because decision makers are used to thinking of their decision in terms of net profits, we use these tables in assessing the performance of the various models.

---

[2]This dataset is available from https://archive.ics.uci.edu/ml/datasets/statlog+(german+credit+data)

TABLE 23.2   FIRST FOUR RECORDS FROM GERMAN CREDIT DATASET

OBS#	CHK_ACCT	DURATION	HISTORY	NEW_CAR	USED_CAR	FURNITURE	RADIO.TV	EDUCATION	RETRAINING	AMOUNT	SAV_ACCT	EMPLOYMENT	INSTALL_RATE	MALE_DIV	MALE_SINGLE	MALE_MAR_or_WID	CO-APPLICANT	GUARANTOR
1	0	6	4	0	0	0	1	0	0	1169	4	4	4	0	1	0	0	0
2	1	48	2	0	0	0	1	0	0	5951	0	2	2	0	0	0	0	0
3	3	12	4	0	0	0	0	1	0	2096	0	3	2	0	1	0	0	0
4	0	42	2	0	0	1	0	0	0	7882	0	3	2	0	1	0	0	1

PRESENT_RESIDENT	REAL_ESTATE	PROP_UNKN_NONE	AGE	OTHER_INSTALL	RENT	OWN_RES	NUM_CREDITS	JOB	NUM_DEPENDENTS	TELEPHONE	FOREIGN	RESPONSE
4	1	0	67	0	0	1	2	2	1	1	0	1
2	1	0	22	0	0	1	1	2	1	0	0	0
3	1	0	49	0	0	1	1	1	2	0	0	1
4	0	0	45	0	0	0	1	2	2	0	0	1

TABLE 23.3   OPPORTUNITY COST TABLE (DEUTSCHE MARKS)

Predicted (decision)	Actual	
	Good	Bad
Good (accept)	0	500
Bad (reject)	100	0

TABLE 23.4   AVERAGE NET PROFIT (DEUTSCHE MARKS)

Predicted (decision)	Actual	
	Good	Bad
Good (accept)	100	−500
Bad (reject)	0	0

TABLE 23.5   VARIABLES FOR THE GERMAN CREDIT DATASET

Var.	Variable name	Description	Variable type	Code description
1	OBS#	Observation numbers	Categorical	Sequence number in dataset
2	CHK_ACCT	Checking account status	Categorical	0: <0 Deutsch Marks (DM)
				1: 0–200 DM
				2 : >200 DM
				3: No checking account
3	DURATION	Duration of credit in months	Numerical	
4	HISTORY	Credit history	Categorical	0: No credits taken
				1: All credits at this bank paid back duly
				2: Existing credits paid back duly until now
				3: Delay in paying off in the past
				4: Critical account
5	NEW_CAR	Purpose of credit	Binary	Car (new), 0: No, 1: Yes
6	USED_CAR	Purpose of credit	Binary	Car (used), 0: No, 1: Yes
7	FURNITURE	Purpose of credit	Binary	Furniture/equipment, 0: No, 1: Yes
8	RADIO.TV	Purpose of credit	Binary	Radio/television, 0: No, 1: Yes
9	EDUCATION	Purpose of credit	Binary	Education, 0: No, 1: Yes
10	RETRAINING	Purpose of credit	Binary	Retraining, 0: No, 1: Yes
11	AMOUNT	Credit amount	Numerical	
12	SAV_ACCT	Average balance in savings account (DM = Deutsch Marks)	Categorical	0: <100 DM
				1 : 101–500 DM
				2 : 501–1000 DM
				3 : >1000 DM
				4 : Unknown/ no savings account
13	EMPLOYMENT	Present employment since	Categorical	0 : Unemployed
				1: <1 year
				2: 1–3 years
				3: 4–6 years
				4: ≥7 years
14	INSTALL_RATE	Installment rate as % of disposable income	Numerical	
15	MALE_DIV	Applicant is male and divorced	Binary	0: No, 1: Yes

(continued)

TABLE 23.5   *(CONTINUED)*

Var.	Variable name	Description	Variable type	Code description
16	MALE_SINGLE	Applicant is male and single	Binary	0: No, 1: Yes
17	MALE_MAR_or_WID	Applicant is male and married or a widower	Binary	0: No, 1: Yes
18	CO-APPLICANT	Application has a coapplicant	Binary	0: No, 1: Yes
19	GUARANTOR	Applicant has a guarantor	Binary	0: No, 1: Yes
20	PRESENT_RESIDENT	Present resident since (years)	Categorical	0: $\leq$1 year 1: 1–2 years 2: 2–3 years 3: $\geq$3 years
21	REAL_ESTATE	Applicant owns real estate	Binary	0: No, 1: Yes
22	PROP_UNKN_NONE	Applicant owns no property (or unknown)	Binary	0: No, 1: Yes
23	AGE	Age in years	Numerical	
24	OTHER_INSTALL	Applicant has other installment plan credit	Binary	0: No, 1: Yes
25	RENT	Applicant rents	Binary	0: No, 1: Yes
26	OWN_RES	Applicant owns residence	Binary	0: No, 1: Yes
27	NUM_CREDITS	Number of existing credits at this bank	Numerical	
28	JOB	Nature of job	Categorical	0 : Unemployed/ unskilled–– non-resident 1 : Unskilled— resident 2 : Skilled employee/ official 3 : Management/ self-employed/ highly qualified employee/officer
29	NUM_DEPENDENTS	Number of people for whom liable to provide maintenance	Numerical	
30	TELEPHONE	Applicant has phone in his or her name	Binary	0: No, 1: Yes
31	FOREIGN	Foreign worker	Binary	0: No, 1: Yes
32	RESPONSE	Credit rating is good	Binary	0: No, 1: Yes

Note: The original dataset had a number of categorical variables, some of which were transformed into a series of binary variables and some ordered categorical variables were left as is, to be treated as numerical.

Assignment

1. Review the predictor variables, and guess what their role in a credit decision might be. Are there any surprises in the data?

2. Divide the data into training and holdout partitions, and develop classification models using the following machine learning techniques in R: logistic regression, classification trees, and neural networks.

3. Choose one model from each technique, and report the confusion matrix and the cost/gain matrix for the holdout data. Which technique has the highest net profit?

4. Let us try and improve our performance. Rather than accepting the default classification of all applicants' credit status, use the estimated probabilities (propensities) from the logistic regression (where *success* means *good*) as a basis for selecting the best credit risks first, followed by poorer-risk applicants. Create a vector containing the net profit for each record in the holdout set. Use this vector to create a cumulative gains chart for the holdout set that incorporates the net profit.

   a. How far into the holdout data should you go to get maximum net profit? (Often, this is specified as a percentile or rounded to deciles.)

   b. If this logistic regression model is used to score to future applicants, what "probability of success" threshold should be used in extending credit?

23.3 TAYKO SOFTWARE CATALOGER[3]

mlba::Tayko is the dataset for this case study.

Background

Tayko is a software catalog firm that sells games and educational software. It started out as a software manufacturer and later added third-party titles to its offerings. It has recently put together a revised collection of items in a new catalog, which it is preparing to roll out in a mailing.

In addition to its own software titles, Tayko's customer list is a key asset. In an attempt to expand its customer base, it has recently joined a consortium of catalog firms that specialize in computer and software products. The consortium affords members the opportunity to mail catalogs to names drawn from a pooled list of customers. Members supply their own customer lists to the pool and can "withdraw" an equivalent number of names in each quarter. Members are allowed to do predictive modeling on the records in the pool so they can do a better job of selecting names from the pool.

The Mailing Experiment

Tayko has supplied its customer list of 200,000 names to the pool, which totals over 5,000,000 names, so it is now entitled to draw 200,000 names for a mailing. Tayko would like to select the names that have the best chance of performing well, so it conducts a test—it draws 20,000 names from the pool and does a test mailing of the new catalog.

This mailing yielded 1065 purchasers, a response rate of 0.053. To optimize the performance of the machine learning techniques, it was decided to work with a stratified sample that contained equal numbers of purchasers and non-purchasers. For ease of presentation, the dataset for this case includes just 1000 purchasers and 1000 nonpurchasers, an apparent response rate of 0.5. Therefore, after using the dataset to predict who will be a purchaser, we must adjust the purchase rate back down by multiplying each case's "probability of purchase" by 0.053/0.5, or 0.107.

Data

There are two outcome variables in this case. Purchase indicates whether or not a prospect responded to the test mailing and purchased something. Spending indicates, for those who made a purchase, how much they spent. The overall procedure in this case will be to develop two models. One will be used to classify

---

[3] Copyright © Datastats, LLC 2019 used with permission.

records as *purchase* or *no purchase*. The second will be used for those cases that are classified as *purchase* and will predict the amount they will spend.

Table 23.6 shows the first few rows of data. Table 23.7 provides a description of the variables available in this case.

TABLE 23.6 — FIRST 10 RECORDS FROM TAYKO DATASET

sequence_number	US	source_a	source_c	source_b	source_d	source_e	source_m	source_o	source_h	source_r	source_s	source_t	source_u	source_p	source_x	source_w	Freq	last_update_days_ago	1st_update_days_ago	Web order	Gender=male	Address_is_res	Purchase	Spending
1	1	0	0	1	0	0	0	0	0	0	0	0	0	0	0	0	2	3662	3662	1	0	1	1	127.87
2	1	0	0	0	0	1	0	0	0	0	0	0	0	0	0	0	0	2900	2900	1	1	0	0	0
3	1	0	0	0	0	0	0	0	0	0	0	1	0	0	0	0	2	3883	3914	0	0	0	1	127.48
4	1	0	1	0	0	0	0	0	0	0	0	0	0	0	0	0	1	829	829	0	1	0	0	0
5	1	0	1	0	0	0	0	0	0	0	0	0	0	0	0	0	1	869	869	0	0	0	0	0
6	1	0	0	0	0	0	0	0	0	1	0	0	0	0	0	0	1	1995	2002	0	0	1	0	0.06
7	1	0	0	0	0	0	0	0	0	0	0	0	0	0	0	1	2	1498	1529	0	0	1	0	0.06
8	1	0	0	1	0	0	0	0	0	0	0	0	0	0	0	0	1	3397	3397	0	1	0	0	0.08
9	1	1	0	0	0	0	0	0	0	0	0	0	0	0	0	0	4	525	2914	1	1	0	1	488.5
10	1	1	0	0	0	0	0	0	0	0	0	0	0	0	0	0	1	3215	3215	0	0	0	1	173.5

TABLE 23.7 — DESCRIPTION OF VARIABLES FOR TAYKO DATASET

Var.	Variable name	Description	Variable type	Code description
1	US	Is it a US address?	Binary	1: Yes 0: No
2–16	Source_ *	Source catalog for the record (15 possible sources)	Binary	1: Yes 0: No
17	Freq.	Number of transactions in last year at source catalog	Numerical	
18	last_update_days_ago	How many days ago last update was made to customer record	Numerical	
19	1st_update_days_ago	How many days ago first update to customer record was made	Numerical	
20	RFM%	Recency–frequency–monetary percentile, as reported by source catalog (see Section 23.1)	Numerical	
21	Web_order	Customer placed at least one order via web	Binary	1: Yes 0: No
22	Gender=mal	Customer is male	Binary	1: Yes 0: No
23	Address_is_res	Address is a residence	Binary	1: Yes 0: No
24	Purchase	Person made purchase in test mailing	Binary	1: Yes 0: No
25	Spending	Amount (dollars) spent by customer in test mailing	Numerical	

Assignment

1. Each catalog costs approximately $2 to mail (including printing, postage, and mailing costs). Estimate the gross profit that the firm could expect from the remaining 180,000 names if it selects them randomly from the pool.

2. Develop a model for classifying a customer as a purchaser or nonpurchaser.
   a. Partition the data randomly into a training set (800 records), validation set (700 records), and holdout set (500 records).
   b. Run stepwise logistic regression using regularization with L1 penalty (setting λ and α as discussed in Section 6.4) to select the best subset of variables and then use this model to classify the data into purchasers and nonpurchasers. Use only the training set for running the model. (Logistic regression is used because it yields an estimated "probability of purchase," which is required later in the analysis.)

3. Develop a model for predicting spending among the purchasers.
   a. Create subsets of the training and validation sets for only purchasers' records by filtering for *Purchase* = 1.
   b. Develop models for predicting spending, using:
      i. Multiple linear regression (use stepwise regression)
      ii. Regression trees
   c. Choose one model on the basis of its performance on the validation data.

4. Return to the original holdout data partition. Note that this holdout data partition includes both purchasers and nonpurchasers.
   a. Add a column to the data frame with the predicted scores from the logistic regression.
   b. Add another column with the predicted spending amount from the prediction model chosen.
   c. Add a column for "adjusted probability of purchase" by multiplying "predicted probability of purchase" by 0.107. *This is to adjust for over-sampling the purchasers* (see earlier description).
   d. Add a column for expected spending: adjusted probability of purchase × predicted spending.
   e. Plot the cumulative gains chart of the expected spending (cumulative expected spending as a function of number of records targeted).
   f. Using this cumulative gains curve, estimate the gross profit that would result from mailing to the 180,000 names on the basis of your machine learning models.

Note: Although Tayko is a hypothetical company, the data in this case (modified slightly for illustrative purposes) were supplied by a real company that sells software through direct sales. The concept of a catalog consortium is based on the Abacus Catalog Alliance.

23.4 POLITICAL PERSUASION[4]

mlba::VoterPersuasion is the dataset for this case study.

Note: Our thanks to Ken Strasma, President of HaystaqDNA and director of targeting for the 2004 Kerry campaign and the 2008 Obama campaign, for the data used in this case and for sharing the information in the following writeup.

Background

When you think of political persuasion, you may think of the efforts that political campaigns undertake to persuade you that their candidate is better than the other candidate. In truth, campaigns are less about persuading people to change their minds and more about persuading those who agree with you to actually go out and vote. Predictive analytics now plays a big role in this effort, but in 2004, it was a new arrival in the political toolbox.

Predictive Analytics Arrives in US Politics

In January of 2004, candidates in the US presidential campaign were competing in the Iowa caucuses, part of a lengthy state-by-state primary campaign that culminates in the selection of the Republican and Democratic candidates for president. Among the Democrats, Howard Dean was leading in national polls. The Iowa caucuses, however, are a complex and intensive process attracting only the most committed and interested voters. Those participating are not a representative sample of voters nationwide. Surveys of those planning to take part showed a close race between Dean and three other candidates, including John Kerry.

Kerry ended up winning by a surprisingly large margin, and the better than expected performance was due to his campaign's innovative and successful use of predictive analytics to learn more about the likely actions of individual voters. This allowed the campaign to target voters in such a way as to optimize performance in the caucuses. For example, once the model showed sufficient support in a precinct to win that precinct's delegate to the caucus, money and time could be redirected to other precincts where the race was closer.

Political Targeting

Targeting of voters is not new in politics. It has traditionally taken three forms:

- Geographic
- Demographic
- Individual

---

[4]Copyright © Datastats, LLC 2019; used with permission.

In geographic targeting, resources are directed to a geographic unit—state, city, county, etc.—on the basis of prior voting patterns or surveys that reveal the political tendency in that geographic unit. It has significant limitations, though. If a county is only, say, 52% in your favor, it may be in the greatest need of attention, but if messaging is directed to everyone in the county, nearly half of it is reaching the wrong people.

In demographic targeting, the messaging is intended for demographic groups—for example, older voters, younger women voters, Hispanic voters, etc. The limitation of this method is that it is often not easy to implement—messaging is hard to deliver just to single demographic groups.

Traditional individual targeting, the most effective form of targeting, was done on the basis of surveys asking voters how they plan to vote. The big limitation of this method is, of course, the cost. The expense of reaching all voters in a phone or door-to-door survey can be prohibitive.

The use of predictive analytics adds power to the individual targeting method and reduces cost. A model allows prediction to be rolled out to the entire voter base, not just those surveyed, and brings to bear a wealth of information. Geographic and demographic data remain part of the picture, but they are used at an individual level.

Uplift

In a classical predictive modeling application for marketing, a sample of data is selected and an offer is made (e.g., on the web) or a message is sent (e.g., by mail), and a predictive model is developed to classify individuals as responding or not-responding. The model is then applied to new data, propensities to respond are calculated, individuals are ranked by their propensity to respond, and the marketer can then select those most likely to respond to mailings or offers.

Some key information is missing from this classical approach: how would the individual respond in the absence of the offer or mailing? Might a high-propensity customer be inclined to purchase irrespective of the offer? Might a person's propensity to buy actually be diminished by the offer? Uplift modeling (see Chapter 14) allows us to estimate the effect of "offer vs. no offer" or "mailing vs. no mailing" at the individual level.

In this case, we will apply uplift modeling to actual voter data that were augmented with the results of a hypothetical experiment. The experiment consisted of the following steps:

1. Conduct a pre-survey of the voters to determine their inclination to vote Democratic.

2. Randomly split the voters into two samples—control and treatment.

3. Send a flyer promoting the Democratic candidate to the treatment group.

4. Conduct another survey of the voters to determine their inclination to vote Democratic.

Data

The data in this case are in the dataset *mlba::VoterPersuasion*. The target variable is MOVED_AD, where a 1 = "opinion moved in favor of the Democratic candidate" and 0 = "opinion did not move in favor of the Democratic candidate." This variable encapsulates the information from the pre- and post-surveys. The important predictor variable is *Flyer*, a binary variable that indicates whether or not a voter received the flyer. In addition, there are numerous other predictor variables from these sources:

1. Government voter files

2. Political party data

3. Commercial consumer and demographic data

4. Census neighborhood data

Government voter files are maintained, and made public, to assure the integrity of the voting process. They contain essential data for identification purposes such as name, address, and date of birth. The dataset used in this case also contains party identification (needed if a state limits participation in party primaries to voters in that party). Parties also staff elections with their own poll watchers, who record whether an individual votes in an election. These data (termed "derived" in the case data) are maintained and curated by each party and can be readily matched to the voter data by name. Demographic data at the neighborhood level are available from the census and can be appended to the voter data by address matching. Consumer and additional demographic data (buying habits, education) can be purchased from marketing firms and appended to the voter data (matching by name and address).

Assignment

The task in this case is to develop an uplift model that predicts the uplift for each voter. Uplift is defined as the increase in propensity to move one's opinion in a Democratic direction. First, review the variables in *mlba::VoterPersuasion*, and understand which data source they are probably coming from. Then, answer the following questions and perform the tasks indicated:

1. Overall, how well did the flyer do in moving voters in a Democratic direction? (Look at the target variable among those who got the flyer, compared with those who did not.)

2. Explore the data to learn more about the relationships between the predictor variables and MOVED_AD (visualization can be helpful). Which of the predictors seem to have good predictive potential? Show supporting charts and/or tables.

3. Partition the data using the partition variable that is in the dataset, make decisions about predictor inclusion, and fit three predictive models accordingly. For each model, give sufficient detail about the method used, its parameters, and the predictors used, so that your results can be replicated.

4. Among your three models, choose the best one in terms of predictive power. Which one is it? Why did you choose it?

5. Using your chosen model, report the propensities for the first three records in the holdout set.

6. Create a derived variable that is the opposite of *Flyer*. Call it *Flyer-reversed*. Using your chosen model, re-score the holdout data using the *Flyer-reversed* variable as a predictor, instead of *Flyer*. Report the propensities for the first three records in the holdout set.

7. For each record, uplift is computed based on the following difference:

$$P(\text{success} \mid \text{Flyer} = 1) - P(\text{success} \mid \text{Flyer} = 0)$$

Compute the uplift for each of the voters in the holdout set, and report the uplift for the first three records.

8. If a campaign has the resources to mail the flyer only to 10% of the voters, what uplift threshold should be used?

23.5 TAXI CANCELLATIONS[5]

mlba::TaxiCancellationCase is the dataset for this case study.

Business Situation

In late 2013, the taxi company Yourcabs.com in Bangalore, India, was facing a problem with the drivers using their platform—not all drivers were showing up for their scheduled calls. Drivers would cancel their acceptance of a call, and, if the cancellation did not occur with adequate notice, the customer would be delayed or even left high and dry.

Bangalore is a key tech center in India, and technology was transforming the taxi industry. Yourcabs.com featured an online booking system (though customers could phone in as well) and presented itself as a taxi booking portal. The Uber ride sharing service started its Bangalore operations in mid-2014.

Yourcabs.com had collected data on its bookings from 2011 to 2013 and posted a contest on Kaggle, in coordination with the Indian School of Business, to see what it could learn about the problem of cab cancellations.

The data presented for this case are a randomly selected subset of the original data, with 10,000 rows, one row for each booking. There are 17 input variables, including user (customer) ID, vehicle model, whether the booking was made online or via a mobile app, type of travel, type of booking package, geographic information, and the date and time of the scheduled trip. The target variable of interest is the binary indicator of whether a ride was canceled. The overall cancellation rate is between 7% and 8%.

Assignment

1. How can a predictive model based on these data be used by Yourcabs.com?

2. How can a profiling model (identifying predictors that distinguish canceled/uncanceled trips) be used by Yourcabs.com?

3. Explore, prepare, and transform the data to facilitate predictive modeling. Here are some hints:

   - In exploratory modeling, it is useful to move fairly soon to at least an initial model without solving *all* data preparation issues. One example is the GPS information—other geographic information is available, so you could defer the challenge of how to interpret/use the GPS information.

---

[5] Copyright © Datastats, LLC and Galit Shmueli 2019; used with permission.

- How will you deal with missing data, such as cases where NULL is indicated?

- Think about what useful information might be held within the date and time fields (the booking timestamp and the trip timestamp).

- Think also about the categorical variables and how to deal with them. Should we turn them all into dummies? Use only some?

4. Fit several predictive models of your choice. Do they provide information on how the predictor variables relate to cancellations?

5. Report the predictive performance of your model in terms of error rates (the confusion matrix). How well does the model perform? Can the model be used in practice?

6. Examine the predictive performance of your model in terms of ranking (lift). How well does the model perform? Can the model be used in practice?

23.6 SEGMENTING CONSUMERS OF BATH SOAP[6]

mlba::BathSoapHousehold is the dataset for this case study.

Business Situation

CRISA is an Asian market research agency that specializes in tracking consumer purchase behavior in consumer goods (both durable and nondurable). In one major research project, CRISA tracks numerous consumer product categories (e.g., "detergents") and, within each category, perhaps dozens of brands. To track purchase behavior, CRISA constituted household panels in over 100 cities and towns in India, covering most of the Indian urban market. The households were carefully selected using stratified sampling to ensure a representative sample; a subset of 600 records is analyzed here. The strata were defined on the basis of socioeconomic status and the market (a collection of cities).

CRISA has both transaction data (each row is a transaction) and household data (each row is a household), and for the household data, it maintains the following information:

- Demographics of the households (updated annually)
- Possession of durable goods (car, washing machine, etc., updated annually; an "affluence index" is computed from this information)
- Purchase data of product categories and brands (updated monthly)

CRISA has two categories of clients: (1) advertising agencies that subscribe to the database services, obtain updated data every month, and use the data to advise their clients on advertising and promotion strategies and (2) consumer goods manufacturers, which monitor their market share using the CRISA database.

Key Problems

CRISA has traditionally segmented markets on the basis of purchaser demographics. They would now like to segment the market based on two key sets of variables more directly related to the purchase process and to brand loyalty:

1. Purchase behavior (volume, frequency, susceptibility to discounts, and brand loyalty)
2. Basis of purchase (price, selling proposition)

Doing so would allow CRISA to gain information about what demographic attributes are associated with different purchase behaviors and degrees of brand loyalty and thus deploy promotion budgets more effectively. More effective

---

[6]Copyright © Cytel, Inc. and Datastats, LLC 2019 used with permission.

market segmentation would enable CRISA's clients (in this case, a firm called IMRB) to design more cost-effective promotions targeted at appropriate segments. Thus, multiple promotions could be launched, each targeted at different market segments at different times of the year. This would result in a more cost-effective allocation of the promotion budget to different market segments. It would also enable IMRB to design more effective customer reward systems and thereby increase brand loyalty.

Data

The data in Table 23.8 profile each household, each row containing the data for one household.

Measuring Brand Loyalty

Several variables in this case measure aspects of brand loyalty. The number of different brands purchased by the customer is one measure of loyalty. However, a consumer who purchases one or two brands in quick succession and then settles on a third for a long streak is different from a consumer who constantly switches back and forth among three brands. Therefore, how often customers switch from one brand to another is another measure of loyalty. Yet a third perspective on the same issue is the proportion of purchases that go to different brands—a consumer who spends 90% of his or her purchase money on one brand is more loyal than a consumer who spends more equally among several brands.

All three of these components can be measured with the data in the purchase summary worksheet.

Assignment

1. Use k-means clustering to identify clusters of households based on:

   a. The variables that describe purchase behavior (including brand loyalty)

   b. The variables that describe the basis for purchase

   c. The variables that describe both purchase behavior and basis of purchase

   Note 1: How should k be chosen? Think about how the clusters would be used. It is likely that the marketing efforts would support two to five different promotional approaches.

   Note 2: How should the percentages of total purchases accounted for by various brands be treated? Isn't a customer who buys all brand A just as loyal as a customer who buys all brand B? What will be the effect on any distance measure of using the brand share variables as is? Consider using a single derived variable.

TABLE 23.8   DESCRIPTION OF VARIABLES FOR EACH HOUSEHOLD

Variable type	Variable name	Description
Member ID	Member id	Unique identifier for each household
Demographics	SEC	Socioeconomic class ($1 =$ high, $5 =$ low)
	FEH	Eating habits($1 =$ vegetarian, $2 =$ vegetarian but eat eggs, $3 =$ nonvegetarian, $0 =$ not specified)
	MT	Native language (see table in worksheet)
	SEX	Gender of homemaker ($1 =$ male, $2 =$ female)
	AGE	Age of homemaker
	EDU	Education of homemaker ($1 =$ minimum, $9 =$ maximum)
	HS	Number of members in household
	CHILD	Presence of children in household (4 categories)
	CS	Television availability ($1 =$ available, $2 =$ unavailable)
	Affluence Index	Weighted value of durables possessed
Purchase summary over the period	No. of Brands	Number of brands purchased
	Brand Runs	Number of instances of consecutive purchase of brands
	Total Volume	Sum of volume
	No. of Trans	Number of purchase transactions (multiple brands purchased in a month are counted as separate transactions)
	Value	Sum of value
	Trans/ Brand Runs	Average transactions per brand run
	Vol/Trans	Average volume per transaction
	Avg. Price	Average price of purchase
Purchase within promotion	Pur Vol	Percent of volume purchased
	No Promo - %	Percent of volume purchased under no promotion
	Pur Vol Promo 6%	Percent of volume purchased under promotion code 6
	Pur Vol Other Promo %	Percent of volume purchased under other promotions
Brandwise purchase	Br. Cd. (57, 144), 55, 272, 286, 24, 481, 352, 5, and 999 (others)	Percent of volume purchased of the brand
Price categorywise purchase	Price Cat 1–4	Percent of volume purchased under the price category
Selling propositionwise purchase	Proposition Cat 5–15	Percent of volume purchased under the product proposition category

2. Select what you think is the best segmentation, and comment on the characteristics (demographic, brand loyalty, and basis for purchase) of these clusters. (This information would be used to guide the development of advertising and promotional campaigns.)

3. Develop a model that classifies the data into these segments. Since this information would most likely be used in targeting direct-mail promotions, it would be useful to select a market segment that would be defined as a *success* in the classification model.

23.7 DIRECT-MAIL FUNDRAISING

mlba::Fundraising and *mlba::FutureFundraising* are the datasets used for this case study.

Background

Note: Be sure to read the information about oversampling and adjustment in Chapter 5 before starting to work on this case.

A national veterans' organization wishes to develop a predictive model to improve the cost-effectiveness of their direct marketing campaign. The organization, with its in-house database of over 13 million donors, is one of the largest direct-mail fundraisers in the United States. According to their recent mailing records, the overall response rate is 5.1%. Out of those who responded (donated), the average donation is $13.00. Each mailing, which includes a gift of personalized address labels and assortments of cards and envelopes, costs $0.68 to produce and send. Using these facts, we take a sample of this dataset to develop a classification model that can effectively capture donors so that the expected net profit is maximized. Weighted sampling is used, underrepresenting the non-responders so that the sample has equal numbers of donors and non-donors.

Data

The dataset *mlba::Fundraising* contains 3120 records with 50% donors (TARGET_B = 1) and 50% non-donors (TARGET_B = 0). The amount of donation (TARGET_D) is also included but is not used in this case. The descriptions for the 22 variables (including two target variables) are listed in Table 23.9.

Assignment

Step 1: Partitioning. Partition the dataset into 60% training and 40% holdout (set the seed to 12345).

Step 2: Model Building. Follow the following steps to build, evaluate, and choose a model.

1. *Select classification tool and parameters.* Run at least two classification models of your choosing. Be sure NOT to use TARGET_D in your analysis. Describe the two models that you chose, with sufficient detail (method, parameters, variables, etc.) so that it can be replicated.

2. *Classification under asymmetric response and cost.* What is the reasoning behind using weighted sampling to produce a training set with equal numbers of donors and non-donors? Why not use a simple random sample from the original dataset?

3. *Calculate net profit.* For each method, calculate the cumulative gains of net profit for both the training and holdout sets based on the actual response

TABLE 23.9   DESCRIPTION OF VARIABLES FOR THE FUNDRAISING DATASET

Variable	Description
ZIP	Zip code group (zip codes were grouped into five groups; 1 = the potential donor belongs to this zip group.)
	00000–19999 $\Rightarrow$ zipconvert_1
	20000–39999 $\Rightarrow$ zipconvert_2
	40000–59999 $\Rightarrow$ zipconvert_3
	60000–79999 $\Rightarrow$ zipconvert_4
	80000–99999 $\Rightarrow$ zipconvert_5
HOMEOWNER	1 = homeowner, 0 = not a homeowner
NUMCHLD	Number of children
INCOME	Household income
GENDER	0 = male, 1 = female
WEALTH	Wealth rating uses median family income and population statistics from each area to index relative wealth within each state The segments are denoted 0–9, with 9 being the highest-wealth group and zero the lowest. Each rating has a different meaning within each state.
HV	Average home value in potential donor's neighborhood in hundreds of dollars
ICmed	Median family income in potential donor's neighborhood in hundreds of dollars
ICavg	Average family income in potential donor's neighborhood in hundreds
IC15	Percent earning less than $15K in potential donor's neighborhood
NUMPROM	Lifetime number of promotions received to date
RAMNTALL	Dollar amount of lifetime gifts to date
MAXRAMNT	Dollar amount of largest gift to date
LASTGIFT	Dollar amount of most recent gift
TOTALMONTHS	Number of months from last donation to July 1998 (the last time the case was updated)
TIMELAG	Number of months between first and second gift
AVGGIFT	Average dollar amount of gifts to date
TARGET_B	Outcome variable: binary indicator for response 1 = donor, 0 = non-donor
TARGET_D	Outcome variable: donation amount (in dollars). We will NOT be using this variable for this case

rate (5.1%). Again, the expected donation, given that they are donors, is $13.00, and the total cost of each mailing is $0.68. (*Hint*: To calculate estimated net profit, we will need to undo the effects of the weighted sampling and calculate the net profit that would reflect the actual response distribution of 5.1% donors and 94.9% non-donors. To do this, divide each row's net profit by the oversampling weights applicable to the actual status of that row. The oversampling weight for actual donors is 50%/5.1% = 9.8. The oversampling weight for actual non-donors is 50%/94.9% = 0.53.)

4. *Draw cumulative gains curves.* Draw the different models' net profit cumulative gains curves for the holdout set in a single plot (net profit on the y-axis, proportion of list or number mailed on the x-axis). Is there a model that dominates?

5. *Select best model.* From your answer in (4), what do you think is the "best" model?

Step 3: Testing. The dataset *mlba::FutureFundraising* contains the attributes for future mailing candidates.

6. Using your "best" model from Step 2 (number 5), which of these candidates do you predict as donors and non-donors? List them in descending order of the probability of being a donor. Starting at the top of this sorted list, roughly how far down would you go in a mailing campaign?

23.8 CATALOG CROSS-SELLING[7]

mlba::CatalogCrossSell is the dataset for this case study.

Background

Exeter, Inc., is a catalog firm that sells products in a number of different catalogs that it owns. The catalogs number in the dozens but fall into nine basic categories:

1. Clothing
2. Housewares
3. Health
4. Automotive
5. Personal electronics
6. Computers
7. Garden
8. Novelty gift
9. Jewelry

The costs of printing and distributing catalogs are high. By far, the biggest cost of operation is the cost of promoting products to people who buy nothing. Having invested so much in the production of artwork and printing of catalogs, Exeter wants to take every opportunity to use them effectively. One such opportunity is in cross-selling—once a customer has "taken the bait" and purchases one product, try to sell them another while you have their attention.

Such cross-promotion might take the form of enclosing a catalog in the shipment of a purchased product, together with a discount coupon to induce a purchase from that catalog. Or, it might take the form of a similar coupon sent by email, with a link to the web version of that catalog.

But which catalog should be enclosed in the box or included as a link in the email with the discount coupon? Exeter would like it to be an informed choice—a catalog that has a higher probability of inducing a purchase than simply choosing a catalog at random.

Assignment

Using the dataset *mlba::CatalogCrossSell*, perform an association rules analysis, and comment on the results. Your discussion should provide interpretations in English of the meanings of the various output statistics (lift, confidence, support)

---

and include a very rough estimate (precise calculations are not necessary) of the extent to which this will help Exeter make an informed choice about which catalog to cross-promote to a purchaser.

Acknowledgment   The data for this case have been adapted from the data in a set of cases provided for educational purposes by the Direct Marketing Education Foundation ("DMEF Academic Data Set Two, Multi Division Catalog Company, Code: 02DMEF"), used with permission.

23.9   TIME SERIES CASE: FORECASTING PUBLIC TRANSPORTATION DEMAND

mlba::Bicup2006 is the dataset for this case study.

Background

Forecasting transportation demand is important for multiple purposes such as staffing, planning, and inventory control. The public transportation system in Santiago de Chile has gone through a major effort of reconstruction. In this context, a business intelligence competition took place in October 2006, which focused on forecasting demand for public transportation. This case is based on the competition, with some modifications.

Problem Description

A public transportation company is expecting an increase in demand for its services and is planning to acquire new buses and to extend its terminals. These investments require a reliable forecast of future demand. To create such forecasts, one can use data on historic demand. The company's data warehouse has data for each 15-minute interval between 6:30 and 22:00, on the number of passengers arriving at the terminal. As a forecasting consultant, you have been asked to create a forecasting method that can generate forecasts for the number of passengers arriving at the terminal.

Available Data

Part of the historic information is available in the dataset *mlba::Bicup2006*. The dataset contains the historic information with known demand for a 3-week period, separated into 15-minute intervals, and dates and times for a future 3-day period (DEMAND = NaN), for which forecasts should be generated (as part of the 2006 competition).

Assignment Goal

Your goal is to create a model/method that produces accurate forecasts. To evaluate your accuracy, partition the given historic data into two periods: a training period (the first 2 weeks) and a test period (the last week). Models should be fitted only to the training data and evaluated on the test data.

Although the competition winning criterion was the lowest mean absolute error (MAE) on the future 3-day data, this is *not* the goal for this assignment. Instead, if we consider a more realistic business context, our goal is to create a model that generates reasonably good forecasts on any time/day of the week. Consider not only predictive metrics such as MAE, mean absolute percentage error (MAPE), and root mean squared error (RMSE), but also look at actual and forecasted values, overlaid on a time plot, as well as a time plot of the forecast errors.

Assignment

For your final model, present the following summary:

1. Name of the method/combination of methods.
2. A brief description of the method/combination.
3. All estimated equations associated with constructing forecasts from this method.
4. The MAPE and MAE for the training period and the test period.
5. Forecasts for the future period (March 22–24), in 15-minute bins.
6. A single chart showing the fit of the final version of the model to the entire period (including training, test, and future). Note that this model should be fitted using the combined training plus test data.

Tips and Suggested Steps

1. Use exploratory analysis to identify the components of this time series. Is there a trend? Is there seasonality? If so, how many "seasons" are there? Are there any other visible patterns? Are the patterns global (the same throughout the series) or local?
2. Consider the frequency of the data from a practical and technical point of view. What are some options?
3. Compare the weekdays and weekends. How do they differ? Consider how these differences can be captured by different methods.
4. Examine the series for missing values or unusual values. Think of solutions.
5. Based on the patterns that you found in the data, which models or methods should be considered?
6. Consider how to handle actual counts of zero within the computation of MAPE.

23.10　LOAN APPROVAL[8]

mlba::UniversalBankCase is the dataset for this case study.

Background

You are a data scientist recently hired by Universal Bank, a mid-sized bank in the southern United States. Most of your work to this point has involved pulling reports from databases, but now you have been given a more interesting task. The bank is facing competition from online lenders that can offer rapid automated loan approvals, and it wants to develop its own predictive model so that it can do likewise. Before building the web infrastructure, which could be costly, the bank wants to pilot a prototype loan approval model, developed by you.

　　The bank wants to launch its model with the approval process for personal loans extended to existing customers. The bank has only been offering these loans for a relatively short time, so has little data on default rates. It does have data on prior loan applications and whether they were approved or disapproved. You have done some preliminary data prep and feature selection work, resulting in the dataset of 5000 records for this project. Each record is for a customer and consists of feature values for that customer along with a record of the human decision on their loan application. Your end goal is to develop a model to predict that human decision and an accompanying report to the bank's chief lending officer.

Regulatory Requirements

You are somewhat familiar with regulatory requirements with respect to discrimination (do a web search for the US Department of Justice Equal Credit Opportunity Act or ECOA). Bank attorneys have told you that the ECOA requirements pertain to the basis for credit decisions and do not mean that the proportion of approved loans must be the same for all groups.

Getting Started

You have the RDS framework in hand (see Chapter 22). You recognize that some aspects of the framework may take more time (e.g., consulting with other stakeholders and learning more about how the data were produced), but you want to get started with at least a draft so that you can discuss next steps with your superiors.

---

[8]Copyright © 2022 Datastats, LLC, and Galit Shmueli. Used by permission.

Assignment

1. Identify any features that might need to be excluded from the modeling task, per the ECOA.

2. Should you simply eliminate these features from the data?

3. Explore the data, with a focus on loan approval rates for different groups.

4. Split the data into training and holdout data, and fit several models of your choice to predict whether a personal loan should be approved, using only permitted features. There are a number of possible performance measures; evaluate the model performance by the metric(s) you consider useful.

5. Assess the usefulness of the model from a pure model performance standpoint.

6. Considering the "protected" categories per the ECOA, evaluate whether the model is fair.

7. Describe steps that might be taken to improve the model fairness. Implement any measures that can be taken without going beyond the dataset at hand. (*Hint:* If you did not calculate a correlation matrix earlier, you should do one now.)

8. Write a very short report summarizing your findings.

References

Aggarwal, C. C. (2016). *Recommender Systems* (Vol. 1). Springer Cham.

Agrawal, R., Imielinski, T., and Swami, A. (1993). Mining associations between sets of items in massive databases. In: *Proceedings of the 1993 ACM-SIGMOD International Conference on Management of Data*, pp. 207-216, New York: ACM Press.

Anderson, D. R., Sweeney, D. J., Williams, T. A., Cam, J. D., Cochran, J. J., Fry, M. J., a Ohlmann, J. W. (2021). *Modern Business Statistics with Microsoft Excel*, 7th ed. Boston, MA: Cengage Learning.

Berry, M. J. A., and Linoff, G. S. (1997). *Data Mining Techniques*. New York: Wiley.

Berry, M. J. A., and Linoff, G. S. (2000). *Mastering Data Mining*. New York: Wiley.

Breiman, L., Friedman, J., Olshen, R., and Stone, C. (1984). *Classification and Regression Trees*. Boca Raton, FL: Chapman Hall/CRC (orig. published by Wadsworth).

Chawla, N. V., Bowyer, K. W., Lawrence, O. H., and Kegelmeyer, W. P. (2002). SMOTE: synthetic minority over-sampling technique. *Journal of Artificial Intelligence Research*, vol. 16, number 1, pp. 321–357.

Chatfield, C. (2003). *The Analysis of Time Series: An Introduction*, 6th ed. Boca Raton, FL: Chapman Hall/CRC.

Coene, J. (2021). *Javascript for R*. Boca Raton, FL: Chapman and Hall/CRC

Delmaster, R., and Hancock, M. (2001). *Data Mining Explained*. Boston, MA: Digital Press.

Efron, B. (1975). The efficiency of logistic regression compared to normal discriminant analysis. *Journal of the American Statistical Association*, vol. 70, number 352, pp. 892–898.

Few, S. (2021). *Now You See It*, 2nd ed. Oakland, CA: Analytics Press.

Few, S. (2012). *Show Me the Numbers*, 2nd ed. Oakland, CA: Analytics Press.

Fleming, G., and Bruce, P. C. (2021). *Responsible Data Science*. Hoboken, NJ: Wiley.

Golbeck, J. (2013). *Analyzing the Social Web*. Waltham, MA: Morgan Kaufmann.

Han, J., and Kamber, M. (2001). *Data Mining: Concepts and Techniques*. San Diego, CA: Academic Press.

Hand, D. J. (2009). Measuring classifier performance: a coherent alternative to the area under the ROC curve. *Machine Learning*, vol. 77, number 1, pp. 103–123.

Harper, F. M., and Konstan, J. A. (2015). The movielens datasets: history and context. *ACM Transactions on Interactive Intelligent Systems (TiiS)*, vol. 5, number 4, pp. 19:1–19:19. DOI: 10.1145/2827872

Harris, H., Murphy, S., and Vaisman, M. (2013). *Analyzing the Analyzers: An Introspective Survey of Data Scientists and Their Work*. Cambridge, MA: O'Reilly Media.

Hastie, T., Tibshirani, R., and Friedman, J. (2001). *The Elements of Statistical Learning*. New York: Springer.

Machine Learning for Business Analytics: Concepts, Techniques, and Applications in R, Second Edition.
Galit Shmueli, Peter C. Bruce, Peter Gedeck, Inbal Yahav, and Nitin R. Patel
© 2023 John Wiley & Sons, Inc. Published 2023 by John Wiley & Sons, Inc.

Hosmer, D. W., and Lemeshow, S. (2000). *Applied Logistic Regression*, 2nd ed. New York: Wiley-Interscience.

Hothorn, T., Hornik K., and Zeileis, A. (2006). Unbiased recursive partitioning: a conditional inference framework. *Journal of Computational and Graphical Statistics*, vol. 15, number 3, pp. 651–674.

Hothorn, T., and Zeileis, A. (2015). Partykit: a modular toolkit for recursive partytioning in R. *The Journal of Machine Learning Research*, vol. 16, number 1, pp. 3905-3909.

Hyndman, R., and Yang, Y. Z. (2018). tsdl: Time Series Data Library. v0.1.0. Available at https://pkg.yangzhuoranyang.com/tsdl/.

Jank, W., and Yahav, I. (2010). E-loyalty networks in online auctions. *The Annals of Applied Statistics*, vol. 4, number 1, pp. 151-178.

Johnson, W., and Wichern, D. (2002). *Applied Multivariate Statistics*. Upper Saddle River, NJ: Prentice Hall.

Kohavi, R., Tang, D., and Xu, Y. (2020). *Trustworthy Online Controlled Experiments: A Practical Guide to a/b Testing*. Cambridge: Cambridge University Press.

Larsen, K. (2005). Generalized naive Bayes classifiers. *SIGKDD Explorations*, vol. 7, number 1, pp. 76-81.

Le, Q. V., Ranzato, M. A., Monga, R., Devin, M., Chen, K., Corrado, G. S., Dean, J., and Ng, A.Y. (2012). Building high-level features using large scale unsupervised learning. In: *Proceedings of the Twenty-Ninth International Conference on Machine Learning*. Editors: John Langford and Joelle Pineau. Edinburgh: Omnipress.

Lobo, J. M., Jiménez-Valverde, A., and Real, R. (2008). AUC: a misleading measure of the performance of predictive distribution models. *Global Ecology and Biogeography*, vol. 17, number 2, pp. 145-151.

Loh, W.-Y., and Shih, Y.-S. (1997). Split selection methods for classification trees. *Statistica Sinica*, vol. 7, pp. 815-840.

Maas, A. L., Daly, R. E., Pham, P. T., Huang, D., Ng, A. Y., and Potts, C. (2011). Learning word vectors for sentiment analysis. In: *Proceedings of the 49th Annual Meeting of the Association for Computational Linguistics: Human Language Technologies - vol. 1*, pp. 142–150. DOI: 10.5555/2002472.2002491.

McCullugh, C. E., Paal, B., and Ashdown, S. P. (1998). An optimisation approach to apparel sizing. *Journal of the Operational Research Society,* vol. 49, number 5, pp. 492–499.

Matz, S. C., Kosinski, S. C., Nave, G., and Stillwell, D. J. (2017). Psychological targeting in digital mass persuasion. *Proceedings of the National Academy of Sciences*, vol. 114, number 48, pp. 12714–12719. DOI: 10.1073/pnas.1710966114.

O'Neil, C. (2016) *Weapons of Math Destruction*. New York: Crown Publishers.

Pregibon, D. (1999). 2001: a statistical odyssey. Invited talk at *The Fifth ACM SIGKDD International Conference on Knowledge Discovery and Data Mining*, p. 4. New York: ACM Press.

Ribeiro, M. T., Singh, S., and Guestrin, C. (2016). Why should I trust you?: explaining the predictions of any classifier. In: *Proceedings of the 22nd ACM SIGKDD International Conference on Knowledge Discovery and Data Mining*. San Francisco, CA: ACM.

Rokach, L., and Maimon, O. Z. (2014). *Data Mining with Decision Trees: Theory and Applications*, 2nd ed. Singapore: World Scientific.

Russell, S. (2019). *Human Compatible: Artificial Intelligence and the Problem of Control*. New York: Penguin Books.

Saddiqi, N. (2017). *Intelligent Credit Scoring: Building and Implementing Better Credit Risk Scorecards*, 2nd ed. Hoboken, NJ: Wiley.

Shmueli, G., and Lichtendahl, K. C. (2016). *Practical Time Series Forecasting with R: A Hands-On Guide*, 2nd ed. Green Cove Springs, FL: Axelrod-Schnall Publishers.

Siegel, E. (2013). *Predictive Analytics*. New York: Wiley.

Sutton, R. S., and Barto, A. G. (2018). *Reinforcement Learning: An Introduction*, 2nd ed. Cambridge, MA: The MIT Press.

R Packages Used in the Book

This book is accompanied by the R package `mlba` which is maintained on GitHub at https://github.com/gedeck/mlba. It can be installed from the GitHub repository using the following command:

```
library(devtools)
install_github("gedeck/mlba/mlba", force=FALSE)
```

It will only reinstall the package if there were changes. Set the argument *force=TRUE* to force installation.

The `mlba` package gives easy access to all datasets used in this book and provides in addition the following function:

```
regressionSummary <- function(predicted, actual) {
  # calculate and return regression metrics RMSE and MAE
  return (list(
    RMSE = caret::RMSE(predicted, actual),
    MAE = caret::MAE(predicted, actual)
  ))
}
```

In addition to `mlba`, the following R packages are used in this book.

Data Loading and Manipulation

`data.table` Extension of *data.frame* suitable for large datasets

`fastDummies` Fast creation of dummy (binary) columns and rows from categorical variables

`mlba` Datasets and utility function for this book

`reshape` Flexibly reshape data

`splitstackshape` Stack and reshape datasets after splitting concatenated values

`tidyverse` Easily install and load the "Tidyverse," a collection of packages to facilitate data handling and visualization (https://www.tidyverse.org/)

Machine Learning for Business Analytics: Concepts, Techniques, and Applications in R, Second Edition.
Galit Shmueli, Peter C. Bruce, Peter Gedeck, Inbal Yahav, and Nitin R. Patel
© 2023 John Wiley & Sons, Inc. Published 2023 by John Wiley & Sons, Inc.

Data Visualization

ggplot2 Create elegant data visualizations using the grammar of graphics

GGally Extension to ggplot2

ggdendro Create dendrograms and tree diagrams using ggplot2

ggmap Spatial visualization with ggplot2

ggnetwork Plot networks with ggplot2

ggrepel Automatically position non-overlapping text labels with ggplot2

gplots Specialized plots using base-R

gridExtra Arrange multiple plots in a "grid" pattern

mosaic Collection of utilities from the "Project MOSAIC" (http://www.mosaic-web.org/). Used in this book for map visualization

plotly Create interactive web graphics via "plotly.js"

rpart.plot Plot decision trees: an enhanced version of "plot.rpart"

scales Scale functions for base-R visualization

treemapify Draw treemaps in "ggplot2"

Training, Validating, and Analyzing Machine Learning Models

adabag Applies multiclass AdaBoost.M1, SAMME, and bagging

caret Classification and regression training; provides a consistent interface to a large variety of machine learning methods

DiscriMiner Discriminant analysis

e1071 Collection of machine learning models from the Department of Statistics, Probability Theory Group (Formerly: E1071), TU Wien; used for naive Bayes models

gains Lift (gains) tables and charts

glmnet Lasso and elastic-net regularized Generalized Linear Models (GLMs)

h2o R interface for the "H2O" scalable machine learning platform

iml Interpretable machine learning

leaps Regression subset selection

MASS Support functions and datasets for Venables and Ripley's "Modern Applied Statistics with S"; used for LDA models

neuralnet Training of neural networks

randomForest Breiman and Cutler's random forests for classification and regression

ROCR Creating ROC and PR curves, gains and lift charts.

rpart Recursive partitioning and regression trees

xgboost Extreme gradient boosting

Deep Learning

The TensorFlow and Keras implementations in R require a Python environment with both installed. Find installation instructions here: https://tensorflow. rstudio.com/

reticulate Interface to "Python" modules, classes, and functions.

tensorflow R interface to "TensorFlow" https://www.tensorflow.org/, an open source software library for numerical computation using data flow graphs

keras R interface to "Keras" https://keras.io, a high-level neural networks API

Other Packages

arules Mining association rules and frequent itemsets

contextual Simulation and analysis of contextual multi-armed bandit policies

recommenderlab Lab for developing and testing recommender algorithms

forecast Functions and models for forecasting time series and linear models

zoo Alternative to *ts* for regular and irregular time series (Z's ordered observations)

lubridate Make dealing with dates a little easier

tm Text mining package

text2vec Text mining framework for R

SnowballC Snowball stemmers based on the C "libstemmer" library

lsa Latent semantic analysis

igraph Network analysis and visualization

Rfacebook Access to Facebook API via R

twitteR R-based Twitter client

Data Files Used in the Book

All datasets used in this book are accessible with the `mlba` package. For example, to load the *Accidents* datset, use

```
accidents.df <- mlba::Accidents
```

You can also download all datasets from https://www.dataminingbook.com.

1. Accidents
2. AccidentsFull
3. AccidentsNN
4. Airfares
5. Amtrak
6. ApplianceShipments
7. AustralianWines
8. AutosElectronics (see Chapter 21 for details on how to load this dataset)
9. Banks
10. BankBiasData
11. BareggTunnel
12. BathSoapHousehold
13. Bicup2006
14. BostonHousing
15. CanadianWorkHours
16. CatalogCrossSell
17. Cereals
18. CharlesBookClub
19. COMPAS_clean
20. Cosmetics
21. CourseTopics
22. DepartmentStoreSales
23. Drug
24. EastWestAirlinesCluster
25. EastWestAirlinesNN
26. eBayAuctions
27. eBayNetwork
28. eBayTreemap
29. EmailABtest
30. Faceplate
31. FarmAds
32. FlightDelays
33. Fundraising
34. FutureFundraising
35. GDP
36. GermanCredit

Machine Learning for Business Analytics: Concepts, Techniques, and Applications in R, Second Edition.
Galit Shmueli, Peter C. Bruce, Peter Gedeck, Inbal Yahav, and Nitin R. Patel
© 2023 John Wiley & Sons, Inc. Published 2023 by John Wiley & Sons, Inc.

Index

Machine Learning for Business Analytics: Concepts, Techniques, and Applications in R, Second Edition.
Galit Shmueli, Peter C. Bruce, Peter Gedeck, Inbal Yahav, and Nitin R. Patel
© 2023 John Wiley & Sons, Inc. Published 2023 by John Wiley & Sons, Inc.